BENEFIT PLANS IN AMERICAN COLLEGES

BENEFIT PLANS
IN AMERICAN COLLEGES

By WILLIAM C. GREENOUGH
and FRANCIS P. KING

NEW YORK AND LONDON 1969

COLUMBIA UNIVERSITY PRESS

FOREWORD

Of all our institutions, we demand most from the educational system—schools, colleges, and universities. The nation's political health, its economic strength, and its capacity to function in a changing world depend on the effectiveness of our educational processes.

This readable book deals with one of the fundamental needs of institutions of higher education, the need to attract first-rate teachers and scholars. Such people must be properly compensated. Good salaries are essential, and so are soundly planned retirement and insurance benefits.

The college professor has come a long way since Andrew Carnegie became a trustee of Cornell University in 1890 and "was shocked to discover that college teachers were paid only about as much as office clerks." Today salaries for college teachers are much improved over the low levels prevailing only a decade ago. And, over the years, significant progress has been made in the development of well-conceived benefit plans for college faculty and staff. Indeed, the colleges and universities have played a pioneering role in the development of such plans.

Many college professors have little time to concern themselves with practical business matters. But they would do well to make an exception when it comes to the adoption of sensible benefit plans. The faculty member may have limited power to control his college's decision concerning one or another benefit plan, but he should be able to tell a good plan from a bad one, and, with his colleagues, to be an effective advocate of the kind of plan best suited to his institution.

In any attempt to get one's bearings in the specialized field of college retirement and insurance plans this book is indispensable—as a thorough discussion of the subject and as a handy reference. The authors' many years of experience have equipped them superbly to prepare such a volume, and they have produced an authoritative work.

A decade has passed since the authors' previous study of the retirement and insurance plans for staff members serving higher education. In my foreword to that volume I noted that the colleges and universities had recently moved to meet the competition for good people with some striking innovations in benefit planning. One was the College Retirement Equities Fund, which made possible new measures of protection of retirement income against increasing living costs during retirement. In the insurance area, plans to meet major medical expenses and provide income during periods of total disability had just been introduced. The present study shows that these benefits have now been widely adopted by the colleges and universities.

The book offers a brief history of college staff benefit planning, and a careful discussion of the philosophy of benefit plans appropriate to the purposes and goals of educational institutions. The structure, goals, and rationale of higher education are quite different from those of many other organizations such as government or business and industrial enterprises, and it is one of the strengths of this book that it clearly recognizes these differences and consistently deals with retirement and benefit plans in terms of the unique aims of the institutions involved. It analyzes the various provisions that compose these plans and provides statistical information on the benefit plans now in effect in institutions of higher learning.

The material on funding of retirement benefits should be of particular interest to those wishing to examine the soundness of their present retirement funding methods, which involve a considerable investment of money over a long period of time and which affect the portability of benefits during working years.

Trustees, administrators, and members of faculty and staff should read this book with their own institution in mind and make notes as to how their institution stands with respect to the quality of its benefit plans.

JOHN W. GARDNER

Washington, D.C.
October 24, 1968

ACKNOWLEDGMENTS

This study could not have been made without the active assistance of over 1,200 college and university business officers. Their willingness to supply detailed information on the retirement and insurance plans in their institutions made the study possible, and we are deeply indebted to them for their considerable work.

We also wish to express our appreciation to the many others who have contributed to the study. The executive officers of the state teacher and public employee retirement systems and of church pension plans, whose participants include staff members of colleges and universities, supplied pension plan information and verified our summaries of their plans. The U.S. Office of Education aided the study through Dr. Alexander Mood of the National Center for Educational Statistics, who made available on punched cards the Center's system of institutional classifications, and Dr. James F. Rogers, specialist for faculty staffing, who gave us many useful comments on various drafts of the questionnaire. Dr. Peggy Heim, associate secretary and economist of the American Association of University Professors, was immensely helpful as we developed the study methods and the questionnaire.

Our colleagues at TIAA deserve special acknowledgement. Thomas C. Edwards, Donald S. Willard, and Thomas F. Cuite read and edited all of the manuscript and rewrote and greatly improved parts of it. James G. MacDonald and Ronald P. McPhee were especially helpful on the chapters discussing group coverages. The descriptions of public retirement plans and self-administered and insured plans were prepared by Thomas F. Cuite, James T. Foran, Gilbert F. Goller, E. H. Joyner, Jr., Alan E. Muller, Lawrence W. Ring, Charles A. Shorter, Jr., and Vincent Taormina.

Vivien Chesley supervised preparation of the descriptions of the TIAA plans and provided statistical assistance and retirement plan information. Ada Horton prepared the descriptions of the church pension plans, statistics summarizing public retirement plan provisions, the footnotes and bibliography, and researched special reference questions. Jo Ann Mahoney, assisted by Patricia Burns, established the general study records and coordinated and supervised the preparation of the questionnaires, the mailings, and the preparation of returned questionnaires for data processing. The typing of successive drafts of the manuscript was carried out with care and patience by Patricia Burns, Lutrella Taylor, Linda Norman, Barbara Lambart, Ann Wagner, and Janet Szalus, who also prepared special statistical materials.

For data processing of the study results we are indebted to Mary Toulis of the Computer Usage Development Corporation and, at TIAA, to Robert Condon, Gerald Doherty, and Sarah Coratello and her staff.

The present study, which was carried out through the facilities of the Educational Research Department of TIAA, is supplemented by two other recent benefit studies, *The Outer Fringe* (1965) and *The Mirror of Brass* (1968), published by the University of Wisconsin Press. The two earlier studies, directed by Dr. Mark H. Ingraham, were accomplished under the joint auspices of the TIAA Educational Research Department and the Association of American Colleges.

WILLIAM C. GREENOUGH
FRANCIS P. KING

New York, New York
July 1968

CONTENTS

1

INTRODUCTION

Part of the compensation of college staff members is provided through participation in benefit plans: retirement plans, group life and health insurance, and plans providing income during disability. The benefits—potential and actual—represent substantial additions to employees' earnings. For the individual and his family the plans furnish a level of protection against financial risks that salary alone cannot provide. As Mark Ingraham observed in his study, *The Outer Fringe*, "Salary is a very good way to pay people . . . Yet salary alone seldom provides the most effective compensation."[1]

For the employer the goal of the benefit program is to strengthen the institution by meeting employee needs at reasonable cost through methods that are subject to budgetary predictability and control. And benefit plans in the aggregate are important to the whole of higher education. The capacity of higher education to attract and retain able personnel and, consequently, to fulfill educational objectives is measured in part by the quality of its benefit plans.

Family financial security depends mainly on regular earned income. Benefit plans are added to deal with specific and extraordinary circumstances. Some part of salary needs to be replaced during retirement, or if there is a long period of disability, or in the event of the early death of the breadwinner. Or it needs to be augmented if there are heavy medical bills to pay.

Salary and benefits constitute the material rewards of work in higher education. But higher education, of course, offers far more than its share of nonmaterial compensation, rewards that cannot be expressed or valued in monetary terms, and which also play a large part in attracting the men and women who form the staffs of educational institutions. When teachers

[1] Ingraham, *The Outer Fringe*, pp. 3–4.

are asked why they chose their job, they usually assign highest importance to the personal satisfactions derived from work with students and professional colleagues, and to opportunities to influence the future through students and research. All these factors count for much in the rewards valued by teachers.[2] The concern of this study with material compensation should not suggest a devaluation of the nonmaterial side.

There is strong competition for the well-trained, creative mind. Ph.D.'s can also find happiness away from the college campus; it is estimated that about 41 per cent of the doctorate holders in the country do not work in academic institutions.[3] The colleges have a competitive edge in providing nonmaterial rewards, but there is a parallel need to meet the material side of the competition. Maintaining reasonably competitive salary levels is imperative. Beyond salary, the colleges have gained much through staff benefit programs of recognized quality.

PURPOSE OF THIS STUDY

The primary objective of this study is to provide information for use by trustees, regents, administrative officers, and faculty committees in their policy-making and operational roles. The report is also designed for use by other concerned persons—individual faculty members, administrative and other personnel, and those with general interests in educational administration.

It is hoped that the report will be used for a variety of purposes: (1) as a guide to the consideration of general principles of benefit planning for educational institutions and to the incorporation of these principles in viable benefit systems, (2) as an outline of the decisions to be made in the installation or review of a benefit plan, (3) as a résumé in nontechnical language of the relevant technical aspects of retirement and insurance plans, and (4) as a source of data on the types of plans in effect, their provisions, and the classes of college and university employees they cover.

The study reports on the present but is concerned with the future. Benefit plan decisions are among those that are closely related to the present and future strength of the institution, the teaching profession, and the educational system as a whole.

[2] Cf. Brown, *The Mobile Professors*, pp. 148–67.
[3] National Academy of Sciences, National Research Council, "Profiles of Ph.D.'s in the Sciences," p. 5.

SCOPE

The study covers the four major staff benefit areas: (1) retirement benefits, (2) benefits for survivors in the event of death during working years,
(3) benefits to cover the expenses of illness or injury, and (4) income benefits during disability.

The 1,530 educational institutions comprising the study universe include
all United States colleges and universities offering a bachelor's degree or
higher. The only four-year institutions excluded from the study are those
which employ no lay teachers or administrative staff (principally seminaries). The list of institutions and their classification was supplied by the
U.S. Office of Education.

The study questionnaire, reprinted in Appendix 1, was mailed January 1,
1968, to each institution's chief business officer. Questionnaire responses
were reviewed for consistency and completeness of response and subse-
quently transformed into punch card form for computer processing. Data
in questionnaires returned after March 18, 1968, are not included in the
study.

The study data were collected for three major personnel categories: (1)
faculty, (2) administrative and other professional staff not classified as
faculty, and (3) other employees. Faculty includes all personnel primarily
assigned to instruction, or to departmental, interdepartmental, or "organized" research, and academic deans and department heads. The administrative group includes administrative officers, their assistants, supervisors,
and other professional or research personnel not classified as faculty. The
third group covers clerical, secretarial, maintenance, service, and other non-
professional employees. Throughout the study the administrative group is
referred to as "administrative personnel" and the third group as "clerical-
service employees." Since employee classifications differ among institutions,
the categories used in a study of so many institutions necessarily encompass numerous variations in employee terminology.

RESPONSE

A total of 1,232 institutions, representing 80 per cent of the survey group,
responded to the survey. By type, 95 per cent of universities and 84 per cent
of liberal arts colleges responded; the response dropped to 65 per cent for

other four-year institutions, mainly professional schools and seminaries. By control, 90 per cent of public institutions and 77 per cent of private institutions responded.

Measured by numbers of employees, responses were received from institutions employing 98 per cent of university employees, 90 per cent of liberal arts college employees, and 86 per cent of the employees of other institutions. Table 1.1 summarizes the response to the study.

PREVIOUS SURVEYS

The present study is the fourth in a series published by Columbia University Press. A 1940 study covered only the retirement plans in higher education.[4] The 1948 study covered retirement and life insurance plans.[5] The 1959 study added data on health insurance and disability income plans.[6] The present study covers the same benefit areas as the 1959 study. All of the previous studies emphasized benefit planning for faculty and administrative officers. The present study reports on benefit coverage for faculty, administrative personnel, and clerical and service employees.

SUMMARY OF PLANS

Table 1.2 summarizes the extent of the benefit plans reported for each employee group. The data are given as percentages of the 1,232 responding institutions and of the total employees in the responding institutions.

COLLEGE LEADERSHIP

The generally high percentages shown in Table 1.2 reflect the considerable attention the college world has given to staff benefit planning. Colleges and universities were among the first employers to concern themselves with staff welfare and with the development of appropriate benefit plans. The retirement system for higher education provided first by the Carnegie Foundation for the Advancement of Teaching in 1906 and later by the Teachers Insurance and Annuity Association (TIAA) preceded by many years the development of significant numbers of retirement plans for employees of business and industry. In 1940 some 350 institutions of higher education had formal retirement plans, and there were only about 1,700

---

[4] Robbins, *College Plans for Retirement Income.*
[5] Greenough, *College Retirement and Insurance Plans.*
[6] Greenough and King, *Retirement and Insurance Plans in American Colleges.*

TABLE 1.1: SUMMARY OF STUDY RESPONSE

	Response				Nonresponse				Total	
	Insts	Per Cent	EEs[a]	Per Cent	Insts	Per Cent	EEs[b]	Per Cent	Insts	EEs
Universities										
Public	93	96.9	351,630	98.2	3	3.1	6,326	1.8	96	357,956
Private	65	92.9	177,406	96.7	5	7.1	6,127	3.3	70	183,533
Liberal arts colleges										
Public	218	87.6	135,406	92.0	31	12.4	11,758	8.0	249	147,164
Private	596	83.1	121,652	88.4	121	16.9	16,029	11.6	717	137,681
Other[c]										
Public	67	91.8	27,665	98.0	6	8.2	552	2.0	73	28,217
Private	193	59.4	24,588	75.9	132	40.6	7,805	24.1	325	32,393
Totals	1,232	80.5	838,347	94.5	298	19.5	48,597	5.5	1,530	886,944

[a] Total full-time faculty, administrative personnel, and clerical-service employees.

[b] Full-time faculty data for nonresponding institutions from Ralph E. Dunham and Patricia S. Wright, *Final Report: Faculty and Other Professional Staff in Institutions of Higher Education, Fall Term, 1963–64.* U.S. Department of Health, Education, and Welfare (1966). The number of nonfaculty in nonresponding institutions was estimated by multiplying the number of faculty by the average ratio, among respondents, of (1) administrative personnel and (2) clerical-service employees to the number of faculty reported.

[c] Includes teachers' colleges, technical schools and institutes, independent professional schools, fine arts schools, and theological or religious schools.

TABLE 1.2: SUMMARY OF BENEFIT PLANS REPORTED
(Per Cent of Institutions Reporting Plans and
Per Cent of Total College and University Employees
in Institutions Reporting Plans)

Type of Plan	Faculty		Administrative		Clerical-Service	
	Per Cent Insts	Per Cent EEs	Per Cent Insts	Per Cent EEs	Per Cent Insts	Per Cent EEs
	N = 1,232	N = 285,414	N = 1,232	N = 108,315	N = 1,232	N = 444,618
Retirement	95.0	99.5	92.6	99.4	74.8	94.7
Life insurance	70.1	87.4	69.6	90.4	62.7	85.1
Basic health insurance	90.0	91.6	89.8	92.8	89.8	90.3
Major medical	81.6	93.6	81.4	94.9	73.2	84.6
Short-term disability income	71.8	81.0	71.9	83.3	72.2	82.6
Long-term disability income	50.9	71.2	51.1	71.8	38.1	58.4

such plans in all of business and industry. Now practically all the colleges and universities have retirement plans and there are well over 150,000 qualified pension, stock option, and bonus plans in industry. These figures give some idea of the leading role the colleges have played in retirement planning. They also show how rapidly the benefit gap has been narrowed, enabling competitive employments to offer far greater economic security than they did three decades ago.

The colleges' leadership in benefit planning can also be measured in quality. For over half a century, TIAA college retirement plans have incorporated full funding, immediate full vesting, and transferability among employers without forfeiture of benefits, and a contractual basis for the assurance of retirement income. Readers of the recent report of the President's Committee on Corporate Pension Funds see in its recommendations for the improvement of business and industrial pension plans the whole array of principles on which these college plans have been based since 1918.[7]

The variable annuity was introduced through college plans. It was invented by TIAA and was first made available through the College Retirement Equities Fund (CREF) in 1952. CREF variable annuities are now an integral part of the retirement plans of 800 colleges and universities.

Likewise, the colleges gave attention to life insurance plans designed specifically to meet staff members' needs for a basic amount of protection. Collective insurance, first offered for college plans in the mid-thirties, introduced the concept of much higher insurance amounts for younger staff members in recognition of the heavier financial burdens of young families with children; insurance amounts then decrease as age advances and in coordination with the growing death benefits of the retirement annuity.

---

[7] President's Committee on Corporate Pension Funds and Other Private Retirement and Welfare Programs, *Public Policy and Private Pension Programs*. Among the Committee's statements were the following:

[*Funding*]: "The adequacy of funding arrangements is vital to the fulfillment of the pension promise. The value of private pension plans as a socially desirable supplement to the public retirement system depends on the degree to which accumulated funds are sufficient to pay the pension benefits of workers as they reach retirement." (p. 47)

[*Mobility*]: ". . . there is cause for concern in the selective impediments to mobility now erected by private pension plans and in the possibility that such plans in the future will not permit a rate of mobility among mature workers sufficient to accommodate a rapid rate of technological change." (pp. viii–ix)

[*Vesting*]: "The values of vesting extend beyond the interests of the participants in pension plans. Benefits to the entire economy are involved, including the strengthening of economic security for retired workers and the effective operation of the Nation's system of labor markets." (p. x)

The importance of health insurance has long been recognized by the colleges. The first hospital insurance plan was started at Baylor University in 1929, and the colleges were quick to participate in other hospital-surgical-medical plans as these were developed in the early thirties. Colleges were early, but not first, in establishing major medical expense insurance plans. They introduced group long-term total disability income plans in a new form, thus ending the long period of general unavailability of disability income coverage during and after the depression of the 1930s.

Background of College Benefit Planning

EARLY HISTORY

A study of college benefit plans starts with the early work of the Carnegie Foundation for the Advancement of Teaching, and with the concern of its founder, Andrew Carnegie, with education and its problems.

When Carnegie became a university trustee in 1890 he was shocked, he later wrote in his autobiography, "to find how small were the salaries of the professors," and concluded that for a professor to save for his old age was almost impossible. The problem made a deep impression on him, and he frequently discussed the matter with the prominent educators of the time.

A dozen years later Henry S. Pritchett, president of Massachusetts Institute of Technology, visited Carnegie at his summer home in Scotland. Asked by Carnegie about his mission in Europe, Pritchett replied, "I am searching for a $25,000 professor at a $7,500 salary." The two men talked about ways to improve the economic standing of college teaching and of the importance to teachers and to higher education of old age provisions. Carnegie had retired a few years before, had sold his steel business, and was engaged in distributing his fortune. He knew that all his millions could not greatly raise teachers' salaries, but he believed that he might help education by providing retirement allowances for teachers in leading colleges and universities. Having decided on this, he announced his gift in April, 1905, in a letter to the twenty-five educators who were to become trustees of the administering organization: [8]

---

[8] Carnegie Foundation for the Advancement of Teaching, *Annual Report*, 1906, pp. 7–8.

New York, April 16, 1905

Gentlemen:

I have reached the conclusion that the least rewarded of all the professions is that of the teacher in our higher educational institutions. New York City generously, and very wisely, provides retiring pensions for teachers in her public schools and also for her policemen. Very few indeed of our colleges are able to do so. The consequences are grievous. Able men hesitate to adopt teaching as a career, and many old professors whose places should be occupied by younger men, cannot be retired.

I have, therefore, transferred to you and your successors, as Trustees, $10,000,000 . . . the revenue from which is to provide retiring pensions for the teachers of Universities, Colleges, and Technical Schools in our country, Canada and Newfoundland under such conditions as you may adopt from time to time. Expert calculation shows that the revenue will be ample for the purpose . . . .

I hope this Fund may do much for the cause of higher education and to remove a source of deep and constant anxiety to the poorest paid and yet one of the highest of all professions.

Gratefully yours,

Andrew Carnegie

"This gift to higher education," a later report noted, "was received with general approval." The report added: "It was universally admitted that no wiser attempt could have been made to aid education than one that sought to deal in a wise and generous way with the question of the teacher's financial betterment." [9]

THE CARNEGIE FOUNDATION

The trustees proceeded at once to establish the Carnegie Foundation, incorporated in the State of New York. During the summer of 1905 they sought information from institutions of higher education throughout the United States which would lead to an assessment of the numbers of institutions eligible to participate in the pension system and of the numbers of pensions required. The first formal meeting of the newly incorporated Foundation was held at the Carnegie residence, 2 East 91st Street in New York City, at 10:00 A.M., November 15, 1905. The Foundation's first report noted that "the occasion brought together a remarkable and interesting gathering" and that "it was felt by those present that there was then being inaugurated an agency which might have a far-reaching effect upon American education." [10]

[9] *Ibid.*, p. 9.   [10] *Ibid.*, p. 10.

Among the men who arrived at 91st Street that morning were Nicholas Murray Butler of Columbia University, Charles W. Eliot of Harvard, Arthur T. Hadley of Yale, Charles C. Harrison of the University of Pennsylvania, David Starr Jordan of Stanford University, Henry C. King of Oberlin College, Henry S. Pritchett of Massachusetts Institute of Technology, Jacob Gould Schurman of Cornell, and Woodrow Wilson of Princeton. Pritchett became the first president of the Foundation.

Very few United States institutions of higher education had established pension plans before the introduction of the Carnegie free pension system. Cornell University, Columbia University, Harvard University, Randolph-Macon Woman's College, the University of California, and Yale University had plans, but they generally provided a retirement income only for long-service staff members who had remained at the institution until retirement.

A "mass of information" on American institutions of higher education was collected by the trustees, who made one of the first national surveys of higher education. It had been necessary to determine the extent of each institution's association with state government, since public institutions were not at first included. The degree of denominational control was studied, since institutions requiring officers, faculty, or students "to belong to any specified sect, or which impose any theological test" were to be excluded. The trustees also sought "to ascertain whether many of the institutions which call themselves colleges and universities are not in reality preparatory schools." [11] In the years to follow, as a result of the interest of the trustees in the character and quality of educational institutions, many of the colleges were to clarify their denominational status and others were to elevate their curriculum from a largely preparatory level.

Having sifted its collected data, the Foundation concluded that 112 institutions "would seem to be eligible to the provisions of this gift," although it noted that some of them were institutions "whose courses of instruction are partly or chiefly of a preparatory character." [12] Among the institutions the trustees found 2,653 teachers of professorial rank averaging $1,800 in annual salary. Assessing potential liabilities, it was estimated that pensions of 50 per cent of active pay might be payable to about 300 retired teachers at an annual cost of $300,000. After adding a plan for disability

[11] *Ibid.*, p. 12.   [12] *Ibid.*, pp. 13–14.

pensions for "those who break down in health and are compelled to give up active work," the total estimated annual expenditures of the Foundation, including administrative costs, were $410,000.[13] The sum was deemed to be well within the income-generating capacity of the Foundation's $10,000,000 endowment.

THE FREE PENSION SYSTEM

Early in 1906 the Foundation was reincorporated with a federal charter to reflect its national scope, and it took a new name, the Carnegie Foundation for the Advancement of Teaching. The addition of the last five words was thought to express better the intentions of Mr. Carnegie "for the upbuilding and the strengthening of the calling of the teacher." [14]

By the end of June, 1906, 52 institutions had been placed on the "accepted list" for free pensions. Retiring allowances, as they were called, had been granted to 33 professors and 4 widows. Allowances were also provided 6 professors from colleges not on the accepted list on the grounds of distinguished service to education.

The trustees' conception of the primary value of a retiring allowance system was that it strengthened the system of education itself. The retiring allowance was to be a certainty, in order to leave the teacher free to devote his working years to the work of teaching without worry about security in his old age. The trustees recognized that "there are few situations in life more full of discomfort and of anxiety than that of the man who sees old age or illness approach, with but slender means to support himself and his family." [15] They were confident that lifting the load of anxiety regarding old age or disability would increase the attractiveness of service in higher education.

The idea developed at that time—that pensions should be treated as deferred compensation fully assured for the future—became the keystone of college retirement planning in all the following years. The concept was incorporated in the successor TIAA system through the principles of the individual annuity contract and the full vesting of all contributions toward retirement income.

As to an age for teacher retirement, the Foundation took care to make clear that this was to be a matter entirely between the teachers and their

---

[13] *Ibid.*, p. 15.   [14] *Ibid.*, p. 18.   [15] *Ibid.*, p. 36.

employing institutions. The principle was early established that the pension system itself must leave this important question to those most immediately concerned.[16]

A DECADE OF EXPERIENCE

The experience and studies of the Foundation's first decade added immeasurably to the understanding of the pension needs of American higher education. The lessons learned led directly to the closing of the free pension system, to the formulation of a sound and enduring pension philosophy for higher education, and to a system for its implementation.

By 1915, 73 colleges and universities had been admitted to the group of "associated" institutions for whose faculty retiring allowances would be paid by the Foundation.[17] The initial $10,000,000 grant by Mr. Carnegie had been augmented by an additional $5,000,000 to enable the admission of public institutions to the faculty pension plan, but it had become apparent that very few more institutions could be brought in. The Foundation's income was sufficient to support free pensions in only a fraction of the growing number of colleges and universities in the country. And, since the associated institutions themselves were beginning to grow in size, it seemed unlikely that the Foundation's income could remain adequate for very long for retired faculty of these institutions.

A comprehensive review of the pension system was inaugurated by the Foundation early in 1915, and the resulting report was submitted for comment to the teachers in the associated institutions in October of that year. Discussions continued during the following year, and in November, 1916, the trustees referred a proposed successor pension plan for study to a special commission consisting of representatives from the American Association of University Professors, the Association of American Universities, the National Association of State Universities, and the Association of American Colleges. This Commission on Insurance and Annuities submitted its report April 27, 1917.

The Commission confirmed the trustees' conclusion that the Foundation's resources were insufficient to carry the burden of a free pension system for American higher education. It noted that the annual income of the Founda-

---

[16] *Ibid.*, p. 51.
[17] Carnegie Foundation for the Advancement of Teaching, *Bulletin* No. 9, 1916, p. xvi.

tion would need to be more than doubled within a generation to carry the estimated financial load just for the limited number of associated institutions, without providing "for much of any growth" or for increased salary levels. "It is clear," the Commission concluded, "that no solution of this matter can be regarded as permanent or as satisfactory for the general body of teachers in the United States and Canada which involves a constantly growing obligation dependent on a limited source." [18]

Another characteristic of the free pension system was noted by the Commission. A system for a limited number of institutions, although seemingly sound at its initiation, had led to the creation of an "educational tariff" favoring a small group, excluding a larger group, and, as the trustees later saw it, tending "to restrict the healthy migration of teachers from one college to another." [19] In considering this aspect of the problem, the Commission underlined the importance of providing pensions broadly and on a contractual basis: the successor system should be able to "furnish to the teacher the security of a contract, so that the man who enters upon the accumulation of an annuity at thirty may have a contract for its fulfillment . . .; [and] to afford these forms of protection in such manner as to leave to the teacher the utmost freedom of action, and to make his migration from one institution to another easy." [20]

Unquestionably the greatest single contribution to pension philosophy by the Carnegie free pensions was the concept of transferability. To qualify for a retiring allowance under the Foundation's rules it was not necessary that a teacher spend any specified length of time in any particular one of the associated institutions. This gave free mobility of academic talent among the associated institutions. In 1918 this concept of mobility was carried over to the much broader TIAA plan, operating within the college world. Then in 1935, thirty years after the Foundation was organized, the federal Social Security Act established transferable pension benefits for most of the American working force.

TIAA

The proposed new retirement system, which became the Teachers Insurance and Annuity Association, was approved by the Commission in its

---

[18] Carnegie Foundation for the Advancement of Teaching, *Annual Report*, 1917, pp. 69–70.
[19] Carnegie Foundation for the Advancement of Teaching, *Annual Report*, 1916, p. 22.
[20] Carnegie Foundation for the Advancement of Teaching, *Annual Report*, 1917, pp. 73–74.

1917 report. The new organization was to be established by the Carnegie
Foundation as a separately organized association to provide insurance and
deferred annuities for college staff members, with the annuity contract being
issued to the individual and based on month-by-month contributions by
the staff member and the employer. The contributions and earnings on them
would establish fully funded reserves. The contract would be the property
of the staff member who, if he wished, would be able to follow his profession in an educational world free of pension barriers.

Teachers entering the associated free pension institutions after November, 1915, and teachers in the other institutions of higher education were
to be eligible for the new contributory system. Teachers already associated
with the free pension group continued to be qualified for retiring allowances
from the Foundation under its established rules.[21]

The Carnegie Foundation's 1918 report noted that Mr. Carnegie had
been in the habit of quoting to his trustees from one of his favorite poets:
"Nae man can tether time or tide." Time had moved fast, the report concluded, between the creation of the Foundation in 1905 and the emergence
of the Association in 1918. The trustees had been called on to solve a problem of far-reaching importance. In their study of it they came in time to a
conception of a pension system widely different from that with which
they had started. "The pension system no longer faces toward the group of
teachers grown old in service," said the 1918 report, "but toward the men
entering the profession, and offers to them the machinery thru [Carnegie's
simplified spelling] which protection against dependence for themselves
and for their families may be had upon terms that are secure, that make for
a larger freedom of the individual, and that are within the reach of men on
modest salary. The change is not merely one of details; the underlying
philosophy of the pension problem has been transformed and its point of
view oriented to conform to this philosophy."[22]

PUBLIC RETIREMENT SYSTEMS

The Foundation's concern with the pension problems of higher education
on a national scale were paralleled by its encouragement of government-
sponsored retirement provisions on the local level for elementary and secondary public school teachers. The first plans for schoolteachers came into

---

[21] Carnegie Foundation for the Advancement of Teaching, *Annual Report*, 1918, p. 25.
[22] *Ibid.*, p. 20.

being in the late 1890s and in the decade that followed. By 1914, thirteen statewide teacher retirement systems were in existence and eleven states had general laws permitting the establishment of local systems.[23] Concerned with the soundness of these systems and with the development of adequate pensions for schoolteachers in other states, the Foundation began a series of studies designed to bring out a full discussion of the good and bad of the local plans. "The publication of facts," an early report stated, "together with the careful but simple discussion of the actuarial principles involved should afford the surest guidance for the future."[24]

These early public plans recognized pension needs, but the 1914 Carnegie report concluded that only in Massachusetts "is there any recognizable relation between the number and amount of the contributions and the size of the pensions."[25] The problems were numerous; contributions were arbitrarily calculated, and benefits were low. Benefits were conditioned on the absence of other "means of comfortable support" or prorated among participants from available funds.[26] Some plans were little more than relief funds.

The Foundation's reports and studies focused strong light on these plans, and on others as they came into being, and minced no words in pointing out deficiencies in basic principle. The studies were concerned mainly with furthering actuarial soundness, adequacy of funding, protection of employee contributions, and the legal assurance of benefits promised. In each of these areas there was much to be done in the early plans, and considerable effort was required to avoid similar pitfalls in the later ones. The Foundation's 1918 report on *Pensions for Public School Teachers*, prepared at the request of the Committee on Salaries, Pensions, and Tenure of the National Education Association, stimulated widespread discussion and did much to influence the legislative proposals of the ensuing years.[27] Many of the plans now covering public schoolteachers benefited from this aspect of the Foundation's concern for retirement security.

STATEMENT OF PRINCIPLES

A statement of principles for college and university retirement planning was published by the Commission on Insurance and Annuities in its 1917

---

[23] Carnegie Foundation for the Advancement of Teaching, *Annual Report*, 1914, pp. 28–36.
[24] *Ibid.*, p. 25.   [25] *Ibid.*, p. 28.   [26] *Ibid.*, pp. 31–33.
[27] The report was published as the Foundation's *Bulletin* No. 12 (1918).

report on the future of pension planning in higher education. The Commission concluded that: [28]

A college retirement system should rest upon the cooperation and mutual contributions of the colleges and the teachers.

For the assurance of the annuity there must be set aside, year by year, enough to build up a reserve adequate to meet the ultimate benefit payments.

The arrangement with the teacher should be put on a contractual basis.

Inasmuch as the annuities were to originate with colleges that were ready to install retirement systems as a matter of institutional policy, the cost of the annuities could and ought to be reduced by eliminating the element of agents' commissions from the premium schedule.

The greatest freedom of movement of the college teacher from one college to another should be provided for.

In the late 1940s a Special Joint Committee of the Association of American Colleges and the American Association of University Professors undertook a thorough study of the principles of academic retirement. The final Report of the Joint Committee and its "Statement of Principles on Academic Retirement" were formally adopted by the annual meetings of the two associations in 1950.[29] The Statement was amended in 1953 to recommend that college retirement plans concern themselves with the purchasing power of retirement annuities as well as with their dollar amount, and again in 1957 to add a brief statement on life insurance plans, medical expense insurance, and long-term total disability income provisions. In 1968 a joint committee of the two associations adopted a revision of the Statement of Principles which incorporated a more detailed discussion of retirement age provisions and of retirement income objectives, and which further spelled out recommendations regarding insurance plans. The Council of the AAUP and the Commission on College Administration of the AAC approved the joint Statement in the spring of 1968, for presentation for formal adoption by the annual meetings of the two associations in 1969. The new Statement of Principles follows.[30]

---

[28] These conclusions are summarized from "The Report of the Commission on Insurance and Annuities," Carnegie Foundation for the Advancement of Teaching, *Annual Report*, 1917.

[29] "Academic Retirement and Related Subjects," *Association of American Colleges Bulletin*, XXXVI (May, 1950), 308–28, and *American Association of University Professors Bulletin*, XXXVI (Spring, 1950), 97–117.

[30] "Statement of Principles on Academic Retirement and Insurance Plans," *American Association of University Professors Bulletin*, XLIV (Autumn, 1968), 295–297.

Statement of Principles on Academic Retirement and Insurance Plans

The purpose of an institution's retirement policy for faculty members and administrators and its program for their insurance benefits and retirement annuities should be to help educators and their families withstand the financial impacts of illness, old age, and death, and to increase the educational effectiveness of the college and university. This policy and program should be designed to attract individuals of the highest abilities to educational work, to sustain the morale of the faculty, to permit faculty members to devote their energies with singleness of purpose to the concerns of the institution and the profession, and to provide for the orderly retirement of faculty members and administrators.

The following practices are recommended:

1. The retirement policy and annuity plan of an institution, as well as its insurance plans, should:

   a. Be clearly defined and easily understandable by both the faculty and the administration of the institution. When the age of retirement is fixed, the faculty member or administrator should be reminded of his approaching retirement at least one year prior to the date on which it is to become effective. When the retirement age is flexible, he should be informed of his impending retirement at least six months prior to the date on which it is to occur, except that if he is to be retired as early as age 65, this period should be at least one year.

   b. Take into account the old age, survivor, disability, and medical benefits of federal Social Security and other applicable public programs.

   c. Permit mobility of faculty members and administrators among institutions without loss of accrued retirement benefits and with little or no gap in annuity and insurance plan participation.

   d. Be reviewed periodically by faculty and administration of the institution, with appropriate recommendations to the institution's governing board, to assure that the plans continue to meet the needs, resources, and objectives of the institution and the faculty.

2. Retirement should normally occur at the end of the academic year in which the faculty member or administrator reaches the age specified for retirement by his institution's plan. Each institution should make clear whether, for these purposes, the summer period attaches to the preceding or the forthcoming academic year. Retirement provisions currently in effect at different institutions vary in the age specified for retirement and in the degree of flexibility relating to extensions of active service. Cogent arguments can be advanced in support of a number of these arrangements. Since conditions vary greatly among institutions, however, no universally applicable formula can be prescribed. Plans in which the retirement age falls within the range of 65 to 70 appear to be in conformity with reasonable practice.

Where the institution has a flexible plan that provides for extension of service beyond its base retirement age, extensions should be by annual appointment and ordinarily should not postpone retirement beyond the end of the academic year in which age 70 is attained. Such extensions should be made upon recommendation of representatives of the faculty and administration through appropriate committee procedures that assure full protection of academic freedom. Representatives of the faculty should be chosen in accordance with procedures adopted by the faculty for committee appointment. (This also applies to the responsibilities noted in 1d, 3, and 4.)

3. Circumstances that may seem to justify a faculty member's retirement before the base retirement age in a flexible plan or the stated age in a fixed plan, or his disassociation from the institution for reasons of disability, should in all cases be considered by representatives of the faculty and administration through appropriate committee procedures. Where issues of tenure are involved in a case of retirement before the base retirement age in a flexible plan or the stated age in a fixed plan, standard procedures of due process should be available.

4. The retirement age for faculty may differ from the age for retirement for administrative duties. Cessation of administrative duties, however, with assignment of teaching responsibilities only, is not interpreted as a retirement.

5. The recall of faculty members from retired status to full or part-time activity should be by annual appointment upon recommendation of representatives of the faculty and administration through appropriate committee procedures. Such recall should be rare; expected duties should be clearly defined; and full-time service should be arranged only in unusual circumstances.

6. Between the age of 60 and retirement, faculty members should be permitted to arrange, on their own initiative, reductions in salary and services acceptable both to them and to their institutions. Such reductions in salary and services should occur without loss of tenure, rank, or eligibility for benefit plan participation.

7. The institution should provide for a plan of retirement annuities. Such a plan should:

a. Require participation after not more than one year of service by all full-time faculty members and administrators who have attained a specified age, not later than 30.

b. Be financed by contributions made during each year of service, including leaves of absence with pay, with the institution contributing as much as or more than each participant. Moreover, an institution's retirement plan should be so organized as to permit voluntary annuity contributions from employees on leaves of absence without pay. In order that participants in a contributory plan may have the tax treatment of a noncontributory plan available to them, the individual should have the option to make his required contributions by salary reduction, in accordance with relevant tax laws.

c. Maintain contributions at a level considered sufficient to give the long-term participant a retirement income that is appropriately related to his level of income prior to retirement, with provision for continuing more than half of such retirement income to a surviving spouse. The recommended objective for a person who participates in the plan for 35 or more years is an after-tax retirement income including federal Social Security benefits equivalent in purchasing power to approximately two-thirds of the yearly disposable income realized from his salary after taxes and other mandatory deductions during his last few years of full-time employment.

d. Ensure that the full accumulations from the individual's and the institution's contributions are fully and immediately vested in the individual, available as a benefit in case of death before annuity payments commence, and with no forfeiture in case of withdrawal or dismissal from the institution.

e. Be such that the individual may withdraw the accumulated funds only in the form of an annuity. To avoid administrative expense, exception might be made for very small accumulations in an inactive account.

8. The institution should help retired faculty members and administrators remain a part of the institution, providing, where possible, such facilities as: a mail address, library privileges, office facilities, faculty club membership, the institution's publications, secretarial help, administration of grants, laboratory rights, faculty dining privileges, and participation in convocations and academic processions. Institutions that confer the emeritus status should do so in accordance with standards determined by the faculty and administration.

9. When a new retirement policy or annuity plan is initiated or an old one changed, reasonable transition provisions, either by special financial arrangements or by the gradual inauguration of the new plan, should be made for those who would otherwise be adversely affected.

10. The institution should maintain a program of group insurance financed in whole or in part by the institution and available to faculty members and administrators as soon as practicable after employment. The program should continue all coverages during leave of absence with pay, and during leave without pay unless equally adequate protection is otherwise provided for the individual. The program should include:

a. Life insurance providing a benefit considered sufficient to sustain the standard of living of the staff member's family for at least one year following his death. Where additional protection is contemplated, the special financial needs of families of younger faculty members should receive particular consideration.

b. Insurance for medical expenses, with emphasis upon protection against the major expenses of illness or injury in preference to minor expenses that cause no serious drain on a family's budget. Such insurance should continue to be available through the institution (1) for the retired staff member and spouse, and (2) for the surviving spouse who does not remarry and dependent children of an active or retired staff member who dies while insured.

c. Insurance providing a monthly income for staff members who remain totally disabled beyond the period normally covered by salary continuation or sick pay. For a person who has been disabled six months or more, the plan should provide an after-tax income including federal Social Security benefits equivalent in purchasing power to approximately two-thirds of the income he realized after taxes and mandatory deductions prior to his disability. Such income should continue during total disability for the normal period of employment at the institution, with adequate provision for a continuing income throughout the retirement years.

2

RETIREMENT: TYPES OF PLANS
AND FUNDING

Over 99 per cent of faculty and administrative personnel and about 95 per cent of clerical-service personnel are employed at institutions reporting a retirement plan. Over 95 per cent of reporting institutions have a plan for faculty, 93 per cent for administrative personnel, and 75 per cent for the clerical-service groups. (See Table 2.1.)

TABLE 2.1: RETIREMENT PLANS IN INSTITUTIONS OF HIGHER EDUCATION

(Per Cent Reporting Plans)

Employee Class Covered	Per Cent Insts	Per Cent EEs
Faculty	$N = 1,232$ 95.0	$N = 285,414$ 99.5
Administrative	$N = 1,232$ 92.6	$N = 108,315$ 99.4
Clerical-Service	$N = 1,232$ 74.8	$N = 444,618$ 94.7

The retirement plan is by far the most significant staff benefit plan. It undoubtedly has more long-range influence on the institution—its educational objectives, its ability to attract the level of talent to which it aspires, and the morale of its staff members—than all the other benefit plans together. Its cost is much greater than that of the other plans; in the "total compensation" budget the retirement plan normally stands second only to salary. Because of the comprehensive nature of a college retirement plan and the various benefit provisions that should be incorporated in it, it should greatly influence the design of the other plans, such as life insurance and disability income insurance. For these reasons a substantial part of this book is concerned with retirement planning in its various aspects.

The institutions reporting no retirement plan for faculty and administrative personnel employ about one-half of 1 per cent of these two employee classes. Institutions reporting no plan for clerical-service groups employ 5 per cent of the total for this group. Virtually all of the institutions without plans are small private colleges, mainly degree-granting professional and theological schools and Catholic liberal arts colleges that have only recently begun to add full-time lay faculty to a religious or diocesan teaching staff.

Types of Plans

Retirement plans in higher education fall into the following categories:
1. Teachers Insurance and Annuity Association and College Retirement Equities Fund (TIAA-CREF).
2. Governmental retirement systems, including state employee systems, state teacher systems, municipal systems, and the U.S. Civil Service retirement system.
3. Self-administered or trusteed retirement plans.
4. Commercial insurance company plans.
5. Church pension plans.

In most institutions, just one of the above plans covers all of the institution's retirement plan participants. In some, however, more than one retirement plan is in operation. For instance, a new faculty member or administrative officer joining the staff of a component institution of the State University of New York (SUNY) has the option of joining the New York State Teachers Retirement System, the New York State Employees Retirement System, or TIAA-CREF. SUNY institutions thus report three retirement systems for faculty and administrative personnel, although an individual is covered by only one plan. An example of concurrent participation is provided by the West Virginia publicly supported institutions. The West Virginia State Teachers Retirement System is supplemented by a TIAA-CREF plan for which all employees earning over $4,800 are eligible.

Table 2.2 shows the distribution of retirement plans in responding institutions according to type of plans reported. Generally speaking, the pub-

TABLE 2.2: TYPES OF RETIREMENT PLANS REPORTED[a]

Type of Plan	Faculty		Administrative		Clerical-Service	
	Per Cent Insts N = 1,170	Per Cent EEs N = 283,986	Per Cent Insts N = 1,141	Per Cent EEs N = 107,705	Per Cent Insts N = 921	Per Cent EEs N = 420,974
State teacher retirement system	17.9	32.0	16.7	17.4	8.9	9.3
State employee retirement system	8.4	15.2	12.9	21.8	22.8	32.6
Single state system for teachers and others	6.7	12.6	6.8	11.7	8.5	11.2
TIAA-CREF	63.8	53.3	61.3	59.1	39.2	24.3
Self-administered or trusteed	7.3	8.8	8.2	20.9	13.2	27.3
Church pension plan	13.8	3.7	12.3	3.0	8.1	1.5
Insurance company	9.6	5.0	10.2	5.0	10.2	7.1
Other	2.4	3.5	2.3	4.0	2.5	3.0

[a] Percentages add to over 100 per cent because more than one plan (for alternative or concurrent participation) was reported by some institutions.

lic retirement systems, and the TIAA-CREF system covering both public and private institutions, constitute the main sources of retirement coverage in higher education. Seventy-two different public retirement systems cover faculty or other staff members at various state universities, colleges, state teachers' colleges, and other institutions.

TIAA-CREF plans for faculty are reported by nearly two-thirds of the institutions, employing a little over half of faculty. Public retirement plans for faculty are reported by a third of the institutions, employing 60 per cent of faculty. Thus there is some overlap between public plans and TIAA-CREF. Public plans are available for half of the administrative personnel; TIAA-CREF plans are available for 60 per cent of the administrative personnel. In the study a decade ago, TIAA-CREF plans were reported by half the institutions, employing 45 per cent of total faculty, and public retirement plans were reported by 31 per cent of the institutions, employing a third of total faculty. The fact that the proportion of institutions with public plans has scarcely changed but faculty covered increased from one-third of the total to 60 per cent shows the extraordinary growth in size of public institutions. The increase in TIAA-CREF plans during the ten-year period was due in part to the adoption of such plans by publicly supported institutions as either successors, alternates, or overrides to a public plan.

For clerical-service employees, TIAA-CREF plans are reported by 39 per cent of institutions, employing 24 per cent of personnel in this category. Public retirement plans for clerical-service employees are reported by 40 per cent of institutions, employing 53 per cent of personnel. One other type, the self-administered or trusteed plan, covers significant numbers of clerical-service employees: 13 per cent of institutions, employing 27 per cent of such personnel.[1]

Principles of Retirement Planning

A college's retirement plan can help or hinder the achievement of the institution's educational objectives. If the plan is to help, it must be based on principles consistent with the educational aims of the institution. In order to make certain that the retirement plan makes a positive contribution to the educational objectives of the college, those responsible for its design

[1] The table below outlines the known distribution of retirement plans among the 298 institutions which did not respond to the survey. The nonrespondents represent 20 per cent of

must have a clear understanding of the many things a retirement plan can accomplish for the institution, for its staff members, and for higher education as a whole.

College boards of trustees, administrative officers, and faculty representatives indicate that well-designed retirement plans help them achieve vital objectives:

1. To effect the orderly retirement of superannuated employees with an income sufficient to meet their future needs.
2. To attract promising new talent.
3. To retain above-average staff members.
4. To part more easily before retirement with those who are not measuring up to the college's standards.

ORDERLY RETIREMENT

Most people seek independence in old age: freedom from financial worries, freedom from dependence on other people, freedom to throw off the harness of work when infirmities make it burdensome, freedom to pursue hobbies and studies. The manner in which a college helps its staff members look forward to security in retirement also influences their effectiveness during their working years.

---

the institutions to which questionnaires were sent, and about 5 per cent of all employees in four-year institutions of higher education.

TYPES OF RETIREMENT PLANS IN NONRESPONDING INSTITUTIONS

Types of Plan	Faculty		Administrative		Clerical-Service	
	Per Cent Insts N = 298	Per Cent EEs N = 16,624	Per Cent Insts N = 298	Per Cent EEs N = 6,207	Per Cent Insts N = 298	Per Cent EEs N = 25,766
State teacher retirement system	6.0	18.4	3.4	7.2	3.0	5.7
State employee retirement system	—	—	2.3	10.8	2.7	12.1
Single state system for teachers and others	4.7	7.3	4.7	6.9	4.7	7.0
TIAA-CREF	19.5	31.7	16.8	29.9	7.7	8.0
Self-administered or trusteed	0.7	5.0	0.4	1.8	0.4	1.8
Church pension plan	13.0	6.4	12.8	6.2	9.0	5.1
Insurance company	1.3	2.4	1.3	2.5	0.4	0.1
Other	0.7	0.8	0.7	0.8	0.7	0.8
No information	54.1	28.0	57.6	33.9	71.4	59.4
Totals	100.0	100.0	100.0	100.0	100.0	100.0

A means for the orderly retirement of superannuated employees is essential, whatever the institution's definition of superannuation. Barring earlier death, departure, or retirement, virtually all employees outlive their period of useful service to the college. Retention of teachers and administrators long after they can perform their work competently is detrimental to the students, and can also lead to the dissatisfaction or departure of younger colleagues who see that promotions do not become available as they should. The institution, as well as the individual, gains from the presence of a systematic method of replacing earnings with retirement income.

ATTRACTING AND HOLDING ABLE MEN

In seeking able men for teaching, research, and administrative positions, colleges are in constant competition not only with other colleges, but also with business and industrial employment and with government. The monetary returns from college employment are still not great compared with those of some other professions. Yet colleges have the services of many of America's outstanding men and women. One reason is that the college staff member can look forward to reasonable security throughout his life.

For more than fifty years, fully vested college retirement plans have proved advantageous in attracting superior staff members, because these plans recognize that many of the able men and women in higher education and in research may, during their lifetime, serve in a number of positions in different colleges, universities, research organizations, or foundations.

The freedom to move is as important as movement itself. Many faculty and other staff members remain at one college for their entire career. But free choice in the matter is important, even if the person has no intention of leaving. Over the years, colleges and individuals change. No one can be certain that he will not want to change employers in the future.

Both colleges and staff members benefit from movement of personnel among institutions. If good professors are poorly placed, the whole system of higher education pays a penalty. Geographic and economic barriers have no place in higher education. As noted by David G. Brown in his study of academic job changes, the labor market for professionals in higher education is defined by high training costs, high skill levels, and high experience levels. As a result, the market is dependent on a broad mobility. "Whereas the local labor market concept has meaning for occupations where retraining workers is cheaper and faster than relocating, in the professions the costs of training and the benefits of experience dictate that employers draw boundaries that are related to what a man can do instead of how convenient it is for him to come." [2]

A great many industrial-type or governmental pension plans provide no vested benefits, or no vesting of benefits until 10 or 15 years of service, or until some such age as 40 or 45. For the individual such plans incorporate either a forfeiture of security if he accepts another position before meeting the vesting requirement, or the alternative of reluctantly remaining where he is so as not to forfeit benefits, an alternative referred to as "economic peonage." Either one is anathema to a college professor.

The factors that help a college attract good men also help to hold them. The maintenance of a healthy "climate" for the work of scholars in American colleges and universities is considered essential. It is the legitimate hope of a young man who has already shown ability in a scholarly field that he will become an authority in his specialty and will perhaps assume responsibility for leading a group of able and progressive associates. In deciding whether to stay with a particular college, he will usually consider whether he can expect to grow in eminence and responsibility at that institution and whether the positions above him will be cleared through a systematic retirement procedure. A plan designed to meet the special needs of college faculties has a good effect on the development of the institution and on the well-being of its staff members.

PARTING BEFORE RETIREMENT

From time to time there are individuals whose professional growth in a particular atmosphere becomes inhibited. For any one of a variety of causes a promising beginner may later fail to live up to his excellent prospects: his abilities may have been misjudged, there may be a lack of opportunity for advancement in his special fields of interest, or there may be a conflict in personalities that interferes with his progress. When such situations develop, it is often mutually advantageous for the person and the college that he

[2] Brown, *The Mobile Professors*, p. 169.

move on to other employment. But individuals employed by colleges with forfeiture retirement plans often say quite frankly that they cannot afford at their age to sacrifice their accrued retirement benefits by leaving the college. So they serve out their time, perhaps conscious that their own advancement and the health of the college would have been aided by a change.

An outstanding man usually can command enough salary in another position to make it worth his while to leave if he so wishes, despite forfeiture of retirement benefits. Therefore the forfeiture plan will not of itself hold him. Some, indeed, will see the economic advantage in "getting out while the getting is good," that is, while the pension loss is still moderate. But a forfeiture plan will have its greatest holding effect on the person whose abilities are limited and who, if offered another job, may find that its advantages do not compensate for the loss of retirement benefits.

IMPLEMENTING OBJECTIVES

The retirement system used by an institution of higher education should be able to carry out the general objectives outlined above. In the remainder of this chapter the systems are discussed in terms that relate to their effect on these objectives. The analysis is devoted to the important differences between types of plans with respect to death, disability, and retirement benefits, contributions, vesting, funding, investment, maintenance of purchasing power, and various options and flexibilities.

A résumé of general annuity principles makes a helpful introduction to a discussion of retirement systems.

The Annuity Concept

Retirement systems are (or should be) basically rather simple. A funded retirement plan is a savings process followed by a lifetime pay-out system. During working years, funds are gradually accumulated by setting aside and investing employer and employee contributions. At retirement the accumulated contributions and their investment earnings become the basis for the retirement annuity.[3]

---

[3] The term pension appears frequently in governmental retirement plans and usually refers to that part of the retirement income based on the contributions or benefit promise of the state or other public employer.

THE ANNUITY

An annuity is a pooling of resources by many people in order that each may be protected against the financial risk of "living too long." Without annuities, retired persons may try to live on only the interest earned by their life's savings, keeping the principal intact; or they may draw on both principal and interest, apprehensive that they may live too long and use up all the principal prematurely. An annuity organization, working with thousands of annuitants, spreads both principal and interest over the lifetimes of all retired persons no matter how long they live. This assures each of them a much larger income than they would receive from interest earnings alone.

INCOME OPTIONS

One use of annuity principles is to provide a lifetime income for two persons. This is necessary when the retiring employee wishes to make sure that a lifetime income continues to his widow after his death. Hence the income options offered by virtually all retirement systems. A frequently selected option provides the surviving husband or wife two-thirds of the income received when both husband and wife were living, the "joint and two-thirds to survivor" option. The various options available in college retirement plans are discussed in Chapter 3.

Accumulating Retirement Funds

To provide adequate benefits, regular contributions to the plan, normally by both employer and employee, should begin as early as practicable in the working career. The AAUP-AAC Statement recommends that retirement plan participation begin not later than age 30. If retirement is at age 65, this provides for thirty-five years of fund accumulation to support a benefit period that must on the average span about sixteen years for a man and about twenty years for a woman.

A timely start with adequate regular contributions is important. To produce a reasonable benefit amount, accumulation periods of less than thirty or so years require disproportionately large contributions because of the shorter period for payment of contributions and for compounding of investment earnings.

The method of defining pension rights—whether in terms of the input (*contributions* as a percentage of salary) or of the output (*benefits* as a percentage of salary)—has an important effect on the plan's funding pattern, that is, how much money is to be paid on behalf of each participant and when. The funding pattern strongly influences the distribution of total compensation among individuals participating in the plan, the overall cost of the plan, and the degree of budgetary control held by the institution in funding its pension liabilities. The two principal approaches to defining pension rights under college and university retirement plans are "defined contribution" (money purchase) and "defined benefit" (unit benefit). The defined *contribution* approach fixes contributions in advance as a percentage of each person's salary. The defined *benefit* approach fixes benefits in advance as a percentage of salary for each year of service, or occasionally as a flat dollar amount.

DEFINED CONTRIBUTION APPROACH

This approach establishes employer and employee contributions as a percentage of current salary, deposits them each month on behalf of the participants, and credits the earnings of the pension fund's investments to the participants' accounts. For example, the contributions might be 12 per cent of salary, 5 per cent being contributed by the employee and 7 per cent by the employer.

Nearly all TIAA-CREF plans in higher education use the defined contribution approach. Many of the church pension systems and insurance company plans, as well as some of the public retirement systems, also use this approach. Contribution patterns for these plans and illustrative benefits are discussed in Chapter 3. Prospectively, the great majority of them do a good job of meeting the AAUP-AAC objective of a disposable retirement income for husband and wife, including Social Security, equal to two-thirds of preretirement disposable earnings.

Under the defined contribution approach a specified and known amount of money, when paid to the participant's vested annuity each month, is clearly his as part of his total compensation. Future investment earnings are credited to the individual's annuity instead of being used to reduce employer costs. His benefit is the retirement income that can be purchased by employer and employee contributions and credited investment earnings.

From the standpoint of both the college and the staff member, full funding of current service benefits occurs at the time the service is rendered. Salary increases do not raise the college's pension liabilities for all service accrued prior to the increase, as is automatically true under final average salary defined benefit arrangements. Budgeting and forecasting of costs are simple: the employer's cost is the rate of employer contributions multiplied by the salary of plan participants.

DEFINED BENEFIT APPROACH

This approach establishes benefits as a predetermined percentage of salary for each year of service. The salary is normally expressed either as the average salary over the period of plan participation, the "career average," or as the average salary over a designated period of service just preceding retirement, the "final average." For example, a formula might provide for a retirement benefit at age 65 equal to 1½ per cent of the person's "final-five" or "high-five" average salary times years of service. After 35 years of service for one employer, this formula would assure an employee a retirement income starting at age 65 equal to 52.5 per cent of the average salary he earned from age 60 to age 65. If expressed in terms of postretirement compared with preretirement disposable income, this formula would also approximate the two-thirds disposable income goal.

Under the defined benefit approach, the participant can accurately predict the ratio of retirement benefits to final average salary but he cannot predict with certainty the number of dollars of annuity income he will receive during retirement, unless his salary prospects before retirement are known to him. The benefit is fixed by formula, and the investment experience of the pension funds affects the employer's cost, not the amount of the individual's benefit.

Nearly all defined benefit plans in the colleges are contributory, with employee contributions being a fixed percentage of current salary, withheld and deposited in the employee's annuity account to help purchase the formula benefit. If the plan is currently funded, employer contributions are made in whatever amounts are considered necessary, usually on recommendation of the plan's actuary, to purchase the portion of the prospective formula benefits not purchased by employee contributions. Since the price of a given amount of deferred annuity benefit increases as the period remaining until retirement shortens, the employer's contributions on behalf of each individual increase greatly with age. The actual amount of yearly employer contributions for individual participants is not announced to them, only averages covering all people at all ages.

CONTRASTING DEFINED CONTRIBUTION
AND DEFINED BENEFIT APPROACHES

Perhaps the most specific way to explain the differences between these two approaches in contribution patterns, in vesting, in funding, and in benefits at and before retirement, is to take a given retirement benefit and see how it can be financed by employer and employee contributions during the working years. Table 2.3 shows the percentage of salary needed at various ages, starting at age 30, to purchase an annuity at age 65 that will equal 1½ per cent of final-five average salary (i.e., 52.5 per cent of final-five average salary) for a person who stays until retirement. The table compares the defined contribution and defined benefit approaches. The employee is assumed to contribute 5 per cent of his salary at all ages under either plan; this is a typical employee contribution rate under both approaches. The illustration uses the same actuarial factors for both approaches, including an assumption that salary increases at a rate of 4 per cent a year.

Under the defined contribution approach a level percentage contribution of 9.5 per cent of salary by the employer at all ages is needed, in addition to the 5 per cent employee contribution, to purchase the benefit. Using this approach, the staff member in a vested plan has a deferred compensation right with respect to 9.5 per cent additional salary each year. The employer joins proportionately, year by year, with the employee in financing his benefits. Under the defined contribution approach, employer contributions are fixed and moderate throughout. The accumulated funds for a person starting in his twenties, thirties, or forties are materially higher throughout his entire period of service until he retires. Death benefits are substantially higher during the working years. Even so, the employer's total contributions over an individual's working lifetime are smaller than under a defined benefit plan because of greater investment earnings arising from the larger accumulations built up in the early years.

Under the defined benefit approach the employer contributions range

TABLE 2.3: COMPARISON OF DEFINED CONTRIBUTION
AND DEFINED BENEFIT APPROACHES

(Contribution Rates at Quinquennial Ages to Purchase the Same Final Benefit[a])

Employee's Attained Age (Male)	Contribution Rate as Per Cent of Salary			Contribution Amount in Dollars		
	Employee Contributions, Either Approach 1	Employer Contributions		Employee Contributions, Either Approach 4	Employer Contributions	
		Defined Contribution Approach 2	Defined Benefit Approach 3		Defined Contribution Approach 5	Defined Benefit Approach 6
30	5%	9.5%	-1.19%	$ 400	$ 759	$ -95
35	5	9.5	0.22	487	924	26
40	5	9.5	2.60	592	1,124	308
45	5	9.5	5.76	720	1,367	830
50	5	9.5	10.03	876	1,663	1,758
55	5	9.5	15.75	1,066	2,024	3,359
60	5	9.5	23.58	1,297	2,462	6,118
64	5	9.5	31.27	1,518	2,880	9,490

[a] Final retirement benefit under both approaches equals 52.5 per cent of final-five average salary (1½ per cent of final average salary times 35 years of service). Death benefits reflect accumulated contributions to date under each plan and thus are higher throughout in the defined contribution approach. For dollar amounts of contribution a starting salary of $8,000 is assumed, commencing at age 30, increasing 4 per cent a year to $28,000 as the final-five average salary.

from "minus 1.19 per cent" (no employer contribution) at age 30 to more than 31 per cent of salary at age 64, as shown in column 3. Under this approach the younger employee's own contributions more than cover the cost of the benefit promised him for that year. Even with full and immediate vesting of employer contributions, the vesting provision has little value below age 40 because the employer contributions are small or nonexistent. Thus at the earlier ages, when job decisions are being made, the retirement plan adds little or nothing in terms of compensation. An individual changing employment takes with him a right to benefits related to his five-year average salary just before leaving, not to his five-year average salary immediately preceding retirement.

As the individual's age increases, employer contributions for him under the final average salary defined benefit approach rise rapidly in order, each year, to fund: (1) the additional cost of the current year's benefits at the higher age, and (2) if salary has been increased that year, the cost of funding the higher average salary formula benefits for all previous years. At the older ages the amounts necessary to buy a given benefit during the smaller number of years to retirement, and the "catch-up" for increases in benefits for prior years' service, become substantial. They may reach a third of salary close to retirement. The contributions as a percentage of salary required during the later years are much larger because small contributions not only purchased relatively small benefits in the early years but also produced smaller investment earnings than would have been provided under a defined contribution approach. This has important budgetary implications, especially during a period of salary inflation.

Columns 4, 5, and 6 of Table 2.3 present the dollar amounts of contribution necessary to fund the same final benefit under the two approaches. The percentage contributions shown in the first three columns are multiplied by a salary scale of $8,000 at age 30, increasing 4 per cent a year to a final-five average of $28,000 between ages 60 and 65 (Scale B, Chapter 3). Under both approaches the employee's 5 per cent of salary contribution results in a rising annual dollar amount of contribution ranging from $400 a year at age 30 to $1,518 at age 64. Under the defined contribution approach the employer contributes 9.5 per cent of salary throughout, resulting in dollar amounts paid by the employer increasing in direct proportion to the individual's increasing contributions as salary increases, and ranging from $759 to $2,880. Under the defined benefit approach, applying the increasing rates of employer contributions necessary for funding the final benefit results in employer contributions of "minus $95" (or zero) at age 30, reaching $9,490 by age 65. The implications of *de minimus* vesting for the younger individual and budgetary problems for the employer with respect to the total cost of its salary and benefit plan administration are significant.[4]

The differences between the two approaches become even more crucial if the retirement plan includes a variable annuity. The younger staff member participating in a defined contribution plan will have a long period of substantial, evenly distributed, employer contributions invested in his variable annuity, and this can be expected to provide substantial accumulated retirement funds. Under the defined benefit approach the absence of employer contributions in the early years and the heavy concentration of employer contributions in the late years bring in a short-term speculative factor—the risk of investing substantial sums in common stocks at a high level of the market.

Funding

In some retirement plans it is possible to accumulate promises but not supporting funds. This is particularly true of "prior service benefits," that is, those promised for service rendered prior to the installation or updating of an institution's retirement plan. But it is also true of benefits currently being earned under many plans, and it is therefore important to examine the degree of funding of the current retirement obligations being undertaken. Some plans are fully funded; others are only partially funded; and some are not funded at all.

[4] On this point the President's 1965 cabinet-level committee on pensions said:
". . . there is cause for concern in the selective impediments to mobility now erected by private pension plans and in the possibility that such plans in the future will not permit a rate of mobility among mature workers sufficient to accommodate a rapid rate of technological change.

Employers should be encouraged to adopt more widely those types of pension plans which do not involve significantly higher costs for older workers, in preference to those types which involve greater differences in cost between new employees in different age groups." (President's Committee on Corporate Pension Funds and Other Private Retirement and Welfare Programs, *Public Policy and Private Pension Programs: A Report to the President on Private Employee Retirement Plans*, pp. viii–ix.)

FULLY FUNDED PLANS

Under fully funded plans, for each portion of service rendered to the institution by the employee, a sum of money is concurrently set aside to provide future retirement income related to that service. A fully funded plan might be defined as one which, if it had to be closed out at any time, would already have enough money in it to meet, with future investment earnings, all obligations for benefits accrued under the plan from its inception to its termination.

A fully funded plan obviously derives more from investment earnings than an unfunded or partially funded plan. For example, at 5 per cent interest compounded annually, a $100 deposit made at a participant's age 35 will have increased to $432 by the time he has reached age 65. If, on the other hand, benefits are not to be funded until retirement, instead of depositing $100 in advance the employer must produce over four times that amount at retirement. A fully funded plan makes full use of the investment earnings capacity of the pension program and helps reduce the ultimate number of employer or employee dollars needed to provide retirement benefits.

Full funding assures an institution and its staff members that all obligations to participants are currently and fully discharged as service is rendered. From the accounting standpoint the full cost of "production" is known and is fully charged to the period when the "production" occurred. Each individual knows that funds are actually in being to support benefits, and that retirement benefits will be forthcoming on schedule. In the colleges and universities, TIAA-CREF is the largest system of fully funded plans.

PARTIALLY FUNDED PLANS

These plans range from those that would be more accurately described as nonfunded to those that are close to being fully funded. A few plans use terminal funding; that is, rather than accumulating funds before retirement, a single sum purchase of an annuity is made at the time each individual retires. Terminal funding confronts the employer with the problem of the very large contributions necessary, without the help of prior investment earnings, to support the benefits. It also confronts him with substantial variations in the number of employees reaching retirement age and therefore in the size of the lump sum payments that must be provided in a given year regardless of the employer's other financial problems at the time.

Most state teacher and public employee systems do not fully fund their current benefit liabilities. Employee contributions are, of course, withheld from salary and paid directly to the system, and this provides for a partial funding of total benefits promised. But, beyond this, the degree of current funding of currently earned benefits varies considerably among public plans. Sometimes public appropriations cover only the actual benefits expected to be paid out during the following legislative biennium, so that even the benefits already being paid are not financed beyond the next legislative session. Other plans bring benefits up to the fully funded level only as individuals reach retirement age, a form of terminal funding. Still others are working toward higher levels of partial funding or full funding of current service benefits. Proposals for the improvement of vesting provisions have frequently exposed to public view the need for sounder financial support of the obligations assumed by a plan.

The readers of the reports of actuarial consultants and auditors of public plans will note the frequency of recommendations for more adequate levels of funding. The reports emphasize the importance to plan stability of limiting, through sound financial planning, the extent to which future legislatures must be asked to provide funds for benefits promised years before their time. For example, ever since its establishment in 1941, the State Universities Retirement System of Illinois has had an accumulating unfunded liability. A recent examination of the system by an independent auditor noted that "At August 31, 1967, unfunded reserve requirements for accrued pension credits approximated $143,600,000 as computed by the actuary retained by the System."[5]

A corrective step, however, was taken in September, 1967, by the Illinois legislature, which amended the Pension Code to require henceforth that current service liabilities be fully funded. Although the new requirement does not reduce the unfunded liability, it should stem any further shifting of accrued liabilities to future generations.

A 1966 actuarial study of the Connecticut State Employees Retirement

---

[5] State Universities Retirement System, Illinois, *Annual Report for the Year Ended August 31, 1967*, p. 7.

System indicates that, if the present "pay-as-you-go" program (no advance funding) continues, "the projected unfunded accrued liability for prior service of active employees and for the roll of pensioners will increase from $279,288,000 as of July 1, 1966 to $627,276,000 on July 1, 1976, to $1,296,403,000 on July 1, 1991 and to $3,203,578,000 on July 1, 2016." [6]

Increases in benefit levels or the removal of ceilings on the amount of salary on which benefits are calculated often lead to increased unfunded liabilities. A consulting actuary's 1964 report on the Public Employees Retirement System of Nevada states: "Since the last valuation date, there have been substantial increases in basic benefit liabilities because of amending the act to remove the $600 salary limit. The only increases in contributions available as an offset to this large increase in cost are the increases in *future* contributions. A small part of the increased costs has been absorbed because of the increased interest earnings on the invested funds. Nevertheless, the net result of removing the salary limitation has been to cause a substantial increase in the unfunded liability of the system." [7]

"Final-average" plans face a continuing concern in maintaining adequate funding levels, since benefits are defined as a percentage of salary levels toward the end of a career, but contributions are normally related to salary year by year. As salary levels rise, considerable underfunding develops unless there are annual upward funding adjustments.

NONFUNDED PLANS

In recent years the number of wholly unfunded college retirement plans, never large, has declined. The University of Kentucky's "change of work" retirement plan was replaced in 1964 by a TIAA-CREF plan. Louisiana State University reports a noncontributory, nonfunded retirement plan for faculty members; other employees participate in the state plan for public employees.

In nonfunded retirement plans neither the individual nor the college makes contributions toward future benefits during the period in which the

---

[6] State of Connecticut, *Report on the State Government Personnel Study* (1967), Vol. III, "Actuarial Report on the State Retirement System," by Russell O. Hooker and Associates, Consulting Actuaries, p. 1.

[7] State of Nevada, Public Employees Retirement Board, "Fourth Actuarial Report" (1965), by Coates, Herfurth and England, Consulting Actuaries, pp. 61–62.

individual renders service to the institution. During retirement the needed funds are provided on a "pay-as-you-go" basis. The benefits must then be financed solely by the college without the help of investment earnings and without individual contributions. This is done from current budget, through special money-raising efforts, and perhaps at the salary expense of the younger people in the group. As there is no prior financing, there are no accumulating investment earnings or capital gains on invested retirement funds to help finance the benefits. Risks are undertaken because of the substantial mortality fluctuations that occur within small groups of retired people. These factors lead to much higher eventual costs per dollar of benefits paid, compared with funded plans.

For the active staff, if no money is being accumulated currently, little is accomplished in the way of assurance of retirement benefits commensurate with service to the institution. In effect, the remaining nonfunded plans offer a scenario from the days preceding the Carnegie free pension system, when, if benefits were payable at all for retired college employees, they were paid from current budget and available only to those who stayed until retirement.

COLLEGE AND UNIVERSITY RETIREMENT SYSTEMS

The remaining part of this chapter describes the principal retirement systems covering employees in higher education: TIAA-CREF, public employee and state teacher systems, self-administered or trusteed plans, insurance company plans, and church plans.

TIAA-CREF

TIAA-CREF is a nationwide retirement system limited to colleges, universities, independent schools, and certain other institutions that are nonprofit and, in addition, are engaged primarily in education or research. The development of TIAA from the efforts of the Carnegie Foundation for the Advancement of Teaching is described in Chapter 1. CREF (College Retirement Equities Fund), established in 1952, is a companion organization to TIAA and has the same nonprofit status and limited eligibility. CREF provides a variable annuity, invented by TIAA as a means of helping to maintain the purchasing power of annuity income through lifetime common stock investments.

Each plan in the TIAA-CREF system is established by resolution of the educational institution's governing board. The institution determines for itself, and states in its resolution, the provisions governing employee eligibility, waiting periods, the employer and employee contribution rates, contributions during leaves of absence, prior service benefits, the age of retirement, and extensions of service, if any, beyond the normal retirement age. In the case of public institutions the plan is established by a board of regents or through enabling legislation and subsequent institutional resolution. The retirement resolution is the working agreement between the institution and the participants in its plan. Resolution provisions differ among institutions. The provisions of plans in the TIAA-CREF system are shown institution by institution in Appendix 4.

THE ANNUITY CONTRACT

The agreement between the participant and the retirement system is provided by the individual TIAA and CREF annuity contracts. The contractual provisions, which are uniform throughout the TIAA-CREF system, specify the payment of annuity and preretirement death benefits, the income options available, the right of the individual to pay additional premiums, the right to change the date for commencing annuity benefits, and the like. The employer and employee contributions for each participant are paid into the individual annuity contracts, which are immediately and fully vested in the participant. Investment of funds, fund accounting, actuarial functions, and payment of benefits are the responsibility of TIAA and CREF. The system thus permits each educational institution to mold its plan to suit its own situation, while safeguarding the right of each participant to the benefits earned during each pay period.

Staff Member Owns Contract. The guarantee of immediate full vesting for each participating staff member is one of the most significant features of the retirement plans using TIAA and CREF annuities. From the day the staff member's first annuity premium is paid he assumes full ownership of all retirement and survivor benefits purchased by his own and his employer's contributions. It is the ownership of the contract that gives the individual the assurance that funds are actually being set aside to support him during his retirement and that no future change of the retirement plan, differences of opinion with an employer, or other such circumstances can deprive him of retirement income already set aside for him.

No Cash or Loan Value. As a corollary to full vesting, TIAA and CREF annuities do not provide cash surrender or loan values. The primary purpose of a retirement plan is to assure the individual that funds will be available to finance the retirement benefit. This assurance applies to employers as well. Employers quite properly would be reluctant to contribute to a fully vested annuity contract that could be turned in for cash or mortgaged at the staff member's request. The institution is assured that the funds it contributes will be used solely for their intended purpose, that of providing retirement income or death benefits for the staff member and his family.[8]

No Forfeitures—No Penalties. Benefits purchased by premiums already paid are not affected if a person suspends further premium payments. Whether premiums are continued or not, whether the policyholder remains in academic work or not, whether the employing institution continues to share in premiums or not—none of these alternatives has any effect on benefits purchased by premiums already paid.

Death Benefit. If the policyholder dies before he begins to receive annuity payments, the full accumulation in the contract is payable to the named beneficiary or to the estate; if to the former, the policyholder may choose among several income payment methods or may leave this choice to be made by the beneficiary. A single sum payment is available if (1) the policyholder's estate, or a corporation, association, or partnership is the beneficiary; (2) the beneficiary is other than the policyholder's widow; or (3) the policyholder's contributing institution has agreed to a single sum settlement for widows.

Choice of Retirement Date. Annuity income usually commences, but need not, at the time the individual retires from the college. The policyholder may have annuity payments begin on the first of any month, but normally not later than age 71. The Association's practice is to allow deferment beyond age 71 if employment continues beyond that age.

Choice of Income Arrangement. The policyholder may choose among

---

[8] Within established rules, small-amount or short-term annuities will be "repurchased" if requested by the individual *and* approved by the institution.

various forms of lifetime income on retirement. Selection among the options may be made at any time before income payments begin. The various options are described in Chapter 3.

Premium Payments. Each premium on a TIAA retirement annuity purchases a definite, guaranteed annuity benefit at the rates in effect when the premium is paid. Dividends, as declared, purchase additional annuity benefits. Each premium on a CREF retirement annuity purchases a definite number of CREF accumulation units (described later in this chapter). The participant's *pro rata* share of CREF dividend income purchases additional accumulation units. The total annuity premium, including the individual's and the college's contributions, may be applied to a TIAA contract, or, if applied to a combined TIAA-CREF annuity, not less than 25 per cent nor more than 75 per cent may be allocated to either TIAA or CREF, the balance being allocated to the other organization, subject to the provisions of the participating institution's retirement plan. Policyholders may, if they wish, pay additional annuity premiums to TIAA or to TIAA-CREF on their own within the same allocation rules, either periodically or as additional single premiums.

TIAA INVESTMENTS

Premiums paid to TIAA annuity contracts are invested primarily in the bonds and direct placement obligations of corporations and in mortgages.

Mortgages provide relatively high yield and make suitable investments for a retirement fund because of the low liquidity requirements of funds being invested for the long term. In 1967, mortgage loans made up 53 per cent of the value of TIAA investments. Residential properties, with mortgages guaranteed by the Veterans Administration or insured by the Federal Housing Administration, secure just under half of these mortgage loans. The remainder are secured by "conventional" mortgages on property used for income-producing purposes, including apartment houses, office buildings, stores, manufacturing facilities, and shopping centers. These mortgages carry a higher prospective yield than do loans with government guarantees or insurance.

Bonds constitute 38 per cent of TIAA investments and include debt obligations of governments, public utilities, and of business and industrial corporations. Loans made directly to corporations account for a substantial portion of TIAA bond investments. These direct placements usually offer a higher yield than publicly offered bonds available at the time the commitment is made. Remaining investments are in income-yielding real estate and in common stocks.

CREF

Before CREF was established in 1952, pension planning had not produced any satisfactory means of giving a retired person some continuing protection against price inflation, not to mention the opportunity to share in the rising standard of living that is taken almost for granted during working years. But it was clear then, as it is now, that a level amount of income is not enough to give real security during retirement years. Between 1940 and 1950, rising prices had cut the purchasing power of anyone living on a fixed income almost in half. Even a more moderate inflation can take its toll. By the middle of 1968 the 2 per cent average yearly rate of price increase since 1950 had cut the purchasing power of fixed-dollar income 30 per cent.

And, in addition to the problem of inflation, the economic position of retired persons living on a fixed income is weakened as earned incomes and living standards all about them generally rise. In terms of one measurement, per capita personal consumption expenditures in dollars of constant purchasing power, the United States living standard was nearly 42 per cent higher in 1967 than in 1950. Retired people living on fixed incomes usually have little or no opportunity to share in such advances of a growing economy. (Figure 3.1 of Chapter 3 illustrates the income growth needed to keep up with changing living standards and price inflation between 1940 and 1968.)

CREF, developed as a response to these problems, provides retirement income based on common stock investments to complement the fixed-dollar retirement income provided by TIAA. The purpose of the combined program is to provide a retirement income that is more responsive to economic change than a fixed-dollar annuity alone and less volatile than a variable annuity alone.

A study of relevant economic data covering the period 1880 to 1951 preceded the establishment of CREF. The aim was to discover how an individual would have fared during retirement if part of his regular preretirement savings had been invested in equities such as common stocks and part in fixed-dollar obligations. The various periods of accumulation and pay-out included war, peace, depression, prosperity, inflation, deflation; the study examined short and long working lifetimes, and short and long retirements.[9]

Figure 2.1 illustrates the most difficult years of any of the accumulation and annuity pay-out periods studied. It covers a working career of 30 years from 1900 to 1930 and a retirement period of 20 years beginning in 1930. The chart assumes that $100 a year was paid to the retirement plan from 1900 to 1930. The fixed-dollar income line represents the retirement income resulting from application of the full $100 a year to a fixed-dollar fund only. The combined income line illustrates the annuity resulting from $50 a year to a fixed-dollar fund and $50 to an equity fund—the variable annuity. The period shown is of special interest because it encompasses the years of the great depression and of World War II. The accumulation bars at the left of the chart show that during the late 1920s the retirement savings of the participant in the combined fund increased greatly because of the speculative upswing of the stock market. At retirement in 1930, the chart shows a rapidly falling annuity for the next two years. At the distressing low of common stock prices in 1932, however, the combined annuity was only moderately smaller than the fixed-dollar annuity; from that point forward it moved generally upward. Except for a short period during the eye of the depression, the individual with a combined annuity was better off throughout the entire period than the individual whose income was based wholly on the fixed-dollar fund.

The economic study reached three major conclusions:

1. It is unwise to commit all of one's retirement savings to dollar obligations, since decreases in the purchasing power of the dollar can seriously reduce the value of a fixed-income annuity. Increases in the purchasing power of the dollar, on the other hand, improve the status of the owner of a fixed-income annuity.

2. It is equally unwise to commit all of one's retirement savings to equity investments, since variations in prices of common stocks are much too pronounced to permit full reliance on them for the stable income needed during retirement. Changes in the value of common stocks and other equities are by no means perfectly correlated with cost of

[9] Greenough, A New Approach to Retirement Income.

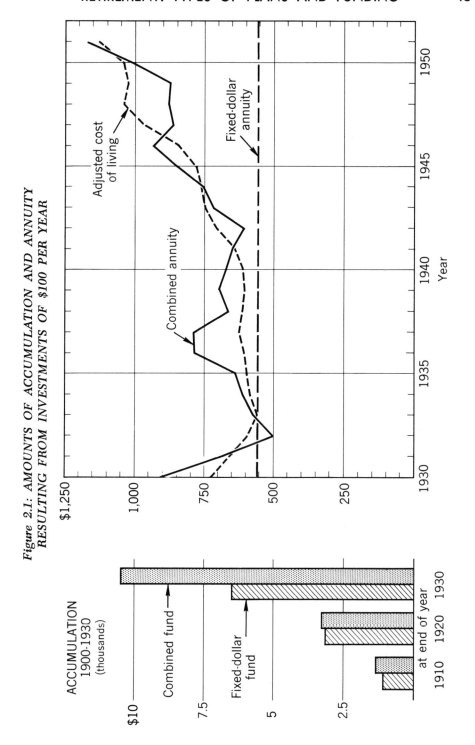

Figure 2.1: AMOUNTS OF ACCUMULATION AND ANNUITY RESULTING FROM INVESTMENTS OF $100 PER YEAR

living changes, but they have provided considerably better protection against inflation than have debt obligations.

3. Contributions to a retirement plan that are invested partly in debt obligations and partly in common stocks through an equities fund providing lifetime unit annuities offer promise of supplying retirement income that is at once reasonably free of violent fluctuations in amount and serious depreciation through price level changes.

The Variable Annuity. To implement a system in which common stock investment could be utilized for the generation and production of retirement income, TIAA constructed a new device, now well known, the variable or unit annuity.[10] The variable annuity incorporates the lifetime income principles of traditional annuities, but, instead of accumulating and paying out funds as a fixed number of dollars, the retirement funds are accumulated and paid out as the current value of units which measure the individual's share of the equity investment portfolio.

Accumulation Units. Payments to CREF purchase "accumulation units" for each participant during his working years, each unit in effect being a small share of ownership in every common stock in the CREF portfolio. The number of units bought with each monthly payment depends on the current value of the accumulation unit. This value is determined once each month by dividing the month-end market value of the CREF accumulation fund by the total number of accumulation units outstanding among all participants. This unit value serves a dual purpose: it marks the month-by-month dollar value of all the accumulation units owned by any participant, and it sets the current price for the purchase of an accumulation unit.

Increases in the prices of the equities in the CREF portfolio result in rising accumulation unit values; decreases result in falling unit values. More units are purchased for a given premium amount when the accumulation unit value is lower, fewer units when it is higher.

Dividends received by CREF on the investments are reinvested and apportioned to individual CREF accounts as additional accumulation units. The accumulation unit was valued initially at $10. Table 2.4 shows the year-end accumulation unit values since then.

Annuity Units. At retirement the accumulation units are converted into

---

[10] Duncan, "A Retirement System Granting Unit Annuities and Investing in Equities," *Transactions of the Society of Actuaries,* IV (1952), 317–44.

TABLE 2.4: *CREF YEAR-END ACCUMULATION UNIT VALUES, 1952–1968*

End of Year	Accumulation Unit Value	End of Year	Accumulation Unit Value
1952	$10.52	1961	$31.86
1953	10.37	1962	26.65
1954	14.85	1963	30.83
1955	18.06	1964	33.96
1956	19.19	1965	39.08
1957	17.75	1966	36.33
1958	24.36	1967	43.78
1959	27.11	1968	45.35
1960	27.38		

a lifetime income of "annuity units." The annuity pays an income that varies year by year as a continuing reflection of the performance of the common stocks in the CREF portfolio.

The annuity calculations are basically the ones actuaries make for a fixed-dollar annuity to determine how many dollars can be paid out each month in order to use up a capital sum and the earnings on it over the lifetimes of a large number of annuitants of any given age. However, the CREF income is expressed as a fixed number of annuity units payable each month for life, rather than as a fixed number of dollars. Once a year this unchanging number of annuity units is multiplied by the latest value of the annuity unit to determine how much income to pay each month during the CREF fiscal year.

The CREF annuity unit is revalued as of each March 31. The new value is reflected in annuity payments beginning on May 1 and remains constant until the following May 1. The value of the annuity unit for each year since 1952 is shown in Table 2.5. By far the most important factor in the yearly revaluations has been the change in market prices of CREF common stocks. Another significant factor is the level of dividend income CREF receives on its investments. Additional factors include expenses and variations in annuitant longevity.

The Transition to Retirement Income. Many people are aware from personal experience of the risk of selecting the "wrong" time to sell a common stock. For retiring CREF participants there is no "wrong" or "right" time at which to begin CREF annuity income. The individual's *pro rata* share of the CREF portfolio is not sold at one point in the market, on the day of retire-

TABLE 2.5: CREF ANNUITY UNIT VALUES, 1952–1968

Annuity Year (May through April)	Annuity Unit Value	Annuity Year (May through April)	Annuity Unit Value
Initial Value	$10.00	1961–1962	$26.25
1953–1954	9.46	1962–1963	26.13
1954–1955	10.74	1963–1964	22.68
1955–1956	14.11	1964–1965	26.48
1956–1957	18.51	1965–1966	28.21
1957–1958	16.88	1966–1967	30.43
1958–1959	16.71	1967–1968	31.92
1959–1960	22.03	1968–1969	29.90
1960–1961	22.18		

ment. Instead there is merely a transition from the pay-in period, when payments to CREF over the years purchased common stocks at varying market prices and dividend levels, to the pay-out variable annuity period, when benefits are paid to the annuitant over the years in accordance with varying market prices and dividend levels. At retirement the individual trades in accumulation units for a lifetime stream of annuity units, which continue to measure the value of his share in CREF investments. Since the same common stocks support both units, a "high" or "low" market level at the moment of retirement has no significant effect on the transition from one type of unit to the other.

CREF Investment Philosophy. Regular investment of annuity premiums in selected equities month after month, year after year, puts into effect the basic investment principle of diversification over time. Under a program of investing premiums regularly over a staff member's working years, the level of common stock prices at any one time is relatively unimportant. As measured by the number and value of an individual's accumulation or annuity units, this long-term investment program permits each deposit to CREF to participate in the developments in American business and industry that span the economic experience of many years, long after any particular deposit is made. During a person's retirement this direct participation in the economy continues (and continues throughout the life of a survivor as well when the individual selects a survivor annuity option) in much the same manner it did during the accumulation period, except that instead of paying premiums he is receiving a lifetime income.

An accompanying aspect of CREF participation is that portfolio diversification among a variety of issues permits college staff members to share in the productivity of companies that make up a cross section of American industry. It would be hard for a CREF participant to glance around a classroom, his living room, or the campus parking lot without seeing a number of products made by a company in which he shares ownership as a CREF policyholder. In mid-1968 there were 83 companies in the CREF portfolio, of which 23 have been there since the first year of operation. Retirement plan contributions of approximately $15,000,000 are currently invested each month.

The principle of dollar cost averaging, under which the average cost of the common shares purchased is less than the corresponding average market price per share, is made unusually effective in a college retirement program because of the regularity of college employment and salaries, and the resulting regularity of monthly contributions over many years received by the Fund on each individual's behalf.

In addition to regularity of premium investment, another stabilizing factor in the operation of CREF is the absence of cash surrender provisions. Because CREF is a part of a retirement system, its need for cash is limited to annuities being paid and is therefore predictable and stable. There can be no sudden rush of cash withdrawals to force the sale of securities during periods of market weakness.

Public Retirement Systems Covering College and University Employees

Over 2,300 separate retirement systems cover state and local employees; 123 of them cover about 90 per cent of total participants.[11] Of these 123 systems, 72 cover one or more classes of employees in the publicly supported four-year colleges and universities—faculty, administrative and other professional staff, and clerical and service personnel.

In some states two public retirement plans cover employees on the same campus. For example, in Montana, faculty and administrative personnel belong to the state teacher system, while the clerical-service staff is covered by the public employee system. In a few states, Oklahoma and Texas, for example, a state teacher plan covers all employee classes. In others, Utah

[11] U.S. Bureau of the Census, *Census of Governments: 1962, Employee-Retirement Systems of State and Local Governments,* pp. 1–3.

and Nevada, for example, a public employee plan covers all classes. In some states the schoolteacher and public employee plans have been merged into a single plan, as in North Carolina.

The general characteristics of the 72 public plans covering faculty and staff in higher education are outlined in this section. It should be noted that only a small proportion of the total members of these systems serve in higher education; the plans have been designed primarily for elementary and secondary schoolteachers and other school employees, and for employees of departments of local and state governments.

Summaries of the provisions of each system and information about the colleges and employee groups covered appear in Appendix 5.

Of the 72 public retirement systems covering college employees, 54 use the defined benefit approach, 5 the defined contribution approach, and 13 combine elements of both approaches. In these 13 plans the total benefit is composed of an annuity based on the employee's own defined contributions plus a pension from employer contributions expressed as a defined benefit.

DEFINED BENEFIT APPROACH

When a formula is used to state part or all of the benefit, it includes the years of membership in the system, the average salary over a stated period of membership, and a percentage factor; for example, 1½ per cent of the highest five years' average salary times years of service.

When the benefit formula calculation has been completed, the result is the amount of single life annuity payable to the retiring staff member. If, instead of the single life annuity, the staff member desires to select an income option which will continue lifetime benefits to a survivor, tables are provided by the retirement system to give information about alternative benefit levels. The tables also show the amount of the actuarially reduced single life annuity if retirement takes place before the "normal" retirement age to which the benefit formula applies.

Salary Factor. The average salary element of the formula benefit calculation in public plans normally takes the form of a "final average" over a stated period of years. Of the 67 formula benefit plans, only 5 use the career average salary (one of them uses the "first 25 years," to which a flat annual benefit is added for each year of service thereafter); 47 use a five-year salary average period; 10 use a three-year period; and 5 a ten-year period. The periods are generally stated so that the resulting salary average encompasses the highest salary period of a career. The most frequent statements are "highest 5 years' average salary" and "highest 5 consecutive years' salary."

Percentage Factor. The percentage factor for each year of service in the 54 plans that use the defined benefit approach exclusively normally ranges among plans from 1 to 2 per cent. Of these plans, 37 apply a single level percentage to the benefit calculation, and 12 apply a lower percentage (or fraction) to part of average salary and a higher percentage to the balance. For example, in 2 of the plans the benefit for each year of service is 1 per cent of the first $4,800 of final average salary (fixed at a former Social Security earnings base) and 2 per cent of the excess. Five plans apply different percentages to different segments of service. For example, the benefits of one such plan are 1 per cent of average highest five years' annual salary for the first ten years of employment and 2 per cent for each year thereafter. (This plan for clerical-service employees states a benefit maximum of $3,000.)

In the 13 plans using the defined benefit formula only with respect to benefits credited from employer contributions, the percentage ranges among plans from 0.6 per cent to 1.1 per cent. A typical benefit statement is the following: "Pension of .67% of final average salary multiplied by each year of service, plus an annuity that is the money purchase [defined contribution] equivalent of employee contributions to the plan."

Table 2.6 shows the formula percentages in use in the public plans covering college employees.

Years of Service Factor. Most of the public plans using a benefit formula (58 of 67) include all years of plan membership in the formula. Nine of the plans state limits on the number of years which will be counted. Of these 9 plans, 1 states a maximum of 20 years; 2 plans, 30 years; 3 plans, 35 years; and the remaining state maximums of 37½, 40, and 45 years, respectively. It should be noted that the plan using the 20-year maximum has a benefit formula of 2½ per cent of final average salary for each year of service up to the maximum.

TABLE 2.6: *PUBLIC EMPLOYEE AND STATE TEACHER RETIREMENT SYSTEMS COVERING INSTITUTIONS OF HIGHER EDUCATION, BENEFIT FORMULA PERCENTAGE FOR SERVICE RETIREMENT*

Benefit based on single percentage of final average salary times
years of service

Less than 1%	1[a]	
1%	4[b]	
1¼ to 1½%	11[c]	
1⅔%	7[d]	
1¾%	4[e]	
2% or above	10[f]	
		37

Benefit based on two or more percentage factors applied to final
average salary times years of service

1. Percentage changes at

$4,200 (1–1½%)	1	
$4,800 (1–1½%; 1–2%; 1–2%; $\frac{1}{90}$–$\frac{1}{60}$)	4[g]	
$5,600 (1¼–1½%)	1	
$6,600 (1½–1%)	1	
Current OASDHI base	5[h]	
		12

2. Percentages applied by service periods

1½% first 5 years, 1¾% 5–10 years, 2% thereafter	1	
1% first 10 years, 2% thereafter	1[i]	
1% first 20 years, 1.66% 20–30 years, 1.75% thereafter	1[j]	
2½% first 20 years, 1½% 20–30 years	1	
		4

3. Percentages applied by service periods and salary levels

Under current OASDHI base—$\frac{1}{120}$ final average salary for each year of service to 30, $\frac{1}{240}$ for each year in excess of 30 (over current OASDHI base, fractions are $\frac{1}{60}$ and $\frac{1}{120}$, respectively)		1

Benefit based on annuity purchased by employee contributions
plus pension based on percentage of final average salary

0.67 to 1% per year of service	10[k]	
0.6% to $3,000 and 1.1% of excess per year of service	2	
0.5% above $1,200 per year of service	1	
		13

Defined contribution plans		5
Total systems		72

[a] Maximum final average salary considered is $7,500.

[b] One system—maximum salary considered is $4,800; alternative is annuity from employee contributions plus $24 per year of service plus $6 per year of service to a maximum of $192. One system considers a maximum of $6,000 salary.

[c] One system considers only salary in excess of $1,200. One system considers a maximum of

EMPLOYEE CONTRIBUTIONS

The great majority of the public plans covering college and university employees provide for a contribution by the employee. Only three of the plans are noncontributory: the clerical-service plan at Michigan State University, and the state employee and teacher systems of the State of New York.

Forty-four of the 72 plans provide for an employee contribution rate that is the same level percentage of salary for all employees. These rates range among plans from 3 to 7 per cent of salary. Twelve plans report that their employee contribution rates differ among employees according to their sex and the age they enter the plan. For instance, one such plan provides for a contribution rate throughout his career of 6.50 per cent for a man who enters the plan at age 25. For a man entering the plan at age 45, however, the contribution rate is set and remains at 8.56 per cent of salary. For women the rate for entry at age 25 is 6.59 per cent, and for entry at age 45, 9.25 per cent.

Eleven of the public plans report a step-rate contribution pattern under which one contribution rate is applied to salary up to a stated amount, and

---

$6,600 final average salary; another system has a maximum final average salary of $8,400. One system considers a maximum of 35 years of service. One system actuarially increases benefits for retirement between 60 and 65. One system has a minimum of $6 monthly per year of service.

[d] One system actuarially increases benefits for retirement between 60 and 65. One system considers a maximum of 45 years of service. One system has a minimum monthly benefit of $150 and a maximum monthly benefit of $500.

[e] One system considers a maximum of 40 years of service. Two systems consider a maximum of $25,000 final average salary. Minimum benefit in three systems is $76 per year of service. Maximum benefit in one system is 75% of final average salary. One system actuarially increases benefits for retirement between 65 and 70.

[f] One system has a minimum benefit of $720 and a maximum benefit of $1,200 for employees with 25 years of service. One system considers a maximum of 20 years of service; one system has a maximum benefit of 80% of final average salary. One system has an additional cash benefit of $300 per year. One system has a maximum benefit of 75% of final average salary and supplements benefits of less than $2,640 annually. Another system has a maximum benefit of 75% of final average salary and uses a smaller percentage for calculating benefits for members with less than 20 years of service.

[g] One system actuarially increases benefits for retirement between 60 and 65 and offers a minimum benefit of $100 per month at age 60 with 20 years of service.

[h] Percentage factors are: $1-1\frac{1}{2}\%$; $1-1\frac{3}{4}\%$; $1\frac{1}{8}-1\frac{3}{4}\%$; $\frac{6}{7}-1\frac{2}{7}\%$; $\frac{6}{7}-1\frac{2}{7}\%$. One system considers only final average salary below $12,180. Two systems provide a different formula for employees not covered by OASDHI.

[i] System considers a maximum of $3,000 final average salary.

[j] System uses different percentages for determining benefits for employees not covered by OASDHI.

[k] Two systems have a minimum total benefit of $\frac{1}{70}$ final average salary. One system offers an additional benefit of $100 per year. Two systems have limits of 30 years and 35 years, respectively, on the length of service considered in determining benefits.

another and usually higher rate applies to the balance of salary. The present or a former Social Security earnings base often marks the stepping point. Four plans use the current base and change accordingly if the base is changed; 7 have set the step at a fixed base which in most instances corresponds with an earlier Social Security earnings base.

TABLE 2.7: PUBLIC EMPLOYEE AND STATE TEACHER RETIREMENT
SYSTEMS COVERING INSTITUTIONS OF HIGHER EDUCATION,
EMPLOYEE CONTRIBUTIONS TO SYSTEM AS PERCENTAGE OF SALARY

Level percentage of salary for all

3%	4[a]	
3½%	2	
4%	9[b]	
4½%	2	
5%	10[c]	
5½ to 5¾%	3	
6%	7[d]	
6½%	2	
7%	5	
	—	
		44

Percentage varies by sex and by age at entry into system		12[e]

Percentage changes at

$4,200 (3–5%)	1	
$4,800 (3–6%; 4–6%)	2	
$5,600 (5–6%)	1	
$6,000 (3–8%)	1	
$6,600 (3–6%)	2	
Current OASDHI base	4[f]	
	—	
		11

Four percentages	
4% to $500 per month; 5%, $500–$1,000; 6%, $1,000–$1,500; 7% above $1,500	1

Percentage changes by years of service	
4% first 8 years, 5% second 8 years, 6% thereafter	1

Noncontributory	3

Total systems	72

[a] In one system, 6% if not in OASDHI. One system will increase to 5% July, 1969.
[b] One system will increase to 5% by 1975 by increments of ¼%.
[c] In one system, 1% additional for survivor benefits.
[d] In one system, ¼% additional for survivor benefits.
[e] Two plans reduce contributions by 2% up to OASDHI base. One plan reduces contributions by half up to OASDHI base. One plan reduces contributions by one-third on salary up to $400 monthly. Employee may elect 4% plan in one system; benefits are adjusted accordingly.
[f] 2–5%; 3–5%; 4½–7%; 4½–7%.

Table 2.7 summarizes the employee contribution rates reported by the public systems covered by the current survey. Table 2.8 shows the amount of salary on which employee contributions and benefits are based in the public plans. In 51 of the 72 public plans the employee contribution rate (or rates) is applied to all of salary. In one plan the employee contributions are not applied to the first $1,200 of annual salary. Seventeen of the plans, or about a quarter of them, set an upper limit to the salary on which employee contributions and benefits are based.

The effect of a limit, of course, is to hold down the final benefit, since benefit formulas are based on an average salary. In recent years a number of states have succeeded in removing or at least raising these limits.

TABLE 2.8: *PUBLIC EMPLOYEE AND STATE TEACHER RETIREMENT SYSTEMS COVERING INSTITUTIONS OF HIGHER EDUCATION, AMOUNT OF SALARY ON WHICH EMPLOYEE CONTRIBUTIONS AND BENEFITS ARE BASED*

Entire salary		51
Entire salary except for first $1,200		1
Salary up to a specified level		
$ 3,333	1[a]	
$ 4,800	1	
$ 6,000–$ 7,500	4	
$ 8,400–$ 8,600	4	
$12,000–$16,000	5[b]	
$25,000	2[c]	
		17
Noncontributory		3
Total systems		72

[a] First 8 years, $3,000; second 8 years, $3,600; thereafter, $3,333.
[b] In one system, contributions are made only on salary between $6,000 and $12,000. In one system, contributions are made only on salary between $1,200 and $15,000. In one system, contributions are on first $7,500 or first $16,000, depending on plan selected.
[c] Both systems permit optional contributions on salary in excess of $25,000.

VESTING

Immediate full vesting of retirement benefits is rare among public retirement systems. Of the 72 public systems covering employees of institutions of higher education, only the 2 Wisconsin systems provide for the immediate full vesting of all contributions. In the other 70 plans, full vesting does not occur until the employee has served a stated period of time or has reached a stated age. Table 2.9 summarizes the vesting provisions of the public plans.

Inspection of Table 2.9 suggests that a substantial number of the "members" of public plans will not receive benefits from their plans because of the prevailing pattern of delayed vesting. Employees who change jobs be-

TABLE 2.9: PUBLIC EMPLOYEE AND STATE TEACHER RETIREMENT SYSTEMS COVERING INSTITUTIONS OF HIGHER EDUCATION, VESTING PROVISIONS ON TERMINATION OF EMPLOYMENT

Immediate vesting		2
Service requirement (years)		
4	3[a]	
5	11	
8	1	
10	22	
12	1	
15	8	
20	7	
25	1[b]	
	—	
		54
Age requirement (age 55)		1
Age and service (20 years *and* age 60)		1
Alternate vesting provisions		
8 years or age 55	1	
20 years or $500 employee contributions	1	
25 years or age 50 and 10 years	1	
25 years or age 55 and 10 years	1	
25 years or age 60 and 10 years	2[c]	
	—	
		6
Gradual vesting of employer contributions (years)		
3–20	1	
10–20	1	
16–20	1	
	—	
		3
No vesting		5
		—
Total systems		72

[a] One system provides vesting after 4 years for those in higher education, after 10 years for all others.

[b] If involuntary separation, 10 years.

[c] One system also vests after 20 years of service except that deferred benefits are reduced by 4% for each year the employee is under age 60. Maximum reduction is 20%.

fore fulfilling the vesting requirement receive only a return of their own money credited with interest at a stated rate. Improvement has taken place over the last decade, but the picture remains one in which delay of vesting characterizes public plans.

Advisory Commission. The negative effect of delay in vesting has drawn the serious attention of the Advisory Commission on Intergovernmental Relations. Immobilization of public employees in a mobile society was early identified by the Commission as a special problem, and a 1963 report of the Commission noted that "many public administrators and agencies are finding the serious lack of provision for intergovernmental transferability of retirement rights to be a hindrance to personnel recruitment." [12]

The 1963 Commission report concluded that "provision should be made for an employee to change jobs without suffering any major loss of retirement credits . . . . In the long run, public employers and employees at all levels of government—Federal, State, and local—will benefit from a better program for the preservation of retirement credits of employees who transfer from one governmental unit to another." [13] The Commission placed its hopes for improvement in a recommendation that "the employee's benefits be vested when he has completed a period of service of not more than five years in the system . . ." [14] This, the Commission concluded, is the most practicable means of relaxing the grip of interstate immobility on public employees. [15] If carried out, the recommendation for five-year vesting in public plans would represent an important step toward the ultimate goal of immediate full vesting.

Vesting and Compensation Surveys. The AAUP in its compensation surveys goes to considerable effort to include the value of staff benefit plans. In facing the problem of whether to include retirement contributions there are, of course, no difficulties in the decision regarding fully vested employer contributions. They are includable at full value as an addition to cash salary. Nor are there difficulties in deciding that a long period of delayed vesting should be given no value whatsoever.

[12] Advisory Commission on Intergovernmental Relations, "Transferability of Public Employee Retirement Credits among Units of Government," p. 5.

[13] *Ibid.,* p. 50.

[14] *Ibid.,* p. 53.

[15] Five-year vesting is also a goal of the NEA National Council on Teacher Retirement. National Education Association, National Council on Teacher Retirement, *Proceedings of the 43rd Annual Meeting, October, 1965,* p. 67.

The AAUP Committee's report underlines the differences between immediate and delayed vesting in evaluating compensation:

Where the contribution by the institution is immediately vested in the faculty member, that is, where it becomes his property no matter whether or when he quits his position, no question arises concerning the inclusion of this contribution as a part of the compensation. But where the accumulated amounts revert to the institution if the faculty member leaves his position, they cannot be regarded as compensation for services but, at best, as compensation for not quitting the job.[16]

The Committee recognizes that, under plans with relatively short periods of delay in vesting, many members of a plan will become vested. A decision at some point along the line was called for and simplicity was required. The Committee's decision was as follows:

We decided . . . to count the *entire* contributions of the institution if they become vested within 5 years, and to count *no* part of the contributions if they become vested only in more than 5 years. This is not only simple, but it also serves to express disapproval of schemes of using retirement plans to create a "captive" faculty. An amount of money that will not "belong" to the potential payee unless he stays on his job for many years is not compensation for services rendered but compensation for submission to captivity.[17]

Another problem for the compensation survey is raised by the defined benefit approach. As noted earlier (see Table 2.3), the employer contribution under these plans is not the same percentage of salary for all employees, but varies among employees by age. For younger employees it may be a fraction of 1 per cent of salary; for employees in their forties it may about equal the employee's own contribution; for older employees it may reach above 20 or 30 per cent of salary. The respondent to a compensation survey, however, normally has at hand only the *average percentage of employer contribution* for the whole group (e.g., 8 per cent of payroll), so only the average is reported. The result is substantial overstatement of total compensation for younger staff members and understatement for older members.

Cash Values after Vesting. A widespread feature of public plans permits a vested employee to cash out his own contributions on termination of service and forfeit the employer's contributions and all future benefits. This

---

[16] "The Economic Status of the Profession, 1959–1960: Annual Report by Committee Z," *American Association of University Professors Bulletin*, XLVI (Summer, 1960), p. 160.
[17] *Ibid.*

is almost as destructive to retirement planning as no vesting at all. Under these plans an employee who is changing jobs may be tempted to sacrifice future annuity benefits in order to obtain cash. A retirement plan should not allow terminating employees to take their accumulated contributions out of the retirement plan to finance current purchases—a house, a car, a trip. Reduced financial security in retirement is a real part of the price being paid for such items. Among public plans the progressive Wisconsin systems have taken a modest forward step; they do not permit members terminating employment at age 55 or over to take cash.

MAINTAINING PURCHASING POWER AND LIVING STANDARDS

Most public retirement plans provide a retirement income that remains unchanged once payments begin. With an annual average increase in living costs of about 2 per cent a year over the last 15 years, the beneficiaries of most public employee and state teacher plans have experienced a substantial loss in purchasing power. A retired person may also be bypassed by increasing living standards (measured by increases in average wages or consumer expenditures per capita in dollars of constant value) if no mechanism of income adjustment is available.

"Final-average" formula plans, widely found in industrial and governmental employment, represent one of the earlier devices that took some cognizance of inflation, although inflation was not usually the reason for adoption of the final-average formula. With a reasonable formula, final-average plans will usually provide a good level of benefits for the first few years of retirement. But the benefits are normally a fixed amount and, as living costs rise, pensioners have to make ends meet on benefits related to an increasingly obsolete base. Very few final-average plans have any built-in protection for inflation that occurs during a person's retirement.

To relieve hard-pressed annuitants, state legislatures from time to time have acted to increase benefit levels for persons already retired. Such supplements are helpful to annuitants, but are almost always late in coming. They may not correspond to living cost changes as they have affected different age classes within the retired group. Since few public systems have progressed in the development of systematic methods of maintaining pension purchasing power, most of the college and university employees retired from public plans still depend on the responsiveness of future legislatures for any needed financial adjustments.

In the plans in which maintenance of retirement benefit purchasing power has been approached on a systematic basis, three principal methods have been used: (1) variable annuities, (2) automatic adjustments linked to increases in the Consumer Price Index of the Bureau of Labor Statistics, and (3) automatic annual percentage increases in benefits.

Variable Annuities. In three states, Wisconsin, New York, and Oregon, regular employee-employer contributions to a public plan may now be made to a public variable annuity fund investing in common stocks. The Wisconsin State Teachers Retirement System and the Wisconsin Retirement Fund for state employees have provided variable annuity programs since 1958. The New York City Teachers Retirement System and the Public Employees Retirement System of Oregon adopted variable annuity programs in 1967 to become effective in 1968. All of these systems have patterned their variable annuity program after the College Retirement Equities Fund, currently used by 118 publicly supported colleges and universities in 28 states.

The Wisconsin State Teachers Retirement System provides that each participant may elect that half of his employee contributions be credited to his account in the system's variable annuity fund. The balance goes to the fixed-dollar fund. If this election is made, state contributions equal to the employee's are also credited to his variable annuity account, with the balance going to the fixed-dollar fund. Additional voluntary deposits may be made by the employee, to either the fixed or the variable fund. The variable annuity of the Wisconsin Retirement Fund for nonteaching public employees is essentially the same. While the Wisconsin systems employ a recently introduced defined benefit aspect, the funding pattern is essentially defined contribution, permitting common stock investment throughout employee service that maximizes opportunity for long-term gains and avoids concentrating the bulk of contributions in the years near retirement.

Under the variable annuity of the New York City Teachers Retirement System an employee may allocate half or all of his designated contributions to the variable annuity. Employer contributions are excluded from the allocation. Unlike the Wisconsin plans, which are managed entirely by public authorities, the New York City plan is administered under contract by a life insurance company and a bank trustee.

A 1967 amendment of the Public Employees Retirement Act of the State of Oregon established a variable annuity account within the Public Employees Retirement System. The account provides for an investment in equities of a portion of the regular employee contributions to the system. An employee may elect that one-fourth or one-half of his own contributions go to the fund.

In New Jersey, members of the Public Employees' Retirement System and the Teachers' Pension and Annuity Fund may make voluntary additional contributions to the Supplemental Annuity Collective Trust, established by the State in 1963, which provides a variable annuity. Regular employee-employer contributions, however, may not be paid to the supplementary plan. The supplemental fund has both fixed and variable divisions, and employees may elect to participate in either one or both. Up to 5 per cent of salary may be applied to the supplemental program by payroll deduction. (A similar supplemental variable annuity plan is provided under the self-administered retirement plan of the University of California.)

Price Index Plans. Three public plans currently covering staff members in institutions of higher education link retirement benefits with the Consumer Price Index of the Bureau of Labor Statistics. They are the Civil Service Retirement System of the federal government, which covers agricultural extension employees at many state universities and civilian employees of the service academies, the New York State Employees Retirement System, and the Teachers' Retirement System of the State of Alaska.

Under the federal plan a cost of living increase becomes effective following retirement after the Consumer Price Index has gone up by 3 per cent and stays up for three consecutive months. The percentage of increase is equal to the percentage increase in the index calculated at its highest level during the three-month period. Thereafter, whenever the national cost of living rises by at least 3 per cent over the Consumer Price Index for the month used as a base for the most recent increase in benefits, and stays up for three consecutive months, an increase equal to the percentage rise is granted.

The index-related plan of the New York State Employees Retirement System was introduced in 1967. This plan provides for the recalculation of a one-year "supplemental retirement allowance" once each year. An increase begins in October of any year of retirement in which the ratio of the average of the twelve monthly Consumer Price Indexes of the Bureau of Labor Statistics (all items, U.S. city average) at the end of the preceding year to the index for the year of retirement, minus 1, expressed as a percentage, is at least 3 per cent. The increase percentage is multiplied by retirement income up to $7,000. Like a number of other provisions of the New York State System, the cost of living provision must be reenacted by the legislature annually.

Under the Teachers' Retirement System of the State of Alaska, a "post-retirement pension adjustment" is payable to a retired teacher when the administrator determines that the cost of living has increased and the financial condition of the fund permits payments of the adjustment. The retirement act specifies that the administrator is authorized to issue regulations necessary to promulgate payment of this benefit but specifies that the amount of the increase shall not exceed 1½ per cent for each year of retirement.

In addition, a teacher who retires under the Alaska plan and has his permanent residence in Alaska is entitled to receive a "place-of-living allowance" not to exceed 10 per cent of the annual retirement benefit. A 10 per cent allowance has been in effect since July 1, 1966. The allowance is paid from the State's general fund.

Automatic Increases. Retirement systems in Hawaii, Kentucky, and Nevada provide for automatic increases in benefits on an annual basis.

The Employees' Retirement System of Hawaii, covering all employees of the University of Hawaii, provides by statute for an annual increase in the retirement benefit after benefits have started. The 1961 Hawaii legislature created a "postretirement benefit" under which the retirement allowance of each pensioner is increased by 1½ per cent on the first day of July of each year after retirement. Each successive year's 1½ per cent increase is applied to the income received during the previous year.

The Hawaii benefit is financed by current employee and employer contributions. Active members pay an additional contribution of ½ per cent of salary, and an equal levy is made on the payrolls of employer governments.

The Kentucky Teachers' Retirement System provides for an annual automatic increase of 1 per cent in retirement benefits. The provision became effective July 1, 1967, on which date the first such increase was made. On July 1 of each year thereafter, 1 per cent of the original annuity amount is to be added to each check.

The Nevada Public Employees Retirement System provides for an automatic annual increase of "1.5 per cent of the amount of such monthly disability allowance or service retirement allowance as originally computed, approved and paid." This increase provision became effective July 1, 1963.

It should be noted that the Kentucky and Nevada provisions do not incorporate any compounding effects. Under both, the increases are financed by current contributions from the state.

Retirement benefits linked, with an upper limit, to the Consumer Price Index, or to a stated annual increase, provide a helpful degree of purchasing power protection. But opportunity for protection is limited. Experience shows that the average increase in the cost of living over even just a few years can compound at a rate higher than 1 or 1½ per cent per year.

The funding of increases triggered by index changes raises a difficult problem. Inflation imposes its burdens quite unequally over time. Increases in benefits cannot be accurately projected, with the result that funds for future increases for today's employees are not now being set aside, thus leaving the financing to be carried by future employees or by future taxpayers.

Automatic increases permit the individual periodically to regain a part, or under some conditions all, of his retirement income's purchasing power. But neither these nor cost of living index-related plans offer him an opportunity to share in the increasing productivity of the economy, that is, in the rising standard of living enjoyed by friends and neighbors who are still a part of the active labor force. Measured in dollars of constant purchasing power, per capita personal consumption expenditures in the United States in 1967 were 25 per cent higher than in 1960. However, the person retired under these plans is better off than the person living on a fixed-income annuity.

INVESTMENTS

Public employee retirement systems have been circumscribed in their range of permitted investments. Over the years the investments of public systems have been concentrated in the debt obligations of states, municipalities, and other public bodies, including the federal government. The lower yields of these issues have been reflected in the lower earnings figures reported by the public retirement systems.

Higher-yield mortgage investments, both guaranteed and conventional, have never played much part in the portfolios of public pension plans. But securities of business and industrial organizations are now playing a much more prominent role. In recent years, statutory investment limitations have been relaxed in a number of states to permit more creative use of the supporting funds for future retirement income. There has been growing recognition that governmental bodies derive little advantage from purchasing tax-exempt public securities, for which there is sufficient market from nongovernmental purchasers. At the same time the higher yields of corporate bonds, including direct placements, have attracted the attention of public retirement system managers. Wisconsin, New York, and Ohio are among the states whose retirement systems have led in the broadening of investment channels.

The distribution of investments among all state systems is shown in Table 2.10. The reduction in the proportion of public debt obligations— from 59 to 27 per cent from 1959 to 1966—is apparent, as is the increase in corporate bonds from 30 to 50 per cent. Corporate stock holdings have increased sixfold over the same period.

TABLE 2.10: DISTRIBUTION OF RETIREMENT FUND INVESTMENTS, ALL PUBLIC RETIREMENT SYSTEMS, 1959, 1962, AND 1966

	Per Cent of Investments		
	1959	*1962*	*1966*
Cash and deposits	1.4	1.2	1.0
Bonds			
Federal government	33.9	26.2	20.0
State and local government	25.3	17.4	7.0
Corporate	30.6	41.4	50.2
Corporate stocks	1.8	2.7	11.6
Mortgages	5.2	8.9	5.1
Other	1.8	2.2	5.1
Total	100.0	100.0	100.0

Source: U.S. Bureau of the Census, *Census of Governments: Employer-Retirement Systems of State and Local Governments* (1962), p. 13, and Murray, "Economic Aspects of Pensions: A Summary Report," in *Old Age Income Assurance*, Part V: *Financial Aspects of Pension Plans*, p. 100. (Joint Economic Committee, Subcommittee on Fiscal Policy, 1967).

More imaginative and productive investment policies for public retirement systems are inhibited by a number of factors. Dr. Roger F. Murray's report on economic aspects of pensions for the National Bureau of Economic Research, submitted as part of a series of papers for the Subcommittee on Fiscal Policy of the Joint Economic Committee, December, 1967, has summarized these factors:

.... The practice of seeking to secure competent investment advice by competitive bidding, the inability to pay adequate salaries for expert staff, and the apparent unwillingness to lay out even very modest sums for investment management are all factors conspiring to produce uninspired and mediocre portfolio management. Despite the great progress of recent years, few systems have adequate staffs, strong investment advisory arrangements, effective finance committees, and the capability of providing first-rate management. These former sleeping giants of the pension-fund field sometimes appear to be only partially awake.

Under the circumstances, it is doubtful that State and local retirement systems will soon break out of the statutory, accounting, and institutional restraints on their effective management of huge aggregations of capital. While the high cost of pension benefits will create increasing pressure to improve rates of return, it is not likely that the public systems will greatly accelerate the pace at which they follow private funds. Nor is it likely that they will be as flexible in approaching investment opportunities as they occur in the future of a dynamic capital market structure.[18]

In the great majority of public plans an investment yield higher than that assumed by the actuaries in calculating contribution rates helps to reduce the employer's cost, but does not directly benefit the employee. The employee's contributions are normally credited a statutory interest rate, usually 2, 3, or 4 per cent.

FUNDING

The funding status of a retirement system indicates its capacity to meet present and future obligations. A pension system is on a fully funded basis only if reserves representing employee service already performed will completely discharge all accrued benefits, and if amounts being contributed to the fund on behalf of current service are sufficient, according to appro-

---

[18] Murray, "Economic Aspects of Pensions: A Summary Report," in *Old Age Income Assurance*, Part V: *Financial Aspects of Pension Plans*, p. 103. (Joint Economic Committee, Subcommittee on Fiscal Policy, 1967).

priate interest, mortality, and expense calculations, to discharge newly accruing pension obligations as they mature.

In the 1959 report we wrote, "In many state retirement systems, the necessary annual state appropriation to the pension reserve is and has been seriously inadequate." The situation has not substantially changed. While employee contributions continue to be paid into the systems, employer contributions continue in many systems at a level below the actuarial requirements, and the unfunded accrued liabilities of many systems continue to show increases. Year after year the deficiencies are pointed out by responsible actuarial analysts. In a few plans, benefit payments to retired people are being paid out of current employee contributions, a really appalling failure of the governmental units to meet any part of the liability that is accumulating.

The factors chiefly responsible for underfunding are: (1) failure to include the full pension costs of current service in the budget; (2) increases in prospective benefits and liberalization of benefit formulas without appropriate provision for required funding revenues; (3) upward salary adjustments to meet changing salary scales and price level increases without corresponding provisions for funding increases under plans tying benefits to final average salary; (4) an unduly large proportion of assets invested in state, local, and federal bonds with a consequent sacrifice in earnings; (5) use of obsolete mortality tables; (6) increases in pensions to retired employees without reserve financing; and (7) legislative decision to finance the system on a pay-as-you-go basis.

THE TAXING POWER

The power to tax and the power of legislative bodies to make appropriations to public retirement systems provides a source of funds for support of pension benefits that is not available to private systems. In those states that meet their obligations as they accrue year by year through substantial funding of their retirement plans, this standby taxing ability is an additional source of strength and can occasionally be used to increase benefits to persons already retired without serious implications for the long-term soundness of the pension plans. The difficulty arises when future potential taxing power is used as an excuse to undertax the current generation for its obligations.

Insurance Company Plans

Life insurance companies play a relatively small role in providing retirement plans for higher education. Table 2.2 shows that about 10 per cent of the institutions report a commercial life insurance company retirement plan. These institutions employ 5 per cent of the faculty and administrative personnel in the responding institutions, and about 7 per cent of total clerical-service employees. Insurance company retirement plans in institutions employing 100 or more full-time faculty are described in Appendix 7.

The retirement plans offered by commercial insurers are provided mainly through individual policies, group annuity contracts, and group deposit administration contracts.

Individual policy plans use *retirement annuity* contracts or *retirement income* contracts as funding instruments, both of which provide for allocation of contributions to individual employee accounts. Group plans use the funding instruments of group annuity contracts or group permanent contracts, or the deposit administration group contracts. Sometimes a plan combines two funding instruments, a trusteed fund and an individual ordinary life or endowment insurance contract. The combination (or split) plan funds part of the retirement benefits through the cash value of the insurance contract and uses the trusteed fund for the remainder.

INDIVIDUAL POLICIES

Retirement plans using individual insurance policies issued by commercial insurance companies normally provide for the designation of a trustee to hold title to the individual contracts issued. The trustee serves as custodian of the contracts, applies for additional contracts, and pays the premiums. The trust function can be performed by a permanent college pension committee established as a trust or by a corporate trustee, such as a bank or other fiduciary. The provisions of the plan are usually incorporated in a trust agreement, and the corporate trustee or pension committee is charged with the responsibility of administering the plan according to the rules set forth. The arrangement is often referred to as an individual contract pension trust, or simply as a pension trust. (Self-administered plans may also use trust agreements.) The individual policies issued under the plan are either retirement annuity policies or retirement income policies. Individual policy pension trusts are found mainly among small business employers, averaging 16 members per plan.[19]

Retirement Annuity Policies. Benefits of retirement annuity policies are normally expressed as units of $10 of monthly income payable at retirement. A predetermined level of benefits is funded through an established level of periodic contributions on behalf of each employee. If increases in the participant's salary are to result in an increase in benefits, additional policies must be purchased. New contracts providing additional benefits are normally written only in units of $5 or $10 per month of annuity income; therefore salary increases can be recognized for retirement purposes only when they are large enough to entitle the employee to an additional unit of $5 or $10 of monthly retirement income. When there have been enough increases in compensation, an additional policy in the appropriate amount is purchased. Over a period of years a large number of policies may be acquired for each individual employee. Because some insurers do not issue a retirement annuity policy that has less than five years to run, entry into a plan or recognition of salary changes may not be permitted for persons over age 59 or 60.

Retirement Income Policies. The principal difference between retirement income and retirement annuity policies is that the former incorporate a life insurance element, at additional cost. Benefits of the retirement income policy are expressed in terms of $1,000 of initial face value of life insurance for each $10 per month of annuity benefit. The policy pays a death benefit before retirement of $1,000 for each $10 unit of monthly income purchased, or the cash value, whichever is larger. Any excess of the death benefit over the cash value represents the insurance element. The employee may have to furnish the insurer with evidence of insurability unless the insurer is willing to waive this requirement. If an employee is uninsurable, retirement annuity policies may be issued. As under a retirement annuity policy, increases in compensation are recognized in a retirement income policy only when they result in the purchase of a minimum increased benefit of $5 or $10.

Other Provisions. The individual contracts may be used with either the the defined benefit or the defined contribution approach. Annuity rates are generally guaranteed on contracts purchased; future contracts are pur-

[19] Institute of Life Insurance, *Life Insurance Fact Book* (1967), p. 35.

chased at rates in effect at the time of purchase. The contracts are not usually vested immediately; such provisions as there are for vesting of retirement and death benefits are commonly written into the trust agreement and are administered by the trustee.

GROUP INSURED PLANS

Under a group insured pension plan the master contract, which covers all aspects of the plan, is between the insurer and the employer. The employee receives a certificate which summarizes benefits and coverage provisions. Many of the 94 commercial insurer plans reported for nonacademic employees are group annuity plans. The principal types of group contracts are group annuity contracts and group deposit administration contracts.

Group Annuity Plans. Group annuity plans provide their benefits through a series of single premium deferred annuities held by the insurance company for the ultimate benefit of the employee who qualifies. No life insurance coverage is included. A minimum group of 10 to 25 employees is usually required, and most insurers require 75 per cent participation if the plan is contributory.

Benefits of group annuity plans are usually expressed by a defined benefit formula. At retirement the employee is entitled to the income from the series of deferred annuities purchased for him; the income equals the benefits expressed by the formula. Some group variable annuity plans are now being written; they, of course, provide benefits that vary with the experience of the investments in the fund.

Although group annuities frequently use the defined benefit approach, they are also used in connection with a defined contribution pattern in which the plan contribution is a stated level percentage of the employee's annual compensation. Age and service requirements for vesting are usually incorporated in the master contract, although group annuities can be written to vest immediately, if this is desired by the employer. Plans using group annuities, however, do not usually provide for the immediate vesting of retirement benefits.

Deposit Administration Plans. Under group deposit administration contracts, *employer* contributions are not allocated to specific employees until the retirement date. The individual's annuity is purchased with money from the deposit administration fund at the time of retirement rather than in separate increments during working years, as under the group annuity. (Annuities may also be purchased as benefits vest.[20]) Premiums and investment earnings are credited to the deposit administration (or "active life") fund. Single premiums required to purchase annuities for retiring participants, or for those whose benefits become vested before retirement, are charged against the fund. The fund is also debited for any death or disability benefits if they are payable.

Under contributory plans the employee contributions are subject to separate accounting. They may be credited to the deposit administration fund, maintained in a separate employee fund, or applied to the purchase of paid-up annuities.

Self-Administered or Trusteed Plans

Self-administered or trusteed retirement plans account for another segment of college retirement planning. For faculty a self-administered or trusteed plan was reported by 7 per cent of institutions employing about 9 per cent of faculty. For administrative personnel this type of plan was reported by 8 per cent of institutions employing 21 per cent of such personnel. Self-administered or trusteed plans were reported for a somewhat higher percentage of clerical-service personnel than for the other employee classes, 13 per cent of institutions employing 27 per cent of total clerical-service personnel in responding institutions. The two largest self-administered plans are the University of California Retirement System and the State Universities Retirement System of Illinois.

The University of California System is administered by a governing board functioning under the authority of the Board of Regents of the University. Funds are held by the treasurer of the Regents. The governing board is responsible for the general administration of the plan, which covers the faculty and other employees of all the campuses of the University.

The State Universities Retirement System of Illinois is administered by a

[20] At the time that an immediate annuity is purchased under a deposit administration plan, interest and annuity rate guarantees are provided by the insurer, along with the establishment of appropriate contingency funds and methods of dividend allocation. Immediate participation guarantee (IPG) contracts, under which benefit payments are charged directly against the unallocated deposit administration account, go one step further and "guarantee that there are no guarantees." No contingency reserves are established, and the actual investment and actuarial experience is credited directly to the deposit administration fund.

Board of Trustees established by law and composed of board members of the participating institutions. The retirement board administers the system and is the custodian of all funds and is responsible for their investment.

Under trusteed plans, employer contributions and those of the employee, if any, are deposited with a trustee, usually a bank or other fiduciary, responsible for the investment of the funds, either as a separate trust or a commingled investment fund. The fiduciary does not guarantee minimum interest rates or assume mortality risks. The employer, or the fiduciary at the employer's direction, employs a consulting actuary to determine the extent of the plan's obligations according to characteristics of the covered group and actuarial assumptions approved by the employer. The employer pays the charges of the trustee for investment management and the fees for actuarial services.

A trust agreement sets forth definitions of terms, eligibility rules, contribution rates, retirement age provisions, the benefit formula, income options, the employee's rights on termination of employment (vesting provisions), death benefits before and after retirement, and the powers and the responsibilities of the retirement committee or board. It also specifies provisions for amendment or termination of the plan and usually states that the trust fund is to be the sole source of benefits.

A retirement committee or board is charged with the general administration of the plan. Although the trust agreement is primarily concerned with the receipt, investment, and disbursement of funds under the plan, it usually states in detail the duties and responsibilities of the retirement committee and the method of succession of individual members of this body. Under its authority are the maintenance of plan records, the determination of levels of contributions, the designation of actuarial consultants, the approval of standards used in actuarial calculations, the employment of accounting and legal services, and the preparation of published material regarding the plan.

Benefit payments are normally made directly from the trust fund to plan participants. Some trusteed plans, however, provide for the purchase from an insurer of an immediate annuity as employees retire.

Under a trusteed plan the employer is responsible for the establishment of the trust agreement, the limits of the power of the trustee, the actuarial assumptions and calculations used, and the general administration and payment of benefits. The smaller trusteed plans generally employ a corporate trustee, as described above. For instance, the Loyola University (Chicago) Employees' Retirement Plan is administered by the Retirement Allowance Committee, consisting of six persons appointed by the president, and is trusteed by a local bank. Larger plans may designate a somewhat different arrangement. In the University of Missouri's self-administered retirement plan the trust fund is held by The Board of Curators of the University of Missouri, the board of trustees of the institution.

Church Pension Systems

A church pension plan for faculty members is reported by 14 per cent of institutions employing 4 per cent of the faculty in institutions reporting plans. For administrative personnel 12 per cent of the institutions employing 3 per cent of such personnel report a church plan. The 8 per cent of institutions reporting a church plan for clerical-service employees employ 1½ per cent of employees in this category. All the institutions with church plans are privately supported, mainly liberal arts colleges and theological schools.

Church plans are generally administered by organizations created by authority of a parent church and operated in close association with it. Although a substantial number of the private colleges report a church plan, the plans usually cover relatively few individuals. Except in theological schools, a common coverage pattern is one in which ordained ministers serving as administrators or teachers belong to the church plan, and other faculty and employees participate in a TIAA-CREF or other plan.

Twelve pension systems provide the church plans reported by the colleges. Four provide separate benefit arrangements for ministers and missionaries as distinguished from lay employees. Eight of the 12 are defined contribution plans, 2 are defined benefit plans, 1 offers a choice of defined benefit or defined contribution, and 1 provides a flat dollar benefit related to years of service. Three of the plans have established variable annuities to accompany fixed-dollar benefits.

Five of the 12 systems provide immediate full vesting of benefits. Of the 7 plans with delayed vesting, 4 vest after five years of service, 1 vests when the employee's contributions plus interest earnings equal $1,000 or more, 1 vests gradually according to age and service with full vesting at age 55 regardless of service, and 1 vests after 20 years and the attainment of age 60. Four of the plans do not permit a vested employee who terminates service before retirement to withdraw employee contributions.

Church plans frequently incorporate packages of benefits including retirement and death benefits, health insurance, long-term disability benefits, and survivor benefits based on the number of children.

Most of the church plans are contributory, although a number of the systems recommend to the employer that he pay the entire premium. The total of employer and employee contribution rates range among the plans from 6 per cent to 13 per cent of salary. One system reduces benefits by a portion of the employee's Social Security benefits.

3

RETIREMENT: PARTICIPATION
AND BENEFITS

This chapter discusses the fundamental decisions to be made by a college in establishing, updating, or improving a retirement plan, including the choice of retirement system. The decisions are not of a highly technical nature, and a knowledge of the niceties of actuarial science and annuities is not necessary. They have to do with college objectives, and should be made by those who are acquainted with the goals of the institution and with the system of higher education as a whole. It is generally good policy to involve members of the board of trustees, administrative officers, and members of faculty and staff in the deliberations.

These are the fundamental decisions to be reviewed by the college:

1. Who should participate in the plan.
2. When should participation begin.
3. When should retirement occur.
4. What should be the benefit objective, and how much should be contributed toward the plan by the participant and the institution to achieve it.
5. What benefits should be established in recognition of service performed before establishment of a new plan, or what supplemental benefits should be provided for those nearing retirement or those already retired under an inadequate plan.

These decisions are essential to the goal of assuring a satisfactory retirement income and to the broader objective of contributing to the welfare of the college, its staff members, and its students. The plan will provide greatest advantages if decisions are made carefully and, once made, are reviewed and reconsidered from time to time. Some one person or group of persons—the president, the business officer, the personnel officer, a faculty-administration committee, or a committee of the board of trustees—should accept continuing responsibility for recommending changes to fit the retirement plan to changing needs and objectives of the college. Today, even more than in prior years, a college's retirement provisions have a strong influence on its ability to attract competent men and women and to part with mediocre ones on reasonable financial terms.

Classes of Employees Covered

Normally all categories of employees of a college or university should be covered by a retirement plan. In the early college retirement plans, faculty and administrative officers were often the only employees included. Currently 75 per cent of the institutions have retirement plans for their clerical-service employees, and these institutions employ 95 per cent of total clerical-service personnel (see Table 2.1).

Most colleges exclude part-time and definitely temporary employees from the retirement plan. Whether to include part-time employees depends largely on their permanence and the local situation. A number of institutions include faculty and other employees who work "half-time or more." Professional schools which depend largely on a part-time faculty often include them in the plan unless their employment is considered temporary.

Entry Age—Voluntary and Compulsory Participation

During a major portion of an individual's working years, participation in a retirement plan should be a condition of employment. Optional participation at ages under 30, and during a stated initial service period, is frequently allowed. Some colleges make participation optional for a year or two for all those in service when a plan is first established. With these exceptions, participation should be compulsory.

The AAUP-AAC Statement recommends that the retirement plan "Require participation after not more than one year of service by all full-time faculty members and administrators who have attained a specified age, not later than 30." If retirement is at age 65 or later, this entry age permits a span of participation of 35 years or more. This is long enough to build up an adequate benefit within the bounds of reasonable cost.

The experience of colleges with no retirement plans or with voluntary plans has shown that it is wishful thinking to believe that all or even a substantial portion of college staff members will make adequate provision for their old age if left to their own devices. Few people realize the large sums of money that must be saved during working years in order to provide an adequate income during the rather considerable number of retirement years that lie ahead. Perhaps the frequently repeated statement that the life span *from birth* in America is now about 67 years for men and 74 years for women tends to obscure the fact that men who have *already reached* age 65 have a life expectancy of some 16 years beyond that age, women about 20 years, and that either can live to well over age 90. Providing financial support for that long a period of time is a major job.

The employing institution has a strong interest in requiring its staff members to participate in the retirement plan. Under a voluntary retirement plan, in which a staff member can join or stay out, a college may make substantial annuity contributions for those who do join and yet not meet its retirement objectives. It is not merely theory that the very persons who lack the determination to save are among the ones who will not join a voluntary plan. Staff members who may be the most valuable to the college during their productive years, well liked and highly regarded by students, alumni, and faculty, may, if left to their own devices, reach retirement age without funds. The college may find itself accused of cruelty if it parts with them at retirement without providing income during their remaining years. Yet to keep a staff member in service after he should be retired is a hindrance to students and colleagues and is unfair to those who do participate in the plan and are retired at the expected age. If a free pension is granted the improvident staff member on an emergency basis, it may relieve his problems but it is unfair to persons who have over the years shared the cost of their retirement benefits with the college, and it establishes an unfortunate precedent.

Does a signed waiver for the record protect the college from the gaps in its retirement planning created by those who fail to participate under a voluntary plan? College officials who have had experience with this say that a waiver signed many years before, no matter how strongly worded, provides scant surcease from embarrassment on the part of the college when a staff member must be retired without adequate income.[1]

When a new plan is installed or an old plan is extended to new groups, it may be impractical to require participation of employees who have worked at the college for some years and whose employment understanding has never included participation in a retirement plan. For this reason, participation is sometimes *required* only when these employees receive an increase in rank or salary. Sometimes participation is made voluntary until a certain date in the future, usually one or two years after the inauguration or extension of the plan, after which all eligible persons must participate. If prior service benefits are being provided, they are normally made contingent on participation in the new plan.

WAITING PERIOD

Participation in the retirement plan should not be deferred beyond the time the individual is really launched on his career. Many college retirement plans, except public employee and state teacher systems, specify a waiting period before participation begins, usually 1, 2, or 3 years of employment with the college. In about 40 per cent of the TIAA-CREF plans there is also a provision that the individual must have attained the age of 30 before participation is required.

A waiting period allows for the fact that the first year or two of employment and the years before age 30 cover the period when newly hired staff members are making some initial decisions regarding their career and the type of employer they wish to work for, and when the college is evaluating them to determine whether to encourage them to stay.

A number of institutions with contributory plans permit voluntary par-

---

[1] One university, which requires participation when a faculty member is granted tenure, leaves it voluntary until then, although participation is strongly encouraged. A waiver is required of those who do not wish to participate during nontenure appointment, part of which reads as follows: "I fully understand that _____ considers nonparticipation in the plan most unwise, urges that I join in the plan, requires membership by tenured faculty, and accepts this waiver only under strong pressure from me that it do so. I further understand that failure to join TIAA-CREF at this time may greatly reduce my retirement benefits and that _____ will not under any circumstances undertake, in respect of any time when this waiver is in effect, to supplement any retirement income I may have should it ultimately prove inadequate, or provide any if I have none. I recognize also that the amount equal to 10 per cent (10%) of my salary which would be contributed to this plan in my behalf by _____ in the absence of this waiver will not be available to me in any other form, nor will it be recoverable within the plan at any later date."

ticipation in the plan before the individual has completed the waiting period. An opportunity for early voluntary participation seems to result generally in participation being chosen by those who have a professional attitude toward college employment and a farsighted one regarding their own affairs, and they are likely to be the persons the employer is most anxious to encourage.

Regardless of the established waiting period, many colleges have found it advantageous to permit immediate participation for staff members employed at ranks above that of instructor and for those who bring with them approved annuity contracts started elsewhere.

Income Goals

STATEMENT OF PRINCIPLES

The AAUP-AAC Statement recommends that the retirement plan and the Social Security program together provide the long-term participant an after-tax retirement income "equivalent in purchasing power to approximately two-thirds of the yearly disposable income realized from his salary after taxes and other mandatory deductions during his last few years of full-time employment." There should be "provision for continuing more than half of such retirement income to a surviving spouse."

This goal is based on participation in a retirement plan—or a succession of plans—for 35 or more years, a period corresponding with the major part of a working career. It posits entry into the plan after not more than one year of service by those who have attained a specified age, "not later than 30." It is important to note that the income objective is stated in terms of (1) a *disposable* income that is (2) capable of maintaining its purchasing power and (3) includes protection for a surviving spouse.

DISPOSABLE INCOME

In previous AAUP-AAC Statements the retirement income goal was expressed in terms of before-tax income and called for a retirement income of 50 per cent of average salary over the 10 years of service preceding retirement. The current Statement, by relating *disposable* retirement income to *disposable* income just before retirement, provides a more realistic measure of retirement income adequacy. It does this by recognizing that personal income taxes and other deductions from salary generally weigh much more heavily on earned income than on retirement income.

During retirement, taxes as a percentage of income, as well as in absolute amounts, are usually lower than during working years. Taxable income is usually lower and persons age 65 or over are entitled to a double income tax exemption. Social Security benefits are not subject to income tax, nor is that portion of the retirement annuity based on employee contributions. In addition there are no more annuity contributions to make or Social Security taxes to pay.

Many of the demands that consume preretirement pay decline during retirement. The children's education is usually completed, and they have often become financially independent. The home mortgage may be paid off. It is usually a time to ease up on personal savings. Professional expenses, such as dues to learned societies, professional journals, and self-paid trips to professional meetings, may be reduced or discontinued. The expenses of travel to and from work and lunches away from home are decreased. A lower level of contributions to charities and churches is expected from older people. For all of these reasons, "two-thirds of disposable income" will go a long way toward maintaining the retirement living standard.

LOWER-INCOME EMPLOYEES

The AAUP-AAC "two-thirds" goal applies generally to professional personnel. For lower-income employees the goal may be insufficient. However, the fact that Social Security benefits are larger as a percentage of salary for lower-paid people aids the institution in achieving income adequacy for them. For lower-paid groups after a career of service, total retirement benefits as a percentage of former disposable income may have to rise somewhat above the percentage for faculty in order to meet a minimum income standard.

MAINTAINING PURCHASING POWER
AND LIVING STANDARDS

The cost of living can go up or down, but under present economic conditions it tends to rise, even over relatively short periods. The extent to which the purchasing power of a fixed income can be eroded over time is perhaps not fully comprehended by persons who have not yet retired, since their salaries or wages tend to increase as living costs increase. The AAUP-AAC recommendation that the retirement plan be designed to maintain purchasing power has been in effect since 1953.

Past experience with fixed incomes provides telling instances of loss of purchasing power. Most periods of severe inflation, like the 1940s and the early 1950s, have occurred during and soon after wars. But even moderate chronic price inflation can undermine a fixed income. For example, prices rose at an average rate of 1.3 per cent per year between 1960 and 1965 (before rising faster in response to economic pressures connected with the Viet Nam war). During these five years of near price stability, the purchas-

Figure 3.1: PERSONAL CONSUMPTION EXPENDITURES PER CAPITA
IN CURRENT PRICES AND CONSTANT DOLLARS

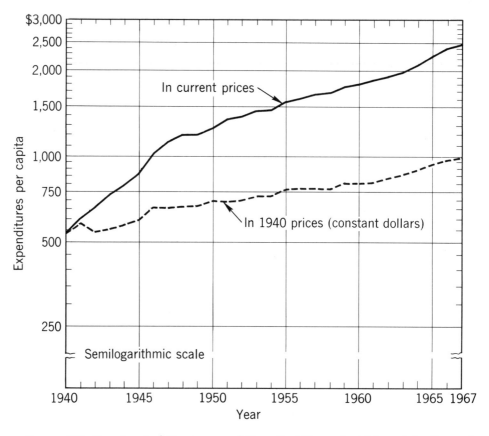

Source: U.S. Department of Commerce and Council of Economic Advisers data, *Economic Report of the President* (February, 1968), pp. 212, 227.

ing power of fixed incomes fell just over 6 per cent. Even if price increases could be held to this moderate rate during the more than 20 years of annuity payments expected for a husband and wife on retirement at age 65, the purchasing power of a fixed income would decline about 25 per cent during their retirement years.

Living *standards* change as well as living *costs*. The American economy has increased its output of goods and services, measured in dollars of constant purchasing power, at an average rate of slightly over 3 per cent a year for the past century or more. During the past twenty years the rate has averaged nearly 4 per cent. This growth has permitted most Americans to live better or at least to consume more. This is illustrated by Figure 3.1, which shows personal consumption expenditures per capita since 1940. The upper line, which measures spending in current prices, shows the number of dollars needed each year to keep up with both rising living standards and increasing prices. The lower line measures spending in terms of 1940 prices and thus suggests how average consumption of goods and services—not distorted by price change—has risen during the period.

Table 3.1 uses similar data to suggest how retirement incomes in four different periods would have had to change to keep pace with the combined effect of changing prices and living standards.

TABLE 3.1: PERSONAL CONSUMPTION EXPENDITURES PER CAPITA AS A PER CENT OF AMOUNT IN FOUR BASE YEARS

An Index of Income Needed to Keep Up with Changing Prices and Living Standards

Year of Retirement	1930	1940	1950	1960
First year	100.0	100.0	100.0	100.0
2 years later	68.6	122.4	109.7	105.7
4 years later	71.6	145.9	115.7	116.0
6 years later	85.2	189.2	125.9	131.3
8 years later	86.8	220.9	132.3	147.4
10 years later	94.5	234.9	143.0	
12 years later	115.7	257.6	151.1	
14 years later	137.9	271.6	165.8	
16 years later	178.8	295.7	187.9	

Source: Computed from U.S. Department of Commerce and Council of Economic Advisors data, *Economic Report of The President* (1968), pp. 212, 227.

Salary increases generally permit the actively employed to meet rising prices and to share in the country's rising productivity. A fixed retirement income cuts the individual off from participating in rising living standards and from any protection against inflation. The variable annuity was developed more than 15 years ago to help make the retirement incomes of college staff members more responsive to changing price levels and living standards through direct participation in the investment experience of common stocks. The variable annuity and other methods being used to help retirement incomes adjust to changing economic conditions are discussed in Chapter 2.

Retirement Plan Contributions

The AAUP-AAC Statement emphasizes the importance of an adequate level of contributions and a substantial employer role in each year's contributions to the employee's annuity. The pertinent sections of the Statement recommend that the retirement plan should:

1. Be financed by contributions made during each year of service, including leaves of absence with pay, with the institution contributing as much as or more than each participant . . . .
2. Maintain contributions at a level considered sufficient to give the long-term participant a retirement income that is appropriately related to his level of income prior to retirement, with provisions for continuing more than half of such income to a surviving spouse.

DEFINED CONTRIBUTION APPROACH

Defined contribution plans, described in Chapter 2, fix contributions in advance as a percentage of each year's salary. The majority of college retirement plans (including virtually all of the TIAA-CREF plans and a number of the insurance company plans, self-administered plans, and church systems) use the defined contribution approach. Eighteen of the 72 public retirement systems covering employees in higher education use this method in whole or part: 13 provide defined contribution benefits from employee contributions and defined benefits from employer contributions, and 5 use the defined contribution approach for both employer and employee contributions.

The level of contributions and the investment earnings on them determine the size of retirement benefits under a defined contribution plan. The
majority of these plans use one of the following contribution patterns:

1. The *level percentage* pattern, with contributions a uniform percentage
of each person's full salary; for example, contributions that are 10 per cent
of salary, or 15 per cent.

2. The *step-rate* pattern, with contributions set at one rate, usually 10
per cent, on the portion of a person's salary within the Social Security earnings base, and at a higher rate, often 15 per cent, above the base. This
differential reflects the fact that Social Security pays an old age income on
salary within the earnings base and not on salary above it.

Contribution Rates and Benefits. There is no way to predict future benefits with precision under any retirement plan that is flexible enough to
meet changing needs and objectives over the years. However, an illustration,
based on assumed salary scales and the Social Security Act as amended in
1967, can be helpful in visualizing the relative level of benefits provided by
various contribution patterns and by Social Security.

The salary scales shown in Table 3.2 are based on three starting salaries,
$4,000, $8,000, and $12,000, each increasing at a rate of 4 per cent a year to
reflect promotions as well as changes in the general level of compensation in
higher education. This is not a prediction of future academic salaries, of
course, but this rate of growth does approximate the annual rate of in-

TABLE 3.2: SALARY SCALES FOR BENEFIT ILLUSTRATIONS
Average Annual Earnings During 5-Year Periods

Age	Salary Scale A	Salary Scale B	Salary Scale C
(Starting salary at age 30)	($4,000)	($8,000)	($12,000)
30–34	$ 4,300	$ 8,700	$13,000
35–39	5,300	10,500	15,800
40–44	6,400	12,800	19,200
45–49	7,800	15,600	23,400
50–54	9,500	19,000	28,400
55–59	11,600	23,100	34,600
60–64	14,000	28,000	42,000

Final 5-Year Average Annual DISPOSABLE Income

	$10,200	$18,400	$25,300

crease experienced by college and university faculty salaries over 35-year periods during most of this century.[2]

Figure 3.2 illustrates the disposable retirement income, expressed as a percentage of preretirement income or "take-home" pay, produced under

Figure 3.2: RETIREMENT INCOME ILLUSTRATION

If Entry Age Is 30 (Male) and Retirement Is at Age 65 (Joint and Two-thirds Option)

*Disposable Retirement Income as a Per Cent of
Final Average Preretirement Disposable Income*

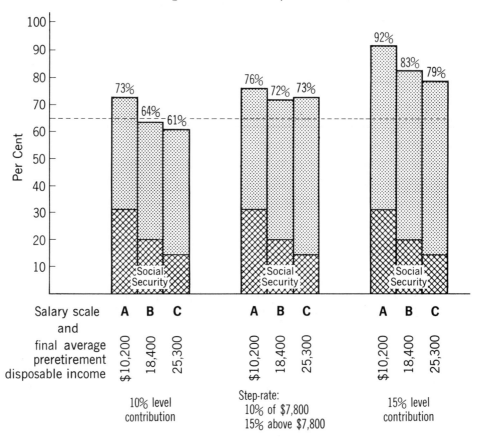

[2] Faculty salaries have grown faster in some periods than others, and salaries have declined in some years. An analysis of data contained in studies by the National Bureau of Economic Research and the Fund for the Advancement of Education show a median rate of 3.7 per cent for 22 career periods of 35 years each, assuming a person advanced from assistant professor to full professor. The comparable median rate for advancement from instructor to full professor was 4.9 per cent.

various contribution patterns, a 10 per cent level plan, a 10–15 per cent step-rate plan, and a 15 per cent level plan. Under all three patterns the individual participates continuously from age 30 to retirement at age 65. His disposable income before retirement is gross income less Social Security taxes, a 5 per cent contribution to the retirement plan, and 1967 federal and state (New York) income taxes. The retirement income is the annuity benefit plus the husband and wife Social Security benefit less federal and state income taxes. The participant's wife is two years younger, and at retirement they choose the joint and two-thirds to survivor option. The examples are based on TIAA 1968 deferred annuity rates and the 1968 dividend scale (not guaranteed). It is assumed that all premiums are paid to TIAA rather than to a combined TIAA-CREF annuity.

In the benefit illustration the step-rate plan comes closest to meeting the AAUP-AAC benefit objective of two-thirds of final average disposable income and to producing benefits that are a fairly uniform percentage of earnings among the three salary scales. The 15 per cent level contribution plan provides superior benefits for all three scales but, of course, costs more than the others.

Control Levers. There are three main levers to use in adjusting retirement costs and benefits under a defined contribution plan: (1) the age at which contributions begin, (2) the age at which annuity payments begin, and (3) the level of contributions. Table 3.3, based on the same assumptions as the illustrations in Figure 3.2, illustrates these three levers. The approximate effect of each of them is as follows:

1. Delaying the start of contributions by 1 year for a person who is in his early thirties decreases the retirement benefit at age 65 by about 3 per cent (depending on salary scale), and by 4 per cent or more for each year's delay in his forties. In order to obtain adequate benefits at a reasonable contribution level, participation in the retirement plan should begin at age 30 or soon thereafter.

2. Each year's postponement of retirement after age 65 increases the retirement benefit by about 10 per cent over the previous year for a person beginning contributions in his thirties or forties. Delaying the retirement age has a powerful effect on benefits because interest accumulates on the total fund for a longer period, contributions may be continued for a longer

TABLE 3.3: VARIATIONS IN DISPOSABLE RETIREMENT INCOME ACCORD-
ING TO AGE OF ENTRY, RETIREMENT AGE, AND CONTRIBUTION RATE
(Salary Scale B: $8,000—$28,000; Joint and Two-Thirds Annuity Option)

	Retirement at Age 65		Retirement at Age 70	
Entry Age	Disposable Retirement Income	% of Final Average Preretirement Disposable Income	Disposable Retirement Income	% of Final Average Preretirement Disposable Income
	10 Per Cent Contribution Rate plus Social Security			
30	$11,763	64	$16,062	73
35	10,495	57	14,605	66
40	9,232	50	13,116	59
	10–15 Per Cent Step-Rate Contribution plus Social Security			
30	$13,343	72	$18,478	84
35	12,051	65	17,032	77
40	10,683	58	15,484	70
	15 Per Cent Contribution Rate plus Social Security			
30	$15,197	83	$20,872	95
35	13,497	73	18,944	86
40	11,758	64	16,954	77

period, and, when payments to the annuitant begin, the larger accumulation
is spread over a shorter assumed life span.

3. The contribution rate, of course, has a direct influence on the size of
benefits. Premiums equal to 15 per cent of salary at a given age will purchase benefits one and one-half times as large as those resulting from
premiums equal to 10 per cent of salary.

These three control levers should be set or adjusted only after careful
consideration of all factors involved. The higher the retirement age, for
example, the greater will be the benefits from a given level of contributions. But, in considering the higher age, the institution must balance the
larger annuity benefits thereby obtained, and the longer service of its staff
members, against the likelihood of having to keep some of its older staff
members on full salary after their capacities have waned, and against the
effect of a high retirement age on the attitudes of younger staff members.

For each institution, the level of contributions, the retirement age, and
the entry age selected usually reflect a balancing of factors that cannot
always be measured in dollars and cents alone. There is no ideal retirement
age or size of retirement benefit that will meet all needs of all individuals,

but the institution by recognizing the factors involved can set its goal to provide adequately and equitably for the great majority of its people.

DEFINED BENEFIT APPROACH

Defined benefit plans fix benefits in advance as a percentage of salary for each year of service. A typical benefit formula is 1½ per cent of final average salary for each year of service. As noted in Chapter 2, the employee's contribution generally runs about 5 per cent of salary but in some plans rises to 8 per cent or more; the employer's cost is the balance necessary to purchase the defined benefit. Under a funded plan the employer's contributions to the plan range from zero for the younger employees to 20 or 30 per cent or more of salary for those nearing retirement. The principal concentration of defined benefit plans covering employees in higher education is among the public employee and state teacher systems.

Flat benefit plans, giving the same benefit to all persons without regard to differences in salary, are rarely found in the colleges. Most of them are negotiated plans for industrial workers paid on an hourly basis. They provide a certain specified retirement benefit, such as $150 a month for each participant after 30 years of service. Or the benefit may be expressed as a monthly retirement benefit for each year of service, for example, $3 or $4 a month multiplied by the number of years of service.

Sharing Contributions

The AAUP-AAC Statement recommends that the retirement plan "Be financed by contributions made during each year of service, including leaves of absence with pay, with the institution contributing as much as or more than each participant." One of the basic questions in designing or reviewing a retirement plan is how much of the plan's cost shall be contributed by the participant and how much by the institution.

The great majority of retirement plans in higher education provide for a sharing of contributions by the employer and the employee. As indicated in Table 3.4, 83 per cent of the plans covering faculty and administrative personnel, and 79 per cent of those covering clerical-service employees, provide for joint contributions. The employer pays the full cost (noncontributory plans) in about 15 per cent of plans for faculty and administrative

TABLE 3.4: SHARING OF RETIREMENT PLAN CONTRIBUTIONS

	Faculty		Administrative		Clerical-Service	
	Per Cent Insts N = 1,170	*Per Cent EEs* N = 283,936	*Per Cent Insts* N = 1,141	*Per Cent EEs* N = 107,705	*Per Cent Insts* N = 921	*Per Cent EEs* N = 420,974
Employer pays full cost	14.3	10.0	14.5	13.3	17.4	18.2
Employer and employee share cost	82.8	88.3	82.5	85.2	78.5	80.0
Employee pays full cost	1.3	0.9	1.3	0.4	1.7	0.8
No response	1.6	0.8	1.7	1.1	2.4	1.0
Total	100.0	100.0	100.0	100.0	100.0	100.0

personnel, and in 17 per cent of plans covering clerical-service employees. Plans in which the employee pays the whole cost are negligible in number and size.

Despite the relatively small proportion of plans in which the college pays the whole cost, the subject of contributory versus noncontributory plans should be carefully considered for its effect on the participants, the institution, and the level of benefits to be provided under the plan.

Some of the reasons advanced in favor of noncontributory retirement plans are:

1. Favorable tax treatment is accorded employer contributions. Under present federal income tax laws an employee's contributions to a retirement plan are included in his taxable income, but employer contributions are not. (The employee is taxed on this deferred portion of compensation when he receives it as part of his annuity income, a time when his taxable income is presumably less.)

2. A noncontributory plan is simpler to administer. There are no salary deductions to make, and the plan automatically assures coverage of all those eligible without arguments with persons who resist participating. No records are required to distinguish employer from employee contributions.

3. A noncontributory plan avoids situations in which departing participants may urge the return of contributions made through salary withholding, despite provisions for noncashability of retirement benefits.

4. There is a high degree of employee approval of a noncontributory

plan. Employees appreciate the employer's willingness to assume the full cost of the plan as a part of employee compensation.

Some of the reasons advanced in favor of contributory retirement plans are:

1. Employee contributions play an important role in building benefits. Unless the college is confident that it can maintain the necessary level of annuity contributions without employee participation, it probably should not adopt the noncontributory basis. Once a noncontributory plan has been established, it is not easy to change to a contributory basis.

2. It seems reasonable for an employee to share in the cost of benefits that are fully vested in him at all times.

3. Contributory plans seem to promote more interest and understanding of the plan among participants, since they are reminded of costs and benefits and have more of a voice in the provisions of the plan because of their direct financial participation.

4. The institution can retain the sharing principle of a contributory plan while giving each participant the tax treatment of a noncontributory plan, if he so chooses, by use of the salary reduction provisions of Section 403(b) of the Internal Revenue Code, described later in this chapter.

A few institutions with contributory plans for faculty have established noncontributory plans for the lower-paid employees, including the clerical-service groups. Their reasons are as follows:

1. At the lower salary levels every take-home dollar counts more. It is a relatively heavier burden for the clerical and service employees to have part of their earnings deducted than it is for employees who are earning perhaps a good deal more.

2. Experience has shown that, when lower-paid employees have contributed to the retirement plan, there are all too frequently occasions on which the employee requests the return of his contributions for other uses. In plans under which employee contributions are returned if the employee leaves, this often means that the employee is encouraged to leave by the availability of the potential cash. A noncontributory plan does not raise this question.

3. Because of the relatively greater weight of Social Security benefits for those at the lower salary levels, a lower contribution to the annuity can support a good level of total benefits.

Taxation of Annuity Contributions

Pension plans in business and industry must "qualify" under standards set forth in the Internal Revenue Code and related Treasury regulations in order to be entitled to: (1) deductibility of employer contributions as a business expense; (2) tax exemption of pension fund earnings and appreciation; and (3) employee exemption from current income tax on employer contributions. The qualification requirements, established primarily to control corporate use of tax incentives, have little meaning when applied to tax-exempt institutions, which of course finance their pension commitments without the incentive of corporate tax deductions, and therefore in 100-cent dollars. To give college employees tax treatment equivalent to that provided under qualified plans, the Bureau of Internal Revenue held in the early 1930s that a college's contributions toward annuities for its employees were not currently taxable income to the employee. This treatment was added to the Internal Revenue Code in the 1942 amendments and was continued in the 1954 Code. Then in 1958 Congress enacted a specific "substitute for educational, charitable, and religious organizations for the 'qualification' required of industrial plans." [3]

This substitute is Section 403(b) of the Code, which sets a uniform limit, or "exclusion allowance," within which contributions by educational, charitable, and religious institutions to fully vested annuity contracts are not taxed currently to the employee, but are taxed instead during his retirement years.

THE EXCLUSION ALLOWANCE

An employee's exclusion allowance is 20 per cent of the "includable compensation" (taxable income) the college pays him for the current calendar year, multiplied by his years of employment by the college, less all past annuity contributions made by the college and not included in his taxable income in prior years. This "20 per cent rule" accommodates the needs of college retirement plans, including the purchase of current service and prior service benefits. It also leaves some room for the payment of supplemental contributions a college may want to make for its older faculty members to offset the effects of past inflation, short-term participation in the retirement

---

[3] U.S., Congress, Senate, Committee on Finance, *Technical Amendments Act of 1958*, S. Rept. 1983, 85th Cong., 2nd sess., 1958, p. 38.

plan, or other factors that may have impaired the adequacy of a person's prospective retirement income.

PAYMENT BY SALARY REDUCTION

The tax advantages that business and industry can offer their employees through profit sharing, stock options, incentive plans, and the like—often over and above a qualified pension plan—are unavailable in the nonprofit sector. This adds to the competitive problems of attracting talented men and women to academic employment. A small amount of the differential was removed by the 1958 legislation and its subsequent regulations, which made it possible for an employee of a college or university to take a limited reduction in salary in order to release funds for the institution to deposit in his annuity contract as before-tax employer contributions. The salary reduction is permissible only to the extent that regular pension contributions by the institution fall short of the employee's exclusion allowance.

The voluntary aspect of the 1958 legislation, the "salary-or-annuity option," is now used by many colleges and universities to give participants in a contributory annuity plan the choice of making their required contributions by salary *re*duction, rather than *de*duction, if they prefer, thus deferring taxes on these contributions until the retirement years.[4] This retains the sharing principle of a contributory plan, and at the same time leaves each participant free to choose the tax treatment of a noncontributory plan if he wishes. A number of institutions also permit staff members to reduce their salaries, within the statutory limit, in order to purchase supplemental annuity benefits on a tax-deferred basis. The granting by Congress of this amount of discretion has been helpful in strengthening the retirement security of many educators.

Table 3.5 summarizes the permitted uses of the option for regular contributions in institutions with contributory plans, and for extra contributions. For faculty and administrative personnel, 37 per cent of the institutions, employing 37 per cent of such personnel, permit optional use of salary reduction for regular plan contributions, and approximately equal numbers do not permit its use. It should be noted in this connection that this use is not available for regular contributions under publicly administered retire-

---

[4] Other terms sometimes used to describe the salary-or-annuity option are "tax-deferred annuity" and the improper and misleading term, "tax-sheltered annuity."

TABLE 3.5: EMPLOYEE CONTRIBUTIONS UNDER SECTION 403(b), INTERNAL REVENUE CODE

Institutional Provision for Use of Section 403(b), Internal Revenue Code for Regular and for Extra Employee Retirement Plan Contributions

	Faculty		Administrative		Clerical-Service	
	Per Cent Insts N = 994	Per Cent EEs N = 255,335	Per Cent Insts N = 969	Per Cent EEs N = 93,264	Per Cent Insts N = 747	Per Cent EEs N = 342,304
Regular contributions[a]						
Not permitted	33.7	43.5	34.7	39.8	43.4	64.5
Required	22.8	15.9	22.1	12.7	20.7	10.1
Optional	37.4	37.0	36.7	41.9	27.6	18.4
No response	6.1	3.6	6.5	5.6	8.3	7.0
Total	100.0	100.0	100.0	100.0	100.0	100.0
	N = 1,170	N = 283,936	N = 1,141	N = 107,705	N = 921	N = 420,974
Extra contributions						
Not permitted	27.7	27.5	27.2	22.4	34.6	40.2
Permitted	67.4	70.5	66.9	71.6	55.0	49.6
No response	4.9	2.0	5.9	6.0	10.4	10.2
Total	100.0	100.0	100.0	100.0	100.0	100.0

[a] Cannot be made under Section 403(b) to publicly administered retirement systems under current regulations.

ment plans. About a fifth of the institutions require salary reduction, but they employ less than a fifth of the respective employee classes. Two-thirds of clerical-service employees are in institutions not permitting use of salary reduction for this employee class for regular plan contributions.

The salary-or-annuity option offers a systematic, tax-deferred method of setting aside additional funds for retirement income over and above the regular employee contributions to the retirement plan. As with regular contributions, the college must approve use of the option for additional annuity payments via salary reduction. After use of the option is approved, the institution and the employee must enter into an agreement under which the employee agrees to a salary reduction and the institution agrees to contribute an amount corresponding to the reduction to a fully vested, nontransferable (i.e., nonassignable) annuity contract for the employee. If existing annuity contracts issued under the institution's retirement plan do not meet these requirements, contributions can be made to separate annuity contracts that do.

As shown in Table 3.5, faculty and administrative personnel may use the salary-or-annuity option for extra annuity contributions in about two-thirds of the institutions reporting a retirement plan. Seventy per cent of faculty are employed by the institutions permitting this use of the option. About half of all clerical-service employees are at institutions that make the option available.

Prior Service and Supplementary Benefits

About one-half of 1 per cent of faculty and administrative personnel in higher education are in institutions which have not yet established a retirement plan for their employees. A somewhat larger proportion, 5 per cent, of the clerical-service employees are in institutions not having a plan for this category. Although these proportions of total staff are small, the number of institutions without plans is fairly substantial; 311 institutions report no plan for clerical-service employees; 91, no plan for administrative personnel; and 62, no plan for faculty. Almost all of these institutions are small private liberal arts colleges, professional schools, or seminaries.

For these institutions the most important goal is to set up a plan for future service. But attention needs to be paid to prior service benefits, that is, supplementary benefits for persons with substantial service when the plan begins and whose remaining years to retirement are too few to permit normal contributions for future service benefits to produce a satisfactory retirement income. Although the cost of prior service benefits is only transitional, its presence has led some colleges to delay establishment of any retirement plan. They have not seen their way clear to meeting the cost of both future and prior service benefits at the same time, for the moment overlooking the fact that the situation only gets worse by waiting and that something needs to be done for long-service people in any event, such as keeping them in service, paying a salary during retirement, or buying an annuity when they retire.

DETERMINING THE BENEFIT

If prior service benefits are to be provided, the college should choose a uniform method of determining the level. Otherwise the governing board is likely to run into difficult problems requiring arbitrary decisions and perhaps leading to greater liberality in some cases than in others just as deserving.

In determining such benefits the colleges frequently use a defined benefit formula. Credited prior service is usually expressed as years of service preceding the effective date of the new plan, less the waiting period, if any, before participation in the new plan is required. A 1 per cent prior service benefit, for instance, would be expressed by the following formula:

$$\text{Monthly prior service benefit} = (1\%) \times \left(\begin{array}{c}\tfrac{1}{12} \text{ annual salary on} \\ \text{effective date of plan}\end{array}\right) \times \left(\begin{array}{c}\text{years of credited} \\ \text{prior service}\end{array}\right)$$

If the college is installing a step-rate plan, an appropriate prior service benefit can be calculated in two parts. For a 10–15 per cent step-rate contribution pattern, for example, the prior service factor might be 1 per cent of current salary within the Social Security earnings base on the effective date of the plan, and $1\tfrac{1}{2}$ per cent of current salary above, times years of credited prior service.

Prior service benefits are usually financed out of current budget as they become payable. Some institutions fund prior service benefits through the purchase of single premium deferred annuity contracts, others through periodic premium deferred annuity contracts. The use of periodic premium payments helps spread the financing over the individual's remaining service period, and the load can be fairly well distributed except for those who must retire soon.

SUPPLEMENTARY BENEFITS

The provisions of existing plans should be reviewed and revised from time to time, where the need is indicated. Under many plans the generally lower salaries of the 1930s, 1940s, and early 1950s, combined with low interest rates for nearly a quarter of a century, and inflation have resulted in inadequate benefits for many people now approaching retirement. Some colleges have taken cognizance of this by establishing supplementary benefits. Since supplementary benefits are granted in recognition of prior service during which retirement benefit accruals proved to be inadequate, they are often determined in the same manner as prior service benefits but with an offset in the benefit formula for benefits accrued to date. The earlier discussion of Section 403(b) of the Internal Revenue Code in this chapter emphasized the manner in which an individual and his college can share in the cost of bringing inadequate benefits up to a reasonable point without placing an unreasonable income tax liability on the individual.

Leave of Absence

The chief purpose of a leave of absence program for faculty and other professional staff members is to assure continuing opportunity for the growth of professional capacities. The 1965 AAUP-AAC conference on leaves of absence observed that "It is our belief that leaves, though serving both the personal needs of individuals and the interests of institutions, are primarily an investment of society for strengthening higher education . . ."[5]

Leaves of absence are usually classified according to whether they are granted with or without pay.

LEAVES WITH PAY

Regular compensation or part of it continues during leaves with pay. Institutional and individual contributions to the retirement plan normally continue, therefore, as a matter of course. The contribution rate is generally applied to the level of salary paid during the leave.

LEAVES WITHOUT PAY

Leaves without pay are granted for a wider variety of purposes than leaves with pay. They may include leaves for study, for research supported by outside grants or other sources independent of the college, or for temporary service under other employers, including governmental organizations, foundations, or private enterprise.

The AAUP-AAC Statement recommends that "An institution's retirement plan should be so organized as to permit voluntary annuity contributions from employees on leaves of absence without pay." The leave of absence conference report suggests that "Those institutions that continue their con-

[5] "A Statement on Leaves of Absence," *American Association of University Professors Bulletin,* LIII (Autumn, 1967), 271. The report of the conference on leaves of absence was prepared by Professor Mark H. Ingraham of the University of Wisconsin, Dean J. Douglas Brown of Princeton University, and Professor Neill Megaw of Williams College and was approved for publication by the conference participants.

tributions toward retirement annuities for faculty members on leaves without pay are generous—wisely generous." [6]

If a staff member on leave without pay becomes a full-time employee of another institution or organization, it is reasonable to expect the new institution to assume the cost of institutional contributions to the individual's retirement annuity and group insurance coverage. The leave of absence conference report recommends that organizations financing leaves for research and study include an amount sufficient to maintain institutional annuity and group insurance contributions. [7]

Retirement Age for Faculty

The story is told of Elihu Root who, as a trustee of Hamilton College, was one day discussing with fellow trustees the retiring age for professors. Someone asked whether there were any members of the faculty approaching that age. Mr. Root replied, "Well, we haven't any going in the opposite direction." [8]

A retirement plan presupposes an age at which retirement will occur. The AAUP-AAC Statement notes that "Retirement provisions currently in effect at different institutions vary in the age specified for retirement and in the degree of flexibility relating to extensions of active service. Cogent arguments can be advanced in support of a number of these arrangements. Since conditions vary greatly among institutions, however, no universally applicable formula can be prescribed. Plans in which the retirement age falls within the range of 65 to 70 appear to be in conformity with reasonable practice."

At what age should college staff members retire? As in other matters of human relations, there is no formula that will deal equitably with all persons concerned. Perhaps sometime we shall have developed yardsticks to measure physiological age as nicely as we now measure chronological age, to measure the intangibles of mental elasticity, artistic and scientific awareness, sensitivity to the problems and concerns of youth, and the variety of capacities that make up the good teacher. But as yet we have no such tests as criteria for retirement. The judgment of the staff member about his own abilities often differs from that of his students, colleagues, or superiors.

[6] *Ibid.*, p. 273.   [7] *Loc. cit.*   [8] Jessup, *Elihu Root* (1938), p. 494.

Although this tends to be true at any age, it seems to be an especially critical problem at the upper ages.

All of us can think of exceptional men and women in public life and among our own friends and colleagues who have retained striking intellectual vigor well beyond the normal age for retirement. Perhaps, however, the conspicuousness of these exceptions merely supports the generally held conclusion that the ravages of time begin taking their toll of most people in their middle sixties or early seventies.

FACULTY RETIREMENT

The question of a proper age for faculty retirement at colleges and universities seems to span only about five years. Nine out of ten colleges state a normal retirement age of 65 or 70 or somewhere between (Table 3.6). The survey defined normal retirement age as "the first age at which retirement would not be classified as 'early' and the age beyond which further service, if permitted, is considered an 'extension of service.'"

Extensions of faculty service beyond the normal retirement age are permitted in 88 per cent of all institutions (Table 3.7). Three-quarters of the institutions that do provide for extensions of service use age 65 as the normal age (Table 3.8).

TABLE 3.6: STATED NORMAL RETIREMENT AGE[a]

	Faculty		Administrative		Clerical-Service	
	Per Cent Insts	Per Cent EEs	Per Cent Insts	Per Cent EEs	Per Cent Insts	Per Cent EEs
Stated Normal Retirement Age	N = 1,170	N = 283,936	N = 1,141	N = 107,705	N = 921	N = 420,974
60 and under	5.9	14.0	6.0	6.3	7.5	9.5
62–63	0.5	1.2	0.5	1.8	0.5	0.9
65	70.6	48.0	76.1	66.4	69.6	56.8
66–68	8.9	16.4	7.5	9.8	6.8	13.6
70	11.0	17.9	6.7	12.0	11.1	15.7
Over 70	0.2	[b]	0.1	[b]	0.1	[b]
None stated	2.1	2.4	2.5	3.6	2.8	3.2
No response	0.8	0.1	0.6	0.1	1.6	0.3
Total	100.0	100.0	100.0	100.0	100.0	100.0

[a] The survey defined normal retirement age as "the first age at which retirement would not be classified as 'early' and the age beyond which further service, if permitted, is considered an 'extension of service.'"
[b] Less than 0.1%.

TABLE 3.7: FIXED AND FLEXIBLE RETIREMENT AGE PROVISIONS

	Faculty		*Administrative*		*Clerical-Service*	
	Per Cent Insts N = 1,170	*Per Cent EEs N = 283,936*	*Per Cent Insts N = 1,141*	*Per Cent EEs N = 107,705*	*Per Cent Insts N = 921*	*Per Cent EEs N = 420,974*
Fixed age, no extensions	8.4	11.4	10.6	10.8	11.7	13.1
Service may be extended beyond normal age	88.0	85.0	85.4	84.5	82.9	83.2
No age stated	2.1	2.4	2.5	3.6	2.8	3.2
No response	1.5	1.2	1.5	1.1	2.6	0.5
Total	100.0	100.0	100.0	100.0	100.0	100.0

TABLE 3.8: INSTITUTIONS PERMITTING EXTENSIONS OF SERVICE BEYOND THE NORMAL RETIREMENT AGE

Distribution of Stated Normal Retirement Ages in Faculty Retirement Plans

Stated Normal Faculty Retirement Age	*Per Cent Insts N = 1,030*	*Per Cent EEs N = 241,573*
Under 60	0.4	3.1
60–64	6.9	14.7
65	76.3	53.8
66–68	8.1	15.7
70	8.3	12.7
Over 70	—	—
Total	100.0	100.0

Institutions not permitting extensions report a somewhat higher retirement age than those that do. Among institutions using a fixed retirement age with no extensions, two-thirds state for faculty an age higher than 65 (Table 3.9).

To flexibility through extensions of service should be added another element of college employment rarely found elsewhere. This is the willingness to employ persons retired from other institutions. The Retired Professors Registry, established in 1957 under the aegis of the AAC, AAUP, Ford Foundation, and TIAA, and now administered by the AAUP, provides a registration and listing service to bring colleges and retired academic talent together for their mutual advantage. The Registry reported for 1967 that 4,600 referrals were made to 600 colleges seeking the services of already retired professors.

Normal or Base Retirement Age. More detailed analysis of the data

TABLE 3.9: *INSTITUTIONS STATING A FIXED RETIREMENT AGE*
WITH NO EXTENSIONS
Distribution of Ages Stated in Faculty Retirement Plans

Stated Fixed Faculty Retirement Age	Per Cent Insts N = 98	Per Cent EEs N = 32,248
Under 65	—	—
65	33.7	9.7
66–68	20.4	27.4
70	43.9	62.6
Over 70	2.0	0.3
Total	100.0	100.0

(Table 3.6) shows that the 70 per cent of institutions reporting a normal or base faculty retirement age of 65 employ 48 per cent of the full-time faculty in the responding institutions. The 11 per cent of institutions reporting age 70 as the normal age employ 18 per cent of faculty. About 9 per cent report ages 66 through 68, and they employ 16 per cent of faculty.

When responses are subdivided, certain differences appear, mainly according to whether the institution is public or private. For instance, the all-institution response shows 6 per cent of institutions employing 14 per cent of faculty reporting a base retirement age of 60 or under (mainly 60). Most of these institutions are public colleges, many of which have recently been teachers colleges having a long-standing association with the public schoolteacher system in their state. Among public liberal arts colleges, 20 per cent state a base retirement age of 60 or under; 2 per cent, 62 or 63; 50 per cent, age 65; 26 per cent, an age over 65; and 2 per cent do not specify a retirement age. Among private liberal arts colleges, 85 per cent state age 65, 13 per cent a higher age, and 2 per cent do not specify an age.

Public universities generally state normal faculty retirement ages that range both higher and lower than their private counterparts. In the public universities, 10 per cent state a base retirement age of 60 or under, about 40 per cent state age 65, 40 per cent a higher age, and about 7 per cent do not specify a retirement age. None of the private universities reports a base retirement age under 65, 70 per cent state age 65, and 30 per cent a higher age.

Extensions of Service. As noted above, a substantial proportion of the colleges and universities provide for extension of faculty service beyond a normal or base retirement age. The AAUP-AAC recommendation on this point is the following:

Where the institution has a flexible plan that provides for extension of service beyond its base retirement age, extensions should be by annual appointment and ordinarily should not postpone retirement beyond the end of the academic year in which age 70 is attained. Such extensions should be made upon recommendation of representatives of the faculty and administration through appropriate committee procedures that assure full protection of academic freedom. Representatives of the faculty should be chosen in accordance with procedures adopted by the faculty for committee appointment.

Table 3.10 shows the distribution of the ages beyond which faculty extensions are no longer permitted. As noted earlier, about half the institutions permitting extensions of faculty service and reporting 65 as the base retirement age use the age 70 limit for extensions, and about a third state no limit. The table indicates that, when the stated normal age is higher than 65, there is increasing likelihood that the institution does not state a specific limit on extensions.

Fixed versus Flexible. Over the years there has been a trend toward flexibility in college faculty retirement ages, that is, away from plans stating a fixed age with no extensions and toward plans providing for extensions of service beyond a base retirement age. For all institutions of higher education, the 1959 study reported that 14 per cent of the plans had a fixed retirement age without extensions. As shown in Table 3.7, 8 per cent of the plans for faculty in higher education now report a fixed retirement age without extensions. Whether the retirement age is fixed or flexible, there should be sufficient precision in the statement of the date retirement is to begin so that no ambiguity arises in individual cases.[9]

[9] The AAUP-AAC Statement recommends that "Retirement should normally occur at the end of the academic year in which the faculty member or administrator reaches the age specified for retirement by his institution's plan. Each institution should make clear, for these purposes, whether the summer period attaches to the preceding or the forthcoming academic year." The statement of a fixed retirement age requires precision as to the exact date of retirement, but is normally brief.

One such statement is the following: "The policy on faculty retirement adopted by the Board of Trustees is as follows: The retirement age shall be 68. It is understood that actual retirement in each case shall take place on the 31st of August following the attainment of the above age. Members of the faculty may retire at age 65 with emeritus status."

Another institution's fixed-age statement is this: "The statutory age at which an officer of instruction must retire is sixty-eight. The date that defines the year of retirement is that of the officer's sixty-eighth birthday. If it falls before June 30, the spring term ending with the Commencement early in the same June is the last term of service. If it falls after June 30, the last term of service is the next spring term."

TABLE 3.10: *INSTITUTIONS PERMITTING EXTENSIONS OF SERVICE*
Age Beyond Which Extensions Are No Longer Permitted in Faculty Retirement Plans

	Per Cent Insts N = 786	Per Cent EEs N = 129,943
Normal age 65, extensions to		
66–69[a]	7.3	8.0
70	49.9	55.9
71 or higher	4.3	6.0
No stated limit	35.8	28.8
No response	2.7	1.3
Total	100.0	100.0
	N = 84	N = 37,856
Normal age 66–68, extensions to		
68–69	2.3	4.0
70	23.8	12.7
71–72	11.9	15.5
73 or higher	2.4	0.2
No stated limit	56.0	65.9
No response	3.6	1.7
Total	100.0	100.0
	N = 85	N = 30,674
Normal age 70 or higher, extensions to		
71	14.1	4.8
73	2.4	0.7
74 or higher	—	—
No stated limit	77.6	88.2
No response	5.9	6.3
Total	100.0	100.0

[a] Usually age 68.

The selection of a fixed age—65, 70, or in between—may deprive the college of some men who are in possession of their full capacities, and it may delay the retirement of others too long. But it avoids claims of favoritism or discrimination. It is easier to administer than a flexible provision, and it opens up on schedule expected promotions for young faculty. It makes it possible for a staff member to anticipate the timing of the many important changes he must make when retiring from a work-centered life.

A flexible system, on the other hand, in which the faculty member may continue service beyond the normal retirement age, allows a college to retain longer those men who are still outstanding in their field and are able to continue valuable service. If realistically administered, extension arrangements help the institution to take account of the different rates at which men age, and can afford the institution useful elasticity in meeting its needs. A flexible system helps the college adjust to changes in the supply of teachers and to periods of rapidly increasing student enrollments. However, flexibility requires considerable decisiveness and tact as well as procedures to assure fair treatment and the preservation of academic freedom.

Extension procedures frequently require a special vote of the board of trustees or other employing authority. The president, a faculty committee, or department head usually must recommend the extension. A statement of the special procedures involved helps make it clear to all that retirement is to occur on a certain date; that, if an extension of service is to be made, the burden of proof of fitness to continue rests on the staff member; that, if service is continued, the decision must be reviewed and approved, probably each year at appropriate decision-making levels at the institution, and is far from automatic.[10]

[10] Retirement age policy statements under flexible plans vary considerably, but generally attempt to outline the conditions under which extensions will be considered and the procedures to be followed. Two examples are given here. In the first one the question of extension is initiated by the institution, which "invites" the individual to continue service, except that any administrative responsibilities cease at age 65. The second example establishes detailed criteria for extensions and involves faculty participation in the decision. Both examples require an *early* decision and transmission of that decision to the individual, a highly recommended practice.

Example 1. Retirement age. A faculty member's regular appointment terminates at the end of the academic year in which his sixty-fifth birthday falls. The academic year is here understood to end June 30. A faculty member on reaching retirement age (65) may be invited to continue on an annual basis during the three following years. Such appointments, full-time or part-time, will be made in relation to the teaching needs of the College and will not involve administrative responsibility or committee assignments. Consideration of continuation beyond the retirement age may be initiated by the Education Committee of the Board of Trustees of the College, the Advisory Committee of the Faculty, or the President. A retiring faculty member will be notified by the President in the Spring preceding the year after which he would normally be retired whether or not he is to be recommended to the Board of Trustees for an annual appointment. Thereafter, he will be notified by December 15 concerning the following year.

Example 2. Subject to further action of the Board of Trustees, faculty members who have reached the age of 65 may continue on the faculty in accordance with the following terms and provisions:

1. A faculty member about to be 65 shall discuss his situation with his respective dean, and indicate whether he wishes to continue teaching full-time through the year in which he reaches age 67. This discussion shall take place before April first of the college year (July 1 to June 30) prior to the college year in which his sixty-fifth birthday will occur. If the faculty member indicates his desire to continue teaching after the close of the college year in which he reaches age 65, the matter shall be considered by the appropriate departmental faculty council and the general faculty council. Recommendations may be made to the board for continuation until the end of the college year in which the faculty member reaches the age of 67.

Length of Extensions. How often and how long is faculty retirement deferred beyond the normal or base age under flexible retirement plans? Table 3.8 shows the established upper limits, but of course many of those who continue beyond the normal age will wish to serve only one or two years. A study of a sample of institutions whose plans provide for normal retirement at age 65, with provisons for extension beyond that age, suggests that about half of faculty members reaching a stated normal retirement age of 65 do retire at that age. Of those whose service was extended, half had retired within 2 years.[11]

Another indication of the ages actually selected for retirement can be derived from an analysis of the annuity starting dates selected by TIAA plan participants. These figures represent male annuitants retiring in 1967 under a wide variety of retirement age provisions, fixed and flexible, and persons

2. In making such recommendations the councils should be guided by the total good of the college, primary consideration to be given to high quality of instruction. Although not necessarily exclusive, the following criteria shall be considered:

(a) Adequate physical stamina and inclination not only to meet classes regularly but to teach with vitality.

(b) An active involvement with current research and developments in the faculty member's field of scholarship. This does not necessarily mean continued publication, but does presuppose personal research or other evidence of interest and concern with his field. Activity with professional societies or other form of continued vital interest would be relevant.

(c) Continuing inclination and ability to present the substantive content of the faculty member's field of scholarship in a manner which is interesting and challenging to students.

(d) Inclination and ability to stand in relation to students with understanding and sympathy, maintaining such out-of-class contacts as are significant in the liberal arts college. This does not imply a judgment on the basis of personal popularity. It does involve a determination that the faculty member perceives himself as a part of an academic community in which cooperation and communication among all members, both students and faculty, is important.

3. Where extensions are made beyond the age of 65, they will be subject to the continuation of good health and the college will not be obligated to continue a faculty member in service after his ability to perform has become impaired.

4. Persons continued beyond the age of 65 shall receive a salary equal to the salary received during the year in which age 65 is reached, adjusted only for changes in salary scale. Recommendations may be made, in appropriate cases, for continuance on the basis of a reduced teaching load, in which cases the salary shall be adjusted on a mutually satisfactory basis. In all cases, college contributions to annuity premiums will be discontinued at age 65, but the faculty member's contribution will continue. Persons will not be eligible to serve as council members during or after the college year in which they may be considered by the councils for service after age 65, and persons beyond the age of 65 will not be eligible for sabbatical leave. Faculty members continued beyond the age of 65 shall be relieved of all administrative duties and committee responsibilities.

5. Administrative officers, other than the president, will ordinarily retire at the close of the fiscal year in which they reach age 65. Exceptions may be made only on special recommendation of the president, in which case annual reappointments may be made through the college year in which the officer reaches 67. In the case of the president, extensions beyond age 65 may be made by the Board of Trustees as the Board may determine.

[11] Teachers Insurance and Annuity Association, "Retirement Practices at Selected Colleges and Universities" 1961.

who delayed starting their TIAA income until after the date they retired. Ninety-four per cent began their TIAA income at age 60 or above. Of these, 6 per cent began it at ages 60 through 64, 26 per cent began it at age 65, and 17 per cent at age 66. Twenty-two per cent started the income at ages 67 through 69, 12 per cent at age 70, and 11 per cent at age 71 or higher.

Early and Late Retirement. Flexibility for the individual in choosing the date on which he wishes his annuity to start is important whether or not the institution has a fixed retirement age or provides for extensions. Neither the individual nor any particular college can know many years beforehand at what age the individual will retire, whether he will work at some other institution, or what revisions will be made in the plan's stated retirement age. Thus it seems advisable to arrange retirement income by means that permit adjustment of the age at which annuity payments are to begin, either to an earlier or a later date than that originally selected.

Gradual Retirement. A procedure permitting gradual reduction of duties shortly before retirement can help the individual adjust to his forthcoming change of status. It can also help the institution in preparing those who are to take over the retiring person's responsibilities. Reductions in teaching load, where provided for, are usually voluntary. A corresponding reduction in salary is appropriate. Publicly supported institutions of higher education in Texas provide for a system of gradual retirement between the ages of 65 and 70 under which both the teaching load and the individual salary are reduced.

At least one institution provides for reduction of duties at the discretion of the board: "At or after age 65 [the mandatory retirement age is 68], the Board of Regents may for good reason and upon recommendation by the Administration reduce a teacher's load and decrease his salary correspondingly. If this is not done, the teacher may continue on full load and salary until age 68, or he may retire voluntarily at any age between 65 and 68."

Another tapering-off arrangement is reported by the University of Michigan. The individual nearing retirement age is permitted one term's leave out of the last three, or he can choose to teach half-time during all three terms. There is no reduction of salary.

The new AAUP-AAC Statement for the first time takes cognizance of a procedure for gradual retirement by providing that "Between the age of 60 and retirement, faculty members should be permitted to arrange, on their own initiative, reductions in salary and services acceptable both to them and to their institutions."

Retirement Age for Other Personnel

ADMINISTRATIVE PERSONNEL

The normal retirement age for administrative officers and other professional nonfaculty personnel tends somewhat more to be age 65 than is true for faculty. Table 3.6 compares the percentage distribution of the normal retirement ages reported for faculty, administrative personnel, and clerical-service employees.

Three out of four of the institutions reporting a retirement plan use 65 as the normal retirement age for administrative personnel; 7.5 per cent use ages 66 through 68; and about 7 per cent state age 70. This compares with 7 out of 10, 9 per cent, and 11 per cent, respectively, for faculty. A greater contrast appears in connection with numbers of people affected. Two out of three of the administrative personnel are subject to a normal retirement age of 65, compared with just under half of faculty.

A fixed-age, no-extension retirement plan for administrative personnel is reported by 11 per cent of the institutions (Table 3.7), a figure slightly larger than the 8 per cent of institutions reporting a fixed age with no extension for faculty. Public institutions tend to make retirement for administrative personnel mandatory at the stated normal age more often than the private institutions, about 15 per cent of public institutions versus about 8 per cent of private institutions. Generally, however, institutions of higher education provide a retirement flexibility for administrators that is not dissimilar from that for faculty.

CLERICAL-SERVICE EMPLOYEES

The stated normal retirement ages reported for clerical-service employees are generally similar to those for faculty. About 70 per cent of the institutions use age 65, 11 per cent age 70 (Table 3.6). Retirement is compulsory at the stated normal retirement age for clerical-service employees in 12 per cent of the institutions, compared with 8 per cent for faculty and 11 per cent for administrative personnel. But flexibility is the pattern here also. Service may be continued beyond the normal retirement age in 83 per cent of the reporting institutions, a figure that is close to the 88 per cent for faculty and 85 per cent for administrative personnel. Retirement for the clerical-service groups is compulsory at the normal age in about 15 per cent of public institutions and in about 8 per cent of private institutions. Generally speaking, the retirement age provisions for all college employees, professional and nonprofessional, do not differ greatly from each other. There may be differences, however, in the criteria established to govern extensions of employment. Extensions of service for the clerical-service personnel may be virtually automatic if health and performance criteria are met.

Income Arrangements at Retirement

In practically all college retirement plans the annuitant may elect an annuity that not only continues throughout his lifetime but continues, usually in a reduced amount, throughout the lifetime of his spouse or other beneficiary. Examples of income arrangements that are generally available are as follows:

1. Single life annuity. This option is generally appropriate for unmarried persons or men or women whose spouses are protected by other sources of income. The single life annuity provides the largest monthly income of any of the options and continues payments as long as the annuitant lives, but all payments cease at the death of the annuitant.

2. Survivor annuity. The survivor annuity provides a lifetime income for the primary annuitant and, if he dies before the second annuitant, usually his wife, she then continues to receive an income for the rest of her life. There is usually a choice, made by the retiring employee, as to what proportion of the income will continue to the survivor on his death.

The *joint and two-thirds benefit to survivor* provides that, at the death of either the retired employee or his wife, the payments are reduced to two-thirds of the amount that would have been paid if both had lived, and continue to the survivor for life. When this option includes a "10-year guarantee," if *both* annuitants die within the first 10 years of payments, the two-thirds amount is continued to a named beneficiary for the balance of the 10-year period. The *full-benefit to survivor* option continues the full income as long as either the retired employee or his wife is living. A *half-benefit to second annuitant* option continues full income to the retired employee as long as he lives, and one-half that income to the wife if she survives the retired employee.

For a man aged 65 whose wife is 2 years younger, the two-thirds to survivor with 10-year guarantee option pays about 13 per cent less than the single life annuity would pay the husband alone. The full benefit option pays about 21 per cent less, and the half-benefit option 12 per cent less.

3. Ten or twenty years certain and life. This option pays the annuitant an income as long as he lives with installments guaranteed to continue during the first 10 or 20 years, as selected, whether he lives or dies. If death occurs during the guaranteed period, payments are continued to a beneficiary for the rest of the period. If the annuitant lives beyond the period, payments continue for the rest of his life.

For a man aged 65, the 10 years certain and life option pays about 5 per cent less than the single life annuity. The 20 years certain and life option pays about 16 per cent less.

4. Installment refund. The installment refund option pays the annuitant an income as long as he lives. If he dies before having received total payments equal to the amount of the full accumulation when annuity payments began, the income is continued to a beneficiary until the sum of all payments equals that accumulation amount. For a man aged 65, this option would pay about 12 per cent less than the single life annuity. The installment refund option is not available in CREF.

MAKING THE CHOICE

It is important for the retiring employee that he remain free to make his choice of income option right up until the time of retirement, and free to put off the start of the annuity. A problem in this connection is encountered in retirement plans requiring that the selection of an income option involving a survivor benefit for the spouse must be made a certain number of years in advance of retirement. Health and family conditions can change rapidly at advanced ages and, furthermore, the individual should not have to decide several years ahead of retirement precisely when and how he wants to start his retirement income. It is unfortunate if, after a college and an individual have paid premiums during the individual's working lifetime on the assumption of appropriate protection for him and his wife during retirement, the income option most suited to his situation may be blocked because of this requirement. Flexibility to meet real needs is quite important from the standpoint of the college, the individual, and the survivors, and retiring employees in good health or bad should be allowed to choose the income option right up until the month before the start of income, or to put off the start of the annuity itself.

Although the income options available to the beneficiary in the event the participant dies before retirement are somewhat more restricted than those available during retirement, especially in publicly administered plans, these options are nonetheless satisfactory on the whole. They generally include the choice of an income option for life, with or without a minimum period of guaranteed payments such as 10 or 20 years, or an income for a fixed period of years.

4

SOCIAL SECURITY

Since its establishment more than 30 years ago, the federal Social Security program has grown from a plan providing retirement income and small lump sum death benefits for employees in industry and business to one covering nearly every employed American and providing retirement income, substantial survivor benefits, disability income, and health insurance. With tax collections of about 30 billion dollars a year going into this Old Age, Survivors, Disability, and Health Insurance (OASDHI) program, and yearly benefit payments of some 21 billion dollars going to individuals, the program strongly influences the economic, social, and political life of the country.[1]

The total Social Security program represents a broad federal, state, and local attack on insecurity. Twelve major programs are provided for under the Social Security Act. Two are operated by the federal government alone: (1) Old Age, Survivors, and Disability Insurance and (2) Health Insurance for the Aged (Medicare). Ten other programs are operated by the states with the aid of federal contributions; they include unemployment insurance, public assistance and welfare services, and children's services.

The federal part of the Social Security program has an all-pervading influence on the important phases of college staff benefit planning. Each section of this study brings out the pertinence of the federal program and its influence on the design of the college plans. A general description of Social Security, its philosophy, its history in the colleges, and some details concerning its operation are presented in this chapter.

---

[1] "Current Operating Statistics," *Social Security Bulletin*, XXXI (May 1968), pp. 29, 32.

Early Social Security Not Open to Colleges

Employees of private educational institutions were not originally included in the Social Security program, nor were employees of governmental units, including staff members of publicly supported colleges and universities. When Social Security legislation was being considered in the mid 1930s, there was strong opposition to inclusion of nonprofit educational, charitable, and religious organizations. The opposition was based on questions of taxation of nonprofit institutions, separation of church and state, the presence of good retirement systems in the colleges, and the cost of the federal program. In the case of coverage for public employees, questions were raised about the constitutionality of a tax on public employees and employers, and fear was expressed that existing public employee retirement systems would be weakened or replaced if employees were brought under Social Security.

Commencing in 1937, TIAA, on behalf of educational institutions, suggested a number of amendments to the Social Security Act which would make it more appropriate for and acceptable to the educational world, and recommended coverage of employees of educational institutions. By 1939 the Association of American Colleges came to favor the inclusion of educational employees in the Social Security system, and in the early 1940s a survey of college administrators by the American Council on Education found that about 80 per cent favored Social Security coverage of their employees. The changing educational viewpoint was expressed in 1941, two days after the United States entered World War II:

Colleges and universities have often led in formulating social policies. Social Security legislation is now shaping our most comprehensive social movement; surely our educational institutions should be in the game rather than on the sidelines; they should be more than mildly interested spectators; they should be instrumental in determining the outcome.[2]

During World War II and the postwar period an additional factor made itself felt. Efforts to attract nonacademic employees under conditions of full employment led the colleges to recognize the importance of having Social Security benefits. Faculty members were also interested in Social Security as a supplement to existing retirement prospects. By 1950 most opposition had melted away in the private sector.

[2] Robbins, *Developments in Social Security and Pension Plans.*

Social Security Extended to Private Colleges

In the Social Security Act Amendments of 1950, participation was made available by institutional referendum to employees of private nonprofit educational institutions and to public employees not covered by a retirement system.

As the nationwide benefit organization for the colleges and their staff members, TIAA held institutes on Social Security for college officers in many cities throughout the country. This helped the colleges and TIAA to cope in a short period of time with technical adjustments, the problem of explaining Social Security for college staff members, and the methods of amending existing benefit plans, in order to come into the newly available Social Security program. By the January, 1951, effective date, three-fourths of the private institutions with TIAA retirement plans had decided to obtain the new coverage.[3] Within a few years practically all employees in the private colleges and universities were covered.

Social Security for Public Employees

The opposition to participation in Social Security by representatives of employees of governments, including strong opposition by public school-teacher groups, was based largely on the fear that the federal program would replace or weaken the existing public retirement plans. In response the 1950 Social Security amendments did not extend coverage to employees of federal, state, or local governments in positions covered by a public retirement program. Those who were not covered by any retirement system were brought into Social Security. Ironically, this meant that the only way in which public employees covered by an existing retirement system could obtain Social Security coverage was by abolishing their existing public system; in a few instances this was done. But the vast majority did not enter Social Security until after the amendments of 1954. These amendments broadened the coverage so that nearly all nongovernmental jobs in the United States were brought under the program, and state and local employees were also made eligible for it. In the case of state and local employees, coverage could be obtained under a federal-state agreement if a referen-

[3] TIAA *Bulletin,* January, 1951, p. 1.

dum was held among the members of the public retirement system and a
majority voted in favor of Social Security coverage.

Within the next few years most public employee groups in most states,
including employees of publicly supported colleges and universities, became
covered by Social Security. At present, the only states in which substantial
numbers of employees of public institutions of higher education are not
included in Social Security are Colorado, Florida, Illinois, Louisiana, Maine,
Massachusetts, Nevada, and Ohio.

A Universal Program

By the late 1950s, Social Security in the United States had become virtually
a universal program, covering employees of business and industry, agricultural workers, employees of nonprofit organizations, self-employed persons, ministers, doctors and other independent professionals, part-time
workers, domestic workers, members of the armed forces, and employees of
most states and municipalities. Among the few specific exclusions are federal
employees covered by the Civil Service Retirement System, members of
the Railroad Retirement System (except for the hospital insurance tax), and
the president and vice-president of the United States and members of Congress.

The Social Security tax has now grown to be the largest source of federal
receipts after the income tax. In the mid-forties, collections from the Social
Security tax accounted for less than 3 per cent of total federal tax collections. In 1967 the Social Security taxes amounted to about 17 per cent of
federal taxes. As a percentage of the gross national product the Social
Security tax collections have also risen, from about 0.6 per cent in the mid-
forties to nearly 3 per cent in the mid-sixties. Over the same twenty years
the collections as a percentage of personal income rose from 0.8 per cent to
slightly over 3 per cent; as a percentage of the wages and salaries of covered
employees the collections rose from 1.7 per cent to 5.2 per cent.[4] These
collections have become increasingly significant as a part of the total economy, with consequences relating to fiscal policy, resource allocation, and
economic growth.

[4] Tax Foundation, *Economic Aspects of the Social Security Tax*, p. 18.

Objectives and Principles of Social Security

The federal Social Security program operates largely through redistribution of income: from young to old; from the healthy to the ill; from the living to the families of the deceased; from the single worker to the family. The program has built a substantial foundation of benefits for working Americans and their dependents and survivors.

Concurrently, developments in the private sector suggest that a large part of job-connected financial security can be supplied independently, without direct government action. Private pension plans covered 10 million people in 1950; they now cover 25 million.[5] Their assets and reserves totaled 12 billion dollars in 1950; they will soon exceed 100 billion.[6] Basic medical benefit plans now cover 160 million Americans;[7] major medical plans provide additional protection for 60 million people.[8] Life insurance coverage now equals 1 trillion dollars, one and one-fourth times the gross national product.[9]

A joint partnership of government and private action can be effective in providing Americans a more secure society. The crucial question has to do with the proper sphere, the proper scope, of each sector. It is generally agreed that the Social Security program should provide a basic level of wage-connected benefits for as many persons as possible. But what is a "basic" level of retirement, survivor, disability, and health insurance benefits? Some believe that the government program should provide no more than a minimum subsistence level of income sufficient to bring beneficiaries without other income somewhat above the poverty line; employer benefit plans and individual savings would provide the rest. Others regard the minimum goal as insufficient and believe that Social Security should be the source of a modest but reasonably comfortable standard of living. Still others would have Social Security do the whole job of providing retirement, disability, and survivor incomes.

By and large, decisions about the extent of Social Security benefits have

[5] U.S. Bureau of the Census, *Statistical Abstract of the United States* (1967), p. 296.
[6] Institute of Life Insurance, *Private and Public Pension Plans in the United States*, p. 3.
[7] Reed, "Private Health Insurance Coverage and Financial Experience, 1940–66," *Social Security Bulletin*, XXX (Nov. 1967), 4.
[8] *Ibid.*, p. 14.
[9] U.S. Bureau of the Census, *Statistical Abstract of the United States* (1967), p. 474.

been made politically and pragmatically, taking into some account the cost of increasing benefits above earlier levels, increased living costs and personal income levels, and current judgment of what constitutes an acceptable "minimum." While there were no Social Security tax or benefit increases during the 1940s, thereafter Congress increased taxes and benefits seven times in the next seventeen years. A comparison of Social Security with the private benefit systems described in this book can help to indicate the optimum balance between the social program providing basic benefits for all employed persons and their families, and the diverse and innovative private sector benefit plans. In the benefit field, as in many other sectors of our economic life, the federal government performs a large and growing "climate-setting" function. Our intention is to emphasize the fact that the private and public sector benefits can and should work admirably together, complementing each other's strengths.

A SYSTEM OF SOCIAL EQUITY

Social Security should not attempt to provide the full benefits needed and desired by all people at various income levels in this country. A substantial part of that job is best done in the private sector, where the individual's and his employer's extra efforts can be directly reflected in the size of his individual benefits. Social Security is primarily a system of "social equity." It is a transfer system different in its treatment of people from the "individual equity" of insurance in the private sector, under which each dollar of premium purchases a specified right to retirement, death, disability, or health benefits. To some degree, Social Security benefits are related to the taxes paid on behalf of an individual, but the emphasis is on income redistribution and on the individual's presumed needs, appropriate criteria for a national program.

Several provisions implement the social equity aspects of the system. The Social Security tax rate is applied uniformly to the entire earnings base. Benefits, although related to the average monthly wage on which taxes have been paid, are weighted in favor of those who earn less than the full earnings base. Benefits are also weighted heavily in favor of persons with dependents. The same tax payments that entitle a single person to "primary" retirement benefits entitle a married person to the same "primary" benefit plus a wife's benefit if he is retired, or survivor benefits worth tens of thousands of dollars for his widow and children if he dies prematurely.

The weighting of benefits under the Social Security program is based on "presumptive need." The employee cannot designate his beneficiary as under an annuity or insurance contract; beneficiaries are defined in the law. The law defines the dependents for whom need is presumed, and defines the limits to which such needs will be covered. Widows with no children under age 18 are not presumed to be dependent until they reach age 60. For an employee who stops working at an age younger than 62, no Social Security retirement benefit is payable before that age, since the program presumes "old age" and lessened ability to work, and is not a benefit program in the strict individual equity connotation. At any age before 72 the "work test" enforces the presumptive need philosophy by providing for decreases in benefits when covered persons or their dependents engage in "substantial" employment.

CONTRIBUTORY FINANCING

Except for a part of Medicare, the OASDHI program is supported by taxes paid by employees and employers and by self-employed persons, plus interest earnings on the relatively small Social Security trust funds.[10] The current excess of income to the system over administrative costs and benefits is credited to the trust funds and invested in government bonds.

The reserve accumulation of this government trust fund is not at all comparable, either in function or in its ratio to accrued benefits, to the reserve funds required for fully funded retirement plans. The Social Security trust funds constitute only a contingency reserve toward future benefit payments, rather than a traditional insurance reserve, since the program is largely a "pay-as-you-go" system.

The gradually escalating payroll tax rate built into Social Security is designed to cover estimated future costs of the old age, survivors, and disability benefits, and of the hospital insurance portion of Medicare. A wide

[10] Contributions are collected by the Internal Revenue Service under the Federal Insurance Contributions Act and paid into the United States Treasury as revenue collections. The amounts collected are appropriated to the Federal Old Age and Survivors Insurance Trust Fund, Federal Disability Insurance Trust Fund, and the Federal Hospital Insurance Trust Fund. The Federal Supplemental Medical Insurance Trust Fund receives the payments of premiums and matching payments under the supplementary medical insurance program.

spectrum of people and organizations—labor unions, management, econo-
mists, sociologists, government officials, and politicians—has always strongly
supported the contributory feature of Social Security. Past increases in
benefits have been accompanied by increases in the scheduled tax rates and
earnings base. Thus it is reasonable to assume that the maximum level of
payroll tax that is generally acceptable will be an important factor determining the general future benefit level of Social Security.

Social Security Taxes and Benefits

EARNINGS BASE

The Social Security earnings base is the amount of covered employee
earnings subject to the Social Security tax. Originally $3,000, the earnings
base has been increased several times en route to its current level of $7,800.
Annual earnings in excess of the base are not subject to the Social Security
tax.

TAXES

Social Security taxes are levied under the Federal Insurance Contributions Act, a part of the Internal Revenue Code of 1954, as amended. The
taxes are levied at the same rate on the employer and the employee.

The 1969 tax rate of 9.6 per cent total (4.8 per cent each for employer
and employee) on salary within the taxable earnings base is scheduled to
remain in effect until January 1, 1971, when it is scheduled to rise to 10.4
per cent. Additional increases are scheduled thereafter to 11.3 per cent in
1973, then 11.4 per cent from 1976 to 1980, and 11.6 per cent from 1980
to 1987, with 11.8 per cent from then on. In terms of dollar amounts of
taxes, employer and employee, this means that Social Security taxes for
a covered person earning $7,800 or more will be $748.80 a year until 1971,
then $811.20 until 1973, and finally $920.40 a year after 1987. The tax rate
for the self-employed is 75 per cent of the combined employer-employee tax
rate. Of course, scheduled future rates and the level of the earnings base
are subject to change by the Congress.

A fact of importance to some colleges is that earnings taxable for Social

Security purposes are not limited to cash salary received, but include the value of board and room, rent, and such other items as are furnished for the convenience of the college. Excluded as taxable earnings are sickness and accident disability benefits, medical and hospitalization expense payments, death benefits for an employee and his dependents, and amounts paid by an employer for insurance and annuities under a system established by the employer.

ELIGIBILITY FOR BENEFITS

Eligibility for Social Security benefits depends on the covered employee's insured status, which is determined by the number of calendar quarters of coverage he has under the program. For some benefits the individual must have a *fully insured* status, for some only a *currently insured* status is required, and for others both fully and currently insured status is required. In addition, there is a *disability* insured status.

Full details of the tests are available at Social Security offices. Most employed people now easily meet the minimum tests, and the present broad coverage means that nearly all future employees, except federal employees, state and local employees in some states, and railroad workers, will meet them.

AVERAGE MONTHLY WAGE

The amount of Social Security benefits for an employee and his dependents depends on the employee's *average monthly wage* in covered employment. This amount for most college staff members is the total taxable earnings (for Social Security purposes) in covered employment after 1950, divided by the total number of months elapsing after 1950 or after the year of the twenty-first birthday, if later, and before the quarter in which the employee reaches retirement age (65 for men, 62 for women) or dies. In calculating the average, up to five of the years of lowest or no earnings may be dropped out. Earnings after age 62 or 65 and before age 72 can be counted if they increase the benefit.[11]

---

[11] There are six different computation methods in use in current OASDHI claims, three of which include only earnings from 1951 on. For a complete description see U.S. Department of Health, Education, and Welfare, *Social Security Handbook.*

OLD AGE AND SURVIVOR BENEFITS

Typical benefit schedules are given in Table 4.1.

TABLE 4.1: MONTHLY INCOME FROM SOCIAL SECURITY

	Old Age Benefits		Survivor Benefits	
Average Monthly Wage	*Primary Amount*	*Husband and Wife Both 65 or Over*	*Mother and 1 Child*	*Maximum Family Benefit*
$400	$154	$230	$230	$322
500	178	266	266	375
600	204	306	306	415
650	218	323	327	434

DISABILITY BENEFITS

Disability income provisions were introduced into the Social Security program in 1956. At first, benefits for total and permanent disability were payable only to covered employees between the ages of 50 and 65. In 1960 the minimum age limit was removed; benefits are now payable to eligible persons of any age up to 65. The initial definition of disability required that the disability be expected to result in death or to continue for a long and indefinite period. This was liberalized in 1965 so that benefits are now payable for medically determinable physical or mental impairments "which can be expected to result in death or which can be expected to last for a continuous period of not less than 12 months." [12] (Chapter 9 discusses further the extent of disability required for benefit eligibility under Social Security and other long-term disability plans.)

The disabled worker's Social Security benefit is the amount he would be allowed if he were age 65 and had applied for retirement benefits. (See Table 4.1.) Dependents of disabled workers are also entitled to benefits: a wife age 62 or older, a wife caring for a child or children under age 18, or a child or children under age 18 or between 18 and 22 if students. Benefits for dependents are the same as if the disabled worker had retired at age 65 at the time of disability.

A "disability freeze" provision, similar in purpose to the disability waiver

[12] U.S. Department of Health, Education, and Welfare, *Social Security Handbook* (1966), pp. 96–97.

of premium provision in private insurance, provides that the period of disability will not be counted against the disabled employee in any future determinations of his insured status or his retirement or other benefit amounts.

Under an "offset" provision a reduction in disability income benefits is made when the employee's combined monthly Social Security benefits and any Workmen's Compensation benefits he is entitled to exceed 80 per cent of his average monthly earnings prior to the onset of disability.

As an incentive for personal rehabilitation the disability program provides for continuation of benefits for a trial employment period of up to nine months.

Medicare

The Social Security Amendments of 1965 established two health insurance programs for persons aged 65 and over, effective July 1, 1966.

PART A. HOSPITAL INSURANCE

Part A of Medicare covers the cost of hospital and related care. It is financed by the payment of part of the Social Security tax into the Hospital Insurance Trust Fund.

In order to be covered under the hospital plan, persons reaching age 65 after 1967 must either be eligible for Social Security retirement benefits or have at least three quarters of Social Security coverage (acquired at any time) for each year between 1965 and the year in which they reach age 65. Under a special transitional provision the hospital insurance plan included persons not eligible for Social Security retirement benefits provided they reached age 65 before 1968.

Part A *covered services* in a hospital or extended care facility (a skilled nursing home or special part of a hospital) include the cost of room and meals (including special diets) in semiprivate accommodations, regular nursing services, and use of operating rooms. They also include the cost of drugs, supplies, appliances, and equipment which are furnished for use in the facility and which are ordinarily furnished to inpatients of the hospital or extended care facility in which treatment is received.

Part A hospital insurance pays all or part of the cost of covered services for the following care: (1) up to 90 days in a participating hospital during each "spell of illness"; (2) a "lifetime reserve" of 60 additional benefit days; (3) up to 100 days of care in a participating extended care facility; (4) up to 100 home health visits by nurses, physical therapists, or certain health workers (but not doctors) from a participating home health agency.

PART B. SUPPLEMENTARY MEDICAL INSURANCE

Part B, which supplements the hospital plan, reimburses for doctors' bills and a number of other services and supplies not covered by Part A. Part B is financed by a $4 per month contribution from those enrolled, plus matching contributions from general tax revenues, paid into the Supplementary Medical Insurance Trust Fund.

An individual is eligible to enroll in the voluntary supplementary medical insurance plan if he is entitled to the hospital insurance protection of Part A. A person who reaches age 65 has seven months in which to sign up for the voluntary plan, starting three months before the first of the month in which the sixty-fifth birthday occurs. The effective date of coverage depends on when the enrollment occurs, but coverage cannot start before the first of the month in which a person reaches age 65.

Part B medical insurance pays 80 per cent of the reasonable charges for all covered services except for a deductible of the first $50 of such expenses in each calendar year. Any covered medical expenses incurred in October, November, or December which are used to meet that year's annual deductible can also be used to meet the following year's deductible amount.

Part B pays benefits for the following covered services: (1) physicians' services; (2) up to 100 home health visits each year by nurses, physical therapists, and other health workers from a qualified home health agency, in addition to the visits provided for under Part A; (3) medical and health services prescribed by a doctor; (4) drugs administered by a doctor as part of his professional services and which cannot be self-administered; (5) laboratory, x-ray, and other radiology services; (6) certain services furnished by a hospital or extended care facility for which Part A hospital insurance cannot pay; (7) outpatient physical therapy services; and (8) hospital outpatient services, including diagnosis and treatment.

SUMMARY

The hospital and medical insurance of Medicare recalls the pattern of basic hospital-surgical-medical coverage under nongovernmental plans. But the federal coverage is broader and more substantial in significant respects. Hospitalization periods are longer than in many basic plans. All phases of a physician's services are covered, in contrast to the common limitation of medical-surgical coverage to doctors' bills for surgery and visits to hospitalized patients. Other important Medicare features include the substantial benefits for nursing or "extended care" facilities and for home health services, both of special value to persons at the higher ages. The liberal coverage of outpatient diagnostic services and tests expresses a public policy encouraging preventive medicine, also of special importance at the higher ages. No dollar limits are set on the benefits payable; limitations take the form of deductibles, coinsurance, and service periods. Virtually all persons over 65 are covered, and the cost to them is limited to the monthly charge for Part B.

The addition of Medicare to the Social Security program represented a substantial change in public policy. For the portion of the United States population most in need of health care and least able to pay for it, a reasonable level of medical care became a matter of direct public concern.

5

GROUP LIFE INSURANCE
PLANS

A group life insurance plan for faculty and administrative personnel is currently reported by 70 per cent of colleges and universities, employing about 90 per cent of such personnel. For clerical-service personnel, 63 per cent of the institutions report a group life plan, and these institutions employ 85 per cent of employees in this category. In the survey of faculty and administrative coverage ten years ago, just half of the colleges and universities, employing two-thirds of the total teaching staff, reported a group life plan.

THE BENEFIT ENVIRONMENT

When considering the establishment or revision of a life insurance plan, a college should recognize the survivor benefits of the Social Security program and the death or survivor benefits of the college's retirement program. A life insurance plan that has been designed with these two income sources in mind stands a better chance of providing a good pattern of benefits at reasonable cost.

With the exception of public employees in just a few states, the federal Social Security program covers practically all employees in higher education. The family survivor benefits consist of a regular monthly income for a widow, regardless of her age, when she has a child or children under age 18 in her care, for children under age 18, or age 18 through 21 if they are students, and for a widow age 60 or over. Table 5.1 illustrates the magnitude of the monthly survivor income benefits of Social Security by showing the cumulative totals of such benefits when payable over five-, ten-, or fifteen-year periods. The totals reach into the tens of thousands.

TABLE 5.1: SOCIAL SECURITY BENEFITS FOR SURVIVORS
Illustration of Monthly Income Amounts and Cumulative Totals

Worker's Average Monthly Wage	Survivors' Monthly Income (Mother and 1 Child)	Cumulative Total if Payable for		
		5 Years	10 Years	15 Years
$400	$230	$13,824	$27,648	$41,472
500	266	15,984	31,968	47,952
600	306	18,360	36,720	55,080
650	327	19,620	39,240	58,860

Worker's Average Monthly Wage	Survivors' Monthly Income (Maximum Family Benefit)	Cumulative Total if Payable for		
		5 Years	10 Years	15 Years
$400	$322	$19,344	$38,688	$58,032
500	375	22,488	44,976	67,464
600	415	24,912	49,824	74,736
650	434	26,064	52,128	78,192

The college's retirement program is another potential source of survivor benefits. In many plans, including all TIAA-CREF plans, the full annuity accumulation is payable as a survivor benefit if the staff member dies before retirement. Although such death benefits are small at first, they build up over the years to substantial amounts. For a widow whose husband dies shortly before retirement such an accumulation should provide an adequate lifetime income. The pattern and importance of these survivor benefits can be illustrated by showing the annuity accumulations that result under typical contribution patterns for TIAA-CREF retirement plans. For example, assuming a starting salary of $8,000 a year at age 30, increasing at 4 per cent a year, the death benefits under various TIAA-CREF plans would be those shown in Table 5.2. Tables 5.1 and 5.2, showing the very large Social Security survivor benefits for a family with young children, and the very large TIAA-CREF survivor benefits for the family of a staff member who dies after a number of years of participation in the retirement plan, give some indication of the significant effect both of these plans should have on the design of any life insurance plan established by the college.

Survivor benefits under the 72 public employee and state teacher retirement systems covering college and university personnel vary greatly as to types of benefits and benefit amounts. The pattern of such survivor benefits is important in the design of the participating institution's group life plan. All of the systems provide for payment to survivors of an amount

TABLE 5.2: ILLUSTRATIVE DEATH BENEFITS UNDER A TIAA-CREF RETIREMENT PLAN

Entry Age: 30	If the Contribution Rate as a Percentage of Salary is[a]		
		Step-Rate	
Attained Age	*10 Per Cent*	*10–15 Per Cent*[b]	*15 Per Cent*
40	$11,442	$12,449	$ 17,163
50	34,705	40,025	52,058
60	79,966	95,048	119,949

[a] Assumes that all premiums are paid to TIAA, none to CREF, at TIAA 1968 rates for deferred annuities with nonguaranteed dividends on the 1968 scale applied throughout. Starting annual salary of $8,000 increasing at 4 per cent per year.
[b] Contribution of 10 per cent on first $7,800 of salary and 15 per cent on remaining salary.

equal to at least the deceased employee's contributions, with all but 7 crediting interest on such contributions. Nearly 30 per cent of the systems pay an additional lump sum benefit, the amount of which frequently depends on length of service. The lump sum benefit may be a stated dollar amount, or it may be expressed as a multiple of salary, such as six months' or a year's salary. About 30 per cent of the systems provide survivor income benefits for widows with children in their care, normally paid in lieu of any lump sum benefits or the return of employee contributions. Eligibility for survivor income benefits is usually based on employee service and age requirements. Three-fourths of the 72 public plans provide a life income for the widow of an employee who dies close to retirement, after attaining, for example, age 55 and 20 years of service.

Life Insurance Benefit Objective

The AAUP-AAC Statement of Principles recommends a program of "Life insurance providing a benefit considered sufficient to sustain the standard of living of the staff member's family for at least one year following his death. Where additional protection is contemplated, the special financial needs of families of younger faculty members should receive particular consideration."

BASIC READJUSTMENT BENEFIT

An insurance amount related to salary is frequently used to provide basic readjustment benefits. Each employee's insurance amount may be specified as one and a half times annual salary, for example. Or a salary-related plan may use salary brackets to assign insurance amounts, for example, $7,000 of insurance for those whose salaries are between $5,000 and $7,000; $9,000 for salaries between $7,000 and $9,000, etc.

ADDITIONAL PROTECTION

A college insurance program that provides more than a basic insurance amount may reasonably provide larger benefits for the younger staff members. Typically their insurance needs are high because they have young children, and their salaries and accumulated death benefits under the retirement plan are low. The lower cost of insurance for younger staff members aids the college in applying its available funds economically at the point where they will do the most good.

If the college life insurance program has properly taken family needs into account, group insurance benefits added to the basic Social Security income and individual insurance proceeds can be of substantial help in relieving pressure for the widow to work while the children are young. When a family has only the Social Security benefits to live on, the widow may have to take a job. If she does, the Social Security "work test" may reduce her Social Security benefits.

An appropriate college program might incorporate insurance of several times salary at the younger ages, decreasing by age to more modest amounts, such as one times salary, for persons over age 50. The various types and patterns of insurance are described below.

Types of Plans

There are three general types of life insurance coverage for employee groups in higher education: group term, collective, and group permanent. Group accidental death and dismemberment insurance is a subsidiary feature that is often added to a group life plan at extra cost.

GROUP TERM INSURANCE

The form of insurance used most frequently in group life plans is one-year renewable term insurance. The group contract is issued to the employer; each insured employee receives a certificate summarizing his coverage.

The group contract sets forth the amounts of insurance, the initial premium rates, the effective dates of insurance, the waiver of premium or benefit pay-out provisions for disabled persons, employee classes covered, the termination of insurance for those who leave the eligible group, provisions for continuation of insurance during certain leaves of absence, and a description of methods of paying benefits.

Group life insurance incorporates a "conversion privilege" that may be exercised by the employee if he terminates employment. Through this provision the terminating employee has the right to convert his group term insurance to an individual policy without evidence of insurability. The "privilege" is seldom used except by persons with impaired health, because insurers normally require that the type of insurance be changed at the time of conversion from low premium term to permanent insurance, which requires much higher premiums per $1,000 of protection. Only about 1¼ per cent of terminating employees exercise the conversion right.[1]

COLLECTIVE LIFE INSURANCE

Collective insurance provides decreasing term insurance which automatically concentrates a greater amount of protection at the younger ages. Each covered staff member receives his own individual life insurance contract rather than a certificate evidencing coverage under the employer's group term insurance contract. The same administrative economies are provided as under group term insurance, but unlike group term, the premium for each participant's insurance remains the same from year to year. The protection at any age is the amount of one-year term insurance purchased by the premium for that year. The insurance is issued in units; one unit of protection is the amount that can be purchased at each age by a premium of $1 per month, as shown in Table 5.5. Dividends as declared are applied as additional insurance protection. If the employee leaves the institution, he may continue his individual policy in force on his own without conversion.

GROUP PERMANENT INSURANCE

Group paid-up and level premium group permanent life insurance plans have been adopted by only a few educational institutions.

Under a group paid-up plan the employee's contributions are applied

[1] Eilers and Crowe (eds.), *Group Insurance Handbook*, p. 110.

each month to purchase increments of paid-up, as distinguished from term, insurance. Employer contributions are applied to purchase term insurance. Employer contributions are not used for the paid-up insurance coverage because they would then be taxable to the employee as income. As the paid-up insurance accumulates with successive employee contributions, the term insurance purchased by employer contributions decreases by a corresponding amount. The amount of each segment of paid-up insurance purchased depends on the size of the employee's contributions and his age. The paid-up insurance is retained by the employee on termination of employment, or he may surrender it for its cash value. On the term portion, he has the usual conversion privilege.

Level premium group permanent life insurance also provides for paid-up insurance, but with separate certificates given, as a rule, for the original amounts of permanent insurance and for any subsequent increases. It is frequently used to provide supplemental life insurance for pension plans of business and industrial organizations.

Several characteristics of group paid-up or permanent insurance account for its infrequent use for group coverage. For a given expenditure, higher levels of protection can be obtained with group term insurance. The paid-up insurance has a high cash value element and is therefore more savings than insurance, compared with term insurance. Many regard this as an expensive way to save. The employee can do as much on his own. Furthermore, administration is more complex under paid-up or permanent plans because much individual record keeping is required, and it is sometimes difficult to give the staff a clear understanding of the plan.

GROUP ACCIDENTAL DEATH AND
DISMEMBERMENT INSURANCE

Accidental death and dismemberment insurance (AD&D) pays specified indemnity amounts if the individual dies as the result of an accident, or if he sustains the accidental loss of certain parts of the body—eyes, arms, legs, or combinations thereof. When provided, AD&D is usually written in conjunction with group life insurance. The principal AD&D insurance amount is paid for loss of life or the loss of both hands, both feet, sight of both eyes, one hand and one foot, one hand and the sight of one eye, or one foot and the sight of one eye. Half of the principal AD&D amount is paid for the loss of one hand, one foot, or the sight of one eye. Not more than the principal amount is paid for all losses sustained by an employee in any one accident. Most insurers do not pay AD&D benefits for death caused by suicide or intentionally self-inflicted injury, war or acts of war, disease or bodily or mental infirmity, ptomaine or bacterial infections (except for infection of accidental cuts or wounds), or participation in the committing of a felony.

Fifty-seven per cent of the colleges have added accidental death and dismemberment provisions to their life insurance plans. Although this represents a slight majority, there is a real question of the propriety of an expenditure for insurance benefits that are payable in connection with accidental death or bodily injury, but not for death from other causes.

AD&D coverage may tend to mislead staff members, who, not fully aware of the limited coverage it provides, may assume that their protection is broader and their coverage is greater than in fact it is. According to census figures, only about 6 per cent of deaths are caused by accidents each year, which is very close to the figures shown by life insurance companies, 6.7 per cent.[2] A sounder basis for a college plan is to make sure that the full amount of a staff member's group insurance is paid for death from sickness as well as from accident.

Underwriting

Some of the common underwriting standards for group life insurance are written into state insurance laws; others are set forth by the insurer. These requirements for group life insurance, which also apply to group health and disability insurance, are:

1. A cohesive group, usually with a minimum of 10 people. The group must be based on a strong and continuing common relationship other than the desire for insurance, normally the employer-employee relationship. New entrants should continually be entering the group as others leave.

2. A central administrative unit for enrollment, record keeping, and collection of participants' contributions when the employees share in the cost of the plan, normally by payroll deduction.

3. Precision in the definition of the employees eligible and of the amount

[2] U.S. Bureau of the Census, *Statistical Abstract of the United States: 1967*, p. 59. (Includes all age groups.) Institute of Life Insurance, *Life Insurance Fact Book*, p. 92. (Includes all ordinary life insurance policyholders.)

of insurance provided. Eligibility should be based on factors pertaining to employment. There should be no doubt about which employee categories are eligible for the plan, and when.

4. A high percentage of enrollment of the eligible group in order to assure a reasonable distribution between healthy and impaired lives. When the employer pays the entire cost of the insurance (noncontributory), all members of the eligible classes are automatically insured. When the employees share in the cost, an enrollment of at least 75 per cent of the eligible employees is normally required.

5. Benefits for each participant that are reasonable in relation to the benefits provided other participants.

Premiums and Experience Rating

In determining the total monthly premium for an insured group, the amount of insurance in force at the respective ages (nearest birthday) of all insured employees is first multiplied by the premium per $1,000 of insurance for each age, and the results are totaled. This total is commonly adjusted to reflect the proportionately smaller administrative expense for larger plans. It is then divided by one-thousandth of the total insurance in force to obtain the average monthly premium rate per $1,000 of insurance for the group as a whole. The college's total monthly premium for a given month is then determined by applying the average premium rate for the plan to the total amount of insurance in force that month. The insurance in force may vary each month according to additions and terminations of employees under the plan, and according to any changes in the amounts for which individual participants are insured. The average monthly premium rate is recalculated once a year, usually on the anniversary date of the plan.

After a plan has gone into operation, its claim experience may influence the level of rates. Whether or not it does will depend on several factors such as the size of the group, the volume of insurance in force, and the practices of the insurer. In general, the experience of relatively small groups (this varies, but may involve groups with up to a few hundred employees), is pooled with the experience of groups of similar size and, under some methods, with part of the experience of larger groups.

This pooling among many groups is the basic insurance or risk-sharing function. Premium rates can be maintained at a fairly constant level for all institutions to the extent they participate in the pool, despite periods of high claim experience for some groups in the pool. For example, the yearly premium might be $700 for a group of 10 participants in which each member is insured for $10,000. The death of one staff member—resulting in a $10,000 benefit—would thus equal about fifteen years of premium payments, and the death of two staff members, thirty years. Without pooling, there would be no risk sharing to make insurance possible.

Large institutions having many hundreds or even thousands of employees tend to have a more predictable and level number of deaths in their group over the years and are thus often "self-rated" or "experience-rated." The net cost of a self-rated plan (premiums less dividends) is based on the experience of the plan, although, depending on the practice of the insurer, a portion of even a large group's claim experience may be pooled with other groups' experience. Insurers are willing to provide self-rating for groups that are sufficiently large to produce a reasonably predictable level of claims. The relative weight assigned to a group's own experience and to the pool differs from insurer to insurer. There is an advantage in self-rating to a large institution if there are few claims, since dividends or retroactive rate adjustments reflect this experience, thus reducing the cost of the plan. Many claims produce the opposite effect in a self-rated plan.

When a group is large enough to have its plan self-rated to some extent, insurers competing to underwrite the plan are usually compared on the basis of "retention" illustrations. The retention is the insurer's charge for the plan beyond the payment of plan benefits, and it includes administrative expenses, contingency reserves, commissions, taxes, and, in some cases, a margin for profit. The balance of gross premium is applied to pay claims, establish claim reserves, and provide dividends or premium refunds.

Other Contract Provisions

WAIVER OF PREMIUM BENEFIT

To continue insurance for employees who become disabled, a waiver of premium provision is usually incorporated in the master contract. Under a typical waiver benefit, a participant who becomes "totally and permanently" disabled for a period of six months before age 60 has his life insurance coverage continued under the group policy without further premium payments during such disability. The charge for the benefit is included in the group life premium rate.

DISABILITY PAY-OUT

A group life insurance contract may provide that, in the event of a total and permanent disability before age 60 that has continued for 6 months, the death benefit of the policy may be paid out to the insured as monthly income, usually over a five-year period. This provision is added at an extra charge of about 8 cents per month per $1,000 of insurance. The defect of the provision is readily apparent: the pay-out correspondingly reduces the amount of life insurance protection for the family at a time when the breadwinner has become uninsurable and needs insurance protection as never before.

SETTLEMENT OPTIONS

The beneficiary of a group insurance policy may choose to take the insurance proceeds as a lump sum or as monthly income under several different options. The options usually include (1) a life annuity with income ceasing at death, (2) a life annuity for the original payee with income continuing to a second payee for the balance of a stated period if death occurs within that period (usually the first 10 or 20 years), (3) an income of a specified monthly amount, as selected, for as long as proceeds plus interest permit, (4) an income for a fixed period of years, usually from 1 to 30 as selected, or (5) a monthly income consisting of interest earned on the proceeds, with the principal remaining intact to be paid at a later date.[3]

College Plan Decisions

The decisions to be made in adopting or reviewing a group life plan include the following:

1. Classes of employees to be covered.
2. Waiting period, if any, before newly eligible persons are brought into the plan.

---

[3] Up to 75 per cent of TIAA life insurance proceeds, but not less than $1,000, may be used to purchase a CREF variable annuity income, with the balance of proceeds purchasing a TIAA fixed-dollar income.

3. Amount of insurance to be provided each class.
4. Whether the institution should pay all or only a part of the cost.
5. Whether any insurance should be continued after a staff member retires.

CLASSES OF EMPLOYEES COVERED

Of the 1,232 responding institutions, 70 per cent report a life insurance plan for faculty and administrative personnel, and 63 per cent for clerical-service employees. The life insurance plans in the colleges and universities normally extend eligibility to substantially all full-time employees in the personnel categories covered.

Regardless of a staff member's job or length of service, his death is bound to cause financial difficulties for his family. Even single persons without dependents should have some insurance. It therefore seems appropriate to include all presumably permanent, full-time employees of the institution in the life insurance plan. Eligibility for the plan usually must be based on conditions pertaining to employment, such as employee job classification or salary. In assigning insurance amounts to eligible employees, however, there is sufficient flexibility within which to recognize various broad categories of need. Insurance may be assigned by age, dependent or marital status, job category, rank, salary level, or combinations of these and other factors.

Each employee's eligibility for the plan depends on the definitions stated in the group policy; eligibility must be clearly defined. The college should use its own precise personnel terminology and make sure that there is no uncertainty in individual cases.

The following are examples of eligibility definitions used by various institutions:

All *regular* staff employees are eligible to enroll. Regular staff employees are those who have not reached normal retirement age, who work 30 hours per week or more, and are employed for a period expected to be six months or longer.

All permanent full-time members of the faculty above the rank of instructor are eligible to participate in the group life insurance program. Other permanent full-time nonclassified staff members with annual salaries of $10,000 or more are also eligible. Permanent service is defined as employment that is expected to last 1 year or more.

If you enter the full-time service of the University, you will become automatically insured in the Group Insurance Plan from date of employment. Full-time service is defined as working at least two-thirds of a normal full-time schedule.

After the plan has started, the participation of newly hired eligible employees may be required by the employer as a condition of employment. Of course, when the institution pays the entire premium, all eligible staff members automatically participate. Employees not originally eligible for coverage who later enter classes covered by the plan should be immediately informed of their eligibility and encouraged or required to participate in the plan as soon as eligibility is attained. Medical evidence of insurability is required by the insurer for individuals electing coverage more than 31 days after becoming eligible.

WAITING PERIOD

Early coverage is advantageous both to the employee and to the institution. Faculty and administrative officers are usually brought into the plan on the first of the month coinciding with or next following the date of initial employment. A somewhat longer waiting period, such as three months, is not unreasonable for classifications of employees normally having a higher turnover rate in the early months of employment.

Table 5.3 shows the waiting period provisions in effect in the colleges and universities. Almost 80 per cent of the faculty plans provide for immediate participation or a waiting period of a month or less, and these plans cover about 85 per cent of faculty in institutions reporting plans. About 60 per cent of plans for clerical-service employees, covering two-thirds of this group of employees in institutions reporting plans, provide for participation at once or in a month or less. A waiting period of six months or more is more frequent in clerical-service plans than in faculty plans, 18 per cent versus 7 per cent.

INSURANCE PATTERNS

Several different patterns of life insurance protection are used in the colleges.[4] A common method of assigning insurance is by salary, either by

[4] About half the states have enacted legislation setting upper limits on the amount of group life insurance that may be assigned an employee under a group life plan. Most of them limit the insurance amount to the greater of $20,000 or 150 per cent of salary up to a maximum of $40,000.

TABLE 5.3: GROUP LIFE INSURANCE PLANS

Waiting Period Before New Employee Is Eligible to Participate in Plan

	Faculty[a]		Clerical-Service	
Waiting Period	Per Cent Insts N = 864	Per Cent EEs N = 249,340	Per Cent Insts N = 772	Per Cent EEs N = 378,167
No waiting period	57.1	62.2	39.5	43.5
1 month or less	21.5	24.3	19.5	23.4
2–3 months	6.1	4.0	15.3	11.5
6 months	3.1	4.3	8.7	7.4
12 months	3.1	1.0	6.0	7.6
Over 12 months	1.1	0.2	3.8	1.7
Until anniversary or semi-anniversary date of plan	4.4	1.5	3.3	1.0
Other	2.2	1.9	2.5	3.1
No response	1.4	0.6	1.4	0.8
Total	100.0	100.0	100.0	100.0

[a] Data for administrative personnel are similar to those for faculty.

brackets or as a multiple of salary. For example, a salary bracket plan might state its benefits as follows:

Basic Annual Salary	Amount of Insurance
Less than $5,000	$ 5,000
$5,000 but less than $9,000	9,000
$9,000 but less than $13,000	13,000
$13,000 but less than $17,000	17,000
$17,000 or more	20,000

Another method of relating insurance to salary is to state the insurance as a multiple of salary, for example, one, one and a half, or two times salary, usually rounded to the next $500 or $1,000.

The insurance amounts may differ for single and for married persons. For example, insurance of one times salary may be assigned to those with no dependents, and of two times salary to those with a spouse or children under 19 years of age.

Age is often a factor in the assignment of insurance amounts. Patterns under which the insurance amount begins regular decreases at a stated age offer flexibility in adapting insurance to changing needs as age advances. By providing larger amounts of insurance for younger staff members, the college can concentrate protection where it is most needed, and at the same time provide a far larger total of protection than is available for the same cost under a plan continuing unreduced amounts to retirement. A decreasing insurance pattern also coordinates well with a fully vested retirement plan by providing the largest insurance amounts during the years when the annuity accumulation is still relatively small, and decreasing amounts as the annuity accumulation becomes more substantial. The insurance amount may be assigned by age alone, as shown below in Example 1, or by age and salary multiple, as in Example 2. Both examples show the provision of larger amounts of insurance for staff members at the younger ages.

EXAMPLE 1.

Age Nearest Birthday	Insurance Amount	Age Nearest Birthday	Insurance Amount
Under 25	$25,000	45 but under 50	$7,000
25 but under 30	20,000	50 but under 55	5,000
30 but under 35	16,000	55 but under 60	3,000
35 but under 40	12,000	60 but under 65	2,000
40 but under 45	9,000	70 or over	1,000

EXAMPLE 2. Amount of life insurance for employees with dependents is determined by multiplying *annual salary* by the factor opposite the attained age (shown at quinquennial ages after 40). For employees without dependents, amount is one times salary at any age.

Age	Factor	Age	Factor
35 and under	4.0	45	3.0
36	3.9	50	2.5
37	3.8	55	2.0
38	3.7	60	1.5
39	3.6	65 or over	1.0
40	3.5		

In relatively few institutions is the same amount of insurance assigned to all plan participants without relating the insurance amounts to salary, age, or some other factor.

Units of Insurance. Another way of relating insurance amounts to age is through a "graded" or "decreasing" pattern expressed in terms of units. For example, one unit might represent $2,500 of coverage through age 50, after which the insurance decreases by $125 each year until it becomes $250 at age 68 and after. An eight-unit plan would provide $20,000 of insurance through age 50, decreasing to $2,000 at age 68 and after, and so on. The same number of units may be assigned to all eligible persons, or the number may differ according to employee classification or salary. For example, one unit of insurance could be assigned for each $2,500 of salary or fraction thereof. Table 5.4 illustrates this type of insurance.

TABLE 5.4: INSURANCE PATTERN DECREASING AFTER AGE 50

Age Nearest Birthday	Amount of Insurance		Age Nearest Birthday	Amount of Insurance	
	One Unit	Eight Units		One Unit	Eight Units
Through 50	$2,500	$20,000	59	1,375	11,000
			60	1,250	10,000
51	2,375	19,000	61	$1,125	$ 9,000
52	2,250	18,000	62	1,000	8,000
53	2,125	17,000	63	875	7,000
54	2,000	16,000	64	750	6,000
55	1,875	15,000	65	625	5,000
56	1,750	14,000	66	500	4,000
57	1,625	13,000	67	375	3,000
58	1,500	12,000			
			68 or over	250	2,000

Collective life insurance provides another pattern of decreasing insurance by providing substantial amounts of protection at the younger ages and decreasing each year as age advances. Table 5.5 illustrates the coverage pattern of a three-unit collective plan.

TABLE 5.5: INSURANCE PATTERN OF A THREE-UNIT COLLECTIVE LIFE INSURANCE PLAN
(Quinquennial Ages)

Age	Monthly Premium	Contractual Insurance Amount	Total Insurance Amount Including 95 Per Cent Dividend[a]
25	$3[b]	$17,580	$34,281
30	3	15,192	31,182
35	3	13,440	26,208
40	3	8,664	17,784
45	3	5,730	11,175
50	3	3,477	7,137
55	3	2,310	4,506
60	3	1,455	2,985
65	3	990	1,932

[a] 1968 dividend scale for TIAA collective insurance, not guaranteed for future years.
[b] Three units at $1 per unit.

Combined Basic and Decreasing Insurance. A combination plan may be used to provide a basic amount of insurance for everyone plus additional amounts generally coordinating with family insurance needs. For example, a combination plan might provide insurance of one times salary for everyone, plus four units of insurance which begins to decrease each year after age 50.

CONTRIBUTIONS

Most states require employers to pay at least part of the cost of a group life insurance plan. Group life insurance plans of associations of state teachers or other association groups, however, may be paid for wholly by the participants. The maximum group life insurance contribution that may be made by the employee is frequently limited by statute or state insurance regulation to no more than 60 cents per month per $1,000 of insurance. Under the minimum standard monthly rate shown in Table 5.6 for the State of New York, 60 cents per month per $1,000 is more than the group insurance premium for persons up to about age 43 and less than the premium for persons above that age. (The minimum standard rate is that required to be charged during the first policy year of a group life plan; lower premium rates may be used for subsequent policy years.) The 60 cent limit may be exceeded as long as the employer pays 25 per cent or more of the total premium for the plan.

TABLE 5.6: MONTHLY PREMIUM PER $1,000 OF GROUP LIFE INSURANCE
STATE OF NEW YORK
(Quinquennial Ages)[a]

Age Nearest Birthday	Monthly Premium	Age Nearest Birthday	Monthly Premium
20	$0.23	60	$ 2.51
25	0.25	65	3.78
30	0.27	70	5.81
35	0.32	75	8.56
40	0.45	80	12.83
45	0.68	85	18.80
50	1.06	90	26.62
55	1.65	95	40.98

[a] Minimum group life renewable term gross premiums, Commissioner's Standard Group Mortality Table with interest at 3 per cent, effective August 1, 1961, exclusive of adjustments based on premium or insurance volume. New York State Insurance Department Regulation Number 32, September 26, 1961.

When the employee shares in the cost, employee contributions may be graded so as to take into account the lower cost of group life insurance for younger staff members. For example, the employee contribution may be established as 20 cents a month per $1,000 for persons under age 30, 30 cents for persons from 30 to 39 years of age, 40 cents for persons from ages 40 to 44, and 60 cents for those aged 45 or more. Ideally, the employee contribution should not be set at an amount per $1,000 of insurance that is higher than the net cost for which the individual can buy term life insurance on his own.

A growing proportion of the colleges provides life insurance coverage without cost to the employee. In 1958, approximately 18 per cent of group life plans for faculty were noncontributory, that is, paid for wholly by the employer. Currently a third of the plans for faculty, administrative personnel, and clerical-service employees are noncontributory. The premium is shared by employer and employee in slightly more than half the plans. The full cost of the life insurance plan is paid by the employee in about 12 per cent of plans. The employee-pay-all plans are concentrated largely in publicly supported institutions and account for about a fourth of the staff members in the institutions having group life plans. A number of these plans are provided through employee associations (e.g., the North Carolina State Employees' Association) rather than through a plan sponsored by the employer. Table 5.7 summarizes the employer and employee roles in paying for group life insurance.

When the premium is shared, the employer normally pays a substantial portion of it so that employee contributions will be within statutory limits,

TABLE 5.7: EMPLOYER-EMPLOYEE CONTRIBUTIONS FOR GROUP LIFE INSURANCE COVERAGE

Employer-Employee Sharing of Cost	Faculty[a]		Clerical-Service	
	Per Cent Insts N = 864	Per Cent EEs N = 249,340	Per Cent Insts N = 772	Per Cent EEs N = 378,167
ER pays full cost	34.4	23.5	33.0	23.9
ER and EE share cost	52.5	51.8	53.0	49.7
EE pays full cost	11.8	24.4	12.6	26.2
No response	1.3	0.3	1.4	0.2
Total	100.0	100.0	100.0	100.0

[a] Data for administrative personnel are similar to those for faculty.

and low enough to make participation attractive. Employee contributions are normally made through regular payroll deduction.

Under contributory plans the employee contribution is usually expressed as a monthly amount per $1,000 of insurance. If insurance is expressed in units, the employee contribution is normally set at an amount *per unit* of insurance. Under collective insurance a common sharing arrangement is for the college and the staff member each to pay 50 cents per month per unit of insurance, which is half the cost.

A plan may provide for a basic amount of insurance and an additional amount of insurance that is optional. The option is exercised at the time each individual enters the class eligible for it. A fourth of the college plans reported the availability of such added group insurance. A third of these plans are noncontributory for the basic amount of insurance.

Good arguments can be advanced for either a contributory or a non-contributory plan. Advantages frequently cited for noncontributory plans include: (1) certainty that all eligible employees are covered; (2) economy of installation and simplicity of administration—there are no payroll deductions and there are fewer accounting operations; (3) employee good-will and approval; and (4) employer contributions toward the first $50,000 of group life insurance are not includable in the employee's taxable income.

Advantages frequently cited for contributory plans include: (1) benefits possibly larger than the employer would finance alone; (2) more effective use of employer contributions, if it is assumed that the employees who do not elect to participate in a contributory plan are most often those with lesser insurance needs; (3) greater control by the staff over plan provisions —staff members who themselves pay part of the cost generally feel entitled to a greater voice in plan changes and improvements; (4) greater employee awareness—employees are more conscious of the existence and provisions of a benefit plan when they contribute each month to its cost.

GROUP INSURANCE DURING RETIREMENT

College life insurance plans are normally designed to continue coverage for participants as long as they remain in active service, but not thereafter. About a third of the plans do continue some group coverage during retirement, however, usually on a reduced basis.

The cost of group life insurance for retired staff members is dramatically high. It costs about eighteen times more per $1,000 of insurance at age 70 than at age 35. Life insurance of $5,000 for one year costs about $300 at age 70 and about $700 at age 80; as age advances, the yearly premium moves closer to the amount of insurance. A college is therefore forced to spend a substantial amount if it wishes to provide even a modest program of life insurance during retirement. Unlike the insurance coverage for the active staff, every dollar of group insurance for the retired staff must inevitably be paid, perhaps only to an estate or to distant relatives.

The college considering the continuation of some life insurance for retired persons might well ask the following questions: (1) If the college is prepared to spend the amount necessary for this additional life insurance, might it not be more appropriate to apply the premium toward greater life or health insurance protection for the active staff? (2) If the life insurance program for the active staff is satisfactory, and it is decided to add to the benefits available during retirement, might it not be better to apply the money to increased retirement benefits or medical protection or a program of laboratory privileges, secretarial help, or faculty club membership?

PLAN OPERATION

When a plan is installed, the insurer normally makes available to the institution an administration manual outlining the procedures necessary to keep the plan running smoothly. Such information includes the procedures for enrolling newly eligible employees, applying for benefit payments, reporting individual changes in insurance amounts, insurance terminations of employees leaving the institution, premium remittance procedures, and general maintenance of records.

The value of any benefit plan is enhanced by full employee understanding of the benefits provided. Newly hired or newly eligible employees should be thoroughly informed about the plan and how it coordinates with the individual's own life insurance protection. Those who have participated in the plan for some time should periodically be reminded of the protection provided. Employee information booklets and the faculty handbook offer means of presenting the plan information. Staff meetings offer added opportunities for review of plan provisions and for question-and-answer sessions.

6

HEALTH INSURANCE: BASIC
HOSPITAL-SURGICAL-MEDICAL
PLANS

Health insurance is the broad term used to describe insurance coverages
providing benefits for the cost of treatment by doctors and other medical
practitioners, for hospitalization or other use of medical facilities and
equipment, and for other medical requirements, such as prescribed drugs
and medicines. The term can also include disability income insurance, but
in this study it is confined to insurance plans directly relating to medical
care.

Like life insurance, health insurance may be obtained by individuals
directly from an insurer or via an insurance agent or, for groups of employees, through group coverage. Group coverage has the greater impact,
accounting for about two-thirds of annual health insurance premiums in
the United States.[1] This chapter and the next one discuss health insurance
in its group form as it covers faculty and staff in higher education. Base
plans (basic hospital-surgical-medical plans) are described in this chapter,
and major medical and combined plans in the next.

Group health insurance in higher education is usually provided by (1) a
basic hospital-surgical-medical plan, (2) a basic plan plus a major medical
expense plan, or (3) a single "comprehensive" plan combining features of
both basic and major medical plans. Only about 3 per cent of the responding
institutions have no health insurance plan at all, that is, neither basic nor
major medical coverage.

Ninety per cent of the responding institutions reported a basic plan for
all employees. Of these, 72 per cent reported basic coverage supplemented

[1] Health Insurance Institute, *1967 Source Book of Health Insurance*, p. 29.

by major medical for faculty and administrators and, for clerical-service personnel, 64 per cent. Sixteen per cent reported for all classes a single plan combining basic and major medical coverage. The remainder of the institutions provide basic coverage only. In 1958, 82 per cent of the responding institutions reported basic coverage for faculty and administrators. At that time only 17 per cent of four-year institutions of higher education had basic coverage supplemented by major medical, 5 per cent reported a single "comprehensive" plan, and approximately 65 per cent had basic coverage only.

Scope of Basic Health Insurance

The medical expenses covered by basic health insurance plans normally include hospital expenses, surgeons' fees and physicians' fees for visits in the hospital. Occasionally a base plan covers physicians' home or office visits, but this is infrequent except in community group practice plans. Nor do base plans normally cover the cost of blood or blood serum, or the cost of medical equipment or appliances.

TYPES OF BENEFITS

Basic group health insurance plans provide employees and their dependents with either an *indemnity* or a *service* benefit for the care specified. An indemnity plan provides for a cash payment to the insured when he or his dependents incur a covered expense. Insurance company hospital-surgical-medical plans and Blue Shield surgical-medical plans are generally of the indemnity type.

Blue Cross hospital plans are by far the most numerous service plan arrangements. In such plans the benefit is in the form of the care or service rendered. Blue Cross compensates participating hospitals for their services on the basis of reimbursement contracts with the hospitals. When an individual is hospitalized, designated services are provided without charge to him; services not covered by the contract are billed to him directly.

ROLE OF BASE PLANS IN MEDICAL PROTECTION

Up to a certain level it is reasonable to pay for routine items of medical care from regular family income and savings. When medical expenses begin to accumulate, however, most people begin to need financial help. Hospitalization is one point of presumed need at which basic plans step in.

Although a base plan meets a real need, a serious illness or accident can result in expenses considerably in excess of base plan benefits. Basic health insurance plans are not the total answer to the need for protection against medical costs, nor is this their claim. They are normally supplemented by major medical expense insurance, discussed in Chapter 7, which can step in above the limits of, and can meet expenses not covered by, basic plans.

Types of Base Plans

BLUE CROSS

Blue Cross organizations provide their hospital service benefits under contract with hospitals. If a Blue Cross participant is cared for in a noncontracting hospital, he usually receives a cash benefit instead of a service benefit. The contract between Blue Cross and the employer sets forth all details of the coverage of employees and dependents. Employees receive a certificate describing their benefits. Most Blue Cross service benefits provide for a specified number of days of care per hospital confinement in semiprivate (two-to-four bed) accommodations. Periods of full benefit, sometimes followed by periods of half benefit (in which the plan pays 50 per cent of the hospital's regular daily semiprivate charge), vary among plans. Typical periods of coverage per confinement are 21 days of full benefit followed by 90 days of half benefit, or 30, 70, 120, or 365 days of full care per confinement.

Blue Cross service benefits in semiprivate accommodations typically include room and board, special diets, general nursing service, use of operating and treatment rooms and equipment, and drugs and medicines required during hospitalization. The following services are also included when rendered as a regular hospital service provided by the hospital: laboratory examinations, x-ray examinations, electrocardiograms, basal metabolism tests, physical therapy, oxygen and its administration, anesthesia and its administration, administration of blood and plasma (but not their cost), and intravenous injections.

Maternity benefits are normally available under Blue Cross plans after nine or ten months' participation under a family certificate. Maternity benefits are usually limited to a specified dollar amount of hospital charges for such care, or to a specified number of days of care, including use of the delivery room, ordinary nursery care, and diaper service for the newborn during the mother's eligible hospital stay.

When a hospital patient uses private instead of semiprivate accommodations, Blue Cross plans normally provide an allowance toward the cost of the private room. In many plans the allowance is a specified dollar amount, but in some plans it is based on the hospital's average semiprivate charge. The difference between allowance and charge is billed to the patient.

As a rule, there are only a few health conditions for which Blue Cross benefits are excluded or limited: chronic alcoholism, drug addiction, mental disorders, and pulmonary tuberculosis. Hospitalization primarily for diagnostic studies, physical therapy, x-ray therapy, radium therapy, or convalescence is also normally excluded from Blue Cross coverage.

Enrollment of new employees in Blue Cross plans is normally made at times specified in the contract. Enrollment of new employees may be monthly, quarterly, or within a specified period following employment, such as 30 or 60 days. To be covered, a new spouse must be enrolled within a specified number of days after marriage.

Children are covered as dependents usually from birth or after a specified number of days following birth, such as 14, to the end of the year in which the child reaches age 19. After age 19, children may obtain individual direct-pay certificates.

A stated percentage of enrollment of eligible employees must be maintained in Blue Cross plans. Typically, a higher percentage enrollment is required of smaller groups. The requirement, which differs among plans, may range from 40 or 50 per cent for groups of 500 or more, to 100 per cent for groups of less than 10.

Persons leaving their employer may change to a direct-pay certificate and are, in some plans, given the opportunity of continuing coverage at the group premium rate for a short time, for example, three months. A few plans require a deductible, such as $25 or $100, for employees continuing coverage on leaving a group.

BLUE SHIELD

Most Blue Shield plans operate in coordination with the local Blue Cross plan, with billing of premiums, enrollment, and other business carried out through consolidated procedures. As under Blue Cross, employee contributions are paid by salary deduction, and an employee who leaves his group may continue Blue Shield coverage by paying the full premiums directly.

Blue Shield plans normally provide scheduled cash payments for specified surgical procedures performed in the hospital, office, or home, and specified amounts for doctors' visits to a hospitalized patient.

Most of the Blue Shield plans provide that participating physicians and surgeons will accept the scheduled benefit amount as payment in full if the subscriber's income is below a certain figure. In some plans this figure is as low as $3,500; in others as high as $8,500.

Many Blue Shield plans provide at the time of each individual's enrollment a choice among surgical fee scales. For example, one scale might range from $5 for minor surgical procedures to $200 for major ones, another from $5 to $500, a higher premium being charged for the higher schedule. For doctors' visits in the hospital, one schedule might provide $10 for the first day and $3 for the next 29 days per admission; a higher benefit and premium scale might provide $15 for the first day, $10 for the second day, and a lesser amount for the remainder of the period up to a total dollar limit.

Some Blue Shield plans include certain additional benefits, such as specified amounts for x-ray diagnosis (sometimes limited to fractures and dislocations), pathological analysis, treatment by radiation therapy in lieu of surgery, and general anesthesia services by a doctor in a hospital.

INSURANCE COMPANY BASE PLANS

The basic health insurance plans provided by insurance companies offer a cafeteria of benefit arrangements; an employer may choose almost any type of plan he wishes, for whatever level and scope of benefits he is willing to buy. The hospital and surgical-medical benefits are normally provided for under a single group contract.

Nearly all private insurers' basic hospital plans are of the indemnity type. Reimbursement is usually for the hospital's actual room and board charges up to a specified daily maximum; sometimes this maximum is stated as the hospital's charge for semiprivate room accommodations. If a private room is used in such instances, reimbursement is usually based, according to the plan, either on the hospital's average semiprivate charge, or on its average semiprivate charge plus a specified dollar amount such as $2 or $4 a day. A few plans provide a fixed daily dollar benefit regardless of the actual hospital room and board charge. Under such plans the daily benefit tends to be relatively low, almost invariably below the average semiprivate room and board charges in the area. The maximum number of days for which benefits are paid usually ranges from 70 to 120, depending on the plan, although longer periods are not uncommon.

For hospital services other than room and board (such as drugs, laboratory tests, x-ray, operating room), many plans pay the cost up to a specified total amount, such as $300 or $500 per confinement. Lower limits are usually placed on benefits for hospital confinements due to normal pregnancies. Additional benefits above a given limit are sometimes provided on a coinsurance basis, with the plan paying 75 or 80 per cent of the regular benefit amount.

Under insurance company plans the maximum amount payable for each surgical procedure is set forth in a schedule similar to that described previously for Blue Shield plans. The maximum benefit for doctors' hospital visits usually accumulates at a fixed rate for each day of hospital confinement; for example, the rate may be $5 a day, with the total benefit payable for each confinement limited to $200.

Under insurance company plans the right of a terminating employee to convert to an individual basic health insurance policy (normally included in Blue Cross-Blue Shield plans) depends on the provisions written into the group contract.

COMMUNITY GROUP PRACTICE PLANS

College and university staff members who belong to community group practice plans are provided hospital care and also doctors' services for home, office, hospital visits, and surgery—all performed by doctors employed by the insuring organization or under contract to it. The coverage normally includes regular medical care, preventive medicine, physical examinations, immunization, diagnosis, eye examinations, laboratory tests, x-ray, and radiation and physiotherapy treatments. Some of the plans provide visiting nurse service and private duty nursing in the hospital. The participant chooses his physician from a panel of the doctors associated with the plan. These comprehensive plans are available in only a few parts of the country. They include the Health Insurance Plan of Greater New York (whose hospital care is provided through Blue Cross), the Ross-Loos Medical Group (Southern California), the Kaiser Foundation Health Plan in various locations in California, Oregon, Washington, Hawaii, and Alaska, the Group Health Cooperative of Puget Sound, the Community Health Association (Detroit), and the Group Health Association (Washington, D.C.).

Reviewing Basic Health Insurance

In seeking basic coverage for the first time or reviewing an existing plan, an institution should consider the following points:

1. The type of plan.
2. The benefits provided.
3. The classes of employees covered.
4. The waiting period, if any, before participation begins.
5. The sharing of contributions between employer and employee.
6. Coverage for retired employees and widows.

TYPES OF PLANS AND BENEFITS

Table 6.1 shows the types of plans in operation in institutions reporting base plans. In 1958, 80 per cent of the four-year institutions with basic plans had Blue Cross-Blue Shield plans, 16 per cent had insurance company plans, and 4 per cent other types of plans. Table 6.1 indicates a considerable increase in insurance company plans in the last decade, from 16 to 34 per cent, and a slight decrease in the proportion of Blue Cross and Blue Shield plans.

CLASSES OF EMPLOYEES COVERED

Virtually all of the institutions reporting basic plans make all employee classes eligible for the coverage. If the institution has a basic health insurance plan, there is good reason to make it available to all full-time employees and even to employees working "half-time" or more. Everyone is of course subject to accidents and illness and to the hospital and doctor bills

TABLE 6.1: TYPES OF BASIC HEALTH INSURANCE PLANS REPORTED[a]

	Faculty[b]		
	All Insts Per Cent N = 1,109	Public Insts Per Cent N = 338	Private Insts Per Cent N = 771
Blue Cross	70.1	69.5	70.2
Blue Shield	65.6	67.1	64.8
Insurance company	34.2	44.7	29.6
Other[c]	6.6	13.3	3.6

[a] Percentages add to over 100 per cent due to more than one plan in effect at the same institution, e.g., nearly all Blue Shield plans accompany a Blue Cross plan.

[b] Data for other employee categories are similar to those for faculty.

[c] Includes community group practice plans.

that result; broad opportunity for protection is important to both institution and staff.

BRINGING EMPLOYEES INTO A NEW PLAN

The coverage under a new plan begins on its effective date provided the required proportion of eligible employees has enrolled. If an employee is not actively at work on the date coverage is to begin, he is covered on the date he returns to work.

Persons in service who do not elect coverage when a plan is inaugurated may join later. In Blue Cross-Blue Shield plans they may join on specified late enrollment dates; in insurance company plans, on providing evidence of insurability; in both, they join during later "open enrollment" periods.

WAITING PERIODS

In most colleges and universities, eligible employees hired after a plan is in operation may join the plan without delay. Some institutions, however, have set up short waiting periods for classes of employees that have a high turnover rate in the early months of employment.

When the employer pays the entire premium, eligible employees are covered automatically as soon as they have completed the waiting period, if any. When the employee who has completed a waiting period is to pay part or all of the premium and is not required to participate in the plan, the group contract states a period within which the newly eligible employee

can elect coverage. Provisions for subsequent enrollment are stated for those
who do not elect coverage when they initially become eligible.

Table 6.2 indicates that base plan participation is made available to more
than 4 out of 5 new college faculty and administrative staff members without
a waiting period or within the first month following employment. The great
majority of clerical-service staff is also brought in during the first month of
employment, but at about a fifth of the institutions they have to wait until
a later date before becoming eligible.

TABLE 6.2: WAITING PERIOD FOR PARTICIPATION IN
BASIC HOSPITAL-SURGICAL-MEDICAL PLANS

	Faculty		Administrative		Clerical-Service	
	Per Cent Insts N = 1,109	Per Cent EEs N = 261,445	Per Cent Insts N = 1,106	Per Cent EEs N = 100,513	Per Cent Insts N = 1,106	Per Cent EEs N = 401,665
No waiting period	56.6	51.7	55.0	54.1	48.0	48.2
Less than 1 month	25.2	35.2	25.2	30.6	23.9	34.3
Stated number of months	10.3	7.9	11.8	9.4	19.3	11.8
Until stated date(s) within first year	3.4	1.2	3.4	1.0	4.0	1.3
Other	2.3	2.4	2.2	3.1	2.5	3.1
No response	2.2	1.6	2.4	1.8	2.3	1.3
Total	100.0	100.0	100.0	100.0	100.0	100.0

Dependent coverage, like employee coverage, becomes effective automatically for eligible dependents of insured employees if the employer
also pays the full premium for dependents. If the employee pays part or all
of the premium for dependent coverage, he can elect it at the time he joins
the plan. If a dependent is hospitalized when first eligible, coverage begins
after confinement ends. Coverage for a new spouse must usually be applied
for within a specified period after the date of the marriage; otherwise, the
addition may be made only at specified times. In most plans, newborn
children are covered automatically under a family certificate, either from
date of birth or after a specified number of days, for example, 14 days.
Under other plans, coverage for a newborn child must be applied for
within a specified period after birth, for example, 60 days.

SHARING THE PREMIUMS

The years since 1958 have seen a considerable increase in the proportion of colleges sharing in the cost of their staff members' basic group health insurance coverage. In 1958, 20 per cent of universities and about 30 per cent of colleges reported making contributions toward the cost of the basic health insurance plan for faculty members. In 1968 the proportion of institutions contributing all or part of the cost had increased to about 54 per cent of universities and 64 per cent of colleges. Comparative figures are not available for the clerical-service employee classifications of a decade ago; however, because institutions contributing to health insurance for one employee group normally do so for others as well, it may be assumed that a similar rise has occurred for these groups.

Table 6.3 shows the distribution of current premium-sharing arrangements for faculty, administrative, and clerical-service employees.

TABLE 6.3: EMPLOYER AND EMPLOYEE CONTRIBUTIONS FOR BASIC HOSPITAL-SURGICAL-MEDICAL COVERAGE OF EMPLOYEES

	Faculty		Administrative		Clerical-Service	
	Per Cent Insts	*Per Cent EEs*	*Per Cent Insts*	*Per Cent EEs*	*Per Cent Insts*	*Per Cent EEs*
Employer-Employee	N =	N =	N =	N =	N =	N =
Sharing of Cost	1,109	261,445	1,106	100,513	1,106	401,665
ER pays full cost	24.2	20.5	24.2	21.9	24.1	20.5
EE and ER share	38.9	40.2	39.1	37.5	41.6	44.4
EE pays full cost	35.3	38.6	35.0	40.2	32.7	34.8
No response	1.6	0.7	1.7	0.4	1.6	0.3
Total	100.0	100.0	100.0	100.0	100.0	100.0

The number of institutions paying the full cost for dependent coverage is considerably less than the number paying the full cost of employee coverage. Twenty-four per cent of the institutions pay the full cost of the faculty members' coverage, while only 7 per cent pay the full cost for faculty dependents. These percentages are about the same for the other employee categories. The sharing of premiums for coverage of faculty dependents is shown in Table 6.4.

The trend since 1958 has raised the proportion of employers who contribute to the cost of basic health insurance coverage for the employee.

TABLE 6.4: *EMPLOYER AND EMPLOYEE CONTRIBUTIONS FOR BASIC HOSPITAL-SURGICAL-MEDICAL COVERAGE OF DEPENDENTS*

	Faculty[a]	
Employer-Employee Sharing of Cost	*Per Cent Insts N = 1,095*	*Per Cent EEs N = 261,039*
ER pays full cost	6.7	5.6
EE and ER share	29.8	34.0
EE pays full cost	61.5	58.6
No response	2.0	1.8
Total	100.0	100.0

[a] Data for other employee categories are similar to those for faculty.

However, it is still lower than the percentages of employers who contribute toward major medical coverage (79 per cent), group life insurance plans (87 per cent), long-term total disability benefits (85 per cent), and retirement plans (98 per cent). In part, the difference is a carry-over from the history of basic coverage. In the pre-World War II era the pioneering Blue Cross-Blue Shield plans began largely on an employee-pay-all basis. A college group could inaugurate a plan as soon as there were enough individuals willing to pay for it, provided the employer volunteered group enrollment facilities. Once started, this contribution pattern tended to continue. The difference can also be ascribed in part to the fact that the colleges have always had a stronger interest in making employer contributions toward covering the major risks—the retirement plan, group life insurance, disability insurance, and major medical expense insurance.

Basic Health Insurance Coverage for Retired Staff

About a third of the colleges and universities cover their retired staff members under their basic group health insurance plan; these institutions employ about half of all staff members. Table 6.5 summarizes group coverage during retirement under basic hospital-surgical-medical plans.

The introduction of Medicare vastly increased health protection resources for persons age 65 and over by providing through the Social Security system a hospital insurance program and a voluntary medical insurance program. Medicare provides a much broader coverage for those over 65 than is nor-

TABLE 6.5: GROUP COVERAGE DURING RETIREMENT UNDER
BASIC HOSPITAL-SURGICAL-MEDICAL PLANS

	Faculty[a]	
	Per Cent Insts N = 1,109	Per Cent EEs N = 261,445
Continuation on retirement		
Before and after 65	30.2	49.6
Before 65 only	3.9	6.2
At or after 65 only	4.5	4.0
Coverage not continued	53.7	36.3
No response	7.7	3.9
Total	100.0	100.0

[a] Data for other employee categories are similar to those for faculty.

mally provided by insured base plans for those who are under 65. Consequently, in deciding whether to make base plan coverage available after retirement, the institution should keep in mind that the Social Security program offers extensive health insurance protection. While post-65 base plan coverage can include "wrap-around" benefits to pay the deductibles and coinsurance of Medicare, the institution should ask itself whether the continuation of major medical protection is not more important.

The institution that provides basic coverage for retired employees must determine how much it will pay toward the premium. One out of five institutions that report retired basic group coverage contributes the entire premium amount, as shown in Table 6.6. The great majority of the plans,

TABLE 6.6: EMPLOYER AND RETIRED EMPLOYEE CONTRIBUTIONS TO
BASIC HOSPITAL-SURGICAL-MEDICAL COVERAGE OF
RETIRED EMPLOYEES

	Faculty[a]	
Employer-Retired Employee Sharing of Cost	Per Cent Insts N = 449	Per Cent EEs N = 158,517
ER pays full cost	20.0	17.0
ER and EE share	28.3	36.7
EE pays full cost	46.1	43.8
No response	5.6	2.5
Total	100.0	100.0

[a] Data for other employee categories are similar to those for faculty.

however, require a contribution from the retired employee. A contributory plan raises the question of finding a dependable method of collecting contributions from retired employees. Active employees' contributions may be withheld from salary, but withholding is not possible for unsalaried retired employees. Address changes, delays in premium payments, changes in premium rates, and the like, may create administrative difficulties.

The full cost of coverage for the dependents of retired employees is paid by 6 per cent of the institutions reporting that they continue basic coverage for retired employees. Table 6.7 shows the premium-sharing arrangements for dependents under these plans.

TABLE 6.7: EMPLOYER AND RETIRED EMPLOYEE CONTRIBUTIONS
FOR BASIC HOSPITAL-SURGICAL-MEDICAL COVERAGE
OF DEPENDENTS OF RETIRED EMPLOYEES

Employer-Retired Employee Sharing of Cost	Faculty[a]	
	Per Cent Insts N = 449	Per Cent EEs N = 158,157
ER pays full cost	6.2	7.7
ER and EE share	26.3	34.3
EE pays full cost	58.4	53.7
No response	9.1	4.3
Total	100.0	100.0

[a] Data for other employee categories are similar to those for faculty.

HEALTH INSURANCE:
MAJOR MEDICAL EXPENSE PLANS

Twenty years ago there were no major medical plans in higher education. Ten years ago, one-third of the universities and about a fifth of the colleges had major medical plans. Currently, major medical plans are reported by over 80 per cent of universities and colleges.

A large majority of institutions follow the "two-plan" approach: a major medical plan in conjunction with a separate basic hospital-surgical-medical plan. At the other institutions there is usually either a basic hospital-surgical-medical plan by itself, or a major medical plan to which some of the first-dollar elements of a base plan have been added. Table 7.1 summarizes major medical coverage currently reported by colleges and universities.

TABLE 7.1: GROUP MAJOR MEDICAL EXPENSE INSURANCE PLANS

	Faculty[a]		Clerical-Service	
	Per Cent Insts N = 1,232	Per Cent EEs N = 285,414	Per Cent Insts N = 1,232	Per Cent EEs N = 444,618
Major medical plan with separate base plan	65.1	74.6	57.6	68.9
Major medical plan as single health insurance plan	15.1	17.7	14.2	14.8
No major medical plan	18.4	6.4	26.8	15.4
No response	1.4	1.3	1.4	0.9
Total	100.0	100.0	100.0	100.0

[a] Data for administrative personnel similar to those for faculty.

Scope of Major Medical Plans

Group major medical expense insurance concentrates on reimbursement for the major expenses of medical care—the higher and more unpredictable costs associated with prolonged illness or serious injury, costs that may amount to thousands of dollars and that can leave a family battered financially unless insurance protection is available. The individual can usually handle the lesser and the more predictable expenses from his earnings or through base plan coverage.

Major medical plans usually reimburse 80 per cent (in a few plans, 75 per cent) of covered expenses that (1) are not reimbursed by a base plan and (2) exceed a deductible amount such as $100, which is paid by the insured person himself.

The maximum benefit amount for each insured individual should be high enough to encompass very large medical expenses. As Table 7.2 shows, 23 per cent of the college plans have a maximum benefit amount of $25,000 for each insured staff member and for each insured member of his family. But 2 per cent have a maximum as low as $5,000, and 38 per cent still have maximum benefit amounts of only $10,000.

TABLE 7.2: MAXIMUM BENEFIT AMOUNT IN GROUP
MAJOR MEDICAL EXPENSE INSURANCE PLANS

	Faculty[a]	
Maximum Benefit Amount	Per Cent Insts N = 1,005	Per Cent EEs N = 267,270
$ 5,000	1.9	1.1
$10,000	38.2	30.1
$15,000	18.2	26.5
$20,000	11.1	16.1
$25,000	23.1	22.2
Other	2.5	1.8
No response	5.0	2.2
Total	100.0	100.0

[a] Data for other employee categories similar to those for faculty.

Origin

The development of major medical insurance occurred during a period of steeply rising medical costs, a period also characterized by rapidly advancing medical techniques that required increasingly expensive equipment and facilities. Major medical coverage provided a means of insuring against the high cost of medical care.

The first group major medical insurance was developed in the forties when the Elfun Society, an association of General Electric employees, designed a form of protection against some part of the higher costs of serious illness or injury not covered by basic plans. This prototype was insured with the Liberty Mutual Insurance Company, and it worked well.

In the years following the Elfun innovation the number of major medical plans grew rapidly and the growth continues. By 1957 the Health Insurance Council reported 12,428,000 employees and dependents covered by group major medical plans. In 1966 the Council estimated that 52,002,000 employees and dependents were covered by group major medical plans.[1]

Major Medical Plans in the Colleges

In the early 1950s only a few institutions of higher education had installed major medical plans. Interest in the coverage was growing, however, as indicated by a 1953 survey of ways in which staff benefit plans could improve the attractiveness of the teaching profession. Financed by the Fund for the Advancement of Education and carried out by TIAA, the survey reported, *inter alia*, the following: [2]

Major Medical Expense—"Catastrophe" Insurance. College authorities have expressed some interest in protecting both faculty members and the institution in cases where highly expensive or protracted medical treatment is necessary. They refer to catastrophic medical emergencies requiring funds greatly in excess of those provided by regular medical and hospital expense plans. These events, affecting a faculty member or one of his family, may entail unusually expensive treatments or medical attention over a longer period of time than provided for in regular medical plans.

So-called major medical expense insurance has been introduced recently by a small number of commercial insurance companies. Application of insurance of this type on a group basis to the college world interests both faculty members and college administrators.

DETAILED STUDY

During the ensuing period, with the encouragement of the Ford Foundation, TIAA carried out a study of major medical and total disability insurance for higher education. The study determined that the great majority of colleges had installed basic hospital-surgical-medical plans, usually on an

---

[1] Health Insurance Institute, *1967 Source Book of Health Insurance Data*, p. 18.
[2] King, *Financing the College Education of Faculty Children*, p. 105.

employee-pay-all basis, and that there was general satisfaction with this coverage as far as it went. Furthermore, college officers and faculty committees hoped that the major medical insurance offerings then available could somehow be simplified or organized into a "recommended" plan for educational institutions. A major aim was to work out a plan with provisions for the colleges that would meet their needs at reasonable cost and would save the time of faculty, administration, and trustees in deciding on the pros and cons of multifold technical points and options.

The study led to a 1956 Ford Foundation appropriation of $5,000,000 for developmental expenses and contingency reserves for new TIAA plans of major medical and long-term disability income insurance for higher education. The study resulted in the establishment of the TIAA Optimum Plan—specifically designed for the educational world and incorporating recommended, standard provisions for educational institutions.

A major objective of the Ford grant was to encourage rapid and widespread adoption of the new medical coverage throughout higher education. The extraordinary growth during the next decade brought about the realization of this goal.

Major Medical Plan Objectives

The primary objective of major medical expense insurance is to assure the individual that, when a more serious accident or illness strikes, he can obtain the kind of medical care he should have without undue financial strain. By keeping this primary objective in mind the college and its staff members can establish the kind of plan that will meet the real needs and yet be economical in its premiums and administration.

A number of additional objectives stand out as important, and a brief recounting of them may be helpful when considering the establishment or revision of a major medical insurance plan.

THE COLLEGE'S NEEDS

The college has these interests among others:

1. It has a direct interest in freeing its staff members, academic and non-academic, from concern over the financial problems of medical care so that they can concentrate more fully on their primary functions.

2. It has a direct interest in seeking an optimum balance between cost and

benefits. If it chooses to cover almost all medical expenses, even in the area which can be readily handled by the individual from his regular earnings, then the plan will be expensive. Substantial savings can be made by emphasizing coverage for the major risks only.

THE STAFF MEMBER'S NEEDS

The college staff member needs:

1. Real protection against the large medical expenses he and his family may face.

2. As broad a scope of coverage as possible.

3. Low premium costs. If the staff members are willing to pay minor expenses themselves, premiums can be much lower than they would otherwise be. Again, it is a question of choosing the optimum point between level of benefits desired and costs.

WHAT THE INSURER CAN DO

An insurer *can* insure against almost all medical expenses merely by charging the cost to the insured group. For instance, it would be possible to give 100 per cent coverage for almost all medical bills. However, when full coverages of one sort or another have been attempted, the premiums have been high initially and have risen still higher. There is some point at which the size of the premium no longer represents an appropriate expenditure by the employer or employee.

This calls for protecting the college plan against certain abuses that can develop, such as exorbitant charges or overutilization of medical care through unnecessary or "luxury" treatments having little or nothing to do with needs. There is no magic method of defraying medical expenses; over a period of time the premiums must meet them. Therefore, in setting up a major medical program, the college must adopt safeguards to help keep premiums within reason while at the same time providing an attractive staff benefit plan.

Features of Major Medical Expense Insurance

The following features are found in most group major medical insurance plans:

1. A broad scope of coverage. Major medical expense coverage includes just about all types of physicians' charges and other necessary medical expenses, whether the individual is in the hospital or not. Thus its coverage extends beyond surgery and hospitalization and includes home and office care, private duty nursing, rental of special equipment, drugs, and so on.

2. A high benefit maximum. Nowadays the maximum per insured employee and each dependent should be no less than $20,000 or $25,000. Far too many college plans still have maximums well below that level.

3. Family coverage. Group major medical plans normally insure employees and their eligible dependents.

4. A cash deductible amount, designed to screen out smaller expenses, which a family should be able to meet from current income or savings. The cash deductible amount is the out-of-pocket amount paid by the individual for covered medical expenses before reimbursement begins under the major medical plan. A cash deductible amount of $100 is typically used in college plans.

5. A coinsurance percentage, designed to give the individual a personal stake in the size of his medical bills, in order, like the deductible amount, to help keep costs reasonable. A coinsurance percentage is the percentage of covered medical expenses above the cash deductible amount that the insured himself pays and for which he is not reimbursed by the major medical plan. The coinsurance is sometimes 25 per cent, but in nine out of ten college plans the rate is 20 per cent. Occasionally major medical plans carried without a basic plan provide an area of full reimbursement (no coinsurance) for a limited amount of hospital charges. For example, the first $500 of covered hospital charges incurred, or the first $500 above a cash deductible amount, or maternity expenses up to a specified amount, are reimbursed in full. Other covered charges, in hospital or not, are reimbursed on the regular deductible and coinsurance basis.

6. A benefit period. This is the period during which major medical benefits are paid for covered expenses incurred after the cash deductible amount has been satisfied. To establish another benefit period, the insured individual must again pay the cash deductible amount.

7. A reinstatement provision, allowing an individual who has received major medical benefits of a substantial amount (usually $1,000 or more) to restore his original maximum benefit amount if he supplies satisfactory

evidence of insurability. Automatic reinstatement of a stated amount each year, for example, $1,000, is also common and does not require evidence of insurability.

8. Certain limitations. Except for a dollar maximum on the daily hospital charges allowable for *private* room and board, there are usually no "inside limits" such as scheduled allowances for specified surgical charges or doctors' visits or numbers of days of hospitalization allowed. However, a few classes of expenses are generally not covered by major medical insurance, such as eye examinations, glasses, hearing aids, expenses incurred in a government hospital, sickness or injury resulting from war, dental treatment except for treatment of injuries sustained in an accident, and pregnancies, except for certain serious complications. Covered expenses under major medical do not include expenses incurred on account of sickness or injury arising out of or in the course of employment to the extent that benefits are payable under the applicable Workmen's Compensation law or similar statute.

Expenses for treatment of mental or nervous disorders are usually covered on the same basis as other expenses when incurred in a hospital. Out-of-hospital treatment for mental or nervous disorders is frequently not covered or, if covered, is sharply limited. In a few plans it is offered on the same basis as reimbursement for other medical costs, but this has proved quite expensive, largely because of the voluntary nature of the individual's choice of treatment.

9. Termination of employment. If a participant's employment is terminated (or if the college discontinues its plan) while a benefit period is in effect, provision is made for the continuation of benefit payments for a specified period.

How the Plan Works

When, within a stated period, an insured employee or dependent incurs covered expenses which exceed by the cash deductible the amount of any benefits payable under a base plan, a *benefit period* is established for that person. The major medical plan then reimburses him during the benefit period for a stipulated percentage, usually 80 per cent, of all subsequent covered expenses that are not reimbursed by a base plan, up to the maximum benefit amount. Of course, the manner in which the deductible, the benefit period, and the maximum benefit amount are applied varies with the type of plan in which the person participates.

Types of Plans

There are three types of major medical plans: *per cause, calendar year,* and *continued expense.*

THE PER CAUSE PLAN

In a *per cause* plan, each illness or accident is treated separately for the purpose of the deductible, the maximum benefit amount, and the benefit period. The expenses used to satisfy a cash deductible must be related to one illness or accident, and must be accumulated within a limited period of time, such as 90 days. All major medical benefits a person receives as a result of one illness or accident are applied against a maximum benefit amount for that cause. Any covered expenses incurred for a different and unrelated cause are treated under a separate deductible, a separate benefit period, and a separate maximum amount. The benefit period for each illness or accident is usually 3 years, unless it ends sooner because the insured person ceases to incur at least a nominal amount of covered expenses from that cause, or because he reaches the maximum.

Because no medical expense for any illness or accident is reimbursed until a person has satisfied the cash deductible for that particular cause, some small claims are eliminated, and this may help to keep administrative costs down. Furthermore, one illness or accident does not diminish the potential benefits for another, unrelated cause. However, this is no longer a matter of practical importance, as it was in the early days of major medical plans when many of them had maximums as low as $2,500 or $5,000. The higher maximums and the reinstatement provisions now available have made the need for unrelated maximums largely theoretical.

The main disadvantage of the *per cause* method is the difficulty of determining whether a particular medical expense is related to one illness or accident or to another. This uncertainty causes many problems for both insurer and insured, and increases administrative expenses. Another disadvantage is the difficulty of explaining the *per cause* concept to participants, particularly when they find that they must pay a new cash deductible amount before they can be reimbursed for any medical bills that are unrelated to an illness or accident for which they are already receiving major medical benefits. The impact of heavy medical expenses on a person's budget is just as serious whether the expenses arise from one or several causes.

THE CALENDAR YEAR PLAN

Under a *calendar year* plan all covered expenses incurred by an individual, regardless of cause, are combined for purposes of his deductible, maximum benefit amount, and benefit period. The expenses used to satisfy his cash deductible may arise from one cause or from several causes. After a person has paid the deductible amount, he receives benefits for any and all subsequent covered expenses incurred during the remainder of that calendar year. All benefits paid to him are applied against a single overall maximum benefit amount.

This all-cause approach to satisfying a deductible recognizes that a person's budget is hit just as hard by medical expenses whether they arise from one or from several causes. However, there are more small claims to be administered under a *calendar year* plan than under any other method because, once the individual has paid his deductible, he receives benefits for all covered expenses incurred, no matter how small or how far apart, during the remainder of the calendar year.

In most *calendar year* plans, expenses incurred in October, November, and December that are used to satisfy the deductible for the current calendar year may be carried over and used again to help satisfy the deductible required for the following calendar year. However, even with this "carry-over" provision, a main disadvantage of the *calendar year* plan is its use of an arbitrary date each year—December 31—as the cutoff for all benefit periods under the plan. This gives little recognition to the fact that a serious illness or accident can strike in any month and that heavy medical expenses can and do run on from one year to the next.

THE CONTINUED EXPENSE PLAN

This plan was designed by TIAA for the colleges in 1956, and it is now available from commercial insurance companies as well. While incorporating important features from both *calendar year* and *per cause* plans, it is designed to eliminate or reduce the inflexibilities and problems that developed with those plans.

The continued expense method works as follows. When, within a period of 3 consecutive months or less, an insured employee or dependent incurs covered expenses which exceed by $100 the amount of any benefits payable under a base plan, a *benefit period* is established for that person. The TIAA Optimum Plan then reimburses him during the benefit period for 80 per cent of all subsequent covered expenses that are not reimbursed by a base plan up to a maximum of $25,000.

His benefit period, figured from the date of the first expense used to satisfy the deductible amount, continues until whichever occurs first: (a) the end of 3 years, or (b) the end of any 3 consecutive calendar months during which his covered expenses, exclusive of any paid by a base plan, have not exceeded $50.

The *continued expense* plan is thus designed to continue uninterrupted benefits during a period that will normally be long enough to meet the major needs of a serious illness or accident. An insured individual can establish successive benefit periods if major medical expenses continue and he has not used up his maximum benefit amount.

The plan is working well in the colleges for the following reasons:

1. By combining all covered medical expenses for purposes of each individual's deductible, benefit period, and maximum benefit amount, the *continued expense* method gives all-cause protection related to the individual's financial needs. At the same time it eliminates the major disadvantage of *per cause* plans: the problem of determining whether every covered medical expense is related to one illness or accident or to another, and then applying a new deductible for each cause.

2. By providing a 3-year potential benefit period the *continued expense* method meets the needs of serious illness or accident without the *calendar year* plan's disadvantage of a yearly benefit cutoff and new deductible requirement.

3. Through its 3-month, $50 continued expense test the plan keeps costs in line by eliminating payments for minor medical expenses once the period of major expenses is completed.

Table 7.3 shows the distribution of *per cause, calendar year,* and *con-*

TABLE 7.3: TYPE OF MAJOR MEDICAL PLAN IN EFFECT
Per Cause, Calendar Year, and Continued Expense

	Faculty[a]	
	Per Cent Insts N = 1,005	Per Cent EEs N = 267,270
Per cause	27.2	23.4
Calendar year	47.1	48.1
Continued expense	22.5	22.5
Other	3.2	6.0
Total	100.0	100.0

[a] Data for other employee categories similar to those for faculty.

tinued expense major medical plans reported in 1968 by colleges and universities in the United States.

Major Medical Rates

The premium rate for a major medical plan is normally stated in terms of a composite, or averaged, monthly rate for all persons in the group—one composite rate for the insured employee and another composite rate for the insured dependent unit (spouse and/or dependent children). Rates are normally subject to change once a year, depending on changes in the composition of the group and its experience. The composite rates reflect a number of factors that affect medical costs:

1. The range of medical expenses covered.
2. The actuarial value of underlying base plan benefits, if any.
3. Sex and age distribution of the individuals to be insured.
4. Earnings levels of the individuals to be insured.
5. Size of the insured group and cost of administration.
6. The general level of medical costs in and around the geographical location of the insured group.
7. The type of plan, whether per cause, calendar year, or continued expense.
8. The deductible and coinsurance amounts, the maximum benefit amount, and the length of the benefit period.

Age and sex are key elements in medical costs. Major medical experience shows that women have a higher frequency of illness than men and, for the same illness, are more inclined to seek medical treatment. For both sexes, incidence and duration of medical expenses increase with age.

Income tends to influence the size and frequency of medical bills; upper-income groups show higher utilization of medical services and higher charges for a given service than lower-income groups.

Major medical underwriting takes into account regional differences in the cost of hospital care and professional services. On the West Coast, for example, utilization of medical services and charges for such services are high, while utilization and charges in the southeast are comparatively low. Within regions, urban or rural location is also taken into account.

If during any year of plan operation the level of major medical claims is higher than that anticipated by the plan's premium rates, an increase in rates for the following year may result. When benefit payments are less than anticipated, a return of premium in the form of a dividend or retroactive rate adjustment generally results.

INCREASING COSTS

The Consumer Price Index shows that medical care costs have increased at a faster rate than any other major category of personal expense. During the past decade, the total increase for medical care costs has been over 40 per cent, compared with slightly less than 19 per cent for all items.

TABLE 7.4: COST OF MEDICAL CARE COMPARED WITH ALL ITEMS
U.S. Consumer Price Index

Year	All Items	Medical Care
1957	100.0	100.0
1962	107.6	119.6
1967	118.7	143.1

Source: United States Department of Labor, Bureau of Labor Statistics. Adjusted to base 100 for starting year.

The index is, of course, an average. Certain areas, particularly urban centers such as Boston, New York, and Los Angeles, have experienced higher medical costs because of their position as centers of developing medical technology and generally higher urban wage scales.

Expenditures for health services and supplies have increased dramatically from 17.1 billion dollars in 1955 to 37.3 billion dollars in 1965, a per capita increase of 86 per cent. The National Advisory Commission on Health Manpower in its 1967 Report estimates that yearly expenditures for health services and supplies will reach 94 billion dollars by 1975.[3] Projections may vary, but no voices are heard predicting a decrease in the future cost or extent of medical care. And, as medical costs rise, the premiums to insure against these costs will rise.

Installing or Revising a Major Medical Plan

The main decisions to be made in designing or revising a major medical plan have to do with choosing the type of plan, with whether to have two plans or one, with the extent of institutional and individual sharing of the cost of the plan, and with designation of groups eligible to participate.

THE TWO-PLAN APPROACH

Four out of five major medical plans in the colleges have been superimposed on basic hospital-surgical-medical plans. In order to avoid duplicate insurance premiums and benefits for the same medical expense, those covered expenses that are reimbursed by a base plan are not reimbursed by the major medical plan, nor are they counted in satisfying the individual's cash deductible, $100 for example, under the major medical plan. When the base plan does not provide benefits for the kind of treatment the individual is receiving, or if he is not covered by a base plan, major medical insurance benefits begin as soon as he has incurred $100 in covered expenses within a specified period.

The college could provide identical medical expense coverage for everyone by eliminating base plan coverage and establishing a single new medical plan. But the flexibility of the two-plan approach has been appealing. If the college keeps a base plan with voluntary participation and makes a major medical plan available as well, each staff member can decide whether he wants both major medical and base plan coverage at a somewhat higher cost for the two plans, or major medical coverage alone.

In the absence of base plan hospital or surgical benefits, major medical benefits begin as soon as the individual has satisfied the cash deductible

---

[3] National Advisory Commission on Health Manpower, *Report*, I, 35.

requirement. Thus major medical costs and benefits are greater for persons who do not participate in base plan coverage. Equitable treatment for all participants in a major medical plan is usually achieved by requiring higher premium contributions from persons not participating in the college's base plan. For example, some colleges contribute for each participant, whether he carries base plan coverage or not, the amount required to pay the full cost of major medical coverage that *is* carried as a supplement to the college's base plan. A participant who carries the base plan thus makes no contribution for major medical coverage. Those who are not in the base plan do contribute something for major medical coverage.

If the college wants to be certain that *all* eligible staff members have major medical coverage, it contributes the full cost for supplementary major medical coverage for each person as above, but instead of requiring a contribution from those not in the base plan it assigns them a higher deductible under the major medical plan. For example, persons with neither basic hospital nor surgical coverage would have a deductible of $400 under the major medical plan; those with only surgical coverage, $300; those with only hospital coverage, $200; and those with both hospital and surgical coverage, $100.

THE SINGLE PLAN APPROACH

A college that either has no base plan, or is dissatisfied with the one it has, may want to establish major medical coverage as its only plan for covering medical expenses, perhaps adding some provisions that expand the usual major medical approach to include some of the more routine reimbursements typical of base plans. This might be done by setting the deductible at less than $100; or by providing benefits for normal maternity; or by not requiring coinsurance for the first $500 of hospital expenses.

EMPLOYEE PARTICIPATION

All categories of permanent employees are normally covered by the institution's group major medical plan. Institutions recognize that heavy medical expenses create serious problems for any family and therefore extend plan eligibility to virtually all the full-time staff and sometimes to staff working half-time or more.

Eligibility for the plan is based on conditions pertaining to employment, and a precise definition of the employee classes eligible for the plan is important. When specifying eligibility, the institution normally uses its established and recognized personnel classifications. Occasionally these may have to be reviewed and revised so as to leave no uncertainty as to coverage in individual cases, and to make sure that eligibility is based on a clearly stated and "automatic" factor. A few examples of classifications used by the colleges are:

All active full-time employees (except temporary employees).
Nonfaculty employees who work less than 32 hours a week will not be considered full-time employees.

Class 1. All active full-time contract employees (except temporary employees).
Class 2. All other active full-time employees (except temporary employees).
(Twenty hour a week work test for nonfaculty employees.)

All active employees on the monthly, semi-monthly, and biweekly payrolls except for the following: (1) student employees, (2) employees whose appointment or employment is for less than three-fifths of normal full-time duty, (3) employees whose appointment is for less than the full academic term of five consecutive months.

When a plan is newly installed, all eligible employees are covered automatically if the entire premium is being paid by the institution. If employees are to pay a part of the premium, at least 75 per cent of the eligible group must elect coverage. Some institutions require participation in the plan even though the institution does not pay the full cost.

There can be real embarrassment to an institution when the finances of an uninsured staff member are shattered because of heavy medical expenditures for his family. Both the institution's reputation as an employer and the other staff members' sense of security are jeopardized. The adverse effect on individual and institution is not as likely if a staff member rejects basic health insurance coverage. The risk lies in failing to require participation in the plan that covers the catastrophic expenses of illness—major medical.

DEPENDENT PARTICIPATION

The major medical coverage of dependents is provided in 97 per cent of the plans in the colleges and universities, as indicated in Table 7.5.

TABLE 7.5: MAJOR MEDICAL COVERAGE OF DEPENDENTS

	Faculty[a]	
	Per Cent Insts N = 1,005	Per Cent EEs N = 267,270
Dependents covered	97.3	99.0
Dependents not covered	0.9	0.2
No response	1.8	0.8
Total	100.0	100.0

[a] Data for other employee categories similar to those for faculty.

Dependent coverage normally includes the spouse of an eligible employee, unmarried children under age 19, and unmarried children from age 19 to their twenty-third birthday who are full-time students and dependent on the employee for support. In order for dependent coverage to be included in a plan, the usual requirement is that at least 75 per cent of the employees who enroll in the plan and who have such dependents must elect it. An employee cannot carry dependent coverage unless he himself is insured under the major medical plan.

WAITING PERIODS

When a plan is first put into operation, all employees in each eligible class who are in active service on the installation date can begin their participation immediately. In this kind of coverage, waiting periods (preliminary service requirements) are usually quite short or nonexistent. Table 7.6 summarizes the waiting periods specified.

Waiting periods are usually reserved for classifications of employees normally having a high turnover rate. For example, eligible employees in the clerical and service groups might be brought into the plan following the completion of 3 months' service, while others become eligible immediately on employment. When the employer pays the entire premium, newly eligible employees are brought into the plan automatically on the first day they become eligible, provided the staff members meet the "actively at work" requirement of the group policy.

TIAA major medical plans provide that a waiting period does not apply to staff members beginning employment within 3 months of the date they

TABLE 7.6: WAITING PERIODS FOR MAJOR MEDICAL PLAN,
PARTICIPATION OF ELIGIBLE EMPLOYEES

	Faculty		Administrative		Clerical-Service	
	Per Cent Insts N = 1,005	Per Cent EEs N = 267,270	Per Cent Insts N = 1,003	Per Cent EEs N = 102,799	Per Cent Insts N = 902	Per Cent EEs N = 376,339
No waiting period	53.0	52.1	51.3	54.2	41.1	41.3
Less than 1 month	25.4	33.9	25.2	31.7	22.9	33.9
Until stated date(s) in first year	1.8	0.8	1.8	0.7	1.9	0.6
Stated number of months	16.2	9.4	18.1	9.1	29.4	19.2
Other	1.8	3.4	1.8	4.0	2.7	4.6
No response	1.8	0.4	1.8	0.3	2.0	0.4
Total	100.0	100.0	100.0	100.0	100.0	100.0

terminated employment at an institution where they participated in another insured group major medical plan.

SHARING THE COST

Slightly over one-third of the institutions pay the entire cost of the employee's major medical coverage. At the opposite pole, about a fifth of the colleges and universities make no contribution to the employee major medical coverage. In 40 per cent of the plans both the employer and employee contribute to the cost of employee protection. Table 7.7 shows the sharing

TABLE 7.7: EMPLOYER AND EMPLOYEE CONTRIBUTIONS
FOR MAJOR MEDICAL COVERAGE OF EMPLOYEES

	Faculty		Administrative		Clerical-Service	
Employer-Employee Sharing of Cost	Per Cent Insts N = 1,005	Per Cent EEs N = 267,270	Per Cent Insts N = 1,003	Per Cent EEs N = 102,799	Per Cent Insts N = 902	Per Cent EEs N = 376,339
ER pays full cost	38.2	32.9	37.8	35.0	35.7	26.4
EE and ER share	40.5	40.0	40.6	43.1	41.7	49.3
EE pays full cost	19.0	26.5	19.1	21.4	20.4	23.9
No response	2.3	0.6	2.5	0.5	2.2	0.4
Total	100.0	100.0	100.0	100.0	100.0	100.0

of premiums for employee coverage in the three major employee categories in the colleges.

While over a third of the employers pay the entire major medical premium for employees, only a sixth pay the full premium for employees' dependents. A sharing of the cost of dependent coverage was indicated by 33 per cent of the institutions, as shown in Table 7.8.

TABLE 7.8: EMPLOYER AND EMPLOYEE CONTRIBUTIONS FOR MAJOR MEDICAL COVERAGE OF DEPENDENTS

	Faculty[a]	
Employer-Employee Sharing of Cost	Per Cent Insts N = 978	Per Cent EEs N = 264,478
ER pays full cost	17.7	15.3
EE and ER share	33.4	34.9
EE pays full cost	47.5	47.7
No response	1.4	2.1
Total	100.0	100.0

[a] Data for other employee categories similar to those for faculty.

LEAVE OF ABSENCE

Major medical protection may be continued for staff members who are on leave of absence, a feature of particular importance to faculty members on sabbatical or other leave with pay, or on leave with or without pay for special service, research, or study. Leaves of absence are also granted to nonfaculty employees. Thus the college needs, for all classes of employees, a clearly stated policy concerning major medical continuation during leaves.

Under a great many major medical plans a staff member's insurance may be continued for 24 months of leave with at least one-quarter pay. It may also be continued for 24 months of any other official leave, with or without pay, if the staff member is engaged in education or research, such as under a foundation grant, Fulbright grant or government project, or full-time study for an advanced degree.

For employees on leave under employer-pay-all plans that continue major medical during leaves, the institution simply continues premiums as before. Under contributory plans the employer may assume the entire premium payment, or may make special arrangements for the continuation of the employee's contributions during his absence, such as accepting a lump sum payment from the employee out of which premiums can be paid as they fall due.

RETIRED STAFF COVERAGE

In 1958, about a quarter of the major medical plans in higher education provided for the continuation of group coverage for retired staff members and their eligible dependents. In 1968, 40 per cent of colleges and universities reported that major medical coverage continued for retired staff members. Between these two dates the inauguration of the federal Medicare program fundamentally altered the health insurance scene for virtually all persons aged 65 or over.

The proportion of institutions currently continuing major medical coverage for retired staff members is shown in Table 7.9.

TABLE 7.9: GROUP MAJOR MEDICAL EXPENSE INSURANCE
COVERAGE OF RETIRED EMPLOYEES

	Faculty[a]	
	Per Cent Insts N = 1,005	Per Cent EEs N = 267,270
Continuation on retirement		
Before and after age 65	33.1	56.8
Before age 65 only	5.7	6.9
At age 65 or after only	6.4	4.0
Coverage not continued	47.9	29.8
No response	6.9	2.5
Total	100.0	100.0

[a] Data for other employee categories similar to those for faculty.

A number of institutions that continue eligibility for group major medical coverage into retirement do so only for employees who have met a minimum service and age requirement. Ten years of service and retirement from the institution at age 60 or over is the most frequent requirement.

In addition to coordination with Medicare, major medical coverage for retired persons usually provides a reduced maximum benefit amount, such as $5,000 or $10,000, for the retired staff member and the same amount for the spouse. There is no provision for reinstatement of benefit amounts except for an automatic yearly reinstatement of a specified amount, such as $1,000 a year. Expenses for all treatment of mental and nervous diseases are excluded during retirement, and transportation expenses are limited to local ambulance service.

Table 7.10 shows how the cost of major medical coverage is shared by employers and retired staff members.

TABLE 7.10: EMPLOYER AND RETIRED EMPLOYEE CONTRIBUTIONS
TO MAJOR MEDICAL COVERAGE OF RETIRED EMPLOYEES

Employer-Retired Employee Sharing of Cost	Faculty[a]	
	Per Cent Insts N = 464	Per Cent EEs N = 182,736
ER pays full cost	33.6	25.1
EE and ER share	28.7	36.0
EE pays full cost	31.0	36.0
No response	6.7	2.9
Total	100.0	100.0

[a] Data for other employee categories similar to those for faculty.

When the institution pays the full cost of retired coverage, all eligible persons are covered and there are no premium collection problems, an obvious convenience in the case of retired staff members who may travel frequently or who may leave the college community to live in another part of the country.

Coverage for dependents is an important part of major medical protection at all ages, and the relatively greater level of medical need at the higher ages affirms the continued importance of full family protection, particularly for those not yet eligible for Medicare. Practically all institutions that continue major medical coverage for retired staff members also continue it for dependents. Just as survivor annuity options are essential to retirement security, provision for the continuation of major medical protection for a surviving spouse is equally appropriate, and more than a third of the institutions with major medical plans report that such protection continues to be available.

The retired employee pays the full cost of dependent coverage in half of the plans providing such coverage. In 20 per cent of the plans the institution pays the whole cost of dependents' protection, and in 30 per cent the institution contributes part of the cost.

TERMINATION OF INSURANCE

Termination of a staff member's insurance and of his dependents' insurance occurs (1) if his employment is terminated (unless he is retiring and is eligible for retired coverage), (2) if the college terminates the group policy or modifies it to exclude the employee classification to which he belongs, or (3) if the employee discontinues required contributions. If an employee or dependent has a benefit period in effect when insurance is terminated, benefits usually continue after termination for a specified period, usually to the end of the benefit period or one year from the date insurance terminated, whichever occurs first.

If an employee at termination of insurance is not in a benefit period but is disabled because of sickness or injury and is unable to work, he generally has 3 months from the date of termination in which to establish a benefit period by satisfying his deductible through covered expenses incurred because of that sickness or injury. Similarly, if a dependent is hospitalized on the date of termination of dependent insurance and has not yet established a benefit period, the dependent has 3 months in which to establish a benefit period. A benefit period having been established, the covered expenses for that sickness or injury are reimbursed on the regular coinsurance basis, but usually for not longer than 1 year from the date insurance terminated.

8

SHORT-TERM DISABILITY INCOME
PLANS

"What happens to my salary if I'm disabled?" is a vital question for the staff member. For the employer, the corollary question involves the staff as a whole: "What is the employer's obligation at such a time, and how can it be met?" This chapter and the next one deal with the problem of income continuation during absence from work because of disability.

For both the employer and the employee the duration and degree of disability is of paramount financial importance. Everyone is subject to short-term absences from work due to disabilities ranging from colds, sprains, laryngitis, and the ubiquitous virus to appendicitis and other conditions or injuries requiring hospitalization. Most disability absences are for a few days or a few weeks, but some are for long periods and they usher in a new set of financial problems. As a point to use in distinguishing between short-term and long-term disabilities, 6 months is usually chosen.

TYPES OF SHORT-TERM DISABILITY INCOME PROGRAMS

Of the 1,232 responding institutions, 72 per cent reported short-term disability income plans for faculty, administrative personnel, and clerical-service employees (Table 1.2). Of the institutions reporting a short-term plan, a substantial proportion indicates that the arrangements for short-term disability income are informal, each disability case being handled "on its merits." Informal arrangements were reported for faculty by 49 per cent of the institutions, and for administrative personnel by 43 per cent. For clerical-service employees the proportion of informal plans is markedly lower, 29 per cent. Informal plans are decreasing, as they are being replaced by formal plans. In 1958, 58 per cent of the institutions reported informal short-term disability arrangements for faculty and administrative personnel.

The proportion of formal plans, usually described as salary continuation or "sick pay" plans, has almost doubled during the last decade. Formal plans are currently reported by 48 per cent of the institutions for faculty, 54 per cent for administrative personnel, and 62 per cent for clerical-service employees. In 1958, only 27 per cent of the institutions reported a formal plan for faculty and administrative personnel.

A relatively small proportion of the short-term disability plans are insured. Thirteen per cent of the institutions reported an insured plan for faculty, 15 per cent for administrative personnel, and 10 per cent for clerical-service employees.

For disabilities arising out of the course of employment, three-quarters of the institutions report coverage under state Workmen's Compensation laws.

TABLE 8.1: SHORT-TERM DISABILITY INCOME PLANS[a]

	Faculty		Administrative		Clerical-Service	
	Per Cent Insts N = 885	Per Cent EEs N = 231,234	Per Cent Insts N = 886	Per Cent EEs N = 90,175	Per Cent Insts N = 889	Per Cent EEs N = 367,330
Informal	49.1	51.8	42.7	36.1	28.7	14.7
Formal	48.0	53.2	54.4	69.3	61.5	82.9
Group insurance	13.4	12.7	14.6	13.7	16.4	17.0
Workmen's Compensation	75.9	78.3	76.4	84.9	78.4	89.0
Other	4.7	7.1	4.9	7.0	5.2	8.4

[a] Percentages total more than 100 due to the presence of more than one program at some institutions.

FORMAL SALARY CONTINUATION
(SICK PAY) PLANS

A formal plan for salary continuation or sick pay states in writing the amount and duration of income and the conditions under which payments will be made. Each staff member knows in advance just how much he may expect in terms of income if he is absent because of illness or injury. And he knows the specified number of days, weeks, or months for which the plan will pay an income. Salary continuation or "sick pay" plans usually involve no exclusion period before benefits begin. Unless the plan is insured, benefits are paid directly from the salary budget, from other current operating funds, or from designated contingency reserves.

The duration of benefits frequently depends on length of service, particularly for clerical-service employees. But length of service sometimes governs duration of benefits for faculty and administrative personnel as well. The following quoted policy statements from college booklets illustrate "sick pay" provisions applied to faculty:

Accumulation of sick leave is at the rate of four weeks for each year of service to a total accumulation of six months when Total Disability Income Insurance goes into effect.

The College will provide for all participating members of the [long-term disability] program benefits comparable to the TIAA coverage during the six consecutive months of total disability prior to the time the TIAA disability program takes over the payments. [All full-time faculty members and administrative officers with three or more years of service are eligible and expected to participate in the long-term plan, with employees paying approximately 25 per cent of the cost.]

Short-term disability income provisions for clerical-service personnel are typified by this excerpt from an institutional policy statement:

Any absence from work due to injury or illness requires a reduction in your paycheck for time missed, unless the absence is covered by accumulated sick leave credits. If you are a full-time permanent employee, you earn one working day of sick leave with pay for each completed month of employment, up to a maximum of 110 working days [of sick leave] . . . .

The sick leave balance you accumulate is carried over from year to year. It is to be used if needed, but not to be taken automatically as it accumulates. In fact, repeated one and two day sick leaves may be grounds for dismissal because of their interference with job performance.

If you take any sick leave it is deducted from accumulated sick leave credited to you. You continue to accumulate sick leave credits while working full time, or while on sick leave with pay. Sick leave credits do not accumulate while you are receiving Workmen's Compensation or disability income insurance benefits, or any leave without pay. If a holiday falls within a paid sick leave, that day is counted as a holiday, and not as a day of sick leave. For disability extending beyond accumulated sick leave, you may draw on vacation earned. Disability income insurance benefits are paid beginning with the seventh month of disability, and this is described in another section of this handbook.

INSURED PLANS PROVIDING SHORT-TERM DISABILITY INCOME

As indicated in Table 8.1, 13 per cent of the short-term disability income plans for college faculty are carried with insurance companies. Insured plans, variously called "accident and sickness," "weekly indemnity," or "wage replacement" insurance, usually pay a weekly income for a maximum period of 13 or 26 weeks or, occasionally, longer. The weekly benefit may be a level amount for all employees or may vary according to the employee's job classification, salary, length of service, or combinations thereof. Benefits usually begin after 4 to 8 days of disability during which the institution may or may not pay regular salary or wages. The exclusion period is designed to cut the plan costs by excluding the 1- or 2-day illnesses which are so common. The exclusion period following a disability due to accident is sometimes shorter than for sickness. Benefits provided normally replace only a half or two-thirds of the employee's take-home earnings. When Workmen's Compensation benefits are provided (occupational disability), an insured plan normally covers only nonoccupational accidents or illnesses.

WORKMEN'S COMPENSATION BENEFITS

State Workmen's Compensation laws provide mandatory benefits for employees suffering work-connected injuries and occupational illnesses. The benefits are paid without regard to fault, and the amounts are fixed by law, usually determined as a portion of weekly wages with stated minimums and maximums. Benefits include medical care costs, disability income for stated periods, and, in some states, specific indemnities for permanent injuries.

Workmen's Compensation laws are usually administered by state commissions responsible for compliance and procedures. The employer is required to secure the insurance through means specified by law. In twenty-two states, coverage is obtained through private carriers; in eight, the coverage is provided through a state insurance fund; in eleven others the employer may choose either a state insurance fund or a private carrier. In several states, self-insurance is permitted.[1]

A few states specifically exempt colleges, universities, and other nonprofit employers from Workmen's Compensation legislation but permit them to participate voluntarily. When no specific language includes or excludes non-

[1] U.S. Department of Labor, Bureau of Labor Standards, "State Workmen's Compensation Laws," *Bulletin* 161 (rev.), 1964.

profit employers, the courts have usually held them to be subject to the Workmen's Compensation statutes. Four out of five private colleges and universities cover their employees under applicable statutes. In public institutions the coverage is 87 per cent for public universities and 70 per cent for public colleges.

COMPULSORY NONOCCUPATIONAL DISABILITY PROGRAMS

In addition to the statutory requirements for Workmen's Compensation benefits, four states require employers to provide benefits during nonoccupational disability: California, New Jersey, New York, and Rhode Island. In California, New Jersey, and New York, the employer may insure this risk with the state fund, provide comparable coverage through a private insurer, or self-insure. The Rhode Island benefits are administered through a state fund as a part of the state unemployment compensation system. The Rhode Island and California programs are financed by a tax paid by employees on wages. The New Jersey and New York plans tax both employer and employee. Benefit amounts are modest, and the duration of benefits is limited to 26 weeks. Nonprofit educational organizations, public and private, in all four of the states are not required to participate but may do so voluntarily.

9

LONG-TERM DISABILITY INCOME
PLANS

Most disability absences fall well within the scope of salary continuation, sick pay, and other short-term disability arrangements. Relatively few last as long as 6 months, the customary dividing line between short- and long-term disabilities. Those that do, however, may last a year, or 5, 10, or 20 or more years, and they bring with them profound financial trouble. For a staff member earning $10,000 a year, for example, 10 years of disability means a loss of $100,000; 20 years means $200,000; and neither example incorporates normal salary increases. A staff member cannot set aside enough to protect against a loss like this, nor should a college's operating or endowment funds be exposed to such risks. The financial impact on the staff member's family will usually be more severe than that caused by his death, because the former breadwinner becomes a dependent member of the household, in some cases requiring continued medical care and special nursing.

The purpose of a long-term disability income plan is to protect staff members against the virtually hopeless financial situation any one of them may face if salary or sick pay ultimately has to be cut off because a disabling illness or injury is apparently going to continue indefinitely. Long-lasting disabilities are a matter of great concern not only for the disabled staff member and his family, but also for colleagues and fellow workers. The immediate problem of one family is a potential problem for every family. A long-term disability income plan improves the quality of the working environment by assuring all covered staff members that income protection will be available if needed.

To be effective, a long-term disability income plan should, after a suitable waiting period, cover all persons for whom the institution has a responsibility. Benefits should be adequate in amount and should be specifically stated in advance. The income should continue throughout disability to at least age 65, at which time the retirement plan can take over; there should be no cutoff of income after 5 years or 10 years, for example, if disability continues. Contributions to the retirement plan should be continued for the disabled staff member during the period of disability; he should not have to accept an inadequate retirement income when the disability benefits cease. Finally, there should be some means of providing upward adjustments in long-term disability income to meet rising living costs and standards over the years.

Development of Group Insurance Plans for Long-Term Disability Income

Until 1957, group insurance plans for long-term total disability from sickness as well as accident were not available to employers, with only the rarest exceptions. The development of a group insurance plan to provide long-term disability income in higher education grew out of the concern of the Ford Foundation and TIAA regarding the almost total lack of any real disability income provisions. A 1956 survey by TIAA indicated that the majority of educational institutions had been confronted with instances of long-term disability within the previous 10 years, but had been unable to handle them in a systematic or satisfactory manner.[1] With the exception of a few self-administered programs and the benefits available under Social Security, the only consistent form of disability income for college staff members was "early" or "disability" retirement. Disability benefits under public employee and state teacher retirement plans were generally available only to employees having long periods of service at the time they became disabled.

In order to facilitate the introduction of the two needed staff benefit plans for higher education—long-term disability income insurance and major medical expense insurance—the Ford Foundation appropriated $5,000,000 to TIAA in 1956. The grant provided for developmental expenses and contingency reserves for the two new programs.

---

[1] Teachers Insurance and Annuity Association, "Proposed Major Medical Expense and Disability Insurances," Report to the Ford Foundation (unpublished), 1956.

Definitions of Total Disability

Three definitions of total disability are in general use in determining whether benefits are payable:

1. Under the Social Security program, disability is defined as "the inability to engage in any substantial gainful activity by reason of any medically determinable physical or mental impairment which can be expected to result in death or which can be expected to last for a continuous period of not less than 12 months." To be eligible the individual must not only be unable to perform the work for which his education, training, or skills have prepared him, but must also be unable to engage in any "substantial" gainful activity. "Substantial" comprises any work generally performed for gain or profit, even if part-time, and even if less demanding or less responsible than the individual's prior work.[2]

2. In many group insurance programs, disability is "the inability of the employee, by reason of sickness or bodily injury, to engage in any occupation for which the employee is reasonably fitted by education, training or experience."

3. An alternative "dual" definition considers disability to be "during the first 24 months of disability, the complete inability of the employee, by reason of sickness or bodily injury, to engage in *his* regular occupation. Thereafter it will mean the inability of the employee, by reason of sickness or bodily injury, to engage in *any* occupation for which he is reasonably fitted by education, training or experience."

Types of Long-Term Disability Income Plans

Colleges provide long-term disability income in one or more of the following ways: (1) federal Social Security disability benefits, (2) group long-term total disability income insurance plans, (3) the disability or "early retirement" provision of some public employee and state teacher retirement systems, (4) self-administered long-term disability plans, and (5) informal, *ad hoc* arrangements.

[2] U.S. Department of Health, Education, and Welfare, *Social Security Handbook* (1966), pp. 96–97.

Table 9.1 shows the proportion of institutions reporting a plan for long-term disability income. Table 9.2 shows the distribution of plans by type.

TABLE 9.1: LONG-TERM TOTAL DISABILITY INCOME PLANS

	Faculty[a]		Clerical-Service	
	Per Cent Insts N = 1,232	Per Cent EEs N = 285,414	Per Cent Insts N = 1,232	Per Cent EEs N = 444,618
Long-term plan	50.9	71.2	38.1	58.4
No plan	49.1	28.8	61.9	41.6
Total	100.0	100.0	100.0	100.0

[a] Data for administrative personnel are similar to those for faculty.

TABLE 9.2: TYPES OF LONG-TERM TOTAL DISABILITY INCOME PLANS[a]

	Faculty		Administrative		Clerical-Service	
	Per Cent Insts N = 627	Per Cent EEs N = 203,206	Per Cent Insts N = 629	Per Cent EEs N = 77,799	Per Cent Insts N = 469	Per Cent EEs N = 259,492
State employee or teacher retirement plan provision	29.5	46.9	30.7	35.1	41.2	57.4
Group insurance plans	71.8	59.5	70.6	59.2	59.3	49.5
Self-administered plans	5.3	13.5	5.1	18.0	5.1	14.0
Other[b]	6.1	10.0	6.4	11.7	6.8	10.8

[a] Percentages total more than 100 per cent because a number of public institutions are covered by state employee or teacher retirement plan provisions and also sponsor insured programs for total disability benefits.
[b] Includes informal plans.

DISABILITY INCOME FROM SOCIAL SECURITY

The disability benefits of the federal Social Security program, when a person is eligible, provide a floor on which to build a program of long-term disability income. Originally limited to persons between the ages of 50 and 65, disability benefits of Social Security are now payable to eligible persons of any age. The individual's benefit, based on his average monthly wage in covered employment, is the amount that would have been paid had he been eligible for retirement at the time disability occurred. In addition, benefits are paid to eligible dependents of the disabled person; these dependents include a wife age 62 or older, a wife of any age if the couple has a child or children entitled to benefits, a child under age 18, age 18 to 22 if a full-time student, or age 18 or older and suffering from a disability that began before the child reached age 18. A disability "freeze" provision aids disabled persons by eliminating the disability period from the calculation of the average monthly wage for any future retirement or disability benefits under the Social Security program.

GROUP INSURANCE PLANS FOR
LONG-TERM DISABILITY INCOME

Since the introduction of the TIAA long-term total disability group insurance plan in 1957, the number of institutions having an insured total disability plan has increased substantially each year. Other insurers have also entered the field. By 1968, 450 insured plans had been installed in colleges and universities.

Since long-term benefits normally begin after 6 months of disability, it is common practice to pay short-term benefits for 6 months. There should be no gap for eligible persons between the time benefits cease under the short-term disability plan and when they commence under the long-term disability program.

Insured long-term disability plans generally provide a monthly income benefit that comes to 50 or 60 per cent of salary inclusive of any disability benefits paid by Social Security, Workmen's Compensation, or other plans paying a disability income.

Plans described as "long-term" disability income plans range from the few remaining plans that pay benefits for only 2 to 5 years to those which continue benefit payments until the insured attains age 65 or other normal retirement age and then make provision for income continuance during retirement.[3] In some instances the plans are written to provide a longer period

---

[3] Twenty-two of the 627 institutions reporting long-term total disability income plans for faculty (and about the same proportion for administrative and clerical-service groups) indicate that benefits are continued during disability only for a stated period, usually 2 or 5 years. All others report that income benefits (disability or retirement) continue for the full term of disability to age 65 and throughout retirement.

Some group life insurance plans provide for the pay-out in monthly installments over a stated period, usually 5 years, of the insurance amount in the event of total disability. In effect, this limited duration "disability pay-out" provision transfers to disabled persons benefits primarily intended for survivors.

of benefits for accidents than for sickness. For example, a plan may stipulate that, if disability is caused by an accident, income benefits are payable until age 65, but for a sickness they are payable for 5 years.

For a disabled person who recovers, successive periods of disability arising from the same or a related cause and separated by less than 3 months of continuous active employment with the employer are usually considered to be one period of disability.

There are only a few categories of disability for which benefits are not payable under group plans: (1) injury or sickness resulting from war, declared or undeclared, (2) intentional self-inflicted injury or sickness, (3) disability resulting from pregnancy, unless the period of continuous disability begins after a stated period throughout which the employee was actively at work following the termination of such pregnancy, and (4) disability during the first year in the plan if the disability results from a condition existing prior to the beginning of coverage.

Income and Waiver Benefits under TIAA Plans. The TIAA disability plan provides two forms of benefits, both beginning after 6 months of continuous total disability. One benefit pays a monthly income to the disabled staff member. The other benefit, a "waiver of premium," continues both the employee and employer contributions to the staff member's TIAA-CREF annuity contract. For a staff member who participates in a non-TIAA-CREF retirement plan, or who has not yet joined his employer's TIAA-CREF plan, the waiver of premium benefit pays premiums to newly issued TIAA-CREF annuities. Both benefits continue during total disability until age 65, when the annuity takes over.

The TIAA plan can provide an income benefit of 60 per cent of the first $1,000 of monthly salary plus 40 per cent of salary in excess of $1,000 a month, subject to the following benefit limits based on the size of the eligible group: $1,000 per month for groups of 2 to 99 employees, $1,200 for groups of 100 to 199 employees, and $1,500 for groups of 200 or more. The income benefit is reduced by the amount of any income benefit under the Social Security program, Workmen's Compensation, or any other group disability program, but is in no event reduced below $50 a month.

The waiver benefit is the amount of the retirement annuity premiums being applied to a person's annuity in the regular operation of the institution's retirement plan at the time total disability begins. The amount is credited to the annuity as regular monthly premiums. The continuation of annuity premiums during total disability to age 65 produces at that age an annuity income of the same amount the individual would have received if he had not become totally disabled and if his salary had remained the same until age 65.

Increasing Benefit Provision. In 1968, TIAA made available to the colleges an automatic increase provision in its disability program. Under it, the monthly income and waiver benefits automatically increase 3 per cent each year for persons who become disabled after their institution adopts this new provision. The purpose, of course, is to help disability benefits adjust to cost of living increases. An automatic yearly increase in his monthly income check and in the amount being set aside in his TIAA-CREF annuity contracts offers the disabled person a reasonable chance of protecting the purchasing power of his benefits.

Premiums. The cost of a group long-term total disability insurance plan is normally stated in terms of a composite monthly premium rate for each $100 of monthly benefit. One rate is stated for the income benefit, another for the waiver benefit. The rate will differ from group to group on the basis of such factors as:

1. Sex and age distribution of insured employees.
2. Salary distribution of insured employees.
3. The rate of contribution to the retirement plan for the waiver benefit.
4. Size of the insured group and cost of administration.
5. Whether the staff members are covered by Social Security.

The total premium for a TIAA program including both income and waiver benefits with a 3 per cent increasing benefit provision generally is between one-third and two-thirds of 1 per cent of the payroll of plan participants. Without the 3 per cent provision, it ranges between one-quarter and one-half of 1 per cent of payroll.

Summary. The opening, a dozen years ago, of the group insurance route to long-term disability income protection in the colleges materially changed the financial prospects for college staff members during periods of disability:

1. Employees no longer need to be subject to the 10- and 15-year waiting periods that are common under the disability provisions of public retirement plans. Under insured plans a 1-year waiting period for new employees is common.

2. A realistic level of benefits can be assured. Benefits are stated as a substantial percentage of salary for all insured staff members regardless of length of service or size of retirement accumulation at the time of disability.

3. The waiver benefit provides for regular contributions toward the accumulation of retirement and death benefits. There is no need to use up retirement savings prematurely in order to provide some disability income.

4. An annual benefit increase provision can help disability income meet increasing living costs.

THE COLLEGE DECISIONS

Once the decision has been made to provide a disability income benefit to cover the normally active years, and a waiver benefit to assure adequacy of income during the succeeding retirement years, the remaining decisions concern employee eligibility for the plan and the sharing of premiums.

Participation. The institution may extend coverage to all classes of substantially full-time employees, academic and nonacademic, or only to specified classes of employees. The definition of classes covered in the disability plan should include all categories of staff members for whom the college feels a long-term responsibility, and this will help it to attract the best in new staff talent. Different waiting periods may be arranged for different classes of employees. Temporary employees are not eligible for the coverage. Often a work test (minimum number of hours of work per week) governs eligibility of staff members other than faculty for participation in the plan. In addition, eligibility may be restricted to staff members earning more than a certain minimum. For lower-paid staff members, Social Security, Workmen's Compensation, and similar benefits for disability usually provide benefits which, as a percentage of salary, generally equal the desired overall income goal.

The definition of eligible classes of employees requires precise language; it is important that there be no uncertainty as to who is and who is not covered. Since the insurance is issued without medical examination (except for late applicants), group underwriting rules require the use of clearly defined and automatic factors such as rank or length of service in determining eligibility. Eligibility definitions become a part of the group contract. The following examples illustrate some of the eligibility rules established by institutions with plans now in effect:

All full-time staff members who have completed two years of employment and are under age 64 years and six months are eligible to participate in this plan.

Eligibility. 1. All active, full-time Employees (except temporary Employees) who are Trustee-appointed faculty or administrative staff members who have completed one year of service. 2. All other active, full-time Employees (except temporary Employees) who have completed two years of service. For the purpose of eligibility, non-faculty Employees who work less than 32 hours a week will not be considered full-time Employees.

All active full-time employees (other than temporary employees) who have completed one year of service and earn an annual salary (exclusive of overtime, etc.) of $4,800 are eligible to participate in the Long Term Disability Plan. Full-time is defined as a normal class assignment or 30 hours work per week.

Waiting Periods. All employees in an eligible class can be covered as soon as they have completed the waiting period (service requirement). Insurers normally require a waiting period of a year or more of service before an otherwise eligible employee may participate in the plan. An alternative to the waiting period is a "preexisting conditions exclusion" which excludes from coverage, usually for 1 year, total disabilities resulting from injuries which occurred or sickness which commenced prior to the date the employee became insured under the group policy.

Colleges frequently use longer waiting periods for clerical-service employees in view of the high turnover rates among these staff members. There is no exact way to determine just how long after employment a college should begin to assume the responsibility of providing long-term disability income for its employees. Not many employers feel obliged to promise substantial long-term disability benefits to new employees the moment they arrive on campus. Furthermore, a waiting period that is too short might encourage job applications from persons in poor health. But, in setting a waiting period, the college should avoid spans of such length that they detract from the appeal of the plan.

To facilitate continuity of coverage for staff members who move from one institution to another, TIAA disability plans automatically eliminate the waiting period for those who become eligible for an institution's plan within 3 months of leaving a similar long-term disability plan.

Sharing the Cost. A larger proportion of institutions pay the full cost of group disability income coverage than pay the full cost of other group plans.

Among the 450 institutions reporting an insured long-term program for faculty and administrative personnel, 47 per cent pay the full cost and 36 per cent provide for sharing of the cost. Seventeen per cent report a plan paid for wholly by the faculty. Of the 278 institutions reporting an insured long-term plan for the clerical and service groups, 44 per cent pay the whole cost, 37 per cent provide for a sharing of the cost, and 19 per cent are employee-pay-all.

When the employer pays the whole cost, all eligible employees are covered automatically and administrative procedures are at their simplest. There is no danger that a total disability will strike an individual who did not sign up because the plan required an employee contribution. The total cost to the institution for an individual is so small as a percentage of payroll, and potential benefits are so great, that there is every reason to achieve universality of protection by means of a noncontributory plan.

If participants are to contribute toward the premium, the institution decides the approximate share of the total premium it will pay, and then selects a method for determining employee contributions. Employee contributions should be based on a formula that is expressed simply, is convenient to administer, will not need frequent changes, and yet produces the desired sharing of the total cost. For example, the employee's contribution can be established as a percentage of salary. It can also be expressed as so much for each $100 of his monthly salary, or as a specified amount for each of several salary groupings. Choice of the best method for establishing employee contributions at a particular college may depend in part on the college's own payroll and accounting procedures.

Leaves of Absence. The college should make sure that plan provisions concerning coverage during leaves of absence are clear and that these provisions meet the needs of employees. Both leaves with pay and leaves without pay should be considered.

Under TIAA plans, coverage may be continued for up to 24 months of sabbatical or other leave with pay, or for leaves without pay if the staff member is engaged in education or research, such as under a foundation grant, Fulbright grant, or government project, or is engaged in full-time study for an advanced degree. Coverage may be continued for up to 24 months of leave for any other purpose if the college is continuing at least one-fourth of the staff member's pay. The level of coverage remains the same as immediately before the start of the leave. Under a contributory plan the college may assume payment of the entire premium during leaves, or it may arrange in advance with the staff member for the continuation of his regular plan contribution.

Termination of Insurance. Termination of a staff member's insurance occurs if his active service is terminated, if he ceases his premium contributions, if he ceases to be in a class of employees eligible for coverage, or if the group policy is terminated. Since benefits are not usually payable beyond the normal retirement age nor, in most instances, during the first 6 months of total disability, insurance and premiums normally terminate 6 months before the active employee's attainment of normal retirement age. Termination of a staff member's insurance should not, and in most college plans does not, affect his benefits for a total disability existing on the date of such termination.

DISABILITY INCOME UNDER
PUBLIC RETIREMENT SYSTEMS

About 190 institutions participate in public employee and state teacher retirement systems that provide some long-term disability income for employees meeting eligibility requirements. Recent years have witnessed considerable improvement in the disability provisions of some plans, although most of them are still characterized by a limiting of benefits to persons with 10 to 15 years of service.

Benefits under the plans vary widely. The plans most likely to provide an adequate disability income are those providing a benefit equal to the retirement benefit the employee would have received had he continued in service (at his salary at onset of disability) to age 60 or 65. Others give credit for future service to age 60 or 65, but actuarially reduce the benefit to account for the extra cost of beginning it at the age of disability. Others apply the benefit formula only to the number of years served up to the date of disability and also actuarially reduce the benefit according to the age at disability. Still other plans equate "early retirement" provisions with "disability retirement," and permit disability retirement only when requirements for early retirement have been met.

Tables 9.3 and 9.4 summarize the eligibility requirements (service and

TABLE 9.3: *PUBLIC EMPLOYEE AND STATE TEACHER RETIREMENT SYSTEMS COVERING INSTITUTIONS OF HIGHER EDUCATION, ELIGIBILITY REQUIREMENTS FOR NONSERVICE-CONNECTED LONG-TERM TOTAL DISABILITY*

No age or service requirement		5[a]
Service requirement only		
5 years	14	
7–8 years	4	
10 years	35[b]	
12 years	1	
15 years	11[c]	
		65
Age requirement only		
Age 55		1
No disability provision		1
Total systems		72

[a] One system reduces benefits if employee has service of less than 10 years. One plan has a 10-year service requirement for life disability annuity; those in service for less than 10 years receive 1 month's benefit for each month of service.

[b] In one system, benefits are actuarially reduced if employee has fewer than 30 years of service. Alternative eligibility requirement of 5 years' service and age 50 in one system. In one system, 10 years' service or $500 on deposit.

[c] In one system, service requirement is 10 years for veterans.

TABLE 9.4: *PUBLIC EMPLOYEE AND STATE TEACHER RETIREMENT SYSTEMS COVERING INSTITUTIONS OF HIGHER EDUCATION, BENEFITS FOR NONSERVICE-CONNECTED LONG-TERM TOTAL DISABILITY*

Retirement benefit employee would have earned had he continued at present salary to retirement age	11
A percentage of the benefit payable at retirement	6
A percentage of the retirement benefit earned by service to date	3
Percentage of final average salary preceding disability	11
Retirement benefit earned to date of disability	34[a]
Flat amount per month	2
Miscellaneous	4
No disability provision	1
Total	72

[a] Twenty-four of the plans actuarially reduce the formula benefit according to the age at which disability benefits begin.

age) and benefits under the long-term total disability provisions of the public retirement systems covering institutions of higher education.

SELF-ADMINISTERED PLANS

Self-administered long-term total disability plans are reported by about 5 per cent of the institutions having long-term plans; about two dozen self-administered plans are in operation in addition to the two large self-administered plans for public employees in higher education, the State Universities Retirement System of Illinois and the University of California Retirement System. As examples of the provisions of self-administered plans, those reported by the following institutions are briefly summarized below: Indiana University, the University of Michigan, and the University of Pennsylvania.

Indiana University. Under the Indiana University plan the eligible staff member who becomes totally disabled "may retire and receive benefits equal to his retirement expectations at age 70." The University provides a disability benefit equal to the difference between the amount of the TIAA-CREF annuity begun at the age disability begins and the annuity the staff member would have received had he continued in service at current salary to age 70. Waiting periods for eligibility range from 5 to 10 years. Long-term disability income for employees other than faculty, administrative officers, and professional librarians is covered under the provisions of the Public Employees' Retirement Fund of Indiana.

University of Michigan. Faculty and other employees are eligible for the long-term total disability plan after completing 5 years of continuous service. Benefits continue throughout disability until age 65, at which time retirement income begins. The plan pays 50 per cent of salary up to a maximum benefit of $400 per month. Up to 75 per cent of salary may be received from the combined benefits of the University program, Social Security, Workmen's Compensation, and other such benefits. The University continues its own and the individual's contributions to the retirement plan during disability.

University of Pennsylvania. Faculty members are eligible for the plan after 1 year of service, other employees after 3 years. Long-term benefits begin after 6 months of disability. Benefits continue during disability to age 65. The benefits vary according to length of service: including amounts

LONG-TERM DISABILITY INCOME PLANS   193

payable under Social Security, Workmen's Compensation, and similar programs, and one-half of the monthly installments of a 5-year pay-out under the University group life insurance plan, the benefit is 30 per cent of monthly salary, but not more than $480 per month for those with less than 6 years' service; 40 per cent but not more than $640 per month for those with 6 to 12 years' service; and 50 per cent but not more than $800 per month for those with 12 years' service and over. During total disability the plan provides for a waiver of premium benefit that continues contributions to the disabled person's TIAA-CREF retirement annuity, which becomes payable following termination of the disability income at age 65.

BIBLIOGRAPHY

"Academic Retirement and Related Subjects," *Association of American Colleges Bulletin*, XXXVI (May, 1950), 308–28. Also in *American Association of University Professors Bulletin*, XXXVI (Spring, 1950), 97–117.

Advisory Commission on Intergovernmental Relations. "Transferability of Public Employee Retirement Credits Among Units of Government." *Report* A-16. Washington, D.C., U.S. Government Printing Office, 1963.

Bernstein, Merton C. *The Future of Private Pensions*. New York, Free Press, 1964.

Blue Cross Guide. Chicago, Blue Cross Association, Annual.

Brown, David G. *The Mobile Professors*. Washington, D.C., American Council on Education, 1967.

Carnegie Foundation for the Advancement of Teaching. *Annual Report(s)*, 1906, 1914, 1916, 1917, and 1918. *Bulletin* No. 9 (1916) and *Bulletin* No. 12 (1918).

Duncan, Robert M. "A Retirement System Granting Unit Annuities and Investing in Equities," *Transactions of the Society of Actuaries*, IV (1952), 317–44.

Dunham, Ralph E., and Patricia S. Wright. *Final Report: Faculty and Other Professional Staff in Institutions of Higher Education, Fall Term, 1963–64*. U.S. Department of Health, Education, and Welfare, Office of Education. Washington, D.C., U.S. Government Printing Office, 1966.

"The Economic Status of the Profession, 1959–60: Annual Report by Committee Z," *American Association of University Professors Bulletin*, XLVI (Summer, 1960), 156–93.

Eilers, Robert D., and Robert M. Crowe, eds. *Group Insurance Handbook*. Homewood, Ill., Richard D. Irwin, 1965.

Greenough, William C. *College Retirement and Insurance Plans*. New York, Columbia University Press, 1948.

———. "A New Approach to Retirement Income." New York, TIAA, 1951.

———, and Francis P. King. *Retirement and Insurance Plans in American Colleges*. New York, Columbia University Press, 1959.

Health Insurance Institute. *1967 Source Book of Health Insurance Data*. New York, Health Insurance Institute, 1967.

Ingraham, Mark H. *The Mirror of Brass*. Madison, University of Wisconsin Press, 1968.

———. *The Outer Fringe*. Madison, University of Wisconsin Press, 1965.

Institute of Life Insurance. *Life Insurance Fact Book*. New York, Institute of Life Insurance, 1967.

————. *Private and Public Pension Plans in the United States*. New York, Institute of Life Insurance, 1967.

Jessup, Philip C. *Elihu Root*. New York, Dodd, Mead, 1938.

King, Francis P. *Financing the College Education of Faculty Children*. New York, Henry Holt, 1954.

Murray, Roger F. "Economic Aspects of Pensions: A Summary Report," in *Old Age Income Assurance: A Compendium of Papers on Problems and Policy Issues in the Public and Private Pension System*, Part V: *Financial Aspects of Pension Plans*, pp. 36–114. (Submitted to the Subcommittee on Fiscal Policy of the Joint Economic Committee, 90th Congress, 1st Session.) Washington, D.C., U.S. Government Printing Office, 1967.

National Academy of Sciences, National Research Council. "Profiles of Ph.D's in the Sciences: Summary Report on Follow-up of Doctorate Cohorts, 1935–1960." *Publication* 1293. Washington, D.C., National Academy of Sciences, 1965.

National Advisory Commission on Health Manpower. *Report*, Vol. I. Washington, D.C., U.S. Government Printing Office, 1967.

National Education Association, National Council on Teacher Retirement. *Proceedings of the 43rd Annual Meeting*. October, 1965.

President's Committee on Corporate Pension Funds and Other Private Retirement and Welfare Programs. *Public Policy and Private Pension Programs: A Report to the President on Private Employee Retirement Plans*. Washington, D.C., U.S. Government Printing Office, 1965.

Reed, Louis S. "Private Health Insurance: Coverage and Financial Experience, 1940–66," *Social Security Bulletin*, XXX (November, 1967), 3–22.

Robbins, Rainard B. *College Plans for Retirement Income*. New York, Columbia University Press, 1940.

————. "Developments in Social Security and Pension Plans." Address before the Eastern Association of College and University Business Officers, White Sulphur Springs, West Virginia, December 9, 1941.

State of Connecticut. *Report on the State Government Personnel Study*, Vol. III, "Actuarial Report on the State Retirement System," by Russell O. Hooker and Associates, Consulting Actuaries. Hartford, 1967.

State of Nevada. *Ninth Biennial Report of the Public Employee Retirement Board*, "Fourth Actuarial Report: A Survey of the Public Employees Retirement System," by Coates, Herfurth, and England, Consulting Actuaries, pp. 47–64. Carson City, 1965.

State Universities Retirement System, Illinois. *Annual Report for the Year Ended August 31, 1967*.

————. Handbook of Information. Urbana, October, 1965.

"A Statement on Leaves of Absence," *American Association of University Professors Bulletin*, LIII (Autumn, 1967), 270–74.

Tax Foundation. *Economic Aspects of the Social Security Tax*. New York, Tax Foundation, 1966.

Teachers Insurance and Annuity Association. *Bulletin,* January, 1951.

————. "Proposed Major Medical Expense and Disability Insurances." Report to the Ford Foundation. New York, unpublished, 1956.

————. "Retirement Practices at Selected Colleges and Universities." New York, unpublished, 1961.

U.S. Bureau of the Census. *Census of Governments: 1962,* Vol. VI, No. 1—"Employee-Retirement Systems of State and Local Governments." Washington, D.C., U.S. Government Printing Office, 1963.

————. *Statistical Abstract of the United States: 1967.* Washington, D.C., U.S. Government Printing Office, 1967.

Council of Economic Advisors, *Economic Report of the President, February, 1968.* Washington, D.C., U.S. Government Printing Office, 1968.

U.S. Department of Health, Education, and Welfare. *Social Security Handbook.* 3rd ed. Washington, D.C., U.S. Government Printing Office, 1966.

————, Social Security Administration, Office of Research and Statistics. "State and Local Government Retirement Systems . . . 1965," by Joseph Krislov. Research Report No. 15. Washington, D.C., U.S. Government Printing Office, 1966.

U.S. Department of Labor, Bureau of Labor Standards. "State Workmen's Compensation Laws." *Bulletin* 161 (rev.) Washington, D.C., U.S. Government Printing Office, 1964.

Appendix 1

QUESTIONNAIRE

The survey questionnaire is reproduced on the next nineteen pages. The questionnaire was mailed to all four-year colleges and universities January 1, 1968.

PLEASE COMPLETE
AND RETURN BEFORE
JANUARY 31, 1968

SURVEY OF
RETIREMENT AND INSURANCE PLANS IN HIGHER EDUCATION

Educational Research Department
TIAA/CREF
730 Third Avenue   New York, N. Y. 10017

TO THE BUSINESS OFFICER:

The purpose of this survey is to assemble current information for a new edition of *Retirement and Insurance Plans in American Colleges.* Previous editions have been the chief source of information on retirement, life insurance, health insurance, and disability plans in U.S. colleges and universities.

A complimentary copy of the published study will be mailed to your institution.

INSTRUCTIONS

1. Please answer all six sections of the questionnaire, giving information as of January 1, 1968. Each section has at least one item to be answered even though your institution may not have a plan. Most answers require single check marks and may be made by hand. It is not necessary to use a typewriter.

2. A business reply envelope and copy of the questionnaire for your files are enclosed for your convenience.

3. Except for TIAA plans, please enclose a copy of the booklets or folders describing the retirement and insurance benefit plans at your institution.

4. If your institution has a Faculty Handbook, please enclose a copy.

5. Public institutions: In the questions asking whether "the institution (or State)" pays toward the cost of a plan, "State" includes municipalities and school districts where appropriate.

CARD 1
2–8

Name and Address of Institution:

Please fill in the following before turning to the retirement and insurance items:

Number of Full-Time Staff Members:
(Use estimates if necessary—Do not include "equivalents")

Catholic institutions: Please indicate only full-time *lay* personnel. Questionnaire answers should be given for lay personnel only.

1. **Faculty**   9–13

(All faculty members, including those primarily assigned to instruction, departmental research, or organized research, and academic deans and department heads)

2. **Administrative Staff and other Professional Staff not Classified as Faculty**   14–18

(Administrative officers, their assistants, supervisors, other professional or research staff members)

3. **Other Employees**   19–23

(Clerical, secretarial, maintenance, service, other non-professional)

4. **Name and Title of Person Supplying Information:**

5. **Area Code, Telephone Number and Extension:**

202

APP. 1

SECTION I—RETIREMENT PLAN

1. Are employees of your institution covered by federal Social Security?   24–1 ☐ YES
   -2 ☐ NO

Retirement plan information is sought for the three general employee categories indicated in the column headings A, B, and C.

	A	B	C
	FACULTY	ADMINISTRATIVE STAFF/OTHER PROFESSIONAL	OTHER EMPLOYEES

2. Does your institution have a retirement plan?

   In each column answered YES, please check the appropriate boxes to show which employee classes are eligible (assuming age, service, or other requirements have been met). (Check as many as apply. Use the extra spaces to designate classes not shown.)

   If your institution has no retirement plan for any employee group, please turn to Section II.

   Please complete the following questions for the columns checked YES in question 2:

A	B	C
25–1 ☐ YES	32–1 ☐ YES	38–1 ☐ YES
-2 ☐ NO	-2 ☐ NO	-2 ☐ NO
26 ☐ Professors	33 ☐ Adm. Officers	39 ☐ Clerical & Secretarial
27 ☐ Assoc. Profs.	34 ☐ Adm. Staff	
28 ☐ Ass't. Profs.	35 ☐ Other Professional or Research	40 ☐ Maintenance & Service
29 ☐ Instrs.		
30 ☐ _____	36 ☐ _____	41 ☐ _____
31 ☐ _____	37 ☐ _____	42 ☐ _____

3. Please check the type(s) of retirement plan(s) covering employees of your institution: (Check as many as apply in each column.)
   Do not include plans now closed to new entrants.

	A	B	C
a. State Teacher Retirement System	43–1 ☐	44–1 ☐	45–1 ☐
b. State Employee Retirement System	46–1 ☐	47–1 ☐	48–1 ☐
c. A Single State Retirement System Covering both Teachers and other State Employees	49–1 ☐	50–1 ☐	51–1 ☐
d. TIAA/CREF	52–1 ☐	53–1 ☐	54–1 ☐
e. Self-Administered or Trusteed	55–1 ☐	56–1 ☐	57–1 ☐
f. Church Pension Plan:_____	58–1 ☐	59–1 ☐	60–1 ☐
g. Insurance Company:_____	61–1 ☐	62–1 ☐	63–1 ☐
h. Other:_____	64–1 ☐	65–1 ☐	66–1 ☐

4. If more than one plan is checked in a column, are plans alternatives or is participation concurrent? (Check as many as apply.)

	A	B	C
Plans are alternatives	67–1 ☐	68–1 ☐	69–1 ☐
Participation is concurrent	70–1 ☐	71–1 ☐	72–1 ☐

5. Does the institution (or State) pay toward the cost of the retirement plan?

A	B	C
73–1 ☐ YES	74–1 ☐ YES	75–1 ☐ YES
-2 ☐ NO	-2 ☐ NO	-2 ☐ NO

SECTION I—RETIREMENT PLAN (Continued)

	A	B	C
	FACULTY	ADMINISTRATIVE STAFF/OTHER PROFESSIONAL	OTHER EMPLOYEES

6. Does the employee pay toward the cost of the retirement plan?

	A	B	C
	76–1 ☐ YES –2 ☐ NO	77–1 ☐ YES –2 ☐ NO	78–1 ☐ YES –2 ☐ NO

IF YES, does your institution permit *regular employee contributions* to the retirement plan to be made by salary REduction under Section 403(b) of the Internal Revenue Code (the "Salary-or-Annuity" Option)? (*Check one.*)

79–80 BL
CARD 2
2–8

No

	A	B	C
	9–1 ☐	10–1 ☐	11–1 ☐

Yes—Required for regular employee contributions

	A	B	C
	–2 ☐	–2 ☐	–2 ☐

Yes—Optional for regular employee contributions

	A	B	C
	–3 ☐	–3 ☐	–3 ☐

7. Does your institution permit employees to make extra annuity contributions (i.e., over and above those required by the retirement plan) by salary REduction under Section 403(b) of the Internal Revenue Code (the "Salary-or-Annuity" Option)?

	A	B	C
	12–1 ☐ YES –2 ☐ NO	13–1 ☐ YES –2 ☐ NO	14–1 ☐ YES –2 ☐ NO

8. Retirement age:

a. What does the retirement plan state as the "normal" retirement age?

	A	B	C
	(AGE) 15–16	(AGE) 17–18	(AGE) 19–20

Normal retirement age is defined here as the first age at which retirement would not be classified as "early" and is the age beyond which further service, if permitted, is considered an "extension of service."

b. Check here if plan does not state any retirement age:

	A	B	C
	21–1 ☐	22–1 ☐	23–1 ☐

c. Is there a years-of-service requirement for retirement under the plan?

	A	B	C
	24–1 ☐ YES –2 ☐ NO	25–1 ☐ YES –2 ☐ NO	26–1 ☐ YES –2 ☐ NO

IF A NORMAL RETIREMENT AGE IS STATED IN THE PLAN, PLEASE ANSWER THE FOLLOWING:

d. Is retirement compulsory without exception at the age stated in question 8a above?

	A	B	C
	27–1 ☐ YES –2 ☐ NO	28–1 ☐ YES –2 ☐ NO	29–1 ☐ YES –2 ☐ NO

e. May service be extended beyond the age stated in question 8a above?

	A	B	C
	30–1 ☐ YES –2 ☐ NO	31–1 ☐ YES –2 ☐ NO	32–1 ☐ YES –2 ☐ NO

SECTION I—RETIREMENT PLAN (*Continued*)

	A	B	C
	FACULTY	ADMINISTRATIVE STAFF/OTHER PROFESSIONAL	OTHER EMPLOYEES

f. If extensions of service are made:

(1) For what periods of time are extensions made? (*Check as many as apply.*)

Periods of less than one academic or calendar year — 33–1 ☐ 34–1 ☐ 35–1 ☐

One academic or calendar year at a time — 36–1 ☐ 37–1 ☐ 38–1 ☐

Periods longer than one academic or calendar year — 39–1 ☐ 40–1 ☐ 41–1 ☐

Other — 42–1 ☐ 43–1 ☐ 44–1 ☐

(2) Are extensions made on a full-time or part-time basis? (*Check one.*)

Full-time — 45–1 ☐ 46–1 ☐ 47–1 ☐

Part-time — –2 ☐ –2 ☐ –2 ☐

Both — –3 ☐ –3 ☐ –3 ☐

(3) What is the age beyond which extensions are no longer permitted?

(AGE) 48–49   (AGE) 50–51   (AGE) 52–53

Check here if there is no stated age limit for extensions: 54–1 ☐ 55–1 ☐ 56–1 ☐

57-80 BL

REMARKS: (*Include any remarks concerning answers to questions, general comments, etc.*)

PLEASE ENCLOSE A COPY OF THE BOOKLETS OR FOLDERS DESCRIBING YOUR RETIREMENT PLAN OR PLANS (EXCEPT FOR TIAA PLANS)

SECTION II—GROUP LIFE INSURANCE

Group life insurance plan information is sought for the three general employee categories indicated in the column headings A, B, and C.

	A	B	C
	FACULTY	ADMINISTRATIVE STAFF/OTHER PROFESSIONAL	OTHER EMPLOYEES

1. Does your institution have a group (or collective) life insurance plan(s)? (*Do not include as life insurance the death benefit provisions of a retirement plan.*)

	A	B	C
	9–1 ☐ YES –2 ☐ NO	16–1 ☐ YES –2 ☐ NO	22–1 ☐ YES –2 ☐ NO

In each column answered YES, please check the appropriate boxes to show which employee classes are eligible (assuming age, service, or other requirements have been met). (*Check as many as apply. Use the extra spaces to designate classes not shown.*)

A	B	C
10 ☐ Professors	17 ☐ Adm. Officers	23 ☐ Clerical & Secretarial
11 ☐ Assoc. Profs.	18 ☐ Adm. Staff	24 ☐ Maintenance & Service
12 ☐ Ass't. Profs.	19 ☐ Other Professional or Research	
13 ☐ Instrs.		
14 ☐ _____	20 ☐ _____	25 ☐ _____
15 ☐ _____	21 ☐ _____	26 ☐ _____

If your institution has no group life insurance coverage for any employee group, please turn to Section III.

Please complete the following questions for the columns checked YES in question 1:

LIFE INSURANCE FOR ACTIVE EMPLOYEES

2. Does the institution (or State) pay toward the cost of the plan?

A	B	C
27–1 ☐ YES –2 ☐ NO	28–1 ☐ YES –2 ☐ NO	29–1 ☐ YES –2 ☐ NO

3. Does the employee pay toward the cost of the plan?

A	B	C
30–1 ☐ YES –2 ☐ NO	31–1 ☐ YES –2 ☐ NO	32–1 ☐ YES –2 ☐ NO

4. May a covered employee choose additional optional insurance coverage under the plan?

A	B	C
33–1 ☐ YES –2 ☐ NO	34–1 ☐ YES –2 ☐ NO	35–1 ☐ YES –2 ☐ NO

IF YES, check here if the individual's *only* contribution is for the optional insurance, i.e., the institution pays the full cost of the basic insurance:

A	B	C
36–1 ☐	37–1 ☐	38–1 ☐

5. Please indicate the waiting period, if any, before a new employee is eligible to participate in the plan: (*Check one.*)

No waiting period

A	B	C
39–1 ☐	40–1 ☐	41–1 ☐

Less than a month or until first day of the month following date of employment

A	B	C
–2 ☐	–2 ☐	–2 ☐

Until the anniversary or semi-anniversary date of the plan

A	B	C
–3 ☐	–3 ☐	–3 ☐

A stated number of months (*Please give number.*)

A	B	C
–4 ☐	–4 ☐	–4 ☐
(MONTHS) 42–43	(MONTHS) 44–45	(MONTHS) 46–47

Other: (*Specify*) _____

A	B	C
–5 ☐	–5 ☐	–5 ☐

SECTION II—GROUP LIFE INSURANCE (Continued)

	A FACULTY	B ADMINISTRATIVE STAFF/OTHER PROFESSIONAL	C OTHER EMPLOYEES

6. Please give a brief description of the insurance amounts: (e.g., 1½ times salary; units of collective insurance; $2,000 to $5,000 depending on salary or rank; $10,000 for all members of class, graded downward after a stated age, etc.)

48–49   50–51   52–53

7. Are accidental death and dismemberment benefits (AD&D) provided under the plan?

54–1 ☐ YES 55–1 ☐ YES 56–1 ☐ YES
-2 ☐ NO   -2 ☐ NO   -2 ☐ NO

LIFE INSURANCE FOR RETIRED EMPLOYEES

8. Are retired employees covered by the group life insurance plan? (Do not consider individual use of a conversion privilege as continued coverage under a group plan.)

57–1 ☐ YES 58–1 ☐ YES 59–1 ☐ YES
-2 ☐ NO   -2 ☐ NO   -2 ☐ NO

If retired employees are not covered by group life insurance, please turn to Section III.

For columns checked YES in question 8 please answer the following:

9. Does the institution (or State) pay toward the cost of retirement coverage?

60–1 ☐ YES 61–1 ☐ YES 62–1 ☐ YES
-2 ☐ NO   -2 ☐ NO   -2 ☐ NO

10. Does the retired employee pay toward the cost of his coverage?

63–1 ☐ YES 64–1 ☐ YES 65–1 ☐ YES
-2 ☐ NO   -2 ☐ NO   -2 ☐ NO

11. Please give a brief description of the insurance amounts for retired employees. (Please state whether insurance is "paid-up" or "term.")

66–67   68–69   70–71

72-80 BL

REMARKS: (Include any remarks concerning answers to questions, general comments, etc.)

PLEASE ENCLOSE A COPY OF THE BOOKLET OR FOLDER DESCRIBING YOUR GROUP LIFE INSURANCE PLAN
(EXCEPT FOR TIAA PLANS)

— 7 —

SECTION III—BASIC GROUP HOSPITAL-SURGICAL-MEDICAL INSURANCE

This section covers basic health insurance plans only—Blue Cross and Blue Shield plans and other plans that provide service or indemnity benefits normally limited to in-hospital board and room charges in semi-private accommodations for a stated number of days, other hospital charges, allowances toward fees for surgery performed in the hospital or the doctor's office, and, under some plans, allowances for doctors' visits in the hospital.

Major medical expense insurance, either carried in conjunction with a separate basic hospital-surgical-medical plan or as the single health insurance plan at the institution, is covered in Section IV.

CARD 4
2-8

Basic group hospital-surgical-medical insurance plan information is sought for the three general employee categories indicated in column headings A, B, and C.

	A	B	C
	FACULTY	ADMINISTRATIVE STAFF/OTHER PROFESSIONAL	OTHER EMPLOYEES

1. Does your institution have a group hospital-surgical-medical plan(s) that is limited to the type of basic coverage described above?

	A	B	C
	9–1 ☐ YES –2 ☐ NO	16–1 ☐ YES –2 ☐ NO	22–1 ☐ YES –2 ☐ NO

In each column answered YES, please check the appropriate boxes to show which employee classes are eligible (assuming age, service, or other requirements have been met). (*Check as many as apply. Use the extra spaces to designate classes not shown.*)

A	B	C
10 ☐ Professors	17 ☐ Adm. Officers	23 ☐ Clerical & Secretarial
11 ☐ Assoc. Profs.	18 ☐ Adm. Staff	
12 ☐ Ass't. Profs.	19 ☐ Other Professional or Research	24 ☐ Maintenance & Service
13 ☐ Instrs.		
14 ☐ _____	20 ☐ _____	25 ☐ _____
15 ☐ _____	21 ☐ _____	26 ☐ _____

If you answered NO in all three columns, please turn to Section IV.

Please complete the following questions for the columns checked YES in question 1:

BASIC GROUP HEALTH INSURANCE FOR ACTIVE EMPLOYEES

2. Does the institution (or State) pay toward the cost of employee coverage?

A	B	C
27–1 ☐ YES –2 ☐ NO	28–1 ☐ YES –2 ☐ NO	29–1 ☐ YES –2 ☐ NO

3. Does the employee pay toward the cost of his coverage?

A	B	C
30–1 ☐ YES –2 ☐ NO	31–1 ☐ YES –2 ☐ NO	32–1 ☐ YES –2 ☐ NO

4. Please indicate the waiting period, if any, before a new employee is eligible to participate in the plan: (*Check one.*)

No waiting period

A	B	C
33–1 ☐	34–1 ☐	35–1 ☐

Less than a month or until first day of the month following date of employment

A	B	C
–2 ☐	–2 ☐	–2 ☐

Until a stated date or dates during first year of employment

A	B	C
–3 ☐	–3 ☐	–3 ☐

A stated number of months (*Please give number.*)

A	B	C
–4 ☐	–4 ☐	–4 ☐

A	B	C
(MONTHS) 36–37	(MONTHS) 38–39	(MONTHS) 40–41

Other: (*Specify*)_____

A	B	C
–5 ☐	–5 ☐	–5 ☐

SECTION III—BASIC GROUP HOSPITAL-SURGICAL-MEDICAL INSURANCE (*Continued*)

	A	B	C
	FACULTY	ADMINISTRATIVE STAFF/OTHER PROFESSIONAL	OTHER EMPLOYEES

5. Basic health insurance plan(s) carried with: (*Check as many as apply.*)

	A	B	C
Blue Cross	42–1 ☐	43–1 ☐	44–1 ☐
Blue Shield	45–1 ☐	46–1 ☐	47–1 ☐
Insurance Company:_____	48–1 ☐	49–1 ☐	50–1 ☐
Other:_____	51–1 ☐	52–1 ☐	53–1 ☐

BASIC GROUP HEALTH INSURANCE FOR DEPENDENTS OF ACTIVE EMPLOYEES

6. Are employees' dependents (e.g., spouse and children) eligible for coverage under the basic group health insurance plan?

A	B	C
54–1 ☐ YES –2 ☐ NO	55–1 ☐ YES –2 ☐ NO	56–1 ☐ YES –2 ☐ NO

If there is no dependent coverage for any employee group, please go to question 9 below.

For columns checked YES in question 6 please answer the following:

7. Does the institution (or State) pay toward the cost of dependent coverage?

A	B	C
57–1 ☐ YES –2 ☐ NO	58–1 ☐ YES –2 ☐ NO	59–1 ☐ YES –2 ☐ NO

8. Does the employee pay toward the cost of his dependents' coverage?

A	B	C
60–1 ☐ YES –2 ☐ NO	61–1 ☐ YES –2 ☐ NO	62–1 ☐ YES –2 ☐ NO

BASIC GROUP HEALTH INSURANCE FOR RETIRED EMPLOYEES

9. Are retired employees eligible to continue in your basic group health insurance plan? (*Do not include conversions to an individual insurance policy or to "direct-pay" Blue Cross-Blue Shield coverage. Answer both a and b.*)

   a. Employees who retire before age 65?

A	B	C
63–1 ☐ YES –2 ☐ NO	64–1 ☐ YES –2 ☐ NO	65–1 ☐ YES –2 ☐ NO

   IF YES, does group participation continue beyond age 65?

A	B	C
66–1 ☐ YES –2 ☐ NO	67–1 ☐ YES –2 ☐ NO	68–1 ☐ YES –2 ☐ NO

   b. Employees who retire at age 65 or after?

A	B	C
69–1 ☐ YES –2 ☐ NO	70–1 ☐ YES –2 ☐ NO	71–1 ☐ YES –2 ☐ NO

If retired employees are not covered by basic group health insurance, please turn to Section IV.

For columns checked YES in questions 9a or b please answer the following:

10. Must an employee meet a "years of active service" and/or an age requirement in order to be eligible for basic group health insurance coverage during retirement?

A	B	C
72–1 ☐ YES –2 ☐ NO	73–1 ☐ YES –2 ☐ NO	74–1 ☐ YES –2 ☐ NO

75–80 BL

SECTION III—BASIC GROUP HOSPITAL-SURGICAL-MEDICAL INSURANCE (*Continued*)   CARD 5
                                                                    2–8

	A FACULTY	B ADMINISTRATIVE STAFF/OTHER PROFESSIONAL	C OTHER EMPLOYEES
IF YES in question 10, please state the requirement:			
a. Years of service	(YEARS) 9–10	(YEARS) 11–12	(YEARS) 13–14
b. Age	(AGE) 15–16	(AGE) 17–18	(AGE) 19–20
11. Does the institution (or State) pay toward the cost of retired employee coverage?	21–1 ☐ YES –2 ☐ NO	22–1 ☐ YES –2 ☐ NO	23–1 ☐ YES –2 ☐ NO
12. Does the retired employee pay toward the cost of his coverage?	24–1 ☐ YES –2 ☐ NO	25–1 ☐ YES –2 ☐ NO	26–1 ☐ YES –2 ☐ NO
13. Are dependents (e.g., spouse and children) of retired employees covered under the plan?	27–1 ☐ YES –2 ☐ NO	28–1 ☐ YES –2 ☐ NO	29–1 ☐ YES –2 ☐ NO
If dependents of retired employees are not covered by basic group health insurance, please turn to Section IV. **For columns checked YES in question 13 please answer the following:**			
14. Does the institution (or State) pay toward the cost of coverage of dependents of retired employees?	30–1 ☐ YES –2 ☐ NO	31–1 ☐ YES –2 ☐ NO	32–1 ☐ YES –2 ☐ NO
15. Does the retired employee pay toward the cost of his dependents' coverage?	33–1 ☐ YES –2 ☐ NO	34–1 ☐ YES –2 ☐ NO	35–1 ☐ YES –2 ☐ NO
16. Does the basic group health insurance coverage continue for dependents after the death of the retired employee?	36–1 ☐ YES –2 ☐ NO	37–1 ☐ YES –2 ☐ NO	38–1 ☐ YES –2 ☐ NO

39–80 BL

REMARKS: (*Include any remarks concerning answers to questions, general comments, etc.*)

PLEASE ENCLOSE A COPY OF THE BOOKLET OR FOLDER DESCRIBING YOUR BASIC GROUP
HOSPITAL-SURGICAL-MEDICAL INSURANCE PLAN

SECTION IV—GROUP MAJOR MEDICAL EXPENSE INSURANCE

This section deals with major medical expense insurance, which normally covers doctors' bills for home, office, and hospital visits, hospital board and room and other charges, prescription drugs, x-ray, blood and blood plasma, and rental of medical appliances. Reimbursement is for covered expenses not reimbursed by a base plan, and normally does not depend on hospital confinement. The plans are usually identified by three features: a deductible amount (frequently $100), coinsurance (usually 80%-20%), and a stated maximum benefit amount (such as $15,000 or $25,000) for each employee and dependent.

Major medical plans are normally carried in conjunction with a separate basic hospital-surgical-medical plan, but sometimes constitute the single health insurance plan at the institution.

CARD 6
2-8

Group major medical expense insurance plan information is sought for the three general employee categories indicated in the column headings A, B, and C.

	A	B	C
	FACULTY	ADMINISTRATIVE STAFF/OTHER PROFESSIONAL	OTHER EMPLOYEES

1. Does your institution have a major medical health insurance plan?

	A	B	C
	9–1 ☐ YES –2 ☐ NO	16–1 ☐ YES –2 ☐ NO	22–1 ☐ YES –2 ☐ NO

In each column answered YES, please check the appropriate boxes to show which employee classes are eligible (assuming age, service, or other requirements have been met). (*Check as many as apply. Use the extra spaces to designate classes not shown.*)

A	B	C
10 ☐ Professors	17 ☐ Adm. Officers	23 ☐ Clerical & Secretarial
11 ☐ Assoc. Profs.	18 ☐ Adm. Staff	
12 ☐ Ass't. Profs.	19 ☐ Other Professional or Research	24 ☐ Maintenance & Service
13 ☐ Instrs.		
14 ☐ _____	20 ☐ _____	25 ☐ _____
15 ☐ _____	21 ☐ _____	26 ☐ _____

If you answered NO in all three columns, please answer only question 26 at the end of this section and then turn to Section V.

Please complete the following questions for the columns checked YES in question 1:

2. Please check the form of coverage in effect at your institution: (*Check one.*)

Major medical plan and a separate basic health insurance plan

A	B	C
27–1 ☐	28–1 ☐	29–1 ☐

Major medical plan as the single health insurance plan at your institution

A	B	C
–2 ☐	–2 ☐	–2 ☐

MAJOR MEDICAL INSURANCE FOR ACTIVE EMPLOYEES

3. Does the institution (or State) pay toward the cost of employee coverage?

A	B	C
30–1 ☐ YES –2 ☐ NO	31–1 ☐ YES –2 ☐ NO	32–1 ☐ YES –2 ☐ NO

4. Does the employee pay toward the cost of his coverage?

A	B	C
33–1 ☐ YES –2 ☐ NO	34–1 ☐ YES –2 ☐ NO	35–1 ☐ YES –2 ☐ NO

SECTION IV—GROUP MAJOR MEDICAL EXPENSE INSURANCE (*Continued*)

	A	B	C
	FACULTY	ADMINISTRATIVE STAFF/OTHER PROFESSIONAL	OTHER EMPLOYEES

5. Please indicate the waiting period, if any, before a new employee is eligible to participate in the plan: (*Check one.*)

    No waiting period   36–1 ☐   37–1 ☐   38–1 ☐

    Less than a month or until first day of the month following date of employment   –2 ☐   –2 ☐   –2 ☐

    Until a stated date or dates during first year of employment (*e.g., September 1, January 1, and March 1, etc.*)   –3 ☐   –3 ☐   –3 ☐

    A stated number of months (*Please give number.*)   –4 ☐   –4 ☐   –4 ☐

(MONTHS)	(MONTHS)	(MONTHS)
39–40	41–42	43–44

    Other: (*Specify*)_____   –5 ☐   –5 ☐   –5 ☐

    If your major medical plan is with TIAA please check here and skip questions 6 through 12 in the checked column(s), beginning again with question 13:   45–1 ☐   46–1 ☐   47–1 ☐

6. Is the plan PER CAUSE or ALL CAUSE? (*Check one.*)

    PER CAUSE—A separate deductible and maximum benefit amount are applied to each separate illness or injury.   48–1 ☐   49–1 ☐   50–1 ☐

    ALL CAUSE—Covered expenses are applied toward a person's deductible and maximum benefit amount, whether from one or more illnesses or injuries.   –2 ☐   –2 ☐   –2 ☐

    OTHER—(*e.g., a combination of All Cause and Per Cause, etc.*): (*Specify*)_____   –3 ☐   –3 ☐   –3 ☐

7. Deductible amount: (*Check one and give amount.*)

    Same for all participants (*Please give amount.*)   51–1 ☐   52–1 ☐   53–1 ☐

$_____	$_____	$_____
(AMOUNT)	(AMOUNT)	(AMOUNT)
54–56	57–59	60–62

    Differs among participants according to the basic insurance coverage carried by the individual (*Please give range of deductibles.*)   –2 ☐   –2 ☐   –2 ☐

$_____ –$_____	$_____ –$_____	$_____ –$_____
(RANGE)	(RANGE)	(RANGE)
63–65 66–68	69–71 72–74	75–77 78–80

    Other: (*e.g., differs according to salary, etc.*)   –3 ☐   –3 ☐   –3 ☐

    (*Specify*)_____

— 12 —

SECTION IV—GROUP MAJOR MEDICAL EXPENSE INSURANCE (Continued)

	A	B	C
	FACULTY	ADMINISTRATIVE STAFF/OTHER PROFESSIONAL	OTHER EMPLOYEES

8. What is the period of time within which covered expenses must be incurred in order to be counted toward satisfying a deductible? (e.g., 3 months, 6 months, calendar year, etc.)

(PERIOD) 9-10	(PERIOD) 11-12	(PERIOD) 13-14

9. Are there categories of expense for which benefits are paid without a deductible or coinsurance requirement?

    a. Without deductible requirement?

15-1 ☐ YES -2 ☐ NO	16-1 ☐ YES -2 ☐ NO	17-1 ☐ YES -2 ☐ NO

    b. Without coinsurance requirement?

18-1 ☐ YES -2 ☐ NO	19-1 ☐ YES -2 ☐ NO	20-1 ☐ YES -2 ☐ NO

10. After benefits begin, what percentage of covered charges are reimbursed by the plan? (e.g., 75%, 80%, etc.)

% 21-22	% 23-24	% 25-26

11. Maximum length of benefit period: When the deductible has been satisfied, how long can the individual continue to receive benefits without having to satisfy a new deductible? (e.g., 3 years, balance of calendar year, etc.)

(PERIOD) 27-28	(PERIOD) 29-30	(PERIOD) 31-32

12. What is the plan's maximum benefit amount? (e.g., $10,000, $15,000, $25,000, etc., per insured person.)

$ (AMOUNT) 33-34	$ (AMOUNT) 35-36	$ (AMOUNT) 37-38

MAJOR MEDICAL INSURANCE FOR DEPENDENTS OF ACTIVE EMPLOYEES

13. Are employees' dependents (e.g., spouse and children) covered under the plan?

    If there is no dependent coverage for any employee group, please go to question 16.

    For columns checked YES in question 13 please answer the following:

39-1 ☐ YES -2 ☐ NO	40-1 ☐ YES -2 ☐ NO	41-1 ☐ YES -2 ☐ NO

14. Does the institution (or State) pay toward the cost of dependent coverage?

42-1 ☐ YES -2 ☐ NO	43-1 ☐ YES -2 ☐ NO	44-1 ☐ YES -2 ☐ NO

15. Does the employee pay toward the cost of his dependents' coverage?

45-1 ☐ YES -2 ☐ NO	46-1 ☐ YES -2 ☐ NO	47-1 ☐ YES -2 ☐ NO

SECTION IV—GROUP MAJOR MEDICAL EXPENSE INSURANCE (Continued)

	A FACULTY	B ADMINISTRATIVE STAFF/OTHER PROFESSIONAL	C OTHER EMPLOYEES

MAJOR MEDICAL INSURANCE FOR RETIRED EMPLOYEES

16. Are employees eligible to continue in the plan during retirement? (Do not include conversions to an individual insurance policy. Answer both a and b.)

    a. Employees who retire before age 65?

	A	B	C
	48–1 ☐ YES –2 ☐ NO	49–1 ☐ YES –2 ☐ NO	50–1 ☐ YES –2 ☐ NO

       IF YES, does group participation continue beyond age 65?

	A	B	C
	51–1 ☐ YES –2 ☐ NO	52–1 ☐ YES –2 ☐ NO	53–1 ☐ YES –2 ☐ NO

    b. Employees who retire at age 65 or after?

	A	B	C
	54–1 ☐ YES –2 ☐ NO	55–1 ☐ YES –2 ☐ NO	56–1 ☐ YES –2 ☐ NO

If retired employees are not covered by the major medical plan, please skip questions 17 through 25 and answer question 26.

For columns checked YES in question 16 please answer the following:

17. Must an employee meet a "years of active service" and/or an age requirement in order to be eligible for major medical coverage during retirement?

	A	B	C
	57–1 ☐ YES –2 ☐ NO	58–1 ☐ YES –2 ☐ NO	59–1 ☐ YES –2 ☐ NO

    IF YES, please state the requirement:

       a. Years of service

	A	B	C
	_____ (YEARS) 60–61	_____ (YEARS) 62–63	_____ (YEARS) 64–65

       b. Age

	A	B	C
	_____ (AGE) 66–67	_____ (AGE) 68–69	_____ (AGE) 70–71

18. Does the institution (or State) pay toward the cost of retired employee coverage?

	A	B	C
	72–1 ☐ YES –2 ☐ NO	73–1 ☐ YES –2 ☐ NO	74–1 ☐ YES –2 ☐ NO

19. Does the retired employee pay toward the cost of his coverage?

	A	B	C
	75–1 ☐ YES –2 ☐ NO	76–1 ☐ YES –2 ☐ NO	77–1 ☐ YES –2 ☐ NO

                                                     78–80 BL
CARD 8
2–8

20. Maximum benefit amount for retired employees: (e.g., $5,000, $10,000, etc., per insured person.)

    a. Under age 65 and retired:

	A	B	C
	$ _____ 9–10	$ _____ 11–12	$ _____ 13–14

    b. Age 65 or over and retired:

	A	B	C
	$ _____ 15–16	$ _____ 17–18	$ _____ 19–20

SECTION IV—GROUP MAJOR MEDICAL EXPENSE INSURANCE (Continued)

	A	B	C
	FACULTY	ADMINISTRATIVE STAFF/OTHER PROFESSIONAL	OTHER EMPLOYEES

21. Deductible amount: Are the deductible amounts for retired employees the same as for active employees?

    IF NO, please show amount of deductible for retired employees:

21-1 ☐ YES	22-1 ☐ YES	23-1 ☐ YES
-2 ☐ NO	-2 ☐ NO	-2 ☐ NO
$ _____	$ _____	$ _____
24-26	27-29	30-32

22. Are dependents (e.g., spouse and eligible children) of retired employees covered under the plan?

33-1 ☐ YES	34-1 ☐ YES	35-1 ☐ YES
-2 ☐ NO	-2 ☐ NO	-2 ☐ NO

If dependents of retired employees are not covered by the plan, please skip the next three questions and answer question 26.

For columns checked YES in question 22 please answer the following:

23. Does the institution (or State) pay toward the cost of coverage of dependents of retired employees?

36-1 ☐ YES	37-1 ☐ YES	38-1 ☐ YES
-2 ☐ NO	-2 ☐ NO	-2 ☐ NO

24. Does the retired employee pay toward the cost of his dependents' coverage?

39-1 ☐ YES	40-1 ☐ YES	41-1 ☐ YES
-2 ☐ NO	-2 ☐ NO	-2 ☐ NO

25. Does the major medical coverage continue for dependents after the death of the retired employee?

42-1 ☐ YES	43-1 ☐ YES	44-1 ☐ YES
-2 ☐ NO	-2 ☐ NO	-2 ☐ NO

MEDICARE BENEFITS OF THE FEDERAL SOCIAL SECURITY PROGRAM

26. Does the institution pay for all, part, or none of the retired individual's share of the cost of Medicare Part B for:

    a. The retired employee?

45-1 ☐ ALL	46-1 ☐ ALL	47-1 ☐ ALL
-2 ☐ PART	-2 ☐ PART	-2 ☐ PART
-3 ☐ NONE	-3 ☐ NONE	-3 ☐ NONE

    b. Spouse of the retired employee?

48-1 ☐ ALL	49-1 ☐ ALL	50-1 ☐ ALL
-2 ☐ PART	-2 ☐ PART	-2 ☐ PART
-3 ☐ NONE	-3 ☐ NONE	-3 ☐ NONE

REMARKS: (Include any remarks concerning answers to questions, general comments, etc.)

51-80 BL

PLEASE ENCLOSE A COPY OF THE BOOKLET OR FOLDER DESCRIBING YOUR MAJOR MEDICAL INSURANCE PLAN
(EXCEPT FOR TIAA PLANS)

SECTION V—SHORT-TERM DISABILITY INCOME (SICK PAY) PROVISIONS

Short-term disabilities are defined here as illnesses or injuries that cause absences from work lasting from a few days to perhaps as long as six months or so. Short-term plans include formal or informal sick pay or salary continuation, Workmen's Compensation, and short-term disability insurance. Long-term disability plans are covered in Section VI.

CARD 9
2-8

Information on short-term disability income provisions is sought for the three general employee categories indicated in column headings A, B, and C.

	A	B	C
	FACULTY	ADMINISTRATIVE STAFF/OTHER PROFESSIONAL	OTHER EMPLOYEES

1. Does your institution have a short-term disability income plan(s)?

A	B	C
9–1 ☐ YES	16–1 ☐ YES	22–1 ☐ YES
–2 ☐ NO	–2 ☐ NO	–2 ☐ NO

In each column answered YES, please check the appropriate boxes to show which employee classes are eligible (assuming age, service, or other requirements have been met). (*Check as many as apply. Use the extra spaces to designate classes not shown.*)

A	B	C
10 ☐ Professors	17 ☐ Adm. Officers	23 ☐ Clerical & Secretarial
11 ☐ Assoc. Profs.	18 ☐ Adm. Staff	
12 ☐ Ass't. Profs.	19 ☐ Other Professional or Research	24 ☐ Maintenance & Service
13 ☐ Instrs.		
14 ☐ _____	20 ☐ _____	25 ☐ _____
15 ☐ _____	21 ☐ _____	26 ☐ _____

If you answered NO in all three columns, please turn to Section VI.

Please complete the following questions for the columns checked YES in question 1:

2. Please check the type(s) of short-term disability income plan(s) covering employees of your institution: (*Check as many as apply.*)

	A	B	C
a. INFORMAL ("*each case on its merits*") salary continuation plan	27–1 ☐	28–1 ☐	29–1 ☐
b. FORMAL sick pay (or salary continuation) plan *Formal—i.e., amount, duration, and conditions of sick pay (or salary continuation) are stated for staff members in printed form.*	30–1 ☐	31–1 ☐	32–1 ☐
c. State Workmen's Compensation coverage	33–1 ☐	34–1 ☐	35–1 ☐
d. Group insurance plan (other than Workmen's Compensation) providing short-term disability income	36–1 ☐	37–1 ☐	38–1 ☐
e. Other: (*Specify*)_____	39–1 ☐	40–1 ☐	41–1 ☐

In answering the remaining questions in this section do not include provisions of Workmen's Compensation. If you checked *only* 2c please turn to Section VI.

SECTION V—SHORT-TERM DISABILITY INCOME (SICK PAY) PROVISIONS (*Continued*)

	A FACULTY	B ADMINISTRATIVE STAFF/OTHER PROFESSIONAL	C OTHER EMPLOYEES

3. Must an employee meet a years of service and/or an age requirement to be eligible for the short-term disability income plan?

    IF YES, please state the requirement:

        a. Years of service

A	B	C
42–1 ☐ YES –2 ☐ NO	43–1 ☐ YES –2 ☐ NO	44–1 ☐ YES –2 ☐ NO
_____ (YEARS) 45–46	_____ (YEARS) 47–48	_____ (YEARS) 49–50

        b. Age

A	B	C
_____ (AGE) 51–52	_____ (AGE) 53–54	_____ (AGE) 55–56

4. Does the duration of disability payments vary according to length of service?

    IF YES, what period of service is required in order to be eligible for the maximum duration of disability payments? (*Give "cumulative days" formula, if any.*)

A	B	C
57–1 ☐ YES –2 ☐ NO	58–1 ☐ YES –2 ☐ NO	59–1 ☐ YES –2 ☐ NO
_____ (SERVICE) 60–61	_____ (SERVICE) 62–63	_____ (SERVICE) 64–65

5. Please indicate the benefit amount (or portion of salary) that is paid during disability, and the duration of the payments:

A	B	C
AMOUNT: 66–	AMOUNT: 67–	AMOUNT: 68–
DURATION: 69–70	DURATION: 71–72	DURATION: 73–74

6. Does the institution (or State) pay toward the cost of the employee's short-term disability coverage?

A	B	C
75–1 ☐ YES –2 ☐ NO	76–1 ☐ YES –2 ☐ NO	77–1 ☐ YES –2 ☐ NO

7. Does the employee pay toward the cost of his short-term disability coverage?

A	B	C
78–1 ☐ YES –2 ☐ NO	79–1 ☐ YES –2 ☐ NO	80–1 ☐ YES –2 ☐ NO

    REMARKS: (*Include any remarks concerning answers to questions, general comments, etc.*)

PLEASE ENCLOSE A COPY OF THE BOOKLET OR FOLDER DESCRIBING YOUR SHORT-TERM SICK PAY, SALARY CONTINUATION, OR DISABILITY INSURANCE PLAN

SECTION VI—LONG-TERM TOTAL DISABILITY INCOME PLAN

This section covers long-term disability income plans providing benefits that begin after a specified period of continuous total disability, such as three to six months or so. Long-term disability income usually starts after benefits under a short-term disability plan (covered in Section V) have terminated.

CARD 0
2–8

Long-term total disability income plan information is sought for the three general employee categories indicated in column headings A, B, and C.

	A	B	C
	FACULTY	ADMINISTRATIVE STAFF/OTHER PROFESSIONAL	OTHER EMPLOYEES

1. Does your institution have a long-term total disability income plan(s)?

A	B	C
9–1 ☐ YES –2 ☐ NO	16–1 ☐ YES –2 ☐ NO	22–1 ☐ YES –2 ☐ NO

In each column answered YES, please check the appropriate boxes to show which employee classes are eligible (assuming age, service, or other requirements have been met). (*Check as many as apply. Use the extra spaces to designate classes not shown.*)

A	B	C
10 ☐ Professors	17 ☐ Adm. Officers	23 ☐ Clerical & Secretarial
11 ☐ Assoc. Profs.	18 ☐ Adm. Staff	
12 ☐ Ass't. Profs.	19 ☐ Other Profes-	24 ☐ Maintenance & Service
13 ☐ Instrs.	sional or Research	
14 ☐ _____	20 ☐ _____	25 ☐ _____
15 ☐ _____	21 ☐ _____	26 ☐ _____

If you answered NO in all three columns, this is the last question to answer. Thank you for your cooperation.

Please complete the following questions for the columns checked YES in question 1:

2. Please check the type(s) of long-term total disability income plan(s) covering employees of your institution. (*Check as many as apply in each of the three employee classifications.*)

a. Disability provision of a state employee or state teacher retirement system

A	B	C
27–1 ☐	28–1 ☐	29–1 ☐

b. Group insurance plan for long-term total disability (*Including TIAA plans*)

A	B	C
30–1 ☐	31–1 ☐	32–1 ☐

c. Self-administered plan for long-term total disability

A	B	C
33–1 ☐	34–1 ☐	35–1 ☐

d. Other: (*Specify*)_____

A	B	C
36–1 ☐	37–1 ☐	38–1 ☐

3. If plan is insured or self-administered, does it provide for continuation of contributions to the retirement annuity during disability?

A	B	C
39–1 ☐ YES –2 ☐ NO	40–1 ☐ YES 2– ☐ NO	41–1 ☐ YES –2 ☐ NO

4. Does the institution (or State) pay toward the cost of employee coverage?

A	B	C
42–1 ☐ YES –2 ☐ NO	43–1 ☐ YES –2 ☐ NO	44–1 ☐ YES –2 ☐ NO

5. Does the employee pay toward the cost of his coverage?

A	B	C
45–1 ☐ YES –2 ☐ NO	46–1 ☐ YES –2 ☐ NO	47–1 ☐ YES –2 ☐ NO

SECTION VI—LONG-TERM TOTAL DISABILITY INCOME PLAN (Continued)

	A	B	C
	FACULTY	ADMINISTRATIVE STAFF/OTHER PROFESSIONAL	OTHER EMPLOYEES

6. Please indicate the waiting period, if any, before a new employee is eligible for participation in the plan. (Check one.)

	A	B	C
No waiting period	48–1 ☐	49–1 ☐	50–1 ☐
Less than one year	–2 ☐	–2 ☐	–2 ☐
One year	–3 ☐	–3 ☐	–3 ☐
More than one year (Please give nearest number of years.)	–4 ☐	–4 ☐	–4 ☐
	(YEARS) 51–52	(YEARS) 53–54	(YEARS) 55–56

If your long-term disability income plan is with TIAA please check here: (For column(s) checked this is the last question. Thank you for your cooperation.)

	A	B	C
	57–1 ☐	58–1 ☐	59–1 ☐

7. Must a person who is already a plan participant meet a years of service and/or an age requirement before he becomes eligible to receive disability income if disabled?

	A	B	C
	60–1 ☐ YES	61–1 ☐ YES	62–1 ☐ YES
	–2 ☐ NO	–2 ☐ NO	–2 ☐ NO

IF YES, please state the requirement:

    a. Years of service

	A	B	C
	(YEARS) 63–64	(YEARS) 65–66	(YEARS) 67–68

    b. Age

	A	B	C
	(AGE) 69–70	(AGE) 71–72	(AGE) 73–74

8. How long must the individual be totally disabled before total disability income begins? (Give period in months.)

	A	B	C
	(MONTHS) 75–76	(MONTHS) 77–78	(MONTHS) 79–80

CARD X
2–8

9. What is the maximum period during which total disability income is paid to the totally disabled employee? (Check one.)

	A	B	C
To age 65	9–1 ☐	10–1 ☐	11–1 ☐
Stated period of time (State nearest years.)	–2 ☐	–2 ☐	–2 ☐
	(YEARS) 12–13	(YEARS) 14–15	(YEARS) 16–17
Other: (Specify)_____	–3 ☐	–3 ☐	–3 ☐

SECTION VI—LONG-TERM TOTAL DISABILITY INCOME PLAN (*Continued*)

	A	B	C
	FACULTY	ADMINISTRATIVE STAFF/OTHER PROFESSIONAL	OTHER EMPLOYEES

10. Please check whether total disability income is payable for work-connected and/or non-work-connected disabilities: (*Check one or both.*)

      Payable for work-connected disabilities   18–1 ☐   19–1 ☐   20–1 ☐

      Payable for disabilities not connected with an individual's work   21–1 ☐   22–1 ☐   23–1 ☐

11. What is the income benefit under the total disability income plan? (*Give amount or formula.*)

    24–1   25–1   26–1

    REMARKS: (*Include any remarks concerning answers to questions, general comments, etc.*)

27–80 BL

PLEASE ENCLOSE A COPY OF THE BOOKLET OR FOLDER DESCRIBING YOUR LONG-TERM TOTAL DISABILITY INCOME PLAN (EXCEPT FOR TIAA PLANS)

THANK YOU FOR YOUR COOPERATION

Appendix 2

INDEX TO
BENEFIT PLAN COVERAGE

This appendix lists the benefit plans reported by the responding institutions for each major employee category: faculty, administrative, and clerical-service. The institutions appear alphabetically by state.

The entries in each of the six columns show, left to right, the employee categories eligible for the plan: 1 indicates faculty; 2, administrative and other professionals; and 3, clerical-service employees. If a benefit plan does not cover an employee category, 0 appears in the place of a 1, 2, or 3.

KEY:

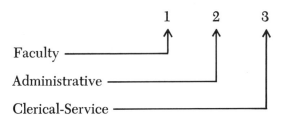

0 indicates employee category not covered.

INSTITUTION	RETIREMENT	LIFE INSURANCE	BASIC HOSPITAL-SURGICAL-MEDICAL	MAJOR MEDICAL	SHORT-TERM DISABILITY	LONG-TERM DISABILITY
	1	2	3	4	5	6
ALABAMA						
Alabama A & M College	123	000	123	000	000	000
Alabama College	123	123	123	123	123	123
Auburn U	123	123	123	123	123	123
Alabama State College	123	000	123	000	123	000
Athens College	120	120	123	123	000	000
Birmingham Southern College	123	123	123	123	123	123
Florence State College	123	120	123	123	000	123
Samford U	123	123	000	123	123	123
Huntingdon College	123	000	123	123	000	000
Jacksonville State U	120	000	123	123	000	120
Judson College	120	123	123	000	123	000
Livingston State College	123	123	123	123	123	123
Mobile College	120	123	123	123	123	000
Oakwood College	123	000	123	000	000	000
St Bernard College	123	000	000	000	000	000
Spring Hill College	120	123	123	123	123	123
Troy State College	123	123	123	123	123	120
Tuskegee Institute	123	123	123	000	123	000
U of Alabama Main Campus	123	123	123	123	123	123
U of South Alabama	123	123	000	123	000	123
ALASKA						
Alaska Methodist U	120	000	123	123	000	000
U of Alaska Main Campus	123	000	123	123	023	000
ARIZONA						
Amer Inst Foreign Trade	123	123	123	123	123	000
Northern Arizona U	123	123	123	123	123	000
Arizona State U	123	123	123	123	123	123
Grand Canyon College	123	123	000	123	123	123
U of Arizona	123	123	123	123	123	123
ARKANSAS						
Arkansas A & M College	123	123	123	000	123	123
Arkansas Baptist College	000	000	000	000	000	000
Arkansas College	123	123	123	123	123	123
Arkansas Polytech College	123	000	123	123	000	000
Arkansas State U Main Campus	123	120	123	120	000	000
Arkansas State Tchrs College	123	000	123	123	000	000
College of the Ozarks	123	123	123	123	123	123
Harding College Main Campus	120	120	000	123	000	120
Henderson State Tchrs College	123	123	123	123	123	123
Hendrix College	123	123	000	123	120	123
John Brown U	123	000	123	123	000	123
Little Rock U	120	123	123	123	123	123
Southern State College	123	123	123	123	123	123
U of Arkansas	123	123	000	123	123	123

Key: 1–Faculty, 2–Administrative, 3–Clerical-Service. 0 indicates no coverage.

INSTITUTION	RETIREMENT	LIFE INSURANCE	BASIC HOSPITAL-SURGICAL-MEDICAL	MAJOR MEDICAL	SHORT-TERM DISABILITY	LONG-TERM DISABILITY
	1	2	3	4	5	6
CALIFORNIA						
California St Col Hayward	123	123	123	123	123	123
Art Center Col of Design	123	000	123	123	000	000
Azusa Pacific College	120	120	123	123	123	123
Bethany Bible College	123	000	123	123	123	000
Biola College Main Campus	123	123	123	123	123	000
Calif Baptist Theol Sem	120	000	123	000	123	000
California Baptist College	123	123	123	123	123	000
Calif Col Arts & Craft	123	000	123	000	123	123
California Podiatry College	000	000	000	000	000	000
California Inst of Tech	123	123	123	123	000	123
California Lutheran College	123	120	123	123	000	120
California Maritime Acad	123	123	123	123	123	123
Calif St Col Dominguez Hls	123	123	123	123	123	123
Calif St Col San Bernardino	123	123	123	123	123	123
Calif St Poly San Luis Ob	123	123	123	123	123	123
Calif St Poly Col Pomona	123	123	123	123	123	123
U S International U	120	000	123	123	123	123
Chapman College	123	000	123	123	000	123
Chico State College	123	123	123	123	123	123
Calif Inst of the Arts	000	123	000	123	123	000
Claremont Grad Sch & U Ctr	120	123	123	123	000	123
Claremont Mens College	120	123	123	123	000	123
College of the Holy Names	100	000	123	000	123	000
Loma Linda U All Campuses	123	000	123	000	123	000
College of Our Lady of Mercy	000	000	123	000	000	000
U of the Pacific	123	123	123	123	123	123
Fresno St Col Main Campus	123	123	123	123	123	123
Fuller Theol Seminary	120	000	123	000	123	000
Pepperdine College	120	123	123	123	023	123
Golden Gate Bapt Theol Sem	120	120	120	000	123	120
Harvey Mudd College	120	123	123	123	000	123
Humboldt State College	123	123	123	123	123	123
Immaculate Heart College	120	000	123	123	123	123
La Verne College	123	123	123	123	123	123
Calif State Col Long Bch	123	123	123	123	123	123
L A Bapt Col & Theol Sem	000	000	123	123	123	000
L A College Optometry	123	123	123	123	123	123
Otis Art Inst L A Cnty	123	000	123	123	123	000
Calif State College L A	123	123	123	123	123	123
Loyola U of Los Angeles	123	120	123	120	123	123
Marymount College	123	000	123	123	123	123
Menlo College	123	123	123	123	123	123
Mills College	123	000	000	123	123	123
Monterey Inst Foreign Stud	120	120	123	123	000	000
Mount St Marys College	123	000	123	123	123	123
Northrop Inst of Tech	123	123	000	123	123	123
Occidental College	123	123	123	123	123	120
Calif St College Fullerton	123	123	123	123	123	123
Pacific Christian College	120	120	120	120	123	000
Pacific College	120	120	000	000	000	000
Pacific Oaks College	123	000	123	120	000	000
Pacific Sch of Religion	123	000	123	123	000	000
Pasadena College	120	120	123	123	000	000
Pasadena Playhs Col Thr Art	000	000	123	000	123	000

Key: 1–Faculty, 2–Administrative, 3–Clerical-Service. 0 indicates no coverage.

INSTITUTION	RETIREMENT	LIFE INSURANCE	BASIC HOSPITAL- SURGICAL- MEDICAL	MAJOR MEDICAL	SHORT- TERM DISABILITY	LONG- TERM DISABILITY
	1	2	3	4	5	6
CALIFORNIA (cont'd)						
Pitzer College	120	123	123	123	000	123
Pomona College	120	123	123	123	000	123
Sacramento State College	123	123	123	123	123	123
St Marys Col California	120	000	123	000	123	000
U of San Diego Col for Women	100	000	123	123	000	000
San Diego St Col Main Campus	123	123	123	123	123	123
San Fernando Vly St College	123	123	123	123	123	123
San Francisco State College	123	123	123	123	123	123
San Jose Bible College	120	000	123	000	123	000
San Jose State College	123	123	123	123	123	123
Scripps College	120	123	123	123	000	123
Sonoma State College	123	123	123	123	123	123
Southern California College	123	123	123	123	000	000
School of Theol at Claremont	120	123	123	123	123	000
Stanford U	123	123	123	123	123	123
Stanislaus State College	123	123	123	123	123	123
Starr King Sch Ministry	100	000	000	000	000	000
U of Cal Berkeley	123	123	123	123	123	123
U of Cal College Medicine	123	123	123	123	123	123
U of Cal Davis	123	123	123	123	123	123
U of Cal Hastings Col Law	123	123	123	123	123	123
U of Cal Irvine	123	123	123	123	123	123
U of Cal San Diego	123	123	123	123	123	123
U of Cal Los Angeles	123	123	123	123	123	123
U of Cal Riverside	123	123	123	123	123	123
U of Cal San Francisco	123	123	123	123	123	123
U of Cal Santa Cruz	123	123	123	123	123	123
U of Cal Santa Barbara	123	123	123	123	123	123
U of Redlands	123	123	123	123	123	123
U of San Diego College for Men	123	123	123	123	000	000
U of San Francisco	120	123	123	123	123	123
U of Southern California	123	123	123	123	123	123
West Coast U Main Campus	000	123	123	123	123	000
Wstrn Bapt Col & Theo Sem	000	000	123	123	123	000
Westmont College	123	123	000	123	123	123
Whittier College	120	000	123	123	123	000
COLORADO						
Adams State College	123	120	123	123	123	000
Colorado College	123	123	000	123	123	123
Colorado School of Mines	123	123	123	123	123	000
Colorado State College	123	120	123	123	123	123
Colorado State U	123	123	123	003	123	000
Fort Lewis College	123	000	123	003	000	000
Iliff School of Theology	120	000	123	123	123	123
Loretto Heights College	120	123	123	123	123	120
Southern Colorado St College	123	120	123	123	000	000
U of Colorado	123	123	023	123	123	123
U of Denver	123	123	123	123	123	120
Wstrn St College Colorado	123	120	123	123	123	000

Key: 1–Faculty, 2–Administrative, 3–Clerical-Service. 0 indicates no coverage.

INSTITUTION	RETIREMENT	LIFE INSURANCE	BASIC HOSPITAL-SURGICAL-MEDICAL	MAJOR MEDICAL	SHORT-TERM DISABILITY	LONG-TERM DISABILITY
	1	2	3	4	5	6
CONNECTICUT						
Albertus Magnus College	100	000	123	000	000	000
Annhurst College	000	123	123	123	123	000
Central Conn State College	123	123	123	123	123	123
Connecticut College	123	123	123	123	123	123
Western Conn State College	123	123	123	123	123	123
Fairfield U	120	120	123	120	000	000
Hartford Sem Foundation	123	123	123	123	000	123
Holy Apostles Seminary	000	000	123	000	123	000
New Haven College	123	123	123	123	000	000
Quinnipiac College	120	120	123	120	120	000
Sacred Heart U	123	120	123	123	123	120
St Joseph College	123	000	123	000	000	000
Southern Conn State College	123	123	123	123	123	123
Trinity College	123	123	123	123	000	123
U of Bridgeport	123	123	123	123	123	123
U of Connecticut	123	123	123	123	000	123
U of Hartford	123	123	123	123	000	123
Wesleyan U	123	123	123	123	123	000
Eastern Conn State College	123	123	123	123	123	123
Yale U	123	123	123	123	123	000
DELAWARE						
Delaware State College	123	000	123	000	123	000
U of Delaware	123	123	123	120	123	123
DISTRICT OF COLUMBIA						
American U	123	123	123	123	123	123
Catholic U of America	123	123	123	000	123	000
Dunbarton Col Holy Cross	120	123	123	000	123	000
Gallaudet College	123	123	123	000	123	000
George Washington U	123	123	123	123	123	123
Howard U	123	123	123	123	123	000
Southeastern U	000	020	020	020	000	000
Trinity College	123	000	123	120	123	120
Wesley Theological Sem	123	000	123	123	123	000
FLORIDA						
Barry College	123	000	123	000	000	000
Bethune Cookman College	123	123	123	123	123	000
Biscayne College	123	123	123	123	123	000
Florida Inst of Tech	000	123	123	123	123	000
Embry-Riddle Aero Inst	120	123	000	123	123	123
Florida A & M U	123	123	123	000	123	123
Florida Atlantic U	123	000	123	123	000	000
Florida Presbyterian College	123	123	123	123	000	123
Florida Southern College	120	120	123	123	123	000
Florida State U	123	123	123	123	123	123
Jacksonville U	123	120	123	120	123	120
New College	120	123	123	123	123	000
Rollins College	123	123	123	123	123	123

Key: 1–Faculty, 2–Administrative, 3–Clerical-Service. 0 indicates no coverage.

INSTITUTION	RETIREMENT	LIFE INSURANCE	BASIC HOSPITAL-SURGICAL-MEDICAL	MAJOR MEDICAL	SHORT-TERM DISABILITY	LONG-TERM DISABILITY
	1	2	3	4	5	6
FLORIDA (cont'd)						
Southeastern Bible College	123	000	123	123	123	000
Stetson U	120	123	123	123	123	120
U of Florida	123	123	123	123	123	123
U of Miami	123	123	123	123	123	123
U of South Florida	123	123	123	123	000	000
U of Tampa	123	123	123	123	000	120
GEORGIA						
Albany State College	123	123	123	123	123	123
Armstrong State College	123	123	000	123	000	000
Atlanta U	123	123	123	123	000	000
Augusta College	123	123	123	123	000	000
Berry College	123	123	123	123	123	120
Clark College	123	123	123	123	000	000
Emory U	123	123	123	120	123	120
Georgia Inst Technology	123	123	123	123	123	123
Georgia Southwestern College	123	123	123	123	000	000
Georgia State College	123	123	123	123	123	123
Georgia Southern College	123	123	123	123	123	000
Interdenominatnl Theo Ctr	123	123	123	123	000	123
La Grange College	123	123	123	123	000	000
Medical College of Georgia	123	123	123	123	000	123
Mercer U	123	123	123	123	123	000
North Georgia College	123	123	123	123	123	123
Oglethorpe College	120	123	123	123	000	000
Paine College	123	123	123	123	123	123
Piedmont College	120	120	123	000	123	000
Savannah State College	123	123	123	123	123	123
Shorter College	120	123	123	000	000	000
Spelman College	123	123	123	123	000	000
Tift College	120	000	123	123	000	000
U of Georgia	123	123	123	123	123	123
Valdosta State College	123	123	123	123	000	123
Wesleyan College	123	000	123	123	123	000
West Georgia College	123	123	123	123	123	123
HAWAII						
Chaminade Col	123	123	123	123	123	000
Church College of Hawaii	123	123	123	123	000	000
U of Hawaii	123	123	123	123	123	000
IDAHO						
Boise College	123	000	123	123	123	123
Idaho State U	123	123	123	123	123	123
Northwest Nazarene College	123	123	123	123	123	123
U of Idaho	123	123	000	123	000	000

Key: 1–Faculty, 2–Administrative, 3–Clerical-Service. 0 indicates no coverage.

INSTITUTION	RETIREMENT	LIFE INSURANCE	BASIC HOSPITAL-SURGICAL-MEDICAL	MAJOR MEDICAL	SHORT-TERM DISABILITY	LONG-TERM DISABILITY
	1	2	3	4	5	6
ILLINOIS						
Aero-Space Institute	000	000	000	000	000	000
Augustana College	123	123	123	123	123	120
Aurora College	123	123	123	123	123	123
Bethany Theological Sem	120	123	123	123	123	120
Blackburn College	120	000	000	000	000	123
Bradley U	123	123	123	123	123	120
Chicago Col of Osteopathy	123	123	123	123	123	120
Chicago Conservatory College	000	123	123	000	000	000
Chicago Kent College of Law	123	123	000	123	000	123
Illinois Tchrs Col Chgo South	123	000	123	123	123	123
Illinois Tchrs Col Chgo North	123	123	123	123	123	123
Chicago Technical College	123	123	123	000	123	000
Chicago Theological Sem	123	123	000	123	123	120
College of Jewish Studies	123	123	123	123	000	000
Columbia College	000	123	123	123	000	000
Concordia Teachers College	123	123	000	123	123	123
DePaul U	123	123	123	123	123	123
Eastern Illinois U	123	123	123	123	123	123
Elmhurst College	123	123	123	123	123	123
Eureka College	123	000	123	123	123	000
Garrett Biblical Inst	123	000	123	123	000	123
George Williams College	123	123	123	123	123	000
Greenville College	123	123	123	123	123	123
Illinois College	120	123	123	120	000	120
Illinois College Optometry	123	123	123	123	123	123
Illinois Inst of Tech	123	123	123	123	000	000
Illinois State U	123	000	123	123	123	123
Illinois Wesleyan U	123	123	003	123	123	123
Knox College	123	123	000	123	123	123
Lake Forest College	123	123	123	123	120	120
Lewis College	120	123	123	000	000	000
Lincoln Christian College	123	123	123	123	123	000
Loyola U	123	123	123	123	123	123
MacMurray College	120	000	123	120	000	120
Maryknoll Seminary	103	103	103	103	000	000
McCormick Theol Sem	123	123	123	120	000	120
McKendree College	120	000	123	123	000	000
Meadville Theol School	120	123	123	123	000	123
Millikin U	123	123	123	123	123	120
Monmouth College	123	123	123	123	123	000
Mundelein College	120	123	123	123	123	000
National College of Educ	123	123	123	123	123	123
North Central College	123	123	123	123	123	123
Northern Illinois U	123	123	123	123	123	123
North Park Col & Theol Sem	123	123	123	123	000	000
Northwestern U	123	123	123	120	123	123
Olivet Nazarene College	123	123	123	123	000	000
Principia College	123	123	000	000	000	000
Quincy College	120	123	123	123	000	000
Rockford College	120	123	123	123	123	123
Roosevelt U	123	123	123	123	000	123
Rosary College	123	000	123	000	123	000
St Procopius College	123	123	123	123	123	000
St Xavier College	123	123	123	123	000	000

Key: 1–Faculty, 2–Administrative, 3–Clerical-Service. 0 indicates no coverage.

INSTITUTION	RETIREMENT	LIFE INSURANCE	BASIC HOSPITAL-SURGICAL-MEDICAL	MAJOR MEDICAL	SHORT-TERM DISABILITY	LONG-TERM DISABILITY
	1	2	3	4	5	6
ILLINOIS (cont'd)						
Seabury Wstrn Theol Sem	100	000	123	100	000	000
Sherwood Music School	000	000	123	000	000	000
Shimer College	123	123	123	123	123	123
Southern Illinois U	123	123	123	123	123	123
Trinity College	100	100	123	000	123	000
U of Chicago	123	123	123	123	123	123
U of Illinois All Campuses	123	123	123	123	123	123
Western Illinois U	123	123	123	123	123	123
Wheaton College	123	123	123	123	123	123
INDIANA						
Anderson College	123	123	123	120	123	120
Ball State U	123	123	123	123	123	123
Bethel College	123	000	123	000	123	000
Butler U	123	123	123	123	123	123
Christian Theological Sem	123	000	000	123	123	000
DePauw U	123	123	123	123	123	123
Earlham College	123	000	123	123	123	120
U of Evansville	123	123	123	120	123	120
Franklin College of Indiana	120	000	123	123	123	123
Goshen College & Biblical Sem	120	120	123	123	123	120
Grace Theol Sem & College	123	123	123	123	123	123
Hanover College	123	000	123	120	000	120
Indiana Central College	123	123	123	123	123	123
Indiana State U	123	123	123	123	123	120
Indiana Inst of Tech	123	123	123	123	123	000
Indiana U	123	123	123	123	123	123
Manchester College	123	123	123	123	123	120
Marian Col Indianapolis	123	000	123	000	123	000
Marion College Marion	123	000	123	123	000	123
Mennonite Biblical Sem	123	123	123	000	123	000
Oakland City College	120	000	123	000	123	000
Purdue U	123	123	003	123	123	123
Rose Polytechnic Inst	123	123	123	123	000	000
St Benedict College	000	000	000	000	000	000
St Francis College	100	123	123	123	123	000
St Joseph Col Main Campus	120	123	123	000	123	123
St Marys College	123	123	123	123	000	023
St Mary of the Woods College	100	000	000	000	123	000
St Meinrad Seminary	000	123	123	000	123	000
Taylor U	123	123	123	123	123	000
Tri-State College	120	123	123	123	123	000
U of Notre Dame	123	123	123	123	123	000
Valparaiso U	123	123	123	123	123	120
Wabash College	123	123	123	123	123	123
IOWA						
Briar Cliff College	123	000	123	000	123	000
Buena Vista College	123	123	123	123	123	000
Central College	120	000	123	123	000	000
Vennard College	000	000	123	000	123	000

Key: 1–Faculty, 2–Administrative, 3–Clerical-Service. 0 indicates no coverage.

INSTITUTION	RETIREMENT	LIFE INSURANCE	BASIC HOSPITAL-SURGICAL-MEDICAL	MAJOR MEDICAL	SHORT-TERM DISABILITY	LONG-TERM DISABILITY
	1	2	3	4	5	6
IOWA (cont'd)						
Clarke College	100	000	123	123	000	000
Coe College	123	123	123	123	123	120
College Ost Med & Surg	120	123	123	000	123	000
Cornell College	123	123	123	123	123	123
Dordt College	123	123	123	123	000	123
Drake U	120	123	123	123	123	120
Graceland College	123	000	123	000	123	000
Grinnell College	120	123	123	123	123	120
U of Northern Iowa	123	123	123	000	123	123
Iowa State U of Sci & Tech	123	123	123	000	123	123
Iowa Wesleyan College	123	000	123	123	123	000
Loras College	123	123	123	123	000	123
Luther College	120	120	123	123	123	120
Morningside College	123	123	123	123	000	123
Mount Mercy College	123	000	123	000	123	000
Northwestern College	123	000	123	000	123	000
Parsons College	123	123	123	123	000	120
St Ambrose College	120	120	123	000	123	000
Simpson College	123	120	123	120	000	000
U of Iowa	123	123	123	123	123	123
U of Dubuque	120	123	123	123	123	000
Upper Iowa U	123	123	123	000	123	123
Wartburg College	123	000	123	123	123	123
Westmar College	120	123	123	123	123	000
William Penn College	000	123	123	000	000	000
KANSAS						
Baker U	120	123	123	120	123	000
Bethany College	120	123	123	123	000	000
Bethel College	120	123	123	123	123	000
College of Emporia	120	000	123	000	123	000
Ft Hays Kansas State College	123	120	123	123	000	000
Friends Bible College	000	000	123	000	000	000
Friends U	120	123	123	123	123	000
Kansas St Col Pittsburg	123	123	123	120	123	023
Kansas St Teachers College	123	000	123	123	123	023
Kansas St U Ag & App Sci	123	123	123	123	000	123
Kansas Wesleyan	123	120	123	000	123	000
Manhattan Bible College	100	000	123	123	000	000
Marymount College	123	000	123	000	000	000
McPherson College	123	123	123	123	123	123
Miltonvale Wesleyan College	123	000	123	123	123	000
Mt St Scholastica College	120	000	123	000	123	000
Ottawa U	120	000	123	123	123	000
Sacred Heart College	123	123	123	123	123	123
St Benedicts College	120	000	123	123	123	000
St Mary College	120	000	123	123	123	000
St Mary of the Plains College	120	123	123	000	003	000
Sterling College	120	120	123	123	123	000
Tabor College	120	120	120	000	000	000
U of Kansas	123	123	123	123	123	023
Wichita State U	123	123	123	123	000	003
Washburn U of Topeka	123	000	123	123	000	123

Key: 1–Faculty, 2–Administrative, 3–Clerical-Service. 0 indicates no coverage.

INSTITUTION	RETIREMENT	LIFE INSURANCE	BASIC HOSPITAL-SURGICAL-MEDICAL	MAJOR MEDICAL	SHORT-TERM DISABILITY	LONG-TERM DISABILITY
	1	2	3	4	5	6
KENTUCKY						
Asbury Theological Seminary	123	123	123	123	123	000
Bellarmine College	123	123	123	123	123	123
Berea College	123	123	123	123	000	000
Brescia College	123	000	123	000	123	000
Centre College of Kentucky	120	123	123	120	000	120
Eastern Kentucky U	123	123	123	000	123	123
Georgetown College	123	123	123	123	000	123
Kentucky State College	123	000	123	000	000	123
Kentucky Wesleyan College	123	123	123	123	000	000
Louisville Presb Theol Sem	123	000	123	000	123	000
Morehead State U	123	123	123	123	123	123
Murray State U	123	000	123	120	123	120
Catherine Spalding College	120	000	123	120	123	120
Pikeville College	123	000	123	000	000	000
Southern Baptist Theo Sem	123	123	123	123	123	123
Transylvania College	123	123	123	123	000	123
Union College	123	000	123	123	000	123
U of Kentucky Main Campus	123	123	123	123	123	120
U of Louisville	123	123	123	123	123	120
Ursuline College	123	000	123	000	000	000
Villa Madonna College	120	000	123	123	123	120
LOUISIANA						
Centenary College	123	123	123	123	123	120
Dillard U	123	123	123	123	123	120
F T Nicholls State College	123	123	123	123	123	000
Louisiana College	123	123	123	123	123	123
La St U Main Campus	123	123	123	123	000	123
La St U Medical Center	123	123	123	123	000	123
La St U at New Orleans	123	123	123	123	123	123
Loyola U	123	123	123	123	000	000
McNeese State College	123	123	123	123	123	123
Ntheast Louisiana St College	123	123	123	123	123	123
Nthwstrn St Col Louisiana	123	123	123	123	000	000
St Marys Dominican College	120	000	123	123	000	000
Southeastern Louisiana College	123	123	123	123	000	123
Tulane U of Louisiana	120	123	123	123	123	123
Xavier U	120	123	123	000	123	000
MAINE						
Aroostook State College	123	123	000	000	123	123
Bates College	120	000	123	000	123	000
Bowdoin College	123	123	123	120	000	120
Colby College	123	123	123	120	000	120
Farmington State College	123	123	000	000	123	123
Ft Kent State College	123	123	000	000	123	123
Gorham State College	123	123	000	000	123	123
Husson College	123	123	123	123	123	123
Nasson College	120	000	123	120	123	120
Ricker College	000	123	123	123	123	123
St Francis College	123	000	123	000	123	000

Key: 1–Faculty, 2–Administrative, 3–Clerical-Service. 0 indicates no coverage.

INSTITUTION	RETIREMENT	LIFE INSURANCE	BASIC HOSPITAL-SURGICAL-MEDICAL	MAJOR MEDICAL	SHORT-TERM DISABILITY	LONG-TERM DISABILITY
	1	2	3	4	5	6
MAINE (cont'd)						
Thomas College	123	123	123	123	123	000
U of Maine	123	123	123	123	123	123
Washington State College	123	123	000	000	123	123
Westbrook College	120	123	123	123	123	123
MARYLAND						
College of Notre Dame of Md	100	000	123	100	000	000
Goucher College	120	123	123	120	123	000
Hood College	123	123	123	123	123	123
Johns Hopkins U	123	123	123	123	123	123
Loyola College	120	120	123	123	000	000
Mount St Marys College	120	000	123	120	000	000
Peabody Cons of Music	123	000	123	000	000	000
St Johns College	123	123	123	123	000	123
St Joseph College	123	000	123	000	000	000
Bowie State College	123	000	123	000	123	000
Salisbury State College	123	000	123	000	123	123
Towson State College	123	000	123	000	000	123
U of Baltimore	123	123	123	123	123	000
U of Maryland	123	120	123	000	123	123
U of Maryland State College	123	123	123	000	123	000
Washington College	123	123	123	123	000	000
Western Maryland College	120	120	123	120	123	000
MASSACHUSETTS						
American Internatl College	123	123	123	123	123	123
Amherst College	123	123	123	123	123	123
Anna Maria College for Women	120	000	123	123	123	000
Assumption College	123	123	123	123	123	123
Babson Inst Bus Admin	123	123	123	123	123	120
Bentley College Acc & Fin	123	123	123	123	123	123
Berkshire Christian College	120	000	123	000	123	000
Boston College	123	120	123	123	123	120
Boston U	123	123	123	123	123	000
Brandeis U	123	123	123	123	123	120
Cardinal Cushing College	120	123	000	123	123	000
Clark U	123	123	123	000	123	000
College of the Holy Cross	123	123	123	123	123	100
College of Our Lady of Elms	100	000	103	000	103	000
Curry College	120	123	123	123	123	123
Eastern Nazarene College	123	123	123	000	000	000
Emerson College	123	000	123	123	123	123
Emmanuel College	120	000	000	120	000	000
Episcopal Theol School	123	123	123	123	000	000
Harvard U	123	123	000	123	123	120
Hebrew Tchrs College	123	000	123	123	000	000
Holy Cross Grk Orth Theo Sc	000	000	123	000	000	000
Lesley College	120	120	123	000	123	000
Lowell Technological Inst	123	123	000	123	123	123
Massachusetts College of Art	123	123	000	123	123	123
Massachusetts Inst of Tech	123	123	120	123	123	120

Key: 1–Faculty, 2–Administrative, 3–Clerical–Service. 0 indicates no coverage.

INSTITUTION	RETIREMENT	LIFE INSURANCE	BASIC HOSPITAL-SURGICAL-MEDICAL	MAJOR MEDICAL	SHORT-TERM DISABILITY	LONG-TERM DISABILITY
	1	2	3	4	5	6
MASSACHUSETTS (cont'd)						
Massachusetts Maritime Acad	123	123	000	123	123	123
Merrimack College	123	123	123	123	000	123
Mount Holyoke College	123	123	123	123	123	120
New England Cons of Music	120	000	123	123	123	000
Newton College Sacred Heart	123	000	000	123	000	000
Nichols College of Bus Adm	123	123	123	123	123	120
Northeastern U	123	123	123	123	123	123
Regis College	123	123	123	123	000	000
Simmons College	123	123	123	123	123	000
Smith College	123	123	000	123	123	000
Southeastern Mass Tech Inst	123	123	123	000	123	123
Springfield College	123	123	123	123	123	120
State College at Bridgewater	123	123	000	123	123	123
State College at Fitchburg	123	123	000	123	123	123
State College at Framingham	123	123	000	123	123	123
State College at Lowell	123	123	000	123	123	123
State College at North Adams	123	123	000	123	123	123
State College at Salem	123	123	000	123	123	123
State College at Westfield	123	123	000	123	123	123
State College at Worcester	123	123	000	123	123	123
State College at Boston	123	123	000	123	123	123
Stonehill College	123	120	123	123	123	123
Suffolk U	123	123	123	123	123	123
Tufts U	123	123	123	123	123	000
U of Mass All Campuses	123	123	123	123	000	123
Wellesley College	123	120	123	123	000	120
Western New England College	123	123	123	123	123	000
Wheaton College	123	123	123	123	123	123
Wheelock College	123	000	123	000	123	120
Williams College	123	123	003	123	123	123
Worcester Poly Inst	123	123	123	123	123	000
MICHIGAN						
Adrian College	120	120	123	000	123	120
Albion College	123	123	123	000	123	120
Alma College	120	123	123	120	123	000
Aquinas College	123	100	123	123	100	100
Calvin College	123	123	123	123	123	120
Central Michigan U	123	123	123	123	123	123
Cranbrook	123	123	123	123	123	000
Detroit Bible College	123	000	123	000	000	000
Detroit College of Law	100	123	123	000	000	000
Detroit Inst of Tech	120	000	123	123	123	123
Eastern Michigan U	123	123	123	123	123	123
Ferris State College	123	123	123	000	123	123
Grace Bible College	000	123	123	123	123	000
Grand Rapids Bapt Col & Sem	000	000	123	000	123	000
Grand Valley State College	123	123	123	123	123	120
Hillsdale College	120	123	123	000	123	000
Hope College	120	000	123	123	123	000
Kalamazoo College	120	123	123	123	123	120
Lawrence Inst Technol	123	123	123	123	000	000
Mackinac College	123	000	123	123	123	120

Key: 1–Faculty, 2–Administrative, 3–Clerical-Service. 0 indicates no coverage.

INSTITUTION	RETIREMENT 1	LIFE INSURANCE 2	BASIC HOSPITAL- SURGICAL- MEDICAL 3	MAJOR MEDICAL 4	SHORT- TERM DISABILITY 5	LONG- TERM DISABILITY 6
MICHIGAN (cont'd)						
Marygrove College	123	000	123	000	123	000
Mercy College of Detroit	123	000	000	000	123	000
Merrill Palmer Institute	123	003	123	120	123	000
Michigan Tech U Main Campus	123	123	123	123	123	000
Michigan State U Main Campus	123	123	123	120	123	120
Northern Michigan U	123	123	123	000	123	000
Olivet College	123	123	123	000	123	000
Owosso College	120	000	123	000	000	000
Sacred Heart Seminary	123	000	123	000	123	000
Saginaw Valley State College	123	123	123	123	123	000
Spring Arbor College	123	123	123	123	123	123
U of Detroit	123	123	123	123	123	000
U of Michigan	123	123	123	120	123	123
Wayne State U	123	123	123	123	123	123
Western Michigan U	123	123	123	123	123	123
Western Theological Seminary	123	123	000	123	123	123
MINNESOTA						
Augsburg College	123	123	123	123	123	120
Bemidji State College	123	123	123	123	000	000
Bethany Luth Col & Theo Sem	123	123	123	123	000	000
Bethel College & Seminary	123	000	123	000	123	000
Carleton College	123	123	123	123	000	123
College of St Benedict	123	123	123	120	000	000
College of St Catherine	123	000	123	123	123	000
College of St Scholastica	123	123	123	000	000	000
College of St Thomas	120	123	123	123	123	000
Concordia College Moorhead	123	123	123	000	123	123
Concordia College St Paul	123	000	000	123	123	123
Gustavus Adolphus College	120	120	123	123	000	120
Hamline U	120	123	123	120	123	120
Macalester College	123	123	123	123	123	000
Mankato State College	123	123	123	123	000	000
Minneapolis School of Art	123	000	123	123	123	000
Minnesota Bible College	000	000	123	123	123	000
Moorhead State College	123	123	123	123	000	000
St Cloud State College	123	123	123	123	000	000
St Johns U	123	123	123	123	123	120
St Marys College	123	000	123	000	123	000
St Olaf College	120	120	123	123	123	120
St Paul Bible College	123	000	123	123	000	000
St Paul Seminary	000	000	000	000	000	000
U of Minn All Campuses	123	123	123	123	123	123
Winona State College	123	123	123	123	123	123
MISSISSIPPI						
Alcorn A & M College	123	123	123	123	123	000
Belhaven College	120	000	123	123	000	000
Millsaps College	120	123	123	123	123	120
Mississippi College	123	123	123	123	123	123
Miss State College for Women	123	123	123	123	123	123

Key: 1–Faculty, 2–Administrative, 3–Clerical-Service. 0 indicates no coverage.

INSTITUTION	RETIREMENT	LIFE INSURANCE	BASIC HOSPITAL-SURGICAL-MEDICAL	MAJOR MEDICAL	SHORT-TERM DISABILITY	LONG-TERM DISABILITY
	1	2	3	4	5	6
MISSISSIPPI (cont'd)						
Mississippi State U	123	123	123	123	123	000
Miss Valley State College	123	123	123	123	123	123
Rust College	123	123	123	123	000	000
Tougaloo College	123	123	123	123	123	000
U of Mississippi Main Campus	123	123	123	123	123	123
William Carey College	123	000	123	123	000	000
MISSOURI						
Central Bible College	120	123	123	000	123	000
Central Missouri State College	123	000	123	123	000	123
Avila College	123	123	123	123	123	000
Immac Conception Seminary	000	000	123	000	000	000
Concordia Seminary	123	000	000	123	123	123
Culver Stockton College	120	003	123	123	123	000
Drury College	120	000	123	123	123	000
Eden Theological Seminary	123	000	123	000	123	000
Fontbonne College	120	123	123	123	123	000
Harris Teachers College	123	000	000	000	123	000
Kansas City Art Institute	120	000	123	000	000	000
Calvary Bible College	000	000	123	123	123	000
Kansas City Col Osteopathy	120	000	123	000	120	120
Kirksville Col Osteopathy	123	123	000	123	123	120
Lincoln U	123	123	123	123	000	123
Lindenwood College	120	023	123	123	000	000
Marillac College	123	123	123	123	123	000
Maryville College Sacred Heart	123	123	123	123	000	000
Missouri School of Religion	123	123	123	123	000	000
Missouri Valley College	120	120	123	120	123	120
Northeast Missouri St Tchrs Col	123	000	123	000	123	000
Northwest Missouri St College	123	000	123	000	123	123
Park College	120	000	123	123	123	123
Rockhurst College	120	123	123	123	123	123
St Louis College of Pharmacy	123	123	123	123	123	123
St Louis U	123	123	123	123	000	120
Southeast Missouri St College	123	000	123	123	123	123
Southwest Missouri St College	123	000	123	123	000	000
Stephens College	123	123	123	120	000	120
Tarkio College	123	123	000	123	123	123
U of Missouri All Campuses	123	123	000	123	123	123
Washington U	123	123	123	123	123	000
Webster College	120	123	000	123	000	000
Westminster College	123	123	123	123	123	000
William Woods College	123	123	123	123	123	123
MONTANA						
Carroll College	120	123	123	123	000	000
College of Great Falls	100	000	123	123	123	000
Eastern Montana College	123	000	123	000	000	000
Montana Col Minrl Sci & Tech	123	000	000	123	000	000
Montana State U	123	000	123	123	000	000
U of Montana	123	000	123	123	000	123

Key: 1–Faculty, 2–Administrative, 3–Clerical-Service. 0 indicates no coverage.

INSTITUTION	RETIREMENT	LIFE INSURANCE	BASIC HOSPITAL-SURGICAL-MEDICAL	MAJOR MEDICAL	SHORT-TERM DISABILITY	LONG-TERM DISABILITY
	1	2	3	4	5	6
MONTANA (cont'd)						
Northern Montana College	123	000	123	123	123	000
Rocky Mountain College	123	123	123	123	123	123
Western Montana College	123	000	123	000	123	000
NEBRASKA						
College of St Mary	000	000	123	000	123	000
Concordia Teachers College	123	000	000	123	123	123
Creighton U	123	123	123	123	123	123
Dana College	123	123	123	123	123	000
Doane College	120	123	123	123	000	000
Duchesne College Sacred Heart	123	123	123	000	000	000
Hastings College	120	120	123	000	123	000
Midland Lutheran College	123	123	123	000	123	000
Municipal U of Omaha	123	123	000	123	000	123
Chadron State College	123	000	123	000	123	000
Kearney State College	123	000	123	123	123	000
Peru State College	123	000	123	000	000	000
Wayne State College	123	000	000	000	000	000
Nebraska Wesleyan U	120	123	123	000	123	120
Union College	123	000	123	123	123	120
U of Nebraska	123	123	000	123	123	120
NEVADA						
U of Nevada Main Campus	123	123	000	123	123	123
NEW HAMPSHIRE						
Belknap College	123	000	000	123	000	000
Colby Jr College for Women	123	000	123	123	123	000
Dartmouth College	123	123	123	123	123	120
Franklin Pierce College	000	123	123	123	123	123
U of N H Keene St College	123	123	123	123	123	123
Mount St Mary College	000	123	000	000	000	000
New England College	123	123	123	123	123	000
U of N H Plymouth St College	123	123	123	123	123	123
Rivier College	123	000	123	123	123	000
St Anselms College	120	000	123	123	000	000
U of New Hampshire	123	123	123	123	123	123
NEW JERSEY						
Alma White College	000	000	000	000	123	000
Bloomfield College	123	123	123	123	000	000
Caldwell College for Women	123	123	123	123	123	000
Centenary College for Women	123	000	123	123	123	000
Don Bosco College	000	000	000	000	000	000
Drew U	123	123	123	123	000	123
Fairlgh Dcknsn U Main Campus	120	120	123	120	000	120
Georgian Court College	100	000	123	000	123	000
Glassboro State College	123	123	123	123	123	123
Immaculate Conception Sem	123	123	123	123	123	000

Key: 1–Faculty, 2–Administrative, 3–Clerical-Service. 0 indicates no coverage.

INSTITUTION	RETIREMENT	LIFE INSURANCE	BASIC HOSPITAL-SURGICAL-MEDICAL	MAJOR MEDICAL	SHORT-TERM DISABILITY	LONG-TERM DISABILITY
	1	2	3	4	5	6
NEW JERSEY (cont'd)						
Jersey City State College	123	123	123	123	123	123
Monmouth College	123	120	123	123	000	000
Montclair State College	123	123	123	123	123	123
Newark College of Engineering	123	123	123	123	123	123
Newark State College	123	123	123	123	123	000
New Brunswick Theol Sem	120	120	120	120	000	000
N J Col of Med & Dentistry	123	123	123	123	123	123
Northeastern Col Bible Inst	000	123	123	000	123	000
Paterson State College	123	123	123	123	123	123
Princeton Theol Seminary	123	123	123	120	123	120
Princeton U	123	123	123	123	123	120
Rider College	123	123	123	123	123	123
Rutgers The State U	123	123	123	123	123	123
St Peters College	123	123	123	123	123	123
Seton Hall U	123	123	123	120	123	123
Stevens Institute of Technology	123	123	123	123	123	123
Trenton State College	123	123	123	123	123	000
Upsala College	123	123	123	123	123	000
Westminster Choir College	120	123	123	123	000	000
NEW MEXICO						
U of Albuquerque	123	123	123	123	123	123
College of the Southwest	000	000	000	000	000	000
Eastern New Mexico U	123	123	123	123	123	000
New Mexico Highlands U	123	123	123	123	123	123
New Mexico State U	123	123	123	123	123	123
U of New Mexico	123	123	000	123	000	000
NEW YORK						
Adelphi U Main Campus	123	123	123	123	123	123
Baptist Bible Sem	000	000	000	123	000	000
Bard College	123	000	123	120	123	120
New York Theol Seminary	123	000	123	000	123	000
Briarcliff College	123	123	123	123	123	000
CUNY Brooklyn College	123	120	123	123	123	123
Canisius College	120	120	123	123	123	120
CUNY City College	123	100	123	123	123	123
Clarkson College of Technology	123	120	123	123	123	120
Colgate Rochester Div Sch	123	000	123	123	000	000
Colgate U	123	123	123	123	003	120
College of Insurance	123	123	123	123	123	000
College of New Rochelle	123	120	123	120	123	000
College of St Rose	120	123	123	120	123	000
Columbia U Main Div	123	123	123	123	123	123
Columbia U Barnard College	123	123	123	120	123	000
Columbia U College Pharmacy	123	123	123	123	000	123
Columbia U Teachers College	123	123	123	123	123	120
Cooper Union	123	123	123	123	123	000
Cornell U Main Campus	123	123	123	123	123	123
D Youville College	120	000	123	000	000	000
Elmira College	123	123	123	123	000	000

Key: 1–Faculty, 2–Administrative, 3–Clerical-Service. 0 indicates no coverage.

INSTITUTION	RETIREMENT	LIFE INSURANCE	BASIC HOSPITAL-SURGICAL-MEDICAL	MAJOR MEDICAL	SHORT-TERM DISABILITY	LONG-TERM DISABILITY
	1	2	3	4	5	6
NEW YORK (cont'd)						
Finch College	120	123	123	123	000	000
Fordham U	123	123	123	123	123	120
Good Counsel College	123	000	000	000	123	000
Hamilton College	123	123	123	123	123	120
Hartwick College	123	120	123	120	123	023
Hobart & Wm Smith College	123	123	123	123	123	000
Hofstra U	123	123	123	123	123	120
Houghton College	123	123	123	000	123	000
CUNY Hunter College	123	123	123	123	123	123
Iona College Main Campus	123	123	123	123	123	000
Ithaca College	123	123	123	123	023	000
Jewish Theol Sem of Amer	123	120	123	120	123	020
Keuka College	120	123	123	120	123	000
Kings College	120	123	000	123	123	000
Ladycliff College	103	000	103	000	103	000
Le Moyne College	123	123	123	123	123	123
Long Island U	123	123	123	120	123	120
Manhattan College	123	123	123	123	123	123
Manhattan School of Music	123	123	123	123	123	000
Marist College	123	120	123	123	123	123
Marymount College	123	000	123	120	123	000
Marymount Manhattan College	123	123	123	123	003	000
Mercy College	123	000	123	123	123	000
Molloy Cath College Women	123	000	123	000	123	000
Mount St Mary College	100	000	123	123	123	000
Nazareth College Rochester	120	000	123	123	123	000
New Sch for Soc Research	123	123	123	123	000	000
New York U	123	123	123	123	123	000
Niagara U	123	123	123	123	123	000
Notre Dame Col Staten Is	120	000	123	120	000	120
Pace College Main Campus	120	123	123	123	123	123
Polytechnic Inst Brooklyn	123	123	123	123	123	000
Pratt Institute	123	123	123	123	123	123
CUNY Queens College	123	123	123	123	123	123
Rensselaer Poly All Campuses	123	123	003	120	123	120
Roberts Wesleyan College	123	123	123	123	023	000
Rochester Inst Technology	123	123	123	123	123	123
Rockefeller U	123	123	123	123	123	000
Rosary Hill College	123	003	123	123	123	000
Russell Sage College	120	123	123	123	123	000
St Bernardine Siena College	120	120	123	123	123	120
St Bernards Sem & College	103	000	103	000	103	000
St Francis College	123	123	123	123	123	123
St Josephs College Women	100	000	123	000	123	000
St Lawrence U	123	123	123	123	123	000
Sarah Lawrence College	123	123	123	123	123	123
Skidmore College	123	123	123	123	123	120
SUNY State U Binghamtn	123	000	123	123	123	000
SUNY State U Albany	123	000	123	123	123	000
SUNY College Brockport	123	000	123	123	123	000
SUNY College Buffalo	123	000	123	123	123	000
SUNY State U Buffalo	123	000	123	123	123	000
SUNY College Cortland	123	000	123	123	123	000
SUNY College Fredonia	123	000	123	123	123	000

Key: 1–Faculty, 2–Administrative, 3–Clerical-Service. 0 indicates no coverage.

INSTITUTION	RETIREMENT	LIFE INSURANCE	BASIC HOSPITAL- SURGICAL- MEDICAL	MAJOR MEDICAL	SHORT- TERM DISABILITY	LONG- TERM DISABILITY
	1	2	3	4	5	6
NEW YORK (cont'd)						
SUNY College Geneseo	123	000	123	123	123	000
SUNY College New Paltz	123	000	123	123	123	000
SUNY College Oneonta	123	000	123	123	123	000
SUNY College Oswego	123	000	123	123	123	000
SUNY College Plattsburgh	123	000	123	123	123	000
SUNY College Potsdam	123	000	123	123	123	000
SUNY State U Stony Brook	123	000	123	123	123	000
SUNY Maritime College	123	000	123	123	123	000
SUNY College of Forestry	123	000	123	123	123	000
SUNY Downstate Med Ctr	123	000	123	123	123	000
SUNY Upstate Med Ctr	123	000	123	123	123	000
Agr & Tech College Alfred	123	000	123	123	123	000
Agr & Tech College Canton	123	000	123	123	123	000
Agr & Tech College Cobleskill	123	000	123	123	123	000
Agr & Tech College Delhi	123	000	123	123	123	000
Agr & Tech College Farmingdale	123	000	123	123	123	000
Agr & Tech College Morrisville	123	000	123	123	123	000
Syracuse U	123	123	000	123	123	000
Albany College of Pharmacy	123	000	123	123	003	000
Albany Law School	123	000	123	123	123	123
Albany Medical College	123	120	123	123	123	120
Union College	123	120	123	123	123	123
Union Theological Seminary	123	123	123	120	123	000
U of Rochester	123	123	123	123	123	000
Vassar College	123	123	123	120	123	120
Wagner College	120	123	123	123	123	120
Webb Inst of Naval Arch	120	000	123	120	123	000
Wells College	123	123	123	123	123	123
Alfred U College of Ceramics	123	000	123	123	123	000
SUNY Col of Agr at Cornell	123	000	123	123	123	000
SUNY Col Home Ec Cornell	123	000	123	123	123	000
SUNY Ind Labr Rel Cornell	123	000	123	123	123	000
SUNY Vet College at Cornell	123	000	123	123	123	000
NORTH CAROLINA						
N C Agric & Tech State U	123	123	123	000	123	000
Appalachian St Tchrs College	123	123	123	123	123	123
Asheville Biltmore College	123	123	123	000	123	000
Atlantic Christian College	123	123	123	123	000	123
Barber-Scotia College	123	000	123	123	000	000
Bennett College	123	123	123	123	000	123
Catawba College	120	123	123	123	123	000
U of N C at Charlotte	123	123	123	123	123	123
Davidson College	123	000	123	123	123	123
Duke U	123	123	123	120	123	000
East Carolina College	123	123	123	123	123	123
Elon College	123	123	123	123	000	000
St Andrew Presby College	120	123	123	123	123	120
Greensboro College	120	120	120	120	123	000
Guilford College	120	123	123	123	120	120
High Point College	123	123	123	123	000	120
Johnson C Smith U	123	123	123	123	000	123
Lenoir-Rhyne College	120	123	123	123	000	000

Key: 1–Faculty, 2–Administrative, 3–Clerical-Service. 0 indicates no coverage.

INSTITUTION	RETIREMENT	LIFE INSURANCE	BASIC HOSPITAL-SURGICAL-MEDICAL	MAJOR MEDICAL	SHORT-TERM DISABILITY	LONG-TERM DISABILITY
	1	2	3	4	5	6
NORTH CAROLINA (cont'd)						
Mars Hill College	120	120	123	120	120	120
Meredith College	123	123	123	000	123	123
Methodist College	120	000	123	000	123	000
N C College at Durham	123	000	123	000	123	000
N C Wesleyan College	120	123	123	123	123	123
Pfeiffer College	123	123	123	123	123	123
Piedmont Bible College	123	123	123	123	123	000
Queens College	123	123	123	123	123	123
Salem College	123	123	123	123	123	120
Shaw U	120	123	123	123	123	000
U of N C at Chapel Hill	123	123	000	123	123	123
N C State U at Raleigh	123	123	123	123	123	123
U of N C at Greensboro	123	123	023	123	123	123
Wake Forest College	123	123	123	123	123	123
Winston-Salem State College	123	123	123	000	123	000
NORTH DAKOTA						
Jamestown College	120	000	123	000	123	000
Mary College	000	000	120	000	123	000
North Dakota State U	123	123	000	123	123	100
Dickinson State College	123	000	123	123	000	000
Mayville State College	123	123	123	123	123	000
Minot State College	123	000	123	123	123	000
Valley City State College	123	123	000	123	000	000
OHIO						
Antioch College	123	123	123	123	123	120
Ashland College	123	123	123	123	123	123
Baldwin-Wallace College	123	123	123	123	123	120
Borromeo Seminary of Ohio	123	123	123	000	123	000
Bluffton College	123	123	123	000	000	000
Bowling Grn St U Main Campus	123	123	123	123	120	120
Capital U	123	000	123	123	123	000
Case Western Reserve U	123	123	123	123	123	000
Central State U	123	120	123	120	000	120
Cincinnati Bible Seminary	123	123	123	000	123	000
Cleveland Inst of Art	120	000	123	000	123	000
Cleveland Inst of Music	123	000	123	000	123	000
Cleveland Marshall Law School	120	120	123	123	123	000
College Mt St Joseph on Ohio	120	000	123	000	123	000
College of St Mary of Springs	120	000	123	000	123	000
College of Steubenville	123	123	123	123	123	123
College of Wooster	123	123	123	120	123	120
Columbus College Art & Design	123	000	123	123	000	000
Defiance College	123	000	123	123	123	123
Denison U	123	123	123	120	123	120
Dyke College	000	123	123	000	123	000
Cleveland State U	123	123	123	123	123	123
Findlay College	123	123	123	123	000	000
Hebrew Un Col Main Campus	123	123	123	123	123	123
Heidelberg College	123	000	123	123	123	123

Key: 1–Faculty, 2–Administrative, 3–Clerical-Service. 0 indicates no coverage.

INSTITUTION	RETIREMENT	LIFE INSURANCE	BASIC HOSPITAL- SURGICAL- MEDICAL	MAJOR MEDICAL	SHORT- TERM DISABILITY	LONG- TERM DISABILITY
	1	2	3	4	5	6
OHIO (cont'd)						
Hiram College	123	123	123	123	123	123
John Carroll U	123	123	123	123	123	123
Kent State U	123	123	123	123	000	123
Kenyon College	123	123	123	123	123	120
Lake Erie College	120	120	123	120	123	000
Malone College	123	120	000	123	123	000
Marietta College	123	123	123	123	123	123
Mary Manse College	000	000	000	000	000	000
Methodist Theo Sch Ohio	120	120	123	000	123	000
Miami U	123	123	123	123	123	123
Mount Union College	120	123	000	123	123	120
Muskingum College	123	000	123	120	123	120
Notre Dame College	123	000	103	000	000	000
Oberlin College	123	123	123	123	123	120
Ohio Northern U	123	123	123	123	123	123
Ohio State U	123	123	123	123	000	000
Ohio U	123	123	003	120	123	123
Ohio Wesleyan U	123	120	123	123	123	120
Otterbein College	120	120	123	120	123	120
Our Lady of Cincinnati College	000	000	123	000	123	123
Rabbinical College Telshe	000	000	000	000	000	000
Rio Grande College	123	123	123	123	123	000
St John College Cleveland	123	123	123	000	123	000
Salmon P Chase College Law	120	000	123	000	000	000
Tiffin U	000	000	123	000	000	123
U of Akron	123	123	123	123	123	123
U of Cincinnati	123	123	123	123	000	123
U of Dayton	123	123	123	000	123	000
Ursuline College for Women	123	123	123	000	123	000
Walsh College	120	000	123	000	000	000
Western College for Women	120	000	123	000	123	123
Wilberforce U	123	123	123	123	123	123
Wilmington College	120	123	123	123	123	123
Winebrenner Theol Seminary	100	100	100	100	123	000
Wittenberg U	123	123	123	123	123	120
Xavier U	123	100	123	123	123	120
Youngstown U	123	123	123	123	123	123
OKLAHOMA						
Bethany Nazarene College	123	123	123	123	123	123
Central Pilgrim College	000	123	123	123	123	000
Central State College	120	123	123	123	123	000
East Central State College	123	123	123	123	123	000
Langston U	123	123	123	123	123	000
Northeastern State College	120	123	123	123	123	000
Oklahoma Christian College	120	120	123	000	123	000
Oklahoma City U	123	123	123	123	123	000
Okla St U All Campuses	123	123	123	123	123	120
Panhandle A & M College	123	123	123	123	000	000
Phillips U	123	000	123	123	000	123
Southwestern State College	123	123	123	123	000	000
U of Oklahoma	123	123	123	123	000	123
U of Tulsa	123	123	123	123	123	000

Key: 1–Faculty, 2–Administrative, 3–Clerical-Serivce. 0 indicates no coverage.

INSTITUTION	RETIREMENT	LIFE INSURANCE	BASIC HOSPITAL- SURGICAL- MEDICAL	MAJOR MEDICAL	SHORT- TERM DISABILITY	LONG- TERM DISABILITY
	1	2	3	4	5	6
OREGON						
Cascade College	000	000	123	123	123	000
Portland State College	123	000	123	123	123	123
George Fox College	123	000	123	123	123	000
Lewis & Clark College	123	123	123	123	000	123
Mount Angel College	000	123	120	120	123	000
Multnomah School of Bible	123	000	123	000	123	000
Northwest Christian College	123	000	123	123	123	123
Oregon College of Educ	123	123	123	123	123	123
Oregon State U	123	000	123	123	123	123
Oregon Tech Institute	123	123	123	123	123	000
Pacific U	120	000	123	123	000	000
Reed College	123	120	123	123	123	123
Southern Oregon College	123	000	123	123	123	000
U of Oregon Main Campus	123	123	123	123	123	123
U of Portland	120	000	123	120	000	120
Warner Pacific College	123	123	123	000	123	123
Willamette U	123	120	123	123	000	120
PENNSYLVANIA						
Acad of the New Church	123	000	123	123	000	000
Albright College	123	120	123	120	123	120
Allegheny College	120	123	123	123	123	123
Allntwn Col St Fr d Sals	123	123	123	000	000	000
Alliance College	120	000	123	123	123	000
Beaver College	120	123	123	120	123	000
Bryn Mawr College	123	123	123	120	123	120
Bucknell U	123	123	123	123	123	123
Cabrini College	123	000	123	000	000	000
Carnegie-Mellon U	123	123	123	123	000	000
Cedar Crest College	123	123	123	123	123	000
Chatham College	123	123	123	123	123	123
Chestnut Hill College	120	000	123	120	000	000
College Misericordia	000	123	000	000	123	000
Crozer Theological Seminary	120	000	120	120	123	120
Curtis Institute of Music	023	000	123	000	000	000
Dickinson College	123	123	123	123	123	000
Dickinson School of Law	103	123	123	000	123	000
Dropsie Col Hbr Cog Lrng	000	123	123	123	000	000
Duquesne U	123	123	123	123	000	123
Eastern Baptist College	120	123	123	123	000	000
Eastern Baptist Theol Sem	123	123	123	123	000	000
Elizabethtown College	123	123	123	120	123	120
Evngelcl Congr Sch Theo	120	120	120	120	123	120
Franklin & Marshall College	123	123	123	123	123	120
Gannon College	123	123	123	123	123	120
Gettysburg College	123	123	000	123	123	123
Gwynedd-Mercy College	100	000	103	000	103	103
Haverford College	120	000	123	123	123	120
Holy Family College	100	100	123	123	123	000
Jefferson Med Col Phila	123	123	123	120	123	120
Juniata College	120	123	123	123	000	000
Kilroe Sem Sacred Heart	000	123	123	000	000	000
Kings College	123	123	123	123	123	000

Key: 1–Faculty, 2–Administrative, 3–Clerical-Service. 0 indicates no coverage.

INSTITUTION	RETIREMENT	LIFE INSURANCE	BASIC HOSPITAL-SURGICAL-MEDICAL	MAJOR MEDICAL	SHORT-TERM DISABILITY	LONG-TERM DISABILITY
	1	2	3	4	5	6
PENNSYLVANIA (cont'd)						
Lafayette College	123	123	123	120	123	120
La Roche College	120	000	100	000	123	000
Lebanon Valley College	123	123	123	123	123	000
Lehigh U	123	123	123	123	123	123
Lincoln U	123	123	123	120	123	120
Luth Theol Sem Gettysburg	123	000	123	000	123	000
Lycoming College	123	000	123	123	123	000
Marywood College	123	000	123	123	000	000
Mercyhurst College	120	123	123	120	000	000
Messiah College	123	000	123	123	123	000
Moore College of Art	123	000	123	000	000	000
Moravian College	120	000	123	123	123	120
Mount Mercy College	100	123	123	123	123	000
Muhlenberg College	123	123	123	123	123	123
Our Lady of Angels College	000	000	000	000	000	000
Pennsylvania Military College	120	123	123	120	123	120
Penn College of Optometry	123	123	123	123	123	123
Penn College of Podiatry	123	123	123	123	000	000
Penn St U Main Campus	123	123	123	123	123	123
Phila College of Bible	123	000	123	000	000	000
Phila College Pharm & Sci	123	123	123	123	123	123
Phila College of Art	120	123	123	123	123	120
Phila Musical Academy	000	000	123	000	000	000
Phila College of Tex & Sci	123	123	123	123	123	123
Pittsburgh Theol Seminary	123	123	123	000	123	000
Reformed Presb Theol Sem	100	000	000	000	000	000
Rosemont College	123	000	123	000	123	000
St Fidelis Col & Sem	123	000	123	000	023	000
St Francis College	120	000	123	120	123	120
St Joseph College	123	123	123	123	123	123
St Vincent College	123	123	123	123	123	000
Bloomsburg State College	123	000	123	123	123	123
California State College	123	000	123	123	123	123
Cheyney State College	123	000	123	123	123	123
Clarion State College	123	000	123	123	123	123
East Stroudsburg St College	123	000	123	123	123	123
Edinboro State College	123	000	123	000	123	123
Indiana U of Pennsylvania	123	000	000	123	123	000
Kutztown State College	123	000	123	123	123	123
Lock Haven State College	123	000	123	123	123	123
Mansfield State College	123	000	123	123	000	000
Millersville State College	123	000	123	123	123	123
Shippensburg State College	123	000	123	123	123	123
Slippery Rock State College	123	000	123	123	123	123
West Chester State College	123	000	123	123	123	123
Susquehanna U	120	123	123	120	123	123
Swarthmore College	123	123	123	120	123	120
Temple U	123	123	123	123	123	123
Lancaster Theol Seminary	100	120	123	123	123	000
Thiel College	123	123	123	123	000	123
U of Pennsylvania	123	123	123	123	123	123
U of Pittsburgh Main Campus	123	123	123	123	123	000
Ursinus College	123	120	123	123	000	000

Key: 1–Faculty, 2–Administrative, 3 -Clerical-Service. 0 indicates no coverage.

INSTITUTION	RETIREMENT	LIFE INSURANCE	BASIC HOSPITAL- SURGICAL- MEDICAL	MAJOR MEDICAL	SHORT- TERM DISABILITY	LONG- TERM DISABILITY
	1	2	3	4	5	6
PENNSYLVANIA (cont'd)						
Villa Maria College	120	000	123	000	000	000
Villanova U	100	123	123	123	000	000
Washington Jefferson College	120	120	123	120	123	120
Waynesburg College	120	120	123	120	123	120
Westminster College	123	123	123	123	123	123
Westminster Theol Seminary	123	123	123	000	123	000
Wilkes College	120	000	123	120	123	120
Womans Med College of Pa	123	123	123	123	000	000
RHODE ISLAND						
Brown U	123	123	123	123	003	000
Bryant College	120	120	123	123	123	000
Barrington College	120	000	123	123	000	000
Providence College	123	123	123	123	123	000
Rhode Island College	123	123	123	123	000	003
R I School of Design	123	123	123	123	123	000
Salve Regina College	120	000	123	123	000	120
Sem of Our Lady of Prov	003	000	000	000	003	000
U of Rhode Island	123	123	123	123	123	123
SOUTH CAROLINA						
Allen U	123	123	123	123	123	000
Benedict College	000	000	123	000	123	000
Citadel Military College	123	120	123	120	123	120
Clemson U	123	123	123	123	123	123
Columbia Bible College	123	123	123	123	123	000
Columbia College	120	123	123	123	123	123
Converse College	120	123	123	123	000	120
Erskine College	123	123	123	123	123	123
Furman U	123	123	123	123	000	123
Limestone College	120	123	123	123	000	000
Medical College of S C	123	000	123	000	000	000
Morris College	000	000	000	000	123	000
Newberry College	123	123	123	123	123	123
U of South Carolina	123	123	123	123	123	123
Winthrop College	123	123	123	123	123	000
Wofford College	120	123	000	123	000	120
SOUTH DAKOTA						
Augustana College	123	123	123	123	123	123
Black Hills State College	123	000	123	123	000	000
Dakota Wesleyan U	123	000	000	123	123	000
Gen Beadle State College	123	000	123	123	123	123
Huron College	120	000	123	000	000	000
Mount Marty College	000	000	123	000	123	000
Northern State College	123	000	123	000	123	000
Sioux Falls College	120	000	123	000	123	000
S Dak Sch Mines & Tech	120	000	123	123	123	000
South Dakota State U	123	123	123	123	123	000
Southern State College	123	000	123	123	123	000

Key: 1–Faculty, 2–Administrative, 3–Clerical-Service. 0 indicates no coverage.

INSTITUTION	RETIREMENT	LIFE INSURANCE	BASIC HOSPITAL-SURGICAL-MEDICAL	MAJOR MEDICAL	SHORT-TERM DISABILITY	LONG-TERM DISABILITY
	1	2	3	4	5	6
SOUTH DAKOTA (cont'd)						
U of South Dakota	123	123	123	000	123	123
Yankton College	123	000	123	123	000	000
TENNESSEE						
Austin Peay State College	123	123	123	123	123	000
Belmont College	123	123	123	123	123	123
Christian Brothers College	123	000	123	123	000	000
David Lipscomb College	123	123	123	123	123	123
East Tenn State U	123	123	123	123	123	123
Fisk U	120	120	123	120	000	000
Free Will Bapt Bible College	123	000	123	123	000	000
George Peabody Col Tchrs	120	123	123	123	123	120
King College	123	000	000	123	123	000
Lambuth College	120	120	120	120	000	000
Lincoln Memorial U	123	000	123	123	000	000
Maryville College	123	123	123	123	000	123
Meharry Medical College	120	000	123	000	123	000
Memphis Academy of Arts	120	000	123	123	123	000
Memphis State U	123	123	123	123	123	000
Middle Tennessee State U	123	123	123	123	123	123
Milligan College	120	120	123	123	123	120
Scarritt College	123	123	123	123	123	123
Siena College	000	000	000	000	000	000
Southern Col of Optometry	123	123	123	123	123	000
Southern Missionary College	123	000	123	000	123	123
Southwestern at Memphis	123	123	000	123	000	000
Tenn Ag & Indus State U	123	123	123	123	000	000
Tenn Technological U	123	123	123	123	000	000
Tenn Wesleyan College	120	123	123	123	123	120
Trevecca Nazarene College	120	123	123	123	123	123
Tusculum College	123	123	123	123	123	123
Union U	123	000	123	123	000	000
U of Chattanooga	123	123	123	123	123	123
U of the South	123	123	123	123	123	000
U of Tenn All Campuses	123	123	123	123	123	120
Vanderbilt U	123	123	123	123	123	123
William J Bryan College	123	123	123	000	123	000
TEXAS						
Abilene Christian College	120	120	123	123	123	000
Texas A & M U	123	123	123	123	123	120
Arlington State College	123	123	123	123	000	123
Austin College	123	123	123	123	000	123
Baylor U Main Campus	120	123	123	123	000	000
East Texas Baptist College	123	123	123	123	000	000
East Texas State U	123	123	000	123	123	123
Episcopal Theol Sem of SW	100	123	123	123	000	100
Hardin Simmons U	123	123	000	123	123	123
Howard Payne College	123	123	123	123	000	000
Incarnate Word College	120	120	123	000	000	000
Mary Hardin Baylor College	123	000	123	123	000	000

Key: 1–Faculty, 2–Administrative, 3–Clerical-Service. 0 indicates no coverage.

INSTITUTION	RETIREMENT	LIFE INSURANCE	BASIC HOSPITAL-SURGICAL-MEDICAL	MAJOR MEDICAL	SHORT-TERM DISABILITY	LONG-TERM DISABILITY
	1	2	3	4	5	6
TEXAS (cont'd)						
Midwestern U	123	000	123	123	000	000
North Texas State U	123	123	123	123	123	123
Our Lady of the Lake College	120	120	123	123	000	000
Pan American College	123	123	123	123	123	000
Prairie View A & M College	123	123	000	123	123	123
Rice U	123	123	000	123	123	123
St Edwards U	123	123	123	123	123	000
St Marys U	123	123	123	123	123	000
Sam Houston State College	123	000	123	123	000	000
Angelo State College	123	000	123	123	000	123
Southwestern Assemb God Col	123	000	123	123	123	000
Southwest Texas State College	123	123	123	123	123	000
Sul Ross State College	123	123	123	123	123	123
Texas College	000	000	000	000	000	000
Texas Lutheran College	123	123	123	123	000	123
Texas Southern U	123	123	123	000	123	123
Texas Technological College	123	123	123	123	000	000
Texas Wesleyan College	123	000	123	123	000	000
U of Texas at El Paso	123	123	123	120	000	123
Texas Womans U	123	123	123	123	000	000
U of Corpus Christi	123	120	120	120	000	000
U of Dallas	120	123	123	123	000	000
U of Houston	123	123	123	120	123	000
U of Texas Main Campus	123	123	123	123	123	123
West Texas State U	123	123	123	123	000	000
UTAH						
Brigham Young U	123	123	123	123	123	000
U of Utah Main Campus	123	123	123	123	000	000
Utah State U Main Campus	123	123	123	123	123	123
Weber State College	123	123	123	123	123	000
Westminster College	123	123	123	123	123	000
VERMONT						
Bennington College	123	123	123	123	123	120
Goddard College	123	123	123	123	000	123
Middlebury College	123	123	123	123	123	120
Norwich U	123	000	123	123	000	000
Castleton State College	123	123	123	123	123	123
Johnson State College	123	123	123	123	123	123
Lyndon State College	123	123	123	123	123	123
Trinity College	100	000	123	000	123	000
U of Vt & St Agric College	123	123	123	123	123	120
Vermont College	123	123	123	123	123	123
Windham College	123	123	123	123	123	000
VIRGINIA						
Bridgewater College	120	123	123	123	123	123
Old Dominion College	123	123	123	123	000	123
Richmond Prof Institute	123	123	123	123	023	023

Key: 1–Faculty, 2–Administrative, 3–Clerical-Service. 0 indicates no coverage.

INSTITUTION	RETIREMENT	LIFE INSURANCE	BASIC HOSPITAL-SURGICAL-MEDICAL	MAJOR MEDICAL	SHORT-TERM DISABILITY	LONG-TERM DISABILITY
	1	2	3	4	5	6
VIRGINIA (cont'd)						
Eastern Mennonite College	123	000	123	123	000	123
Emory & Henry College	120	123	123	123	123	120
Hampden Sydney College	123	123	123	123	123	123
Hampton Institute	123	123	123	123	123	000
Hollins College	123	123	123	123	123	123
Longwood College	123	123	123	123	123	000
Lynchburg College	123	000	123	123	000	000
Madison College	123	123	123	123	123	123
Mary Baldwin College	123	000	123	123	000	000
Medical College of Virginia	123	123	123	123	000	000
Radford College	123	123	123	123	123	123
Randolph Macon College	123	123	003	123	123	000
Randolph Macon Womans Col	123	123	123	123	123	120
Roanoke College	123	123	123	123	123	123
St Pauls College	123	000	123	123	000	000
Sweet Briar College	123	123	123	123	123	123
U of Richmond	123	120	123	123	123	123
U of Virginia Main Campus	123	123	123	123	123	123
U of Va Mary Wash College	123	123	123	123	000	123
Virginia Military Inst	123	123	123	123	123	000
Virginia Polytechnic Inst	123	123	123	123	123	123
Va State College Main Campus	123	123	123	123	000	123
Virginia Union U	123	000	123	123	000	123
Washington & Lee U	123	123	123	123	123	123
WASHINGTON						
Central Washington State Col	123	123	123	123	123	120
U of Puget Sound	123	120	023	120	123	120
Eastern Washington State Col	123	123	123	123	123	123
Ft Wright College Holy Names	123	000	000	000	123	000
Northwest College	123	000	123	123	123	000
Pacific Lutheran U	123	123	000	123	123	123
Seattle U	120	120	123	120	123	120
U of Washington	123	123	120	123	123	123
Walla Walla College	123	000	000	123	123	000
Washington State U	123	123	123	123	000	123
Western Washington State Col	123	000	123	123	123	123
Whitman College	120	123	123	123	123	123
Whitworth College	120	000	123	123	120	123
WEST VIRGINIA						
Alderson Broaddus College	120	120	123	000	000	000
Bethany College	123	123	000	123	003	123
Bluefield State College	123	000	000	000	000	000
Concord College	123	000	123	123	123	123
Davis & Elkins College	120	123	123	123	123	123
Fairmont State College	123	000	123	123	000	123
Glenville State College	123	000	123	123	123	123
Marshall U	123	000	123	120	123	123
Morris Harvey College	123	000	123	120	123	000
Salem College	123	123	123	123	123	000

Key: 1–Faculty, 2–Administrative, 3–Clerical-Service. 0 indicates no coverage.

INSTITUTION	RETIREMENT	LIFE INSURANCE	BASIC HOSPITAL- SURGICAL- MEDICAL	MAJOR MEDICAL	SHORT- TERM DISABILITY	LONG- TERM DISABILITY
	1	2	3	4	5	6
WEST VIRGINIA (cont'd)						
Shepherd College	123	000	123	123	123	123
West Liberty State College	123	000	123	120	000	120
W Virginia Inst of Tech	123	000	123	123	123	123
West Virginia State College	123	000	123	123	000	000
West Virginia U	123	000	123	123	000	123
West Virginia Wesleyan College	123	120	123	123	000	120
Wheeling College	123	000	123	120	123	000
WISCONSIN						
Beloit College	123	123	003	120	000	120
Cardinal Stritch College	000	000	123	123	123	000
Carroll College	120	120	123	123	123	123
Carthage College	123	000	123	123	123	000
Holy Family College	000	000	003	000	123	000
Lawrence U Main Campus	123	123	123	120	123	120
Marian College Fond du Lac	003	000	000	000	000	000
Marquette U	123	123	003	120	000	000
Milwaukee School of Engrg	123	123	123	123	123	123
Mount Mary College	120	000	123	000	000	000
Mount St Paul College	123	000	123	000	000	000
Mount Senario College	120	000	123	000	123	000
Northland College	123	123	123	123	123	000
Ripon College	123	123	000	123	123	123
St Norbert College	120	123	123	123	123	123
Stout State U	123	123	123	123	123	123
U of Wisconsin All Campuses	123	123	123	123	000	000
Viterbo College	120	123	123	123	123	000
Wisconsin State U Eau Claire	123	123	123	123	000	000
Wisconsin State U La Crosse	123	123	123	123	123	123
Wisconsin State U Oshkosh	123	123	123	123	123	123
Wisconsin State U River Falls	123	123	123	123	123	123
Wisconsin State U Stevns Pnt	123	123	123	123	123	123
Wisconsin State U Superior	123	123	123	123	123	123
Wisconsin State U Whitewater	123	123	123	123	123	123
Wisconsin State U Platteville	123	123	123	123	123	123
WYOMING						
U of Wyoming	123	123	123	123	123	123
PUERTO RICO						
Catholic U of Puerto Rico	000	100	023	020	000	000
College of the Sacred Heart	123	000	000	000	123	000
Inter American U of P R	120	120	120	120	000	000

Key: 1–Faculty, 2–Administrative, 3–Clerical-Service. 0 indicates no coverage.

Appendix 3

TABLES

The following tables present in detail information derived from the survey questionnaire. Each table heading includes the number of the question on which the table is based.

In the tables the responding institutions are classified by type as universities, liberal arts colleges, and other, which includes teachers' colleges, technical institutes, independent professional schools, and theological and religious schools. All offer at least the bachelor's degree. By control the institutions are classified as public or private. The responses are given by numbers of institutions and numbers of full-time employees reported, which in effect weights responses by size of institution. Each table is divided into subsections showing the responses for faculty, administrative and other professional personnel, and clerical-service employees.

Limited space prevents publication of all the tables prepared from the questionnaire. Questionnaire information not found in this appendix is generally summarized in the text.

Percentages are rounded to the nearest tenth; an asterisk indicates a percentage of less than one tenth of a per cent.

TABLE 1. FEDERAL SOCIAL SECURITY COVERAGE OF COLLEGE AND UNIVERSITY EMPLOYEES
(Questionnaire Sect. I Q.1)

| | ALL INSTITUTIONS | | UNIVERSITIES | | | | LIBERAL ARTS COLLEGES | | | | OTHER | | | |
| | | | PUBLIC | | PRIVATE | | PUBLIC | | PRIVATE | | PUBLIC | | PRIVATE | |
	INSTs	EEs	INSTs	EEs	INSTs	EEs	INSTs	EEs	INSTs	EEs	INSTs	EEs	INSTs	EEs
Total	1232 100.0	838347 100.0	93 100.0	351630 100.0	65 100.0	177406 100.0	218 100.0	135406 100.0	596 100.0	121652 100.0	67 100.0	27665 100.0	193 100.0	24588 100.0
No Response	10 .8	1307 .2	— —	— —	— —	— —	— —	— —	7 1.2	1268 1.0	— —	— —	3 1.6	39 .2
Employees Covered by Social Security	1160 94.2	740655 88.3	78 83.9	283555 80.6	65 100.0	177406 100.0	194 89.0	112082 82.8	587 98.5	119725 98.5	47 70.1	23346 84.4	189 97.9	24541 99.8
Employees Not Covered By Social Security	62 5.0	96385 11.5	15 16.1	68075 19.4	— —	— —	24 11.0	23324 17.2	2 .3	659 .5	20 29.9	4319 15.6	1 .5	8 *

TABLE 2. RETIREMENT PLANS IN COLLEGES AND UNIVERSITIES
(Questionnaire Sect. I Q.2)

	ALL INSTITUTIONS		UNIVERSITIES				LIBERAL ARTS COLLEGES				OTHER			
			PUBLIC		PRIVATE		PUBLIC		PRIVATE		PUBLIC		PRIVATE	
	INSTs	EEs	INSTs	EEs	INSTs	EEs	INSTs	EEs	INSTs	EEs	INSTs	EEs	INSTs	EEs
FACULTY														
Total	1232 100.0	285414 100.0	93 100.0	111008 100.0	65 100.0	48174 100.0	218 100.0	63175 100.0	596 100.0	44090 100.0	67 100.0	10715 100.0	193 100.0	8252 100.0
Retirement Plan in Effect	1170 95.0	283936 99.5	93 100.0	111008 100.0	65 100.0	48174 100.0	218 100.0	63175 100.0	569 95.5	43300 98.2	67 100.0	10715 100.0	158 81.9	7564 91.7
No Retirement Plan	62 5.0	1478 .5	— —	— —	— —	— —	— —	— —	27 4.5	790 1.8	— —	— —	35 18.1	688 8.3
ADMINISTRATIVE														
Total	1232 100.0	108315 100.0	93 100.0	47992 100.0	65 100.0	28488 100.0	218 100.0	10488 100.0	596 100.0	15898 100.0	67 100.0	2155 100.0	193 100.0	3294 100.0
Retirement Plan in Effect	1141 92.6	107705 99.4	93 100.0	47992 100.0	64 98.5	28428 99.8	218 100.0	10488 100.0	550 92.3	15559 97.9	67 100.0	2155 100.0	149 77.2	3083 93.6
No Retirement Plan	91 7.4	610 .6	— —	— —	1 1.5	60 .2	— —	— —	46 7.7	339 2.1	— —	— —	44 22.8	211 6.4
CLERICAL-SERVICE														
Total	1232 100.0	444618 100.0	93 100.0	192630 100.0	65 100.0	100744 100.0	218 100.0	61743 100.0	596 100.0	61664 100.0	67 100.0	14795 100.0	193 100.0	13042 100.0
Retirement Plan in Effect	921 74.8	420974 94.7	93 100.0	192630 100.0	60 92.3	98069 97.3	215 98.6	61215 99.1	371 62.2	43747 70.9	66 98.5	14637 98.9	116 60.1	10676 81.9
No Retirement Plan	311 25.2	23644 5.3	— —	— —	5 7.7	2675 2.7	3 1.4	528 .9	225 37.8	17917 29.1	1 1.5	158 1.1	77 39.9	2366 18.1

TABLE 3. TYPES OF RETIREMENT PLANS COVERING COLLEGE AND UNIVERSITY STAFF MEMBERS
(Questionnaire Sect. I Q.3)

	ALL INSTITUTIONS		UNIVERSITIES				LIBERAL ARTS COLLEGES				OTHER			
			PUBLIC		PRIVATE		PUBLIC		PRIVATE		PUBLIC		PRIVATE	
	INSTs	EEs	INSTs	EEs	INSTs	EEs	INSTs	EEs	INSTs	EEs	INSTs	EEs	INSTs	EEs
FACULTY														
Total	1170	283936	93	111008	65	48174	218	63175	569	43300	67	10715	158	7564
	100.0	100.0	100.0	100.0	100.0	100.0	100.0	100.0	100.0	100.0	100.0	100.0	100.0	100.0
State Teacher Retirement System	210	90762	39	42219	1	2000	137	40992	4	775	29	4776	–	–
	17.9	32.0	41.9	38.0	1.5	4.2	62.8	64.9	.7	1.8	43.3	44.6	–	–
State Employee Retirement System	98	43066	14	17770	1	2000	49	18432	–	–	34	4864	–	–
	8.4	15.2	15.1	16.0	1.5	4.2	22.5	29.2	–	–	50.7	45.4	–	–
Single State System for Teachers and Others	78	35835	20	18432	–	–	45	14682	–	–	13	2721	–	–
	6.7	12.6	21.5	16.6	–	–	20.6	23.2	–	–	19.4	25.4	–	–
TIAA/CREF	746	151349	36	39473	57	44269	55	20097	478	37867	26	3966	94	5677
	63.8	53.3	38.7	35.6	87.7	91.9	25.2	31.8	84.0	87.5	38.8	37.0	59.5	75.1
Self-Administered or Trusteed	85	25051	6	13761	6	4555	9	3042	33	2329	5	467	26	897
	7.3	8.8	6.5	12.4	9.2	9.5	4.1	4.8	5.8	5.4	7.5	4.4	16.5	11.9
Church Pension Plan	162	10364	–	–	4	922	–	–	109	7859	–	–	49	1583
	13.8	3.7	–	–	6.2	1.9	–	–	19.2	18.2	–	–	31.0	20.9
Insurance Company	112	14314	4	3981	5	3261	6	915	63	4115	3	811	31	1231
	9.6	5.0	4.3	3.6	7.7	6.8	2.8	1.4	11.1	9.5	4.5	7.6	19.6	16.3
Other	28	9875	5	5557	1	2000	4	1029	11	755	1	311	6	223
	2.4	3.5	5.4	5.0	1.5	4.2	1.8	1.6	1.9	1.7	1.5	2.9	3.8	2.9
ADMINISTRATIVE														
Total	1141	107705	93	47992	64	28428	218	10488	550	15559	67	2155	149	3083
	100.0	100.0	100.0	100.0	100.0	100.0	100.0	100.0	100.0	100.0	100.0	100.0	100.0	100.0
State Teacher Retirement System	190	18690	30	11096	1	750	133	5228	4	588	22	1028	–	–
	16.7	17.4	32.3	23.1	1.6	2.6	61.0	49.8	.7	3.8	32.8	47.7	–	–
State Employee Retirement System	147	23481	34	18298	1	750	69	2980	–	–	43	1453	–	–
	12.9	21.8	36.6	38.1	1.6	2.6	31.7	28.4	–	–	64.2	67.4	–	–
Single State System for Teachers and Others	78	12580	20	9370	–	–	45	2825	–	–	13	385	–	–
	6.8	11.7	21.5	19.5	–	–	20.6	26.9	–	–	19.4	17.9	–	–
TIAA/CREF	700	63614	32	19842	56	24591	51	2265	452	13616	24	1052	85	2248
	61.3	59.1	34.4	41.3	87.5	86.5	23.4	21.6	82.2	87.5	35.8	48.8	57.0	72.9
Self-Administered or Trusteed	93	22479	8	7006	12	12638	9	1505	32	954	5	52	27	324
	8.2	20.9	8.6	14.6	18.8	44.5	4.1	14.3	5.8	6.1	7.5	2.4	18.1	10.5
Church Pension Plan	140	3266	–	–	2	95	–	–	103	2663	–	–	35	508
	12.3	3.0	–	–	3.1	.3	–	–	18.7	17.1	–	–	23.5	16.5
Insurance Company	116	5410	4	272	7	2981	6	125	66	1383	3	94	30	555
	10.2	5.0	4.3	.6	10.9	10.5	2.8	1.2	12.0	8.9	4.5	4.4	20.1	18.0
Other	26	4275	6	3002	1	750	4	126	10	317	1	23	4	57
	2.3	4.0	6.5	6.3	1.6	2.6	1.8	1.2	1.8	2.0	1.5	1.1	2.7	1.8

Percentages add to over 100 because more than one plan (for alternative or concurrent participation) was reported by some institutions.

TABLE 3. TYPES OF RETIREMENT PLANS COVERING COLLEGE AND UNIVERSITY STAFF MEMBERS

(continued)

| | ALL INSTITUTIONS | | UNIVERSITIES | | | | LIBERAL ARTS COLLEGES | | | | OTHER | | | |
| | | | PUBLIC | | PRIVATE | | PUBLIC | | PRIVATE | | PUBLIC | | PRIVATE | |
	INSTs	EEs	INSTs	EEs	INSTs	EEs	INSTs	EEs	INSTs	EEs	INSTs	EEs	INSTs	EEs
CLERICAL-SERVICE														
Total	921	420974	93	192630	60	98069	215	61215	371	43747	66	14637	116	10676
	100.0	100.0	100.0	100.0	100.0	100.0	100.0	100.0	100.0	100.0	100.0	100.0	100.0	100.0
State Teacher Retirement System	82	39158	16	24289	—	—	62	13752	2	477	2	640	—	—
	8.9	9.3	17.2	12.6	—	—	28.8	22.5	.5	1.1	3.0	4.4	—	—
State Employee Retirement System	210	137242	46	94154	1	4000	114	28913	1	241	48	9934	—	—
	22.8	32.6	49.5	48.9	1.7	4.1	53.0	47.2	.3	.6	72.7	67.9	—	—
Single State System for Teachers and Others	78	46996	20	29592	—	—	45	13541	—	—	13	3863	—	—
	8.5	11.2	21.5	15.4	—	—	20.9	22.1	—	—	19.7	26.4	—	—
TIAA/CREF	361	102379	14	29204	37	38708	16	2083	241	29036	3	478	50	2870
	39.2	24.3	15.1	15.2	61.7	39.5	7.4	3.4	65.0	66.4	4.5	3.3	43.1	26.9
Self-Administered or Trusteed	122	115099	10	37257	19	53478	12	10830	45	8874	5	651	31	4009
	13.2	27.3	10.8	19.3	31.7	54.5	5.6	17.7	12.1	20.3	7.6	4.4	26.7	37.6
Church Pension Plan	75	6491	—	—	1	492	—	—	54	3503	—	—	20	2496
	8.1	1.5	—	—	1.7	.5	—	—	14.6	8.0	—	—	17.2	23.4
Insurance Company	94	29807	1	782	10	20122	4	439	51	6422	2	288	26	1754
	10.2	7.1	1.1	.4	16.7	20.5	1.9	.7	13.7	14.7	3.0	2.0	22.4	16.4
Other	23	12484	4	9300	1	500	4	1184	10	1161	1	180	3	159
	2.5	3.0	4.3	4.8	1.7	.5	1.9	1.9	2.7	2.7	1.5	1.2	2.6	1.5

Percentages add to over 100 because more than one plan (for alternative or concurrent participation) was reported by some institutions.

TABLE 4. EMPLOYER-EMPLOYEE CONTRIBUTION TOWARD THE COST OF THE RETIREMENT PLAN

(Questionnaire Sect. I Q.5,6)

	ALL INSTITUTIONS		UNIVERSITIES PUBLIC		UNIVERSITIES PRIVATE		LIBERAL ARTS COLLEGES PUBLIC		LIBERAL ARTS COLLEGES PRIVATE		OTHER PUBLIC		OTHER PRIVATE	
	INSTs	EEs	INSTs	EEs	INSTs	EEs	INSTs	EEs	INSTs	EEs	INSTs	EEs	INSTs	EEs
FACULTY														
Total	1170	283936	93	111008	65	48174	218	63175	569	43300	67	10715	158	7564
	100.0	100.0	100.0	100.0	100.0	100.0	100.0	100.0	100.0	100.0	100.0	100.0	100.0	100.0
No Response	19	2256	2	1146	1	310	—	—	10	746	—	—	6	54
	1.6	.8	2.2	1.0	1.5	.6	—	—	1.8	1.7	—	—	3.8	.7
Employer Pays Full Cost	167	28383	8	10747	5	4238	12	3127	74	6465	18	2202	50	1604
	14.3	10.0	8.6	9.7	7.7	8.8	5.5	4.9	13.0	14.9	26.9	20.6	31.6	21.2
Employer and Employee Share Cost	969	250734	83	99115	59	43626	198	58149	481	35840	48	8433	100	5571
	82.8	88.3	89.2	89.3	90.8	90.6	90.8	92.1	84.5	82.8	71.6	78.7	63.3	73.7
Employee Pays Full Cost	15	2563	—	—	—	—	8	1899	4	249	1	80	2	335
	1.3	.9	—	—	—	—	3.7	3.0	.7	.6	1.5	.7	1.3	4.4
ADMINISTRATIVE														
Total	1141	107705	93	47992	64	28428	218	10488	550	15559	67	2155	149	3083
	100.0	100.0	100.0	100.0	100.0	100.0	100.0	100.0	100.0	100.0	100.0	100.0	100.0	100.0
No Response	19	1151	3	787	1	48	—	—	12	295	—	—	3	21
	1.7	1.1	3.2	1.6	1.6	.2	—	—	2.2	1.9	—	—	2.0	.7
Employer Pays Full Cost	165	14358	8	3737	6	5860	12	785	73	2439	18	848	48	689
	14.5	13.3	8.6	7.8	9.4	20.6	5.5	7.5	13.3	15.7	26.9	39.4	32.2	22.3
Employer and Employee Share Cost	942	91737	82	43468	57	22520	197	9330	461	12759	48	1293	97	2367
	82.5	85.2	88.2	90.6	89.0	79.2	90.4	88.9	83.8	82.0	71.6	60.0	65.1	76.8
Employee Pays Full Cost	15	459	—	—	—	—	9	373	4	66	1	14	1	6
	1.3	.4	—	—	—	—	4.1	3.6	.7	.4	1.5	.6	.7	.2
CLERICAL-SERVICE														
Total	921	420974	93	192630	60	98069	215	61215	371	43747	66	14637	116	10676
	100.0	100.0	100.0	100.0	100.0	100.0	100.0	100.0	100.0	100.0	100.0	100.0	100.0	100.0
No Response	22	4388	3	2563	1	239	1	74	11	1267	1	74	5	171
	2.4	1.0	3.2	1.3	1.7	.2	.5	.1	3.0	2.9	1.5	.5	4.3	1.6
Employer Pays Full Cost	160	76823	9	20551	12	33042	13	3121	71	11083	15	4209	40	4817
	17.4	18.2	9.7	10.7	20.0	33.7	6.0	5.1	19.1	25.3	22.7	28.8	34.5	45.1
Employer and Employee Share Cost	723	336479	81	169516	47	64788	193	55679	282	30523	49	10285	71	5688
	78.5	80.0	87.1	88.0	78.3	66.1	89.8	91.0	76.0	69.8	74.3	70.2	61.2	53.3
Employee Pays Full Cost	16	3284	—	—	—	—	8	2341	7	874	1	69	—	—
	1.7	.8	—	—	—	—	3.7	3.8	1.9	2.0	1.5	.5	—	—

TABLE 5. PAYMENT OF REGULAR EMPLOYEE CONTRIBUTIONS TO RETIREMENT PLAN APP. 3
BY SALARY REDUCTION UNDER SECTION 403(b) INTERNAL REVENUE CODE
("SALARY-OR-ANNUITY" OPTION)
(Questionnaire Sect. I Q.6)

| | ALL INSTITUTIONS | | UNIVERSITIES | | | | LIBERAL ARTS COLLEGES | | | | OTHER | | | |
| | | | PUBLIC | | PRIVATE | | PUBLIC | | PRIVATE | | PUBLIC | | PRIVATE | |
	INSTs	EEs	INSTs	EEs	INSTs	EEs	INSTs	EEs	INSTs	EEs	INSTs	EEs	INSTs	EEs
FACULTY														
Total	994	255335	85	100261	60	43936	206	60048	492	36671	49	8513	102	5906
	100.0	100.0	100.0	100.0	100.0	100.0	100.0	100.0	100.0	100.0	100.0	100.0	100.0	100.0
No Response	61	9091	4	2178	2	2258	6	1146	37	2673	1	196	11	640
	6.1	3.6	4.7	2.2	3.3	5.1	2.9	1.9	7.5	7.3	2.0	2.3	10.8	10.8
Not Permitted by Institution	335	111241	45	60494	9	5335	98	32101	132	8616	25	3345	26	1350
	33.7	43.5	52.9	60.3	15.0	12.1	47.6	53.4	26.8	23.5	51.0	39.2	25.5	22.9
Required for Regular Employee Contributions	227	40476	9	8051	2	948	70	19505	110	8046	16	3180	20	746
	22.8	15.9	10.6	8.0	3.3	2.2	34.0	32.5	22.4	21.9	32.7	37.4	19.6	12.6
Optional for Regular Employee Contributions	371	94527	27	29538	47	35395	32	7296	213	17336	7	1792	45	3170
	37.4	37.0	31.8	29.5	78.4	80.6	15.5	12.2	43.3	47.3	14.3	21.1	44.1	53.7
ADMINISTRATIVE														
Total	969	93264	85	44255	58	22568	206	9703	473	13058	49	1307	98	2373
	100.0	100.0	100.0	100.0	100.0	100.0	100.0	100.0	100.0	100.0	100.0	100.0	100.0	100.0
No Response	63	5262	6	2507	2	1468	7	249	36	738	1	26	11	274
	6.5	5.6	7.1	5.7	3.4	6.5	3.4	2.6	7.6	5.7	2.0	2.0	11.2	11.5
Not Permitted by Institution	336	37147	49	23300	9	4406	100	5321	126	2876	26	643	26	601
	34.7	39.8	57.6	52.6	15.5	19.5	48.5	54.8	26.6	22.0	53.1	49.1	26.5	25.3
Required for Regular Employee Contributions	214	11850	8	4439	2	1095	70	3035	99	2634	16	364	19	283
	22.1	12.7	9.4	10.0	3.4	4.9	34.0	31.3	20.9	20.2	32.7	27.9	19.4	11.9
Optional for Regular Employee Contributions	356	39005	22	14009	45	15599	29	1098	212	6810	6	274	42	1215
	36.7	41.9	25.9	31.7	77.7	69.1	14.1	11.3	44.9	52.1	12.2	21.0	42.9	51.3
CLERICAL-SERVICE														
Total	747	342304	83	171229	48	65027	201	58020	293	31983	50	10354	72	5691
	100.0	100.0	100.0	100.0	100.0	100.0	100.0	100.0	100.0	100.0	100.0	100.0	100.0	100.0
No Response	62	23797	10	11584	2	3598	12	2048	27	2217	3	2284	8	2066
	8.3	7.0	12.0	6.8	4.2	5.5	6.0	3.5	9.2	6.9	6.0	22.1	11.1	36.3
Not Permitted by Institution	324	220843	57	135215	18	30874	107	37842	91	10434	28	5212	23	1266
	43.4	64.5	68.7	79.0	37.5	47.5	53.2	65.2	31.1	32.6	56.0	50.3	31.9	22.2
Required for Regular Employee Contributions	155	34740	5	7425	2	3156	67	15717	52	5482	16	2513	13	447
	20.7	10.1	6.0	4.3	4.2	4.9	33.3	27.1	17.7	17.1	32.0	24.3	18.1	7.9
Optional for Regular Employee Contributions	206	62924	11	17005	26	27399	15	2413	123	13850	3	345	28	1912
	27.6	18.4	13.3	9.9	54.1	42.1	7.5	4.2	42.0	43.4	6.0	3.3	38.9	33.6

TABLE 6. EXTRA ANNUITY CONTRIBUTIONS TO RETIREMENT PLAN BY EMPLOYEES UNDER "SALARY-OR-ANNUITY" OPTION OF SECTION 403(b) INTERNAL REVENUE CODE

(Questionnaire Sect. I Q.7)

	ALL INSTITUTIONS		UNIVERSITIES PUBLIC		UNIVERSITIES PRIVATE		LIBERAL ARTS COLLEGES PUBLIC		LIBERAL ARTS COLLEGES PRIVATE		OTHER PUBLIC		OTHER PRIVATE	
	INSTs	EEs	INSTs	EEs	INSTs	EEs	INSTs	EEs	INSTs	EEs	INSTs	EEs	INSTs	EEs
FACULTY														
Total	1170 100.0	283936 100.0	93 100.0	111008 100.0	65 100.0	48174 100.0	218 100.0	63175 100.0	569 100.0	43300 100.0	67 100.0	10715 100.0	158 100.0	7564 100.0
No Response	57 4.9	5566 2.0	3 3.2	1444 1.3	2 3.1	1193 2.5	4 1.8	476 .8	32 5.6	1617 3.7	3 4.5	434 4.1	13 8.2	402 5.3
Extra Contributions Permitted	789 67.4	200296 70.5	63 67.8	75750 68.2	57 87.7	44750 92.9	137 62.9	35778 56.6	386 67.9	31828 73.5	52 77.6	7120 66.4	94 59.5	5070 67.0
Extra Contributions Not Permitted	324 27.7	78074 27.5	27 29.0	33814 30.5	6 9.2	2231 4.6	77 35.3	26921 42.6	151 26.5	9855 22.8	12 17.9	3161 29.5	51 32.3	2092 27.7
ADMINISTRATIVE														
Total	1141 100.0	107705 100.0	93 100.0	47992 100.0	64 100.0	28428 100.0	218 100.0	10488 100.0	550 100.0	15559 100.0	67 100.0	2155 100.0	149 100.0	3083 100.0
No Response	67 5.9	6415 6.0	5 5.4	1478 3.1	2 3.1	3734 13.1	5 2.3	198 1.9	40 7.3	813 5.2	3 4.5	74 3.4	12 8.1	118 3.8
Extra Contributions Permitted	764 66.9	77181 71.6	62 66.6	32306 67.3	55 86.0	23421 82.4	138 63.3	6203 59.1	369 67.1	11627 74.8	52 77.6	1645 76.4	88 59.0	1979 64.2
Extra Contributions Not Permitted	310 27.2	24109 22.4	26 28.0	14208 29.6	7 10.9	1273 4.5	75 34.4	4087 39.0	141 25.6	3119 20.0	12 17.9	436 20.2	49 32.9	986 32.0
CLERICAL-SERVICE														
Total	921 100.0	420974 100.0	93 100.0	192630 100.0	60 100.0	98069 100.0	215 100.0	61215 100.0	371 100.0	43747 100.0	66 100.0	14637 100.0	116 100.0	10676 100.0
No Response	96 10.4	42937 10.2	10 10.8	8102 4.2	9 15.0	23513 24.0	17 7.9	3043 5.0	44 11.9	4903 11.2	5 7.6	2826 19.3	11 9.5	550 5.2
Extra Contributions Permitted	506 55.0	208735 49.6	51 54.8	112115 58.2	32 53.3	35083 35.8	111 51.6	25926 42.4	204 54.9	22780 52.1	48 72.7	9486 64.8	60 51.7	3345 31.3
Extra Contributions Not Permitted	319 34.6	169302 40.2	32 34.4	72413 37.6	19 31.7	39473 40.2	87 40.5	32246 52.6	123 33.2	16064 36.7	13 19.7	2325 15.9	45 38.8	6781 63.5

TABLE 7. SUMMARY OF PROVISIONS FOR FIXED AND FLEXIBLE RETIREMENT AGE COLLEGE AND UNIVERSITY RETIREMENT PLANS APP. 3

(Questionnaire Sect. I Q.8)

| | ALL INSTITUTIONS | | UNIVERSITIES | | | | LIBERAL ARTS COLLEGES | | | | OTHER | | | |
| | | | PUBLIC | | PRIVATE | | PUBLIC | | PRIVATE | | PUBLIC | | PRIVATE | |
	INSTs	EEs	INSTs	EEs	INSTs	EEs	INSTs	EEs	INSTs	EEs	INSTs	EEs	INSTs	EEs
FACULTY														
Total	1170	283936	93	111008	65	48174	218	63175	569	43300	67	10715	158	7564
	100.0	100.0	100.0	100.0	100.0	100.0	100.0	100.0	100.0	100.0	100.0	100.0	100.0	100.0
No Response	18	3404	—	—	1	2350	2	508	10	485	—	—	5	61
	1.5	1.2	—	—	1.5	4.9	.9	.8	1.8	1.1	—	—	3.2	.8
Retirement Age Fixed at Age Stated	98	32248	14	15545	5	4196	32	9015	32	2850	1	48	14	594
	8.4	11.4	15.1	14.0	7.7	8.7	14.7	14.3	5.6	6.6	1.5	.4	8.9	7.9
Service May Be Extended Beyond Age Stated	1030	241573	73	90384	59	41628	179	52837	519	39418	65	10433	135	6873
	88.0	85.0	78.4	81.4	90.8	86.4	82.1	83.6	91.2	91.0	97.0	97.4	85.4	90.8
No Retirement Age Stated	24	6711	6	5079	—	—	5	815	8	547	1	234	4	36
	2.1	2.4	6.5	4.6	—	—	2.3	1.3	1.4	1.3	1.5	2.2	2.5	.5
ADMINISTRATIVE														
Total	1141	107705	93	47992	64	28428	218	10488	550	15559	67	2155	149	3083
	100.0	100.0	100.0	100.0	100.0	100.0	100.0	100.0	100.0	100.0	100.0	100.0	100.0	100.0
No Response	17	1139	—	—	1	790	3	206	11	130	—	—	2	13
	1.5	1.1	—	—	1.6	2.8	1.4	2.0	2.0	.8	—	—	1.3	.4
Retirement Age Fixed at Age Stated	121	11653	13	5865	6	2587	42	1387	40	1358	1	12	19	444
	10.6	10.8	14.0	12.2	9.4	9.1	19.3	13.2	7.3	8.7	1.5	.6	12.8	14.4
Service May Be Extended Beyond Age Stated	975	91076	75	38832	57	25051	168	8786	484	13768	65	2022	126	2617
	85.4	84.5	80.6	80.9	89.0	88.1	77.0	83.8	88.0	88.6	97.0	93.8	84.6	84.9
No Retirement Age Stated	28	3837	5	3295	—	—	5	109	15	303	1	121	2	9
	2.5	3.6	5.4	6.9	—	—	2.3	1.0	2.7	1.9	1.5	5.6	1.3	.3
CLERICAL-SERVICE														
Total	921	420974	93	192630	60	98069	215	61215	371	43747	66	14637	116	10676
	100.0	100.0	100.0	100.0	100.0	100.0	100.0	100.0	100.0	100.0	100.0	100.0	100.0	100.0
No Response	24	2099	—	—	—	—	3	657	17	1401	—	—	4	41
	2.6	.5	—	—	—	—	1.4	1.1	4.6	3.2	—	—	3.4	.4
Retirement Age Fixed at Age Stated	108	55340	17	35973	4	9470	32	4485	30	4216	10	581	15	615
	11.7	13.1	18.3	18.7	6.7	9.7	14.9	7.3	8.1	9.6	15.2	4.0	12.9	5.8
Service May Be Extended Beyond Age Stated	763	350237	70	145765	56	88599	175	55417	311	36807	55	13647	96	10002
	82.9	83.2	75.2	75.6	93.3	90.3	81.4	90.5	83.8	84.2	83.3	93.2	82.8	93.6
No Retirement Age Stated	26	13298	6	10892	—	—	5	656	13	1323	1	409	1	18
	2.8	3.2	6.5	5.7	—	—	2.3	1.1	3.5	3.0	1.5	2.8	.9	.2

TABLE 8. DISTRIBUTION OF STATED RETIREMENT AGES UNDER PLANS NOT PERMITTING EXTENSIONS OF SERVICE BEYOND NORMAL RETIREMENT AGE
(Questionnaire Sect. I Q.8)

	ALL INSTITUTIONS		UNIVERSITIES				LIBERAL ARTS COLLEGES				OTHER			
			PUBLIC		PRIVATE		PUBLIC		PRIVATE		PUBLIC		PRIVATE	
	INSTs	EEs	INSTs	EEs	INSTs	EEs	INSTs	EEs	INSTs	EEs	INSTs	EEs	INSTs	EEs
FACULTY														
Total	98	32248	14	15545	5	4196	32	9015	32	2850	1	48	14	594
	100.0	100.0	100.0	100.0	100.0	100.0	100.0	100.0	100.0	100.0	100.0	100.0	100.0	100.0
65	33	3142	1	752	—	—	3	382	18	1469	—	—	11	539
	33.7	9.7	7.1	4.8	—	—	9.4	4.2	56.2	51.5	—	—	78.6	90.7
66-67	7	709	—	—	—	—	5	556	2	153	—	—	—	—
	7.1	2.2	—	—	—	—	15.6	6.2	6.3	5.4	—	—	—	—
68	13	8136	2	3590	2	2846	4	1275	5	425	—	—	—	—
	13.3	25.2	14.3	23.1	40.0	67.8	12.5	14.1	15.6	14.9	—	—	—	—
69	—	—	—	—	—	—	—	—	—	—	—	—	—	—
	—	—	—	—	—	—	—	—	—	—	—	—	—	—
70	43	20150	11	11203	3	1350	20	6802	6	717	1	48	2	30
	43.9	62.6	78.6	72.1	60.0	32.2	62.5	75.5	18.8	25.2	100.0	100.0	14.3	5.1
Over 70	2	111	—	—	—	—	—	—	1	86	—	—	1	25
	2.0	.3	—	—	—	—	—	—	3.1	3.0	—	—	7.1	4.2
ADMINISTRATIVE														
Total	121	11653	13	5865	6	2587	42	1387	40	1358	1	12	19	444
	100.0	100.0	100.0	100.0	100.0	100.0	100.0	100.0	100.0	100.0	100.0	100.0	100.0	100.0
65	70	5137	6	2361	3	1240	18	389	27	877	—	—	16	270
	57.8	44.1	46.1	40.3	50.0	47.9	42.9	28.0	67.5	64.6	—	—	84.2	60.8
66-67	10	1459	—	—	2	1300	6	95	2	64	—	—	—	—
	8.3	12.5	—	—	33.3	50.3	14.3	6.8	5.0	4.7	—	—	—	—
68	11	1048	2	665	—	—	4	179	5	204	—	—	—	—
	9.1	9.0	15.4	11.3	—	—	9.5	12.9	12.5	15.0	—	—	—	—
69	—	—	—	—	—	—	—	—	—	—	—	—	—	—
	—	—	—	—	—	—	—	—	—	—	—	—	—	—
70	29	4002	5	2839	1	47	14	724	6	213	1	12	2	167
	24.0	34.3	38.5	48.4	16.7	1.8	33.3	52.3	15.0	15.7	100.0	100.0	10.5	37.6
Over 70	1	7	—	—	—	—	—	—	—	—	—	—	1	7
	.8	.1	—	—	—	—	—	—	—	—	—	—	5.3	1.6

TABLE 8. DISTRIBUTION OF STATED RETIREMENT AGES
UNDER PLANS NOT PERMITTING EXTENSIONS OF SERVICE BEYOND NORMAL RETIREMENT AGE
(continued)

| | ALL INSTITUTIONS | | UNIVERSITIES | | | | LIBERAL ARTS COLLEGES | | | | OTHER | | | |
| | | | PUBLIC | | PRIVATE | | PUBLIC | | PRIVATE | | PUBLIC | | PRIVATE | |
	INSTs	EEs	INSTs	EEs	INSTs	EEs	INSTs	EEs	INSTs	EEs	INSTs	EEs	INSTs	EEs
CLERICAL-SERVICE														
Total	108	55340	17	35973	4	9470	32	4485	30	4216	10	581	15	615
	100.0	100.0	100.0	100.0	100.0	100.0	100.0	100.0	100.0	100.0	100.0	100.0	100.0	100.0
65	54	20891	6	8011	2	8122	11	1464	21	2701	—	—	14	593
	50.0	37.8	35.3	22.3	50.0	85.8	34.4	32.6	70.0	64.1	—	—	93.3	96.4
66-67	7	1779	—	—	1	1100	6	679	—	—	—	—	—	—
	6.5	3.2	—	—	25.0	11.6	18.8	15.1	—	—	—	—	—	—
68	4	9001	2	8630	—	—	—	—	2	371	—	—	—	—
	3.7	16.3	11.8	24.0	—	—	—	—	6.7	8.8	—	—	—	—
69	—	—	—	—	—	—	—	—	—	—	—	—	—	—
	—	—	—	—	—	—	—	—	—	—	—	—	—	—
70	42	23647	9	19332	1	248	15	2342	7	1144	10	581	—	—
	38.9	42.7	52.9	53.7	25.0	2.6	46.8	52.3	23.3	27.1	100.0	100.0	—	—
Over 70	1	22	—	—	—	—	—	—	—	—	—	—	1	22
	.9	*	—	—	—	—	—	—	—	—	—	—	6.7	3.6

PROVIDING FOR EXTENSIONS OF SERVICE BEYOND "NORMAL" RETIREMENT AGE
(Questionnaire Sect. I Q.8)

| | ALL INSTITUTIONS | | UNIVERSITIES | | | | LIBERAL ARTS COLLEGES | | | | OTHER | | | |
| | | | PUBLIC | | PRIVATE | | PUBLIC | | PRIVATE | | PUBLIC | | PRIVATE | |
	INSTs	EEs	INSTs	EEs	INSTs	EEs	INSTs	EEs	INSTs	EEs	INSTs	EEs	INSTs	EEs
FACULTY														
Total	1030	241573	73	90384	59	41628	179	52837	519	39418	65	10433	135	6873
	100.0	100.0	100.0	100.0	100.0	100.0	100.0	100.0	100.0	100.0	100.0	100.0	100.0	100.0
Under 60	4	7585	1	586	–	–	1	6800	–	–	2	199	–	–
	.4	3.1	1.4	.6	–	–	.6	12.9	–	–	3.1	1.9	–	–
60-64	71	35515	12	17613	–	–	45	15710	1	45	13	2147	–	–
	6.9	14.7	16.4	19.5	–	–	25.1	29.7	.2	.1	20.0	20.6	–	–
65	786	129943	37	39578	45	25599	101	21191	463	34526	16	2609	124	6440
	76.3	53.8	50.7	43.8	76.2	61.5	56.4	40.0	89.1	87.6	24.6	25.0	91.9	93.8
66-67	29	13658	6	5854	2	3500	12	3795	5	327	2	104	2	78
	2.8	5.7	8.2	6.5	3.4	8.4	6.7	7.2	1.0	.8	3.1	1.0	1.5	1.1
68	55	24198	4	8998	9	9579	3	1191	30	2754	3	1474	6	202
	5.3	10.0	5.5	10.0	15.3	23.0	1.7	2.3	5.8	7.0	4.6	14.1	4.4	2.9
69	–	–	–	–	–	–	–	–	–	–	–	–	–	–
	–	–	–	–	–	–	–	–	–	–	–	–	–	–
70	85	30674	13	17755	3	2950	17	4150	20	1766	29	3900	3	153
	8.3	12.7	17.8	19.6	5.1	7.1	9.5	7.9	3.9	4.5	44.6	37.4	2.2	2.2
ADMINISTRATIVE														
Total	975	91076	75	38832	57	25051	168	8786	484	13768	65	2022	126	2617
	100.0	100.0	100.0	100.0	100.0	100.0	100.0	100.0	100.0	100.0	100.0	100.0	100.0	100.0
Under 60	4	272	1	44	–	–	1	200	–	–	2	28	–	–
	.4	.3	1.3	.1	–	–	.6	2.3	–	–	3.1	1.4	–	–
60-64	69	8309	11	5273	–	–	43	2638	1	25	14	373	–	–
	7.1	9.1	14.7	13.6	–	–	25.6	30.0	.2	.2	21.5	18.4	–	–
65	792	65600	47	25594	47	19656	105	3997	442	12575	32	1251	119	2527
	81.2	72.0	62.7	65.9	82.4	78.5	62.4	45.5	91.4	91.4	49.2	62.0	94.4	96.5
66-67	24	3898	5	2176	–	–	10	1557	5	114	2	23	2	28
	2.5	4.3	6.7	5.6	–	–	6.0	17.7	1.0	.8	3.1	1.1	1.6	1.1
68	40	4071	4	1365	7	1751	2	176	21	595	3	156	3	28
	4.1	4.5	5.3	3.5	12.3	7.0	1.2	2.0	4.3	4.3	4.6	7.7	2.4	1.1
69	–	–	–	–	–	–	–	–	–	–	–	–	–	–
	–	–	–	–	–	–	–	–	–	–	–	–	–	–
70	46	8926	7	4380	3	3644	7	218	15	459	12	191	2	34
	4.7	9.8	9.3	11.3	5.3	14.5	4.2	2.5	3.1	3.3	18.5	9.4	1.6	1.3

TABLE 9. DISTRIBUTION OF STATED "NORMAL" RETIREMENT AGES UNDER PLANS PROVIDING FOR EXTENSIONS OF SERVICE BEYOND "NORMAL" RETIREMENT AGE

(continued)

| | ALL INSTITUTIONS | | UNIVERSITIES | | | | LIBERAL ARTS COLLEGES | | | | OTHER | | | |
| | | | PUBLIC | | PRIVATE | | PUBLIC | | PRIVATE | | PUBLIC | | PRIVATE | |
	INSTs	EEs	INSTs	EEs	INSTs	EEs	INSTs	EEs	INSTs	EEs	INSTs	EEs	INSTs	EEs
CLERICAL-SERVICE														
Total	763	350237	70	145765	56	88599	175	55417	311	36807	55	13647	96	10002
	100.0	100.0	100.0	100.0	100.0	100.0	100.0	100.0	100.0	100.0	100.0	100.0	100.0	100.0
Under 60	4	3951	1	609	—	—	1	3200	—	—	2	142	—	—
	.5	1.1	1.4	.4	—	—	.6	5.8	—	—	3.6	1.0	—	—
60-64	70	39951	11	24423	—	—	44	13463	1	20	14	2045	—	—
	9.2	11.4	15.7	16.8	—	—	25.1	24.3	.3	.1	25.5	15.0	—	—
65	577	217604	38	69616	48	77597	101	21846	286	33659	14	5253	90	9633
	75.6	62.2	54.4	47.8	85.7	87.6	57.8	39.4	92.0	91.4	25.5	38.5	93.8	96.4
66-67	22	21671	5	10380	—	—	9	10686	4	299	2	181	2	125
	2.9	6.2	7.1	7.1	—	—	5.1	19.3	1.3	.8	3.6	1.3	2.1	1.2
68	30	24534	4	14018	5	7210	3	616	11	1298	4	1292	3	100
	3.9	7.0	5.7	9.6	8.9	8.1	1.7	1.1	3.5	3.5	7.3	9.5	3.1	1.0
69	—	—	—	—	—	—	—	—	—	—	—	—	—	—
	—	—	—	—	—	—	—	—	—	—	—	—	—	—
70	60	42526	11	26719	3	3792	17	5606	9	1531	19	4734	1	144
	7.9	12.1	15.7	18.3	5.4	4.3	9.7	10.1	2.9	4.2	34.5	34.7	1.0	1.4

OF SERVICE BEYOND NORMAL RETIREMENT AGE ARE NO LONGER PERMITTED
(NORMAL RETIREMENT AGE OF 65 OR HIGHER) — BY RETIREMENT AGE
(Questionnaire Sect. I Q.8)

| | ALL INSTITUTIONS | | UNIVERSITIES | | | | LIBERAL ARTS COLLEGES | | | | OTHER | | | |
| | | | PUBLIC | | PRIVATE | | PUBLIC | | PRIVATE | | PUBLIC | | PRIVATE | |
	INSTs	EEs	INSTs	EEs	INSTs	EEs	INSTs	EEs	INSTs	EEs	INSTs	EEs	INSTs	EEs
FACULTY														
Normal Ret. at 65	786	129943	37	39578	45	25599	101	21191	463	34526	16	2609	124	6440
	100.0	100.0	100.0	100.0	100.0	100.0	100.0	100.0	100.0	100.0	100.0	100.0	100.0	100.0
Exts. to 66-69	58	10457	3	3909	—	—	11	2066	30	3703	2	564	12	215
	7.4	8.0	8.1	9.9	—	—	10.9	9.7	6.5	10.7	12.5	21.6	9.7	3.3
Exts. to 70	392	72589	23	24630	27	15049	66	13857	218	14379	9	1435	49	3239
	49.9	55.9	62.2	62.2	60.0	58.8	65.3	65.4	47.1	41.6	56.3	55.0	39.5	50.3
Exts. to 71 or Higher	34	7796	2	3047	2	1198	6	1396	18	1746	1	196	5	213
	4.3	6.0	5.4	7.7	4.4	4.7	6.0	6.6	3.9	5.1	6.3	7.5	4.0	3.3
No Stated Limit	281	37414	9	7992	16	9352	14	3125	186	14062	3	384	53	2499
	35.8	28.8	24.3	20.2	35.6	36.5	13.9	14.7	40.2	40.7	18.8	14.7	42.7	38.8
No Response	21	1687	—	—	—	—	4	747	11	636	1	30	5	274
	2.7	1.3	—	—	—	—	4.0	3.5	2.4	1.8	6.3	1.1	4.0	4.3
Normal Ret. 66-69	84	37856	10	14852	11	13079	15	4986	35	3081	5	1578	8	280
	100.0	100.0	100.0	100.0	100.0	100.0	100.0	100.0	100.0	100.0	100.0	100.0	100.0	100.0
Exts. to 68-69	2	1520	—	—	1	1500	—	—	—	—	—	—	1	20
	2.4	4.0	—	—	9.1	11.5	—	—	—	—	—	—	12.5	7.1
Exts. to 70	20	4805	1	593	3	1888	4	1272	9	957	—	—	3	95
	23.8	12.7	10.0	4.0	27.3	14.4	26.7	25.5	25.7	31.1	—	—	37.5	33.9
Exts. to 71-72	10	5860	1	527	2	4835	1	80	5	360	—	—	1	58
	11.9	15.5	10.0	3.5	18.2	37.0	6.7	1.6	14.3	11.7	—	—	12.5	20.7
Exts. to 73 or Higher	2	85	—	—	—	—	—	—	1	15	—	—	1	70
	2.4	.2	—	—	—	—	—	—	2.9	.5	—	—	12.5	25.0
No Stated Limit	47	24952	7	13279	5	4856	10	3634	18	1568	5	1578	2	37
	56.0	65.9	70.0	89.4	45.5	37.1	66.7	72.9	51.4	50.9	100.0	100.0	25.0	13.2
No Response	3	634	1	453	—	—	—	—	2	181	—	—	—	—
	3.6	1.7	10.0	3.1	—	—	—	—	5.7	5.9	—	—	—	—
Normal Ret. 70 or Higher	85	30674	13	17755	3	2950	17	4150	20	1766	29	3900	3	153
	100.0	100.0	100.0	100.0	100.0	100.0	100.0	100.0	100.0	100.0	100.0	100.0	100.0	100.0
Exts. to 71	12	1473	—	—	—	—	4	727	—	—	8	746	—	—
	14.1	4.8	—	—	—	—	23.5	17.5	—	—	27.6	19.1	—	—
Exts. to 73	2	225	—	—	—	—	1	145	—	—	1	80	—	—
	2.4	.7	—	—	—	—	5.9	3.5	—	—	3.4	2.1	—	—
No Stated Limit	66	27049	11	16008	3	2950	12	3278	17	1586	20	3074	3	153
	77.6	88.2	84.6	90.2	100.0	100.0	70.6	79.0	85.0	89.8	69.0	78.8	100.0	100.0
No Response	5	1927	2	1747	—	—	—	—	3	180	—	—	—	—
	5.9	6.3	15.4	9.8	—	—	—	—	15.0	10.2	—	—	—	—

Extensions beyond normal retirement age are usually made for one calendar or academic year at a time, either full- or part-time.

TABLE 10. INSTITUTIONS PERMITTING EXTENSIONS: AGE BEYOND WHICH EXTENSIONS OF SERVICE BEYOND NORMAL RETIREMENT AGE ARE NO LONGER PERMITTED (NORMAL RETIREMENT AGE OF 65 OR HIGHER) — BY RETIREMENT AGE

(continued)

	ALL INSTITUTIONS		UNIVERSITIES PUBLIC		PRIVATE		LIBERAL ARTS COLLEGES PUBLIC		PRIVATE		OTHER PUBLIC		PRIVATE	
	INSTs	EEs	INSTs	EEs	INSTs	EEs	INSTs	EEs	INSTs	EEs	INSTs	EEs	INSTs	EEs
ADMINISTRATIVE														
Normal Ret. at 65	792	65600	47	25594	47	19656	105	3997	442	12575	32	1251	119	2527
	100.0	100.0	100.0	100.0	100.0	100.0	100.0	100.0	100.0	100.0	100.0	100.0	100.0	100.0
Exts. to 66-69	56	4584	4	1431	1	1127	10	269	31	1546	2	95	8	116
	7.1	7.0	8.5	5.6	2.1	5.7	9.5	6.7	7.0	12.3	6.3	7.6	6.7	4.6
Exts. to 70	349	28573	25	11087	26	9558	60	2165	189	4432	7	194	42	1137
	44.1	43.6	53.2	43.3	55.3	48.6	57.1	54.2	42.8	35.2	21.9	15.5	35.3	45.0
Exts. to 71 or Higher	36	1814	1	350	3	619	6	184	21	612	1	26	4	23
	4.5	2.8	2.1	1.4	6.4	3.1	5.7	4.6	4.8	4.9	3.1	2.1	3.4	.9
No Stated Limit	325	29950	16	12594	17	8352	23	1273	190	5734	21	931	58	1066
	41.0	45.7	34.0	49.2	36.2	42.5	21.9	31.8	43.0	45.6	65.6	74.4	48.7	42.2
No Response	26	679	1	132	—	—	6	106	11	251	1	5	7	185
	3.3	1.0	2.1	.5	—	—	5.7	2.7	2.5	2.0	3.1	.4	5.9	7.3
Normal Ret. 66-69	64	7969	9	3541	7	1751	12	1733	26	709	5	179	5	56
	100.0	100.0	100.0	100.0	100.0	100.0	100.0	100.0	100.0	100.0	100.0	100.0	100.0	100.0
Exts. to 69	1	11	—	—	—	—	—	—	—	—	—	—	1	11
	1.6	.1	—	—	—	—	—	—	—	—	—	—	20.0	19.6
Exts. to 70	16	1505	1	457	4	640	3	211	7	189	—	—	1	8
	25.0	18.9	11.1	12.9	57.1	36.6	25.0	12.2	26.9	26.7	—	—	20.0	14.3
Exts. to 72	5	114	—	—	—	—	—	—	4	97	—	—	1	17
	7.8	1.4	—	—	—	—	—	—	15.4	13.7	—	—	20.0	30.4
Exts. to 73	1	10	—	—	—	—	—	—	—	—	—	—	1	10
	1.6	.1	—	—	—	—	—	—	—	—	—	—	20.0	17.9
No Stated Limit	39	6207	7	2979	3	1111	9	1522	14	406	5	179	1	10
	60.9	77.9	77.8	84.1	42.9	63.4	75.0	87.8	53.8	57.3	100.0	100.0	20.0	17.9
No Response	2	122	1	105	—	—	—	—	1	17	—	—	—	—
	3.1	1.5	11.1	3.0	—	—	—	—	3.8	2.4	—	—	—	—
Normal Ret. 70 or Higher	46	8926	7	4380	3	3644	7	218	15	459	12	191	2	34
	100.0	100.0	100.0	100.0	100.0	100.0	100.0	100.0	100.0	100.0	100.0	100.0	100.0	100.0
Exts. to 71	12	100	—	—	—	—	4	45	—	—	8	55	—	—
	26.1	1.1	—	—	—	—	57.1	20.6	—	—	66.7	28.8	—	—
Exts. to 73	2	24	—	—	—	—	1	10	—	—	1	14	—	—
	4.3	.3	—	—	—	—	14.3	4.6	—	—	8.3	7.3	—	—
Exts. to 76 or Higher	1	116	—	—	—	—	1	116	—	—	—	—	—	—
	2.2	1.3	—	—	—	—	14.3	53.2	—	—	—	—	—	—
No Stated Limit	28	7926	6	3738	3	3644	—	—	14	388	3	122	2	34
	60.9	88.8	85.7	85.3	100.0	100.0	—	—	93.3	84.5	25.0	63.9	100.0	100.0
No Response	3	760	1	642	—	—	1	47	1	71	—	—	—	—
	6.5	8.5	14.3	14.7	—	—	14.3	21.6	6.7	15.5	—	—	—	—

Extensions beyond normal retirement age are usually made for one calendar or academic year at a time, either full- or part-time.

APP. 3   TABLE 10. INSTITUTIONS PERMITTING EXTENSIONS: AGE BEYOND WHICH EXTENSIONS OF SERVICE BEYOND NORMAL RETIREMENT AGE ARE NO LONGER PERMITTED (NORMAL RETIREMENT AGE OF 65 OR HIGHER) — BY RETIREMENT AGE

(continued)

| | ALL INSTITUTIONS | | UNIVERSITIES | | | | LIBERAL ARTS COLLEGES | | | | OTHER | | | |
| | | | PUBLIC | | PRIVATE | | PUBLIC | | PRIVATE | | PUBLIC | | PRIVATE | |
	INSTs	EEs	INSTs	EEs	INSTs	EEs	INSTs	EEs	INSTs	EEs	INSTs	EEs	INSTs	EEs
CLERICAL-SERVICE														
Normal Ret. at 65	577	217604	38	69616	48	77597	101	21846	286	33659	14	5253	90	9633
	100.0	100.0	100.0	100.0	100.0	100.0	100.0	100.0	100.0	100.0	100.0	100.0	100.0	100.0
Exts. to 66-69	41	22701	3	8883	3	5820	10	2533	17	3582	1	1675	7	208
	7.1	10.4	7.9	12.8	6.3	7.5	9.9	11.6	5.9	10.6	7.1	31.9	7.8	2.2
Exts. to 70	254	100100	23	35553	25	34434	64	13308	109	11633	5	667	28	4505
	44.0	46.0	60.5	51.1	52.1	44.4	63.4	60.9	38.1	34.6	35.7	12.7	31.1	46.8
Exts. to 71 or Higher	32	12629	1	2100	3	4393	8	1835	16	2246	1	1851	3	204
	5.5	5.8	2.6	3.0	6.3	5.7	7.9	8.4	5.6	6.7	7.1	35.2	3.3	2.1
No Stated Limit	229	79373	10	22767	17	32950	12	2836	137	15610	6	1040	47	4170
	39.7	36.5	26.3	32.7	35.4	42.5	11.9	13.0	47.9	46.4	42.9	19.8	52.2	43.3
No Response	21	2801	1	313	–	–	7	1334	7	588	1	20	5	546
	3.6	1.3	2.6	.4	–	–	6.9	6.1	2.4	1.7	7.1	.4	5.6	5.7
Normal Ret. 66-69	52	46205	9	24398	5	7210	12	11302	15	1597	6	1473	5	225
	100.0	100.0	100.0	100.0	100.0	100.0	100.0	100.0	100.0	100.0	100.0	100.0	100.0	100.0
Exts. to 69	2	1430	1	1394	–	–	–	–	–	–	–	–	1	36
	3.8	3.1	11.1	5.7	–	–	–	–	–	–	–	–	20.0	16.0
Exts. to 70	12	6571	1	1253	3	3918	2	353	4	680	1	350	1	17
	23.1	14.2	11.1	5.1	60.0	54.3	16.7	3.1	26.7	42.6	16.7	23.8	20.0	7.6
Exts. to 72	3	143	–	–	–	–	–	–	2	54	–	–	1	89
	5.8	.3	–	–	–	–	–	–	13.3	3.4	–	–	20.0	39.6
Exts. to 73	1	50	–	–	–	–	–	–	–	–	–	–	1	50
	1.9	.1	–	–	–	–	–	–	–	–	–	–	20.0	22.2
No Stated Limit	33	36857	6	20597	2	3292	10	10949	9	863	5	1123	1	33
	63.5	79.8	66.7	84.4	40.0	45.7	83.3	96.9	60.0	54.0	83.3	76.2	20.0	14.7
No Response	1	1154	1	1154	–	–	–	–	–	–	–	–	–	–
	1.9	2.5	11.1	4.7	–	–	–	–	–	–	–	–	–	–
Normal Ret. 70 or Higher	60	42526	11	26719	3	3792	17	5606	9	1531	19	4734	1	144
	100.0	100.0	100.0	100.0	100.0	100.0	100.0	100.0	100.0	100.0	100.0	100.0	100.0	100.0
Exts. to 73	2	154	–	–	–	–	1	85	–	–	1	69	–	–
	3.3	.4	–	–	–	–	5.9	1.5	–	–	5.3	1.5	–	–
Exts. to 76 or Higher	2	1526	–	–	–	–	2	1526	–	–	–	–	–	–
	3.3	3.6	–	–	–	–	11.8	27.2	–	–	–	–	–	–
No Stated Limit	55	39186	10	25059	3	3792	14	3995	9	1531	18	4665	1	144
	91.7	92.1	90.9	93.8	100.0	100.0	82.4	71.3	100.0	100.0	94.7	98.5	100.0	100.0
No Response	1	1660	1	1660	–	–	–	–	–	–	–	–	–	–
	1.7	3.9	9.1	6.2	–	–	–	–	–	–	–	–	–	–

Extensions beyond normal retirement age are usually made for one calendar or academic year at a time, either full- or part-time.

TABLE 11. GROUP LIFE INSURANCE PLANS IN COLLEGES AND UNIVERSITIES
(Questionnaire Sect. II Q.1)

	ALL INSTITUTIONS		UNIVERSITIES PUBLIC		UNIVERSITIES PRIVATE		LIBERAL ARTS COLLEGES PUBLIC		LIBERAL ARTS COLLEGES PRIVATE		OTHER PUBLIC		OTHER PRIVATE	
	INSTs	EEs	INSTs	EEs	INSTs	EEs	INSTs	EEs	INSTs	EEs	INSTs	EEs	INSTs	EEs
FACULTY														
Total	1232 / 100.0	285414 / 100.0	93 / 100.0	111008 / 100.0	65 / 100.0	48174 / 100.0	218 / 100.0	63175 / 100.0	596 / 100.0	44090 / 100.0	67 / 100.0	10715 / 100.0	193 / 100.0	8252 / 100.0
Group Plan in Effect	864 / 70.1	249340 / 87.4	85 / 91.4	104592 / 94.2	64 / 98.5	48070 / 99.8	144 / 66.1	48416 / 76.6	419 / 70.3	35787 / 81.2	44 / 65.7	6895 / 64.3	108 / 56.0	5580 / 67.6
No Group Life Plan	368 / 29.9	36074 / 12.6	8 / 8.6	6416 / 5.8	1 / 1.5	104 / .2	74 / 33.9	14759 / 23.4	177 / 29.7	8303 / 18.8	23 / 34.3	3820 / 35.7	85 / 44.0	2672 / 32.4
ADMINISTRATIVE														
Total	1232 / 100.0	108315 / 100.0	93 / 100.0	47992 / 100.0	65 / 100.0	28488 / 100.0	218 / 100.0	10488 / 100.0	596 / 100.0	15898 / 100.0	67 / 100.0	2155 / 100.0	193 / 100.0	3294 / 100.0
Group Plan in Effect	858 / 69.6	97895 / 90.4	85 / 91.4	44961 / 93.7	64 / 98.5	28467 / 99.9	143 / 65.6	7940 / 75.7	414 / 69.5	13047 / 82.1	44 / 65.7	1126 / 52.3	108 / 56.0	2354 / 71.5
No Group Life Plan	374 / 30.4	10420 / 9.6	8 / 8.6	3031 / 6.3	1 / 1.5	21 / .1	75 / 34.4	2548 / 24.3	182 / 30.5	2851 / 17.9	23 / 34.3	1029 / 47.7	85 / 44.0	940 / 28.5
CLERICAL-SERVICE														
Total	1232 / 100.0	444618 / 100.0	93 / 100.0	192630 / 100.0	65 / 100.0	100744 / 100.0	218 / 100.0	61743 / 100.0	596 / 100.0	61664 / 100.0	67 / 100.0	14795 / 100.0	193 / 100.0	13042 / 100.0
Group Plan in Effect	772 / 62.7	378167 / 85.1	84 / 90.3	177570 / 92.2	63 / 96.9	100048 / 99.3	135 / 61.9	43057 / 69.7	352 / 59.1	42440 / 68.8	42 / 62.7	6960 / 47.0	96 / 49.7	8092 / 62.0
No Group Life Plan	460 / 37.3	66451 / 14.9	9 / 9.7	15060 / 7.8	2 / 3.1	696 / .7	83 / 38.1	18686 / 30.3	244 / 40.9	19224 / 31.2	25 / 37.3	7835 / 53.0	97 / 50.3	4950 / 38.0

TABLE 12. EMPLOYER-EMPLOYEE CONTRIBUTION TOWARD COST OF GROUP LIFE INSURANCE PLAN
(Questionnaire Sect. II Q.2,3)

	ALL INSTITUTIONS		UNIVERSITIES PUBLIC		UNIVERSITIES PRIVATE		LIBERAL ARTS COLLEGES PUBLIC		LIBERAL ARTS COLLEGES PRIVATE		OTHER PUBLIC		OTHER PRIVATE	
	INSTs	EEs	INSTs	EEs	INSTs	EEs	INSTs	EEs	INSTs	EEs	INSTs	EEs	INSTs	EEs
FACULTY														
Total	864	249340	85	104592	64	48070	144	48416	419	35787	44	6895	108	5580
	100.0	100.0	100.0	100.0	100.0	100.0	100.0	100.0	100.0	100.0	100.0	100.0	100.0	100.0
No Response	11	836	—	—	—	—	3	462	4	238	—	—	4	136
	1.3	.3	—	—	—	—	2.1	1.0	1.0	.7	—	—	3.7	2.4
Employer Pays Full Cost	297	58552	14	16617	16	7377	25	14610	188	15786	9	1636	45	2526
	34.4	23.5	16.5	15.9	25.0	15.3	17.4	30.2	44.9	44.1	20.5	23.7	41.7	45.3
Employer and Employee Share Cost	454	129012	41	47064	45	39702	66	15868	218	19406	27	4133	57	2839
	52.5	51.8	48.2	45.0	70.3	82.6	45.8	32.8	52.0	54.2	61.3	60.0	52.7	50.9
Employee Pays Full Cost	102	60940	30	40911	3	991	50	17476	9	357	8	1126	2	79
	11.8	24.4	35.3	39.1	4.7	2.1	34.7	36.0	2.1	1.0	18.2	16.3	1.9	1.4
ADMINISTRATIVE														
Total	858	97895	85	44961	64	28467	143	7940	414	13047	44	1126	108	2354
	100.0	100.0	100.0	100.0	100.0	100.0	100.0	100.0	100.0	100.0	100.0	100.0	100.0	100.0
No Response	13	367	—	—	—	—	3	75	5	142	—	—	5	150
	1.5	.4	—	—	—	—	2.1	.9	1.2	1.1	—	—	4.6	6.4
Employer Pays Full Cost	293	20955	14	6058	16	6113	24	1480	186	5927	9	249	44	1128
	34.1	21.4	16.5	13.5	25.0	21.5	16.8	18.6	44.9	45.4	20.5	22.1	40.7	47.8
Employer and Employee Share Cost	451	58230	41	25918	45	21312	67	2476	214	6889	27	572	57	1063
	52.6	59.5	48.2	57.6	70.3	74.8	46.8	31.2	51.7	52.8	61.3	50.8	52.8	45.2
Employee Pays Full Cost	101	18343	30	12985	3	1042	49	3909	9	89	8	305	2	13
	11.8	18.7	35.3	28.9	4.7	3.7	34.3	49.3	2.2	.7	18.2	27.1	1.9	.6
CLERICAL-SERVICE														
Total	772	378167	84	177570	63	100048	135	43057	352	42440	42	6960	96	8092
	100.0	100.0	100.0	100.0	100.0	100.0	100.0	100.0	100.0	100.0	100.0	100.0	100.0	100.0
No Response	11	713	—	—	—	—	3	423	4	256	—	—	4	34
	1.4	.2	—	—	—	—	2.2	1.0	1.1	.6	—	—	4.2	.4
Employer Pays Full Cost	255	90451	15	32753	17	27090	23	6098	152	18400	9	1287	39	4823
	33.0	23.9	17.9	18.4	27.0	27.1	17.0	14.2	43.2	43.4	21.4	18.5	40.6	59.6
Employer and Employee Share Cost	409	188072	39	75272	43	68376	62	13649	188	23411	26	4389	51	2975
	53.0	49.7	46.4	42.4	68.2	68.3	46.0	31.7	53.4	55.1	61.9	63.1	53.1	36.8
Employee Pays Full Cost	97	98931	30	69545	3	4582	47	22887	8	373	7	1284	2	260
	12.6	26.2	35.7	39.2	4.8	4.6	34.8	53.1	2.3	.9	16.7	18.4	2.1	3.2

TABLE 13. GROUP LIFE INSURANCE PLANS: PROVISION OF ADDITIONAL OPTIONAL AMOUNTS OF INSURANCE COVERAGE
(Questionnaire Sect. II Q.4)

	ALL INSTITUTIONS		UNIVERSITIES PUBLIC		UNIVERSITIES PRIVATE		LIBERAL ARTS COLLEGES PUBLIC		LIBERAL ARTS COLLEGES PRIVATE		OTHER PUBLIC		OTHER PRIVATE	
	INSTs	EEs	INSTs	EEs	INSTs	EEs	INSTs	EEs	INSTs	EEs	INSTs	EEs	INSTs	EEs
FACULTY														
Total	864 / 100.0	249340 / 100.0	85 / 100.0	104592 / 100.0	64 / 100.0	48070 / 100.0	144 / 100.0	48416 / 100.0	419 / 100.0	35787 / 100.0	44 / 100.0	6895 / 100.0	108 / 100.0	5580 / 100.0
No Response	27 / 3.1	2695 / 1.1	1 / 1.2	530 / .5	— / —	— / —	3 / 2.1	584 / 1.2	16 / 3.8	983 / 2.7	2 / 4.5	459 / 6.7	5 / 4.6	139 / 2.5
Additional Optional Coverage Available	208 / 24.1	79037 / 31.7	25 / 29.4	38363 / 36.7	12 / 18.8	11050 / 23.0	57 / 39.6	19974 / 41.3	70 / 16.7	4780 / 13.4	26 / 59.1	3535 / 51.2	18 / 16.7	1335 / 23.9
Additional Optional Coverage Not Available	629 / 72.8	167608 / 67.2	59 / 69.4	65699 / 62.8	52 / 81.2	37020 / 77.0	84 / 58.3	27858 / 57.5	333 / 79.5	30024 / 83.9	16 / 36.4	2901 / 42.1	85 / 78.7	4106 / 73.6
ADMINISTRATIVE														
Total	858 / 100.0	97895 / 100.0	85 / 100.0	44961 / 100.0	64 / 100.0	28467 / 100.0	143 / 100.0	7940 / 100.0	414 / 100.0	13047 / 100.0	44 / 100.0	1126 / 100.0	108 / 100.0	2354 / 100.0
No Response	29 / 3.4	508 / .5	1 / 1.2	74 / .2	— / —	— / —	3 / 2.1	91 / 1.1	17 / 4.1	277 / 2.1	2 / 4.5	43 / 3.8	6 / 5.6	23 / 1.0
Additional Optional Coverage Available	205 / 23.9	28098 / 28.7	26 / 30.6	12744 / 28.3	12 / 18.8	7750 / 27.2	57 / 39.9	4709 / 59.4	65 / 15.7	1622 / 12.4	27 / 61.4	506 / 44.9	18 / 16.7	767 / 32.6
Additional Optional Coverage Not Available	624 / 72.7	69289 / 70.8	58 / 68.2	32143 / 71.5	52 / 81.2	20717 / 72.8	83 / 58.0	3140 / 39.5	332 / 80.2	11148 / 85.5	15 / 34.1	577 / 51.3	84 / 77.7	1564 / 66.4
CLERICAL-SERVICE														
Total	772 / 100.0	378167 / 100.0	84 / 100.0	177570 / 100.0	63 / 100.0	100048 / 100.0	135 / 100.0	43057 / 100.0	352 / 100.0	42440 / 100.0	42 / 100.0	6960 / 100.0	96 / 100.0	8092 / 100.0
No Response	27 / 3.5	4558 / 1.2	1 / 1.2	500 / .3	— / —	— / —	4 / 3.0	1025 / 2.4	15 / 4.3	1275 / 3.0	2 / 4.8	1733 / 24.9	5 / 5.2	25 / .3
Additional Optional Coverage Available	185 / 24.0	129887 / 34.3	26 / 31.0	66193 / 37.3	12 / 19.0	30873 / 30.9	55 / 40.7	24135 / 56.0	54 / 15.3	4744 / 11.2	26 / 61.9	2933 / 42.1	12 / 12.5	1009 / 12.5
Additional Optional Coverage Not Available	560 / 72.5	243722 / 64.5	57 / 67.8	110877 / 62.4	51 / 81.0	69175 / 69.1	76 / 56.3	17897 / 41.6	283 / 80.4	36421 / 85.8	14 / 33.3	2294 / 33.0	79 / 82.3	7058 / 87.2

TABLE 14. GROUP LIFE INSURANCE PLANS:
WAITING PERIOD BEFORE NEW EMPLOYEE IS ELIGIBLE TO PARTICIPATE IN PLAN
(Questionnaire Sect. II Q.5)

	ALL INSTITUTIONS		UNIVERSITIES PUBLIC		UNIVERSITIES PRIVATE		LIBERAL ARTS COLLEGES PUBLIC		LIBERAL ARTS COLLEGES PRIVATE		OTHER PUBLIC		OTHER PRIVATE	
	INSTs	EEs	INSTs	EEs	INSTs	EEs	INSTs	EEs	INSTs	EEs	INSTs	EEs	INSTs	EEs
FACULTY														
Total	864	249340	85	104592	64	48070	144	48416	419	35787	44	6895	108	5580
	100.0	100.0	100.0	100.0	100.0	100.0	100.0	100.0	100.0	100.0	100.0	100.0	100.0	100.0
No Response	12	1485	1	234	—	—	3	707	5	419	—	—	3	125
	1.4	.6	1.2	.2	—	—	2.1	1.5	1.2	1.2	—	—	2.8	2.2
No Waiting Period	493	154728	57	63828	38	36165	96	27869	225	19336	39	5770	38	1760
	57.0	62.1	67.0	61.0	59.4	75.2	66.6	57.6	53.7	54.0	88.7	83.6	35.2	31.6
1 Month or Less	186	60706	23	32049	9	4045	27	14125	90	7658	3	866	34	1963
	21.5	24.3	27.1	30.6	14.1	8.4	18.8	29.2	21.5	21.4	6.8	12.6	31.5	35.2
3 Months	39	6643	—	—	8	3576	1	660	22	1829	—	—	8	578
	4.5	2.7	—	—	12.5	7.4	.7	1.4	5.3	5.1	—	—	7.4	10.4
6 Months	27	10697	2	5555	2	508	12	4024	7	468	1	80	3	62
	3.1	4.3	2.4	5.3	3.1	1.1	8.3	8.3	1.7	1.3	2.3	1.2	2.8	1.1
Until Anniv. or Semi-Anniv. Date of Plan	38	3819	—	—	3	1116	1	238	26	1963	—	—	8	502
	4.4	1.5	—	—	4.7	2.3	.7	.5	6.2	5.5	—	—	7.4	9.0
Other	69	11262	2	2926	4	2660	4	793	44	4114	1	179	14	590
	8.0	4.5	2.4	2.8	6.3	5.5	2.8	1.6	10.5	11.5	2.2	2.5	13.0	10.6
ADMINISTRATIVE														
Total	858	97895	85	44961	64	28467	143	7940	414	13047	44	1126	108	2354
	100.0	100.0	100.0	100.0	100.0	100.0	100.0	100.0	100.0	100.0	100.0	100.0	100.0	100.0
No Response	14	408	1	37	—	—	3	151	7	202	—	—	3	18
	1.6	.4	1.2	.1	—	—	2.1	1.9	1.7	1.5	—	—	2.8	.8
No Waiting Period	473	65660	57	30368	32	20899	96	6096	214	6649	38	885	36	763
	55.2	67.1	67.0	67.5	50.0	73.4	67.1	76.8	51.7	51.1	86.4	78.6	33.4	32.4
1 Month or Less	187	17805	22	10525	10	2403	26	1087	92	2928	3	154	34	708
	21.8	18.2	25.9	23.4	15.6	8.4	18.2	13.7	22.2	22.4	6.8	13.7	31.5	30.1
3 Months	45	2336	1	600	8	660	1	125	25	622	1	49	9	280
	5.2	2.4	1.2	1.3	12.5	2.3	.7	1.6	6.0	4.8	2.3	4.4	8.3	11.9
6 Months	30	3150	2	2370	3	253	12	306	8	176	1	14	4	31
	3.5	3.2	2.4	5.3	4.7	.9	8.4	3.9	1.9	1.3	2.3	1.2	3.7	1.3
Until Anniv. or Semi-Anniv. Date of Plan	39	1670	—	—	3	567	1	31	26	684	—	—	9	388
	4.5	1.7	—	—	4.7	2.0	.7	.4	6.3	5.2	—	—	8.3	16.5
Other	70	6866	2	1061	8	3685	4	144	42	1786	1	24	13	166
	8.2	7.0	2.4	2.4	12.5	12.9	2.8	1.8	10.1	13.7	2.3	2.1	12.0	7.1

TABLE 14. GROUP LIFE INSURANCE PLANS:
WAITING PERIOD BEFORE NEW EMPLOYEE IS ELIGIBLE TO PARTICIPATE IN PLAN
(continued)

| | ALL INSTITUTIONS | | UNIVERSITIES PUBLIC | | UNIVERSITIES PRIVATE | | LIBERAL ARTS COLLEGES PUBLIC | | LIBERAL ARTS COLLEGES PRIVATE | | OTHER PUBLIC | | OTHER PRIVATE | |
	INSTs	EEs	INSTs	EEs	INSTs	EEs	INSTs	EEs	INSTs	EEs	INSTs	EEs	INSTs	EEs
CLERICAL-SERVICE														
Total	772	378167	84	177570	63	100048	135	43057	352	42440	42	6960	96	8092
	100.0	100.0	100.0	100.0	100.0	100.0	100.0	100.0	100.0	100.0	100.0	100.0	100.0	100.0
No Response	11	3169	1	561	—	—	5	2106	2	480	—	—	3	22
	1.4	.8	1.2	.3	—	—	3.7	4.9	.6	1.1	—	—	3.1	.3
No Waiting Period	305	164233	48	88329	14	28614	84	29963	110	10831	35	5869	14	627
	39.5	43.5	57.1	49.7	22.2	28.6	62.2	69.6	31.3	25.5	83.3	84.3	14.6	7.7
1 Month or Less	151	88583	22	65609	8	8255	22	4976	68	7583	2	453	29	1707
	19.6	23.4	26.2	37.0	12.7	8.3	16.3	11.6	19.3	17.9	4.8	6.5	30.2	21.1
3 Months	101	36186	2	2620	16	23339	2	1100	63	7610	1	176	17	1341
	13.1	9.6	2.4	1.5	25.4	23.3	1.5	2.6	17.9	17.9	2.4	2.5	17.7	16.6
6 Months	67	27947	5	11824	7	6519	12	2262	33	4746	1	69	9	2527
	8.7	7.4	6.0	6.7	11.1	6.5	8.9	5.3	9.4	11.2	2.4	1.0	9.4	31.2
Until Anniv. or Semi-Anniv. Date of Plan	26	3905	1	850	1	365	2	393	15	1764	1	74	6	459
	3.4	1.0	1.2	.5	1.6	.4	1.5	.9	4.3	4.2	2.4	1.1	6.3	5.7
Other	111	54144	5	7777	17	32956	8	2257	61	9426	2	319	18	1409
	14.4	14.3	6.0	4.4	27.0	32.9	5.9	5.2	17.3	22.2	4.8	4.6	18.8	17.4

SUMMARY OF INSURANCE AMOUNTS PROVIDED
(Questionnaire Sect. II Q.6)

	ALL INSTITUTIONS		UNIVERSITIES				LIBERAL ARTS COLLEGES				OTHER			
			PUBLIC		PRIVATE		PUBLIC		PRIVATE		PUBLIC		PRIVATE	
	INSTs	EEs	INSTs	EEs	INSTs	EEs	INSTs	EEs	INSTs	EEs	INSTs	EEs	INSTs	EEs
FACULTY														
Total	864	249340	85	104592	64	48070	144	48416	419	35787	44	6895	108	5580
	100.0	100.0	100.0	100.0	100.0	100.0	100.0	100.0	100.0	100.0	100.0	100.0	100.0	100.0
No Response	76	18174	6	3186	3	1933	23	10417	31	2083	2	222	11	333
	8.8	7.3	7.1	3.0	4.7	4.0	16.0	21.5	7.4	5.8	4.5	3.2	10.2	6.0
Multiple of Salary	241	92005	29	39145	30	24914	48	13226	84	8614	26	4064	24	2042
	27.9	36.9	34.0	37.5	46.8	51.8	33.2	27.3	20.0	24.1	59.1	58.9	22.2	36.6
Decreasing, Max $10,000 or Less	16	3291	1	1401	1	325	3	639	10	908	–	–	1	18
	1.9	1.3	1.2	1.3	1.6	.7	2.1	1.3	2.4	2.5	–	–	.9	.3
Decreasing, Max of $11,000-$29,000	19	14292	7	12008	–	–	4	1169	8	1115	–	–	–	–
	2.2	5.7	8.2	11.5	–	–	2.8	2.4	1.9	3.1	–	–	–	–
Decreasing, Max of $30,000 or Over	9	5699	4	4091	–	–	2	834	2	474	1	300	–	–
	1.0	2.3	4.7	3.9	–	–	1.4	1.7	.5	1.3	2.3	4.4	–	–
Salary Bracket, $10,000 or Less	246	42577	10	10452	6	3495	35	16075	146	10354	3	413	46	1788
	28.5	17.1	11.8	10.0	9.4	7.3	24.3	33.3	34.9	29.0	6.8	6.0	42.6	32.0
Salary Bracket, Over $10,000	141	59140	27	33709	15	12933	24	5478	50	4540	11	1806	14	674
	16.3	23.7	31.8	32.2	23.4	26.9	16.7	11.3	11.9	12.7	25.0	26.2	13.0	12.1
Collective Insurance	116	14162	1	600	9	4470	5	578	88	7699	1	90	12	725
	13.4	5.7	1.2	.6	14.1	9.3	3.5	1.2	21.0	21.5	2.3	1.3	11.1	13.0
ADMINISTRATIVE														
Total	858	97895	85	44961	64	28467	143	7940	414	13047	44	1126	108	2354
	100.0	100.0	100.0	100.0	100.0	100.0	100.0	100.0	100.0	100.0	100.0	100.0	100.0	100.0
No Response	72	6036	6	2316	3	1194	23	1745	28	650	2	47	10	84
	8.4	6.2	7.1	5.2	4.7	4.2	16.1	22.0	6.8	5.0	4.5	4.2	9.3	3.6
Multiple of Salary	245	50329	29	22606	31	20201	48	3071	86	3043	26	620	25	788
	28.6	51.4	34.0	50.2	48.3	70.9	33.5	38.6	20.8	23.3	59.1	55.0	23.1	33.4
Decreasing, Max $10,000 or Less	15	1071	1	642	1	40	3	101	9	283	–	–	1	5
	1.7	1.1	1.2	1.4	1.6	.1	2.1	1.3	2.2	2.2	–	–	.9	.2
Decreasing, Max of $11,000-$29,000	19	4428	7	3775	–	–	4	121	8	532	–	–	–	–
	2.2	4.5	8.2	8.4	–	–	2.8	1.5	1.9	4.1	–	–	–	–
Decreasing, Max of $30,000 or Over	9	2250	4	1830	–	–	2	157	2	213	1	50	–	–
	1.0	2.3	4.7	4.1	–	–	1.4	2.0	.5	1.6	2.3	4.4	–	–
Salary Bracket, $10,000 or Less	241	9424	10	2579	6	959	32	1593	145	3439	3	144	45	710
	28.1	9.6	11.8	5.7	9.4	3.4	22.4	20.1	35.0	26.4	6.8	12.8	41.7	30.2
Salary Bracket, Over $10,000	144	18464	27	10913	14	3890	26	1034	51	1958	11	253	15	416
	16.8	18.9	31.8	24.3	21.9	13.7	18.2	13.0	12.3	15.0	25.0	22.5	13.9	17.7
Collective Insurance	113	5893	1	300	9	2183	5	118	85	2929	1	12	12	351
	13.2	6.0	1.2	.7	14.1	7.7	3.5	1.5	20.5	22.4	2.3	1.1	11.1	14.9

TABLE 15. GROUP LIFE INSURANCE PLANS:
SUMMARY OF INSURANCE AMOUNTS PROVIDED
(continued)

	ALL INSTITUTIONS		UNIVERSITIES PUBLIC		PRIVATE		LIBERAL ARTS COLLEGES PUBLIC		PRIVATE		OTHER PUBLIC		PRIVATE	
	INSTs	EEs	INSTs	EEs	INSTs	EEs	INSTs	EEs	INSTs	EEs	INSTs	EEs	INSTs	EEs
CLERICAL-SERVICE														
Total	772	378167	84	177570	63	100048	135	43057	352	42440	42	6960	96	8092
	100.0	100.0	100.0	100.0	100.0	100.0	100.0	100.0	100.0	100.0	100.0	100.0	100.0	100.0
No Response	71	22757	6	7556	3	3922	25	8829	24	1751	3	420	10	279
	9.2	6.0	7.1	4.3	4.8	3.9	18.5	20.5	6.8	4.1	7.1	6.0	10.4	3.4
Multiple of Salary	223	173775	31	82769	28	56251	47	18424	70	10526	26	3099	21	2706
	28.9	45.9	37.0	46.6	44.4	56.2	34.9	42.8	19.9	24.8	62.0	44.6	21.9	33.4
Decreasing, Max $10,000 or Less	12	4806	2	3060	1	375	3	607	6	764	–	–	–	–
	1.6	1.3	2.4	1.7	1.6	.4	2.2	1.4	1.7	1.8	–	–	–	–
Decreasing, Max of $11,000-$29,000	12	15111	7	13626	–	–	2	969	3	516	–	–	–	–
	1.6	4.0	8.3	7.7	–	–	1.5	2.3	.9	1.2	–	–	–	–
Decreasing, Max of $30,000 or Over	6	5722	2	4172	–	–	2	1119	1	81	1	350	–	–
	.8	1.5	2.4	2.3	–	–	1.5	2.6	.3	.2	2.4	5.0	–	⊥
Salary Bracket, $10,000 or Less	292	84973	19	33350	18	18219	38	10077	165	18517	3	468	49	4342
	37.7	22.5	22.6	18.8	28.6	18.2	28.1	23.4	46.9	43.7	7.1	6.7	51.0	53.7
Salary Bracket, Over $10,000	87	55230	16	32187	8	13483	13	2500	35	4334	8	2549	7	177
	11.3	14.6	19.0	18.1	12.7	13.5	9.6	5.8	9.9	10.2	19.0	36.6	7.3	2.2
Collective Insurance	69	15793	1	850	5	7798	5	532	48	5951	1	74	9	588
	8.9	4.2	1.2	.5	7.9	7.8	3.7	1.2	13.6	14.0	2.4	1.1	9.4	7.3

(Questionnaire Sect. II Q.7)

	ALL INSTITUTIONS		UNIVERSITIES				LIBERAL ARTS COLLEGES				OTHER			
			PUBLIC		PRIVATE		PUBLIC		PRIVATE		PUBLIC		PRIVATE	
	INSTs	EEs	INSTs	EEs	INSTs	EEs	INSTs	EEs	INSTs	EEs	INSTs	EEs	INSTs	EEs
FACULTY														
Total	864	249340	85	104592	64	48070	144	48416	419	35787	44	6895	108	5580
	100.0	100.0	100.0	100.0	100.0	100.0	100.0	100.0	100.0	100.0	100.0	100.0	100.0	100.0
No Response	61	15257	3	2912	2	734	21	8928	27	2226	1	289	7	168
	7.1	6.1	3.5	2.8	3.1	1.5	14.6	18.4	6.4	6.2	2.3	4.2	6.5	3.0
AD&D Benefit	489	130802	53	58884	32	26239	85	19962	221	17893	34	4709	64	3115
	56.6	52.5	62.4	56.3	50.0	54.6	59.0	41.3	52.8	50.0	77.2	68.3	59.2	55.8
No AD&D Benefit	314	103281	29	42796	30	21097	38	19526	171	15668	9	1897	37	2297
	36.3	41.4	34.1	40.9	46.9	43.9	26.4	40.3	40.8	43.8	20.5	27.5	34.3	41.2
ADMINISTRATIVE														
Total	858	97895	85	44961	64	28467	143	7940	414	13047	44	1126	108	2354
	100.0	100.0	100.0	100.0	100.0	100.0	100.0	100.0	100.0	100.0	100.0	100.0	100.0	100.0
No Response	61	5692	3	3178	2	155	21	1680	26	609	1	18	8	52
	7.1	5.8	3.5	7.1	3.1	.5	14.7	21.2	6.3	4.7	2.3	1.6	7.4	2.2
AD&D Benefit	488	55052	53	23625	32	18858	85	4312	221	6330	34	727	63	1200
	56.9	56.3	62.4	52.5	50.0	66.3	59.4	54.3	53.4	48.5	77.2	64.6	58.3	51.0
No AD&D Benefit	309	37151	29	18158	30	9454	37	1948	167	6108	9	381	37	1102
	36.0	37.9	34.1	40.4	46.9	33.2	25.9	24.5	40.3	46.8	20.5	33.8	34.3	46.8
CLERICAL-SERVICE														
Total	772	378167	84	177570	63	100048	135	43057	352	42440	42	6960	96	8092
	100.0	100.0	100.0	100.0	100.0	100.0	100.0	100.0	100.0	100.0	100.0	100.0	100.0	100.0
No Response	55	21839	3	5788	2	5685	23	8469	20	1562	1	208	6	127
	7.1	5.8	3.6	3.3	3.2	5.7	17.0	19.7	5.7	3.7	2.4	3.0	6.2	1.6
AD&D Benefit	449	214836	53	102735	32	55675	79	25433	194	22050	31	4844	60	4099
	58.2	56.8	63.1	57.8	50.8	55.6	58.6	59.0	55.1	51.9	73.8	69.6	62.5	50.6
No AD&D Benefit	268	141492	28	69047	29	38688	33	9155	138	18828	10	1908	30	3866
	34.7	37.4	33.3	38.9	46.0	38.7	24.4	21.3	39.2	44.4	23.8	27.4	31.3	47.8

TABLE 17. GROUP LIFE INSURANCE PLANS: COVERAGE OF RETIRED EMPLOYEES
(Questionnaire Sect. II Q.8)

| | ALL INSTITUTIONS | | UNIVERSITIES | | | | LIBERAL ARTS COLLEGES | | | | OTHER | | | |
| | | | PUBLIC | | PRIVATE | | PUBLIC | | PRIVATE | | PUBLIC | | PRIVATE | |
	INSTs	EEs	INSTs	EEs	INSTs	EEs	INSTs	EEs	INSTs	EEs	INSTs	EEs	INSTs	EEs
FACULTY														
Total	864	249340	85	104592	64	48070	144	48416	419	35787	44	6895	108	5580
	100.0	100.0	100.0	100.0	100.0	100.0	100.0	100.0	100.0	100.0	100.0	100.0	100.0	100.0
No Response	13	1578	1	520	—	—	2	604	8	371	—	—	2	83
	1.5	.6	1.2	.5	—	—	1.4	1.2	1.9	1.0	—	—	1.9	1.5
Plan Covers Retired Employees	318	131821	49	62647	34	28297	76	22506	103	11423	34	5772	22	1176
	36.8	52.9	57.6	59.9	53.1	58.9	52.8	46.5	24.6	31.9	77.3	83.7	20.4	21.1
Plan Does Not Cover Retired Employees	533	115941	35	41425	30	19773	66	25306	308	23993	10	1123	84	4321
	61.7	46.5	41.2	39.6	46.9	41.1	45.8	52.3	73.5	67.1	22.7	16.3	77.7	77.4
ADMINISTRATIVE														
Total	858	97895	85	44961	64	28467	143	7940	414	13047	44	1126	108	2354
	100.0	100.0	100.0	100.0	100.0	100.0	100.0	100.0	100.0	100.0	100.0	100.0	100.0	100.0
No Response	13	808	1	418	—	—	2	138	8	241	—	—	2	11
	1.5	.8	1.2	.9	—	—	1.4	1.7	1.9	1.8	—	—	1.9	.5
Plan Covers Retired Employees	321	57847	49	28192	35	19891	75	3602	103	4542	36	976	23	644
	37.4	59.1	57.6	62.7	54.7	69.9	52.4	45.4	24.9	34.8	81.8	86.7	21.3	27.4
Plan Does Not Cover Retired Employees	524	39240	35	16351	29	8576	66	4200	303	8264	8	150	83	1699
	61.1	40.1	41.2	36.4	45.3	30.1	46.2	52.9	73.2	63.4	18.2	13.3	76.8	72.1
CLERICAL-SERVICE														
Total	772	378167	84	177570	63	100048	135	43057	352	42440	42	6960	96	8092
	100.0	100.0	100.0	100.0	100.0	100.0	100.0	100.0	100.0	100.0	100.0	100.0	100.0	100.0
No Response	14	3015	1	467	—	—	4	2035	7	497	—	—	2	16
	1.8	.8	1.2	.3	—	—	3.0	4.7	2.0	1.2	—	—	2.1	.2
Plan Covers Retired Employees	296	205596	48	101465	32	63635	71	17835	92	14554	34	6150	19	1957
	38.3	54.4	57.1	57.1	50.8	63.6	52.6	41.4	26.1	34.3	81.0	88.4	19.8	24.2
Plan Does Not Cover Retired Employees	462	169556	35	75638	31	36413	60	23187	253	27389	8	810	75	6119
	59.9	44.8	41.7	42.6	49.2	36.4	44.4	53.9	71.9	64.5	19.0	11.6	78.1	75.6

TABLE 18. EMPLOYER-EMPLOYEE CONTRIBUTION TOWARD COST OF GROUP LIFE INSURANCE RETIRED COVERAGE
(Questionnaire Sect. II Q.9,10)

	ALL INSTITUTIONS		UNIVERSITIES PUBLIC		UNIVERSITIES PRIVATE		LIBERAL ARTS COLLEGES PUBLIC		LIBERAL ARTS COLLEGES PRIVATE		OTHER PUBLIC		OTHER PRIVATE	
	INSTs	EEs	INSTs	EEs	INSTs	EEs	INSTs	EEs	INSTs	EEs	INSTs	EEs	INSTs	EEs
FACULTY														
Total	318	131821	49	62647	34	28297	76	22506	103	11423	34	5772	22	1176
	100.0	100.0	100.0	100.0	100.0	100.0	100.0	100.0	100.0	100.0	100.0	100.0	100.0	100.0
No Response	9	1391	–	–	–	–	2	533	4	485	2	351	1	22
	2.8	1.1	–	–	–	–	2.6	2.4	3.9	4.2	5.9	6.1	4.5	1.9
Employer Pays Full Cost	110	42731	11	15152	18	15480	14	4815	43	5138	12	1458	12	688
	34.6	32.3	22.4	24.2	52.9	54.6	18.4	21.4	41.7	45.0	35.3	25.3	54.6	58.5
Employer and Employee Share Cost	109	37281	15	15917	11	9324	24	4811	43	4697	13	2225	3	307
	34.3	28.3	30.6	25.4	32.4	33.0	31.6	21.4	41.8	41.1	38.2	38.5	13.6	26.1
Employee Pays Full Cost	64	35015	18	21158	2	1158	29	10828	9	715	4	1063	2	93
	20.1	26.6	36.8	33.8	5.9	4.1	38.2	48.1	8.7	6.3	11.8	18.4	9.1	7.9
No Contribution (Paid Up)	26	15403	5	10420	3	2335	7	1519	4	388	3	675	4	66
	8.2	11.7	10.2	16.6	8.8	8.3	9.2	6.7	3.9	3.4	8.8	11.7	18.2	5.6
ADMINISTRATIVE														
Total	321	57847	49	28192	35	19891	75	3602	103	4542	36	976	23	644
	100.0	100.0	100.0	100.0	100.0	100.0	100.0	100.0	100.0	100.0	100.0	100.0	100.0	100.0
No Response	8	198	–	–	–	–	1	15	4	155	2	24	1	4
	2.5	.3	–	–	–	–	1.3	.4	3.9	3.4	5.6	2.5	4.3	.6
Employer Pays Full Cost	114	22313	11	8701	19	9893	14	606	43	2310	14	330	13	473
	35.5	38.7	22.4	30.9	54.3	49.8	18.7	16.8	41.7	50.9	38.9	33.8	56.6	73.5
Employer and Employee Share Cost	109	15980	15	7079	11	5946	24	714	43	1778	13	335	3	128
	34.0	27.6	30.6	25.1	31.4	29.9	32.0	19.8	41.8	39.1	36.1	34.3	13.0	19.9
Employee Pays Full Cost	64	11640	18	8525	2	605	29	2061	9	198	4	227	2	24
	19.9	20.1	36.8	30.2	5.7	3.0	38.7	57.3	8.7	4.4	11.1	23.3	8.7	3.7
No Contribution (Paid Up)	26	7716	5	3887	3	3447	7	206	4	101	3	60	4	15
	8.1	13.3	10.2	13.8	8.6	17.3	9.3	5.7	3.9	2.2	8.3	6.1	17.4	2.3
CLERICAL-SERVICE														
Total	296	205596	48	101465	32	63635	71	17835	92	14554	34	6150	19	1957
	100.0	100.0	100.0	100.0	100.0	100.0	100.0	100.0	100.0	100.0	100.0	100.0	100.0	100.0
No Response	9	8400	1	6900	–	–	1	492	5	742	2	266	–	–
	3.0	4.1	2.1	6.8	–	–	1.4	2.8	5.4	5.1	5.9	4.3	–	–
Employer Pays Full Cost	110	80458	12	33194	18	33809	14	3227	40	7403	13	1349	13	1476
	37.2	39.1	25.0	32.7	56.1	53.2	19.7	18.1	43.5	50.9	38.2	21.9	68.4	75.4
Employer and Employee Share Cost	97	52059	14	20011	10	18957	23	4251	34	5239	13	3143	3	458
	32.8	25.3	29.2	19.7	31.3	29.8	32.4	23.8	37.0	36.0	38.3	51.2	15.8	23.4
Employee Pays Full Cost	59	42117	16	28900	2	2570	28	8985	9	748	3	912	1	2
	19.9	20.5	33.3	28.5	6.3	4.0	39.5	50.4	9.8	5.1	8.8	14.8	5.3	.1
No Contribution (Paid Up)	21	22562	5	12460	2	8299	5	880	4	422	3	480	2	21
	7.1	11.0	10.4	12.3	6.3	13.0	7.0	4.9	4.3	2.9	8.8	7.8	10.5	1.1

TABLE 19. BASIC GROUP HOSPITAL–SURGICAL–MEDICAL INSURANCE PLANS IN COLLEGES AND UNIVERSITIES
(Questionnaire Sect. III Q.1)

| | ALL INSTITUTIONS | | UNIVERSITIES | | | | LIBERAL ARTS COLLEGES | | | | OTHER | | | |
| | | | PUBLIC | | PRIVATE | | PUBLIC | | PRIVATE | | PUBLIC | | PRIVATE | |
	INSTs	EEs	INSTs	EEs	INSTs	EEs	INSTs	EEs	INSTs	EEs	INSTs	EEs	INSTs	EEs
FACULTY														
Total	1232 / 100.0	285414 / 100.0	93 / 100.0	111008 / 100.0	65 / 100.0	48174 / 100.0	218 / 100.0	63175 / 100.0	596 / 100.0	44090 / 100.0	67 / 100.0	10715 / 100.0	193 / 100.0	8252 / 100.0
Base Plan in Effect	1109 / 90.0	261445 / 91.6	82 / 88.2	98928 / 89.1	60 / 92.3	44235 / 91.8	204 / 93.6	60525 / 95.8	541 / 90.8	40682 / 92.3	52 / 77.6	9693 / 90.5	170 / 88.1	7382 / 89.5
No Base Plan in Effect	123 / 10.0	23969 / 8.4	11 / 11.8	12080 / 10.9	5 / 7.7	3939 / 8.2	14 / 6.4	2650 / 4.2	55 / 9.2	3408 / 7.7	15 / 22.4	1022 / 9.5	23 / 11.9	870 / 10.5
ADMINISTRATIVE														
Total	1232 / 100.0	108315 / 100.0	93 / 100.0	47992 / 100.0	65 / 100.0	28488 / 100.0	218 / 100.0	10488 / 100.0	596 / 100.0	15898 / 100.0	67 / 100.0	2155 / 100.0	193 / 100.0	3294 / 100.0
Base Plan in Effect	1106 / 89.8	100513 / 92.8	83 / 89.2	44069 / 91.8	60 / 92.3	26475 / 92.9	205 / 94.0	10208 / 97.3	537 / 90.1	14609 / 91.9	52 / 77.6	2040 / 94.7	169 / 87.6	3112 / 94.5
No Base Plan in Effect	126 / 10.2	7802 / 7.2	10 / 10.8	3923 / 8.2	5 / 7.7	2013 / 7.1	13 / 6.0	280 / 2.7	59 / 9.9	1289 / 8.1	15 / 22.4	115 / 5.3	24 / 12.4	182 / 5.5
CLERICAL-SERVICE														
Total	1232 / 100.0	444618 / 100.0	93 / 100.0	192630 / 100.0	65 / 100.0	100744 / 100.0	218 / 100.0	61743 / 100.0	596 / 100.0	61664 / 100.0	67 / 100.0	14795 / 100.0	193 / 100.0	13042 / 100.0
Base Plan in Effect	1106 / 89.8	401665 / 90.3	84 / 90.3	172378 / 89.5	61 / 93.8	86150 / 85.5	205 / 94.0	59726 / 96.7	540 / 90.6	57553 / 93.3	52 / 77.6	14079 / 95.2	164 / 85.0	11779 / 90.3
No Base Plan in Effect	126 / 10.2	42953 / 9.7	9 / 9.7	20252 / 10.5	4 / 6.2	14594 / 14.5	13 / 6.0	2017 / 3.3	56 / 9.4	4111 / 6.7	15 / 22.4	716 / 4.8	29 / 15.0	1263 / 9.7

TABLE 20. EMPLOYER-EMPLOYEE CONTRIBUTION TOWARD COST OF EMPLOYEE COVERAGE: BASIC GROUP HOSPITAL-SURGICAL-MEDICAL INSURANCE
(Questionnaire Sect. III Q.2,3)

	ALL INSTITUTIONS		UNIVERSITIES PUBLIC		UNIVERSITIES PRIVATE		LIBERAL ARTS COLLEGES PUBLIC		LIBERAL ARTS COLLEGES PRIVATE		OTHER PUBLIC		OTHER PRIVATE	
	INSTs	EEs	INSTs	EEs	INSTs	EEs	INSTs	EEs	INSTs	EEs	INSTs	EEs	INSTs	EEs
FACULTY														
Total	1109	261445	82	98928	60	44235	204	60525	541	40682	52	9693	170	7382
	100.0	100.0	100.0	100.0	100.0	100.0	100.0	100.0	100.0	100.0	100.0	100.0	100.0	100.0
No Response	18	1944	—	—	—	—	2	1314	12	550	—	—	4	80
	1.6	.7	—	—	—	—	1.0	2.2	2.2	1.4	—	—	2.4	1.1
Employer Pays Full Cost	268	53493	15	17135	9	5159	32	14943	134	9887	27	4523	51	1846
	24.2	20.5	18.3	17.3	15.0	11.7	15.7	24.7	24.8	24.3	52.0	46.7	30.0	25.0
Employer and Employee Share Cost	431	105197	30	41874	22	12859	100	29650	203	15123	15	3132	61	2559
	38.9	40.2	36.6	42.3	36.7	29.1	49.0	48.9	37.5	37.2	28.8	32.3	35.8	34.7
Employee Pays Full Cost	392	100811	37	39919	29	26217	70	14618	192	15122	10	2038	54	2897
	35.3	38.6	45.1	40.4	48.3	59.2	34.3	24.2	35.5	37.1	19.2	21.0	31.8	39.2
ADMINISTRATIVE														
Total	1106	100513	83	44069	60	26475	205	10208	537	14609	52	2040	169	3112
	100.0	100.0	100.0	100.0	100.0	100.0	100.0	100.0	100.0	100.0	100.0	100.0	100.0	100.0
No Response	19	356	—	—	—	—	2	130	12	176	—	—	5	50
	1.7	.4	—	—	—	—	1.0	1.3	2.2	1.2	—	—	3.0	1.6
Employer Pays Full Cost	268	21996	15	9104	9	5241	32	1941	135	3639	27	1234	50	837
	24.2	21.9	18.1	20.7	15.0	19.8	15.6	19.0	25.1	24.9	52.0	60.5	29.6	26.9
Employer and Employee Share Cost	432	37654	32	16277	22	8623	100	5729	202	5356	15	478	61	1191
	39.1	37.5	38.6	36.9	36.7	32.6	48.8	56.1	37.7	36.7	28.8	23.4	36.0	38.3
Employee Pays Full Cost	387	40507	36	18688	29	12611	71	2408	188	5438	10	328	53	1034
	35.0	40.2	43.3	42.4	48.3	47.6	34.6	23.6	35.0	37.2	19.2	16.1	31.4	33.2
CLERICAL-SERVICE														
Total	1106	401665	84	172378	61	86150	205	59726	540	57553	52	14079	164	11779
	100.0	100.0	100.0	100.0	100.0	100.0	100.0	100.0	100.0	100.0	100.0	100.0	100.0	100.0
No Response	18	1361	—	—	—	—	2	600	11	535	—	—	5	226
	1.6	.3	—	—	—	—	1.0	1.0	2.0	.9	—	—	3.0	1.9
Employer Pays Full Cost	267	82227	16	36432	10	13153	31	10458	132	13462	27	6118	51	2604
	24.1	20.5	19.0	21.1	16.4	15.3	15.1	17.5	24.4	23.4	51.9	43.5	31.1	22.1
Employer and Employee Share Cost	459	178238	35	74514	27	35676	103	33978	216	24416	16	4427	62	5227
	41.6	44.4	41.7	43.3	44.3	41.4	50.2	56.9	40.1	42.4	30.8	31.4	37.9	44.4
Employee Pays Full Cost	362	139839	33	61432	24	37321	69	14690	181	19140	9	3534	46	3722
	32.7	34.8	39.3	35.6	39.3	43.3	33.7	24.6	33.5	33.3	17.3	25.1	28.0	31.6

TABLE 21. EMPLOYER-EMPLOYEE CONTRIBUTION TOWARD COST
OF DEPENDENT COVERAGE: BASIC GROUP HOSPITAL-SURGICAL-MEDICAL INSURANCE
(Questionnaire Sect. III Q.7,8)

	ALL INSTITUTIONS		UNIVERSITIES PUBLIC		UNIVERSITIES PRIVATE		LIBERAL ARTS COLLEGES PUBLIC		LIBERAL ARTS COLLEGES PRIVATE		OTHER PUBLIC		OTHER PRIVATE	
	INSTs	EEs	INSTs	EEs	INSTs	EEs	INSTs	EEs	INSTs	EEs	INSTs	EEs	INSTs	EEs
FACULTY														
Total	1095	261039	82	98928	60	44235	202	60380	534	40466	52	9693	165	7337
	100.0	100.0	100.0	100.0	100.0	100.0	100.0	100.0	100.0	100.0	100.0	100.0	100.0	100.0
No Response	22	4707	1	3550	—	—	—	—	14	670	—	—	7	487
	2.0	1.8	1.2	3.6	—	—	—	—	2.6	1.7	—	—	4.2	6.6
Employer Pays Full Cost	73	14712	2	873	1	194	4	9971	40	2976	3	138	23	560
	6.7	5.6	2.4	.9	1.7	.4	2.0	16.5	7.5	7.4	5.8	1.4	13.9	7.6
Employer and Employee Share Cost	326	88770	24	37816	17	10599	69	21991	152	12053	23	4748	41	1563
	29.8	34.0	29.3	38.2	28.3	24.0	34.2	36.4	28.5	29.8	44.2	49.0	24.8	21.3
Employee Pays Full Cost	674	152850	55	56689	42	33442	129	28418	328	24767	26	4807	94	4727
	61.5	58.6	67.1	57.3	70.0	75.6	63.8	47.1	61.4	61.1	50.0	49.6	57.1	64.5
ADMINISTRATIVE														
Total	1093	100298	83	44069	60	26475	203	10077	530	14541	52	2040	165	3096
	100.0	100.0	100.0	100.0	100.0	100.0	100.0	100.0	100.0	100.0	100.0	100.0	100.0	100.0
No Response	21	2214	1	1759	—	—	—	—	13	228	—	—	7	227
	1.9	2.2	1.2	4.0	—	—	—	—	2.5	1.6	—	—	4.2	7.3
Employer Pays Full Cost	71	2210	2	213	1	86	4	700	40	968	3	20	21	223
	6.5	2.2	2.4	.5	1.7	.3	2.0	6.9	7.5	6.7	5.8	1.0	12.7	7.2
Employer and Employee Share Cost	323	32347	24	15985	17	6982	69	3419	150	4104	23	1198	40	659
	29.6	32.3	28.9	36.3	28.3	26.4	34.0	33.9	28.3	28.2	44.2	58.7	24.2	21.3
Employee Pays Full Cost	678	63527	56	26112	42	19407	130	5958	327	9241	26	822	97	1987
	62.0	63.3	67.5	59.2	70.0	73.3	64.0	59.2	61.7	63.5	50.0	40.3	58.9	64.2
CLERICAL-SERVICE														
Total	1089	401095	84	172378	61	86150	203	59510	530	57237	52	14079	159	11741
	100.0	100.0	100.0	100.0	100.0	100.0	100.0	100.0	100.0	100.0	100.0	100.0	100.0	100.0
No Response	22	10161	1	6900	—	—	—	—	15	1369	—	—	6	1892
	2.0	2.5	1.2	4.0	—	—	—	—	2.8	2.4	—	—	3.8	16.1
Employer Pays Full Cost	65	9310	2	1055	—	—	4	5222	38	2415	3	107	18	511
	6.0	2.3	2.4	.6	—	—	2.0	8.8	7.2	4.2	5.8	.8	11.3	4.4
Employer and Employee Share Cost	329	130610	25	60114	19	24693	67	17810	156	19133	22	6375	40	2485
	30.2	32.6	29.8	34.9	31.1	28.7	33.0	29.9	29.4	33.4	42.3	45.3	25.2	21.2
Employee Pays Full Cost	673	251014	56	104309	42	61457	132	36478	321	34320	27	7597	95	6853
	61.8	62.6	66.6	60.5	68.9	71.3	65.0	61.3	60.6	60.0	51.9	53.9	59.7	58.3

TABLE 22. BASIC GROUP HOSPITAL-SURGICAL-MEDICAL PLAN: WAITING PERIOD BEFORE EMPLOYEE IS ELIGIBLE TO PARTICIPATE IN PLAN

(Questionnaire Sect. III Q.4)

| | ALL INSTITUTIONS | | UNIVERSITIES | | | | LIBERAL ARTS COLLEGES | | | | OTHER | | | |
| | | | PUBLIC | | PRIVATE | | PUBLIC | | PRIVATE | | PUBLIC | | PRIVATE | |
	INSTs	EEs	INSTs	EEs	INSTs	EEs	INSTs	EEs	INSTs	EEs	INSTs	EEs	INSTs	EEs
FACULTY														
Total	1109	261445	82	98928	60	44235	204	60525	541	40682	52	9693	170	7382
	100.0	100.0	100.0	100.0	100.0	100.0	100.0	100.0	100.0	100.0	100.0	100.0	100.0	100.0
No Response	24	4090	4	2826	–	–	2	140	11	449	2	600	5	75
	2.2	1.6	4.9	2.9	–	–	1.0	.2	2.0	1.1	3.8	6.2	2.9	1.0
No Waiting Period	628	135050	39	49907	33	26288	114	27223	322	23066	35	5405	85	3161
	56.6	51.7	47.6	50.4	55.0	59.4	55.8	44.9	59.6	56.7	67.3	55.7	50.1	42.9
Less than a Month	279	92148	33	40967	17	10312	62	26983	118	9569	7	1850	42	2467
	25.2	35.2	40.2	41.4	28.3	23.3	30.4	44.6	21.8	23.5	13.5	19.1	24.7	33.4
Until Stated Date(s) During First Year	38	3262	–	–	1	254	3	719	26	2161	–	–	8	128
	3.4	1.2	–	–	1.7	.6	1.5	1.2	4.8	5.3	–	–	4.7	1.7
Stated No. of Months	114	20646	4	3929	4	4614	21	5004	52	4063	8	1838	25	1198
	10.3	7.9	4.9	4.0	6.7	10.4	10.3	8.3	9.6	10.0	15.4	19.0	14.7	16.2
Other	26	6249	2	1299	5	2767	2	456	12	1374	–	–	5	353
	2.3	2.4	2.4	1.3	8.3	6.3	1.0	.8	2.2	3.4	–	–	2.9	4.8
ADMINISTRATIVE														
Total	1106	100513	83	44069	60	26475	205	10208	537	14609	52	2040	169	3112
	100.0	100.0	100.0	100.0	100.0	100.0	100.0	100.0	100.0	100.0	100.0	100.0	100.0	100.0
No Response	26	1790	4	1298	–	–	2	38	13	235	2	41	5	178
	2.4	1.8	4.8	2.9	–	–	1.0	.4	2.4	1.6	3.8	2.0	3.0	5.7
No Waiting Period	608	54412	39	23103	29	15444	114	4823	306	8423	34	1342	86	1277
	55.0	54.1	47.0	52.5	48.3	58.3	55.6	47.2	57.0	57.7	65.4	65.8	50.9	41.0
Less than a Month	279	30779	33	17023	16	4373	63	4752	117	3183	7	275	43	1173
	25.2	30.6	39.8	38.6	26.7	16.5	30.7	46.6	21.8	21.8	13.5	13.5	25.4	37.7
Until Stated Date(s) During First Year	38	997	–	–	1	74	3	83	27	808	–	–	7	32
	3.4	1.0	–	–	1.7	.3	1.5	.8	5.0	5.5	–	–	4.1	1.0
Stated No. of Months	131	9437	5	1754	9	4864	21	457	64	1589	9	382	23	391
	11.8	9.4	6.0	4.0	15.0	18.4	10.2	4.5	11.9	10.9	17.3	18.7	13.6	12.6
Other	24	3098	2	891	5	1720	2	55	10	371	–	–	5	61
	2.2	3.1	2.4	2.0	8.3	6.5	1.0	.5	1.9	2.5	–	–	3.0	2.0

WAITING PERIOD BEFORE EMPLOYEE IS ELIGIBLE TO PARTICIPATE IN PLAN
(continued)

	ALL INSTITUTIONS		UNIVERSITIES PUBLIC		PRIVATE		LIBERAL ARTS COLLEGES PUBLIC		PRIVATE		OTHER PUBLIC		PRIVATE	
	INSTs	EEs	INSTs	EEs	INSTs	EEs	INSTs	EEs	INSTs	EEs	INSTs	EEs	INSTs	EEs
CLERICAL-SERVICE														
Total	1106	401665	84	172378	61	86150	205	59726	540	57553	52	14079	164	11779
	100.0	100.0	100.0	100.0	100.0	100.0	100.0	100.0	100.0	100.0	100.0	100.0	100.0	100.0
No Response	25	5352	4	2464	–	–	2	82	13	631	2	388	4	1787
	2.3	1.3	4.8	1.4	–	–	1.0	.1	2.4	1.1	3.8	2.8	2.4	15.2
No Waiting Period	531	193670	40	83135	23	45454	112	26411	252	25256	32	10146	72	3268
	48.0	48.2	47.6	48.3	37.7	52.8	54.6	44.2	46.7	43.9	61.6	72.1	43.9	27.7
Less than a Month	264	137659	32	75741	15	16490	64	28093	104	10745	8	1794	41	4796
	23.9	34.3	38.1	43.9	24.6	19.1	31.2	47.1	19.3	18.7	15.4	12.7	25.0	40.7
Until Stated Date(s) During First Year	44	5257	–	–	2	909	3	715	31	3519	–	–	8	114
	4.0	1.3	–	–	3.3	1.1	1.5	1.2	5.7	6.1	–	–	4.9	1.0
Stated No. of Months	214	47247	6	8508	16	15794	22	4041	127	15567	10	1751	33	1586
	19.3	11.8	7.1	4.9	26.2	18.3	10.7	6.8	23.5	27.0	19.2	12.4	20.1	13.5
Other	28	12480	2	2530	5	7503	2	384	13	1835	–	–	6	228
	2.5	3.1	2.4	1.5	8.2	8.7	1.0	.6	2.4	3.2	–	–	3.7	1.9

(Questionnaire Sect. III Q.5)

| | ALL INSTITUTIONS | | UNIVERSITIES | | | | LIBERAL ARTS COLLEGES | | | | OTHER | | | |
| | | | PUBLIC | | PRIVATE | | PUBLIC | | PRIVATE | | PUBLIC | | PRIVATE | |
	INSTs	EEs	INSTs	EEs	INSTs	EEs	INSTs	EEs	INSTs	EEs	INSTs	EEs	INSTs	EEs
FACULTY														
Total	1109	261445	82	98928	60	44235	204	60525	541	40682	52	9693	170	7382
	100.0	100.0	100.0	100.0	100.0	100.0	100.0	100.0	100.0	100.0	100.0	100.0	100.0	100.0
Blue Cross	777	188693	53	56540	49	40133	141	48793	373	28949	41	8199	120	6079
	70.1	72.2	64.6	57.2	81.7	90.7	69.1	80.6	68.9	71.2	78.8	84.6	70.6	82.3
Blue Shield	727	178770	51	53378	47	37730	136	47087	346	26808	40	8123	107	5644
	65.6	68.4	62.2	54.0	78.3	85.3	66.7	77.8	64.0	65.9	76.9	83.8	62.9	76.5
Insurance Co.	379	102975	34	49881	14	9463	97	26274	172	12508	20	3576	42	1273
	34.2	39.4	41.5	50.4	23.3	21.4	47.5	43.4	31.8	30.7	38.5	36.9	24.7	17.2
Other	73	36617	6	9682	3	3304	34	21390	18	1557	5	498	7	186
	6.6	14.0	7.3	9.8	5.0	7.5	16.7	35.3	3.3	3.8	9.6	5.1	4.1	2.5
ADMINISTRATIVE														
Total	1106	100513	83	44069	60	26475	205	10208	537	14609	52	2040	169	3112
	100.0	100.0	100.0	100.0	100.0	100.0	100.0	100.0	100.0	100.0	100.0	100.0	100.0	100.0
Blue Cross	776	78925	53	30710	49	25215	141	8145	368	10527	41	1816	124	2512
	70.2	78.5	63.9	69.7	81.7	95.2	68.8	79.8	68.5	72.1	78.8	89.0	73.4	80.7
Blue Shield	724	76682	52	30653	47	24018	136	7939	340	9872	40	1794	109	2406
	65.5	76.3	62.7	69.6	78.3	90.7	66.3	77.8	63.3	67.6	76.9	87.9	64.5	77.3
Insurance Co.	377	31343	35	16028	14	4317	98	5711	172	4373	20	414	38	500
	34.1	31.2	42.2	36.4	23.3	16.3	47.8	55.9	32.0	29.9	38.5	20.3	22.5	16.1
Other	70	9258	6	3457	3	1389	34	3795	16	428	5	72	6	117
	6.3	9.2	7.2	7.8	5.0	5.2	16.6	37.2	3.0	2.9	9.6	3.5	3.6	3.8
CLERICAL-SERVICE														
Total	1106	401665	84	172378	61	86150	205	59726	540	57553	52	14079	164	11779
	100.0	100.0	100.0	100.0	100.0	100.0	100.0	100.0	100.0	100.0	100.0	100.0	100.0	100.0
Blue Cross	783	304670	55	116582	49	77570	144	47436	371	41880	42	10966	122	10236
	70.8	75.9	65.5	67.6	80.3	90.0	70.2	79.4	68.7	72.8	80.8	77.9	74.4	86.9
Blue Shield	731	297590	54	115448	47	76580	137	46152	345	38784	41	10865	107	9761
	66.1	74.1	64.3	67.0	77.0	88.9	66.8	77.3	63.9	67.4	78.8	77.2	65.2	82.9
Insurance Co.	378	158665	35	82329	15	19325	95	31581	177	17620	20	6289	36	1521
	34.2	39.5	41.7	47.8	24.6	22.4	46.3	52.9	32.8	30.6	38.5	44.7	22.0	12.9
Other	67	46835	5	16050	4	6021	32	22368	16	1626	5	570	5	200
	6.1	11.7	6.0	9.3	6.6	7.0	15.6	37.5	3.0	2.8	9.6	4.0	3.0	1.7

Percentages add to over 100 due to more than one plan in effect at the same institution, e.g., nearly all Blue Shield plans accompany a Blue Cross plan.

TABLE 24. BASIC GROUP HOSPITAL-SURGICAL-MEDICAL INSURANCE PLANS: INSTITUTIONS PROVIDING FOR CONTINUATION OF GROUP COVERAGE FOR EMPLOYEES RETIRING BEFORE AGE 65 AND AT AGE 65 OR AFTER

(Questionnaire Sect. III Q.9)

	ALL INSTITUTIONS		UNIVERSITIES				LIBERAL ARTS COLLEGES				OTHER			
			PUBLIC		PRIVATE		PUBLIC		PRIVATE		PUBLIC		PRIVATE	
	INSTs	EEs	INSTs	EEs	INSTs	EEs	INSTs	EEs	INSTs	EEs	INSTs	EEs	INSTs	EEs
FACULTY														
Total	1109	261445	82	98928	60	44235	204	60525	541	40682	52	9693	170	7382
	100.0	100.0	100.0	100.0	100.0	100.0	100.0	100.0	100.0	100.0	100.0	100.0	100.0	100.0
No Response	85	10233	1	3550	3	1972	3	876	53	2889	2	441	23	505
	7.7	3.9	1.2	3.6	5.0	4.5	1.5	1.4	9.8	7.1	3.8	4.5	13.5	6.8
Continuation on Ret. Before and After 65	335	129695	45	58249	20	12795	101	39260	106	10938	37	7233	26	1220
	30.2	49.6	54.9	58.9	33.3	28.9	49.4	65.0	19.6	26.9	71.1	74.6	15.3	16.5
Continuation on Ret. Before 65 Only	43	16080	6	7500	6	5238	5	499	22	1953	3	800	1	90
	3.9	6.2	7.3	7.6	10.0	11.8	2.5	.8	4.1	4.8	5.8	8.3	.6	1.2
Continuation on Ret. at 65 or After Only	50	10540	3	2212	6	4082	3	815	30	2573	3	461	5	397
	4.5	4.0	3.7	2.2	10.0	9.2	1.5	1.3	5.5	6.3	5.8	4.8	2.9	5.4
No Continuation Either Before or After 65	596	94897	27	27417	25	20148	92	19075	330	22329	7	758	115	5170
	53.7	36.3	32.9	27.7	41.7	45.6	45.1	31.5	61.0	54.9	13.5	7.8	67.7	70.1
ADMINISTRATIVE														
Total	1106	100513	83	44069	60	26475	205	10208	537	14609	52	2040	169	3112
	100.0	100.0	100.0	100.0	100.0	100.0	100.0	100.0	100.0	100.0	100.0	100.0	100.0	100.0
No Response	81	3885	1	1759	3	747	3	176	51	854	2	127	21	222
	7.3	3.9	1.2	4.0	5.0	2.8	1.5	1.7	9.5	5.8	3.8	6.2	12.4	7.1
Continuation on Ret. Before and After 65	335	49662	45	24878	20	11582	101	6348	106	4666	37	1467	26	721
	30.3	49.4	54.3	56.4	33.3	43.7	49.2	62.2	19.7	31.9	71.1	71.9	15.4	23.2
Continuation on Ret. Before 65 Only	45	7980	7	2724	6	4001	6	171	22	834	3	230	1	20
	4.1	7.9	8.4	6.2	10.0	15.1	2.9	1.7	4.1	5.7	5.8	11.3	.6	.6
Continuation on Ret. At 65 or After Only	50	3437	3	1111	6	1048	3	135	30	853	3	81	5	209
	4.5	3.4	3.6	2.5	10.0	4.0	1.5	1.3	5.6	5.8	5.8	4.0	3.0	6.7
No Continuation Either Before or After 65	595	35549	27	13597	25	9097	92	3378	328	7402	7	135	116	1940
	53.8	35.4	32.5	30.9	41.7	34.4	44.9	33.1	61.1	50.8	13.5	6.6	68.6	62.4
CLERICAL-SERVICE														
Total	1106	401665	84	172378	61	86150	205	59726	540	57553	52	14079	164	11779
	100.0	100.0	100.0	100.0	100.0	100.0	100.0	100.0	100.0	100.0	100.0	100.0	100.0	100.0
No Response	88	17471	1	6900	5	4194	3	972	56	4096	2	603	21	706
	8.0	4.3	1.2	4.0	8.2	4.9	1.5	1.6	10.4	7.1	3.8	4.3	12.8	6.0
Continuation on Ret. Before and After 65	320	185954	45	92118	17	27570	100	38857	96	15085	37	10091	25	2233
	28.9	46.3	53.6	53.4	27.9	32.0	48.7	65.0	17.8	26.2	71.1	71.7	15.2	19.0
Continuation on Ret. Before 65 Only	45	18206	7	7567	5	6040	6	929	23	3025	3	555	1	90
	4.1	4.5	8.3	4.4	8.2	7.0	2.9	1.6	4.3	5.3	5.8	3.9	.6	.8
Continuation on Ret. At 65 or After Only	49	15536	3	4422	6	5678	3	1125	29	3101	3	392	5	818
	4.4	3.9	3.6	2.6	9.8	6.6	1.5	1.9	5.4	5.4	5.8	2.8	3.0	6.9
No Continuation Either Before or After 65	604	164498	28	61371	28	42668	93	17843	336	32246	7	2438	112	7932
	54.6	41.0	33.3	35.6	45.9	49.5	45.4	29.9	62.1	56.0	13.5	17.3	68.4	67.3

TABLE 25. BASIC GROUP HOSPITAL-SURGICAL-MEDICAL INSURANCE: EMPLOYER-EMPLOYEE CONTRIBUTION TOWARD COST OF EMPLOYEE GROUP COVERAGE DURING RETIREMENT
(Questionnaire Sect. III Q.11,12)

| | ALL INSTITUTIONS | | UNIVERSITIES | | | | LIBERAL ARTS COLLEGES | | | | OTHER | | | |
| | | | PUBLIC | | PRIVATE | | PUBLIC | | PRIVATE | | PUBLIC | | PRIVATE | |
	INSTs	EEs	INSTs	EEs	INSTs	EEs	INSTs	EEs	INSTs	EEs	INSTs	EEs	INSTs	EEs
FACULTY														
Total	449	158517	54	67961	32	22115	110	41234	171	16455	45	8935	37	1817
	100.0	100.0	100.0	100.0	100.0	100.0	100.0	100.0	100.0	100.0	100.0	100.0	100.0	100.0
No Response	25	4009	1	333	2	2312	1	75	19	1135	1	132	1	22
	5.6	2.5	1.9	.5	6.2	10.5	.9	.2	11.1	6.9	2.2	1.5	2.7	1.2
Employer Pays Full Cost	90	26954	10	10964	5	3026	15	6470	30	3259	19	2476	11	759
	20.0	17.0	18.5	16.1	15.6	13.7	13.6	15.7	17.5	19.8	42.3	27.7	29.7	41.8
Employer and Employee Share Cost	127	58177	12	19522	13	9424	49	23281	38	3666	10	2082	5	202
	28.3	36.7	22.2	28.7	40.7	42.6	44.6	56.4	22.2	22.3	22.2	23.3	13.5	11.1
Employee Pays Full Cost	207	69377	31	37142	12	7353	45	11408	84	8395	15	4245	20	834
	46.1	43.8	57.4	54.7	37.5	33.2	40.9	27.7	49.2	51.0	33.3	47.5	54.1	45.9
ADMINISTRATIVE														
Total	450	61657	55	28713	32	16631	111	6779	170	6638	45	1905	37	991
	100.0	100.0	100.0	100.0	100.0	100.0	100.0	100.0	100.0	100.0	100.0	100.0	100.0	100.0
No Response	24	3897	1	109	2	3225	1	25	18	505	1	19	1	14
	5.3	6.3	1.8	.4	6.2	19.4	.9	.4	10.6	7.6	2.2	1.0	2.7	1.4
Employer Pays Full Cost	91	13150	10	7898	5	1250	15	1318	30	1319	19	897	12	468
	20.2	21.3	18.2	27.5	15.6	7.5	13.5	19.4	17.6	19.9	42.3	47.1	32.4	47.2
Employer and Employee Share Cost	127	19180	13	6689	13	6617	49	3969	37	1422	10	369	5	114
	28.2	31.1	23.6	23.3	40.7	39.8	44.2	58.6	21.8	21.4	22.2	19.4	13.5	11.5
Employee Pays Full Cost	208	25430	31	14017	12	5539	46	1467	85	3392	15	620	19	395
	46.3	41.3	56.4	48.8	37.5	33.3	41.4	21.6	50.0	51.1	33.3	32.5	51.4	39.9
CLERICAL-SERVICE														
Total	435	222678	55	104107	28	39288	110	41486	161	22775	45	11641	36	3381
	100.0	100.0	100.0	100.0	100.0	100.0	100.0	100.0	100.0	100.0	100.0	100.0	100.0	100.0
No Response	28	5270	1	693	2	2509	1	100	20	1701	2	177	2	90
	6.4	2.4	1.8	.7	7.1	6.4	.9	.2	12.4	7.5	4.4	1.5	5.6	2.7
Employer Pays Full Cost	86	38428	10	18793	4	4371	15	5238	27	3937	18	4468	12	1621
	19.8	17.3	18.2	18.1	14.3	11.1	13.6	12.6	16.8	17.3	40.1	38.4	33.3	47.9
Employer and Employee Share Cost	121	81599	14	31782	10	14878	48	25811	36	5498	10	3505	3	125
	27.8	36.6	25.5	30.5	35.7	37.9	43.7	62.3	22.4	24.1	22.2	30.1	8.3	3.7
Employee Pays Full Cost	200	97381	30	52839	12	17530	46	10337	78	11639	15	3491	19	1545
	46.0	43.7	54.5	50.7	42.9	44.6	41.8	24.9	48.4	51.1	33.3	30.0	52.8	45.7

TABLE 26. BASIC GROUP HOSPITAL-SURGICAL-MEDICAL INSURANCE PLAN:
EMPLOYER-EMPLOYEE CONTRIBUTION TOWARD COST OF GROUP COVERAGE
OF DEPENDENTS OF COVERED RETIRED EMPLOYEES
(Questionnaire Sect. III Q.14,15)

| | ALL INSTITUTIONS | | UNIVERSITIES | | | | LIBERAL ARTS COLLEGES | | | | OTHER | | | |
| | | | PUBLIC | | PRIVATE | | PUBLIC | | PRIVATE | | PUBLIC | | PRIVATE | |
	INSTs	EEs	INSTs	EEs	INSTs	EEs	INSTs	EEs	INSTs	EEs	INSTs	EEs	INSTs	EEs
FACULTY														
Total	449	158517	54	67961	32	22115	110	41234	171	16455	45	8935	37	1817
	100.0	100.0	100.0	100.0	100.0	100.0	100.0	100.0	100.0	100.0	100.0	100.0	100.0	100.0
No Response	41	6862	1	1214	3	2599	4	606	28	1941	3	349	2	153
	9.1	4.3	1.9	1.8	9.4	11.8	3.6	1.5	16.4	11.8	6.7	3.9	5.4	8.4
Employer Pays Full Cost	28	12151	3	4806	2	2200	3	3171	10	1317	2	101	8	556
	6.2	7.7	5.6	7.1	6.3	9.9	2.7	7.7	5.8	8.0	4.4	1.1	21.6	30.6
Employer and Employee Share Cost	118	54347	13	19375	11	8149	40	20698	31	2552	18	3371	5	202
	26.3	34.3	24.1	28.5	34.4	36.8	36.4	50.2	18.1	15.5	40.0	37.7	13.5	11.1
Employee Pays Full Cost	262	85157	37	42566	16	9167	63	16759	102	10645	22	5114	22	906
	58.4	53.7	68.4	62.6	49.9	41.5	57.3	40.6	59.7	64.7	48.9	57.3	59.5	49.9
ADMINISTRATIVE														
Total	450	61657	55	28713	32	16631	111	6779	170	6638	45	1905	37	991
	100.0	100.0	100.0	100.0	100.0	100.0	100.0	100.0	100.0	100.0	100.0	100.0	100.0	100.0
No Response	41	5269	1	981	3	3339	4	121	28	697	3	94	2	37
	9.1	8.5	1.8	3.4	9.4	20.1	3.6	1.8	16.5	10.5	6.7	4.9	5.4	3.7
Employer Pays Full Cost	29	4546	3	1985	2	1050	3	500	10	568	2	15	9	428
	6.4	7.4	5.5	6.9	6.3	6.3	2.7	7.4	5.9	8.6	4.4	.8	24.3	43.2
Employer and Employee Share Cost	117	18802	13	8111	11	6002	40	2726	30	890	18	959	5	114
	26.0	30.5	23.6	28.2	34.4	36.1	36.0	40.2	17.6	13.4	40.0	50.4	13.5	11.5
Employee Pays Full Cost	263	33040	38	17636	16	6240	64	3432	102	4483	22	837	21	412
	58.5	53.6	69.1	61.5	49.9	37.5	57.7	50.6	60.0	67.5	48.9	43.9	56.8	41.6
CLERICAL-SERVICE														
Total	435	222678	55	104107	28	39288	110	41486	161	22775	45	11641	36	3381
	100.0	100.0	100.0	100.0	100.0	100.0	100.0	100.0	100.0	100.0	100.0	100.0	100.0	100.0
No Response	41	8508	1	2200	3	2910	4	648	28	2320	3	274	2	156
	9.4	3.8	1.8	2.1	10.7	7.4	3.6	1.6	17.4	10.2	6.7	2.4	5.6	4.6
Employer Pays Full Cost	28	13602	3	5515	2	3350	3	2022	9	1487	2	83	9	1145
	6.4	6.1	5.5	5.3	7.1	8.5	2.7	4.9	5.6	6.5	4.4	.7	25.0	33.9
Employer and Employee Share Cost	110	65216	13	28750	8	11768	39	15314	28	3927	18	5318	4	139
	25.3	29.3	23.6	27.6	28.6	30.0	35.5	36.9	17.4	17.2	40.0	45.7	11.1	4.1
Employee Pays Full Cost	256	135352	38	67642	15	21260	64	23502	96	15041	22	5966	21	1941
	58.9	60.8	69.1	65.0	53.6	54.1	58.2	56.6	59.6	66.1	48.9	51.2	58.3	57.4

TABLE 27. GROUP MAJOR MEDICAL EXPENSE INSURANCE
(Questionnaire Sect. IV Q.1)

| | ALL INSTITUTIONS | | UNIVERSITIES | | | | LIBERAL ARTS COLLEGES | | | | OTHER | | | |
| | | | PUBLIC | | PRIVATE | | PUBLIC | | PRIVATE | | PUBLIC | | PRIVATE | |
	INSTs	EEs	INSTs	EEs	INSTs	EEs	INSTs	EEs	INSTs	EEs	INSTs	EEs	INSTs	EEs
FACULTY														
Total	1232	285414	93	111008	65	48174	218	63175	596	44090	67	10715	193	8252
	100.0	100.0	100.0	100.0	100.0	100.0	100.0	100.0	100.0	100.0	100.0	100.0	100.0	100.0
Major Medical Plan in Effect	1005	267270	88	106229	64	47574	190	58519	479	38690	58	10061	126	6197
	81.6	93.6	94.6	95.7	98.5	98.8	87.2	92.6	80.4	87.8	86.6	93.9	65.3	75.1
No Major Medical Plan	227	18144	5	4779	1	600	28	4656	117	5400	9	654	67	2055
	18.4	6.4	5.4	4.3	1.5	1.2	12.8	7.4	19.6	12.2	13.4	6.1	34.7	24.9
ADMINISTRATIVE														
Total	1232	108315	93	47992	65	28488	218	10488	596	15898	67	2155	193	3294
	100.0	100.0	100.0	100.0	100.0	100.0	100.0	100.0	100.0	100.0	100.0	100.0	100.0	100.0
Major Medical Plan in Effect	1003	102799	88	46521	64	28463	190	9670	478	13484	58	2054	125	2607
	81.4	94.9	94.6	96.9	98.5	99.9	87.2	92.2	80.2	84.8	86.6	95.3	64.8	79.1
No Major Medical Plan	229	5516	5	1471	1	25	28	818	118	2414	9	101	68	687
	18.6	5.1	5.4	3.1	1.5	.1	12.8	7.8	19.8	15.2	13.4	4.7	35.2	20.9
CLERICAL-SERVICE														
Total	1232	444618	93	192630	65	100744	218	61743	596	61664	67	14795	193	13042
	100.0	100.0	100.0	100.0	100.0	100.0	100.0	100.0	100.0	100.0	100.0	100.0	100.0	100.0
Major Medical Plan in Effect	902	376339	84	168793	57	89060	184	54849	407	44489	57	12278	113	6870
	73.2	84.6	90.3	87.6	87.7	88.4	84.4	88.8	68.3	72.1	85.1	83.0	58.5	52.7
No Major Medical Plan	330	68279	9	23837	8	11684	34	6894	189	17175	10	2517	80	6172
	26.8	15.4	9.7	12.4	12.3	11.6	15.6	11.2	31.7	27.9	14.9	17.0	41.5	47.3

TABLE 28. GROUP MAJOR MEDICAL EXPENSE INSURANCE PLANS: PLAN ACCOMPANIED BY SEPARATE BASIC HEALTH INSURANCE PLAN OR OPERATING AS THE SINGLE HEALTH INSURANCE PLAN AT INSTITUTION

(Questionnaire Sect. IV Q.2)

	ALL INSTITUTIONS		UNIVERSITIES PUBLIC		UNIVERSITIES PRIVATE		LIBERAL ARTS COLLEGES PUBLIC		LIBERAL ARTS COLLEGES PRIVATE		OTHER PUBLIC		OTHER PRIVATE	
	INSTs	EEs	INSTs	EEs	INSTs	EEs	INSTs	EEs	INSTs	EEs	INSTs	EEs	INSTs	EEs
FACULTY														
Total	988 / 100.0	263681 / 100.0	86 / 100.0	104482 / 100.0	64 / 100.0	47574 / 100.0	188 / 100.0	57340 / 100.0	468 / 100.0	38095 / 100.0	57 / 100.0	9999 / 100.0	125 / 100.0	6191 / 100.0
With Separate Base Plan	802 / 81.2	212974 / 80.8	71 / 82.6	84820 / 81.2	55 / 85.9	41135 / 86.5	155 / 82.4	43226 / 75.4	382 / 81.6	30820 / 80.9	46 / 80.7	8753 / 87.5	93 / 74.4	4220 / 68.2
As Single Health Ins Plan	186 / 18.8	50707 / 19.2	15 / 17.4	19662 / 18.8	9 / 14.1	6439 / 13.5	33 / 17.6	14114 / 24.6	86 / 18.4	7275 / 19.1	11 / 19.3	1246 / 12.5	32 / 25.6	1971 / 31.8
ADMINISTRATIVE														
Total	986 / 100.0	101425 / 100.0	86 / 100.0	45747 / 100.0	64 / 100.0	28463 / 100.0	188 / 100.0	9346 / 100.0	466 / 100.0	13214 / 100.0	57 / 100.0	2048 / 100.0	125 / 100.0	2607 / 100.0
With Separate Base Plan	801 / 81.2	88696 / 87.4	72 / 83.7	40167 / 87.8	55 / 85.9	25578 / 89.9	155 / 82.4	8418 / 90.1	380 / 81.5	10655 / 80.6	46 / 80.7	1956 / 95.5	93 / 74.4	1922 / 73.7
As Single Health Ins Plan	185 / 18.8	12729 / 12.6	14 / 16.3	5580 / 12.2	9 / 14.1	2885 / 10.1	33 / 17.6	928 / 9.9	86 / 18.5	2559 / 19.4	11 / 19.3	92 / 4.5	32 / 25.6	685 / 26.3
CLERICAL-SERVICE														
Total	885 / 100.0	371947 / 100.0	82 / 100.0	166820 / 100.0	57 / 100.0	89060 / 100.0	180 / 100.0	53018 / 100.0	398 / 100.0	44034 / 100.0	56 / 100.0	12220 / 100.0	112 / 100.0	6795 / 100.0
With Separate Base Plan	710 / 80.2	306314 / 82.4	70 / 85.4	139268 / 83.5	49 / 86.0	71680 / 80.5	147 / 81.7	43124 / 81.3	319 / 80.2	36126 / 82.0	45 / 80.4	11524 / 94.3	80 / 71.4	4592 / 67.6
As Single Health Ins Plan	175 / 19.8	65633 / 17.6	12 / 14.6	27552 / 16.5	8 / 14.0	17380 / 19.5	33 / 18.3	9894 / 18.7	79 / 19.8	7908 / 18.0	11 / 19.6	696 / 5.7	32 / 28.6	2203 / 32.4

TABLE 29. EMPLOYER-EMPLOYEE CONTRIBUTION TOWARD COST OF GROUP MAJOR MEDICAL EXPENSE INSURANCE PLAN FOR ACTIVE EMPLOYEES
(Questionnaire Sect. IV Q.3,4)

| | ALL INSTITUTIONS | | UNIVERSITIES | | | | LIBERAL ARTS COLLEGES | | | | OTHER | | | |
| | | | PUBLIC | | PRIVATE | | PUBLIC | | PRIVATE | | PUBLIC | | PRIVATE | |
	INSTs	EEs	INSTs	EEs	INSTs	EEs	INSTs	EEs	INSTs	EEs	INSTs	EEs	INSTs	EEs
FACULTY														
Total	1005	267270	88	106229	64	47574	190	58519	479	38690	58	10061	126	6197
	100.0	100.0	100.0	100.0	100.0	100.0	100.0	100.0	100.0	100.0	100.0	100.0	100.0	100.0
No Response	23	1686	–	–	1	104	2	386	15	1078	1	20	4	98
	2.3	.6	–	–	1.6	.2	1.1	.7	3.1	2.8	1.7	.2	3.2	1.6
Employer Pays Full Cost	384	87851	22	24866	26	18624	37	17866	210	19044	27	4144	62	3307
	38.2	32.9	25.0	23.4	40.6	39.1	19.5	30.5	43.8	49.2	46.6	41.2	49.2	53.4
Employer and Employee Share Cost	407	107009	37	45564	33	26710	60	13899	215	16192	18	2505	44	2139
	40.5	40.0	42.0	42.9	51.5	56.2	31.6	23.8	45.0	41.9	31.0	24.9	34.9	34.5
Employee Pays Full Cost	191	70724	29	35799	4	2136	91	26368	39	2376	12	3392	16	653
	19.0	26.5	33.0	33.7	6.3	4.5	47.8	45.0	8.1	6.1	20.7	33.7	12.7	10.5
ADMINISTRATIVE														
Total	1003	102799	88	46521	64	28463	190	9670	478	13484	58	2054	125	2607
	100.0	100.0	100.0	100.0	100.0	100.0	100.0	100.0	100.0	100.0	100.0	100.0	100.0	100.0
No Response	25	565	–	–	1	21	2	77	17	444	1	4	4	19
	2.5	.5	–	–	1.6	.1	1.1	.8	3.6	3.3	1.7	.2	3.2	.7
Employer Pays Full Cost	379	35975	22	13932	26	10462	37	2355	207	6595	27	1152	60	1479
	37.8	35.0	25.0	29.9	40.6	36.8	19.5	24.4	43.3	48.9	46.6	56.1	48.0	56.8
Employer and Employee Share Cost	407	44269	37	18550	33	15734	60	3208	214	5703	18	276	45	798
	40.6	43.1	42.0	39.9	51.5	55.2	31.6	33.2	44.7	42.3	31.0	13.4	36.0	30.6
Employee Pays Full Cost	192	21990	29	14039	4	2246	91	4030	40	742	12	622	16	311
	19.1	21.4	33.0	30.2	6.3	7.9	47.8	41.6	8.4	5.5	20.7	30.3	12.8	11.9
CLERICAL-SERVICE														
Total	902	376339	84	168793	57	89060	184	54849	407	44489	57	12278	113	6870
	100.0	100.0	100.0	100.0	100.0	100.0	100.0	100.0	100.0	100.0	100.0	100.0	100.0	100.0
No Response	20	1443	–	–	–	–	2	556	13	675	1	54	4	158
	2.2	.4	–	–	–	–	1.1	1.0	3.2	1.5	1.8	.4	3.5	2.3
Employer Pays Full Cost	322	99269	17	34354	21	24536	34	11068	171	20263	27	5815	52	3233
	35.7	26.4	20.2	20.4	36.8	27.5	18.5	20.2	42.0	45.6	47.3	47.4	46.0	47.0
Employer and Employee Share Cost	376	185545	38	77616	32	59769	62	21995	184	19717	18	3577	42	2871
	41.7	49.3	45.3	45.9	56.2	67.2	33.7	40.1	45.2	44.3	31.6	29.1	37.2	41.8
Employee Pays Full Cost	184	90082	29	56823	4	4755	86	21230	39	3834	11	2832	15	608
	20.4	23.9	34.5	33.7	7.0	5.3	46.7	38.7	9.6	8.6	19.3	23.1	13.3	8.9

TABLE 30. GROUP MAJOR MEDICAL EXPENSE INSURANCE PLAN:
EMPLOYER-EMPLOYEE CONTRIBUTION TOWARD COST OF DEPENDENT COVERAGE
(Questionnaire Sect. IV Q.14,15)

	ALL INSTITUTIONS		UNIVERSITIES				LIBERAL ARTS COLLEGES				OTHER			
			PUBLIC		PRIVATE		PUBLIC		PRIVATE		PUBLIC		PRIVATE	
	INSTs	EEs	INSTs	EEs	INSTs	EEs	INSTs	EEs	INSTs	EEs	INSTs	EEs	INSTs	EEs
FACULTY														
Total	978	264478	87	105691	64	47574	186	57346	462	37735	57	10041	122	6091
	100.0	100.0	100.0	100.0	100.0	100.0	100.0	100.0	100.0	100.0	100.0	100.0	100.0	100.0
No Response	14	5621	1	4500	1	325	1	75	8	607	—	—	3	114
	1.4	2.1	1.1	4.3	1.6	.7	.5	.1	1.7	1.6	—	—	2.5	1.9
Employer Pays Full Cost	173	40394	7	7749	15	8995	6	10318	109	11364	3	138	33	1830
	17.7	15.3	8.0	7.3	23.4	18.9	3.2	18.0	23.6	30.1	5.3	1.4	27.0	30.0
Employer and Employee Share Cost	327	92341	29	41092	27	22763	36	8833	171	13405	29	4532	35	1716
	33.4	34.9	33.3	38.9	42.2	47.8	19.4	15.4	37.0	35.5	50.8	45.1	28.7	28.2
Employee Pays Full Cost	464	126122	50	52350	21	15491	143	38120	174	12359	25	5371	51	2431
	47.5	47.7	57.6	49.5	32.8	32.6	76.9	66.5	37.7	32.8	43.9	53.5	41.8	39.9
ADMINISTRATIVE														
Total	975	102250	87	46441	64	28463	186	9551	461	13174	57	2050	120	2571
	100.0	100.0	100.0	100.0	100.0	100.0	100.0	100.0	100.0	100.0	100.0	100.0	100.0	100.0
No Response	14	741	1	500	1	40	1	2	8	163	—	—	3	˙36
	1.4	.7	1.1	1.1	1.6	.1	.5	*	1.7	1.2	—	—	2.5	1.4
Employer Pays Full Cost	172	17798	7	5219	15	7062	6	763	109	3780	3	20	32	954
	17.6	17.4	8.0	11.2	23.4	24.8	3.2	8.0	23.6	28.7	5.3	1.0	26.7	37.1
Employer and Employee Share Cost	326	37226	29	17650	27	11787	36	1467	170	4667	29	1037	35	618
	33.4	36.4	33.3	38.0	42.2	41.5	19.4	15.4	36.9	35.5	50.8	50.6	29.2	24.0
Employee Pays Full Cost	463	46485	50	23072	21	9574	143	7319	174	4564	25	993	50	963
	47.6	45.5	57.6	49.7	32.8	33.6	76.9	76.6	37.8	34.6	43.9	48.4	41.6	37.5
CLERICAL-SERVICE														
Total	868	371578	83	167353	56	88882	179	53469	385	42917	56	12224	109	6733
	100.0	100.0	100.0	100.0	100.0	100.0	100.0	100.0	100.0	100.0	100.0	100.0	100.0	100.0
No Response	15	2993	1	1500	1	375	2	220	8	775	—	—	3	123
	1.7	.8	1.2	.9	1.8	.4	1.1	.4	2.1	1.8	—	—	2.8	1.8
Employer Pays Full Cost	124	40576	5	12245	10	11163	4	4846	78	10174	3	107	24	2041
	14.3	10.9	6.0	7.3	17.9	12.6	2.2	9.1	20.3	23.7	5.4	.9	22.0	30.3
Employer and Employee Share Cost	296	143154	28	61286	26	48620	37	9071	144	16602	27	5552	34	2023
	34.1	38.5	33.7	36.6	46.4	54.7	20.7	17.0	37.4	38.7	48.2	45.4	31.2	30.0
Employee Pays Full Cost	433	184855	49	92322	19	28724	136	39332	155	15366	26	6565	48	2546
	49.9	49.8	59.1	55.2	33.9	32.3	76.0	73.5	40.2	35.8	46.4	53.7	44.0	37.9

TABLE 31. GROUP MAJOR MEDICAL EXPENSE INSURANCE PLAN:
WAITING PERIOD BEFORE NEW EMPLOYEE IS ELIGIBLE TO PARTICIPATE IN PLAN
(Questionnaire Sect. IV Q.5)

	ALL INSTITUTIONS		UNIVERSITIES PUBLIC		PRIVATE		LIBERAL ARTS COLLEGES PUBLIC		PRIVATE		OTHER PUBLIC		PRIVATE	
	INSTs	EEs	INSTs	EEs	INSTs	EEs	INSTs	EEs	INSTs	EEs	INSTs	EEs	INSTs	EEs
FACULTY														
Total	1005	267270	88	106229	64	47574	190	58519	479	38690	58	10061	126	6197
	100.0	100.0	100.0	100.0	100.0	100.0	100.0	100.0	100.0	100.0	100.0	100.0	100.0	100.0
No Response	18	1194	—	—	1	194	—	—	13	823	1	20	3	157
	1.8	.4	—	—	1.6	.4	—	—	2.7	2.1	1.7	.2	2.4	2.5
No Waiting Period	533	139042	48	58816	36	27737	101	25224	256	19496	33	5232	59	2537
	53.0	52.1	54.6	55.4	56.1	58.4	53.1	43.1	53.5	50.4	57.0	52.0	46.8	41.0
1 Month or Less	307	96728	37	42693	18	12084	65	27173	139	10854	8	2016	40	1908
	30.5	36.2	42.0	40.2	28.1	25.4	34.2	46.4	29.0	28.1	13.8	20.0	31.7	30.8
2-3 Months	77	13844	2	2994	4	1441	14	3086	28	2751	16	2793	13	779
	7.7	5.2	2.3	2.8	6.3	3.0	7.4	5.3	5.8	7.1	27.6	27.8	10.3	12.6
6 Months	10	1898	—	—	—	--	5	1378	2	433	—	—	3	87
	1.0	.7	—	—	—	—	2.6	2.4	.5	1.1	—	—	2.4	1.4
12 Months	18	2418	—	—	—	—	2	944	15	1449	—	—	1	25
	1.8	.9	—	—	—	—	1.1	1.6	3.1	3.7	—	—	.8	.4
Other	42	12146	1	1726	5	6118	3	714	26	2884	—	—	7	704
	4.2	4.5	1.1	1.6	7.8	12.9	1.6	1.2	5.4	7.5	—	—	5.6	11.4
ADMINISTRATIVE														
Total	1003	102799	88	46521	64	28463	190	9670	478	13484	58	2054	125	2607
	100.0	100.0	100.0	100.0	100.0	100.0	100.0	100.0	100.0	100.0	100.0	100.0	100.0	100.0
No Response	18	342	—	—	1	86	—	—	13	236	1	4	3	16
	1.8	.3	—	—	1.6	.3	—	—	2.7	1.8	1.7	.2	2.4	.6
No Waiting Period	514	55644	46	26430	30	15681	102	4546	247	6687	32	1302	57	998
	51.3	54.2	52.3	56.8	46.8	55.0	53.7	47.0	51.7	49.6	55.2	63.4	45.6	38.3
1 Month or Less	306	35184	37	18091	17	7651	65	4638	139	3804	8	307	40	693
	30.5	34.2	42.0	38.9	26.6	26.9	34.2	48.0	29.1	28.2	13.8	14.9	32.0	26.6
2-3 Months	92	4585	4	1289	8	1025	14	233	34	1069	17	441	15	528
	9.2	4.5	4.5	2.8	12.5	3.6	7.3	2.4	7.1	7.9	29.3	21.5	12.0	20.3
6 Months	13	511	—	—	1	60	5	148	4	152	—	—	3	151
	1.3	.5	—	—	1.6	.2	2.6	1.5	.8	1.1	—	—	2.4	5.8
12 Months	17	569	—	—	—	—	1	20	15	542	—	—	1	7
	1.7	.6	—	—	—	—	.5	.2	3.1	4.0	—	—	.8	.3
Other	43	5964	1	711	7	3960	3	85	26	994	—	—	6	214
	4.3	5.8	1.1	1.5	10.9	13.9	1.6	.8	5.4	7.4	—	—	4.8	8.2

TABLE 31. GROUP MAJOR MEDICAL EXPENSE INSURANCE PLAN:
WAITING PERIOD BEFORE NEW EMPLOYEE IS ELIGIBLE TO PARTICIPATE IN PLAN
(continued)

| | ALL INSTITUTIONS | | UNIVERSITIES | | | | LIBERAL ARTS COLLEGES | | | | OTHER | | | |
| | | | PUBLIC | | PRIVATE | | PUBLIC | | PRIVATE | | PUBLIC | | PRIVATE | |
	INSTs	EEs	INSTs	EEs	INSTs	EEs	INSTs	EEs	INSTs	EEs	INSTs	EEs	INSTs	EEs
CLERICAL-SERVICE														
Total	902	376339	84	168793	57	89060	184	54849	407	44489	57	12278	113	6870
	100.0	100.0	100.0	100.0	100.0	100.0	100.0	100.0	100.0	100.0	100.0	100.0	100.0	100.0
No Response	18	1526	—	—	1	178	1	496	11	580	1	54	4	218
	2.0	.4	—	—	1.8	.2	.5	.9	2.7	1.3	1.8	.4	3.5	3.2
No Waiting Period	371	155155	42	82135	14	26216	95	22314	154	14588	30	7983	36	1919
	41.1	41.3	50.0	48.7	24.6	29.4	51.7	40.7	37.9	32.8	52.6	65.0	31.9	27.9
1 Month or Less	254	136840	33	74448	15	21674	60	27245	101	9822	8	1877	37	1774
	28.2	36.4	39.3	44.1	26.3	24.3	32.6	49.7	24.8	22.1	14.0	15.3	32.7	25.8
2-3 Months	139	33258	5	7200	10	11047	15	2730	71	8764	17	2290	21	1227
	15.4	8.8	6.0	4.3	17.6	12.4	8.2	5.0	17.4	19.7	29.8	18.7	18.6	17.9
6 Months	32	8432	—	—	3	4068	5	797	19	3180	—	—	5	387
	3.5	2.2	—	—	5.3	4.6	2.7	1.5	4.6	7.1	—	—	4.4	5.6
12 Months	25	12751	—	—	5	9625	1	47	16	2498	—	—	3	581
	2.8	3.4	—	—	8.8	10.9	.5	.1	3.9	5.6	—	—	2.7	8.5
Other	63	28377	4	5010	9	16252	7	1220	35	5057	1	74	7	764
	7.0	7.5	4.8	3.0	15.8	18.2	3.8	2.2	8.6	11.4	1.8	.6	6.2	11.1

TABLE 32. GROUP MAJOR MEDICAL EXPENSE INSURANCE PLANS: PER CAUSE OR ALL CAUSE
(Questionnaire Sect. IV Q.6)

| | ALL INSTITUTIONS | | UNIVERSITIES | | | | LIBERAL ARTS COLLEGES | | | | OTHER | | | |
| | | | PUBLIC | | PRIVATE | | PUBLIC | | PRIVATE | | PUBLIC | | PRIVATE | |
	INSTs	EEs	INSTs	EEs	INSTs	EEs	INSTs	EEs	INSTs	EEs	INSTs	EEs	INSTs	EEs
FACULTY														
Total	1005	267270	88	106229	64	47574	190	58519	479	38690	58	10061	126	6197
	100.0	100.0	100.0	100.0	100.0	100.0	100.0	100.0	100.0	100.0	100.0	100.0	100.0	100.0
No Response	42	4434	1	346	3	1135	4	1023	22	1592	1	20	11	318
	4.2	1.7	1.1	.3	4.7	2.4	2.1	1.7	4.6	4.1	1.7	.2	8.7	5.1
Per Cause	263	62034	23	23548	13	9907	64	15412	115	8608	19	3150	29	1409
	26.2	23.2	26.1	22.2	20.3	20.8	33.7	26.3	24.0	22.2	32.8	31.3	23.0	22.7
All Cause	678	185024	58	70480	44	34858	119	40431	334	27912	38	6891	85	4452
	67.4	69.2	66.0	66.3	68.7	73.3	62.6	69.2	69.7	72.2	65.5	68.5	67.5	71.9
Other	22	15778	6	11855	4	1674	3	1653	8	578	—	—	1	18
	2.2	5.9	6.8	11.2	6.3	3.5	1.6	2.8	1.7	1.5	—	—	.8	.3
ADMINISTRATIVE														
Total	1003	102799	88	46521	64	28463	190	9670	478	13484	58	2054	125	2607
	100.0	100.0	100.0	100.0	100.0	100.0	100.0	100.0	100.0	100.0	100.0	100.0	100.0	100.0
No Response	41	1255	1	132	3	433	4	211	22	393	1	4	10	82
	4.1	1.2	1.1	.3	4.7	1.5	2.1	2.2	4.6	2.9	1.7	.2	8.0	3.1
Per Cause	263	24718	23	10596	13	6796	64	3212	115	3097	19	378	29	639
	26.2	24.0	26.1	22.8	20.3	23.9	33.7	33.2	24.1	23.0	32.8	18.4	23.2	24.5
All Cause	677	73268	58	33282	44	20647	119	6088	333	9698	38	1672	85	1881
	67.5	71.3	66.0	71.5	68.7	72.5	62.6	63.0	69.6	71.9	65.5	81.4	68.0	72.2
Other	22	3558	6	2511	4	587	3	159	8	296	—	—	1	5
	2.2	3.5	6.8	5.4	6.3	2.1	1.6	1.6	1.7	2.2	—	—	.8	.2
CLERICAL-SERVICE														
Total	902	376339	84	168793	57	89060	184	54849	407	44489	57	12278	113	6870
	100.0	100.0	100.0	100.0	100.0	100.0	100.0	100.0	100.0	100.0	100.0	100.0	100.0	100.0
No Response	37	5033	1	313	3	1370	5	1681	17	1324	1	54	10	291
	4.1	1.3	1.2	.2	5.3	1.5	2.7	3.1	4.2	3.0	1.8	.4	8.8	4.2
Per Cause	250	91233	23	39504	13	14473	66	21259	106	10876	17	3531	25	1590
	27.7	24.2	27.4	23.4	22.8	16.3	35.9	38.8	26.0	24.4	29.8	28.8	22.1	23.1
All Cause	593	261385	54	114281	37	70768	109	31027	277	31647	39	8693	77	4969
	65.8	69.5	64.3	67.7	64.9	79.5	59.2	56.5	68.1	71.2	68.4	70.8	68.2	72.4
Other	22	18688	6	14695	4	2449	4	882	7	642	—	—	1	20
	2.4	5.0	7.1	8.7	7.0	2.7	2.2	1.6	1.7	1.4	—	—	.9	.3

TABLE 33. GROUP MAJOR MEDICAL EXPENSE INSURANCE PLANS:
AMOUNT OF DEDUCTIBLE WHERE SAME FOR ALL PARTICIPANTS — DISTRIBUTION
(Questionnaire Sect. IV Q.7)

| | ALL INSTITUTIONS | | UNIVERSITIES | | | | LIBERAL ARTS COLLEGES | | | | OTHER | | | |
| | | | PUBLIC | | PRIVATE | | PUBLIC | | PRIVATE | | PUBLIC | | PRIVATE | |
	INSTs	EEs	INSTs	EEs	INSTs	EEs	INSTs	EEs	INSTs	EEs	INSTs	EEs	INSTs	EEs
FACULTY														
Total	838	221568	75	85252	51	36950	173	54529	382	30269	54	9670	103	4898
	100.0	100.0	100.0	100.0	100.0	100.0	100.0	100.0	100.0	100.0	100.0	100.0	100.0	100.0
No Response	35	2756	1	530	1	170	6	488	17	1183	2	155	8	230
	4.2	1.2	1.3	.6	2.0	.5	3.5	.9	4.5	3.9	3.7	1.6	7.8	4.7
Less Than $100	131	41607	19	20121	7	5599	27	8193	43	3283	17	3321	18	1090
	15.6	18.8	25.3	23.6	13.7	15.2	15.6	15.0	11.3	10.8	31.5	34.3	17.5	22.3
$100	574	140045	41	51921	36	24409	101	31642	293	23154	32	5595	71	3324
	68.6	63.3	54.7	60.9	70.6	66.0	58.3	58.1	76.6	76.6	59.2	57.9	68.9	67.9
$101-$250	44	17150	7	6916	4	3970	14	4585	13	1161	2	467	4	51
	5.3	7.7	9.3	8.1	7.8	10.7	8.1	8.4	3.4	3.8	3.7	4.8	3.9	1.0
Over $250	54	20010	7	5764	3	2802	25	9621	16	1488	1	132	2	203
	6.4	9.0	9.3	6.8	5.9	7.6	14.5	17.6	4.2	4.9	1.9	1.4	1.9	4.1
ADMINISTRATIVE														
Total	837	85066	75	38009	51	23545	173	8876	381	10686	54	1913	103	2037
	100.0	100.0	100.0	100.0	100.0	100.0	100.0	100.0	100.0	100.0	100.0	100.0	100.0	100.0
No Response	33	838	1	74	1	47	6	71	16	475	2	31	7	140
	3.9	1.0	1.3	.2	2.0	.2	3.5	.8	4.2	4.4	3.7	1.6	6.8	6.9
Less Than $100	133	13798	18	6296	7	2925	30	2005	43	1365	17	959	18	248
	15.9	16.2	24.0	16.6	13.7	12.4	17.3	22.6	11.3	12.8	31.5	50.2	17.5	12.2
$100	576	56981	42	24114	36	18086	100	4491	293	7916	32	796	73	1578
	68.8	67.1	56.0	63.4	70.6	76.9	57.8	50.6	76.9	74.1	59.2	41.6	70.8	77.4
$101-$250	44	7763	7	4969	4	1562	14	634	13	473	2	108	4	17
	5.3	9.1	9.3	13.1	7.8	6.6	8.1	7.1	3.4	4.4	3.7	5.6	3.9	.8
Over $250	51	5686	7	2556	3	925	23	1675	16	457	1	19	1	54
	6.1	6.7	9.3	6.7	5.9	3.9	13.3	18.9	4.2	4.3	1.9	1.0	1.0	2.7
CLERICAL-SERVICE														
Total	757	298618	71	126736	45	68543	168	50712	328	35783	53	11706	92	5138
	100.0	100.0	100.0	100.0	100.0	100.0	100.0	100.0	100.0	100.0	100.0	100.0	100.0	100.0
No Response	33	4033	1	500	1	248	9	1067	15	1634	2	178	5	406
	4.4	1.4	1.4	.4	2.2	.4	5.4	2.1	4.6	4.6	3.8	1.5	5.4	7.9
Less Than $100	125	67163	17	29263	7	18247	26	9668	41	4156	16	4853	18	976
	16.5	22.5	23.9	23.1	15.6	26.6	15.5	19.1	12.5	11.6	30.2	41.5	19.6	19.0
$100	514	181199	39	72962	32	44329	98	28605	247	27067	33	4650	65	3586
	67.9	60.6	55.0	57.5	71.1	64.7	58.3	56.4	75.4	75.6	62.2	39.7	70.6	69.8
$101-$250	38	25336	7	15155	3	2598	13	4486	10	1043	2	2025	3	29
	5.0	8.5	9.9	12.0	6.7	3.8	7.7	8.8	3.0	2.9	3.8	17.3	3.3	.6
Over $250	47	20887	7	8856	2	3121	22	6886	15	1883	—	—	1	141
	6.2	7.0	9.9	7.0	4.4	4.6	13.1	13.6	4.6	5.3	—	—	1.1	2.7

TABLE 34. GROUP MAJOR MEDICAL EXPENSE INSURANCE PLAN: PERIOD OF TIME IN WHICH COVERED EXPENSES MUST BE INCURRED IN ORDER TO BE COUNTED TOWARD SATISFYING A DEDUCTIBLE
(Questionnaire Sect. IV Q.8)

| | ALL INSTITUTIONS | | UNIVERSITIES | | | | LIBERAL ARTS COLLEGES | | | | OTHER | | | |
| | | | PUBLIC | | PRIVATE | | PUBLIC | | PRIVATE | | PUBLIC | | PRIVATE | |
	INSTs	EEs	INSTs	EEs	INSTs	EEs	INSTs	EEs	INSTs	EEs	INSTs	EEs	INSTs	EEs
FACULTY														
Total	1005	267270	88	106229	64	47574	190	58519	479	38690	58	10061	126	6197
	100.0	100.0	100.0	100.0	100.0	100.0	100.0	100.0	100.0	100.0	100.0	100.0	100.0	100.0
No Response	99	15108	5	5980	3	1093	13	3405	59	3542	5	677	14	411
	9.9	5.7	5.7	5.6	4.7	2.3	6.8	5.8	12.3	9.2	8.6	6.7	11.1	6.6
Calendar Year	359	104431	40	50402	19	13907	79	20955	139	10018	46	7435	36	1714
	35.7	39.1	45.5	47.5	29.7	29.2	41.6	35.9	29.0	25.9	79.4	74.0	28.6	27.7
3 Months	374	107140	31	37927	37	29112	41	17291	212	19375	4	698	49	2737
	37.2	40.0	35.2	35.7	57.8	61.2	21.6	29.5	44.4	50.0	6.9	6.9	38.8	44.1
6 Months	41	11165	3	4909	2	2367	3	373	24	2083	2	940	7	493
	4.1	4.2	3.4	4.6	3.1	5.0	1.6	.6	5.0	5.4	3.4	9.3	5.6	8.0
12 Months (1 Year)	116	25892	7	5837	2	735	51	15468	38	2984	1	311	17	557
	11.5	9.7	8.0	5.5	3.1	1.5	26.8	26.4	7.9	7.7	1.7	3.1	13.5	9.0
Over 12 Months	7	1671	1	581	—	—	2	696	4	394	—	—	—	—
	.7	.6	1.1	.5	—	—	1.1	1.2	.8	1.0	—	—	—	—
Other	9	1863	1	593	1	360	1	331	3	294	—	—	3	285
	.9	.7	1.1	.6	1.6	.8	.5	.6	.6	.8	—	—	2.4	4.6
ADMINISTRATIVE														
Total	1003	102799	88	46521	64	28463	190	9670	478	13484	58	2054	125	2607
	100.0	100.0	100.0	100.0	100.0	100.0	100.0	100.0	100.0	100.0	100.0	100.0	100.0	100.0
No Response	97	4950	5	2417	3	330	13	656	59	1283	5	128	12	136
	9.7	4.8	5.7	5.2	4.7	1.2	6.8	6.8	12.3	9.5	8.6	6.2	9.6	5.2
Calendar Year	359	37058	40	17783	19	8951	80	4551	138	3336	46	1689	36	748
	35.8	36.0	45.5	38.2	29.7	31.4	42.1	47.0	28.9	24.7	79.4	82.2	28.8	28.7
3 Months	374	48155	31	20802	37	17509	40	1451	212	6993	4	106	50	1294
	37.2	47.0	35.2	44.7	57.8	61.5	21.1	15.0	44.5	52.0	6.9	5.2	40.0	49.7
6 Months	41	4615	3	2239	2	1300	3	72	24	734	2	108	7	162
	4.1	4.5	3.4	4.8	3.1	4.6	1.6	.7	5.0	5.4	3.4	5.3	5.6	6.2
12 Months (1 Year)	116	7118	7	2781	2	313	51	2752	38	1011	1	23	17	238
	11.6	6.9	8.0	6.0	3.1	1.1	26.8	28.5	7.9	7.5	1.7	1.1	13.6	9.1
Over 12 Months	7	254	1	42	—	—	2	143	4	69	—	—	—	—
	.7	.2	1.1	.1	—	—	1.1	1.5	.8	.5	—	—	—	—
Other	9	649	1	457	1	60	1	45	3	58	—	—	3	29
	.9	.6	1.1	1.0	1.6	.2	.5	.5	.6	.4	—	—	2.4	1.1

TABLE 34. GROUP MAJOR MEDICAL EXPENSE INSURANCE PLAN:
PERIOD OF TIME IN WHICH COVERED EXPENSES MUST BE INCURRED
IN ORDER TO BE COUNTED TOWARD SATISFYING A DEDUCTIBLE
(continued)

| | ALL INSTITUTIONS | | UNIVERSITIES | | | | LIBERAL ARTS COLLEGES | | | | OTHER | | | |
| | | | PUBLIC | | PRIVATE | | PUBLIC | | PRIVATE | | PUBLIC | | PRIVATE | |
	INSTs	EEs	INSTs	EEs	INSTs	EEs	INSTs	EEs	INSTs	EEs	INSTs	EEs	INSTs	EEs
CLERICAL-SERVICE														
Total	902	376339	84	168793	57	89060	184	54849	407	44489	57	12278	113	6870
	100.0	100.0	100.0	100.0	100.0	100.0	100.0	100.0	100.0	100.0	100.0	100.0	100.0	100.0
No Response	94	20805	5	9458	3	1316	15	4503	54	3847	5	768	12	913
	10.4	5.5	6.0	5.6	5.3	1.5	8.2	8.2	13.3	8.6	8.8	6.3	10.6	13.3
Calendar Year	343	171620	42	85673	17	32220	81	29966	124	11421	47	10206	32	2134
	38.1	45.6	49.9	50.8	29.8	36.2	44.0	54.8	30.5	25.7	82.4	83.1	28.3	31.1
3 Months	299	126069	25	49222	31	47059	34	5981	163	20920	2	411	44	2476
	33.1	33.5	29.8	29.2	54.3	52.8	18.5	10.9	40.0	47.1	3.5	3.3	38.9	36.0
6 Months	38	20052	3	9810	2	6096	2	185	22	2812	2	713	7	436
	4.2	5.3	3.6	5.8	3.5	6.8	1.1	.3	5.4	6.3	3.5	5.8	6.2	6.3
12 Months (1 Year)	112	33345	7	12897	3	1749	49	13520	37	4417	1	180	15	582
	12.4	8.9	8.3	7.6	5.3	2.0	26.6	24.6	9.1	9.9	1.8	1.5	13.3	8.5
Over 12 Months	7	1437	1	480	—	—	2	449	4	508	—	—	—	—
	.8	.4	1.2	.3	—	—	1.1	.8	1.0	1.1	—	—	—	—
Other	9	3011	1	1253	1	620	1	245	3	564	—	—	3	329
	1.0	.8	1.2	.7	1.8	.7	.5	.4	.7	1.3	—	—	2.7	4.8

TABLE 35. GROUP MAJOR MEDICAL EXPENSE INSURANCE PLANS:
MAXIMUM LENGTH OF BENEFIT PERIOD FOLLOWING SATISFACTION OF THE DEDUCTIBLE

(Questionnaire Sect. IV Q.11)

| | ALL INSTITUTIONS | | UNIVERSITIES | | | | LIBERAL ARTS COLLEGES | | | | OTHER | | | |
| | | | PUBLIC | | PRIVATE | | PUBLIC | | PRIVATE | | PUBLIC | | PRIVATE | |
	INSTs	EEs	INSTs	EEs	INSTs	EEs	INSTs	EEs	INSTs	EEs	INSTs	EEs	INSTs	EEs
FACULTY														
Total	1005	267270	88	106229	64	47574	190	58519	479	38690	58	10061	126	6197
	100.0	100.0	100.0	100.0	100.0	100.0	100.0	100.0	100.0	100.0	100.0	100.0	100.0	100.0
No Response	127	24366	6	10159	2	813	35	8542	62	4046	4	351	18	455
	12.6	9.1	6.8	9.6	3.1	1.7	18.4	14.6	12.9	10.5	6.9	3.5	14.3	7.3
Balance of Calendar Year	368	107778	43	52058	20	15006	81	21205	137	9865	46	7435	41	2209
	36.7	40.4	48.9	49.0	31.3	31.5	42.6	36.2	28.6	25.5	79.3	73.9	32.5	35.7
1 Year	101	16114	6	4694	2	1210	23	5006	50	3617	4	903	16	684
	10.0	6.0	6.8	4.4	3.1	2.5	12.1	8.6	10.4	9.3	6.9	9.0	12.7	11.0
2 Years	117	35356	16	13400	8	5656	34	11251	45	3998	3	512	11	539
	11.6	13.2	18.2	12.6	12.5	11.9	17.9	19.2	9.4	10.3	5.2	5.1	8.7	8.7
3 Years	274	75573	16	23228	28	21416	14	11522	179	16588	1	860	36	1959
	27.3	28.3	18.2	21.9	43.7	45.1	7.4	19.7	37.4	42.9	1.7	8.5	28.6	31.6
Other	18	8083	1	2690	4	3473	3	993	6	576	—	—	4	351
	1.8	3.0	1.1	2.5	6.3	7.3	1.6	1.7	1.3	1.5	—	—	3.2	5.7
ADMINISTRATIVE														
Total	1003	102799	88	46521	64	28463	190	9670	478	13484	58	2054	125	2607
	100.0	100.0	100.0	100.0	100.0	100.0	100.0	100.0	100.0	100.0	100.0	100.0	100.0	100.0
No Response	124	6214	6	3255	2	265	35	1202	61	1289	4	77	16	126
	12.4	6.0	6.8	7.0	3.1	.9	18.4	12.4	12.8	9.6	6.9	3.7	12.8	4.8
Balance of Calendar Year	369	38962	43	19195	20	9189	82	4616	137	3456	46	1689	41	817
	36.7	38.0	48.9	41.3	31.3	32.3	43.2	47.8	28.7	25.6	79.3	82.3	32.8	31.3
1 Year	101	5883	6	2656	2	698	23	803	50	1301	4	111	16	314
	10.1	5.7	6.8	5.7	3.1	2.5	12.1	8.3	10.5	9.6	6.9	5.4	12.8	12.0
2 Years	117	11766	16	6384	8	1826	34	2027	45	1251	3	83	11	195
	11.7	11.4	18.2	13.7	12.5	6.4	17.9	21.0	9.4	9.3	5.2	4.0	8.8	7.5
3 Years	274	37434	16	14966	28	14793	13	777	179	5786	1	94	37	1018
	27.3	36.4	18.2	32.2	43.7	52.0	6.8	8.0	37.3	42.9	1.7	4.6	29.6	39.1
Other	18	2540	1	65	4	1692	3	245	6	401	—	—	4	137
	1.8	2.5	1.1	.1	6.3	5.9	1.6	2.5	1.3	3.0	—	—	3.2	5.3

MAXIMUM LENGTH OF BENEFIT PERIOD FOLLOWING SATISFACTION OF THE DEDUCTIBLE
(continued)

| | ALL INSTITUTIONS | | UNIVERSITIES | | | | LIBERAL ARTS COLLEGES | | | | OTHER | | | |
| | | | PUBLIC | | PRIVATE | | PUBLIC | | PRIVATE | | PUBLIC | | PRIVATE | |
	INSTs	EEs	INSTs	EEs	INSTs	EEs	INSTs	EEs	INSTs	EEs	INSTs	EEs	INSTs	EEs
CLERICAL-SERVICE														
Total	902	376339	84	168793	57	89060	184	54849	407	44489	57	12278	113	6870
	100.0	100.0	100.0	100.0	100.0	100.0	100.0	100.0	100.0	100.0	100.0	100.0	100.0	100.0
No Response	121	24335	5	9804	3	1486	37	7702	58	4689	3	232	15	422
	13.4	6.5	6.0	5.8	5.3	1.7	20.1	14.0	14.3	10.5	5.3	1.9	13.3	6.1
Balance of Calendar Year	353	174972	45	86580	18	33459	82	30355	124	11744	47	10206	37	2628
	39.2	46.5	53.6	51.2	31.6	37.6	44.6	55.4	30.5	26.4	82.4	83.2	32.8	38.4
1 Year	94	22921	6	10559	1	239	23	5300	46	5082	4	777	14	964
	10.4	6.1	7.1	6.3	1.8	.3	12.5	9.7	11.3	11.4	7.0	6.3	12.4	14.0
2 Years	113	50489	16	24836	8	10085	32	8364	44	6232	2	419	11	553
	12.5	13.4	19.0	14.7	14.0	11.3	17.4	15.2	10.8	14.0	3.5	3.4	9.7	8.0
3 Years	203	87064	11	29984	23	36494	7	2445	129	15697	1	644	32	1800
	22.5	23.1	13.1	17.8	40.3	40.9	3.8	4.5	31.6	35.4	1.8	5.2	28.3	26.2
Other	18	16558	1	7030	4	7297	3	683	6	1045	–	–	4	503
	2.0	4.4	1.2	4.2	7.0	8.2	1.6	1.2	1.5	2.3	–	–	3.5	7.3

(Questionnaire Sect. IV Q.12)

	ALL INSTITUTIONS		UNIVERSITIES PUBLIC		UNIVERSITIES PRIVATE		LIBERAL ARTS COLLEGES PUBLIC		LIBERAL ARTS COLLEGES PRIVATE		OTHER PUBLIC		OTHER PRIVATE	
	INSTs	EEs	INSTs	EEs	INSTs	EEs	INSTs	EEs	INSTs	EEs	INSTs	EEs	INSTs	EEs
FACULTY														
Total	1005	267270	88	106229	64	47574	190	58519	479	38690	58	10061	126	6197
	100.0	100.0	100.0	100.0	100.0	100.0	100.0	100.0	100.0	100.0	100.0	100.0	100.0	100.0
No Response	50	5762	1	346	3	983	9	2585	26	1343	2	222	9	283
	5.0	2.2	1.1	.3	4.7	2.1	4.7	4.4	5.4	3.5	3.4	2.2	7.1	4.6
$5,000	19	2874	2	833	—	—	7	1286	7	545	1	176	2	34
	1.9	1.1	2.3	.8	—	—	3.7	2.2	1.5	1.4	1.7	1.7	1.6	.5
$10,000	384	80366	27	27614	13	9248	97	26251	182	13440	12	2033	53	1780
	38.2	30.1	30.7	26.0	20.3	19.4	50.9	44.9	38.1	34.7	20.7	20.2	42.0	28.7
$15,000	183	70732	23	33937	25	21456	22	4182	80	6502	12	3059	21	1596
	18.2	26.5	26.1	31.9	39.1	45.2	11.6	7.1	16.7	16.8	20.7	30.4	16.7	25.8
$20,000	112	43107	21	23968	2	590	40	12818	17	1383	29	4217	3	131
	11.1	16.1	23.9	22.6	3.1	1.2	21.1	21.9	3.5	3.6	50.1	42.0	2.4	2.1
$25,000	232	59431	13	18331	19	13962	10	10218	157	14814	—	—	33	2106
	23.1	22.2	14.8	17.3	29.7	29.3	5.3	17.5	32.8	38.3	—	—	26.2	34.0
Over $25,000	16	4349	1	1200	2	1335	3	992	5	270	2	354	3	198
	1.6	1.6	1.1	1.1	3.1	2.8	1.6	1.7	1.0	.7	3.4	3.5	2.4	3.2
Other	9	649	—	—	—	—	2	187	5	393	—	—	2	69
	.9	.2	—	—	—	—	1.1	.3	1.0	1.0	—	—	1.6	1.1
ADMINISTRATIVE														
Total	1003	102799	88	46521	64	28463	190	9670	478	13484	58	2054	125	2607
	100.0	100.0	100.0	100.0	100.0	100.0	100.0	100.0	100.0	100.0	100.0	100.0	100.0	100.0
No Response	48	1598	1	132	3	312	9	638	26	397	2	47	7	72
	4.8	1.6	1.1	.3	4.7	1.1	4.7	6.6	5.4	2.9	3.4	2.3	5.6	2.8
$5,000	20	1542	3	998	—	—	7	272	7	219	1	42	2	11
	2.0	1.5	3.4	2.1	—	—	3.7	2.8	1.5	1.6	1.7	2.0	1.6	.4
$10,000	384	22699	27	10785	13	2462	97	3955	182	4651	12	261	53	585
	38.3	22.1	30.8	23.2	20.3	8.6	51.0	40.8	38.1	34.5	20.7	12.7	42.4	22.4
$15,000	183	34112	23	11754	25	18110	22	598	79	2559	12	325	22	766
	18.2	33.1	26.1	25.3	39.1	63.7	11.6	6.2	16.5	19.0	20.7	15.8	17.6	29.4
$20,000	111	14057	20	8916	2	113	41	3383	17	480	29	1142	2	23
	11.1	13.7	22.7	19.2	3.1	.4	21.6	35.0	3.6	3.6	50.1	55.7	1.6	.9
$25,000	232	25827	13	12336	19	6856	9	606	157	4988	—	—	34	1041
	23.1	25.1	14.8	26.5	29.7	24.1	4.7	6.3	32.8	37.0	—	—	27.2	39.9
Over $25,000	21	2879	1	1600	2	610	3	173	9	157	2	237	4	102
	2.1	2.8	1.1	3.4	3.1	2.1	1.6	1.8	1.9	1.2	3.4	11.5	3.2	3.9
Other	4	85	—	—	—	—	2	45	1	33	—	—	1	7
	.4	.1	—	—	—	—	1.1	.5	.2	.2	—	—	.8	.3

TABLE 36. GROUP MAJOR MEDICAL EXPENSE INSURANCE: MAXIMUM BENEFIT AMOUNT   APP. 3
(continued)

| | ALL INSTITUTIONS | | UNIVERSITIES | | | | LIBERAL ARTS COLLEGES | | | | OTHER | | | |
| | | | PUBLIC | | PRIVATE | | PUBLIC | | PRIVATE | | PUBLIC | | PRIVATE | |
	INSTs	EEs	INSTs	EEs	INSTs	EEs	INSTs	EEs	INSTs	EEs	INSTs	EEs	INSTs	EEs
CLERICAL-SERVICE														
Total	902	376339	84	168793	57	89060	184	54849	407	44489	57	12278	113	6870
	100.0	100.0	100.0	100.0	100.0	100.0	100.0	100.0	100.0	100.0	100.0	100.0	100.0	100.0
No Response	53	7939	1	313	4	1734	13	3456	26	1524	2	240	7	672
	5.9	2.1	1.2	.2	7.0	1.9	7.1	6.3	6.4	3.4	3.5	2.0	6.2	9.8
$5,000	20	7260	3	3107	1	1239	7	1774	7	646	—	—	2	494
	2.2	1.9	3.6	1.8	1.8	1.4	3.8	3.2	1.7	1.5	—	—	1.8	7.2
$10,000	360	109439	27	51490	12	14709	93	21681	167	16184	11	3176	50	2199
	39.8	29.1	32.1	30.5	21.1	16.5	50.6	39.5	41.1	36.4	19.3	25.9	44.1	31.9
$15,000	173	112844	23	51117	22	45934	22	2986	73	8815	14	2813	19	1179
	19.2	29.9	27.4	30.3	38.5	51.6	12.0	5.4	17.9	19.8	24.6	22.9	16.8	17.2
$20,000	108	70709	21	39560	2	569	40	22766	15	2307	28	5454	2	53
	12.0	18.8	25.0	23.4	3.5	.6	21.7	41.7	3.7	5.2	49.1	44.4	1.8	.8
$25,000	164	60144	8	20206	14	23127	3	900	111	14034	—	—	28	1877
	18.2	16.0	9.5	12.0	24.6	26.0	1.6	1.6	27.3	31.5	—	—	24.8	27.3
Over $25,000	16	7042	1	3000	2	1748	3	789	5	610	2	595	3	300
	1.8	1.9	1.2	1.8	3.5	2.0	1.6	1.4	1.2	1.4	3.5	4.8	2.7	4.4
Other	8	962	—	—	—	—	3	497	3	369	—	—	2	96
	.9	.3	—	—	—	—	1.6	.9	.7	.8	—	—	1.8	1.4

INSTITUTIONS PROVIDING FOR CONTINUATION OF GROUP COVERAGE FOR RETIRING EMPLOYEES
(Questionnaire Sect. IV Q.16)

	ALL INSTITUTIONS		UNIVERSITIES				LIBERAL ARTS COLLEGES				OTHER			
			PUBLIC		PRIVATE		PUBLIC		PRIVATE		PUBLIC		PRIVATE	
	INSTs	EEs	INSTs	EEs	INSTs	EEs	INSTs	EEs	INSTs	EEs	INSTs	EEs	INSTs	EEs
FACULTY														
Total	1005	267270	88	106229	64	47574	190	58519	479	38690	58	10061	126	6197
	100.0	100.0	100.0	100.0	100.0	100.0	100.0	100.0	100.0	100.0	100.0	100.0	100.0	100.0
No Response	69	6650	1	538	2	1187	7	1750	41	2289	3	324	15	562
	6.9	2.5	1.1	.5	3.1	2.5	3.7	3.0	8.6	5.9	5.2	3.2	11.9	9.1
Continuation on Retirement														
At Any Age	333	151622	54	73865	30	28726	76	29340	105	11603	42	6373	26	1715
	33.1	56.8	61.4	69.5	46.8	60.4	40.0	50.1	21.9	30.0	72.3	63.4	20.6	27.7
Before Age 65 Only (To Age 65)	57	18562	11	10549	6	3725	3	268	30	2853	3	1031	4	136
	5.7	6.9	12.5	9.9	9.4	7.8	1.6	.5	6.3	7.4	5.2	10.2	3.2	2.2
At or After Age 65	64	10804	3	2729	6	3613	2	129	40	3261	3	461	10	611
	6.4	4.0	3.4	2.6	9.4	7.6	1.1	.2	8.4	8.4	5.2	4.6	7.9	9.9
No Continuation	482	79632	19	18548	20	10323	102	27032	263	18684	7	1872	71	3173
	47.9	29.8	21.6	17.5	31.3	21.7	53.6	46.2	54.8	48.3	12.1	18.6	56.4	51.1
ADMINISTRATIVE														
Total	1003	102799	88	46521	64	28463	190	9670	478	13484	58	2054	125	2607
	100.0	100.0	100.0	100.0	100.0	100.0	100.0	100.0	100.0	100.0	100.0	100.0	100.0	100.0
No Response	68	2097	1	80	2	530	7	354	41	759	3	98	14	276
	6.8	2.0	1.1	.2	3.1	1.9	3.7	3.7	8.6	5.6	5.2	4.8	11.2	10.6
Continuation on Retirement														
At Any Age	333	62432	54	33618	30	18088	76	4592	105	3832	42	1377	26	925
	33.2	60.7	61.4	72.3	46.8	63.6	40.0	47.5	22.0	28.4	72.3	67.1	20.8	35.5
Before Age 65 Only (To Age 65)	56	8696	11	3372	6	3771	3	40	29	1189	3	239	4	85
	5.6	8.5	12.5	7.2	9.4	13.2	1.6	.4	6.1	8.8	5.2	11.6	3.2	3.3
At or After Age 65	64	4373	3	1825	6	1115	2	14	41	1090	3	81	9	248
	6.4	4.3	3.4	3.9	9.4	3.9	1.1	.1	8.6	8.1	5.2	3.9	7.2	9.5
No Continuation	482	25201	19	7626	20	4959	102	4670	262	6614	7	259	72	1073
	48.0	24.5	21.6	16.4	31.3	17.4	53.6	48.3	54.7	49.1	12.1	12.6	57.6	41.1
CLERICAL-SERVICE														
Total	902	376339	84	168793	57	89060	184	54849	407	44489	57	12278	113	6870
	100.0	100.0	100.0	100.0	100.0	100.0	100.0	100.0	100.0	100.0	100.0	100.0	100.0	100.0
No Response	70	9746	1	1440	3	1723	10	2798	39	2799	3	294	14	692
	7.8	2.6	1.2	.9	5.3	1.9	5.4	5.1	9.6	6.3	5.3	2.4	12.4	10.1
Continuation on Retirement														
At Any Age	283	208634	49	102992	24	54096	71	29495	79	11435	41	9211	19	1405
	31.4	55.5	58.3	61.0	42.1	60.8	38.6	53.7	19.4	25.7	71.8	75.0	16.8	20.5
Before Age 65 Only (To Age 65)	46	25505	10	10415	4	10766	3	362	22	3227	3	666	4	69
	5.1	6.8	11.9	6.2	7.0	12.1	1.6	.7	5.4	7.3	5.3	5.4	3.5	1.0
At or After Age 65	56	15236	3	5118	6	5382	2	58	34	3463	3	392	8	823
	6.2	4.0	3.6	3.0	10.5	6.0	1.1	.1	8.4	7.8	5.3	3.2	7.1	12.0
No Continuation	447	117218	21	48828	20	17093	98	22136	233	23565	7	1715	68	3881
	49.5	31.1	25.0	28.9	35.1	19.2	53.3	40.4	57.2	52.9	12.3	14.0	60.2	56.4

TABLE 38. GROUP MAJOR MEDICAL EXPENSE INSURANCE PLANS: SERVICE AND/OR AGE REQUIREMENT FOR ELIGIBILITY FOR RETIRED GROUP COVERAGE BEGINNING AT AGE 65 OR AFTER
(Questionnaire Sect. IV Q.17)

	ALL INSTITUTIONS		UNIVERSITIES PUBLIC		UNIVERSITIES PRIVATE		LIBERAL ARTS COLLEGES PUBLIC		LIBERAL ARTS COLLEGES PRIVATE		OTHER PUBLIC		OTHER PRIVATE	
	INSTs	EEs	INSTs	EEs	INSTs	EEs	INSTs	EEs	INSTs	EEs	INSTs	EEs	INSTs	EEs
FACULTY														
Total	403	163898	57	76594	38	33526	78	29469	147	15037	45	6834	38	2438
	100.0	100.0	100.0	100.0	100.0	100.0	100.0	100.0	100.0	100.0	100.0	100.0	100.0	100.0
No Response	11	4957	2	1554	1	2835	2	188	5	359	—	—	1	21
	2.7	3.0	3.5	2.0	2.6	8.5	2.6	.6	3.4	2.4	—	—	2.6	.9
Service and/or Age Requirement Stated	204	78469	32	40113	21	15742	29	9185	78	8060	22	3539	22	1830
	50.6	47.9	56.1	52.4	55.3	46.9	37.2	31.2	53.1	53.6	48.9	51.8	57.9	75.0
No Requirement	188	80472	23	34927	16	14949	47	20096	64	6618	23	3295	15	587
	46.7	49.1	40.4	45.6	42.1	44.6	60.2	68.2	43.5	44.0	51.1	48.2	39.5	24.1
ADMINISTRATIVE														
Total	403	67406	57	35443	38	19733	78	4606	148	4973	45	1458	37	1193
	100.0	100.0	100.0	100.0	100.0	100.0	100.0	100.0	100.0	100.0	100.0	100.0	100.0	100.0
No Response	11	3418	2	2067	1	1127	2	34	5	185	—	—	1	5
	2.7	5.1	3.5	5.8	2.6	5.7	2.6	.7	3.4	3.7	—	—	2.7	.4
Service and/or Age Requirement Stated	206	40165	32	19989	22	13817	29	1669	80	2663	22	1093	21	934
	51.1	59.6	56.1	56.4	57.9	70.0	37.2	36.2	54.0	53.6	48.9	75.0	56.8	78.3
No Requirement	186	23823	23	13387	15	4789	47	2903	63	2125	23	365	15	254
	46.2	35.3	40.4	37.8	39.5	24.3	60.2	63.1	42.6	42.7	51.1	25.0	40.5	21.3
CLERICAL-SERVICE														
Total	344	225236	52	108110	31	60476	73	29553	115	15120	44	9603	29	2374
	100.0	100.0	100.0	100.0	100.0	100.0	100.0	100.0	100.0	100.0	100.0	100.0	100.0	100.0
No Response	11	11195	3	5369	1	5370	2	176	4	271	—	—	1	9
	3.2	5.0	5.8	5.0	3.2	8.9	2.7	.6	3.5	1.8	—	—	3.4	.4
Service and/or Age Requirement Stated	182	115333	26	48959	23	42736	32	7802	63	8081	22	5817	16	1938
	52.9	51.2	50.0	45.3	74.2	70.6	43.8	26.4	54.8	53.4	50.0	60.6	55.2	81.6
No Requirement	151	98708	23	53782	7	12370	39	21575	48	6768	22	3786	12	427
	43.9	43.8	44.2	49.7	22.6	20.5	53.5	73.0	41.7	44.8	50.0	39.4	41.4	18.0

CONTRIBUTION TOWARD COST OF EMPLOYEE GROUP COVERAGE DURING RETIREMENT
(Questionnaire Sect. IV Q.18,19)

| | ALL INSTITUTIONS | | UNIVERSITIES | | | | LIBERAL ARTS COLLEGES | | | | OTHER | | | |
| | | | PUBLIC | | PRIVATE | | PUBLIC | | PRIVATE | | PUBLIC | | PRIVATE | |
	INSTs	EEs	INSTs	EEs	INSTs	EEs	INSTs	EEs	INSTs	EEs	INSTs	EEs	INSTs	EEs
FACULTY														
Total	464	182736	68	87143	44	37251	82	29837	179	18055	48	7865	43	2585
	100.0	100.0	100.0	100.0	100.0	100.0	100.0	100.0	100.0	100.0	100.0	100.0	100.0	100.0
No Response	31	5286	4	1763	1	883	4	347	19	1960	1	311	2	22
	6.7	2.9	5.9	2.0	2.3	2.4	4.9	1.2	10.6	10.9	2.1	4.0	4.7	.9
Employer Pays Full Cost	156	45797	9	10982	22	15594	16	6454	73	8793	19	2517	17	1457
	33.6	25.1	13.2	12.6	50.0	41.9	19.5	21.6	40.8	48.7	39.5	32.0	39.5	56.3
Employer and Employee Share Cost	133	65759	21	28771	14	16066	28	14684	48	4359	14	1495	8	384
	28.7	36.0	30.9	33.0	31.8	43.1	34.1	49.2	26.8	24.1	29.2	19.0	18.6	14.9
Employee Pays Full Cost	144	65894	34	45627	7	4708	34	8352	39	2943	14	3542	16	722
	31.0	36.0	50.0	52.4	15.9	12.6	41.5	28.0	21.8	16.3	29.2	45.0	37.2	27.9
ADMINISTRATIVE														
Total	463	76261	68	38815	44	23504	82	4664	179	6232	48	1697	42	1349
	100.0	100.0	100.0	100.0	100.0	100.0	100.0	100.0	100.0	100.0	100.0	100.0	100.0	100.0
No Response	32	2436	4	976	1	560	4	70	20	801	1	23	2	6
	6.9	3.2	5.9	2.5	2.3	2.4	4.9	1.5	11.2	12.9	2.1	1.4	4.8	.4
Employer Pays Full Cost	156	24101	9	8956	22	9293	16	1269	73	2894	19	902	17	787
	33.7	31.6	13.2	23.1	50.0	39.5	19.5	27.2	40.8	46.4	39.5	53.1	40.5	58.4
Employer and Employee Share Cost	133	24261	21	10650	14	9312	28	2363	48	1484	14	277	8	175
	28.7	31.8	30.9	27.4	31.8	39.6	34.1	50.7	26.8	23.8	29.2	16.3	19.0	13.0
Employee Pays Full Cost	142	25463	34	18233	7	4339	34	962	38	1053	14	495	15	381
	30.7	33.4	50.0	47.0	15.9	18.5	41.5	20.6	21.2	16.9	29.2	29.2	35.7	28.2
CLERICAL-SERVICE														
Total	392	250841	62	118525	35	71242	76	29915	139	18447	47	10269	33	2443
	100.0	100.0	100.0	100.0	100.0	100.0	100.0	100.0	100.0	100.0	100.0	100.0	100.0	100.0
No Response	29	10504	5	4777	1	2699	3	259	17	2581	1	160	2	8
	7.4	4.2	8.1	4.0	2.9	3.8	3.9	.9	12.2	14.0	2.1	1.8	6.1	.3
Employer Pays Full Cost	124	56623	8	12629	16	25642	15	4635	51	7761	19	4536	15	1420
	31.7	22.6	12.9	10.7	45.7	36.0	19.7	15.5	36.7	42.1	40.5	44.2	45.4	58.1
Employer and Employee Share Cost	122	99305	19	41730	12	29332	28	19104	42	5443	16	3484	5	212
	31.1	39.5	30.6	35.2	34.3	41.2	36.8	63.8	30.2	29.5	34.0	33.9	15.2	8.7
Employee Pays Full Cost	117	84409	30	59389	6	13569	30	5917	29	2662	11	2069	11	803
	29.8	33.7	48.4	50.1	17.1	19.0	39.6	19.8	20.9	14.4	23.4	20.1	33.3	32.9

TABLE 40. GROUP MAJOR MEDICAL EXPENSE INSURANCE PLANS: EMPLOYER-EMPLOYEE
CONTRIBUTION TOWARD THE COST OF DEPENDENT COVERAGE OF COVERED RETIRED EMPLOYEES
(Questionnaire Sect. IV Q.23,24)

| | ALL INSTITUTIONS | | UNIVERSITIES | | | | LIBERAL ARTS COLLEGES | | | | OTHER | | | |
| | | | PUBLIC | | PRIVATE | | PUBLIC | | PRIVATE | | PUBLIC | | PRIVATE | |
	INSTs	EEs	INSTs	EEs	INSTs	EEs	INSTs	EEs	INSTs	EEs	INSTs	EEs	INSTs	EEs
FACULTY														
Total	409	175294	64	85380	42	36497	73	28527	151	15495	44	7138	35	2257
	100.0	100.0	100.0	100.0	100.0	100.0	100.0	100.0	100.0	100.0	100.0	100.0	100.0	100.0
No Response	2	177	—	—	—	—	—	—	2	177	—	—	—	—
	.5	.1	—	—	—	—	—	—	1.3	1.1	—	—	—	—
Employer Pays Full Cost	83	28690	4	6006	16	11794	4	4036	47	5927	2	99	10	828
	20.3	16.4	6.3	7.0	38.0	32.3	5.5	14.1	31.1	38.3	4.5	1.4	28.6	36.7
Employer and Employee Share Cost	125	60078	17	24575	13	15822	22	12358	42	4015	24	3078	7	230
	30.6	34.3	26.6	28.8	31.0	43.4	30.1	43.4	27.8	25.9	54.6	43.1	20.0	10.2
Employee Pays Full Cost	199	86349	43	54799	13	8881	47	12133	60	5376	18	3961	18	1199
	48.6	49.2	67.1	64.2	31.0	24.3	64.4	42.5	39.8	34.7	40.9	55.5	51.4	53.1
ADMINISTRATIVE														
Total	408	73791	64	37839	42	23388	73	4457	151	5215	44	1638	34	1254
	100.0	100.0	100.0	100.0	100.0	100.0	100.0	100.0	100.0	100.0	100.0	100.0	100.0	100.0
No Response	3	101	—	—	1	40	—	—	2	61	—	—	—	—
	.7	.1	—	—	2.4	.2	—	—	1.3	1.2	—	—	—	—
Employer Pays Full Cost	83	13856	4	3585	16	7218	4	657	47	1850	2	11	10	535
	20.3	18.8	6.3	9.5	38.0	30.9	5.5	14.7	31.1	35.5	4.5	.7	29.4	42.7
Employer and Employee Share Cost	125	26035	17	10356	13	12036	22	1196	42	1403	24	896	7	148
	30.6	35.3	26.6	27.4	31.0	51.4	30.1	26.8	27.8	26.9	54.6	54.7	20.6	11.8
Employee Pays Full Cost	197	33799	43	23898	12	4094	47	2604	60	1901	18	731	17	571
	48.4	45.8	67.1	63.1	28.6	17.5	64.4	58.5	39.8	36.4	40.9	44.6	50.0	45.5
CLERICAL-SERVICE														
Total	339	238642	56	113268	34	69712	67	28765	114	14877	43	9777	25	2243
	100.0	100.0	100.0	100.0	100.0	100.0	100.0	100.0	100.0	100.0	100.0	100.0	100.0	100.0
No Response	4	776	—	—	1	375	—	—	3	401	—	—	—	—
	1.2	.3	—	—	2.9	.5	—	—	2.6	2.7	—	—	—	—
Employer Pays Full Cost	61	35416	4	8515	13	18522	3	2760	31	4462	2	82	8	1075
	18.0	14.8	7.1	7.5	38.3	26.6	4.5	9.6	27.2	30.0	4.7	.8	32.0	47.9
Employer and Employee Share Cost	112	82354	14	28279	12	35120	22	8919	35	4839	24	5074	5	123
	33.0	34.5	25.0	25.0	35.3	50.4	32.8	31.0	30.7	32.5	55.8	51.9	20.0	5.5
Employee Pays Full Cost	162	120096	38	76474	8	15695	42	17086	45	5175	17	4621	12	1045
	47.8	50.4	67.9	67.5	23.5	22.5	62.7	59.4	39.5	34.8	39.5	47.3	48.0	46.6

FOR RETIRED EMPLOYEE
(Questionnaire Sect. IV Q.26)

| | ALL INSTITUTIONS | | UNIVERSITIES | | | | LIBERAL ARTS COLLEGES | | | | OTHER | | | |
| | | | PUBLIC | | PRIVATE | | PUBLIC | | PRIVATE | | PUBLIC | | PRIVATE | |
	INSTs	EEs	INSTs	EEs	INSTs	EEs	INSTs	EEs	INSTs	EEs	INSTs	EEs	INSTs	EEs
FACULTY														
Total	1232	285414	93	111008	65	48174	218	63175	596	44090	67	10715	193	8252
	100.0	100.0	100.0	100.0	100.0	100.0	100.0	100.0	100.0	100.0	100.0	100.0	100.0	100.0
No Response	172	19605	3	5408	3	2823	21	4060	92	4707	6	1260	47	1347
	14.0	6.9	3.2	4.9	4.6	5.9	9.6	6.4	15.4	10.7	9.0	11.8	24.4	16.3
Institution Pays All	62	16573	5	4722	2	2360	14	5113	19	1813	16	2144	6	421
	5.0	5.8	5.4	4.3	3.1	4.9	6.4	8.1	3.2	4.1	23.9	20.0	3.1	5.1
Institution Pays Part	36	12644	3	1910	–	–	9	8452	13	1077	10	1197	1	8
	2.9	4.4	3.2	1.7	–	–	4.1	13.4	2.2	2.4	14.9	11.2	.5	.1
Institution Pays None	962	236592	82	98968	60	42991	174	45550	472	36493	35	6114	139	6476
	78.1	82.9	88.2	89.1	92.3	89.2	79.9	72.1	79.2	82.8	52.2	57.0	72.0	78.5
ADMINISTRATIVE														
Total	1232	108315	93	47992	65	28488	218	10488	596	15898	67	2155	193	3294
	100.0	100.0	100.0	100.0	100.0	100.0	100.0	100.0	100.0	100.0	100.0	100.0	100.0	100.0
No Response	174	5322	3	2389	3	147	21	692	94	1438	6	180	47	476
	14.1	4.9	3.2	5.0	4.6	.5	9.6	6.6	15.8	9.0	9.0	8.4	24.4	14.5
Institution Pays All	64	9220	5	2286	3	3984	14	1143	19	756	16	842	7	209
	5.2	8.5	5.4	4.8	4.6	14.0	6.4	10.9	3.2	4.8	23.9	39.1	3.6	6.3
Institution Pays Part	36	1365	3	523	–	–	9	365	13	335	10	136	1	6
	2.9	1.3	3.2	1.1	–	–	4.1	3.5	2.2	2.1	14.9	6.3	.5	.2
Institution Pays None	958	92408	82	42794	59	24357	174	8288	470	13369	35	997	138	2603
	77.8	85.3	88.2	89.1	90.8	85.5	79.9	79.0	78.8	84.1	52.2	46.2	71.5	79.0
CLERICAL-SERVICE														
Total	1232	444618	93	192630	65	100744	218	61743	596	61664	67	14795	193	13042
	100.0	100.0	100.0	100.0	100.0	100.0	100.0	100.0	100.0	100.0	100.0	100.0	100.0	100.0
No Response	206	33373	4	10432	5	4727	21	3324	117	9534	6	2596	53	2760
	16.7	7.5	4.3	5.4	7.7	4.7	9.6	5.4	19.6	15.5	9.0	17.5	27.5	21.2
Institution Pays All	60	21609	5	5654	3	5577	14	4552	16	1323	16	4278	6	225
	4.9	4.9	5.4	2.9	4.6	5.5	6.4	7.4	2.7	2.1	23.9	28.9	3.1	1.7
Institution Pays Part	33	11290	3	3522	–	–	7	4171	12	1198	10	2394	1	5
	2.7	2.5	3.2	1.8	–	–	3.2	6.8	2.0	1.9	14.9	16.2	.5	*
Institution Pays None	933	378346	81	173022	57	90440	176	49696	451	49609	35	5527	133	10052
	75.7	85.1	87.1	89.9	87.7	89.8	80.8	80.4	75.7	80.5	52.2	37.4	68.9	77.1

TABLE 42. SHORT-TERM DISABILITY INCOME (SICK PAY) PLANS IN COLLEGES AND UNIVERSITIES
(Questionnaire Sect. V Q.1)

| | ALL INSTITUTIONS | | UNIVERSITIES | | | | LIBERAL ARTS COLLEGES | | | | OTHER | | | |
| | | | PUBLIC | | PRIVATE | | PUBLIC | | PRIVATE | | PUBLIC | | PRIVATE | |
	INSTs	EEs	INSTs	EEs	INSTs	EEs	INSTs	EEs	INSTs	EEs	INSTs	EEs	INSTs	EEs
FACULTY														
Total	1232	285414	93	111008	65	48174	218	63175	596	44090	67	10715	193	8252
	100.0	100.0	100.0	100.0	100.0	100.0	100.0	100.0	100.0	100.0	100.0	100.0	100.0	100.0
Short-Term Plan in Effect	885	231234	73	88304	53	43560	163	51998	406	32141	60	8867	130	6364
	71.8	81.0	78.5	79.5	81.5	90.4	74.8	82.3	68.1	72.9	89.6	82.8	67.4	77.1
No Short-Term Plan	347	54180	20	22704	12	4614	55	11177	190	11949	7	1848	63	1888
	28.2	19.0	21.5	20.5	18.5	9.6	25.2	17.7	31.9	27.1	10.4	17.2	32.6	22.9
ADMINISTRATIVE														
Total	1232	108315	93	47992	65	28488	218	10488	596	15898	67	2155	193	3294
	100.0	100.0	100.0	100.0	100.0	100.0	100.0	100.0	100.0	100.0	100.0	100.0	100.0	100.0
Short-Term Plan in Effect	886	90175	74	37692	53	27229	163	8771	405	11875	61	1859	130	2749
	71.9	83.3	79.6	78.5	81.5	95.6	74.8	83.6	68.0	74.7	91.0	86.3	67.4	83.5
No Short-Term Plan	346	18140	19	10300	12	1259	55	1717	191	4023	6	296	63	545
	28.1	16.7	20.4	21.5	18.5	4.4	25.2	16.4	32.0	25.3	9.0	13.7	32.6	16.5
CLERICAL-SERVICE														
Total	1232	444618	93	192630	65	100744	218	61743	596	61664	67	14795	193	13042
	100.0	100.0	100.0	100.0	100.0	100.0	100.0	100.0	100.0	100.0	100.0	100.0	100.0	100.0
Short-Term Plan in Effect	889	367330	73	155934	54	94369	163	50423	407	45274	61	10316	131	11014
	72.2	82.6	78.5	81.0	83.1	93.7	74.8	81.7	68.3	73.4	91.0	69.7	67.9	84.5
No Short-Term Plan	343	77288	20	36696	11	6375	55	11320	189	16390	6	4479	62	2028
	27.8	17.4	21.5	19.0	16.9	6.3	25.2	18.3	31.7	26.6	9.0	30.3	32.1	15.5

TABLE 43. TYPES OF SHORT-TERM DISABILITY INCOME PLANS IN EFFECT IN COLLEGES AND UNIVERSITIES
(Questionnaire Sect. V Q.2)

	ALL INSTITUTIONS		UNIVERSITIES PUBLIC		UNIVERSITIES PRIVATE		LIBERAL ARTS COLLEGES PUBLIC		LIBERAL ARTS COLLEGES PRIVATE		OTHER PUBLIC		OTHER PRIVATE	
	INSTs	EEs	INSTs	EEs	INSTs	EEs	INSTs	EEs	INSTs	EEs	INSTs	EEs	INSTs	EEs
FACULTY														
Total	885	231234	73	88304	53	43560	163	51998	406	32141	60	8867	130	6364
	*	*	*	*	*	*	*	*	*	*	*	*	*	*
Informal	432	119524	34	50932	36	31784	55	14094	211	16832	25	3124	71	2758
	49.1	51.8	46.6	57.7	67.9	73.0	34.4	27.3	52.1	52.4	41.7	35.2	55.0	43.4
Formal	422	122761	43	47322	16	11404	110	39735	160	13120	49	7912	44	3268
	48.0	53.2	58.9	53.6	30.2	26.2	68.8	77.1	39.5	40.8	81.7	89.2	34.1	51.5
Workmen's Comp.	668	180615	63	81067	40	31872	110	31662	314	24446	43	6261	98	5307
	75.9	78.3	86.3	91.8	75.5	73.2	68.8	61.4	77.5	76.1	71.7	70.6	76.0	83.6
Group Insurance	118	29229	14	14884	2	2138	26	7158	48	3393	6	571	22	1085
	13.4	12.7	19.2	16.9	3.8	4.9	16.3	13.9	11.9	10.6	10.0	6.4	17.1	17.1
Other	41	16404	3	4402	4	1920	19	8377	11	1529	1	120	3	56
	4.7	7.1	4.1	5.0	7.5	4.4	11.9	16.2	2.7	4.8	1.7	1.4	2.3	.9
ADMINISTRATIVE														
Total	886	90175	74	37692	53	27229	163	8771	405	11875	61	1859	130	2749
	*	*	*	*	*	*	*	*	*	*	*	*	*	*
Informal	376	32506	21	11051	29	12021	39	1847	203	5765	20	913	64	909
	42.7	36.1	28.4	29.3	54.7	44.1	24.4	21.4	50.2	48.6	32.8	49.1	49.6	33.1
Formal	479	62374	58	32040	21	14001	127	7448	167	5448	55	1774	51	1663
	54.4	69.3	78.4	85.0	39.6	51.4	79.4	86.2	41.3	45.9	90.2	95.4	39.5	60.5
Workmen's Comp.	673	76431	64	33937	43	23053	111	6956	313	8531	43	1586	99	2368
	76.4	84.9	86.5	90.0	81.1	84.7	69.4	80.5	77.5	71.9	70.5	85.3	76.7	86.2
Group Insurance	129	12337	14	7916	1	20	26	2305	55	1355	7	220	26	521
	14.6	13.7	18.9	21.0	1.9	.1	16.3	26.7	13.6	11.4	11.5	11.8	20.2	19.0
Other	43	6263	3	718	7	3000	18	1530	10	856	1	116	4	43
	4.9	7.0	4.1	1.9	13.2	11.0	11.3	17.7	2.5	7.2	1.6	6.2	3.1	1.6
CLERICAL-SERVICE														
Total	889	367330	73	155934	54	94369	163	50423	407	45274	61	10316	131	11014
	*	*	*	*	*	*	*	*	*	*	*	*	*	*
Informal	254	54098	8	19606	13	12238	19	3435	153	16063	5	725	56	2031
	28.7	14.7	11.0	12.6	24.1	13.0	11.9	6.9	37.7	35.5	8.2	7.0	43.1	18.5
Formal	544	304130	66	138667	37	78499	134	45588	200	23413	55	9634	52	8329
	61.5	82.9	90.4	88.9	68.5	83.2	83.8	91.1	49.3	51.7	90.2	93.4	40.0	75.7
Workmen's Comp.	693	326574	64	147124	46	84957	112	40227	325	36149	43	8297	103	9820
	78.4	89.0	87.7	94.4	85.2	90.0	70.0	80.4	80.0	79.9	70.5	80.4	79.2	89.2
Group Insurance	145	62308	14	32071	4	5712	25	14337	66	6814	6	841	30	2533
	16.4	17.0	19.2	20.6	7.4	6.1	15.6	28.7	16.3	15.1	9.8	8.2	23.1	23.0
Other	46	30976	3	8807	6	14549	18	6119	14	1349	—	—	5	152
	5.2	8.4	4.1	5.6	11.1	15.4	11.3	12.2	3.4	3.0	—	—	3.8	1.4

Percentages total more than 100 due to the presence of more than one program at some institutions.

TABLE 44. SHORT-TERM DISABILITY INCOME PLAN:
SERVICE AND/OR AGE REQUIREMENT FOR ELIGIBILITY FOR PLAN PARTICIPATION
(Questionnaire Sect. V Q.3)

	ALL INSTITUTIONS		UNIVERSITIES PUBLIC		UNIVERSITIES PRIVATE		LIBERAL ARTS PUBLIC		LIBERAL ARTS PRIVATE		OTHER PUBLIC		OTHER PRIVATE	
	INSTs	EEs	INSTs	EEs	INSTs	EEs	INSTs	EEs	INSTs	EEs	INSTs	EEs	INSTs	EEs
FACULTY														
Total	500 / 100.0	147084 / 100.0	53 / 100.0	60923 / 100.0	21 / 100.0	15100 / 100.0	127 / 100.0	44141 / 100.0	189 / 100.0	14982 / 100.0	53 / 100.0	8183 / 100.0	57 / 100.0	3755 / 100.0
No Response	32 / 6.4	8972 / 6.1	3 / 5.7	4913 / 8.1	1 / 4.8	443 / 2.9	9 / 7.1	2359 / 5.3	18 / 9.5	1237 / 8.3	1 / 1.9	20 / .2	— / —	— / —
Service and/or Age Requirement	94 / 18.8	20110 / 13.7	1 / 1.9	565 / .9	2 / 9.5	1395 / 9.2	34 / 26.8	12983 / 29.4	39 / 20.6	3864 / 25.8	7 / 13.2	451 / 5.5	11 / 19.3	852 / 22.7
No Service or Age Requirement	374 / 74.8	118002 / 80.2	49 / 92.4	55445 / 91.0	18 / 85.7	13262 / 87.9	84 / 66.1	28799 / 65.3	132 / 69.9	9881 / 65.9	45 / 84.9	7712 / 94.3	46 / 80.7	2903 / 77.3
ADMINISTRATIVE														
Total	544 / 100.0	68108 / 100.0	63 / 100.0	34037 / 100.0	28 / 100.0	16890 / 100.0	135 / 100.0	7627 / 100.0	196 / 100.0	5945 / 100.0	56 / 100.0	1778 / 100.0	66 / 100.0	1831 / 100.0
No Response	36 / 6.6	3184 / 4.7	4 / 6.3	1274 / 3.7	2 / 7.1	1032 / 6.1	10 / 7.4	392 / 5.1	17 / 8.7	472 / 7.9	1 / 1.8	4 / .2	2 / 3.0	10 / .5
Service and/or Age Requirement	113 / 20.8	11994 / 17.6	4 / 6.3	2438 / 7.2	4 / 14.3	5192 / 30.7	35 / 25.9	2227 / 29.2	48 / 24.5	1455 / 24.5	8 / 14.3	165 / 9.3	14 / 21.2	517 / 28.2
No Service or Age Requirement	395 / 72.6	52930 / 77.7	55 / 87.4	30325 / 89.1	22 / 78.6	10666 / 63.2	90 / 66.7	5008 / 65.7	131 / 66.8	4018 / 67.6	47 / 83.9	1609 / 90.5	50 / 75.8	1304 / 71.3
CLERICAL-SERVICE														
Total	611 / 100.0	318126 / 100.0	68 / 100.0	143941 / 100.0	41 / 100.0	82931 / 100.0	141 / 100.0	46526 / 100.0	235 / 100.0	25753 / 100.0	55 / 100.0	9634 / 100.0	71 / 100.0	9341 / 100.0
No Response	36 / 5.9	20713 / 6.5	4 / 5.9	12272 / 8.5	2 / 4.9	4307 / 5.2	10 / 7.1	2877 / 6.2	17 / 7.2	1176 / 4.6	1 / 1.8	54 / .6	2 / 2.8	27 / .3
Service and/or Age Requirement	147 / 24.1	73987 / 23.3	9 / 13.2	14889 / 10.3	15 / 36.6	37825 / 45.6	38 / 27.0	10723 / 23.0	57 / 24.3	5563 / 21.6	9 / 16.4	675 / 7.0	19 / 26.8	4312 / 46.2
No Service or Age Requirement	428 / 70.0	223426 / 70.2	55 / 80.9	116780 / 81.2	24 / 58.5	40799 / 49.2	93 / 65.9	32926 / 70.8	161 / 68.5	19014 / 73.8	45 / 81.8	8905 / 92.4	50 / 70.4	5002 / 53.5

TABLE 45. SHORT-TERM DISABILITY INCOME PLAN:
VARIATION OF LENGTH OF DISABILITY PAYMENTS ACCORDING TO LENGTH OF SERVICE
(Questionnaire Sect. V Q.4)

| | ALL INSTITUTIONS | | UNIVERSITIES | | | | LIBERAL ARTS COLLEGES | | | | OTHER | | | |
| | | | PUBLIC | | PRIVATE | | PUBLIC | | PRIVATE | | PUBLIC | | PRIVATE | |
	INSTs	EEs	INSTs	EEs	INSTs	EEs	INSTs	EEs	INSTs	EEs	INSTs	EEs	INSTs	EEs
FACULTY														
Total	500 / 100.0	147084 / 100.0	53 / 100.0	60923 / 100.0	21 / 100.0	15100 / 100.0	127 / 100.0	44141 / 100.0	189 / 100.0	14982 / 100.0	53 / 100.0	8183 / 100.0	57 / 100.0	3755 / 100.0
No Response	32 / 6.4	11934 / 8.1	4 / 7.5	6760 / 11.1	2 / 9.5	2443 / 16.2	5 / 3.9	1531 / 3.5	19 / 10.1	1167 / 7.8	— / —	— / —	2 / 3.5	33 / .9
Duration Varies by Length of Service	267 / 53.4	83597 / 56.8	29 / 54.8	34330 / 56.3	10 / 47.6	6621 / 43.8	89 / 70.1	26873 / 60.8	67 / 35.4	6243 / 41.7	48 / 90.6	7875 / 96.2	24 / 42.1	1655 / 44.1
Duration Not Related to Length of Service	201 / 40.2	51553 / 35.1	20 / 37.7	19833 / 32.6	9 / 42.9	6036 / 40.0	33 / 26.0	15737 / 35.7	103 / 54.5	7572 / 50.5	5 / 9.4	308 / 3.8	31 / 54.4	2067 / 55.0
ADMINISTRATIVE														
Total	544 / 100.0	68108 / 100.0	63 / 100.0	34037 / 100.0	28 / 100.0	16890 / 100.0	135 / 100.0	7627 / 100.0	196 / 100.0	5945 / 100.0	56 / 100.0	1778 / 100.0	66 / 100.0	1831 / 100.0
No Response	36 / 6.6	1895 / 2.8	3 / 4.8	840 / 2.5	1 / 3.6	51 / .3	6 / 4.4	322 / 4.2	20 / 10.2	432 / 7.3	— / —	— / —	6 / 9.1	250 / 13.7
Duration Varies by Length of Service	310 / 57.0	49976 / 73.4	42 / 66.6	25143 / 73.8	19 / 67.8	14818 / 87.7	98 / 72.6	4856 / 63.7	74 / 37.8	2658 / 44.7	52 / 92.9	1728 / 97.2	25 / 37.9	773 / 42.2
Duration Not Related to Length of Service	198 / 36.4	16237 / 23.8	18 / 28.6	8054 / 23.7	8 / 28.6	2021 / 12.0	31 / 23.0	2449 / 32.1	102 / 52.0	2855 / 48.0	4 / 7.1	50 / 2.8	35 / 53.0	808 / 44.1
CLERICAL-SERVICE														
Total	611 / 100.0	318126 / 100.0	68 / 100.0	143941 / 100.0	41 / 100.0	82931 / 100.0	141 / 100.0	46526 / 100.0	235 / 100.0	25753 / 100.0	55 / 100.0	9634 / 100.0	71 / 100.0	9341 / 100.0
No Response	44 / 7.2	13186 / 4.1	3 / 4.4	7065 / 4.9	1 / 2.4	1552 / 1.9	5 / 3.5	1966 / 4.2	30 / 12.8	2443 / 9.5	— / —	— / —	5 / 7.0	160 / 1.7
Duration Varies by Length of Service	372 / 60.9	224834 / 70.7	48 / 70.6	100086 / 69.5	31 / 75.6	68178 / 82.2	106 / 75.2	26643 / 57.3	108 / 45.9	14379 / 55.8	52 / 94.5	9273 / 96.3	27 / 38.0	6275 / 67.2
Duration Not Related to Length of Service	195 / 31.9	80106 / 25.2	17 / 25.0	36790 / 25.6	9 / 22.0	13201 / 15.9	30 / 21.3	17917 / 38.5	97 / 41.3	8931 / 34.7	3 / 5.5	361 / 3.7	39 / 55.0	2906 / 31.1

TABLE 46. SHORT-TERM DISABILITY INCOME PLANS:
EMPLOYER-EMPLOYEE CONTRIBUTIONS TOWARD COST OF PLAN
(Questionnaire Sect. V Q.6,7)

	ALL INSTITUTIONS		UNIVERSITIES PUBLIC		UNIVERSITIES PRIVATE		LIBERAL ARTS COLLEGES PUBLIC		LIBERAL ARTS COLLEGES PRIVATE		OTHER PUBLIC		OTHER PRIVATE	
	INSTs	EEs	INSTs	EEs	INSTs	EEs	INSTs	EEs	INSTs	EEs	INSTs	EEs	INSTs	EEs
FACULTY														
Total	500	147084	53	60923	21	15100	127	44141	189	14982	53	8183	57	3755
	100.0	100.0	100.0	100.0	100.0	100.0	100.0	100.0	100.0	100.0	100.0	100.0	100.0	100.0
No Response	88	26491	6	7426	6	4173	31	11412	37	2924	1	20	7	536
	17.6	18.0	11.3	12.2	28.6	27.6	24.4	25.9	19.6	19.5	1.9	.2	12.3	14.3
Employer Pays Full Cost	327	97550	35	39370	15	10927	75	27154	119	9912	47	7622	36	2565
	65.4	66.4	66.1	64.6	71.4	72.4	59.1	61.5	62.9	66.2	88.7	93.2	63.2	68.3
Employer and Employee Share Cost	44	6973	4	3331	–	–	6	1290	23	1485	1	300	10	567
	8.8	4.7	7.5	5.5	–	–	4.7	2.9	12.2	9.9	1.9	3.7	17.5	15.1
Employee Pays Full Cost	41	16070	8	10796	–	–	15	4285	10	661	4	241	4	87
	8.2	10.9	15.1	17.7	–	–	11.8	9.7	5.3	4.4	7.5	2.9	7.0	2.3
ADMINISTRATIVE														
Total	544	68108	63	34037	28	16890	135	7627	196	5945	56	1778	66	1831
	100.0	100.0	100.0	100.0	100.0	100.0	100.0	100.0	100.0	100.0	100.0	100.0	100.0	100.0
No Response	98	8718	8	2897	6	2318	35	2297	37	1018	2	30	10	158
	18.0	12.8	12.7	8.5	21.4	13.7	25.9	30.1	18.9	17.1	3.6	1.7	15.2	8.6
Employer Pays Full Cost	352	47788	43	23765	21	13822	79	3342	123	4103	48	1626	38	1130
	64.8	70.2	68.3	69.9	75.0	81.9	58.6	43.8	62.7	69.0	85.7	91.4	57.5	61.7
Employer and Employee Share Cost	53	4024	4	1888	1	750	6	203	26	589	2	73	14	521
	9.7	5.9	6.3	5.5	3.6	4.4	4.4	2.7	13.3	9.9	3.6	4.1	21.2	28.5
Employee Pays Full Cost	41	7578	8	5487	–	–	15	1785	10	235	4	49	4	22
	7.5	11.1	12.7	16.1	–	–	11.1	23.4	5.1	4.0	7.1	2.8	6.1	1.2
CLERICAL-SERVICE														
Total	611	318126	68	143941	41	82931	141	46526	235	25753	55	9634	71	9341
	100.0	100.0	100.0	100.0	100.0	100.0	100.0	100.0	100.0	100.0	100.0	100.0	100.0	100.0
No Response	104	45304	8	11889	6	15793	36	11397	43	4006	2	212	9	2007
	17.0	14.2	11.8	8.3	14.6	19.0	25.5	24.5	18.3	15.6	3.6	2.2	12.7	21.5
Employer Pays Full Cost	407	219611	48	101989	34	63138	84	22335	149	17706	48	8607	44	5836
	66.7	69.1	70.5	70.8	83.0	76.2	59.7	48.0	63.4	68.7	87.3	89.3	62.0	62.4
Employer and Employee Share Cost	60	14912	4	4608	1	4000	5	912	34	3416	2	530	14	1446
	9.8	4.7	5.9	3.2	2.4	4.8	3.5	2.0	14.5	13.3	3.6	5.5	19.7	15.5
Employee Pays Full Cost	40	38299	8	25455	–	–	16	11882	9	625	3	285	4	52
	6.5	12.0	11.8	17.7	–	–	11.3	25.5	3.8	2.4	5.5	3.0	5.6	.6

TABLE 47. LONG-TERM TOTAL DISABILITY INCOME PLANS IN COLLEGES AND UNIVERSITIES
(Questionnaire Sect. VI Q.1)

| | ALL INSTITUTIONS | | UNIVERSITIES | | | | LIBERAL ARTS COLLEGES | | | | OTHER | | | |
| | | | PUBLIC | | PRIVATE | | PUBLIC | | PRIVATE | | PUBLIC | | PRIVATE | |
	INSTs	EEs	INSTs	EEs	INSTs	EEs	INSTs	EEs	INSTs	EEs	INSTs	EEs	INSTs	EEs
FACULTY														
Total	1232	285414	93	111008	65	48174	218	63175	596	44090	67	10715	193	8252
	100.0	100.0	100.0	100.0	100.0	100.0	100.0	100.0	100.0	100.0	100.0	100.0	100.0	100.0
Long-Term Plan in Effect	627	203206	74	91344	41	29312	133	46369	287	26983	36	5809	56	3389
	50.9	71.2	79.6	82.3	63.1	60.8	61.0	73.4	48.2	61.2	53.7	54.2	29.0	41.1
No Plan in Effect	605	82208	19	19664	24	18862	85	16806	309	17107	31	4906	137	4863
	49.1	28.8	20.4	17.7	36.9	39.2	39.0	26.6	51.8	38.8	46.3	45.8	71.0	58.9
ADMINISTRATIVE														
Total	1232	108315	93	47992	65	28488	218	10488	596	15898	67	2155	193	3294
	100.0	100.0	100.0	100.0	100.0	100.0	100.0	100.0	100.0	100.0	100.0	100.0	100.0	100.0
Long-Term Plan in Effect	629	77799	74	39896	41	18549	135	7506	286	9433	37	825	56	1590
	51.1	71.8	79.6	83.1	63.1	65.1	61.9	71.6	48.0	59.3	55.2	38.3	29.0	48.3
No Plan in Effect	603	30516	19	8096	24	9939	83	2982	310	6465	30	1330	137	1704
	48.9	28.2	20.4	16.9	36.9	34.9	38.1	28.4	52.0	40.7	44.8	61.7	71.0	51.7
CLERICAL-SERVICE														
Total	1232	444618	93	192630	65	100744	218	61743	596	61664	67	14795	193	13042
	100.0	100.0	100.0	100.0	100.0	100.0	100.0	100.0	100.0	100.0	100.0	100.0	100.0	100.0
Long-Term Plan in Effect	469	259492	65	142816	28	44824	128	44590	174	18639	37	6446	37	2177
	38.1	58.4	69.9	74.1	43.1	44.5	58.7	72.2	29.2	30.2	55.2	43.6	19.2	16.7
No Plan in Effect	763	185126	28	49814	37	55920	90	17153	422	43025	30	8349	156	10865
	61.9	41.6	30.1	25.9	56.9	55.5	41.3	27.8	70.8	69.8	44.8	56.4	80.8	83.3

TABLE 48. TYPES OF LONG-TERM TOTAL DISABILITY PLANS IN EFFECT IN COLLEGES AND UNIVERSITIES

(Questionnaire Sect. VI Q.2)

	ALL INSTITUTIONS		UNIVERSITIES PUBLIC		UNIVERSITIES PRIVATE		LIBERAL ARTS COLLEGES PUBLIC		LIBERAL ARTS COLLEGES PRIVATE		OTHER PUBLIC		OTHER PRIVATE	
	INSTs	EEs	INSTs	EEs	INSTs	EEs	INSTs	EEs	INSTs	EEs	INSTs	EEs	INSTs	EEs
FACULTY														
Total	627	203206	74	91344	41	29312	133	46369	287	26983	36	5809	56	3389
	100.0	100.0	100.0	100.0	100.0	100.0	100.0	100.0	100.0	100.0	100.0	100.0	100.0	100.0
State Employee or Teacher Retirement Plan Provision	185	95212	43	46973	1	2000	111	41118	1	330	29	4791	—	—
	29.5	46.9	58.1	51.4	2.4	6.8	83.5	88.7	.3	1.2	80.6	82.5	—	—
Group Insurance Plan (Incl. TIAA Plans)	450	120992	44	49184	35	19996	49	22298	264	25102	10	1404	48	3008
	71.8	59.5	59.5	53.8	85.4	68.2	36.8	48.1	92.0	93.0	27.8	24.2	85.7	88.8
Self-Administered Plan	33	27522	9	15856	4	7564	9	3247	7	578	2	104	2	173
	5.3	13.5	12.2	17.4	9.8	25.8	6.8	7.0	2.4	2.1	5.6	1.8	3.6	5.1
Other	38	20235	6	14331	2	3614	2	541	17	1082	3	369	8	298
	6.1	10.0	8.1	15.7	4.9	12.3	1.5	1.2	5.9	4.0	8.3	6.4	14.3	8.8
ADMINISTRATIVE														
Total	629	77799	74	39896	41	18549	135	7506	286	9433	37	825	56	1590
	100.0	100.0	100.0	100.0	100.0	100.0	100.0	100.0	100.0	100.0	100.0	100.0	100.0	100.0
State Employee or Teacher Retirement Plan Provision	193	27333	47	19309	1	750	113	6531	1	61	31	682	—	—
	30.7	35.1	63.5	48.4	2.4	4.0	83.7	87.0	.3	.6	83.8	82.7	—	—
Group Insurance Plan (Incl. TIAA Plans)	444	46087	40	18719	35	13099	49	3764	262	8842	9	235	49	1428
	70.6	59.2	54.1	46.9	85.4	70.6	36.3	50.1	91.6	93.7	24.3	28.5	87.5	89.8
Self-Administered Plan	32	13995	9	9841	4	2396	9	1510	6	189	2	23	2	36
	5.1	18.0	12.2	24.7	9.8	12.9	6.7	20.1	2.1	2.0	5.4	2.8	3.6	2.3
Other	40	9100	7	4642	2	3784	2	114	19	383	3	28	7	149
	6.4	11.7	9.5	11.6	4.9	20.4	1.5	1.5	6.6	4.1	8.1	3.4	12.5	9.4
CLERICAL-SERVICE														
Total	469	259492	65	142816	28	44824	128	44590	174	18639	37	6446	37	2177
	100.0	100.0	100.0	100.0	100.0	100.0	100.0	100.0	100.0	100.0	100.0	100.0	100.0	100.0
State Employee or Teacher Retirement Plan Provision	193	149063	49	100348	1	4000	111	40412	1	241	31	4062	—	—
	41.2	57.4	75.4	70.3	3.6	8.9	86.7	90.6	.6	1.3	83.8	63.0	—	—
Group Insurance Plan (Incl. TIAA Plans)	278	128565	28	56636	24	33850	34	17815	151	16218	7	2155	34	1891
	59.3	49.5	43.1	39.7	85.7	75.5	26.6	40.0	86.8	87.0	18.9	33.4	91.9	86.9
Self-Administered Plan	24	36240	6	19652	2	5112	9	10602	4	583	2	181	1	110
	5.1	14.0	9.2	13.8	7.1	11.4	7.0	23.8	2.3	3.1	5.4	2.8	2.7	5.1
Other	32	28075	6	20468	1	5370	2	274	18	1359	3	460	2	144
	6.8	10.8	9.2	14.3	3.6	12.0	1.6	.6	10.3	7.3	8.1	7.1	5.4	6.6

Percentages add to more than 100 due to presence of more than one plan in some institutions.

TABLE 49. LONG-TERM TOTAL DISABILITY INCOME PLAN: EMPLOYER-EMPLOYEE CONTRIBUTION TOWARD COST OF PLAN
(Questionnaire Sect. VI Q.4,5)

| | ALL INSTITUTIONS | | UNIVERSITIES | | | | LIBERAL ARTS COLLEGES | | | | OTHER | | | |
| | | | PUBLIC | | PRIVATE | | PUBLIC | | PRIVATE | | PUBLIC | | PRIVATE | |
	INSTs	EEs	INSTs	EEs	INSTs	EEs	INSTs	EEs	INSTs	EEs	INSTs	EEs	INSTs	EEs
FACULTY														
Total	627	203206	74	91344	41	29312	133	46369	287	26983	36	5809	56	3389
	100.0	100.0	100.0	100.0	100.0	100.0	100.0	100.0	100.0	100.0	100.0	100.0	100.0	100.0
No Response	16	5668	5	4511	1	138	3	501	6	423	–	–	1	95
	2.6	2.8	6.8	4.9	2.4	.5	2.3	1.1	2.1	1.6	–	–	1.8	2.8
Employer Pays Full Cost	240	60794	9	17742	21	14372	12	9589	162	16089	6	1320	30	1682
	38.3	29.9	12.2	19.4	51.3	49.0	9.0	20.7	56.5	59.6	16.7	22.7	53.6	49.6
Employer and Employee Share Cost	287	99462	41	47438	14	9513	87	28632	102	9257	25	3524	18	1098
	45.7	49.0	55.3	52.0	34.1	32.5	65.4	61.7	35.5	34.3	69.4	60.7	32.1	32.4
Employee Pays Full Cost	84	37282	19	21653	5	5289	31	7647	17	1214	5	965	7	514
	13.4	18.3	25.7	23.7	12.2	18.0	23.3	16.5	5.9	4.5	13.9	16.6	12.5	15.2
ADMINISTRATIVE														
Total	629	77799	74	39896	41	18549	135	7506	286	9433	37	825	56	1590
	100.0	100.0	100.0	100.0	100.0	100.0	100.0	100.0	100.0	100.0	100.0	100.0	100.0	100.0
No Response	15	2193	5	1997	1	20	3	42	5	104	–	–	1	30
	2.4	2.8	6.8	5.0	2.4	.1	2.2	.6	1.7	1.1	–	–	1.8	1.9
Employer Pays Full Cost	241	26949	9	8854	21	10643	14	665	161	5758	6	273	30	756
	38.3	34.6	12.2	22.2	51.3	57.3	10.4	8.9	56.4	61.1	16.2	33.1	53.6	47.6
Employer and Employee Share Cost	291	31288	43	19465	14	2310	87	5414	103	3161	26	376	18	562
	46.3	40.3	58.0	48.8	34.1	12.5	64.4	72.0	36.0	33.5	70.3	45.6	32.1	35.3
Employee Pays Full Cost	82	17369	17	9580	5	5576	31	1385	17	410	5	176	7	242
	13.0	22.3	23.0	24.0	12.2	30.1	23.0	18.5	5.9	4.3	13.5	21.3	12.5	15.2
CLERICAL-SERVICE														
Total	469	259492	65	142816	28	44824	128	44590	174	18639	37	6446	37	2177
	100.0	100.0	100.0	100.0	100.0	100.0	100.0	100.0	100.0	100.0	100.0	100.0	100.0	100.0
No Response	17	10084	4	7911	1	492	4	686	5	600	–	–	3	395
	3.6	3.9	6.2	5.5	3.6	1.1	3.1	1.5	2.9	3.2	–	–	8.1	18.1
Employer Pays Full Cost	150	70988	10	28560	14	24521	14	5417	88	10320	7	1197	17	973
	32.0	27.4	15.4	20.0	50.0	54.8	10.9	12.1	50.6	55.3	18.9	18.6	46.0	44.7
Employer and Employee Share Cost	240	128543	36	75344	10	10735	88	32415	67	6608	26	2952	13	489
	51.2	49.5	55.3	52.8	35.7	23.9	68.8	72.8	38.5	35.5	70.3	45.8	35.1	22.5
Employee Pays Full Cost	62	49877	15	31001	3	9076	22	6072	14	1111	4	2297	4	320
	13.2	19.2	23.1	21.7	10.7	20.2	17.2	13.6	8.0	6.0	10.8	35.6	10.8	14.7

TABLE 50. LONG-TERM TOTAL DISABILITY INCOME PLAN: LENGTH OF TIME INDIVIDUAL APP. 3
MUST BE TOTALLY DISABLED BEFORE TOTAL DISABILITY INCOME BEGINS
(Questionnaire Sect. VI Q.8)

| | ALL INSTITUTIONS | | UNIVERSITIES | | | | LIBERAL ARTS COLLEGES | | | | OTHER | | | |
| | | | PUBLIC | | PRIVATE | | PUBLIC | | PRIVATE | | PUBLIC | | PRIVATE | |
	INSTs	EEs	INSTs	EEs	INSTs	EEs	INSTs	EEs	INSTs	EEs	INSTs	EEs	INSTs	EEs
FACULTY														
Total	627	203206	74	91344	41	29312	133	46369	287	26983	36	5809	56	3389
	100.0	100.0	100.0	100.0	100.0	100.0	100.0	100.0	100.0	100.0	100.0	100.0	100.0	100.0
No Response	164	60532	25	25616	3	4947	85	25429	19	1488	23	2802	9	250
	26.2	29.8	33.8	28.0	7.3	16.9	63.9	54.8	6.6	5.5	63.9	48.2	16.1	7.4
Less Than 3 Months	51	26041	11	18615	1	349	14	4139	16	974	4	1742	5	222
	8.1	12.8	14.9	20.4	2.4	1.2	10.5	8.9	5.6	3.6	11.1	30.1	8.9	6.6
3 Months	69	19459	11	10235	4	3005	7	2406	39	3149	2	450	6	214
	11.0	9.6	14.9	11.2	9.8	10.3	5.3	5.2	13.6	11.7	5.6	7.7	10.7	6.3
4-5 Months	5	7835	2	7190	–	–	2	572	1	73	–	–	–	–
	.8	3.9	2.7	7.9	–	–	1.5	1.2	.3	.3	–	–	–	–
6 Months	326	86963	23	28445	33	21011	24	13538	206	20661	7	815	33	2493
	52.0	42.8	30.9	31.1	80.5	71.6	18.0	29.3	71.8	76.5	19.4	14.0	58.9	73.6
7-11 Months	3	530	–	–	–	–	1	285	2	245	–	–	–	–
	.5	.2	–	–	–	–	.8	.6	.7	.9	–	–	–	–
12 Months	7	1359	1	900	–	–	–	–	4	393	–	–	2	66
	1.1	.7	1.4	1.0	–	–	–	–	1.4	1.5	–	–	3.6	1.9
Over 12 Months	2	487	1	343	–	–	–	–	–	–	–	–	1	144
	.3	.2	1.4	.4	–	–	–	–	–	–	–	–	1.8	4.2
ADMINISTRATIVE														
Total	629	77799	74	39896	41	18549	135	7506	286	9433	37	825	56	1590
	100.0	100.0	100.0	100.0	100.0	100.0	100.0	100.0	100.0	100.0	100.0	100.0	100.0	100.0
No Response	167	23010	25	15639	3	1215	87	5196	19	433	25	425	8	102
	26.6	29.6	33.8	39.2	7.3	6.6	64.4	69.2	6.6	4.6	67.6	51.5	14.3	6.4
Less Than 3 Months	52	6937	12	5961	1	37	13	438	17	281	4	169	5	51
	8.3	8.9	16.2	14.9	2.4	.2	9.6	5.8	5.9	3.0	10.8	20.5	8.9	3.2
3 Months	69	8490	11	4978	4	1834	7	280	39	1227	2	91	6	80
	11.0	10.9	14.9	12.5	9.8	9.9	5.2	3.7	13.6	13.0	5.4	11.0	10.7	5.0
4-5 Months	5	742	2	565	–	–	2	127	1	50	–	–	–	–
	.8	1.0	2.7	1.4	–	–	1.5	1.7	.3	.5	–	–	–	–
6 Months	324	37719	22	12234	33	15463	25	1412	204	7200	6	140	34	1270
	51.4	48.4	29.6	30.7	80.5	83.3	18.6	18.9	71.5	76.3	16.2	17.0	60.7	79.9
7-11 Months	3	109	–	–	–	–	1	53	2	56	–	–	–	–
	.5	.2	–	–	–	–	.7	.7	.7	.6	–	–	–	–
12 Months	7	644	1	380	–	–	–	–	4	186	–	–	2	78
	1.1	.8	1.4	1.0	–	–	–	–	1.4	2.0	–	–	3.6	4.9
Over 12 Months	2	148	1	139	–	–	–	–	–	–	–	–	1	9
	.3	.2	1.4	.3	–	–	–	–	–	–	–	–	1.8	.6

| | ALL INSTITUTIONS | | UNIVERSITIES | | | | LIBERAL ARTS COLLEGES | | | | OTHER | | | |
| | | | PUBLIC | | PRIVATE | | PUBLIC | | PRIVATE | | PUBLIC | | PRIVATE | |
	INSTs	EEs	INSTs	EEs	INSTs	EEs	INSTs	EEs	INSTs	EEs	INSTs	EEs	INSTs	EEs
CLERICAL-SERVICE														
Total	469	259492	65	142816	28	44824	128	44590	174	18639	37	6446	37	2177
	100.0	100.0	100.0	100.0	100.0	100.0	100.0	100.0	100.0	100.0	100.0	100.0	100.0	100.0
No Response	168	92115	24	44629	3	7082	93	35901	16	1606	26	2745	6	152
	35.8	35.5	36.9	31.2	10.7	15.8	72.7	80.5	9.2	8.6	70.3	42.6	16.2	7.0
Less Than 3 Months	47	35847	11	29079	1	678	13	3292	14	1328	4	1319	4	151
	10.0	13.8	16.9	20.4	3.6	1.5	10.1	7.5	8.0	7.1	10.8	20.5	10.8	6.9
3 Months	60	38304	11	24703	4	8438	6	1567	33	3181	1	176	5	239
	12.8	14.8	16.9	17.3	14.3	18.8	4.7	3.5	19.0	17.1	2.7	2.7	13.5	11.0
4-5 Months	4	1538	–	–	–	–	3	1315	1	223	–	–	–	–
	.9	.6	–	–	–	–	2.3	2.9	.6	1.2	–	–	–	–
6 Months	182	89365	18	42989	20	28626	12	2407	106	11721	6	2206	20	1416
	38.8	34.4	27.8	30.1	71.4	63.9	9.4	5.4	60.9	62.9	16.2	34.2	54.1	65.0
7-11 Months	1	82	–	–	–	–	–	–	1	82	–	–	–	–
	.2	*	–	–	–	–	–	–	.6	.4	–	–	–	–
12 Months	5	1999	1	1416	–	–	–	–	3	498	–	–	1	85
	1.1	.8	1.5	1.0	–	–	–	–	1.7	2.7	–	–	2.7	3.9
Over 12 Months	2	242	–	–	–	–	1	108	–	–	–	–	1	134
	.4	.1	–	–	–	–	.8	.2	–	–	–	–	2.7	6.2

TABLE 51. LONG-TERM TOTAL DISABILITY INCOME PLANS:
BENEFITS PAYABLE FOR WORK-CONNECTED AND/OR NONWORK-CONNECTED DISABILITIES
(Questionnaire Sect. VI Q.10)

| | ALL INSTITUTIONS | | UNIVERSITIES | | | | LIBERAL ARTS COLLEGES | | | | OTHER | | | |
| | | | PUBLIC | | PRIVATE | | PUBLIC | | PRIVATE | | PUBLIC | | PRIVATE | |
	INSTs	EEs	INSTs	EEs	INSTs	EEs	INSTs	EEs	INSTs	EEs	INSTs	EEs	INSTs	EEs
FACULTY														
Total	627	203206	74	91344	41	29312	133	46369	287	26983	36	5809	56	3389
	100.0	100.0	100.0	100.0	100.0	100.0	100.0	100.0	100.0	100.0	100.0	100.0	100.0	100.0
No Response	20	7582	2	2911	1	2835	5	1131	8	505	1	62	3	138
	3.2	3.7	2.7	3.2	2.4	9.7	3.8	2.4	2.8	1.9	2.8	1.1	5.4	4.1
Payable for Work-Connected Disabilities Only	21	3122	1	333	–	–	2	696	7	538	10	1544	1	11
	3.3	1.5	1.4	.4	–	–	1.5	1.5	2.4	2.0	27.8	26.6	1.8	.3
Payable for Nonwork-Connected Disabilities Only	44	12245	3	5027	3	774	12	4226	22	1502	2	476	2	240
	7.0	6.0	4.1	5.5	7.3	2.6	9.0	9.1	7.7	5.6	5.6	8.2	3.6	7.1
Payable for Both	542	180257	68	83073	37	25703	114	40316	250	24438	23	3727	50	3000
	86.5	88.8	91.8	90.9	90.3	87.7	85.7	87.0	87.1	90.5	63.8	64.1	89.2	88.5
ADMINISTRATIVE														
Total	629	77799	74	39896	41	18549	135	7506	286	9433	37	825	56	1590
	100.0	100.0	100.0	100.0	100.0	100.0	100.0	100.0	100.0	100.0	100.0	100.0	100.0	100.0
No Response	21	2821	2	1018	1	1127	5	452	9	175	1	6	3	43
	3.3	3.6	2.7	2.6	2.4	6.1	3.7	6.0	3.1	1.9	2.7	.7	5.4	2.7
Payable for Work-Connected Disabilities Only	21	527	1	109	–	–	2	37	7	168	10	142	1	71
	3.3	.7	1.4	.3	–	–	1.5	.5	2.4	1.8	27.0	17.2	1.8	4.5
Payable for Nonwork-Connected Disabilities Only	43	4122	3	2890	3	171	12	407	21	479	2	92	2	83
	6.8	5.3	4.1	7.2	7.3	.9	8.9	5.4	7.3	5.1	5.4	11.2	3.6	5.2
Payable for Both	544	70329	68	35879	37	17251	116	6610	249	8611	24	585	50	1393
	86.6	90.4	91.8	89.9	90.3	93.0	85.9	88.1	87.2	91.2	64.9	70.9	89.2	87.6
CLERICAL-SERVICE														
Total	469	259492	65	142816	28	44824	128	44590	174	18639	37	6446	37	2177
	100.0	100.0	100.0	100.0	100.0	100.0	100.0	100.0	100.0	100.0	100.0	100.0	100.0	100.0
No Response	18	20132	2	12828	1	5370	5	1181	5	567	1	58	4	128
	3.8	7.8	3.1	9.0	3.6	12.0	3.9	2.6	2.9	3.0	2.7	.9	10.8	5.9
Payable for Work-Connected Disabilities Only	19	2955	1	693	–	–	2	459	6	492	10	1311	–	–
	4.1	1.1	1.5	.5	–	–	1.6	1.0	8.4	2.6	27.0	20.3	–	–
Payable for Nonwork-Connected Disabilities Only	36	10765	1	3500	3	1571	12	4019	17	1150	1	350	2	175
	7.7	4.1	1.5	2.5	10.7	3.5	9.4	9.0	9.8	6.2	2.7	5.4	5.4	8.0
Payable for Both	396	225640	61	125795	24	37883	109	38931	146	16430	25	4727	31	1874
	84.4	87.0	93.9	88.0	85.7	84.5	85.1	87.4	83.9	88.2	67.6	73.4	83.8	86.1

Appendix 4

TIAA-CREF RETIREMENT PLANS

This appendix summarizes the principal provisions of the TIAA-CREF college and university retirement plans as of January, 1968. The entries describe the plans as they apply to new entrants, without reference to prior service or supplemental benefits or to alternative plans. Since the summaries are based on a punch card information system, many of the entries are abbreviated.

The columns show the following information:

INSTITUTION: The name of each institution and the staff member categories covered by the TIAA-CREF plan.

PROVISIONS APPLY TO: The categories of full-time staff members to which the information in the succeeding columns applies. A few institutions also include certain categories of part-time employees. The categories listed do not always correspond with the precise terminology of an institution's retirement plan resolution. For instance, the entry DESIG PRO CL (Designated Professional Classes) may include research personnel, librarians, and administrative assistants at one institution but only librarians and research personnel at another.

REQ &/OR VOL: Whether participation in the plan is required, voluntary, or is voluntary for a time and then required.

WAITING PERIOD

TIME, AGE, OTHER: The length of employment, attained age, or other waiting period required before participation begins. The abbreviation IMMED indicates that the individual is eligible to participate in the plan immediately upon employment. Since most institutions waive their regular waiting period for newly employed staff members bringing TIAA-CREF contracts with them, there is no entry describing this waiver provision.

Examples of waiting periods:

REQ 3Y	Required after 3 years' service
VOL 1Y	Voluntary after 1 year
REQ 1Y & 30	Required after 1 year's service and attainment of age 30
REQ 3Y or 35	Required after 3 years' service or attainment of age 35, whichever occurs first

TIAA-CREF CONTRIBUTIONS

SALARY: Entry made only when contribution rates differ on different portions of a person's salary. Shows the portion of salary on which the contribution rates in the columns to the right apply. If there is no entry in this column, the same rate of contribution applies to all of the individual's salary. Most of the entries in this column are for step-rate plans, which usually provide for one contribution rate on the portion of the participant's salary within the Social Security earnings base and a higher contribution rate on the portion of salary above that base.

AGE: Entry made only when contributions are graded by age. Each age shown is the age at which the contribution rates in the columns to the right first take effect. Where contributions are graded by age, no age entry is made until the first change in rates occurs. No entry indicates that there is no grading of contributions by age.

YRS: Entry made only when contributions are graded by years of plan participation. Shows the years of participation required before the contribution rates in the columns to the right apply. No entry indicates that there is no grading of contributions by years of participation.

INST: The institution's regular contributions to each participant's annuity, most frequently expressed as a percentage of salary. (Salary on which TIAA-CREF contributions are made is usually base salary.)

INDIV: The individual's contribution to his annuity, most frequently expressed as a percentage of salary. The # sign indicates that contributions of all participants are made by a salary *re*duction rather than salary *de*duction.

END AT: The point at which annuity contributions cease under the plan. The entry RET indicates that contributions continue throughout service, including any extensions, until retirement. An age entry is made where contributions cease at a stated age even though retirement may not have occurred.

NORM RET AGE: At institutions not permitting extensions of service, the age shown here is the mandatory retirement age. At institutions permitting extensions, the age shown is the age beyond which extensions must be made in order for service to continue.

MAX EXT TO: The age beyond which extensions of service, if any, are no longer made. Where no extensions of service are made beyond the normal retirement age, the entry NX is shown. Where extensions of service are provided for but no maximum age is given, the entry NL is shown.

ABBREVIATIONS:

ACAD	academic	NX	no extensions
ACCUM	accumulated	OASDI	Federal Social Security
APMT	appointment	OFF	officers
ASSOC	associate	PARTIC	participation
ASST	assistant	PERM	permanent
ATTAIN	attainment	PERS	personnel
BAL	balance of salary	PRO	professional
CL	classes	PROBAT	probationary
CLASS	classification	PROF	professors
CLER	clerical	RECOM	recommendation
CONTRIB	contributions	REQ	required
COV	covered	RET	retirement
DESIG	designated	RSCH	research
EDUC	educationally	SAL	salary
ELEC	elected	SEC	secretarial
ELIG	eligible	SERV	service
EQ	equal	SUPPL	supplements other plan
EQUIV	equivalent	VOL	voluntary
EXT	extensions	VOL AD	voluntary additional
FAC	faculty		contribution of desig-
FEM	female		nated amount by in-
IMMED	immediately		dividual increases
INDIV	individual		institution's contribution
INST	institution		by designated amount*
INSTR	instructors	YRS OR Y	years or yearly
M	monthly	#	all participants' contri-
MAINT	maintenance		butions are made by
NA	not applicable		salary reduction
NL	no limit	—	no information
NONACAD	nonacademic		

* Participants in all TIAA-CREF plans may make extra contributions on their own at any time without accompanying institutional contributions.

INSTITUTION	PROVISIONS APPLY TO	REQ &/OR VOL	WAITING PERIOD			TIAA-CREF CONTRIBUTIONS						NOR RET AGE	MAX EXT TO
			TIME	AGE	OTHER	SALARY	AGE	YRS	INST	INDIV	END AT		
ABADAN INSTITUTE OF TECHNOLOGY, IRAN PLAN COVERS- FAC, OFF	ALL ELIGIBLE	REQ	IMMED						10.00%	5.00%	RET	65	70
ADELPHI U, N Y PLAN COVERS- ALL EMPLOYEES	ALL ELIGIBLE	VOL	2Y						6.00%	6.00%	RET	65	70
ADRIAN COL, MICH PLAN COVERS- FAC, OFF	ALL ELIGIBLE	VOL	IMMED			UP TO			10.00%	10.00%	RET	65	70
ALABAMA, U OF SUPPL PLAN COVERS- FAC, OFF	ASSOC PROF & ABOVE & EQUIV OFF	REQ	IMMED			FIRST $7000 BAL	EMPLOYED UNDER AGE 40		3.00% .00%	3.00% .00%	RET	70	NX
						FIRST $7000 BAL	EMPLOYED AT AGE 40 OR OVER		5.00% .00%	5.00% .00%			
	ASST PROF	VOL	3Y			FIRST $7000 BAL	EMPLOYED UNDER AGE 40		3.00% .00%	3.00% .00%	RET	70	NX
						FIRST $7000 BAL	EMPLOYED AT AGE 40 OR OVER		5.00% .00%	5.00% .00%			
	INSTR	VOL	6Y OR		TENURE	FIRST $7000 BAL	EMPLOYED UNDER AGE 40		3.00% .00%	3.00% .00%	RET	70	NX
						FIRST $7000 BAL	EMPLOYED AT AGE 40 OR OVER		5.00% .00%	5.00% .00%			
ALASKA METHODIST U PLAN COVERS- FAC, OFF	ALL ELIGIBLE	REQ VOL	3Y & 30 1Y						5.00%	5.00%	RET	65	70
ALBANY COL OF PHARMACY, NY PLAN COVERS- FAC, OFF, MAINT & SERV	ALL ELIGIBLE	VOL	3Y						7.00%	5.00%	65	65	NL
ALBANY LAW SCH, N Y PLAN COVERS- ALL EMPLOYEES	FAC	REQ	IMMED						8.00%	7.00% #	RET	65	NL
	OTHER	REQ	1Y						8.00%	7.00% #	RET	65	NL
ALBERTUS MAGNUS COL, CONN PLAN COVERS- FAC	ALL ELIGIBLE	REQ VOL	3Y & 30 1Y						5.00%	5.00%	RET	68	70
ALBION COL, MICH PLAN COVERS- ALL EMPLOYEES	FAC, OFF	REQ	2Y			FIRST $6600 BAL			5.00% 10.00%	5.00% # 5.00% #	RET	65	7C
	OTHER	REQ	3Y & 30						3.00%	2.00%	RET	65	70
ALBRIGHT COL, PA PLAN COVERS- ALL EMPLOYEES	FAC, OFF, CLER	REQ	1Y & 30			FIRST $7800 BAL			5.00% 10.00%	5.00% 5.00%	RET	65	NX
	OTHER	VOL	1Y & 30			FIRST $7800 BAL			5.00% 10.00%	5.00% 5.00%	RET	65	70
ALBUQUERQUE, U OF, N M CONTINUED ON NEXT PAGE	ALL ELIGIBLE	VOL	3Y OR		ON RECOM				5.00%	5.00%	RET	67	70

INSTITUTION	PROVISIONS APPLY TO	REQ &/OR VOL	WAITING PERIOD			TIAA-CREF CONTRIBUTIONS					END AT	NOR RET AGE	MAX EXT TO
			TIME AGE	OTHER		SALARY AGE	YRS	INST	INDIV				
PLAN COVERS- FAC													
ALFRED U, N Y	ASST PROF & ABOVE & EQUIV OFF	REQ	4Y OR	TENURE		FIRST $7800		5.00%	5.00%		65	65	70
PLAN COVERS- FAC, OFF		VOL	IMMED			BAL		12.00%	5.00%				
	OTHER	REQ	5Y			FIRST $7800		5.00%	5.00%		65	65	70
		VOL	IMMED			BAL		12.00%	5.00%				
ALLEGHENY COL, PA	ALL ELIGIBLE	VOL	1Y					9.00%	6.00%		RET	65	NL
PLAN COVERS- FAC, OFF													
ALLENTOWN COL, PA	ALL ELIGIBLE	REQ	2Y & 30			FIRST $7800		3.87%	3.87%		RET	65	70
PLAN COVERS- ALL EMPLOYEES		VOL	2Y			BAL		7.50%	7.50%				
ALLIANCE COL, PA	ALL ELIGIBLE	VOL	IMMED					5.00%	5.00%		RET	65	70
PLAN COVERS- FAC, OFF													
ALMA COL, MICH	ALL ELIGIBLE	VOL	IMMED					6.00%	6.00%		RET	65	NL
PLAN COVERS- FAC, OFF						ON TENURE		10.00%	2.00%				
AMERICAN COL FOR GIRLS TURKEY	ALL ELIGIBLE	REQ	3Y & 30			FIRST $7800		3.60%	.00%		RET	65	NL
PLAN COVERS- FAC, OFF & DESIG CL						BAL		8.00%	.00%				
AMERICAN SCH OF CLASSICAL STUDIES, GREECE	ALL ELIGIBLE	REQ	IMMED					10.00%	.00%		RET	65	70
PLAN COVERS- ALL EMPLOYEES													
AMERICAN U, D C	FAC	REQ	IMMED					10.00%	5.00%		RET	70	NX
PLAN COVERS- ALL EMPLOYEES													
	OFF & DESIG NONACAD CL	VOL	IMMED					10.00%	5.00%		RET	70	NX
	OTHER	VOL	1Y					10.00%	5.00%		RET	70	NX
AMERICAN U IN CAIRO	ALL ELIGIBLE	REQ	3Y & 30					9.00%	6.00%		RET	60	65
PLAN COVERS- FAC, OFF		VOL	1Y										
AMERICAN U OF BEIRUT LEBANON	ALL ELIGIBLE	REQ	IMMED			FIRST $4800		*	3.00%		RET	65	70
PLAN COVERS- FAC, OFF, CLER & SEC						BAL		*	5.00%				
						*INSTITUTION, AT RETIREMENT OR OTHER TERMINATION OF SERVICE, PURCHASES TIAA ANNUAL BENEFIT EQUAL TO 30% OF THE INDIVIDUAL'S ACCUMULATED CONTRIBUTIONS.							
AMHERST COL, MASS	FAC, OFF	REQ	2Y			FIRST $7800		7.00%	5.00%		RET	65	70
PLAN COVERS- FAC, OFF, CLER & SEC						BAL		10.00%	5.00%				
	OTHER	REQ	5Y & 30			FIRST $7800		7.00%	5.00%		RET	65	70
						BAL		10.00%	5.00%				
ANDERSON COL, IND	FAC	REQ	7Y					5.00%	5.00%		RET	65	70
PLAN COVERS- ALL EMPLOYEES CONTINUED ON NEXT PAGE		VOL	2Y										

INSTITUTION	PROVISIONS APPLY TO	REQ &/OR VOL	WAITING PERIOD		TIAA-CREF CONTRIBUTIONS					NOR RET AGE	MAX EXT TO
			TIME AGE	OTHER	SALARY AGE	YRS	INST	INDIV	END AT		
	OFF & DESIG NONACAD CL	REQ	7Y				5.00%	5.00%	RET	65	70
		VOL	2Y								
	OTHER	VOL	2Y				5.00%	5.00%	RET	65	70
ANNA MARIA COL, MASS PLAN COVERS— FAC, OFF	ALL ELIGIBLE	REQ	2Y OR 30				5.00%	5.00%	RET	65	NL
		VOL	IMMED								
ANTIOCH COL, OHIO PLAN COVERS— ALL EMPLOYEES	FAC	REQ	2Y				10.00%	.00%	RET	65	NL
	OFF & DESIG NONACAD CL	REQ	2Y				5.00%	5.00%	RET	65	NL
	OTHER	VOL	3Y & 35				3.00%	2.00%	RET	65	NL
AQUINAS COL, MICH PLAN COVERS— ALL EMPLOYEES	FAC, OFF	VOL	2Y				5.00%	5.00%	RET	65	NL
						2	10.00%	.00%			
	OTHER	REQ	2Y				5.00%	.00%	RET	65	NL
ARKANSAS COL PLAN COVERS— FAC, OFF, CLER & SEC	ALL ELIGIBLE	REQ	3Y & 30		FIRST $4800		10.00%	.00%	RET	65	NL
					BAL		15.00%	.00%			
ARKANSAS POLYTECHNIC COL PLAN COVERS— FAC, OFF	ALL ELIGIBLE	REQ	IMMED				6.00%	6.00%	RET	65	72
ARKANSAS STATE TEACHERS COL PLAN COVERS— FAC, OFF	ALL ELIGIBLE	REQ	IMMED				6.00%	6.00%	RET	65	72
ARKANSAS STATE U PLAN COVERS— FAC, OFF	ALL ELIGIBLE	REQ	IMMED				6.00%	6.00%	RET	65	72
ARKANSAS, U OF PLAN COVERS— ALL EMPLOYEES	ALL ELIGIBLE	VOL	IMMED				6.00%	6.00%	67	67	NL
ART CENTER COL OF DESIGN CALIF PLAN COVERS— ALL EMPLOYEES	ALL ELIGIBLE	VOL	3Y & 30		FIRST $6600		1.38%	1.38%	RET	68	73
					BAL		5.00%	5.00%			
ASBURY COL, KY PLAN COVERS— FAC, OFF	ALL ELIGIBLE	REQ	3Y & 25				5.00%	5.00%	RET	65	70
ASBURY THEOLOGICAL SEM, KY PLAN COVERS— ALL EMPLOYEES	FAC, OFF	REQ	3Y & 30				5.00%	5.00%	RET	68	NL
		VOL	IMMED								
	OTHER	VOL	1Y				5.00%	5.00%	RET	68	NL
ASHLAND COL, OHIO PLAN COVERS— ALL EMPLOYEES	FAC	REQ	2Y & 30				6.00%	4.00%	RET	70	NX
		VOL	IMMED								
	OTHER	VOL	2Y				6.00%	4.00%	RET	70	NX
ASSUMPTION COL, MASS	ALL ELIGIBLE	REQ	2Y				5.00%	5.00%	RET	65	70

CONTINUED ON NEXT PAGE

INSTITUTION	PROVISIONS APPLY TO	REQ &/OR VOL	WAITING PERIOD TIME AGE	WAITING PERIOD OTHER	TIAA-CREF CONTRIBUTIONS SALARY AGE	YRS	INST	INDIV	END AT	NOR RET AGE	MAX EXT TO
PLAN COVERS– FAC, OFF, CLER & SEC		VOL	1Y								
ATHENS COL, ALA	ALL ELIGIBLE	REQ	2Y & 30				5.00%	5.00%	RET	70	75
PLAN COVERS– FAC, OFF		VOL	1Y								
ATHENS COL, GREECE	ALL ELIGIBLE	REQ		ON RECOM	UP TO 10.00%			.00%	RET	65	NX
PLAN COVERS– ALL EMPLOYEES		VOL	IMMED								
ATLANTA U, GA	ALL ELIGIBLE	REQ	4Y				5.00%	5.00%	RET	65	70
PLAN COVERS– FAC, OFF, CLER & SEC		VOL	2Y								
AUGSBURG COL, MINN	FAC	REQ		TENURE			10.00%	.00%	RET	65	70
PLAN COVERS– ALL EMPLOYEES											
	OFF	REQ	4Y				10.00%	.00%	RET	65	70
	OTHER	REQ	8Y				8.00%	.00%	RET	65	68
AUGUSTANA COL, ILL	FAC	REQ	IMMED				8.00%	.00%	RET	68	70
PLAN COVERS– ALL EMPLOYEES											
	OTHER	REQ	3Y				8.00%	.00%	RET	68	70
AUGUSTANA COL, S D	FAC, OFF	REQ	3Y OR 30				3.00%	3.00% #	RET	65	70
PLAN COVERS– ALL EMPLOYEES		VOL	IMMED			2	4.00%	4.00% #			
						5	5.00%	5.00% #			
						10	6.00%	5.00% #			
						15	7.00%	5.00% #			
	OTHER	REQ	3Y & 30 &	ON RECOM			3.00%	3.00% #	RET	65	70
		VOL	1Y & 30			2	4.00%	4.00% #			
						5	5.00%	5.00% #			
						10	6.00%	5.00% #			
						15	7.00%	5.00% #			
						20	8.00%	5.00% #			
AURORA COL, ILL	ALL ELIGIBLE	REQ	5Y & 30				5.00%	5.00%	70	65	NL
PLAN COVERS– ALL EMPLOYEES											
	VOL PARTIC	VOL	1Y		UP TO 5.00%			5.00%	70	65	NL
AUSTIN COL, TEX	ASSOC PROF & ABOVE & EQUIV OFF	REQ	3Y & 30				7.00%	5.00%	RET	65	70
PLAN COVERS– ALL EMPLOYEES		VOL	IMMED								
	ASST PROF & INSTR & EQUIV OFF	REQ	3Y & 30				7.00%	5.00%	RET	65	70
		VOL	1Y								
	OTHER	REQ	3Y & 35				7.00%	3.00%	RET	65	70
		VOL	1Y								
AZUSA PACIFIC COL, CALIF	FAC, OFF	REQ	IMMED				5.00%	.00%	RET	65	NL
PLAN COVERS– FAC, OFF											
	PART TIME	REQ	2Y				5.00%	.00%	RET	65	NL
BABSON INSTITUTE OF BUSINESS ADMIN, MASS	FAC, OFF	REQ	2Y		FIRST $6600		5.80%	.80%	65	65	NL
PLAN COVERS– ALL EMPLOYEES CONTINUED ON NEXT PAGE		VOL		ON RECOM	BAL		10.00%	5.00%			

CONTINUED ON NEXT PAGE

INSTITUTION	PROVISIONS APPLY TO	REQ &/OR VOL	WAITING PERIOD			TIAA-CREF CONTRIBUTIONS					END AT	NOR RET AGE	MAX EXT TO
			TIME	AGE	OTHER	SALARY	AGE	YRS	INST	INDIV			
	OTHER	VOL			ON RECOM	FIRST $6600 BAL			5.80% 10.00%	.80% 5.00%	65	65	NL
BAKER U, KAN PLAN COVERS— ALL EMPLOYEES	FAC, OFF	REQ VOL	1Y IMMED						5.00%	5.00%	RET	68	72
	OTHER	VOL			ON RECOM				5.00%	5.00%	RET	68	72
BALDWIN-WALLACE COL, OHIO PLAN COVERS— ALL EMPLOYEES	FAC, OFF	REQ VOL	2Y 1Y			FIRST $6600 BAL			6.00% 9.00%	4.00% 6.00%	RET	65	NL
	OTHER	VOL	3Y						5.00%	3.00%	RET	65	NL
BALL STATE U, IND SUPPL PLAN COVERS— FAC, OFF	FAC	REQ	2Y			FOR ALL PARTICIPANTS: COLLEGE PAYS FULL PREMIUM TO PURCHASE BENEFIT OF $1500 A YEAR AT AGE 66. MAXIMUM CONTRIBUTION IS $1000 A YEAR.					RET	66	NX
	MAJOR OFF	REQ	2Y								RET	66	NX
	OTHER OFF	VOL	2Y &	25							RET	66	NX
BALTIMORE COL OF COMMERCE MD PLAN COVERS— FAC, OFF & DESIG CL	ALL ELIGIBLE	REQ	1Y						5.00%	5.00%	RET	65	NL
	PART TIME	VOL	2Y						5.00%	5.00%	RET	65	NL
BANK STREET COL OF EDUCATION, N Y PLAN COVERS— ALL EMPLOYEES	FAC, OFF	REQ	2Y &	30					5.00%	5.00%	RET	65	NL
	OTHER	VOL	2Y &	30					5.00%	5.00%	RET	65	NL
BAPTIST COL AT CHARLESTON S C PLAN COVERS— FAC, OFF	ALL ELIGIBLE	REQ VOL	3Y & IMMED	30					5.00%	5.00%	RET	65	70
BARD COL, N Y PLAN COVERS— ALL EMPLOYEES	FAC, OFF	REQ VOL	3Y 1Y						12.50%	2.50%	RET	65	NL
	FEM CLER & MAINT	REQ	3Y &	30					10.00%	.00%	RET	65	NL
	OTHER	REQ	3Y &	30					10.00%	.00%	RET	68	NL
BARNARD COL, N Y PLAN COVERS— FAC, OFF	PROF & EQUIV OFF	REQ	IMMED						15.00%	.00%	RET	65	68
	ASST & ASSOC PROF & OFF	REQ	IMMED						10.00%	5.00%	RET	65	68
	OTHER	REQ	3Y						10.00%	5.00%	RET	65	68
BARRINGTON COL, R I PLAN COVERS— FAC, OFF	ALL ELIGIBLE	REQ	3Y &	30					5.00%	5.00%	RET	65	70
BARRY COL, FLA PLAN COVERS— CONTINUED ON NEXT PAGE	ALL ELIGIBLE	REQ VOL	3Y & 1Y	30					5.00%	5.00%	RET	65	70

CONTINUED ON NEXT PAGE

INSTITUTION	PROVISIONS APPLY TO	REQ &/OR VOL	WAITING PERIOD TIME	AGE	OTHER	TIAA-CREF CONTRIBUTIONS SALARY	AGE	YRS	INST	INDIV	END AT	NOR RET AGE	MAX EXT TO
ALL EMPLOYEES													
BATES COL, ME PLAN COVERS— FAC, OFF	ALL ELIGIBLE	REQ VOL	 2Y		RANK OF ASST PROF				5.00%	5.00%	RET	70	NX
BAYLOR U COL OF MEDICINE TEX PLAN COVERS— FAC, OFF	PROF	REQ VOL	3Y & 1Y	35					12.50%	5.00% #	RET	65	70
	ASSOC PROF	REQ VOL	3Y & 1Y	35					10.00%	5.00% #	RET	65	70
	ASST PROF & EQUIV OFF	REQ VOL	3Y & 1Y	35					7.50%	5.00% #	RET	65	70
BEAVER COL, PA PLAN COVERS— FAC, OFF	FAC	REQ VOL	3Y IMMED			FIRST $7800 BAL			5.00% 5.00%	5.00% 5.00%	RET	65	NL
						FIRST $7800 BAL		VOL AD VOL AD	.00% 2.50%	.00% 2.50%			
	OTHER	VOL	IMMED			FIRST $7800 BAL			5.00% 5.00%	5.00% 5.00%	RET	65	NL
						FIRST $7800 BAL		VOL AD VOL AD	.00% 2.50%	.00% 2.50%			
BEIRUT COL FOR WOMEN LEBANON PLAN COVERS— FAC, OFF	ALL ELIGIBLE	REQ VOL	2Y & 1Y	30					5.00%	5.00%	RET	65	70
BELKNAP COL, N H PLAN COVERS— ALL EMPLOYEES	FAC, OFF, CLER	REQ VOL	1Y & 1Y	25					5.00%	5.00%	RET	65	NL
	OTHER	REQ VOL	5Y 1Y						5.00%	5.00%	RET	65	NL
BELLARMINE COL, KY PLAN COVERS— ALL EMPLOYEES	FAC, OFF	REQ VOL	5Y & 2Y		RANK OF ASST PROF	FIRST $7800 BAL			5.00% 7.50%	5.00% 7.50%	RET	65	70
	OTHER	VOL	2Y						3.30%	3.30%	RET	65	70
BELOIT COL, WIS PLAN COVERS— FAC, OFF	ASST PROF & ABOVE & EQUIV OFF	REQ	2Y				35 50	4 10	5.00% 10.00% 15.00%	.00% .00% .00%	RET	65	NX
BENNETT COL, N C PLAN COVERS— ALL EMPLOYEES	FAC	REQ VOL	1Y & IMMED	30					7.00%	5.00%	RET	65	70
	OTHER	VOL	3Y &	35					7.00%	5.00%	RET	65	70
BENNINGTON COL, VT PLAN COVERS— FAC, OFF	ALL ELIGIBLE	REQ VOL	2Y & IMMED	30		FIRST $7800 BAL			5.00% 10.00%	5.00% 5.00%	RET	65	70
BENTLEY COL OF ACCOUNTING AND FINANCE, MASS PLAN COVERS— ALL EMPLOYEES	ALL ELIGIBLE	REQ	2Y &	30 &	JULY 1	FIRST $7800 BAL			8.00% 12.00%	2.00% 3.00%	65	65	70

INSTITUTION	PROVISIONS APPLY TO	REQ &/OR VOL	WAITING PERIOD TIME AGE	WAITING PERIOD OTHER	TIAA-CREF CONTRIBUTIONS SALARY AGE	YRS	INST	INDIV	END AT	NOR RET AGE	MAX EXT TO
BEREA COL, KY PLAN COVERS— ALL EMPLOYEES	ALL ELIGIBLE	REQ VOL	2Y 2Y	$7800 SAL	FIRST $7800 BAL		5.00% 7.50%	5.00% 5.00%	RET	65	68
BERRY COL, GA PLAN COVERS— ALL EMPLOYEES	FAC, OFF, CLER OTHER	REQ VOL VOL	3Y & 30 IMMED 2Y			UP TO	5.00% 5.00%	5.00% 5.00%	RET RET	65 65	70 70
BETHANY BIBLE COL, CALIF PLAN COVERS— ALL EMPLOYEES	ALL ELIGIBLE	REQ VOL	3Y & 30 3Y & 27				10.00%	.00%	RET	65	70
BETHANY COL, KAN PLAN COVERS— FAC, OFF	ALL ELIGIBLE	REQ VOL	2Y & 30 1Y				6.00%	4.00%	RET	68	70
BETHANY COL, W VA PLAN COVERS— FAC	ALL ELIGIBLE	REQ		TENURE			7.50%	2.50%	RET	65	70
BETHANY THEOLOGICAL SEM ILL PLAN COVERS— FAC	CLERGYMEN OTHER	REQ REQ	IMMED IMMED				8.00% 6.00%	2.00% 4.00%	RET RET	65 65	70 70
BETHEL COL, KAN PLAN COVERS— FAC, OFF	FAC, OFF PART TIME	REQ VOL REQ	2Y & 30 2Y	ON RECOM			7.50% 7.50%	2.50% 2.50%	RET RET	65 65	70 70
BIOLA COL, CALIF PLAN COVERS— FAC, OFF	ALL ELIGIBLE	REQ VOL	3Y	30 & TENURE			3.00%	3.00%	RET	65	70
BIRMINGHAM—SOUTHERN COL ALA PLAN COVERS— ALL EMPLOYEES	FAC OFF OTHER	REQ REQ REQ	IMMED IMMED IMMED				7.50% 7.50% 7.50%	7.50% 7.50% 7.50%	RET RET RET	68 65 65	NL NL NL
BISCAYNE COL, FLA PLAN COVERS— FAC, OFF	ALL ELIGIBLE	REQ VOL	2Y & 30 2Y				6.00%	4.00%	RET	65	70
BLACKBURN COL, ILL PLAN COVERS— FAC, OFF	ALL ELIGIBLE	REQ	5Y OR	TENURE			7.50%	2.50%	RET	65	68
BLOOMFIELD COL, N J PLAN COVERS— ALL EMPLOYEES	ALL ELIGIBLE	REQ VOL	2Y IMMED				5.00%	5.00%	RET	67	NL
BLUEFIELD STATE COL, W VA SUPPL PLAN COVERS— ALL EMPLOYEES CONTINUED ON NEXT PAGE	ALL ELIGIBLE	REQ		30 & $4800 SAL	FIRST $4800 BAL FIRST $4800	35	.00% 5.00% .00%	.00% 5.00% .00%	RET	65	NL

CONTINUED ON NEXT PAGE

INSTITUTION	PROVISIONS APPLY TO	REQ &/OR VOL	WAITING PERIOD			TIAA-CREF CONTRIBUTIONS					END AT	NOR RET AGE	MAX EXT TO
			TIME AGE		OTHER	SALARY	AGE	YRS	INST	INDIV			
						BAL	35		6.00%	6.00%			
						FIRST $4800	45		.00%	.00%			
						BAL	45		7.50%	7.50%			
BLUFFTON COL, OHIO PLAN COVERS— ALL EMPLOYEES	ALL ELIGIBLE	REQ	3Y						7.00%	5.00%	RET	65	70
BOSTON COL, MASS PLAN COVERS— ALL EMPLOYEES	FAC, OFF	VOL	3Y						8.00%	5.00%	RET	65	NL
	OTHER	VOL	5Y						6.00%	2.00%	RET	65	NL
BOSTON U, MASS PLAN COVERS— FAC, OFF	ASST PROF & ABOVE & EQUIV OFF	REQ			CONTRIB ACCUM FOR 1ST 3 YRS BEFORE PAID TO CONTRACT	FIRST $6600			3.00%	3.00%	65	65	70
						BAL			5.00%	5.00%			
						FIRST $6600	40		5.00%	3.00%			
						BAL	40		7.00%	5.00%			
						FIRST $6600	45		7.00%	3.00%			
						BAL	45		10.00%	5.00%			
						FIRST $6600	50		7.00%	3.00%			
						BAL	50		13.00%	5.00%			
	OTHER FAC	REQ	3Y & 35 &		ON RECOM	FIRST $6600			3.00%	3.00%	65	65	70
						BAL			5.00%	5.00%			
						FIRST $6600	40		5.00%	3.00%			
						BAL	40		7.00%	5.00%			
						FIRST $6600	45		7.00%	3.00%			
						BAL	45		10.00%	5.00%			
						FIRST $6600	50		7.00%	3.00%			
						BAL	50		13.00%	5.00%			
BOWDOIN COL, ME PLAN COVERS— FAC, OFF & DESIG CL	FAC	REQ	3Y & 30						11.11%	.00%	RET	70	NL
		VOL	3Y OR 30										
	OFF	REQ	3Y & 30			FIRST $7800			11.11%	.00%	RET	65	NX
		VOL	3Y OR 30			BAL			17.65%	.00%			
	OTHER	REQ	3Y & 30						11.11%	.00%	RET	70	NL
		VOL	3Y OR 30										
BOWMAN GRAY SCH OF MEDICINE, WAKE FOREST U NC PLAN COVERS— FAC, OFF	ASST PROF & ABOVE & EQUIV OFF	VOL	IMMED			FIRST $6000			7.50%	5.00%	65	70	NL
						BAL			7.50%	.00%			
						NO CONTRIBUTIONS ARE MADE ON SALARY ABOVE $12000.							
BRADLEY U, ILL PLAN COVERS— ALL EMPLOYEES	ALL ELIGIBLE	VOL	1Y						5.00%	5.00%	RET	65	NL
BRANDEIS U, MASS PLAN COVERS— ALL EMPLOYEES	ASSOC PROF & ABOVE & EQUIV OFF	REQ	IMMED						8.00%	5.00%	RET	65	68
	ASST PROF & INSTR	REQ	1Y &	30 OR TENURE					8.00%	5.00%	RET	65	68
	OTHER	VOL	30						6.00%	3.00%	RET	65	70

INSTITUTION	PROVISIONS APPLY TO	REQ &/OR VOL	WAITING PERIOD TIME AGE	OTHER	TIAA-CREF CONTRIBUTIONS SALARY AGE	YRS	INST	INDIV	END AT	NOR RET AGE	MAX EXT TO
BRIARCLIFF COL, N Y PLAN COVERS— ALL EMPLOYEES	FAC, OFF	REQ	1Y & 30		FIRST $7800 BAL		5.00% 10.00%	5.00% 5.00%	RET	65	70
	OTHER	VOL	3Y & 30				3.00%	3.00%	RET	65	70
BRIDGEPORT, U OF, CONN PLAN COVERS— ALL EMPLOYEES	FAC, OFF	REQ	4Y & 30				5.00%	5.00%	RET	65	70
		VOL	1Y								
	OTHER	VOL	1Y				5.00%	5.00%	RET	65	70
BRIDGEWATER COL, VA PLAN COVERS— FAC, OFF	ALL ELIGIBLE	REQ	3Y & 30				5.00%	5.00%	RET	65	70
		VOL	1Y								
BRIGHAM YOUNG U, UTAH PLAN COVERS— ALL EMPLOYEES	FAC	REQ	4Y				5.00%	5.00%	RET	65	70
		VOL	IMMED								
	OTHER	REQ	4Y				5.00%	5.00%	RET	65	70
		VOL	2Y								
BROOKLYN COL OF PHARMACY N Y PLAN COVERS— FAC, OFF, CLER & SEC	ALL ELIGIBLE	VOL	IMMED				10.00%	.00%	RET	65	NX
BROOKLYN LAW SCH, N Y PLAN COVERS— FAC	ALL ELIGIBLE	REQ	3Y & 30				10.00%	5.00%	RET	65	NL
BROWN U, R I PLAN COVERS— ALL EMPLOYEES	ASSOC PROF & ABOVE	REQ	IMMED				10.00%	5.00%	RET	65	70
	ASST PROF	REQ	3Y OR 40				10.00%	5.00%	RET	65	70
		VOL	2Y								
	INSTR	REQ	5Y OR 40				10.00%	5.00%	RET	65	70
		VOL	2Y								
	OFF	REQ	1Y				10.00%	5.00%	RET	65	70
		VOL	IMMED								
	DESIG PRO CL	REQ	3Y				10.00%	5.00%	RET	65	70
		VOL	IMMED								
	OTHER	VOL	1Y				6.00%	4.00%	RET	65	70
BRYAN COL, TENN PLAN COVERS— ALL EMPLOYEES	FAC	REQ	3Y & 30				5.00%	5.00%	RET	65	70
		VOL	1Y								
	OTHER	REQ	3Y & 35				5.00%	5.00%	RET	65	70
		VOL	1Y								
BRYANT COL, R I PLAN COVERS— FAC, OFF	ALL ELIGIBLE	REQ	3Y				5.00%	5.00%	RET	65	NL
BRYN MAWR COL, PA PLAN COVERS— FAC, OFF, CLER & SEC	ALL ELIGIBLE	REQ	IMMED				10.00%	.00%	RET	65	67

INSTITUTION	PROVISIONS APPLY TO	REQ &/OR VOL	WAITING PERIOD			TIAA-CREF CONTRIBUTIONS						NOR RET AGE	MAX EXT TO
			TIME AGE		OTHER	SALARY AGE	YRS	INST	INDIV	END AT			
BUCKNELL U, PA PLAN COVERS- FAC, OFF	ALL ELIGIBLE	REQ	30					10.00%	5.00%	RET		70	NL
BUENA VISTA COL, IA PLAN COVERS- ALL EMPLOYEES	PROF	REQ	IMMED					5.00%	5.00%	RET		65	70
	ASSOC PROF	REQ	1Y					5.00%	5.00%	RET		65	70
	ASST PROF & INSTR	REQ	2Y					5.00%	5.00%	RET		65	70
	OTHER	REQ	3Y					5.00%	5.00%	RET		65	70
CALIFORNIA COL OF ARTS AND CRAFTS PLAN COVERS- FAC, OFF, CLER & SEC	ALL ELIGIBLE	REQ	3Y & 30			FIRST $6600 BAL		5.00% 7.50%	5.00% 7.50%	RET		68	70
CALIFORNIA INSTITUTE OF TECHNOLOGY PLAN COVERS- FAC, OFF & DESIG CL	ASST PROF & ABOVE	REQ	IMMED			INSTITUTE AND INDIVIDUAL CONTRIBUTIONS ARE SCALED TO SALARY BRACKETS AND RANGE FROM: FOR FACULTY:				RET		68	70
	INSTR	REQ VOL	2Y IMMED			10% TO 20% BY THE INSTITUTE AND .00% TO 5% BY THE INDIVIDUAL.				RET		68	70
	OTHER	REQ			$15000 SAL	FOR OFFICERS AND OTHERS: 10% TO 20% BY THE INSTITUTE AND .00% TO 2.5% BY THE INDIVIDUAL.				RET		68	70
CALIFORNIA LUTHERAN COL PLAN COVERS- FAC, OFF, CLER & SEC	ALL ELIGIBLE	VOL	3Y					6.00%	4.00%	65		65	70
CALIFORNIA WESTERN U PLAN COVERS- FAC, OFF	ALL ELIGIBLE	REQ VOL	3Y 1Y					5.00%	5.00%	RET		65	70
CALVIN COL, MICH PLAN COVERS- FAC, OFF	ASST PROF & ABOVE & EQUIV OFF	REQ	IMMED					10.00%	.00%	RET		70	NX
	OTHER	REQ	2Y OR 43					10.00%	.00%	RET		70	NX
CAMPBELL COL, N C PLAN COVERS- ALL EMPLOYEES	ALL ELIGIBLE	REQ VOL	3Y OR 30 IMMED					5.00%	5.00%	RET		70	NL
CANISIUS COL, N Y PLAN COVERS- FAC, OFF	ALL ELIGIBLE	VOL	IMMED					5.00%	5.00%	RET		65	70
CAPITAL U, OHIO PLAN COVERS- FAC, OFF	ALL ELIGIBLE	REQ VOL	6Y & 32 OR TENURE 3Y					9.00%	3.00%	RET		70	NL
CARDINAL CUSHING COL MASS PLAN COVERS- FAC, OFF & DESIG CL	FAC	REQ VOL	2Y & 30 30					5.00%	5.00%	RET		65	72
	OTHER	REQ	2Y & 30					5.00%	5.00%	RET		65	72
CARNEGIE-MELLON U, PA PLAN COVERS- FAC, OFF	ALL ELIGIBLE	REQ	35			FIRST $4800 BAL		5.00% 7.50%	5.00% 7.50%	RET		68	70
CARROLL COL, MONT	FAC	REQ	3Y &		OCT 1			5.00%	5.00%	65		65	72

CONTINUED ON NEXT PAGE

INSTITUTION	PROVISIONS APPLY TO	REQ &/OR VOL	TIME AGE OTHER	SALARY AGE YRS INST INDIV	END AT	NOR RET AGE	MAX EXT TO
PLAN COVERS- FAC, OFF		VOL	1Y & 30				
	OTHER	REQ	3Y & $7500 SAL	5.00% 5.00%	65	65	72
		VOL	1Y & 30 & $7500 SAL & OCT 1				
CARROLL COL, WIS PLAN COVERS- FAC, OFF, CLER & SEC	ALL ELIGIBLE	VOL	IMMED	10.00% 5.00%	RET	65	70
CARTHAGE COL, WIS PLAN COVERS- FAC, OFF	ALL ELIGIBLE	VOL	2Y	7.00% 5.00%	RET	65	NL
CASTLETON STATE COL, VT PLAN COVERS- FAC, OFF	FAC	REQ	2Y	FIRST $6600 10.00% .00%	RET	65	70
		VOL	IMMED	BAL 15.00% .00%			
	OTHER	VOL	IMMED	FIRST $6600 10.00% .00% BAL 15.00% .00%	RET	65	70
CATAWBA COL, N C PLAN COVERS- FAC, OFF	ALL ELIGIBLE	REQ	3Y	5.00% 5.00%	RET	65	70
		VOL	1Y				
CATHERINE SPALDING COL, KY PLAN COVERS- FAC, OFF	ALL ELIGIBLE	VOL	3Y & 30	5.00% 5.00%	RET	65	NX
CATHOLIC U OF AMERICA, D C PLAN COVERS- ALL EMPLOYEES	FAC, OFF	REQ	2Y & 30 & $6000 SAL	FIRST $7800 4.50% 4.50%	RET	65	70
		VOL	2Y & $6000 SAL	BAL 7.50% 7.50%			
	CLERGYMEN	REQ	2Y & 30	7.50% 7.50%	RET	65	70
		VOL	2Y				
	OTHER	REQ	2Y & 30	FIRST $7800 2.00% 2.00%	RET	65	70
		VOL	2Y	BAL 5.00% 5.00%			
CEDAR CREST COL, PA PLAN COVERS- ALL EMPLOYEES	FAC, OFF	REQ	2Y	FIRST $4800 5.00% 5.00% BAL 9.00% 5.00%	RET	67	NX
	OTHER	VOL	2Y	FIRST $4800 5.00% 5.00% BAL 9.00% 5.00%	RET	67	NX
CENTENARY COL FOR WOMEN, N J PLAN COVERS- FAC, OFF, CLER & SEC	ALL ELIGIBLE	VOL	IMMED	7.50% 7.50%	RET	67	NL
CENTENARY COL OF LOUISIANA PLAN COVERS- FAC, OFF, CLER & SEC	FAC, OFF	REQ	3Y	5.00% 5.00%	RET	65	NL
		VOL	1Y				
	OTHER	VOL	1Y	5.00% 5.00%	RET	65	NL
CENTRAL BIBLE COL, MO PLAN COVERS- FAC, OFF	ALL ELIGIBLE	REQ	2Y & 30	6.00% 4.00%	RET	65	NX
CENTRAL COL, IA PLAN COVERS- FAC, OFF CONTINUED ON NEXT PAGE	PROF	REQ	TENURE	FIRST $7800 5.00% 5.00% BAL 7.00% 7.00%	RET	68	70

INSTITUTION	PROVISIONS APPLY TO	REQ &/OR VOL	WAITING PERIOD			TIAA-CREF CONTRIBUTIONS					END AT	NOR RET AGE	MAX EXT TO
			TIME	AGE	OTHER	SALARY	AGE	YRS	INST	INDIV			
	OFF	VOL	3Y			FIRST $7800			3.00%	3.00%	RET	68	70
						BAL			5.00%	5.00%			
	OTHER FAC	VOL			TENURE	FIRST $7800			3.00%	3.00%	RET	68	70
						BAL			5.00%	5.00%			
CENTRAL METHODIST COL, MO PLAN COVERS- FAC, OFF	ALL ELIGIBLE	VOL	IMMED					UP TO	5.00%	5.00%	RET	70	NX
CENTRAL WASHINGTON STATE COL PLAN COVERS- FAC, OFF	ALL ELIGIBLE	REQ	2Y OR		RANK OF ASSOC PROF	FIRST $4800			2.50%	2.50%	RET	65	70
						BAL			5.00%	5.00%			
						FIRST $4800	35		4.50%	4.50%			
						BAL	35		7.50%	7.50%			
CENTRE COL OF KENTUCKY PLAN COVERS- FAC, OFF	ALL ELIGIBLE	REQ	2Y						10.00%	.00%	RET	65	70
		VOL	1Y										
CHADRON STATE COL, NEB PLAN COVERS- ALL EMPLOYEES	FAC, OFF	REQ	IMMED						6.00%	6.00%	RET	65	68
	OTHER	REQ	IMMED						3.00%	3.00%	RET	65	68
CHAMINADE COL, HAWAII PLAN COVERS- ALL EMPLOYEES	ALL ELIGIBLE	VOL	1Y						5.00%	5.00%	RET	65	70
CHATHAM COL, PA PLAN COVERS- FAC, OFF & DESIG CL	FAC	REQ	1Y OR		RANK OF PROF				10.00%	5.00%	RET	65	NL
	MAJOR OFF	VOL	IMMED						10.00%	5.00%	RET	65	NL
	OTHER OFF	VOL	2Y						10.00%	5.00%	RET	65	NL
	OTHER	VOL	5Y						10.00%	5.00%	RET	65	NL
CHATTANOOGA, U OF, TENN PLAN COVERS- FAC, OFF, CLER & SEC	FAC	REQ			TENURE				12.00%	.00%	RET	65	70
	OTHER	VOL	3Y &		ON RECOM				12.00%	.00%	RET	65	70
CHESTNUT HILL COL, PA PLAN COVERS- FAC, OFF	ALL ELIGIBLE	REQ	2Y &	30		FIRST $7800			7.50%	3.10%	RET	65	NL
		VOL	1Y			BAL			7.50%	7.50%			
CHICAGO COL OF OSTEOPATHY ILL PLAN COVERS- FAC	ALL ELIGIBLE	VOL	2Y &		$4800 SAL				5.00%	5.00%	RET	65	70
						FIRST $6600	FOR THOSE NOT ENGAGED IN FEE		5.00%	5.00%			
						BAL	PRACTICE		10.00%	5.00%			
CHICAGO-KENT COL OF LAW ILL PLAN COVERS- ALL EMPLOYEES	ALL ELIGIBLE	REQ	5Y &	35		FIRST $4800			4.00%	.00%	RET	65	NL
						BAL			8.00%	.00%			

INSTITUTION	PROVISIONS APPLY TO	REQ &/OR VOL	WAITING PERIOD			TIAA-CREF CONTRIBUTIONS			END AT	NOR RET AGE	MAX EXT TO
			TIME AGE		OTHER	SALARY AGE YRS	INST	INDIV			
CHICAGO MEDICAL SCH, ILL — PLAN COVERS— ALL EMPLOYEES	ALL ELIGIBLE	VOL	1Y				5.00%	5.00%	RET	65	70
CHICAGO THEOLOGICAL SEM, ILL — PLAN COVERS— FAC, OFF	ALL ELIGIBLE	REQ	IMMED			FIRST $4800 BAL	5.00% 7.50%	5.00% 5.00%	RET	65	NX
CHICAGO, U OF, ILL — PLAN COVERS— FAC	ASST PROF & ABOVE	REQ	IMMED				7.50%	5.00%	65	65	NL
	OTHER	VOL	2Y				7.50%	5.00%	65	65	NL
CHURCH COL OF HAWAII — PLAN COVERS— FAC, OFF	ALL ELIGIBLE	VOL	IMMED				5.00%	5.00%	RET	65	70
CINCINNATI, U OF, OHIO — PLAN COVERS— FAC, OFF & DESIG CL	FAC	REQ	IMMED			FIRST $7800 BAL	6.25% 10.00%	1.60% 6.00%	RET	67	NX
	OFF	REQ	IMMED			FIRST $7800 BAL	6.25% 10.00%	1.60% 6.00%	RET	65	NX
	OTHER	REQ	IMMED			FIRST $7800 BAL	6.25% 10.00%	1.60% 6.00%	RET	67	NX
CLAREMONT MENS COL, CALIF — PLAN COVERS— FAC, OFF	ASST PROF & ABOVE	REQ	IMMED				12.00%	4.00%	RET	65	68
	OTHER	VOL			VARIES		12.00%	4.00%	RET	65	68
CLAREMONT U CENTER, CALIF — PLAN COVERS— FAC, OFF	ALL ELIGIBLE	REQ	IMMED				12.00%	4.00%	RET	65	68
CLARK COL, GA — PLAN COVERS— FAC, OFF	ALL ELIGIBLE	REQ VOL	2Y & 30 IMMED				8.00%	2.00%	RET	68	NX
CLARK U, MASS — PLAN COVERS— ALL EMPLOYEES	FAC, OFF	REQ VOL	3Y		ON RECOM	FIRST $4800 BAL	5.00% 10.00%	5.00% 5.00%	RET	65	NX
	OTHER	VOL	5Y				2.50%	2.50%	RET	65	NX
CLARKSON COL OF TECHNOLOGY N Y — PLAN COVERS— FAC, OFF, CLER & SEC	ALL ELIGIBLE	REQ VOL	3Y & 30		RANK OF ASSOC PROF		7.50%	2.50%	RET	65	70
CLEVELAND INSTITUTE OF ART OHIO — PLAN COVERS— FAC, OFF	ALL ELIGIBLE	REQ	3Y & 30			FIRST $7500 BAL	5.00% .00%	5.00% .00%	65	65	NL
CLEVELAND INSTITUTE OF MUSIC, OHIO — PLAN COVERS— ALL EMPLOYEES	ALL ELIGIBLE	VOL	2Y & 30			FIRST $7800 BAL	5.00% 10.00%	2.50% 5.00%	65	65	NL
COE COL, IA — PLAN COVERS— CONTINUED ON NEXT PAGE	ASST PROF & ABOVE & EQUIV OFF	REQ	IMMED				7.00%	5.00%	RET	65	70

INSTITUTION	PROVISIONS APPLY TO	REQ &/OR VOL	WAITING PERIOD TIME AGE OTHER	SALARY AGE	YRS	INST	INDIV	END AT	NOR RET AGE	MAX EXT TO
ALL EMPLOYEES										
	INSTR	VOL	IMMED			7.00%	5.00%	RET	65	70
	OTHER	REQ	5Y & 30			5.00%	3.00%	RET	65	70
COKER COL, S C	ALL ELIGIBLE	REQ	2Y			7.50%	7.50%	RET	65	NL
PLAN COVERS— FAC, OFF, CLER & SEC		VOL	1Y							
COLBY COL, ME	PROF	REQ	IMMED	FIRST $7800		5.00%	5.00%	RET	65	70
PLAN COVERS— FAC, OFF & DESIG CL				BAL		15.00%	5.00%			
	ASST & ASSOC PROF & OFF	REQ	IMMED	FIRST $7800		5.00%	5.00%	RET	65	70
				BAL		10.00%	5.00%			
	OTHER	REQ	3Y	FIRST $7800		5.00%	5.00%	RET	65	70
				BAL		10.00%	5.00%			
COLBY JR COL FOR WOMEN, N H	ALL ELIGIBLE	REQ	1Y			8.00%	4.00%	RET	65	70
PLAN COVERS— ALL EMPLOYEES										
COLGATE-ROCHESTER DIVINITY SCH, N Y	FAC, OFF	REQ	IMMED			13.00%	.00%	RET	65	68
PLAN COVERS— ALL EMPLOYEES										
	OTHER	VOL	IMMED			10.00%	.00%	RET	65	68
COLGATE U, N Y	FAC, OFF	REQ	3Y			10.00%	5.00%	RET	68	NL
PLAN COVERS— ALL EMPLOYEES		VOL	1Y							
	DESIG NONACAD CL	REQ	3Y			7.00%	3.00%	RET	65	NL
	OTHER	VOL	1Y			3.00%	3.00%	RET	65	NL
COL MISERICORDIA, PA	ALL ELIGIBLE	REQ	3Y & 30			5.00%	5.00%	RET	65	70
PLAN COVERS— FAC		VOL	1Y							
COLORADO COL	FAC, OFF	REQ	1Y & 30			7.50%	7.50% #	65	65	NL
PLAN COVERS— ALL EMPLOYEES		VOL	1Y							
	OTHER	VOL	2Y & 30			5.00%	5.00% #	65	65	NL
COLORADO, U OF	ASSOC PROF & ABOVE	REQ	IMMED	FIRST $7800		5.00%	5.00% #	RET	68	NX
PLAN COVERS— FAC, OFF				BAL		7.00%	7.00% #			
	ASST PROF & INSTR	REQ	1Y	FIRST $7800		5.00%	5.00% #	RET	68	NX
				BAL		7.00%	7.00% #			
	OTHER	REQ	IMMED	FIRST $7800		5.00%	5.00% #	65	65	68
				BAL		7.00%	7.00% #			
COLUMBIA COL, S C	ALL ELIGIBLE	VOL	3Y		UP TO	5.00%	5.00%	RET	65	70
PLAN COVERS— FAC, OFF										
COLUMBIA U, N Y	ASST PROF & ABOVE & EQUIV OFF	REQ	IMMED			10.00%	5.00%	RET	68	NX
PLAN COVERS— FAC, OFF				50 15		15.00%	.00%			
				60 20		20.00%	.00%			
	INSTR & EQUIV OFF	REQ	3Y			10.00%	5.00%	RET	68	NX
				50 15		15.00%	.00%			

CONTINUED ON NEXT PAGE

INSTITUTION	PROVISIONS APPLY TO	REQ &/OR VOL	WAITING PERIOD TIME	AGE	OTHER	SALARY	AGE	YRS	INST	INDIV	END AT	NOR RET AGE	MAX EXT TO
							60	20	20.00%	.00%			
	OTHER	VOL	3Y &	30					10.00%	5.00%	RET	68	NX
							50	15	15.00%	.00%			
							60	20	20.00%	.00%			
CONCORD COL, W VA SUPPL PLAN COVERS— ALL EMPLOYEES	ALL ELIGIBLE	REQ		30 &	$4800 SAL	FIRST $4800 BAL			.00% 5.00%	.00% 5.00%	RET	65	NL
						FIRST $4800 BAL	35 35		.00% 6.00%	.00% 6.00%			
						FIRST $4800 BAL	45 45		.00% 7.50%	.00% 7.50%			
CONCORDIA COL, MINN PLAN COVERS— ALL EMPLOYEES	ALL ELIGIBLE	REQ VOL	3Y & 1Y	30					5.00%	5.00%	RET	65	72
CONNECTICUT COL PLAN COVERS— ALL EMPLOYEES	ASST PROF & ABOVE	REQ	3Y						10.00%	5.00%	RET	65	70
	OTHER	VOL	3Y						10.00%	5.00%	RET	65	70
CONVERSE COL, S C PLAN COVERS— FAC, OFF	ALL ELIGIBLE	VOL	1Y						5.00%	5.00%	65	65	70
COOPER UNION, N Y PLAN COVERS— ALL EMPLOYEES	FAC, OFF	REQ			CONTRIB ACCUM FOR 1ST 3 YRS BEFORE PAID TO CONTRACT	FIRST $7800 BAL			5.60% 10.00%	.60% 5.00%		65	65	70
	OTHER	VOL	1M		CONTRIB ACCUM FOR 1ST 3 YRS BEFORE PAID TO CONTRACT	FIRST $7800 BAL			5.60% 10.00%	.60% 5.00%		65	65	70
CORNELL COL, IA PLAN COVERS— ALL EMPLOYEES	ALL ELIGIBLE	VOL	1Y						10.00%	5.00%	RET	65	70
CORNELL U, N Y PLAN COVERS— FAC, OFF & DESIG CL	FAC	REQ			RANK OF ASST PROF				10.00%	5.00%	RET	65	68
	DESIG PRO CL	REQ	1Y						10.00%	5.00%	RET	65	68
	OTHER	REQ			CLASS IN SPECIF GRADES OR $5076 SAL				10.00%	5.00%	RET	65	68
CORNELL U MEDICAL COL, N Y PLAN COVERS— FAC, OFF	ALL ELIGIBLE	VOL			RANK OF ASST PROF	FIRST $20000 BAL			5.00% .00%	5.00% .00%	RET	65	NL
CREIGHTON U, NEB PLAN COVERS— FAC, OFF & DESIG CL	FAC, OFF	VOL	1Y &	30		FIRST $12000 BAL			5.00% .00%	5.00% .00%	RET	65	70
	OTHER	VOL	5Y &	30		FIRST $12000 BAL			5.00% .00%	5.00% .00%	RET	65	70
CURRY COL, MASS PLAN COVERS— FAC, OFF	ASST PROF & ABOVE & EQUIV OFF	REQ VOL	2Y IMMED						5.00%	5.00%	RET	65	70
	OTHER	REQ	4Y						5.00%	5.00%	RET	65	70

CONTINUED ON NEXT PAGE

INSTITUTION	PROVISIONS APPLY TO	REQ &/OR VOL	WAITING PERIOD			TIAA-CREF CONTRIBUTIONS					END AT	NOR RET AGE	MAX EXT TO
			TIME	AGE	OTHER	SALARY	AGE	YRS	INST	INDIV			
		VOL	2Y										
DAKOTA WESLEYAN U, S D PLAN COVERS- ALL EMPLOYEES	FAC, OFF	REQ	2Y &	30					5.00%	5.00%	RET	65	70
	OTHER	VOL	2Y &	30					5.00%	5.00%	RET	65	70
DALLAS, U OF, TEX PLAN COVERS- FAC, OFF	ALL ELIGIBLE	REQ	3Y &	30					5.00%	5.00%	RET	65	NL
DANA COL, NEB PLAN COVERS- ALL EMPLOYEES	FAC, OFF	REQ	1Y &	40					3.00%	3.00%	65	65	70
		VOL	2Y &	30			40		7.00%	3.00%			
	OTHER	VOL	2Y &	30					3.00%	3.00%	65	65	70
							40		7.00%	3.00%			
DARTMOUTH COL, N H PLAN COVERS- FAC, OFF	ALL ELIGIBLE	REQ	3Y OR		RANK OF ASST PROF		40		10.00% 16.00%	.00% .00%	65	65	70
DAVIDSON COL, N C PLAN COVERS- FAC, OFF & DESIG CL	ALL ELIGIBLE	REQ	1Y			FIRST $7800 BAL			10.00% 15.00%	.00% .00%	RET	65	70
DAVIS AND ELKINS COL, PLAN COVERS- FAC, OFF	ALL ELIGIBLE	REQ	IMMED						7.50%	2.50%	65	65	70
DAYTON, U OF, OHIO PLAN COVERS- ALL EMPLOYEES	FAC, OFF	REQ	3Y &	30					5.00%	5.00%	65	65	NL
		VOL	1Y										
	DESIG PRO CL	REQ	3Y &	30					5.00%	5.00%	65	65	NL
		VOL	1Y										
	OTHER	REQ	5Y &	35					3.00%	3.00%	65	65	NL
		VOL	2Y &	32									
DEFIANCE COL, OHIO PLAN COVERS- ALL EMPLOYEES	FAC, OFF	REQ	1Y						5.00%	5.00%	70	70	NL
	OTHER	VOL	1Y						5.00%	5.00%	70	70	NL
DELAWARE, U OF SUPPL PLAN COVERS- FAC, OFF & DESIG CL	FAC, OFF	REQ		35		FOR ALL PARTICIPANTS: FIRST $16000 BAL			5.00% .00%	5.00% .00%	RET	65	70
						FIRST $16000 BAL			VOL AD 2.50% VOL AD .00%	2.50% .00%			
	DESIG PRO CL	VOL			ON RECOM	VOLUNTARY CONTRIBUTIONS ON SALARY FROM $16000 TO $20000 ARE MATCHED BY THE COLLEGE.					RET	65	70
DENISON U, OHIO PLAN COVERS- ALL EMPLOYEES	PROF	REQ		27					15.00%	.00%	65	65	70
	ASSOC PROF	REQ		27					15.00%	.00%	65	65	NX
	ASST PROF	REQ		27					15.00%	.00%	65	65	NX
	INSTR	REQ	2Y &	27					15.00%	.00%	65	65	NX
	OFF	REQ	2Y &	27					15.00%	.00%	65	65	67
CONTINUED ON NEXT PAGE													

INSTITUTION	PROVISIONS APPLY TO	REQ &/OR VOL	WAITING PERIOD TIME AGE OTHER	TIAA-CREF CONTRIBUTIONS SALARY AGE YRS	INST	INDIV	END AT	NOR RET AGE	MAX EXT TO
	OTHER	VOL	2Y & 30		5.00%	5.00%	65	65	75
DENVER, U OF, COLO PLAN COVERS— FAC, OFF, CLER & SEC	ASSOC PROF & ABOVE	REQ	IMMED		8.00%	4.00%	RET	68	7C
	ASST PROF	REQ	1Y		8.00%	4.00%	RET	68	7C
		VOL	IMMED						
	INSTR	REQ	5Y		8.00%	4.00%	RET	68	7C
		VOL	1Y						
	OTHER	VOL	3Y		8.00%	4.00%	RET	65	7C
DE PAUL U, ILL PLAN COVERS— FAC, OFF, CLER & SEC	FAC, OFF	VOL	1Y		5.00%	5.00%	RET	65	7C
	OTHER	VOL	10Y		5.00%	5.00%	RET	65	7C
DEPAUW U, IND PLAN COVERS— ALL EMPLOYEES	FAC, OFF	REQ	2Y & 30	FIRST $4800 BAL	5.00% 8.00%	5.00% 5.00%	RET	65	NL
	OTHER	VOL	2Y	FIRST $4800 BAL	5.00% 8.00%	5.00% 5.00%	RET	65	NL
DETROIT BIBLE COL, MICH PLAN COVERS— ALL EMPLOYEES	ALL ELIGIBLE	VOL	1Y		5.00%	5.00%	RET	65	NL
DETROIT INSTITUTE OF TECHNOLOGY, MICH PLAN COVERS— FAC, OFF	ALL ELIGIBLE	VOL	1Y & 30		5.00%	5.00%	RET	65	7C
DETROIT, U OF, MICH PLAN COVERS— ALL EMPLOYEES	FAC, OFF	REQ	2Y & 30	FIRST $4800 BAL	3.00% 6.00%	3.00% 6.00%	65	65	7C
		VOL	30						
	OTHER	REQ	10Y & 40	FIRST $4800 BAL	3.00% 6.00%	3.00% 6.00%	65	65	NX
		VOL	3Y & 30						
				NO CONTRIBUTIONS ARE MADE ON SALARY ABOVE $12000.					
DICKINSON COL, PA PLAN COVERS— ALL EMPLOYEES	FAC	REQ	1Y		10.00%	5.00%	RET	65	7C
	OTHER	VOL	1Y		10.00%	5.00%	RET	65	70
DICKINSON SCH OF LAW, PA PLAN COVERS— FAC	ALL ELIGIBLE	REQ	3Y & 30	FIRST $7800 BAL	5.00% 10.00%	5.00% 5.00%	70	65	70
		VOL	1Y						
DICKINSON STATE COL, N D SUPPL PLAN COVERS— FAC, OFF & DESIG CL	ASSOC PROF & ABOVE & EQUIV OFF	REQ	IMMED	FIRST $20000 BAL	5.00% .00%	5.00% .00%	RET	65	7C
	OTHER	REQ	2Y	FIRST $20000 BAL	5.00% .00%	5.00% .00%	RET	65	7C
DOANE COL, NEB PLAN COVERS— FAC, OFF	ALL ELIGIBLE	REQ	RANK OF ASST PROF		5.00%	5.00%	RET	65	NL

INSTITUTION	PROVISIONS APPLY TO	REQ &/OR VOL	WAITING PERIOD TIME AGE OTHER	TIAA-CREF CONTRIBUTIONS SALARY AGE	YRS	INST	INDIV	END AT	NOR RET AGE	MAX EXT TO
DORDT COL, IA PLAN COVERS— ALL EMPLOYEES	ALL ELIGIBLE	VOL	IMMED			4.00%	2.00%	RET	65	NL
DRAKE U, IA PLAN COVERS— FAC, OFF & DESIG CL	PROF	REQ				5.00%	5.00%	RET	70	NX
	ASSOC PROF	REQ	2Y			5.00%	5.00%	RET	70	NX
	ASST PROF	REQ	2Y			5.00%	5.00%	RET	70	NX
	OFF	REQ	IMMED			5.00%	5.00%	RET	65	NX
	OTHER	REQ	3Y			5.00%	5.00%	RET	65	70
DREW U, N J PLAN COVERS— ALL EMPLOYEES	ASST PROF & ABOVE	REQ	IMMED	FIRST $7800 BAL		6.00% 10.00%	5.00% 5.00%	RET	65	70
	MAJOR OFF	REQ	IMMED	FIRST $7800 BAL		6.00% 10.00%	5.00% 5.00%	RET	65	NX
	OTHER	VOL	3Y & 30	FIRST $7800 BAL		6.00% 10.00%	5.00% 5.00%	RET	65	NX
DRURY COL, MO PLAN COVERS— FAC, OFF	ALL ELIGIBLE	REQ VOL	TENURE IMMED			5.00%	5.00%	RET	65	70
DUBUQUE, U OF, IA PLAN COVERS— ALL EMPLOYEES	ALL ELIGIBLE	VOL	IMMED			5.00%	5.00%	RET	65	68
DUKE U, N C PLAN COVERS— FAC, OFF & DESIG CL	FAC, OFF	REQ	2Y & 30 OR RANK OF ASSOC PROF	FIRST $7800 BAL		7.00% 14.00%	5.00% 5.00%	RET	70	NX
	OTHER	REQ	5Y & 30	FIRST $7800 BAL		7.00% 14.00%	5.00% 5.00%	RET	65	NX
DUNBARTON COL OF HOLY CROSS, D C PLAN COVERS— FAC	ALL ELIGIBLE	REQ	2Y & 30			7.50%	7.50%	RET	65	70
DUQUESNE U, PA PLAN COVERS— FAC, OFF, CLER & SEC	FAC, OFF	REQ	1Y & 26		5 10	5.00% 6.00% 7.00%	5.00% 5.00% 5.00%	RET	65	70
					15 20	8.00% 9.00%	5.00% 5.00%			
					25	10.00%	5.00%			
	DESIG NONACAD CL	VOL	3Y & 26			5.00%	5.00%	RET	65	70
	OTHER	VOL	10Y & 26			5.00%	5.00%	RET	65	70
D YOUVILLE COL, N Y PLAN COVERS— FAC, OFF	ALL ELIGIBLE	VOL	1Y			5.00%	5.00%	RET	65	70
EARLHAM COL, IND PLAN COVERS— FAC, OFF	ALL ELIGIBLE	REQ VOL	2Y & 35 2Y	FIRST $4800 BAL		1.50% 2.50%	1.50% # 2.50% #	RET	65	NL
CONTINUED ON NEXT PAGE				FIRST $4800	1	4.00%	4.00% #			

INSTITUTION	PROVISIONS APPLY TO	REQ &/OR VOL	WAITING PERIOD			TIAA-CREF CONTRIBUTIONS						NOR RET AGE	MAX EXT TO
			TIME	AGE	OTHER	SALARY	AGE	YRS	INST	INDIV	END AT		
						BAL		1	5.00%	5.00% #			
						FIRST $4800		2	6.00%	6.00% #			
						BAL		2	7.00%	7.00% #			
EASTERN BAPTIST COL AND THEOLOGICAL SEM, PA PLAN COVERS- FAC, OFF & DESIG CL	FAC	VOL	IMMED						5.00%	1.00%	RET	70	NL
	OTHER	VOL	IMMED						5.00%	1.00%	RET	65	NL
EASTERN NAZARENE COL, MASS PLAN COVERS- ALL EMPLOYEES	ALL ELIGIBLE	REQ VOL	2Y & 1Y	30					7.50%	5.00%	RET	65	70
EASTERN WASHINGTON STATE COL PLAN COVERS- FAC, OFF & DESIG CL	ALL ELIGIBLE	REQ VOL	2Y		RANK OF ASSOC PROF	FIRST $4800 BAL			4.50% 7.50%	4.50% 7.50%	RET	67	NX
EDGEWOOD COL OF THE SACRED HEART, WIS PLAN COVERS- ALL EMPLOYEES	ALL ELIGIBLE	VOL	3Y						10.00%	.00%	RET	65	70
EISENHOWER COL, N Y PLAN COVERS- ALL EMPLOYEES	FAC	VOL	IMMED			FIRST $7800 BAL			5.00% 10.00%	5.00% 5.00%	RET	65	70
	OTHER	VOL	1Y &	30		FIRST $7800 BAL			5.00% 10.00%	5.00% 5.00%	RET	65	70
ELIZABETHTOWN COL, PA PLAN COVERS- FAC, OFF	ALL ELIGIBLE	REQ VOL	2Y &	30	ON RECOM				5.00%	5.00%	65	65	70
ELMHURST COL, ILL PLAN COVERS- ALL EMPLOYEES	FAC, OFF	VOL	IMMED						5.00%	5.00%	RET	65	70
	OTHER	VOL	3Y						5.00%	5.00%	RET	65	70
ELMIRA COL, N Y PLAN COVERS- ALL EMPLOYEES	FAC	REQ VOL	1Y & 1Y	27		FIRST $7800 BAL			10.60% 15.00%	.00% .00%	RET	65	NL
	DESIG PRO CL	REQ VOL	1Y & 1Y	27		FIRST $7800 BAL			10.60% 15.00%	.00% .00%	RET	65	NL
	OTHER	REQ			VARIES	FIRST $7800 BAL			2.60% 7.00%	2.60% 7.00%	RET	65	NL
ELON COL, N C PLAN COVERS- FAC, OFF	ALL ELIGIBLE	REQ VOL	3Y & 1Y	30					8.00%	4.00%	RET	65	72
EMERSON COL, MASS PLAN COVERS- FAC, OFF	ALL ELIGIBLE	REQ	2Y &	30					7.00%	3.00%	RET	65	70
EMMANUEL COL, MASS PLAN COVERS- FAC	ALL ELIGIBLE	VOL	3Y						5.00%	5.00%	RET	65	70

INSTITUTION	PROVISIONS APPLY TO	REQ &/OR VOL	WAITING PERIOD			TIAA-CREF CONTRIBUTIONS					END AT	NOR RET AGE	MAX EXT TO
			TIME	AGE	OTHER	SALARY	AGE	YRS	INST	INDIV			
EMORY AND HENRY COL, VA PLAN COVERS— FAC, OFF	ALL ELIGIBLE	REQ VOL	3Y & 1Y	30					7.00%	5.00%	RET	65	70
EMORY U, GA PLAN COVERS— ALL EMPLOYEES	FAC, OFF	REQ			RANK OF ASST PROF	FIRST $7800 BAL			7.00% 8.00%	5.00% 5.00%	RET	68	NX
	OTHER	REQ	5Y &	28					2.00%	2.00%	RET	65	68
EPISCOPAL THEOLOGICAL SCH MASS PLAN COVERS— FAC, OFF, CLER & SEC	ALL ELIGIBLE	REQ	2Y &	30		FIRST $6600 BAL			10.00% 15.00%	.00% .00%	RET	65	70
ERSKINE COL, S C PLAN COVERS— FAC, OFF, CLER & SEC	FAC	REQ VOL	2Y & 1Y	30		WITH DR. DEGREE		6 10	5.00% 7.50% 7.50%	5.00% 5.00% 5.00%	RET	65	70
	OFF	REQ VOL	2Y & 1Y	30					7.50%	5.00%	RET	65	70
	OTHER	REQ VOL	2Y & 1Y	30				10	5.00% 7.50%	5.00% 5.00%	RET	65	70
EVANGEL COL, MO PLAN COVERS— FAC, OFF	ALL ELIGIBLE	REQ VOL	2Y & 2Y	30					5.50%	4.00%	65	65	NL
EVANSVILLE, U OF PLAN COVERS— FAC, OFF & DESIG CL	FAC, OFF	REQ VOL	3Y & 2Y	30					5.00%	5.00%	RET	65	70
	OTHER	REQ VOL	5Y & 2Y &	30 30					5.00%	3.00%	RET	65	70
FAIRFIELD U, CONN PLAN COVERS— FAC, OFF	MEN	VOL	3Y						5.00%	5.00%	RET	65	NL
	FEM FAC	VOL	3Y						5.00%	5.00%	RET	60	NL
FAIRLEIGH DICKINSON U, N J PLAN COVERS— FAC, OFF & DESIG CL	ALL ELIGIBLE	REQ VOL	2Y &	28	ON RECOM				5.00%	5.00%	RET	65	NX
FAIRMONT STATE COL, W VA SUPPL PLAN COVERS— ALL EMPLOYEES	ALL ELIGIBLE	VOL		30 &	$4800 SAL	FIRST $4800 BAL FIRST $4800 BAL FIRST $4800 BAL	 35 35 45 45		.00% 5.00% .00% 6.00% .00% 7.50%	.00% 5.00% .00% 6.00% .00% 7.50%	RET	65	NL
FINCH COL, N Y PLAN COVERS— FAC, OFF	ALL ELIGIBLE	REQ	4Y						8.00%	5.00%	RET	65	NL
FINDLAY COL, OHIO PLAN COVERS— FAC, OFF CONTINUED ON NEXT PAGE	ALL ELIGIBLE	REQ VOL		30	CONTRIB ACCUM FIRST YEAR BEFORE PAID TO CONTRACT CONTRIB ACCUM				5.00%	5.00%	RET	65	70

CONTINUED ON NEXT PAGE

INSTITUTION	PROVISIONS APPLY TO	REQ &/OR VOL	WAITING PERIOD			TIAA-CREF CONTRIBUTIONS						NOR RET AGE	MAX EXT TO
			TIME	AGE	OTHER	SALARY	AGE	YRS	INST	INDIV	END AT		
					FIRST YEAR BEFORE PAID TO CONTRACT								
FLORIDA PRESBYTERIAN COL PLAN COVERS— ALL EMPLOYEES	ASST PROF & ABOVE & EQUIV OFF	REQ VOL	1Y IMMED						10.00%	.00%	RET	65	70
	OTHER	REQ	2Y						10.00%	.00%	RET	65	70
FLORIDA SOUTHERN COL PLAN COVERS— FAC, OFF	ALL ELIGIBLE	REQ	2Y & 30					10	5.00% 10.00%	5.00% .00%	RET	65	70
FLORIDA, U OF COL OF MEDICINE SUPPL PLAN COVERS— FAC	ALL ELIGIBLE	VOL	IMMED			CONTRIBUTIONS APPLY TO SALARY FROM CLINIC PRACTICE			6.00%	6.00%	RET	65	70
FONTBONNE COL, MO PLAN COVERS— FAC, OFF	ALL ELIGIBLE	REQ	3Y & 30						5.00%	5.00%	RET	65	70
FORDHAM U, N Y PLAN COVERS— FAC, OFF	ALL ELIGIBLE	REQ VOL	3Y & 30 1Y			FIRST $7800 BAL			5.00% 8.00%	5.00% 5.00%	RET	65	NX
FORT HAYS KANSAS STATE COL PLAN COVERS— FAC	ALL ELIGIBLE	REQ	2Y						5.00%	5.00%	RET	70	NX
FRANKLIN AND MARSHALL COL, PA PLAN COVERS— ALL EMPLOYEES	ASST PROF & ABOVE	REQ	IMMED			FIRST $6600 BAL			10.00% 15.00%	.00% 5.00%	65	65	NX
	INSTR	REQ	1Y			FIRST $6600 BAL			10.00% 15.00%	.00% 5.00%	65	65	NX
	OFF	REQ		30		FIRST $6600 BAL			10.00% 15.00%	.00% 5.00%	65	65	NX
	OTHER	REQ	3Y & 30			FIRST $6600 BAL			10.00% 15.00%	.00% 5.00%	65	65	NX
FRANKLIN COL OF INDIANA PLAN COVERS— FAC, OFF, CLER & SEC	ALL ELIGIBLE	REQ	1Y & 30			FIRST $6600 BAL			5.00% 10.00%	5.00% # 5.00% #	RET	65	70
FRIENDS U, KAN PLAN COVERS— ALL EMPLOYEES	ALL ELIGIBLE	VOL	IMMED						5.00%	5.00%	RET	65	70
FURMAN U, S C PLAN COVERS— FAC, OFF, CLER & SEC	FAC	REQ VOL	3Y		TENURE				10.00%	.00%	RET	68	NX
	OFF	REQ	3Y		TENURE				10.00%	.00%	RET	68	NX
	FEM FAC	REQ VOL	3Y		TENURE				10.00%	.00%	RET	65	NX
	FEM CLER & SEC	VOL	5Y & 30						5.00%	.00%	RET	65	NX

INSTITUTION	PROVISIONS APPLY TO	REQ &/OR VOL	WAITING PERIOD		TIAA-CREF CONTRIBUTIONS				END AT	NOR RET AGE	MAX EXT TO
			TIME AGE	OTHER	SALARY AGE	YRS	INST	INDIV			
GANNON COL, PA	FAC, OFF	REQ	5Y & 30				5.00%	3.00%	RET	65	NL
PLAN COVERS- ALL EMPLOYEES		VOL	1Y & 25								
					FIRST $7800	VOL AD	.00%	2.00%			
					BAL	VOL AD	4.00%	2.00%			
	OTHER	VOL	1Y & 30				3.00%	3.00%	RET	65	NL
						VOL AD	2.00%	2.00%			
GARRETT BIBLICAL INSTITUTE, ILL	FAC, OFF	REQ	IMMED				9.00%	6.00%	RET	65	NX
PLAN COVERS- FAC, OFF, CLER & SEC											
	CLERGYMEN	REQ	IMMED				12.00%	8.00%	RET	65	NX
	OTHER	VOL	5Y				9.00%	6.00%	RET	65	NX
GENEVA COL, PA	ALL ELIGIBLE	REQ	30				5.00%	5.00%	RET	70	75
PLAN COVERS- ALL EMPLOYEES		VOL	IMMED								
GEORGE FOX COL, ORE	ALL ELIGIBLE	REQ	3Y & 30				5.00%	5.00%	RET	65	70
PLAN COVERS- FAC, OFF		VOL	1Y								
GEORGE PEABODY COL FOR TEACHERS, TENN	FAC, OFF	VOL	IMMED		FIRST $6600		5.00%	5.00%	RET	68	70
PLAN COVERS- FAC, OFF, CLER & SEC					BAL		10.00%	5.00%			
	OTHER	VOL	5Y		FIRST $6600		5.00%	5.00%	RET	68	70
					BAL		10.00%	5.00%			
GEORGE WASHINGTON U, D C	ASSOC PROF & ABOVE & EQUIV OFF	REQ	IMMED				10.00%	5.00%	RET	65	70
PLAN COVERS- ALL EMPLOYEES											
	ASST PROF & INSTR & EQUIV OFF	REQ	2Y				10.00%	5.00%	RET	65	70
	OTHER	VOL	IMMED				10.00%	5.00%	RET	65	70
GEORGE WILLIAMS COL, ILL	ALL ELIGIBLE	VOL	IMMED				7.00%	5.00%	RET	NL	NX
PLAN COVERS- FAC, OFF											
GEORGETOWN COL, KY	FAC, OFF	REQ	3Y & 30				6.00%	6.00%	RET	65	NL
PLAN COVERS- FAC, OFF & DESIG CL		VOL	IMMED								
	OTHER	VOL	1Y				6.00%	6.00%	RET	65	NL
GETTYSBURG COL, PA	FAC, OFF	REQ	3Y & 30				6.00%	4.00%	RET	70	NX
PLAN COVERS- ALL EMPLOYEES		VOL	1Y								
	OTHER	REQ	5Y & 35				6.00%	4.00%	RET	70	NX
GLENVILLE STATE COL, W VA SUPPL	ALL ELIGIBLE	VOL	30 & $4800 SAL		FIRST $4800		.00%	.00%	RET	65	NL
PLAN COVERS- ALL EMPLOYEES					BAL		5.00%	5.00%			
					FIRST $4800	35	.00%	.00%			
					BAL	35	6.00%	6.00%			
					FIRST $4800	45	.00%	.00%			

CONTINUED ON NEXT PAGE

INSTITUTION	PROVISIONS APPLY TO	REQ &/OR VOL	WAITING PERIOD			TIAA-CREF CONTRIBUTIONS						NOR RET AGE	MAX EXT TO
			TIME	AGE	OTHER	SALARY	AGE	YRS	INST	INDIV	END AT		
						BAL	45		7.50%	7.50%			
GODDARD COL, VT	FAC, OFF	REQ	3Y &	30					5.00%	5.00%	RET	65	70
PLAN COVERS- ALL EMPLOYEES		VOL	1Y										
	OTHER	VOL	1Y						5.00%	5.00%	RET	65	70
GOLDEN GATE COL, CALIF	ASSOC PROF & ABOVE	REQ		30					7.00%	5.00%	RET	65	70
PLAN COVERS- FAC, OFF, CLER & SEC	ASST PROF & INSTR	REQ	1Y &	30					7.00%	5.00%	RET	65	70
	OFF	REQ	1Y &	30					7.00%	5.00%	RET	65	70
	OTHER	REQ	5Y &	30					7.00%	5.00%	RET	65	70
GONZAGA U, WASH	FAC	REQ	1Y						5.00%	5.00%	RET	65	75
PLAN COVERS- FAC, OFF	OTHER	VOL	1Y						5.00%	5.00%	RET	65	75
GOOD COUNSEL COL, N Y	ALL ELIGIBLE	REQ	3Y						5.00%	5.00%	RET	65	70
PLAN COVERS- FAC		VOL	1Y										
GOSHEN COL, IND	ALL ELIGIBLE	REQ	3Y &	30					5.00%	.00%	RET	70	72
PLAN COVERS- FAC													
GOUCHER COL, MD	FAC	REQ	IMMED						10.00%	5.00%	RET	65	NX
PLAN COVERS- FAC, OFF	OTHER	VOL	1Y						10.00%	5.00%	RET	65	NX
GRADUATE THEOLOGICAL UNION CALIF	FAC, OFF	REQ	3Y &	30					VARIES		RET	65	70
PLAN COVERS- ALL EMPLOYEES		VOL	1Y										
	OTHER	VOL	1Y						5.00%	5.00%	RET	65	70
GRAND VALLEY STATE COL MICH	ALL ELIGIBLE	REQ	2Y						5.00%	.00%	RET	65	68
PLAN COVERS- FAC, OFF & DESIG CL							30		10.00%	.00%			
GREAT FALLS, COL OF, MONT	ALL ELIGIBLE	REQ	3Y						2.00%	3.00%	RET	65	70
PLAN COVERS- FAC													
GREENSBORO COL, N C	ALL ELIGIBLE	VOL	2Y						5.00%	5.00%	RET	65	70
PLAN COVERS- FAC, OFF								VOL AD	2.00%	2.00%			
GREENVILLE COL, ILL	FAC, OFF	REQ	3Y &	30					6.00%	4.00%	RET	65	NL
PLAN COVERS- ALL EMPLOYEES		VOL	2Y										
	OTHER	VOL	5Y &	30					6.00%	4.00%	RET	65	NL
GRINNELL COL, IA	FAC, OFF	REQ	IMMED						10.00%	.00%	RET	68	70
PLAN COVERS- ALL EMPLOYEES													

CONTINUED ON NEXT PAGE

INSTITUTION	PROVISIONS APPLY TO	REQ &/OR VOL	WAITING PERIOD			TIAA-CREF CONTRIBUTIONS					END AT	NOR RET AGE	MAX EXT TO
			TIME AGE		OTHER	SALARY	AGE	YRS	INST	INDIV			
	OTHER	REQ	3Y & 30						4.00%	.00%	65	65	NX
GUILFORD COL, N C PLAN COVERS- FAC, OFF	FAC ON TENURE	REQ	5Y						10.00%	.00%	RET	65	NL
	OTHER	VOL	3Y						5.00%	5.00%	RET	65	NL
GWYNEDD-MERCY COL, PA PLAN COVERS- FAC	ALL ELIGIBLE	REQ VOL	5Y & 30 2Y						5.00%	5.00%	RET	65	70
HAMILTON COL, N Y PLAN COVERS- FAC, OFF, CLER & SEC	ASSOC PROF & ABOVE	REQ	IMMED						10.00%	.00%	RET	65	70
	ASST PROF	REQ VOL	IMMED		TENURE	ON TENURE			5.00% 10.00%	5.00% .00%	RET	65	NX
	INSTR	VOL	IMMED						5.00%	5.00%	RET	65	NX
	MAJOR OFF	REQ	IMMED						10.00%	.00%	RET	65	NX
	OTHER OFF	VOL	IMMED						5.00%	5.00%	RET	65	NX
	OTHER	VOL	1Y						5.00%	5.00%	RET	65	70
HAMLINE U, MINN PLAN COVERS- FAC, OFF	ASST PROF & ABOVE	REQ	3Y & 30						10.00%	.00%	65	65	68
	OTHER	REQ	3Y & 30						10.00%	.00%	65	65	68
HAMPDEN-SYDNEY COL, VA PLAN COVERS- FAC, OFF, CLER & SEC	ALL ELIGIBLE	REQ VOL	3Y & 30 1Y						7.50%	5.00%	RET	70	NL
HAMPTON INSTITUTE, VA PLAN COVERS- FAC, OFF & DESIG CL	ALL ELIGIBLE	REQ VOL	1Y IMMED						5.00%	5.00%	65	65	70
HANOVER COL, IND PLAN COVERS- FAC, OFF & DESIG CL	FAC	REQ	3Y OR		TENURE				5.00%	5.00%	RET	65	NX
	OTHER	REQ	3Y						5.00%	5.00%	RET	65	NX
HARDING COL, ARK PLAN COVERS- ALL EMPLOYEES	FAC	REQ VOL	1Y & 30 1Y						5.00%	5.00%	RET	65	70
	OTHER	VOL	1Y						5.00%	5.00%	RET	65	70
HARRISBURG AREA COMMUNITY COL, PA PLAN COVERS- ALL EMPLOYEES	ALL ELIGIBLE	REQ	IMMED						5.00%	5.00%	RET	65	NL
HARTFORD, U OF PLAN COVERS- ALL EMPLOYEES	FAC	REQ VOL	1Y & 30 27						5.00%	5.00%	RET	65	70
	OTHER	VOL	1Y & 27						5.00%	5.00%	RET	65	70
HARVARD U, MASS PLAN COVERS- FAC, OFF SUPPLEMENTAL PLAN: SEE HARVARD ENTRY, APP. 6.	ALL ELIGIBLE	REQ	1Y OR		APMT MORE THAN 1 YR		55 60		12.50% 15.00% 20.00%	.00% .00% .00%	66	66	NX
HARTWICK COL, N Y PLAN COVERS- CONTINUED ON NEXT PAGE	FAC, OFF	REQ	IMMED			FIRST $7800 BAL			6.60% 11.00%	5.00% 5.00%	RET	65	70

INSTITUTION	PROVISIONS APPLY TO	REQ &/OR VOL	WAITING PERIOD TIME AGE	OTHER	TIAA-CREF CONTRIBUTIONS SALARY AGE	YRS	INST	INDIV	END AT	NOR RET AGE	MAX EXT TO
ALL EMPLOYEES	OTHER	REQ	5Y				5.00%	1.00%	RET	65	70
						2	5.00%	2.00%			
						3	5.00%	3.00%			
						4	5.00%	4.00%			
						5	5.00%	5.00%			
HARVEY MUDD COL, CALIF PLAN COVERS— FAC, OFF	ALL ELIGIBLE	REQ	IMMED				12.00%	4.00%	RET	65	68
HASTINGS COL, NEB PLAN COVERS— FAC, OFF	ALL ELIGIBLE	REQ	3Y				5.00%	5.00%	RET	65	70
		VOL	2Y								
HAVERFORD COL, PA PLAN COVERS— FAC, OFF	ALL ELIGIBLE	REQ	1Y &	$3300 SAL			12.00%	.00%	RET	65	NL
HAWAII LOA COL PLAN COVERS— ALL EMPLOYEES	ASST PROF & ABOVE & EQUIV OFF	REQ	IMMED				10.00%	5.00%	RET	65	70
	INSTR	REQ	2Y				10.00%	5.00%	RET	65	70
	OTHER	VOL	5Y				10.00%	5.00%	RET	65	70
HEIDELBERG COL, OHIO PLAN COVERS— ALL EMPLOYEES	FAC, OFF	REQ	3Y				6.00%	6.00%	RET	65	70
		VOL	1Y		50		9.00%	6.00%			
	OTHER	REQ	3Y & 30				5.00%	3.00%	RET	65	70
HENDERSON STATE COL, ARK PLAN COVERS— FAC, OFF	ALL ELIGIBLE	REQ	IMMED				6.00%	6.00%	RET	65	72
HENDRIX COL, ARK PLAN COVERS— FAC, OFF, CLER & SEC	ASSOC PROF & ABOVE & EQUIV OFF	REQ	3Y				12.00%	.00%	RET	65	70
	OTHER	VOL	3Y				6.00%	6.00%	RET	65	70
HIGH POINT COL, N C PLAN COVERS— ALL EMPLOYEES	ALL ELIGIBLE	REQ	5Y & 30				7.00%	5.00%	RET	65	70
		VOL	2Y & 30								
HILLSDALE COL, MICH PLAN COVERS— FAC, OFF	ALL ELIGIBLE	REQ	3Y				9.00%	5.00%	RET	65	70
		VOL	IMMED								
HIRAM COL, OHIO PLAN COVERS— ALL EMPLOYEES	ASST PROF & ABOVE & EQUIV OFF	REQ	IMMED				5.00%	5.00%	70	70	NL
	INSTR	REQ	1Y				5.00%	5.00%	70	70	NL
	CLER & SEC	VOL	1Y				5.00%	5.00%	70	70	NL
	OTHER	VOL	1Y				3.00%	3.00%	70	70	NL
						VOL AD	2.00%	2.00%			
HIRAM SCOTT COL, NEB PLAN COVERS— FAC, OFF	ALL ELIGIBLE	REQ	IMMED				8.00%	3.00%	RET	65	NL
HOBART COL, N Y	ASST PROF & ABOVE	REQ		TENURE			5.00%	5.00%	RET	70	72

CONTINUED ON NEXT PAGE

INSTITUTION	PROVISIONS APPLY TO	REQ &/OR VOL	WAITING PERIOD			TIAA-CREF CONTRIBUTIONS					END AT	NOR RET AGE	MAX EXT TO
			TIME AGE		OTHER	SALARY	AGE	YRS	INST	INDIV			
PLAN COVERS— ALL EMPLOYEES													
	OTHER	VOL	IMMED						5.00%	5.00%	RET	70	72
HOFSTRA U, N Y	FAC ON TENURE	REQ	1Y &	30		FIRST $6600 BAL			8.30% 12.50%	3.30% 7.50%	RET	65	68
PLAN COVERS— ALL EMPLOYEES	OFF	REQ	1Y &	30		FIRST $6600 BAL			5.80% 10.00%	3.30% 7.50%	RET	65	68
						FIRST $6600 BAL		5 5	8.30% 12.50%	3.30% 7.50%			
	OTHER FAC	REQ	1Y &	30		FIRST $6600 BAL			5.80% 10.00%	3.30% 7.50%	RET	65	68
	OTHER	VOL				FIRST $6600 BAL NO CONTRIBUTIONS ARE MADE ON SALARY ABOVE $20000.			5.80% 10.00%	3.30% 7.50%	RET	65	68
HOLLINS COL, VA	FAC, OFF	REQ	3Y						5.00%	5.00%	RET	65	70
PLAN COVERS— ALL EMPLOYEES		VOL	IMMED										
	OTHER	VOL	IMMED						5.00%	5.00%	RET	65	70
HOLY CROSS , COL OF THE MASS	ALL ELIGIBLE	REQ	1Y &	30		FIRST $7800			5.00%	5.00%	RET	65	NX
PLAN COVERS— FAC		VOL	1Y			BAL			10.00%	5.00%			
HOOD COL, MD	ASST PROF & ABOVE	REQ	3Y &	35					7.50%	7.50%	RET	65	70
PLAN COVERS— ALL EMPLOYEES		VOL	IMMED										
	OFF	REQ	3Y &	35					7.50%	7.50%	RET	65	NX
		VOL	3Y										
	OTHER FAC	REQ	3Y &	35					7.50%	7.50%	RET	65	70
		VOL	3Y										
	OTHER	VOL	3Y						7.50%	7.50%	RET	65	70
HOPE COL, MICH	ALL ELIGIBLE	REQ	3Y &	30					5.00%	5.00%	RET	65	70
PLAN COVERS— FAC, OFF		VOL	IMMED										
HOUGHTON COL, N Y	FAC, OFF	REQ			TENURE				5.00%	5.00%	RET	70	NL
PLAN COVERS— ALL EMPLOYEES		VOL	IMMED										
	OTHER	REQ	5Y						5.00%	5.00%	RET	70	NL
		VOL	IMMED										
HOUSTON BAPTIST COL, TEX	ALL ELIGIBLE	REQ	3Y &	30					10.00%	5.00% #	RET	65	NL
PLAN COVERS— FAC, OFF		VOL	1Y										
	FAC ON TENURE	REQ	3Y &	30					15.00%	.00%	RET	65	NL
		VOL	1Y										
HOWARD U, D C	ASST PROF & ABOVE & EQUIV OFF	REQ	IMMED			FIRST $4800 BAL			5.00% 8.00%	5.00% 5.00%		70	68	NL
PLAN COVERS— ALL EMPLOYEES	OTHER	REQ	1Y &	30 &	CONTRIB ACCUM FOR 1ST 5 YRS BEFORE PAID TO CONTRACT	FIRST $4800 BAL			5.00% 8.00%	5.00% 5.00%		70	68	NL

INSTITUTION	PROVISIONS APPLY TO	REQ &/OR VOL	WAITING PERIOD			TIAA-CREF CONTRIBUTIONS					END AT	NOR RET AGE	MAX EXT TO
			TIME AGE		OTHER	SALARY	AGE	YRS	INST	INDIV			
HUNTINGDON COL, ALA PLAN COVERS- FAC, OFF & DESIG CL	ALL ELIGIBLE	VOL	IMMED						10.00%	5.00%	RET	65	72
HUNTINGTON COL, IND PLAN COVERS- ALL EMPLOYEES	FAC	REQ VOL	2Y & IMMED	30					5.00%	5.00%	RET	65	70
	OTHER	REQ VOL	2Y & 2M	30					5.00%	5.00%	RET	65	70
HURON COL, S D PLAN COVERS- FAC, OFF	ALL ELIGIBLE	REQ	2Y &	30					5.00%	5.00%	65	65	NL
HUSSON COL, ME PLAN COVERS- ALL EMPLOYEES	FAC, OFF	REQ VOL	1Y & 1Y	35		FIRST $7800 BAL			3.00% 6.00%	3.00% 4.00%	RET	65	NL
	OTHER	VOL	2Y &	30		FIRST $7800 BAL			3.00% 6.00%	3.00% 4.00%	RET	65	NL
IDAHO, COL OF PLAN COVERS- FAC, OFF	ALL ELIGIBLE	REQ VOL	3Y 1Y						4.50%	4.50%	RET	65	70
ILIFF SCH OF THEOLOGY COLO PLAN COVERS- FAC, OFF, CLER & SEC	FAC	REQ VOL	1Y IMMED						5.00%	5.00%	RET	65	70
	OTHER	VOL			$6000 SAL				5.00%	5.00%	RET	65	70
ILLINOIS COL PLAN COVERS- FAC, OFF	ALL ELIGIBLE	REQ	2Y						5.00%	5.00%	RET	65	70
						FIRST $7800 BAL		5 VOL AD 5 VOL AD	.00% 2.50%	.00% 2.50%			
						FIRST $7800 BAL	36 36	5 5	5.00% 7.50%	5.00% 7.50%			
ILLINOIS INSTITUTE OF TECHNOLOGY PLAN COVERS- ALL EMPLOYEES	ASST PROF & ABOVE & EQUIV OFF	REQ	1Y &		$8000 SAL				8.00%	5.00%	65	65	NL
	OTHER	REQ	5Y						6.00%	5.00%	65	65	NL
ILLINOIS WESLEYAN U PLAN COVERS- FAC, OFF	ALL ELIGIBLE	REQ VOL	3Y OR IMMED		TENURE			3	5.00% 10.00%	5.00% .00%	RET	65	NL
IMMACULATA COL, PA PLAN COVERS- FAC	ALL ELIGIBLE	REQ VOL	2Y & 1Y	30					5.00%	5.00%	RET	65	70
IMMACULATE HEART COL CALIF PLAN COVERS- FAC, OFF	ALL ELIGIBLE	REQ VOL	1Y & 1Y	30		FIRST $7800 BAL			5.00% 8.00%	5.00% 7.00%	RET	65	7C
INDIANA CENTRAL COL PLAN COVERS- ALL EMPLOYEES CONTINUED ON NEXT PAGE	FAC, OFF	REQ VOL	2Y & 1Y &	30 30					6.00%	5.00%	RET	65	NX

CONTINUED ON NEXT PAGE

INSTITUTION	PROVISIONS APPLY TO	REQ &/OR VOL	WAITING PERIOD TIME AGE	OTHER	TIAA-CREF CONTRIBUTIONS SALARY	AGE	YRS	INST	INDIV	END AT	NOR RET AGE	MAX EXT TO
	OTHER	VOL	2Y & 30					6.00%	5.00%	RET	65	NX
INDIANA INSTITUTE OF TECHNOLOGY PLAN COVERS- ALL EMPLOYEES	FAC, OFF	REQ	3Y & 30					5.00%	5.00%	RET	65	70
		VOL	3Y									
	CLER & SEC, MAINT & SERV	VOL	5Y & 32					5.00%	5.00%	RET	65	70
INDIANA STATE U PLAN COVERS- FAC, OFF	ALL ELIGIBLE	REQ	2Y & 30 OR TENURE		FIRST $7800			6.00%	5.00%	RET	66	70
		VOL	2Y		BAL			10.00%	5.00%			
INDIANA U PLAN COVERS- FAC, OFF & DESIG CL	ASST PROF & ABOVE	REQ	1Y OR	TENURE	FIRST $7800 BAL			11.00% 15.00%	.00% .00%	70	70	NL
	OFF	REQ	IMMED		FIRST $7800 BAL			11.00% 15.00%	.00% .00%	70	70	NL
	JR OFF	REQ	1Y		FIRST $7800 BAL			11.00% 15.00%	.00% .00%	70	70	NL
	OTHER	REQ	3Y		FIRST $7800 BAL CONTRIBUTIONS MATCHED AT HIGHER RATES, SCALED BY AGE, FOR THOSE EMPLOYED AFTER AGE 50.			11.00% 15.00%	.00% .00%	70	70	NL
INSTITUTE FOR ADVANCED STUDY, N J PLAN COVERS- ALL EMPLOYEES	FAC, OFF	REQ	IMMED		*INSTITUTE CONTRIBUTES ADDITIONAL MONTHLY PREMIUMS TO PROVIDE ANNUAL BENEFIT OF $15000.			5.00%*	5.00%	RET	70	NX
	OTHER	REQ	2Y & 28		FOR NONACADEMIC EMPLOYEES, INSTITUTE PURCHASES BENEFIT OF 1% OF 1ST $4200 OF SALARY FOR EACH YEAR OF SERVICE. ON SALARY ABOVE $4200, THE INSTITUTE WILL CONTRIBUTE 10% IF THE INDIVIDUAL CONTRIBUTES 5%.					RET RET	65 65	NX NX
INSTITUTE OF PAPER CHEMISTRY, WIS PLAN COVERS- ALL EMPLOYEES	FAC, OFF	REQ	IMMED		ALL PARTICIPANTS: FIRST $4800 NEXT $5200 BAL			5.00% 7.50% 10.00%	5.00% 5.00% 5.00%	65	65	69
	OTHER	VOL	5Y &	ON RECOM						65	65	69
INSURANCE, COL OF, N Y PLAN COVERS- ALL EMPLOYEES	FAC	VOL	IMMED		FIRST $4800 BAL			8.00% 12.00%	.00% .00%	RET	65	70
					FIRST $4800 BAL	40 40		10.00% 15.00%	.00% .00%			
					FIRST $4800 BAL	50 50		12.00% 18.00%	.00% .00%			
	OTHER	VOL	1Y & 30		FIRST $4800 BAL			8.00% 12.00%	.00% .00%	RET	65	70
CONTINUED ON NEXT PAGE					FIRST $4800 BAL	40 40		10.00% 15.00%	.00% .00%			

INSTITUTION	PROVISIONS APPLY TO	REQ &/OR VOL	WAITING PERIOD			TIAA-CREF CONTRIBUTIONS						NOR RET AGE	MAX EXT TO
			TIME AGE		OTHER	SALARY AGE		YRS	INST	INDIV	END AT		
						FIRST $4800 50 BAL 50			12.00% 18.00%	.00% .00%			
INTER AMERICAN U OF PUERTO RICO PLAN COVERS- FAC, OFF	ALL ELIGIBLE	VOL	1Y						5.00%	5.00%	RET	65	70
IONA COL, N Y PLAN COVERS- FAC	ALL ELIGIBLE	REQ	3Y						5.00%	5.00%	RET	68	70
IOWA STATE U OF SCIENCE AND TECHNOLOGY PLAN COVERS- ALL EMPLOYEES	FAC	REQ			$6600 SAL	FIRST $4800 BAL			6.66% 10.00%	3.33% 5.00%	RET	70	NX
	MAJOR OFF	REQ			$6600 SAL	FIRST $4800 BAL			6.66% 10.00%	3.33% 5.00%	RET	70	NX
	OTHER	REQ	1Y &		$6600 SAL	FIRST $4800 BAL			6.66% 10.00%	3.33% 5.00%	RET	70	NX
IOWA, U OF PLAN COVERS- ALL EMPLOYEES	FAC, OFF	REQ			$4800 SAL	FIRST $4800 BAL			6.66% 10.00%	3.33% 5.00%	68	68	69
	OTHER	REQ			$4800 SAL	FIRST $4800 BAL			6.66% 10.00%	3.33% 5.00%	RET	70	NX
IOWA WESLEYAN COL PLAN COVERS- FAC, OFF, CLER & SEC	ALL ELIGIBLE	VOL	IMMED						8.00%	6.00%	RET	65	70
ITHACA COL, NY PLAN COVERS- FAC, OFF	ALL ELIGIBLE	VOL	3Y OR		RANK OF ASSOC PROF				5.00%	5.00%	RET	65	70
JACKSONVILLE U, FLA PLAN COVERS- FAC, OFF	ALL ELIGIBLE	VOL	1Y & 30						5.00%	5.00%	RET	NL	NX
JAMESTOWN COL, N D PLAN COVERS- ALL EMPLOYEES	ALL ELIGIBLE	REQ VOL	1Y & 30 1Y						5.00%	5.00%	RET	65	70
JEFFERSON MEDICAL COL, PA PLAN COVERS- FAC, OFF	ALL ELIGIBLE	REQ	IMMED			FIRST $6600 BAL			4.00% 4.00%	.00% 5.00%	RET	65	70
JEWISH THEOLOGICAL SEM OF AMERICA, N Y PLAN COVERS- ALL EMPLOYEES	FAC, OFF	VOL	2Y						7.00%	6.00%	RET	65	68
	OTHER	VOL	5Y						5.00%	5.00%	RET	65	68
JOHN CARROLL U, OHIO PLAN COVERS- ALL EMPLOYEES	FAC	REQ	1Y & 30			FIRST $4800 BAL			3.60% 5.40%	3.00% 4.50%	RET	65	70
	OTHER	REQ	5Y & 30			FIRST $4800 BAL			3.60% 5.40%	3.00% 4.50%	RET	65	70
JOHN J PERSHING COL, NEB PLAN COVERS- CONTINUED ON NEXT PAGE	FAC, OFF	REQ VOL	5Y & 35 IMMED						5.00%	5.00%	RET	65	70

CONTINUED ON NEXT PAGE

INSTITUTION	PROVISIONS APPLY TO	REQ &/OR VOL	WAITING PERIOD			TIAA–CREF CONTRIBUTIONS					END AT	NOR RET AGE	MAX EXT TO
			TIME	AGE	OTHER	SALARY	AGE	YRS	INST	INDIV			
FAC, OFF & DESIG CL	OTHER	VOL	5Y						5.00%	5.00%	RET	65	70
JOHNSON C SMITH U, N C PLAN COVERS— FAC, OFF, CLER & SEC	FAC, OFF	REQ	3Y &	30					5.00%	5.00%	RET	68	70
	CLER & SEC	VOL	3Y						5.00%	5.00%	RET	68	70
JOHNSON STATE COL, VT PLAN COVERS— FAC, OFF	FAC	REQ	IMMED			FIRST $6600 BAL			10.00% 15.00%	.00% .00%	RET	65	70
	OTHER	REQ	IMMED			FIRST $6600 BAL			10.00% 15.00%	.00% .00%	RET	65	70
JUDSON COL, ALA PLAN COVERS— FAC, OFF, CLER & SEC	ALL ELIGIBLE	REQ VOL	3Y & 1Y	30				VOL AD	3.00% 2.00%	3.00% 2.00%	RET	65	70
JUNIATA COL, PA PLAN COVERS— FAC, OFF, CLER & SEC	ALL ELIGIBLE	REQ VOL	3Y & 1Y &	30 30					5.00%	5.00%	RET	65	70
KALAMAZOO COL, MICH PLAN COVERS— FAC, OFF	ALL ELIGIBLE	REQ	2Y						10.00%	5.00%	RET	65	NL
KANSAS CITY ART INSTITUTE AND SCH OF DESIGN, MO PLAN COVERS— FAC, OFF	ALL ELIGIBLE	VOL	2Y						5.00%	5.00%	RET	65	70
KANSAS CITY COL OF OSTEOPATHY AND SURGERY, MO PLAN COVERS— FAC, OFF	ALL ELIGIBLE	REQ VOL	2Y & 2Y	30		FIRST $15000 BAL			5.00% .00%	5.00% .00%	NA	NA	
KANSAS STATE COL OF PITTSBURG PLAN COVERS— FAC	ALL ELIGIBLE	REQ	2Y						5.00%	5.00%	RET	70	NX
KANSAS STATE TEACHERS COL PLAN COVERS— FAC	ALL ELIGIBLE	REQ	2Y						5.00%	5.00%	RET	70	NX
KANSAS STATE U PLAN COVERS— FAC	ALL ELIGIBLE	REQ	2Y						5.00%	5.00%	RET	70	NX
KANSAS, U OF PLAN COVERS— FAC	ALL ELIGIBLE	REQ	2Y						5.00%	5.00%	RET	70	NX
KANSAS WESLEYAN U PLAN COVERS— ALL EMPLOYEES	ASSOC PROF & ABOVE & EQUIV OFF	REQ	IMMED						7.00%	3.00%	RET	65	70
	OTHER FAC	REQ	1Y OR 35						7.00%	3.00%	RET	65	70
	OTHER	VOL	1Y & 35						7.00%	3.00%	RET	65	70
KEARNEY STATE COL, NEB PLAN COVERS— ALL EMPLOYEES	FAC, OFF	REQ	IMMED						6.00%	6.00%	RET	65	68

CONTINUED ON NEXT PAGE

INSTITUTION	PROVISIONS APPLY TO	REQ &/OR VOL	WAITING PERIOD			TIAA-CREF CONTRIBUTIONS				END AT	NOR RET AGE	MAX EXT TO
			TIME	AGE	OTHER	SALARY AGE YRS	INST	INDIV				
	CLER & SEC	REQ	3Y &	30			3.00%	3.00%		RET	65	68
	OTHER	REQ	2Y &	40			3.00%	3.00%		RET	65	68
KEENE STATE COL, N H	ALL ELIGIBLE	REQ	2Y			FIRST $6600	5.00%	5.00%		RET	65	69
PLAN COVERS- FAC, OFF		VOL			RANK OF ASST PROF	BAL	10.00%	7.00%				
KENTUCKY SOUTHERN COL	ASST PROF & ABOVE & EQUIV OFF	REQ	3Y &	30		FIRST $6600	5.00%	5.00%		RET	65	70
PLAN COVERS- ALL EMPLOYEES		VOL	1Y &	30		BAL	7.50%	7.50%				
	OTHER	REQ	5Y &	32		FIRST $6600	5.00%	5.00%		RET	65	70
		VOL	3Y &	32		BAL	7.50%	7.50%				
KENTUCKY, U OF	ALL ELIGIBLE	REQ	1Y &	30			10.00%	5.00%		RET	65	70
PLAN COVERS- FAC, OTHERS WITH EDUC RELATED DUTIES		VOL	1Y									
KENTUCKY WESLEYAN COL	ALL ELIGIBLE	VOL	4Y &	30			5.00%	5.00%		RET	65	70
PLAN COVERS- FAC, OFF												
KENYON COL, OHIO	FAC, OFF	VOL	1Y				7.50%	5.00%		RET	68	NL
PLAN COVERS- ALL EMPLOYEES												
	OTHER	VOL	3Y				7.50%	5.00%		RET	68	NL
KEUKA COL, N Y	ALL ELIGIBLE	VOL	1Y				8.00%	5.00%	65		65	66
PLAN COVERS- FAC												
KING COL, TENN	FAC, OFF, CLER	REQ	2Y &	30			5.00%	5.00%		RET	65	70
PLAN COVERS- ALL EMPLOYEES												
	MAINT & SERV	VOL	2Y &	30			5.00%	5.00%		RET	65	70
KINGS COL, THE, N Y	ALL ELIGIBLE	VOL	1Y &	30			5.00%	5.00%		RET	65	70
PLAN COVERS- FAC, OFF												
KINGS COL, PA	FAC	REQ	2Y &	30			5.00%	5.00%		RET	65	70
PLAN COVERS- FAC, OFF, CLER & SEC		VOL	1Y									
	OFF & CLER	REQ	5Y				5.00%	5.00%		RET	65	70
		VOL	1Y									
KIRKSVILLE COL OF OSTEOPATHY AND SURGERY, MO	ALL ELIGIBLE	REQ	2Y &	30 &	$4800 SAL	FIRST $15000	5.00%	5.00%		RET	65	70
PLAN COVERS- ALL EMPLOYEES						BAL	.00%	.00%				
KNOX COL, ILL	ASSOC PROF & ABOVE & EQUIV OFF	REQ	2Y				13.00%	2.00%		RET	68	70
PLAN COVERS- ALL EMPLOYEES		VOL	1Y									
	OTHER FAC & OFF	REQ	2Y				5.00%	5.00%		RET	68	70
		VOL	1Y									
	OTHER	REQ	5Y				3.00%	2.00%		RET	68	70
LADYCLIFF COL, N Y	ALL ELIGIBLE	REQ	3Y &	30			5.00%	5.00%		RET	65	70
PLAN COVERS-		VOL	1Y									

CONTINUED ON NEXT PAGE

INSTITUTION	PROVISIONS APPLY TO	REQ &/OR VOL	WAITING PERIOD			TIAA-CREF CONTRIBUTIONS				END AT	NOR RET AGE	MAX EXT TO
			TIME AGE		OTHER	SALARY AGE	YRS	INST	INDIV			
FAC, OFF, CLER & SEC												
LAFAYETTE COL, PA PLAN COVERS- FAC, OFF, CLER & SEC	ASST PROF & ABOVE	REQ	IMMED					7.00%	5.00%	RET	65	70
	INSTR	REQ	3Y					7.00%	5.00%	RET	65	70
		VOL	2Y									
	OFF	REQ	IMMED					7.00%	5.00%	RET	65	70
	OTHER	VOL	2Y					7.00%	5.00%	RET	65	70
LAGRANGE COL, GA PLAN COVERS- ALL EMPLOYEES	FAC, OFF	VOL	2Y					2.00% 5.00%	2.00% 5.00%	RET	68	NL
LAKE ERIE COL, OHIO PLAN COVERS- FAC, OFF	ALL ELIGIBLE	REQ VOL	2Y & 30 2Y					10.00%	5.00%	RET	65	NL
LAKE FOREST COL, ILL PLAN COVERS- ALL EMPLOYEES	PROF	REQ	IMMED					15.00%	.00%	RET	65	68
	ASSOC PROF	REQ	IMMED					12.50%	.00%	RET	65	68
	ASST PROF	REQ	IMMED					10.00%	.00%	RET	65	68
	OFF	VOL	3Y					UP TO 15.00%	.00%	RET	65	68
	OTHER	VOL	3Y					5.00%	5.00%	RET	65	68
LAKELAND COL, WIS PLAN COVERS- FAC, OFF	ALL ELIGIBLE	REQ VOL	3Y & 30 1Y					5.00%	5.00%	RET	68	70
LAMBUTH COL, TENN PLAN COVERS- FAC, OFF	ALL ELIGIBLE	VOL	2Y					UP TO 7.00%	7.00%	RET	65	70
LA ROCHE COL, PA PLAN COVERS- FAC, OFF	ALL ELIGIBLE	REQ VOL	3Y & 30 2Y					5.00%	5.00%	RET	65	70
LA VERNE COL, CALIF PLAN COVERS- ALL EMPLOYEES	FAC, OFF	REQ	2Y					5.00%	5.00%	RET	65	70
	OTHER	VOL	2Y					5.00%	5.00%	RET	65	70
LAWRENCE U, WIS PLAN COVERS- FAC, OFF & DESIG CL	ASST PROF & ABOVE & EQUIV OFF	REQ	IMMED			FIRST $7800 BAL		7.00% 10.00%	3.00% 5.00%	65	65	NL
	INSTR	REQ	2Y			FIRST $7800 BAL		7.00% 10.00%	3.00% 5.00%	65	65	NL
	OTHER	REQ	5Y			FIRST $7800 BAL		7.00% 10.00%	3.00% 5.00%	65	65	NL
LEA COLLEGE, MINN PLAN COVERS- FAC, OFF, CLER & SEC	PROF	VOL	IMMED					10.00%	3.00%	RET	65	70
	ASSOC PROF	VOL	IMMED					9.00%	3.00%	RET	65	70
	ASST PROF	VOL	IMMED					8.00%	3.00%	RET	65	70
	INSTR	VOL	IMMED					7.00%	3.00%	RET	65	70

CONTINUED ON NEXT PAGE

INSTITUTION	PROVISIONS APPLY TO	REQ &/OR VOL	WAITING PERIOD			TIAA-CREF CONTRIBUTIONS					END AT	NOR RET AGE	MAX EXT TO
			TIME	AGE	OTHER	SALARY	AGE	YRS	INST	INDIV			
	OTHER	VOL	IMMED					UP TO	10.00%	3.00%	RET	65	70
LEBANON VALLEY COL, PA PLAN COVERS- ALL EMPLOYEES	FAC, OFF	REQ	1Y						5.00%	5.00%	RET	65	70
	OTHER	VOL	5Y &	30					3.00%	3.00%	RET	65	70
LEHIGH U, PA PLAN COVERS- FAC, OFF	ALL ELIGIBLE	REQ VOL	1Y &	30 OR 3Y	RANK OF ASSOC PROF	FIRST $4800 BAL			5.75% 12.00%	.00% .00%	65	65	NL
						FIRST $4800 BAL	35 35		7.75% 14.00%	.00% .00%			
						FIRST $4800 BAL	45 45		9.75% 16.00%	.00% .00%			
						FIRST $4800 BAL	55 55		11.75% 18.00%	.00% .00%			
LE MOYNE COL, N Y PLAN COVERS- ALL EMPLOYEES	FAC, OFF	VOL	IMMED						6.50%	3.50%	RET	65	NL
	OTHER	VOL	2Y &	30 OR 5Y					6.50%	3.50%	RET	65	NL
LENOIR RHYNE COL, N C PLAN COVERS- FAC, OFF, CLER & SEC	ALL ELIGIBLE	REQ VOL	3Y & 2Y	30					6.00%	4.00%	68	68	NL
LESLEY COL, MASS PLAN COVERS- FAC, OFF, CLER & SEC	ALL ELIGIBLE	REQ	1Y &	30		FIRST $7800 BAL			5.00% 10.00%	5.00% 5.00%	RET	65	70
LEWIS AND CLARK COL, ORE PLAN COVERS- ALL EMPLOYEES	ALL ELIGIBLE	VOL	1Y &	30					5.00%	5.00%	RET	65	70
LIMESTONE COL, S C PLAN COVERS- FAC, OFF	ALL ELIGIBLE	REQ VOL	3Y & 1Y	30					5.00%	5.00%	RET	65	NL
LINCOLN MEMORIAL U, TENN PLAN COVERS- ALL EMPLOYEES	FAC, OFF	REQ	2Y &	30					10.00%	.00%	RET	65	70
	OTHER	REQ	5Y						10.00%	.00%	RET	65	70
LINCOLN U, PA PLAN COVERS- ALL EMPLOYEES	ASST PROF & ABOVE	REQ VOL	3Y OR IMMED		TENURE				5.00%	5.00%	RET	65	70
	OTHER	VOL	IMMED						5.00%	5.00%	RET	65	70
LINFIELD COL, ORE PLAN COVERS- FAC, OFF	ALL ELIGIBLE	VOL	3Y &		TENURE	FIRST $4800 BAL			10.00% .00%	.00% .00%	65	65	NL
LITTLE ROCK U, ARK PLAN COVERS- FAC, OFF	ALL ELIGIBLE	REQ VOL	1Y IMMED					1	5.00% 10.00%	5.00% .00%	RET	65	70
LIVINGSTONE COL, N C PLAN COVERS- FAC, OFF	ALL ELIGIBLE	REQ VOL	3Y & 1Y	30					5.00%	5.00%	RET	65	70

INSTITUTION	PROVISIONS APPLY TO	REQ &/OR VOL	WAITING PERIOD			TIAA-CREF CONTRIBUTIONS					END AT	NOR RET AGE	MAX EXT TO
			TIME	AGE	OTHER	SALARY	AGE	YRS	INST	INDIV			
LONG ISLAND U, N Y PLAN COVERS— ALL EMPLOYEES	PROF	REQ	1Y &	30 &	TENURE	FIRST $4800			5.00%	5.00%	RET	68	70
		VOL	1Y &	30		BAL			11.00%	5.00%			
	ASSOC PROF	REQ	2Y &	30 &	TENURE	FIRST $4800			5.00%	5.00%	RET	68	70
		VOL	2Y &	30		BAL			11.00%	5.00%			
	ASST PROF	REQ	2Y &	30 &	TENURE	FIRST $4800			5.00%	5.00%	RET	68	70
		VOL	2Y &	30		BAL			11.00%	5.00%			
	INSTR	REQ	3Y &	30 &	TENURE	FIRST $4800			5.00%	5.00%	RET	68	70
		VOL	3Y &	30		BAL			11.00%	5.00%			
	MAJOR OFF	VOL	3Y &	30		FIRST $4800 BAL			5.00% 11.00%	5.00% 5.00%	RET	68	70
	OTHER OFF	VOL	3Y &	30		FIRST $4800 BAL			5.00% 11.00%	5.00% 5.00%	RET	65	70
	OTHER	VOL	3Y &	30					4.00%	4.00%	RET	65	70
LORAS COL, IA PLAN COVERS— FAC, OFF	ALL ELIGIBLE	REQ	3Y &	30					5.00%	5.00%	RET	65	70
LOUISVILLE, U OF, KY PLAN COVERS— ALL EMPLOYEES	FAC	REQ	1Y &	30 &	RANK OF ASST PROF	FIRST $10000 BAL			10.00% .00%	5.00% .00%	RET	65	70
		VOL	1Y										
	MAJOR OFF	REQ	1Y &	30		FIRST $10000 BAL			10.00% .00%	5.00% .00%	RET	65	70
		VOL	1Y										
	OTHER OFF	REQ	1Y &	30		FIRST $10000 BAL			10.00% .00%	5.00% .00%	RET	65	70
		VOL	1Y										
	OTHER	REQ	5Y &	35		FIRST $10000 BAL			5.00% .00%	2.50% .00%	RET	65	70
						FIRST $10000 BAL		15	10.00% .00%	5.00% .00%			
LOYOLA U OF LOS ANGELES CALIF PLAN COVERS— FAC, OFF	ALL ELIGIBLE	REQ	2Y						5.00%	5.00%	RET	68	NL
		VOL	IMMED										
LUTHER COL, IA PLAN COVERS— FAC, OFF	ALL ELIGIBLE	REQ	3Y						10.00%	.00%	RET	65	NL
LYCOMING COL, PA PLAN COVERS— FAC, OFF	ALL ELIGIBLE	REQ	1Y &	30					6.00%	5.00%	RET	65	NL
LYNDON STATE COL, VT PLAN COVERS— FAC, OFF	FAC	REQ	IMMED			FIRST $7800 BAL			10.00% 15.00%	.00% .00%	RET	65	70
	OTHER	VOL	IMMED			FIRST $7800 BAL			10.00% 15.00%	.00% .00%	RET	65	70
MACALESTER COL, MINN PLAN COVERS— FAC, OFF & DESIG CL	FAC	REQ			TENURE	FIRST $7800 BAL			7.50% 10.00%	2.50% 5.00%	RET	67	70
	OTHER	REQ			PERM APMT	FIRST $7800 BAL			7.50% 10.00%	2.50% 5.00%	RET	67	70

INSTITUTION	PROVISIONS APPLY TO	REQ &/OR VOL	WAITING PERIOD			TIAA-CREF CONTRIBUTIONS					END AT	NOR RET AGE	MAX EXT TO
			TIME	AGE	OTHER	SALARY	AGE	YRS	INST	INDIV			
MACKINAC COL, MICH PLAN COVERS− ALL EMPLOYEES	ALL ELIGIBLE	REQ	3Y &	30		FIRST $6600 BAL			5.00% 7.50%	5.00% 7.50%	RET	65	70
		VOL	1Y										
MACMURRAY COL, ILL PLAN COVERS− FAC, OFF & DESIG CL	FAC, OFF	VOL	IMMED						7.50%	7.50%	RET	68	NX
	OTHER	VOL	IMMED						7.50%	7.50%	RET	68	NX
MAINE, U OF PLAN COVERS− FAC, OFF	ALL ELIGIBLE	REQ		30					8.00%	6.00%	RET	65	NX
		VOL	3Y										
MALONE COL, OHIO PLAN COVERS− ALL EMPLOYEES	FAC, OFF	REQ	2Y						5.00%	5.00%	RET	65	70
		VOL	IMMED										
	OTHER	REQ	3Y &	30					5.00%	5.00%	RET	65	70
		VOL	1Y										
MANCHESTER COL, IND PLAN COVERS− ALL EMPLOYEES	FAC, OFF	REQ	2Y &	35					5.00%	5.00%	RET	65	70
						FIRST $7800 BAL		5 5	5.00% 10.00%	5.00% 5.00%			
	OTHER	VOL	5Y						5.00%	5.00%	RET	65	70
MANHATTAN COL, N Y PLAN COVERS− ALL EMPLOYEES	FAC, OFF	REQ	2Y			FIRST $7800 BAL			5.00% 10.00%	5.00% 5.00%	RET	65	70
	OTHER	REQ	5Y &	35					5.00%	3.00%	RET	65	NX
MANHATTAN SCH OF MUSIC N Y PLAN COVERS− ALL EMPLOYEES	FAC	REQ	2Y						5.00%	5.00%	RET	65	NL
		VOL	1Y										
	OTHER	REQ	3Y						5.00%	5.00%	RET	65	NL
		VOL	2Y										
MANHATTANVILLE COL, N Y PLAN COVERS− FAC, OFF, CLER & SEC	FAC, OFF	REQ	1Y						7.50%	7.50%	RET	65	70
	OTHER	VOL	3Y						5.00%	5.00%	RET	65	NL
MARIAN COL, IND PLAN COVERS− ALL EMPLOYEES	FAC, OFF	REQ	3Y &	30					5.00%	5.00%	RET	65	NL
		VOL	2Y										
	CLER & SEC	VOL	2Y						5.00%	5.00%	RET	65	NL
	MAINT & SERV	VOL	5Y						5.00%	5.00%	RET	65	NL
MARIETTA COL, OHIO PLAN COVERS− FAC, OFF & DESIG CL	ALL ELIGIBLE	REQ	3Y &		$3000 SAL				5.00%	5.00%	65	65	70
MARION COL, IND PLAN COVERS− FAC	ALL ELIGIBLE	REQ	5Y &	30					5.00%	5.00%	RET	65	70
		VOL	2Y										
MARIST COL, N Y PLAN COVERS− CONTINUED ON NEXT PAGE	FAC, OFF	REQ	1Y						5.00%	5.00%	RET	65	70

INSTITUTION	PROVISIONS APPLY TO	REQ &/OR VOL	WAITING PERIOD TIME	AGE	OTHER	TIAA-CREF CONTRIBUTIONS SALARY	AGE	YRS	INST	INDIV	END AT	NOR RET AGE	MAX EXT TO
ALL EMPLOYEES	CLER & SEC, MAINT & SERV	REQ	3Y &	30					5.00%	5.00%	RET	65	70
		VOL	2Y &	25									
MARLBORO COL, VT PLAN COVERS— FAC, OFF & DESIG CL	ALL ELIGIBLE	REQ	3Y OR 30 &		TENURE				5.00%	5.00%	RET	65	70
MARQUETTE U, WIS PLAN COVERS— ALL EMPLOYEES	ASSOC PROF & ABOVE	REQ	2Y &		TENURE	FIRST $4800 BAL			3.00% 6.00%	3.00% 6.00%	65	65	NL
	OTHER FAC & OFF	REQ	3Y			FIRST $4800 BAL			3.00% 6.00%	3.00% 6.00%	65	65	NL
	OTHER DESIG PRO CL	REQ	3Y &	30		FIRST $4800 BAL			3.00% 6.00%	3.00% 6.00%	65	65	NL
	OTHER	REQ	10Y &	40		FIRST $4800 BAL			3.00% 6.00%	3.00% 6.00%	65	65	NL
		VOL	3Y &	30		NO CONTRIBUTIONS ARE MADE ON SALARY ABOVE $12000.							
MARS HILL COL, N C PLAN COVERS— ALL EMPLOYEES	ASSOC PROF & ABOVE	REQ	1Y						5.00%	5.00%	70	65	75
	OTHER	REQ	3Y &	28					5.00%	5.00%	70	65	75
MARSHALL U, W VA SUPPL PLAN COVERS— ALL EMPLOYEES	ALL ELIGIBLE	VOL		30 &	$4800 SAL	FIRST $4800 BAL			.00% 5.00%	.00% 5.00%	RET	65	NL
						FIRST $4800 BAL	35 35		.00% 6.00%	.00% 6.00%			
						FIRST $4800 BAL	45 45		.00% 7.50%	.00% 7.50%			
MARY BALDWIN COL, VA PLAN COVERS— ALL EMPLOYEES	FAC, OFF, CLER	REQ	3Y &	30					7.50%	2.50%	RET	65	70
		VOL			ON RECOM								
	OTHER	REQ	5Y &	30					5.00%	.00%	RET	65	70
		VOL			ON RECOM								
MARYLAND INSTITUTE COL OF ART, MD PLAN COVERS— ALL EMPLOYEES	ALL ELIGIBLE	REQ	3Y &	30					5.00%	5.00%	RET	65	70
		VOL	1Y										
MARYMOUNT COL, KAN PLAN COVERS— ALL EMPLOYEES	ALL ELIGIBLE	REQ	2Y &	30					5.00%	5.00%	RET	65	NL
MARYMOUNT COL, N Y, CALIF PLAN COVERS— FAC	ALL ELIGIBLE	VOL	3Y						7.00%	5.00%	RET	65	70
MARYMOUNT MANHATTAN COL N Y PLAN COVERS— FAC	ALL ELIGIBLE	REQ	3Y &	30					5.00%	5.00%	RET	65	70
		VOL	3Y										
MARYVILLE COL, TENN CONTINUED ON NEXT PAGE	ALL ELIGIBLE	REQ	2Y						5.00%	5.00%	RET	65	NL

CONTINUED ON NEXT PAGE

INSTITUTION	PROVISIONS APPLY TO	REQ &/OR VOL	WAITING PERIOD TIME AGE	OTHER	TIAA-CREF CONTRIBUTIONS SALARY AGE	YRS	INST	INDIV	END AT	NOR RET AGE	MAX EXT TO
PLAN COVERS— FAC, OFF & DESIG CL											
MARYVILLE COL OF THE SACRED HEART, MO PLAN COVERS— FAC, OFF, CLER & SEC	FAC	VOL	3Y				5.00%	5.00%	RET	65	70
	OTHER	VOL	3Y & 30				5.CC%	5.00%	RET	65	70
MARYWOOD COL, PA PLAN COVERS— FAC, OFF, CLER & SEC	FAC	VOL	1Y				5.00%	5.00%	RET	65	70
	OTHER	VOL	3Y				5.CC%	5.CC%	RET	65	70
MAYVILLE STATE COL, N D SUPPL PLAN COVERS— FAC, OFF & DESIG CL	ASSOC PROF & ABOVE & EQUIV OFF	REQ	IMMED		FIRST $20000 BAL		5.00% .00%	5.00% .00%	RET	65	70
	OTHER	REQ	2Y		FIRST $20000 BAL		5.00% .00%	5.00% .00%	RET	65	70
MCKENDREE COL, ILL PLAN COVERS— FAC, OFF	ALL ELIGIBLE	REQ VOL	3Y & 30 2Y				5.00%	5.00%	RET	65	70
MCPHERSON COL, KAN PLAN COVERS— FAC, OFF, MAINT & SERV	FAC, OFF	REQ	2Y & 35 OR AFTER 4 YRS				10.00%	.00%	RET	65	70
	MAINT & SERV	REQ	3Y & 35 OR 5 YEARS				5.00%	.CC%	RET	65	70
MEHARRY MEDICAL COL, TENN PLAN COVERS— FAC, OFF	ASST PROF & ABOVE & EQUIV OFF	REQ VOL	3Y & 30 3Y				5.00%	5.CC%	RET	68	70
	INSTR	VOL	3Y				5.00%	5.00%	RET	68	70
MEMPHIS ACADEMY OF ARTS, TENN PLAN COVERS— FAC, OFF	ALL ELIGIBLE	REQ VOL	3Y & 30 1Y				5.00%	5.00%	RET	65	70
MERCER U, GA PLAN COVERS— FAC, OFF & DESIG CL	FAC, OFF	REQ VOL	3Y & 35 IMMED				12.00%	.00%	RET	65	NL
	OTHER	REQ VOL	3Y & 35 3Y				12.00%	.CC%	RET	65	NL
MERCER U SCH OF PHARMACY GA PLAN COVERS— FAC, OFF & DESIG CL	FAC, OFF	REQ VOL	3Y & 35 IMMED				7.00%	5.00%	RET	65	NL
	OTHER	REQ VOL	3Y & 35 3Y				7.CC%	5.CC%	RET	65	NL
MERCY COL OF DETROIT, MICH PLAN COVERS— FAC, OFF & DESIG CL	ALL ELIGIBLE	VOL	3Y & 30				5.00%	5.00%	RET	65	70
MERCYHURST COL, PA PLAN COVERS— FAC, OFF	ALL ELIGIBLE	REQ VOL	3Y & 30 1Y				5.00%	5.00%	RET	65	70

INSTITUTION	PROVISIONS APPLY TO	REQ &/OR VOL	WAITING PERIOD			TIAA-CREF CONTRIBUTIONS					END AT	NOR RET AGE	MAX EXT TO
			TIME AGE		OTHER	SALARY AGE	YRS	INST	INDIV				
MEREDITH COL, N C PLAN COVERS- FAC, OFF, CLER & SEC	ALL ELIGIBLE	REQ	2Y & 30					5.00%	5.00%	RET	67	72
MERRILL-PALMER INSTITUTE MICH PLAN COVERS- FAC, OFF & DESIG CL	ALL ELIGIBLE	REQ VOL	5Y 1Y			FIRST $7800 BAL		7.50% 12.50%	5.00% 5.CC%	RET	65	70
MERRIMACK COL, MASS PLAN COVERS- ALL EMPLOYEES	FAC, OFF	REQ VOL	2Y & 30 2Y					5.00%	5.00%	RET	65	70
	CLER & SEC, MAINT & SERV	VOL	2Y					5.00%	5.CC%	RET	65	70
MESSIAH COL, PA PLAN COVERS- FAC, OFF	SINGLE	REQ VOL	3Y 1Y					3.00%	3.00%	RET	65	71
	MARRIED	REQ VOL	3Y 1Y					5.00%	5.00%	RET	65	71
METHODIST COL, N C PLAN COVERS- FAC, OFF	ALL ELIGIBLE	REQ VOL	2Y 1Y OR		ON RECOM			5.00%	5.00%	RET	68	70
METHODIST THEOLOGICAL SCH IN OHIO PLAN COVERS- FAC, OFF	ALL ELIGIBLE	VOL	IMMED					10.CC%	5.CC%	RET	65	NX
MICHIGAN STATE U PLAN COVERS- FAC, OFF & DESIG CL	ASST PROF & ABOVE & EQUIV OFF	REQ VOL	2Y & 35 IMMED					10.CC%	5.CC%	RET	65	70
	INSTR	REQ VOL	2Y & 35 2Y					10.00%	5.00%	RET	65	70
	OTHER	REQ VOL	2Y & 35 IMMED					10.00%	5.CC%	RET	65	70
MICHIGAN, U OF PLAN COVERS- FAC, OFF & DESIG CL	FAC	REQ VOL	35 IMMED			FIRST $7800 BAL FIRST $7800 BAL		5.00% 10.00% VOL AD 5.00% VOL AD .00%	.00% 5.00% 5.00% .00%	RET	70	NX
	OFF & DESIG NONACAD CL	REQ VOL	IMMED	35 &	$15000 SAL & $15000 SAL	FIRST $7800 BAL FIRST $7800 BAL		5.00% 10.00% VOL AD 5.00% VOL AD .00%	.00% 5.00% 5.CC% .CC%	RET	70	NX
	OTHER	VOL	IMMED	&	$10000- $14999 SAL	FIRST $7800 BAL FIRST $7800 BAL		5.00% 10.00% VOL AD 5.00% VOL AD .00%	.00% 5.00% 5.00% .00%	RET	70	NX
MIDDLEBURY COL, VT PLAN COVERS- ALL EMPLOYEES	ASSOC PROF & ABOVE	REQ	IMMED			FIRST $7800 BAL		5.00% 10.00%	5.00% 5.00%	RET	65	70
CONTINUED ON NEXT PAGE	ASST PROF & INSTR	REQ	2Y			FIRST $7800		5.00%	5.C0%	RET	65	70

INSTITUTION	PROVISIONS APPLY TO	REQ &/OR VOL	WAITING PERIOD TIME	AGE	OTHER	TIAA-CREF CONTRIBUTIONS SALARY AGE YRS	INST	INDIV	END AT	NOR RET AGE	MAX EXT TO
						BAL	10.00%	5.00%			
	OFF	REQ	2Y			FIRST			RET	65	70
						$7800	5.00%	5.00%			
						BAL	10.00%	5.00%			
	OTHER	VOL	5Y &	35			5.00%	3.00%	RET	65	70
MIDWESTERN COL, IA PLAN COVERS— FAC, OFF	ALL ELIGIBLE	REQ	2Y &	30			5.00%	5.00%	RET	65	70
		VOL	1Y								
MILES COL, ALA PLAN COVERS— FAC, OFF, CLER & SEC	ALL ELIGIBLE	REQ	3Y &	30			5.00%	5.00%	RET	65	70
		VOL	1Y								
MILLIKIN U, ILL PLAN COVERS— FAC, OFF	ALL ELIGIBLE	REQ			TENURE		5.00%	5.00%	65	65	70
		VOL	1Y								
MILLS COL, CALIF PLAN COVERS— ALL EMPLOYEES	ASST PROF & ABOVE	REQ	IMMED				10.00%	5.00%	RET	65	NL
	OTHER FAC & OFF	REQ	3Y				10.00%	5.00%	RET	65	NL
	CLER & SEC	REQ	5Y &	35			5.00%	5.00%	RET	65	70
	OTHER	REQ	3Y &	30			5.00%	5.00%	RET	65	70
MILLS COL OF EDUCATION N Y PLAN COVERS— ALL EMPLOYEES	FAC, OFF	REQ	3Y				10.00%	5.00%	RET	65	70
		VOL	1Y								
	PART TIME	VOL	5Y &		ON RECOM		10.00%	5.00%	RET	65	70
	OTHER	VOL	3Y &	30			5.00%	3.00%	RET	65	70
MILLSAPS COL, MISS PLAN COVERS— FAC, OFF	ALL ELIGIBLE	REQ	3Y &	30			10.00%	.00%	RET	65	68
		VOL	IMMED								
MILTON COL, WIS PLAN COVERS— FAC, OFF	ALL ELIGIBLE	REQ	2Y &	30			5.00%	5.00%	RET	70	75
		VOL	1Y								
MILTONVALE WESLEYAN COL KAN PLAN COVERS— ALL EMPLOYEES	ALL ELIGIBLE	REQ	5Y &	30			2.00%	5.00%	RET	65	70
		VOL	2Y								
	OTHER	VOL	2Y				2.00%	5.00%	RET	65	70
MILWAUKEE SCH OF ENGINEERING, WIS PLAN COVERS— FAC, OFF	ALL ELIGIBLE	VOL	3Y &	30			5.00%	5.00%	RET	65	75
MINOT STATE COL, N D SUPPL PLAN COVERS— FAC, OFF & DESIG CL	ASSOC PROF & ABOVE & EQUIV OFF	REQ	IMMED			FIRST			RET	65	70
						$20000	5.00%	5.00%			
						BAL	.00%	.00%			
	OTHER	REQ	2Y			FIRST			RET	65	70
						$20000	5.00%	5.00%			
						BAL	.00%	.00%			
MISSOURI VALLEY COL, MO CONTINUED ON NEXT PAGE	ALL ELIGIBLE	REQ	1Y &	30			5.00%	5.00%	RET	65	75

INSTITUTION	PROVISIONS APPLY TO	REQ &/OR VOL	WAITING PERIOD			TIAA-CREF CONTRIBUTIONS					END AT	NOR RET AGE	MAX EXT TO
			TIME	AGE	OTHER	SALARY	AGE	YRS	INST	INDIV			
PLAN COVERS— FAC, OFF, CLER & SEC		VOL	1Y										
MOBILE COL, ALA PLAN COVERS— FAC, OFF	ALL ELIGIBLE	REQ	3Y OR	35					5.00%	5.00%	RET	65	70
		VOL	IMMED										
MOLLOY CATHOLIC COL FOR WOMEN, N Y PLAN COVERS— ALL EMPLOYEES	ALL ELIGIBLE	REQ	2Y &	30					5.00%	5.00%	RET	65	70
		VOL	2Y										
MONMOUTH COL, ILL PLAN COVERS— ALL EMPLOYEES	ASSOC PROF & ABOVE	REQ	2Y &	30		FIRST $7800			5.00%	5.00%	RET	65	70
		VOL	1Y			BAL			10.00%	5.00%			
	ASST PROF	REQ	2Y &	30		FIRST $7800			5.00%	5.00%	RET	65	70
		VOL	1Y			BAL			6.00%	5.00%			
	OFF & CLER	REQ	2Y &	30					5.00%	5.00%	RET	65	68
		VOL	1Y										
	OTHER FAC	REQ	2Y &	30					5.00%	5.00%	RET	65	70
		VOL	1Y										
	OTHER	REQ	5Y &	30					5.00%	5.00%	RET	65	68
		VOL	5Y										
MONMOUTH COL, N J PLAN COVERS— ALL EMPLOYEES	FAC, OFF	REQ	1Y &	30					5.00%	5.00%	65	65	70
	OTHER	VOL	3Y &	30					5.00%	5.00%	65	65	70
MORAVIAN COL, PA PLAN COVERS— ALL EMPLOYEES	FAC, OFF	REQ	2Y &	30					10.00%	.00%	RET	65	NL
		VOL	2Y OR		ON RECOM								
	CLERGYMEN	REQ	2Y &	30					4.00%	.00%	RET	65	NL
		VOL	2Y OR		ON RECOM								
	OTHER	REQ	2Y &	30					5.00%	5.00%	RET	65	NL
MOREHOUSE COL, GA PLAN COVERS— FAC, OFF, CLER & SEC	ALL ELIGIBLE	REQ	4Y			FIRST			5.00%	5.00%	RET	65	NX
MORNINGSIDE COL, IA PLAN COVERS— ALL EMPLOYEES	ALL ELIGIBLE	REQ	3Y						8.00%	2.00%	RET	65	NL
		VOL	IMMED										
MORRIS BROWN COL, GA PLAN COVERS— FAC, OFF	ASST PROF & ABOVE & EQUIV OFF	REQ	IMMED			FIRST			5.00%	5.00%	RET	65	NX
	OTHER	REQ	3Y			FIRST			5.00%	5.00%	RET	65	NX
MOUNT HOLYOKE COL, MASS PLAN COVERS— FAC, OFF	ASST PROF & ABOVE	REQ			APMT MORE THAN 1 YR				10.00%	5.00%	RET	65	NL
		VOL	3Y										
	INSTR	VOL	3Y						10.00%	5.00%	RET	65	NL
	OFF	REQ	IMMED						10.00%	5.00%	RET	65	NL
	VISITING PROF	VOL	1Y						10.00%	5.00%	RET	65	NL

INSTITUTION	PROVISIONS APPLY TO	REQ &/OR VOL	WAITING PERIOD TIME AGE OTHER	TIAA-CREF CONTRIBUTIONS SALARY AGE YRS	INST	INDIV	END AT	NOR RET AGE	MAX EXT TO
MOUNT MARY COL, WIS PLAN COVERS— FAC	ALL ELIGIBLE	VOL	3Y & 30		5.00%	5.00%	RET	65	70
MOUNT MERCY COL, PA PLAN COVERS— FAC	ALL ELIGIBLE	REQ	1Y		5.00%	5.00%	RET	65	70
MOUNT ST JOSEPH-ON-THE-OHIO, COL OF, OHIO PLAN COVERS— FAC, OFF	ALL ELIGIBLE	REQ VOL	2Y & 30 2Y		5.45%	4.55%	RET	65	NL
MOUNT ST MARY COL, N Y PLAN COVERS— FAC	ALL ELIGIBLE	VOL	1Y		5.00%	5.00%	RET	65	70
MOUNT ST MARYS COL, CALIF PLAN COVERS— FAC	ALL ELIGIBLE	REQ VOL	3Y & 30 1Y		5.00%	5.00%	RET	65	70
	FAC	REQ VOL	3Y & 30 1Y		5.00%	5.00%	RET	65	70
	OTHER	VOL	1Y & 30		5.00%	5.00%	RET	65	70
MOUNT ST MARYS COL, MD PLAN COVERS— FAC, OFF	ALL ELIGIBLE	VOL	3Y		5.00%	5.00%	RET	65	70
MOUNT ST VINCENT, COL OF N Y PLAN COVERS— FAC	ALL ELIGIBLE	REQ VOL	1Y IMMED		5.00%	5.00%	RET	65	70
MOUNT SINAI SCH OF MEDICINE, N Y PLAN COVERS— FAC, OFF	ALL ELIGIBLE	VOL	IMMED		10.00%	5.00%	RET	65	NL
MOUNT UNION COL, OHIO PLAN COVERS— FAC, OFF & DESIG CL	ALL ELIGIBLE	VOL	1Y		10.00%	.00%	RET	NL	NX
MOUNT VERNON NAZARENE COL OHIO PLAN COVERS— ALL EMPLOYEES	ALL ELIGIBLE	REQ VOL	2Y & 30 1Y		7.50%	5.00%	RET	65	70
MUHLENBERG COL, PA PLAN COVERS— ALL EMPLOYEES	FAC, OFF	REQ	2Y	FIRST $4800 BAL	10.00% 15.00%	.00% .00%	RET	65	70
	OTHER	REQ	5Y	FIRST $4800 BAL	10.00% 15.00%	.00% .00%	RET	65	70
MUNDELEIN COL, ILL PLAN COVERS— ALL EMPLOYEES	FAC	REQ VOL	3Y & 30 1Y		5.00%	5.00%	65	65	70
	OTHER	VOL	1Y & 30 & ON RECOM		5.00%	5.00%	65	65	70
MUSKINGUM COL, OHIO PLAN COVERS— FAC, OFF	FAC	REQ	VARIES		8.00%	5.00%	RET	68	70
CONTINUED ON NEXT PAGE									

INSTITUTION	PROVISIONS APPLY TO	REQ &/OR VOL	WAITING PERIOD TIME AGE	OTHER	TIAA-CREF CONTRIBUTIONS SALARY AGE YRS	INST	INDIV	END AT	NOR RET AGE	MAX EXT TO
	OTHER	REQ		VARIES		5.00%	5.00%	RET	65	NX
NASSON COL, ME PLAN COVERS- FAC, OFF	ASST PROF & ABOVE & EQUIV OFF	REQ VOL	3Y & 30 3Y			10.00%	.00%	RET	65	NL
NATIONAL COL OF EDUCATION, ILL PLAN COVERS- ALL EMPLOYEES	ALL ELIGIBLE	VOL	2Y & 30		FIRST $6600 BAL	7.00% 10.00%	4.00% 7.00%	RET	65	NX
NAZARETH COL OF ROCHESTER N Y PLAN COVERS- FAC	ALL ELIGIBLE	REQ VOL	3Y 2Y			5.00%	5.00%	RET	65	70
NEBRASKA, U OF PLAN COVERS- ALL EMPLOYEES	FAC, OFF	REQ	1Y & 30			6.00%	6.00%	RET	65	68
	AGRIC EXTENSION STAFF	REQ	1Y & 30			2.50%	2.50%	RET	65	NX
	OTHER	REQ	3Y & 30 OR 2Y & 40		FIRST $6600 2 BAL 2	2.50% 4.50% 6.00%	2.50% 4.50% 6.00%	RET	65	NX
NEBRASKA WESLEYAN U PLAN COVERS- FAC, OFF	ALL ELIGIBLE	REQ VOL	2Y 1Y			6.00%	6.00%	RET	70	NL
NEW COL, FLA PLAN COVERS- FAC, OFF & DESIG CL	PROF & EQUIV OFF	VOL	1Y			15.00%	5.00%	RET	65	70
	ASSOC PROF & EQUIV OFF	VOL	1Y			10.00%	5.00%	RET	65	70
	ASST PROF & EQUIV OFF	VOL	1Y			7.50%	5.00%	RET	65	70
	OTHER	VOL	1Y			5.00%	5.00%	RET	65	70
NEW ENGLAND COL, N H PLAN COVERS- FAC, OFF, CLER & SEC	ALL ELIGIBLE	REQ VOL	1Y IMMED			5.00%	5.00%	RET	65	70
NEW HAMPSHIRE, U OF PLAN COVERS- FAC, OFF	ALL ELIGIBLE	REQ VOL	2Y	RANK OF ASST PROF	FIRST $6600 BAL	5.00% 10.00%	5.00% 7.00%	RET	65	69
NEW HAVEN COL, CONN PLAN COVERS- ALL EMPLOYEES	FAC, OFF	REQ	1Y & 25			7.00%	5.00%	RET	65	70
	OTHER	REQ	3Y & 30			5.00%	3.00%	RET	65	70
NEW JERSEY COL OF MEDICINE AND DENTISTRY PLAN COVERS- FAC, OFF	ALL ELIGIBLE	REQ		CONTRIB ACCUM FIRST YEAR BEFORE PAID TO CONTRACT		9.31%* *LESS COST OF GROUP LIFE AND DISABILITY INSURANCE.	5.00%	RET	65	NL
NEW ROCHELLE, COL OF, N Y PLAN COVERS- FAC	ALL ELIGIBLE	REQ	2Y & 30			10.00%	5.00%	RET	65	70

INSTITUTION	PROVISIONS APPLY TO	REQ &/OR VOL	WAITING PERIOD TIME AGE	OTHER	TIAA-CREF CONTRIBUTIONS SALARY AGE	YRS	INST	INDIV	END AT	NOR RET AGE	MAX EXT TO
NEW SCH FOR SOCIAL RESEARCH, N Y PLAN COVERS- FAC, OFF, CLER & SEC	FAC, OFF	VOL		RANK OF ASST PROF			10.00%	.00%	RET	70	NX
	OTHER	VOL	3Y			7	5.00% 10.00%	5.00% .00%	RET	65	70
NEW YORK, CITY U OF PLAN COVERS- FAC GRADUATE STUDIES DIVISION BARUCH COLLEGE BROOKLYN COLLEGE CITY COLLEGE HUNTER COLLEGE JOHN JAY COLLEGE OF CRIMINAL JUSTICE LEHMAN COLLEGE QUEENS COLLEGE RICHMOND COLLEGE YORK COLLEGE	ALL ELIGIBLE	REQ		CONTRIB ACCUM FIRST YEAR BEFORE PAID TO CONTRACT	FIRST $7800 BAL		9.00% 12.00%	3.00% 3.00%	RET	70	NX
NEW YORK COL OF MUSIC PLAN COVERS- ALL EMPLOYEES	ALL ELIGIBLE	VOL	5Y		FIRST $6600 BAL		3.00% .00%	3.00% .00%	RET	65	NL
NEW YORK INSTITUTE OF TECHNOLOGY PLAN COVERS- FAC, OFF	ALL ELIGIBLE	REQ	5Y & 30				5.00%	5.00%	RET	65	70
NEW YORK LAW SCH PLAN COVERS- FAC	ALL ELIGIBLE	REQ VOL	2Y & 30 1Y				5.00%	5.00%	RET	65	NX
NEW YORK MEDICAL COL PLAN COVERS- FAC, OFF	FAC	REQ VOL	3Y OR 35 IMMED		FIRST $7800 BAL		6.00% 12.00%	5.00% 5.00%	RET	65	70
	OTHER	VOL	IMMED		FIRST $7800 BAL		6.00% 12.00%	5.00% 5.00%	RET	65	70
NEW YORK SCH OF PSYCHIATRY PLAN COVERS- FAC	ALL ELIGIBLE	VOL	IMMED				12.00%	.00%	RET	65	70
NEW YORK, STATE U OF PLAN COVERS- FAC, OTHERS WITH EDUC RELATED DUTIES	FAC	REQ		CONTRIB ACCUM FIRST YEAR BEFORE PAID TO CONTRACT	FIRST $7800 BAL		12.00% 15.00%	.00% .00%	RET	70	NX

STATE U OF NY AT ALBANY
STATE U OF NY AT BINGHAMTON
STATE U OF NY AT BUFFALO
STATE U OF NY AT
  STONY BROOK
CENTER FOR INTERNATIONAL
  STUDIES AND WORLD
  AFFAIRS
DOWNSTATE MEDICAL CENTER
UPSTATE MEDICAL CENTER
COL AT BROCKPORT
COL AT BUFFALO
COL AT CORTLAND
COL AT FREDONIA
COL AT GENESEO
COL AT NASSAU
COL AT NEW PALTZ
COL AT ONEONTA
COL AT OSWEGO
COL AT PLATTSBURGH
COL AT POTSDAM
	OTHER	REQ		CONTRIB ACCUM FIRST YEAR BEFORE PAID TO CONTRACT	FIRST $7800
					BAL
							12.00%
							15.00%
								.00%
								.00%
									RET	65	NX

CONTINUED ON NEXT PAGE

INSTITUTION	PROVISIONS APPLY TO	REQ &/OR VOL	WAITING PERIOD TIME AGE	OTHER	TIAA-CREF CONTRIBUTIONS SALARY AGE YRS	INST	INDIV	END AT	NOR RET AGE	MAX EXT TO
COL OF FORESTRY AT SYRACUSE U MARITIME COL COL OF CERAMICS AT ALFRED U COL OF AGR AT CORNELL U COL OF HOME ECONOMICS AT CORNELL U SCH OF INDUSTRIAL AND LABOR RELATIONS AT CORNELL U VETERINARY COL AT CORNELL U										
NEW YORK THEOLOGICAL SEM PLAN COVERS— ALL EMPLOYEES	ASST PROF & ABOVE & EQUIV OFF	VOL	IMMED		FIRST $7800 BAL	8.60% 13.00%	.00% .00%	RET	65	68
	INSTR	VOL		ON RECOM	FIRST $7800 BAL	8.60% 13.00%	.00% .00%	RET	65	68
	OTHER	VOL		VARIES		5.00%	.00%	RET	65	68
NEW YORK U PLAN COVERS— FAC, OFF & DESIG CL	ASST PROF & ABOVE & EQUIV OFF	REQ	IMMED		FIRST $4800 BAL	7.50% 10.00%	2.50% 5.00%	RET	68	NX
	INSTR	REQ	3Y OR 30		FIRST $4800 BAL	7.50% 10.00%	2.50% 5.00%	RET	68	NX
		VOL	1Y							
	DESIG PRO CL	REQ	5Y		FIRST $4800 BAL	7.50% 10.00%	2.50% 5.00%	RET	65	68
		VOL	IMMED							
	OTHER DESIG PRO CL	REQ	10Y & 35		FIRST $4800 BAL	7.50% 10.00%	2.50% 5.00%	RET	65	68
		VOL	1Y							
	OTHER	VOL	5Y		FIRST $4800 BAL	7.50% 10.00%	2.50% 5.00%	RET	65	68
NEWBERRY COL, S C PLAN COVERS— FAC, OFF, CLER & SEC	ALL ELIGIBLE	REQ	3Y & 30			5.00%	5.00%	RET	65	70
		VOL	1Y							
NEWTON COL OF THE SACRED HEART, MASS PLAN COVERS— FAC	ALL ELIGIBLE	VOL	1Y & 28			5.00%	5.00%	RET	65	70
NIAGARA U, N Y PLAN COVERS— ALL EMPLOYEES	ALL ELIGIBLE	VOL	3Y & 30			5.00%	5.00%	RET	65	70
NICHOLS COL OF BUSINESS ADMINISTRATION, MASS PLAN COVERS— FAC, OFF	ALL ELIGIBLE	REQ	1Y & 30			5.00%	5.00%	RET	65	70
NORTH CAROLINA, U OF SCHOOL OF MEDICINE SUPPL PLAN COVERS— FAC	ALL ELIGIBLE	REQ	IMMED			10.00%	.00%	RET	65	70
			CONTRIBUTIONS APPLY TO SALARY FROM CLINIC PRACTICE PLUS 5% OF 1/2 THE DIFFERENCE BETWEEN TOTAL SALARY AND CLINIC SALARY.							
NORTH CAROLINA WESLEYAN COL PLAN COVERS— FAC, OFF	ALL ELIGIBLE	REQ	2Y & 30			5.00%	5.00%	RET	65	70
		VOL	1Y							

INSTITUTION	PROVISIONS APPLY TO	REQ &/OR VOL	WAITING PERIOD			TIAA-CREF CONTRIBUTIONS					END AT	NOR RET AGE	MAX EXT TO
			TIME	AGE	OTHER	SALARY AGE	YRS	INST	INDIV				
NORTH CENTRAL BIBLE COL MINN PLAN COVERS— FAC, OFF	ALL ELIGIBLE	REQ	IMMED						3.00%	3.00%	RET	65	NL
NORTH CENTRAL COL, ILL PLAN COVERS— ALL EMPLOYEES	ALL ELIGIBLE	VOL	1Y						5.00%	5.00%	RET	68	70
NORTH DAKOTA STATE U SUPPL PLAN COVERS— FAC, OFF & DESIG CL	ASSOC PROF & ABOVE & EQUIV OFF	REQ	IMMED			FIRST $20000 BAL			5.00% .00%	5.00% .00%	RET	65	70
	OTHER	REQ	2Y			FIRST $20000 BAL			5.00% .00%	5.00% .00%	RET	65	70
NORTH DAKOTA, U OF SUPPL PLAN COVERS— FAC, OFF & DESIG CL	ASSOC PROF & ABOVE & EQUIV OFF	REQ	IMMED			FIRST $20000 BAL			5.00% .00%	5.00% .00%	RET	65	70
	OTHER	REQ	2Y			FIRST $20000 BAL			5.00% .00%	5.00% .00%	RET	65	70
NORTH PARK COL, ILL PLAN COVERS— ALL EMPLOYEES	FAC, OFF	REQ	3Y				5 10		5.00% 7.50% 10.00%	5.00% 2.50% .00%	RET	65	NL
	OTHER	REQ	5Y						5.00%	5.00%	RET	65	NL
		VOL	3Y										
NORTHEASTERN U, MASS PLAN COVERS— ALL EMPLOYEES	FAC	REQ	3Y &	35					5.00%	5.00%	RET	65	70
		VOL	3Y &		ON RECOM								
	OFF	REQ	3Y &	35 &	CONTRIB ACCUM FOR 1ST 5 YRS BEFORE PAID TO CONTRACT				5.00%	5.00%	RET	65	70
		VOL	3Y &	30 &	CONTRIB ACCUM FOR 1ST 5 YRS BEFORE PAID TO CONTRACT								
	DESIG NONACAD CL	REQ	3Y &	35					5.00%	5.00%	RET	65	70
		VOL	3Y &		ON RECOM								
	OTHER	REQ	3Y &	35 &	CONTRIB ACCUM FOR 1ST 5 YRS BEFORE PAID TO CONTRACT				5.00%	5.00%	RET	65	70
		VOL	3Y &	30 &	CONTRIB ACCUM FOR 1ST 5 YRS BEFORE PAID TO CONTRACT								
NORTHERN IOWA, U OF PLAN COVERS— ALL EMPLOYEES	FAC, OFF	REQ	IMMED			FIRST $4800 BAL			6.66% 10.00%	3.33% 5.00%	68	68	70
	OTHER	VOL	1Y &		$4800 SAL	FIRST $4800 BAL			6.66% 10.00%	3.33% 5.00%	70	70	NX
NORTHLAND COL, WIS PLAN COVERS— ALL EMPLOYEES CONTINUED ON NEXT PAGE	FAC, OFF	REQ	2Y &	35					5.00%	5.00%	RET	65	68

CONTINUED ON NEXT PAGE

INSTITUTION	PROVISIONS APPLY TO	REQ &/OR VOL	WAITING PERIOD			TIAA-CREF CONTRIBUTIONS						NOR RET AGE	MAX EXT TO
			TIME	AGE	OTHER	SALARY	AGE	YRS	INST	INDIV	END AT		
NORTHWESTERN U, ILL PLAN COVERS— ALL EMPLOYEES	CLER & SEC, MAINT & SERV	VOL	2Y						5.00%	5.00%	RET	65	68
	ASST PROF	REQ VOL		30 25					10.00%	5.00%	RET	68	NX
	INSTRS	REQ VOL	2Y &	30 25					10.00%	5.00%	RET	68	NX
	OTHERS	VOL	5Y &	35 &	$5100				10.00%	5.00%	RET	68	70
NORWICH U, VT PLAN COVERS— FAC, OFF	ALL ELIGIBLE	VOL							5.00%	5.00%	RET	65	NX
NOTRE DAME, COL OF, CALIF PLAN COVERS— FAC, OFF, CLER & SEC	ALL ELIGIBLE	VOL	IMMED						4.00%	4.00%	RET	65	75
NOTRE DAME COL OF STATEN ISLAND, N Y PLAN COVERS— FAC	FAC	REQ VOL	3Y 1Y						5.00%	5.00%	RET	65	NL
	MAINT & SERV	VOL	1Y						5.00%	5.00%	RET	65	NL
NOTRE DAME OF MARYLAND, COL OF PLAN COVERS— FAC, OFF, CLER & SEC	ALL ELIGIBLE	VOL	1Y						5.00%	5.00%	RET	65	70
NOTRE DAME, U OF, IND PLAN COVERS— FAC, OFF & DESIG CL	FAC	REQ VOL	1Y & 1Y	30		FIRST $6600 BAL			5.00% 10.00%	5.00% 5.00%	RET	65	70
	OTHER	REQ		35 &	$7500 SAL	FIRST $6600 BAL			5.00% 10.00%	5.00% 5.00%	RET	65	70
NOVA U, FLA PLAN COVERS— FAC, OFF	ALL ELIGIBLE	REQ VOL	1Y & IMMED	30					10.00%	5.00%	RET	65	70
OAKLAND CITY COL, IND PLAN COVERS— FAC, OFF	ALL ELIGIBLE	REQ	3Y &	25					5.00%	5.00%	RET	65	70
OBERLIN COL, OHIO PLAN COVERS— ALL EMPLOYEES	FAC, OFF	REQ VOL	1Y &	30	ON RECOM		45 55		10.00% 12.50% 15.00%	5.00% 5.00% 5.00%	RET	66	NX
	DESIG NONACAD CL	REQ	3Y &	30					7.00%	3.00%	RET	65	66
	OTHER	REQ	3Y &	30					5.00%	.00%	RET	65	66
OCCIDENTAL COL, CALIF PLAN COVERS— ALL EMPLOYEES	PROF & EQUIV OFF	REQ	1Y						10.00%	6.00%	RET	65	NL
	ASSOC PROF & EQUIV OFF	REQ	1Y						9.00%	6.00%	RET	65	NL
	ASST PROF & EQUIV OFF	REQ	1Y						8.00%	6.00%	RET	65	NL
	INSTR & EQUIV OFF	REQ	1Y						6.00%	6.00%	RET	65	NL
	OTHER	VOL	3Y						5.00%	5.00%	RET	65	NL
OGLETHORPE COL, GA PLAN COVERS— FAC, OFF	ALL ELIGIBLE	REQ VOL	3Y & 1Y	30		FIRST $7000 BAL			7.00% .00%	5.00% .00%	RET	65	70

INSTITUTION	PROVISIONS APPLY TO	REQ &/OR VOL	WAITING PERIOD			TIAA-CREF CONTRIBUTIONS					END AT	NOR RET AGE	MAX EXT TO
			TIME	AGE	OTHER	SALARY	AGE	YRS	INST	INDIV			
OHIO DOMINICAN COL PLAN COVERS— FAC, OFF	ALL ELIGIBLE	REQ VOL	2Y & 2Y	30					5.00%	5.00%	RET	67	70
OHIO NORTHERN U PLAN COVERS— FAC, OFF, MAINT & SERV	FAC, OFF	REQ	1Y			FIRST $6600 BAL			5.00% 7.50%	5.00% 7.50%	70	70	NL
	OTHER	REQ	3Y						7.50%	.00%	7C	70	NL
OHIO WESLEYAN U PLAN COVERS— FAC, OFF	ALL ELIGIBLE	REQ	1Y						13.00%	.00%	RET	65	70
OKLAHOMA BAPTIST U SUPPL PLAN COVERS— FAC	ALL ELIGIBLE	REQ			TENURE				$300Y	.00%Y	RET	65	70
OKLAHOMA CHRISTIAN COL PLAN COVERS— FAC, OFF	ALL ELIGIBLE	REQ VOL	1Y & 1Y	30					5.00%	5.00%	RET	65	70
OKLAHOMA CITY U PLAN COVERS— ALL EMPLOYEES	FAC, OFF	REQ VOL	3Y		 ON RECOM				5.00%	5.00%	RET	65	NX
	OTHER	VOL	3Y						5.00%	5.00%	RET	65	NX
OLIVET COL, MICH PLAN COVERS— ALL EMPLOYEES	ALL ELIGIBLE	VOL		25					6.00%	4.00%	RET	65	70
OLIVET NAZARENE COL, ILL PLAN COVERS— ALL EMPLOYEES	ALL ELIGIBLE	REQ VOL	1Y IMMED						5.00%	5.00%	RET	65	NL·
ORAL ROBERTS U, OKLA PLAN COVERS— ALL EMPLOYEES	FAC, OFF	VOL	1Y						7.50%	7.50%	RET	65	70
	DESIG PRO CL	VOL	1Y						7.50%	7.50%	RET	65	70
	OTHER	VOL	2Y &	30					7.50%	7.50%	RET	65	70
OREGON GRADUATE CENTER PLAN COVERS— ALL EMPLOYEES	FAC, OFF	REQ VOL	 IMMED	35		FIRST $7800 BAL			5.00% 10.00%	5.00% 5.00%	RET	65	70
	OTHER	REQ VOL	2Y & 1Y	35					7.00%	3.00%	RET	65	70
OREGON STATE BOARD OF HIGHER EDUCATION SUPPL PLAN COVERS— FAC EASTERN OREGON COL OREGON COL OF EDUCATION OREGON STATE U OREGON, U OF PORTLAND STATE COL SOUTHERN OREGON COL	ALL ELIGIBLE	REQ	6M			IF MONTHLY SALARY IS: FIRST $4800 UNDER $500 BAL FIRST $4800 $500–$999 BAL FIRST $4800 $1000–$1499 BAL FIRST $4800 $1500 OR OVER BAL			.00% 4.00% .00% 5.00% .00% 6.00% .00% 7.00%	.00% 4.00% .00% 5.00% .00% 6.00% .00% 7.00%	RET	65	70

INSTITUTION	PROVISIONS APPLY TO	REQ &/OR VOL	WAITING PERIOD			TIAA-CREF CONTRIBUTIONS					END AT	NOR RET AGE	MAX EXT TO
			TIME AGE		OTHER	SALARY AGE	YRS	INST	INDIV				
OTTAWA U, KAN PLAN COVERS— FAC, OFF	ALL ELIGIBLE	REQ			TENURE			5.00%	5.00%		RET	68	NX
OTTERBEIN COL, OHIO PLAN COVERS— FAC, OFF	ASST PROF & ABOVE	REQ			TENURE		15	5.00% 10.00%	5.00% 5.00%		RET	70	NL
		VOL	1Y										
	INSTR	VOL	2Y				15	5.00% 10.00%	5.00% 5.00%		RET	70	NL
	OTHER	REQ	2Y					5.00%	5.00%		RET	70	NL
		VOL	1Y										
OUR LADY OF CINCINNATI COL OHIO PLAN COVERS— FAC	ALL ELIGIBLE	REQ	3Y &	30				5.00%	5.00%		RET	65	70
		VOL	3Y										
OUR LADY OF THE ELMS, COL OF, MASS PLAN COVERS— FAC	ALL ELIGIBLE	REQ	2Y &	30		FIRST $7800 BAL		5.00% 10.00%	5.00% 5.00%		RET	65	70
		VOL	IMMED										
OUR LADY OF THE LAKE COL TEX PLAN COVERS— FAC, OFF	ALL ELIGIBLE	REQ	3Y &	35				5.00%	5.00%		RET	65	70
		VOL	1Y										
OZARKS, SCH OF THE, MO PLAN COVERS— ALL EMPLOYEES	ALL ELIGIBLE	REQ	2Y &	30				6.00%	4.00%		RET	65	70
		VOL	2Y										
PACE COL, N Y PLAN COVERS— FAC, OFF, CLER & SEC	FAC, OFF	REQ	1Y &	30 OR 40		FIRST $7800 BAL		5.00% 10.00%	5.00% 5.00%		RET	65	68
	DESIG NONACAD CL	REQ	1Y &	30 OR 40		FIRST $7800 BAL		5.00% 10.00%	5.00% 5.00%		RET	65	68
	OTHER	VOL	5Y &	30 OR 40		FIRST $7800 BAL		5.00% 10.00%	5.00% 5.00%		RET	68	70
PACIFIC CHRISTIAN COL CALIF PLAN COVERS— FAC, OFF	ALL ELIGIBLE	REQ	2Y			FIRST $7800 BAL		10.00% 15.00%	.00% .00%		RET	70	NL
PACIFIC COL, CALIF PLAN COVERS— FAC, OFF	FAC	REQ	1Y					3.00%	3.00%		RET	65	72
	OFF	REQ	IMMED					3.00%	3.00%		RET	65	72
	PART TIME	VOL	IMMED					3.00%	3.00%		RET	65	72
PACIFIC LUTHERAN U, WASH PLAN COVERS— ALL EMPLOYEES	FAC, OFF	REQ	1Y &	30				10.00%	5.00%		RET	65	70
	OTHER	VOL	3Y &	30				5.00%	3.00%		RET	65	70
PACIFIC OAKS COL, CALIF PLAN COVERS— ALL EMPLOYEES	ALL ELIGIBLE	REQ	3Y					3.00%	3.00%		RET	65	70
		VOL	1Y										

INSTITUTION	PROVISIONS APPLY TO	REQ &/OR VOL	TIME AGE	OTHER	SALARY AGE	YRS	INST	INDIV	END AT	NOR RET AGE	MAX EXT TO
PACIFIC SCH OF RELIGION CALIF PLAN COVERS— ALL EMPLOYEES	FAC, OFF	REQ	IMMED		FIRST $10000 BAL		12.50% 7.50%	.00% .00%	RET	68	70
	OTHER	REQ	3Y				5.00%	2.00%	RET	65	NX
PACIFIC U, ORE PLAN COVERS— ALL EMPLOYEES	ALL ELIGIBLE	REQ VOL	5Y & 30 1Y				6.00%	6.00%	RET	65	68
PACIFIC, U OF THE, CALIF PLAN COVERS— FAC, OFF, CLER & SEC	ALL ELIGIBLE	REQ	1Y & 30		FIRST $7800 BAL		5.00% 7.50%	5.00% 7.50%	RET	70	72
PARK COL, MO PLAN COVERS— FAC, OFF & DESIG CL	FAC	REQ VOL	 IMMED	TENURE			5.00%	5.00%	RET	65	NL
	OTHER	REQ VOL	5Y IMMED				5.00%	5.00%	RET	65	NL
PARSONS COL, IA PLAN COVERS— ALL EMPLOYEES	ALL ELIGIBLE	REQ		$5000 SAL			10.00%	3.00%	RET	65	70
PARSONS SCH OF DESIGN, N Y PLAN COVERS— FAC, OFF, CLER & SEC	ALL ELIGIBLE	REQ VOL	3Y & 30 2Y				5.00%	5.00%	RET	65	70
PASADENA COL, CALIF PLAN COVERS— FAC	ALL ELIGIBLE	REQ	IMMED				5.00%	5.00%	RET	66	NX
PEABODY INSTITUTE OF THE CITY OF BALTIMORE, MD PLAN COVERS— FAC, OFF, CLER & SEC	ALL ELIGIBLE	REQ	3Y &	$2000 SAL	FIRST $6000 BAL		10.00% .00%	.00% .00%	RET	65	NL
PENNSYLVANIA COL OF OPTOMETRY PLAN COVERS— ALL EMPLOYEES	ALL ELIGIBLE	REQ VOL	2Y & 30 2Y		FIRST $4800 BAL		.00% 9.00%	.00% .00%	RET	65	NL
PENNSYLVANIA, U OF PLAN COVERS— FAC, OFF	ALL ELIGIBLE	VOL PARTICIPATION IS A CONDITION FOR TENURE	3Y OR	RANK OF ASST PROF	 30 40		6.00% 8.00% 9.00%	4.00% 5.00% 5.00%	RET	68	NX
PEPPERDINE COL, CALIF PLAN COVERS— FAC, OFF	ALL ELIGIBLE	REQ VOL	 1Y & 32	TENURE			5.00%	5.00%	RET	65	NL
PERU STATE COL, NEB PLAN COVERS— ALL EMPLOYEES	FAC, OFF	REQ	IMMED				6.00%	6.00%	RET	65	68
	OTHER	REQ	3Y & 30 OR				3.00%	3.00%	RET	65	68
PFEIFFER COL, N C PLAN COVERS— FAC, OFF, MAINT & SERV	FAC, OFF	REQ	2Y & 30 OR TENURE				9.00%	5.00%	RET	66	NX
	OTHER	REQ	1Y				5.00%	5.00%	RET	66	NX
PHARMACEUTICAL SCIENCES, COL OF, COLUMBIA U, N Y CONTINUED ON NEXT PAGE	ALL ELIGIBLE	REQ	2Y &	$5000 SAL	FIRST $6600		5.00%	5.00%	RET	65	NL

INSTITUTION	PROVISIONS APPLY TO	REQ &/OR VOL	WAITING PERIOD TIME	AGE	OTHER	TIAA-CREF CONTRIBUTIONS SALARY	AGE	YRS	INST	INDIV	END AT	NOR RET AGE	MAX EXT TO
PLAN COVERS- FAC, OFF & DESIG CL						BAL			10.00%	5.00%			
PHILADELPHIA COL OF ART PA	ALL ELIGIBLE	REQ	3Y &	30		FIRST $7800			5.00%	5.00%	RET	65	70
PLAN COVERS- FAC, OFF		VOL	3Y			BAL			10.00%	5.00%			
PHILADELPHIA COL OF TEXTILES AND SCIENCE, PA	FAC, OFF	REQ	5Y &	30		FIRST $7800			5.00%	5.00%	RET	65	70
PLAN COVERS- ALL EMPLOYEES		VOL	3Y			BAL			5.00%	5.00%			
						FIRST $7800		VOL AD	.00%	.00%			
						BAL		VOL AD	2.50%	2.50%			
	DESIG NONACAD CL	REQ	5Y &	30		FIRST $7800			5.00%	5.00%	RET	65	70
		VOL	3Y			BAL			5.00%	5.00%			
						FIRST $7800		VOL AD	.00%	.00%			
						BAL		VOL AD	2.50%	2.50%			
	CLER & SEC	REQ	5Y &	30		FIRST $7800			5.00%	5.00%	RET	65	70
		VOL	3Y			BAL			5.00%	5.00%			
						FIRST $7800		VOL AD	.00%	.00%			
						BAL		VOL AD	2.50%	2.50%			
	OTHER	REQ	10Y &	30		FIRST $7800			5.00%	5.00%	RET	65	70
		VOL	3Y			BAL			5.00%	5.00%			
						FIRST $7800		VOL AD	.00%	.00%			
						BAL		VOL AD	2.50%	2.50%			
PIEDMONT COL, GA	ALL ELIGIBLE	REQ	3Y &	30					4.00%	4.00%	RET	65	70
PLAN COVERS- FAC, OFF		VOL	IMMED										
PIKEVILLE COL, KY	ALL ELIGIBLE	VOL	1Y						5.00%	5.00%	RET	65	70
PLAN COVERS- ALL EMPLOYEES													
PITTSBURGH, U OF, PA	ASSOC PROF & ABOVE	REQ	IMMED						5.00%	5.00%	RET	70	NX
PLAN COVERS- FAC, OFF & DESIG CL							35		6.25%	6.25%			
							45		7.50%	7.50%			
	ASST PROF & INSTR	VOL	IMMED						5.00%	5.00%	RET	70	NX
							35		6.25%	6.25%			
							45		7.50%	7.50%			
	OFF	REQ	IMMED						5.00%	5.00%	RET	65	NX
							35		6.25%	6.25%			
							45		7.50%	7.50%			
	DESIG PRO CL	VOL	3Y						5.00%	5.00%	RET	65	NX
	MAINT & SERV	VOL	1Y						$11M	$3M	RET	65	NX
	DESIG NONACAD CL	VOL	1Y						$12M	$12M	RET	65	NX
	OTHER	VOL	3Y						$10M	$10M	RET	65	NX
PITZER COL	ASST PROF & ABOVE	REQ	IMMED						12.00%	4.00%	RET	65	70
PLAN COVERS- FAC, OFF													
	OTHER	VOL	2Y						12.00%	4.00%	RET	65	70
PLYMOUTH STATE COL, N H	ALL ELIGIBLE	REQ	IMMED			FIRST $7800			5.00%	5.00%	RET	65	69
PLAN COVERS- CONTINUED ON NEXT PAGE						BAL			10.00%	7.00%			

CONTINUED ON NEXT PAGE

INSTITUTION	PROVISIONS APPLY TO	REQ &/OR VOL	WAITING PERIOD				TIAA-CREF CONTRIBUTIONS						NOR RET AGE	MAX EXT TO
			TIME	AGE	OTHER		SALARY	AGE	YRS	INST	INDIV	END AT		
FAC, OFF														
PMC COLLEGES, PA PLAN COVERS— FAC, OFF	ALL ELIGIBLE	REQ VOL	1Y & 1Y	30						5.00% 	5.00%	RET	65	70
POINT PARK COL, PA PLAN COVERS— FAC, OFF, CLER & SEC	ALL ELIGIBLE	REQ VOL	3Y & 3Y	30			FIRST $6600 BAL			5.00% 12.00%	5.00% 5.00%	RET	65	NL
POLYTECHNIC INSTITUTE OF BROOKLYN, N Y PLAN COVERS— ALL EMPLOYEES	ASST PROF & ABOVE & EQUIV OFF OTHER	REQ VOL	IMMED 5Y							7.50% 7.50%	5.00% 5.00%	RET RET	65 65	70 70
POMONA COL, CALIF PLAN COVERS— FAC, OFF	ASST PROF & ABOVE OTHER	REQ VOL	IMMED 2Y							12.00% 12.00%	4.00% 4.00%	RET RET	65 65	68 68
PORTLAND, U OF, ORE PLAN COVERS— FAC, OFF	ALL ELIGIBLE	VOL	3Y &	30						7.00%	5.00%	RET	65	NL
PRATT INSTITUTE, N Y PLAN COVERS— ALL EMPLOYEES	ALL ELIGIBLE	REQ VOL	2Y & 2Y	30						10.00%	5.00%	RET	65	70
PRESBYTERIAN COL, S C PLAN COVERS— FAC, OFF	ALL ELIGIBLE	VOL	3Y &	30					6	5.00% 7.50%	5.00% 5.00%	65	65	70
PRESCOTT COL, ARIZ PLAN COVERS— ALL EMPLOYEES	ALL ELIGIBLE	REQ VOL	3Y OR							5.00%	5.00%	RET	65	70
PRINCETON U, N J PLAN COVERS— FAC, OFF & DESIG CL	ASST PROF & ABOVE INSTR MAJOR OFF OTHER	REQ VOL REQ REQ REQ	1Y & IMMED 2Y & 1Y & 	30 30 30 30 &	 VARIES			40 50 40 50 40 50 40 50		9.00% 12.00% 15.00% 9.00% 12.00% 15.00% 9.00% 12.00% 15.00% 9.00% 12.00% 15.00%	3.00% 4.00% 5.00% 3.00% 4.00% 5.00% 3.00% 4.00% 5.00% 3.00% 4.00% 5.00%	RET RET RET RET	68 68 65 65	NL NL NL NL
PRINCIPIA, THE, MO PLAN COVERS— FAC, OFF, CLER & SEC	ALL ELIGIBLE	REQ VOL	2Y		ON RECOM					UP TO 7.50% INDIVIDUAL CONTRIBUTION MUST BE MINIMUM REQUIRED TO BUY A SINGLE LIFE ANNUITY OF $25 MONTHLY AT AGE 65.	7.50%	RET	65	NX
PROVIDENCE COL, R I PLAN COVERS— FAC, OFF & DESIG CL	FAC OTHER	VOL VOL	3Y & 5Y &	30 30						UP TO 13.60% 10.00%	.00% 5.00%	RET RET	65 65	70 70
PUGET SOUND COL OF THE BIBLE, WASH PLAN COVERS— ALL EMPLOYEES CONTINUED ON NEXT PAGE	FAC, OFF	REQ	IMMED				FIRST $7800 BAL			5.00% 7.50%	5.00% 7.50%	RET	65	70

INSTITUTION	PROVISIONS APPLY TO	REQ &/OR VOL	WAITING PERIOD			TIAA-CREF CONTRIBUTIONS						NOR RET AGE	MAX EXT TO
			TIME AGE		OTHER	SALARY	AGE	YRS	INST	INDIV	END AT		
	OTHER	REQ	2Y & 30			FIRST $7800 BAL			5.00% 7.50%	5.00% 7.50%	RET	65	70
PUGET SOUND, U OF, WASH PLAN COVERS— ALL EMPLOYEES	FAC, OFF	REQ	IMMED						12.00%	.00%	65	65	NL
	OTHER	REQ	2Y						10.00%	.00%	65	65	NL
PURDUE U, IND PLAN COVERS— FAC, OFF	ASST PROF & ABOVE & EQUIV OFF	REQ	IMMED			FIRST $7800 BAL			11.00% 15.00%	.00% .00%	65	65	68
	OTHER	REQ	3Y			FIRST $7800 BAL			11.00% 15.00%	.00% .00%	65	65	68
QUEENS COL, N C PLAN COVERS— FAC, OFF, CLER & SEC	FAC, OFF	REQ	1Y & 30						12.50%	2.50%	RET	65	70
		VOL	1Y										
	OTHER	REQ	4Y & 30						12.50%	2.50%	RET	65	70
		VOL	1Y										
QUINCY COL, ILL PLAN COVERS— FAC	ALL ELIGIBLE	REQ	3Y			FIRST $6000 BAL			8.00% .00%	6.00% .00%	RET	65	70
RADCLIFFE COL, MASS PLAN COVERS— OFF, CLER & SEC, MAINT & SERV	OFF & CLER	REQ	3Y						12.00%	.00%	RET	65	70
(FAC COVERED BY HARVARD U PLAN)	MAINT & SERV	REQ	3Y						9.00%	3.00%	RET	65	70
RANDOLPH-MACON COL, VA PLAN COVERS— ALL EMPLOYEES	ALL ELIGIBLE	REQ	1Y & 30						5.00%	5.00%	RET	65	70
		VOL	1Y										
RANDOLPH-MACON WOMANS COL, VA PLAN COVERS— FAC, OFF, CLER & SEC	ALL ELIGIBLE	REQ	2Y & 30						10.00%	.00%	RET	68	NL
REDLANDS, U OF, CALIF PLAN COVERS— ALL EMPLOYEES	FAC	REQ	3Y						10.00%	.00%	RET	65	NX
		VOL	1Y										
	OTHER	VOL	1Y						10.00%	.00%	RET	65	NX
REED COL, ORE PLAN COVERS— ALL EMPLOYEES	FAC, OFF	REQ	1Y & 30 OR 2Y & 26				65		10.00% 5.00%	.00% .00%	RET	65	70
	OTHER	REQ	3Y & 26				65		10.00% 5.00%	.00% .00%	RET	65	70
REGIS COL, COLO PLAN COVERS— FAC, OFF	ALL ELIGIBLE	REQ	3Y						5.00%	5.00%	RET	65	NL
REGIS COL, MASS PLAN COVERS— FAC, OFF, CLER & SEC	FAC, OFF	VOL	1Y & 30						5.00%	5.00%	RET	65	70
	OTHER	VOL	3Y & 30						5.00%	3.00%	RET	65	70
RHODE ISLAND COL	ALL ELIGIBLE	REQ	2Y & 30						9.00%	5.00%	RET	65	70

CONTINUED ON NEXT PAGE

INSTITUTION	PROVISIONS APPLY TO	REQ &/OR VOL	WAITING PERIOD — TIME AGE	OTHER	TIAA-CREF CONTRIBUTIONS — SALARY AGE YRS	INST	INDIV	END AT	NOR RET AGE	MAX EXT TO
PLAN COVERS— FAC, OFF		VOL	2Y							
RHODE ISLAND SCH OF DESIGN PLAN COVERS— FAC, OFF	ASSOC PROF & ABOVE & EQUIV OFF	REQ	IMMED		FIRST $7800 BAL	10.00% 15.00%	.00% .00%	RET	65	NL
	ASST PROF	REQ VOL	3Y OR 40 2Y		FIRST $7800 BAL	10.00% 15.00%	.00% .00%	RET	65	NL
	OTHER	REQ VOL	4Y OR 40 2Y		FIRST $7800 BAL	10.00% 15.00%	.00% .00%	RET	65	NL
RHODE ISLAND, U OF PLAN COVERS— FAC, OFF	ALL ELIGIBLE	REQ VOL	2Y & 30 2Y			9.00%	5.00%	RET	65	70
RICE U, TEX PLAN COVERS— ALL EMPLOYEES	ASST PROF & ABOVE & EQUIV OFF	REQ	IMMED			5.00%	5.00%	RET	70	NX
	INSTR	REQ VOL	5Y OR 35 2Y & 30			5.00%	5.00%	RET	70	NX
	DESIG NONACAD CL	REQ VOL	5Y OR 35 & $4200 SAL 2Y & 30 & $4200 SAL			5.00%	5.00%	RET	70	NX
	OTHER	VOL	5Y & 35			5.00%	5.00%	RET	70	NX
RICHMOND, U OF, VA PLAN COVERS— FAC, OFF & DESIG CL	FAC, OFF	REQ	2Y			7.50%	5.00%	RET	70	NL
	OTHER	REQ	5Y			7.50%	5.00%	RET	70	NL
RIDER COL, N J PLAN COVERS— ALL EMPLOYEES	FAC	REQ VOL	3Y 1Y			7.00%	5.00%	RET	65	71
	OTHER	VOL	3Y & 25			7.00%	5.00%	RET	65	71
RINGLING SCH OF ART, FLA PLAN COVERS— FAC, OFF, CLER & SEC	FAC	REQ VOL	3Y & 30 1Y			5.00%	5.00%	RET	65	NL
	OFF & DESIG NONACAD CL	REQ VOL	3Y & 30 1Y			5.00%	5.00%	RET	65	NL
	OTHER	VOL	3Y			5.00%	5.00%	RET	65	NL
RIPON COL, WIS PLAN COVERS— FAC, OFF, MAINT & SERV	FAC, OFF	VOL	2Y OR	ON RECOM		5.00%	5.00%	RET	65	NL
	OTHER	REQ	5Y			5.00%	5.00%	RET	65	NL
RIVIER COL, N H PLAN COVERS— FAC, OFF	ALL ELIGIBLE	REQ VOL	3Y & 30 1Y			5.00%	5.00%	RET	65	70
ROANOKE COL, VA PLAN COVERS— FAC, OFF, CLER & SEC	FAC	REQ	1Y & 30			5.00%	5.00%	RET	65	70
	OFF	REQ	1Y & 30			5.00%	5.00%	RET	65	NX
	OTHER	VOL	1Y & 30			5.00%	5.00%	RET	65	NX
ROBERT COL, TURKEY CONTINUED ON NEXT PAGE	ALL ELIGIBLE	REQ	3Y & 30		FIRST $7800	3.60%	.00%	RET	65	NL

CONTINUED ON NEXT PAGE

INSTITUTION	PROVISIONS APPLY TO	REQ &/OR VOL	WAITING PERIOD			TIAA-CREF CONTRIBUTIONS					NOR RET AGE	MAX EXT TO
			TIME	AGE	OTHER	SALARY AGE	YRS	INST	INDIV	END AT		
PLAN COVERS— FAC, OFF & DESIG CL						BAL		8.00%	.00%			
ROBERTS WESLEYAN COL, N Y PLAN COVERS— ALL EMPLOYEES	ALL ELIGIBLE	REQ	1Y &	35				5.00%	5.00%	RET	65	70
		VOL	1Y &	30								
ROCHESTER INSTITUTE OF TECHNOLOGY, N Y PLAN COVERS— ALL EMPLOYEES	ALL ELIGIBLE	REQ	3M &	35				7.00%	5.00%	68	65	70
		VOL	3M									
ROCHESTER, U OF, N Y PLAN COVERS— FAC, OFF	FAC	REQ			RANK OF ASST PROF			10.00%	5.00%	RET	65	70
	OFF	REQ	1Y					10.00%	5.00%	RET	65	70
ROCKEFELLER U, N Y PLAN COVERS— ALL EMPLOYEES	PROF	REQ	IMMED					20.00%	.00%	RET	65	70
	ASSOC PROF	REQ	IMMED					15.00%	.00%	RET	65	70
	ASST PROF	REQ	IMMED					13.00%	.00%	RET	65	68
	OFF	REQ	IMMED					20.00%	.00%	RET	65	70
	DESIG PRO CL	REQ	2Y					10.00%	.00%	RET	65	68
	OTHER	REQ	2Y &	30				6.00%	4.00%	65	65	NL
							10	8.00%	2.00%			
		VOL	2Y				15	10.00%	.00%			
ROCKFORD COL, ILL PLAN COVERS— FAC, OFF	FAC	REQ	2Y					5.00%	5.00%	RET	65	NL
	OTHER	VOL	2Y					5.00%	5.00%	RET	65	NL
ROCKHURST COL, MO PLAN COVERS— FAC, OFF	ALL ELIGIBLE	VOL	3Y &	40 OR 5 YEARS				10.00%	.00%	RET	65	70
ROCKY MOUNTAIN COL, MONT PLAN COVERS— ALL EMPLOYEES	ALL ELIGIBLE	REQ	3Y					5.00%	5.00%	RET	65	70
ROLLINS COL, FLA PLAN COVERS— FAC, OFF, CLER & SEC	FAC, OFF	REQ	3Y &	30				6.00%	6.00%	RET	65	70
		VOL	1Y &	30								
	OTHER	VOL	3Y &	30				4.00%	4.00%	RET	65	70
ROOSEVELT U, ILL PLAN COVERS— FAC, OFF, CLER & SEC	ASST PROF & ABOVE & EQUIV OFF	REQ	1Y					5.00%	5.00%	RET	65	70
		VOL	IMMED				1	12.00%	.00%			
						65		3.50%	3.50%			
						65	VOL AD	1.50%	1.50%			
	INSTR & EQUIV OFF	VOL	1Y					3.50%	3.50%	RET	65	70
							VOL AD	1.50%	1.50%			
	OTHER	REQ	6Y &	40				3.50%	3.50%	RET	65	70
							VOL AD	1.50%	1.50%			
		VOL	1Y					10.00%	.00%			
						40	6					
						65		3.50%	3.50%			
						65	VOL AD	1.50%	1.50%			
ROSARY COL, ILL PLAN COVERS— FAC	ALL ELIGIBLE	REQ	3Y &	30				5.00%	5.00%	RET	65	70
		VOL	2Y									

INSTITUTION	PROVISIONS APPLY TO	REQ &/OR VOL	WAITING PERIOD TIME AGE	OTHER	TIAA-CREF CONTRIBUTIONS SALARY AGE	YRS	INST	INDIV	END AT	NOR RET AGE	MAX EXT TO
ROSARY HILL COL, N Y PLAN COVERS- ALL EMPLOYEES	ALL ELIGIBLE	REQ VOL	3Y & 30 2Y				5.00%	5.00%	RET	65	70
ROSE POLYTECHNIC INSTITUTE, IND PLAN COVERS- ALL EMPLOYEES	ASST PROF & ABOVE & EQUIV OFF	REQ	IMMED		FIRST $6600 BAL		7.00% 7.00%	.00% 4.20%	RET	67	70
	OTHER	REQ	3Y		FIRST $6600 BAL		7.00% 7.00%	.00% 4.20%	RET	67	70
ROSEMONT COL, PA PLAN COVERS- FAC, OFF	ALL ELIGIBLE	REQ VOL	2Y & 30 2Y				5.00%	5.00%	RET	65	70
RUSSELL SAGE COL, N Y PLAN COVERS- FAC, OFF	ALL ELIGIBLE	VOL	3Y & 30		FIRST $10000 BAL		7.00% .00%	5.00% .00%	RET	65	NL
RUTGERS, THE STATE U, N J PLAN COVERS- FAC	ALL ELIGIBLE	REQ		CONTRIB ACCUM FIRST YEAR BEFORE PAID TO CONTRACT *AMOUNT WHICH WOULD BE CON- TRIBUTED IF PARTICIPANT WAS IN PUBLIC RETIREMENT SYSTEM OF NEW JERSEY PLAN.			*	5.00%	RET	65	NX
SACRED HEART COL, KAN PLAN COVERS- FAC, OFF	ALL ELIGIBLE	REQ VOL	3Y & 30 1Y				5.00%	5.00%	RET	65	68
SACRED HEART U, CONN PLAN COVERS- ALL EMPLOYEES	FAC, OFF	REQ	1Y & 30				5.00%	5.00%	RET	65	70
	OTHER	REQ	3Y & 30				5.00%	5.00%	RET	65	70
SAGINAW VALLEY COL, MICH PLAN COVERS- ALL EMPLOYEES	FAC, OFF	REQ VOL	3Y & 30 IMMED		FIRST $7800 BAL		5.00% 10.00%	5.00% 5.00%	RET	65	70
	OTHER	REQ VOL	5Y & 35 IMMED		FIRST $7800 BAL		5.00% 10.00%	5.00% 5.00%	RET	65	70
ST ANDREWS PRESBYTERIAN COL, N C PLAN COVERS- FAC, OFF	ALL ELIGIBLE	REQ VOL	3Y IMMED				5.00%	5.00%	RET	65	70
ST BENEDICTS COL, KAN PLAN COVERS- FAC	ALL ELIGIBLE	REQ VOL	3Y & 30 OR TENURE 3Y				UP TO 5.00%	5.00%	RET	65	70
ST BERNARD COL, ALA PLAN COVERS- FAC	ALL ELIGIBLE	REQ VOL	4Y & 30 1Y &	ON RECOM			5.00%	5.00%	RET	65	NL
ST BONAVENTURE U, N Y PLAN COVERS- FAC, OFF	ALL ELIGIBLE	VOL	2Y				10.00%	.00%	RET	65	NX
ST CATHERINE, COL OF, MINN PLAN COVERS- FAC	ALL ELIGIBLE	VOL		TENURE			5.00%	5.00%	RET	65	68

INSTITUTION	PROVISIONS APPLY TO	REQ &/OR VOL	WAITING PERIOD			TIAA-CREF CONTRIBUTIONS						NOR RET AGE	MAX EXT TO
			TIME	AGE	OTHER	SALARY	AGE	YRS	INST	INDIV	END AT		
ST EDWARDS U, TEX PLAN COVERS— ALL EMPLOYEES	ALL ELIGIBLE	REQ VOL	 2Y		TENURE				5.00%	5.00%	RET	65	70
ST ELIZABETH, COL OF, N J PLAN COVERS— FAC, OFF	ALL ELIGIBLE	REQ VOL	3Y & 2Y	30					5.00%	5.00%	RET	65	70
ST FRANCIS COL, IND PLAN COVERS— FAC	ALL ELIGIBLE	VOL	3Y						5.00%	5.00%	RET	65	70
ST FRANCIS COL, N Y PLAN COVERS— ALL EMPLOYEES	ASSOC PROF & ABOVE & EQUIV OFF	REQ VOL	1Y &	30	 ON RECOM	FIRST $4800 BAL FIRST $4800 BAL		 1 1	 5.00% 15.00% 10.00% 15.00%	 5.00% .00% .00% .00%	RET	65	70
	FEM FAC & OFF	VOL	1Y &	30		FIRST $4800 BAL FIRST $4800 BAL		 1 1	 5.00% 15.00% 10.00% 15.00%	 5.00% .00% .00% .00%	RET	65	70
	OTHER FAC	REQ	1Y &	30		FIRST $4800 BAL FIRST $4800 BAL		 1 1	 5.00% 15.00% 10.00% 15.00%	 5.00% .00% .00% .00%	RET	65	70
	OTHER	VOL	3Y			FIRST $4800 BAL			 5.00% .00%	 5.00% .00%	RET	65	70
ST JOHN FISHER COL, N Y PLAN COVERS— FAC, OFF	ALL ELIGIBLE	REQ VOL	3Y & 2Y	30					7.50%	2.50%	RET	65	70
ST JOHNS COL, MD, N M PLAN COVERS— FAC, OFF, CLER & SEC	FAC OTHER	REQ VOL VOL	2Y IMMED IMMED						5.00% 5.00%	5.00% # 5.00% #	RET RET	65 65	NX NX
ST JOHNS U, N Y PLAN COVERS— ALL EMPLOYEES	FAC, OFF OTHER	VOL VOL	1Y & 3Y &	30 30					6.00% 5.00%	5.00% 5.00%	RET RET	65 65	70 70
ST JOSEPH COL, CONN PLAN COVERS— FAC	ALL ELIGIBLE	VOL	1Y &	30					5.00%	5.00%	RET	65	70
ST JOSEPH COL, MD PLAN COVERS— FAC	ALL ELIGIBLE	VOL	2Y						5.00%	5.00%	RET	65	70
ST JOSEPHS COL, IND PLAN COVERS— FAC, OFF & DESIG CL	ALL ELIGIBLE	VOL	2Y						10.00%	2.00%	RET	65	70
ST JOSEPHS COL FOR WOMEN, N Y PLAN COVERS— ALL EMPLOYEES	ALL ELIGIBLE	VOL			ON RECOM				6.00%	6.00%	RET	65	NX

INSTITUTION	PROVISIONS APPLY TO	REQ &/OR VOL	WAITING PERIOD			TIAA-CREF CONTRIBUTIONS						NOR RET AGE	MAX EXT TO
			TIME	AGE	OTHER	SALARY	AGE	YRS	INST	INDIV	END AT		
ST LAWRENCE U, N Y PLAN COVERS— FAC, OFF & DESIG CL	ALL ELIGIBLE	REQ	IMMED						8.00%	6.00%	RET	65	NL
ST LOUIS COL OF PHARMACY, MO PLAN COVERS— ALL EMPLOYEES	FAC	VOL	1Y &		SEPT. 1	FIRST $3000 NEXT $1000			ALL PARTICIPANTS: 7.00% 3.00% 6.00%	 4.00%	65	65	NX
	OTHER	VOL	1Y &	30 &	SEPT. 1	BAL			5.00%	5.00%	65	65	NX
ST LOUIS U, MO PLAN COVERS— ALL EMPLOYEES	FAC	VOL	3Y OR		ON RECOM				5.00%	5.00%	RET	68	NX
ST MARY COL, KAN PLAN COVERS— FAC, OFF	ALL ELIGIBLE	REQ	2Y &	30					5.00%	5.00%	RET	65	70
ST MARY-OF-THE-WOODS, IND PLAN COVERS— FAC	ALL ELIGIBLE	REQ	1Y &	30					5.00%	5.00%	RET	65	NX
ST MARYS COL, IND PLAN COVERS— FAC, OFF	ALL ELIGIBLE	REQ VOL	2Y & 1Y	30					5.00%	5.00%	RET	65	70
ST MARYS COL OF CALIFORNIA PLAN COVERS— FAC, OFF	ALL ELIGIBLE	REQ VOL	2Y & 1Y	30					7.50%	5.00%	RET	65	70
ST MARYS DOMINICAN COL, LA PLAN COVERS— FAC, OFF	ALL ELIGIBLE	REQ VOL	5Y 3Y						5.00%	5.00%	RET	65	70
ST NORBERT COL, WIS PLAN COVERS— FAC, OFF	ALL ELIGIBLE	VOL	1Y OR	30					8.00%	5.00%	RET	65	70
ST OLAF COL, MINN PLAN COVERS— FAC, OFF	ALL ELIGIBLE	REQ VOL	1Y & 2Y	35			35	1	5.00% 10.00%	5.00% # 5.00% #	RET	65	70
ST PAUL SCH OF THEOLOGY—METHODIST, MO PLAN COVERS— ALL EMPLOYEES	FAC, OFF	REQ VOL	3Y & 1Y	30					8.00%	8.00%	RET	65	70
	CLERGYMEN	REQ VOL	3Y & 1Y	30					10.00%	8.00%	RET	65	70
	OTHER	VOL	1Y						8.00%	8.00%	RET	65	70
ST PROCOPIUS COL, ILL PLAN COVERS— ALL EMPLOYEES	FAC, OFF	REQ VOL	5Y 2Y						5.00%	5.00%	RET	65	70
	OTHER	VOL	2Y						5.00%	5.00%	RET	65	70
ST ROSE, COL OF, N Y PLAN COVERS— FAC	ALL ELIGIBLE	VOL	1Y						7.00%	5.00%	RET	65	70
ST THOMAS, COL OF, MINN CONTINUED ON NEXT PAGE	ALL ELIGIBLE	REQ			$6000 SAL CONTRIB ACCUM 1ST 5 YRS BEFORE PAID TO CONTRACT				4.00%	4.00%	70	70	NL

CONTINUED ON NEXT PAGE

INSTITUTION	PROVISIONS APPLY TO	REQ &/OR VOL	WAITING PERIOD			TIAA-CREF CONTRIBUTIONS						NOR RET AGE	MAX EXT TO
			TIME AGE		OTHER	SALARY AGE		YRS	INST	INDIV	END AT		
PLAN COVERS— FAC, OFF													
ST VINCENT COL, PA PLAN COVERS— ALL EMPLOYEES	FAC, OFF	REQ VOL	2Y & 2Y	30					5.00%	5.00%	RET	65	NL
	OTHER	REQ VOL	2Y & 2Y	30					2.50%	2.50%	RET	65	NL
ST XAVIER COL, ILL PLAN COVERS— ALL EMPLOYEES	FAC, OFF	VOL	1Y &	30		FIRST $6600 BAL			5.00% 7.50%	5.00% 7.50%	RET	68	70
	OTHER	VOL	3Y &	30		FIRST $6600 BAL			5.00% 7.50%	5.00% 7.50%	RET	65	70
SALEM COL, N C PLAN COVERS— ALL EMPLOYEES	FAC, OFF	REQ	2Y &	30					5.00%	5.00%	RET	65	70
	OTHER	REQ	5Y &	35					5.00%	5.00%	RET	65	NX
SALEM COL, W VA PLAN COVERS— FAC, OFF, CLER & SEC	ALL ELIGIBLE	REQ VOL	2Y & 1Y	30					5.00%	5.00%	RET	65	70
SALVE REGINA COL, R I PLAN COVERS— FAC	ALL ELIGIBLE	REQ VOL	3Y & 3Y	30		FIRST $7800 BAL			5.00% 10.00%	5.00% 5.00%	RET	65	70
	PART TIME	VOL			ON RECOM	FIRST $7800 BAL			5.00% 10.00%	5.00% 5.00%	RET	65	70
SAN DIEGO, U OF, COL FOR MEN, CALIF PLAN COVERS— FAC, OFF, CLER & SEC	ALL ELIGIBLE	VOL	IMMED					1 2 3	2.00% 3.00% 4.00% 5.00%	2.00% 3.00% 4.00% 5.00%	65	65	70
SAN DIEGO, U OF, COL FOR WOMEN, CALIF PLAN COVERS— FAC	ALL ELIGIBLE	VOL		30					5.00%	5.00%	65	65	70
SAN DIEGO, U OF, SCH OF LAW, CALIF PLAN COVERS— FAC, OFF	ALL ELIGIBLE	VOL	1Y					1 2 3 4 5	5.00% 6.00% 7.00% 8.00% 9.00% 10.00%	.00% .00% .00% .00% .00% .00%	65	65	70
SAN FRANCISCO COL FOR WOMEN, CALIF PLAN COVERS— FAC	ALL ELIGIBLE	REQ	3Y &	30					5.00%	5.00%	RET	65	70
SAN FRANCISCO, U OF, CALIF PLAN COVERS— FAC	ALL ELIGIBLE	REQ	IMMED						5.00%	5.00%	RET	65	NL

INSTITUTION	PROVISIONS APPLY TO	REQ &/OR VOL	TIME AGE	OTHER	SALARY AGE	YRS	INST	INDIV	END AT	NOR RET AGE	MAX EXT TO
SANTA FE, COL OF, N M — PLAN COVERS— FAC	ALL ELIGIBLE	REQ	2Y				5.00%	5.00%	RET	65	NL
SARAH LAWRENCE COL, N Y — PLAN COVERS— FAC, OFF, CLER & SEC	FAC	REQ	4Y				10.00%	.00%	RET	68	NL
	OTHER	REQ	4Y				10.00%	.00%	RET	65	NX
SCRIPPS COL, CALIF — PLAN COVERS— FAC, OFF	ALL ELIGIBLE	REQ	IMMED				12.00%	4.00%	RET	65	70
SEATTLE PACIFIC COL, WASH — PLAN COVERS— ALL EMPLOYEES	ALL ELIGIBLE	REQ / VOL	3Y / 1Y				5.00%	5.00%	RET	65	70
SEATTLE U, WASH — PLAN COVERS— FAC, OFF	ALL ELIGIBLE	REQ / VOL	3Y & 30 / 2Y				5.00%	5.00%	RET	65	70
SETON HALL U, N J — PLAN COVERS— FAC, OFF	ALL ELIGIBLE	REQ / VOL	3Y & 30 / 3Y				6.00%	4.00%	RET	65	70
SETON HILL COL, PA — PLAN COVERS— FAC	ALL ELIGIBLE	REQ / VOL	3Y & 30 / 3Y				8.00%	5.00%	RET	65	70
SHAW U, N C — PLAN COVERS— FAC, OFF & DESIG CL	MEN	REQ	3Y OR 30				5.00%	5.00%	RET	65	70
	FEM	REQ	3Y OR 30				5.00%	5.00%	RET	62	70
SHEPHERD COL, W VA SUPPL — PLAN COVERS— ALL EMPLOYEES	ALL ELIGIBLE	VOL		30 & $4800 SAL	FIRST $4800 / BAL		.00% / 5.00%	.00% / 5.00%	RET	65	NL
					FIRST $4800 / BAL	35 / 35	.00% / 6.00%	.00% / 6.00%			
					FIRST $4800 / BAL	45 / 45	.00% / 7.50%	.00% / 7.50%			
SHIMER COL, ILL — PLAN COVERS— FAC, OFF, CLER & SEC	ALL ELIGIBLE	REQ / VOL	5Y / 1Y		FIRST $5000 / BAL		5.00% / 10.00%	5.00% / 5.00%	RET	68	70
SHORTER COL, GA — PLAN COVERS— FAC, OFF, CLER & SEC	ALL ELIGIBLE	VOL	IMMED				5.00%	5.00%	RET	65	NL
SIENA COL, N Y — PLAN COVERS— FAC	ALL ELIGIBLE	REQ / VOL	2Y & 30 / 2Y				7.50%	7.50%	RET	65	NL
SIMMONS COL, MASS — PLAN COVERS— ALL EMPLOYEES — CONTINUED ON NEXT PAGE	FAC, OFF	REQ	3Y & 30				9.00%	3.00%	RET	66	NL

INSTITUTION	PROVISIONS APPLY TO	REQ &/OR VOL	WAITING PERIOD TIME AGE	WAITING PERIOD OTHER	SALARY	AGE	YRS	INST	INDIV	END AT	NOR RET AGE	MAX EXT TO
	OTHER	VOL	3Y & 30					9.00%	3.00%	RET	66	NL
SIMPSON COL, IA PLAN COVERS— ALL EMPLOYEES	ASSOC PROF & ABOVE	VOL	IMMED					8.00%	5.00%	RET	65	70
	OTHER	VOL	1Y					8.00%	5.00%	RET	65	70
SIOUX FALLS COL, S D PLAN COVERS— FAC, OFF	ALL ELIGIBLE	REQ	3Y					4.00%	4.00%	RET	65	70
		VOL	1Y									
SKIDMORE COL, N Y PLAN COVERS— FAC, OFF	ASST PROF & ABOVE & EQUIV OFF	REQ	IMMED		FIRST $7800 BAL			4.00% 5.00%	3.00% 4.00%	RET	68	NX
					FIRST $7800 BAL	30 30		5.00% 6.00%	4.00% 5.00%			
					FIRST $7800 BAL	40 40		6.00% 7.00%	4.00% 6.00%			
					FIRST $7800 BAL	50 50		6.00% 8.00%	4.00% 7.00%			
	OTHER	REQ	2Y		FIRST $7800 BAL			4.00% 5.00%	3.00% 4.00%	RET	68	NX
					FIRST $7800 BAL	30 30		5.00% 6.00%	4.00% 5.00%			
					FIRST $7800 BAL	40 40		6.00% 7.00%	4.00% 6.00%			
					FIRST $7800 BAL	50 50		6.00% 8.00%	4.00% 7.00%			
SMITH COL, MASS PLAN COVERS— FAC, OFF & DESIG CL	ASST PROF & ABOVE & EQUIV OFF	REQ	1Y					15.00%	.00%	RET	65	68
	INSTR & EQUIV OFF	REQ	3Y					15.00%	.00%	RET	65	68
	DESIG NONACAD CL	VOL	3Y & 35					9.00%	.00%	RET	65	NX
SOUTH ALABAMA, U OF PLAN COVERS— FAC, OFF	ASSOC PROF & ABOVE & EQUIV OFF	VOL	IMMED		FIRST $7000 BAL	EMPLOYED UNDER AGE 40		3.00% .00%	3.00% .00%	RET	70	NX
					FIRST $7000 BAL	EMPLOYED AGE 40 OR OVER		5.00% .00%	5.00% .00%			
	ASST PROF	VOL	3Y		FIRST $7000 BAL	EMPLOYED UNDER AGE 40		3.00% .00%	3.00% .00%	RET	70	NX
					FIRST $7000 BAL	EMPLOYED AGE 40 OR OVER		5.00% .00%	5.00% .00%			
	INSTR	VOL	6Y OR	TENURE	FIRST $7000 BAL	EMPLOYED UNDER AGE 40		3.00% .00%	3.00% .00%	RET	70	NX
					FIRST $7000 BAL	EMPLOYED AGE 40 OR OVER		5.00% .00%	5.00% .00%			
SOUTH, U OF THE, TENN PLAN COVERS— FAC, OFF & DESIG CL	ALL ELIGIBLE	VOL	2Y OR 30					9.00%	6.00% #	RET	68	70

INSTITUTION	PROVISIONS APPLY TO	REQ &/OR VOL	WAITING PERIOD			TIAA-CREF CONTRIBUTIONS						NOR RET AGE	MAX EXT TO
			TIME	AGE	OTHER	SALARY	AGE	YRS	INST	INDIV	END AT		
SOUTH-EASTERN BIBLE COL FLA PLAN COVERS— ALL EMPLOYEES	ALL ELIGIBLE	REQ	IMMED						5.00%	5.00%	RET	65	NX
SOUTHERN CALIFORNIA COL PLAN COVERS— FAC, OFF	ALL ELIGIBLE	REQ VOL	2Y & 2Y	30					5.00%	5.00%	65	65	NL
SOUTHERN CALIFORNIA, U OF PLAN COVERS— ALL EMPLOYEES	ALL ELIGIBLE	VOL		30					8.00%	5.00%	RET	65	70
SOUTHERN STATE COL, ARK PLAN COVERS— FAC, OFF	ALL ELIGIBLE	REQ	IMMED						6.00%	6.00%	RET	65	72
SOUTHERN UTAH, COL OF PLAN COVERS— FAC, OFF	ALL ELIGIBLE	REQ	IMMED						5.00%	5.00%#	RET	65	70
SOUTHWESTERN AT MEMPHIS TENN PLAN COVERS— ALL EMPLOYEES	FAC	VOL	3Y					 5 15	6.00% 7.50% 9.00%	6.00% 6.00% 6.00%	RET	70	NX
	OTHER	VOL	3Y					 5 15	6.00% 7.50% 9.00%	6.00% 6.00% 6.00%	RET	65	NX
SOUTHWESTERN COL, KAN PLAN COVERS— FAC, OFF	ALL ELIGIBLE	REQ VOL	1Y & 1Y	30					5.00%	5.00%	RET	68	70
SPELMAN COL, GA PLAN COVERS— FAC, OFF, CLER & SEC	ALL ELIGIBLE	REQ	4Y						5.00%	5.00%	RET	65	70
SPRING ARBOR COL, MICH PLAN COVERS— ALL EMPLOYEES	FAC, OFF	REQ VOL	3Y & 	30 30			55		5.00% VOL AD 1.00%	5.00% 1.00%	65	65	NL
	OTHER	VOL	3Y &	30			55		5.00% VOL AD 1.00%	5.00% 1.00%	65	65	NL
SPRINGFIELD COL, MASS PLAN COVERS— FAC, OFF	ALL ELIGIBLE	REQ VOL	5Y IMMED						8.00%	5.00%	RET	67	NX
STANFORD U, CALIF PLAN COVERS— FAC, OFF & DESIG CL	ASSOC PROF & ABOVE	VOL	IMMED			FIRST $3600 BAL			 8.50% 10.00%	 3.50% 5.00%	65	65	NL
	ASST PROF	VOL	2Y			FIRST $3600 BAL			 8.50% 10.00%	 3.50% 5.00%	65	65	NL
	INSTR	VOL	5Y			FIRST $3600 BAL			 8.50% 10.00%	 3.50% 5.00%	65	65	NL
	OTHER	REQ VOL	2Y & 1Y	35 &	$8400 SAL $8400 SAL	FIRST $3600 BAL			 8.50% 10.00%	 3.50% 5.00%	65	65	NL
STEPHENS COL, MO PLAN COVERS— FAC	ALL ELIGIBLE	REQ VOL	3Y &	30	ON RECOM				10.00%	.00%	RET	65	NL

INSTITUTION	PROVISIONS APPLY TO	REQ &/OR VOL	WAITING PERIOD			TIAA-CREF CONTRIBUTIONS					END AT	NOR RET AGE	MAX EXT TO
			TIME	AGE	OTHER	SALARY	AGE	YRS	INST	INDIV			
STETSON U, FLA PLAN COVERS— FAC	ALL ELIGIBLE	REQ			TENURE				10.00%	.00%	RET	65	70
STEVENS INSTITUTE OF TECHNOLOGY, N J PLAN COVERS— FAC, OFF & DESIG CL	MEN	VOL	IMMED						6.00%	5.00%	RET	70	72
							30		7.00%	5.00%			
							40		8.00%	5.00%			
							50		9.00%	5.00%			
							60		10.00%	5.00%			
	FEM	VOL	IMMED						6.00%	5.00%	RET	68	70
							30		7.00%	5.00%			
							40		8.00%	5.00%			
							50		9.00%	5.00%			
							60		10.00%	5.00%			
STILLMAN COL, ALA PLAN COVERS— FAC, OFF & DESIG CL	ALL ELIGIBLE	REQ	3Y						3.00%	3.00%	RET	65	70
STONEHILL COL, MASS PLAN COVERS— FAC, OFF, MAINT & SERV	ALL ELIGIBLE	VOL	1Y						5.00%	5.00%	RET	65	70
SUFFOLK U, MASS PLAN COVERS— FAC, OFF, MAINT & SERV	FAC, OFF	REQ	2Y & 30 OR 1Y & 40			FIRST $7800 BAL			5.00% 10.00%	5.00% 5.00%	RET	65	NL
	OTHER	REQ	5Y & 30 OR 1Y & 40			FIRST $7800 BAL			5.00% 10.00%	5.00% 5.00%	RET	65	NL
SUSQUEHANNA U, PA PLAN COVERS— FAC	ALL ELIGIBLE	VOL	IMMED						5.00%	5.00%	RET	65	NL
SWARTHMORE COL, PA PLAN COVERS— ALL EMPLOYEES	FAC, OFF	REQ	3Y						5.00%	5.00%	RET	65	70
		VOL	IMMED				50		7.50%	7.50%			
							60		10.00%	10.00%			
							65		5.00%	5.00%			
	OTHER	REQ	3Y						2.50%	2.50%	RET	65	70
		VOL			AFTER PROBAT PERIOD			3 UP TO	5.00%	5.00%			
SWEET BRIAR COL, VA PLAN COVERS— FAC, OFF, CLER & SEC	FAC	REQ	1Y			FIRST $6600 BAL			10.00% 10.00%	.00% 5.00%		65	NL
	OTHER	REQ	1Y & 30			FIRST $6600 BAL			10.00% 10.00%	.00% 5.00%		65	NL
SYRACUSE U, N Y PLAN COVERS— ALL EMPLOYEES	ASST PROF & ABOVE	REQ	4Y						9.00%	6.00%	RET	65	NX
		VOL	IMMED										
	INSTR	REQ	4Y						9.00%	6.00%	RET	65	NX
		VOL	2Y										
	OTHER	VOL	3Y						9.00%	6.00%	RET	65	NX
TABOR COL, KAN PLAN COVERS— FAC, OFF	ALL ELIGIBLE	REQ	IMMED						7.00%	3.00%	RET	65	72
	PART TIME	VOL	IMMED						7.00%	3.00%	RET	65	72
TAMPA, U OF, FLA	ALL ELIGIBLE	REQ	3Y						5.00%	5.00%	RET	65	70

CONTINUED ON NEXT PAGE

INSTITUTION	PROVISIONS APPLY TO	REQ &/OR VOL	WAITING PERIOD TIME	AGE	OTHER	TIAA-CREF CONTRIBUTIONS SALARY AGE	YRS	INST	INDIV	END AT	NOR RET AGE	MAX EXT TO
PLAN COVERS— FAC, OFF												
TARKIO COL, MO	ASST PROF & ABOVE & EQUIV OFF	REQ	3Y &	30				5.00%	5.00%	RET	65	70
PLAN COVERS— FAC, OFF		VOL	IMMED				1	6.00%	5.00%			
							3	7.00%	5.00%			
							5	8.00%	5.00%			
							7	9.00%	5.00%			
							9	10.00%	5.00%			
	OTHER FAC & OFF	REQ	3Y &	30				5.00%	5.00%	RET	65	70
		VOL	IMMED									
TAYLOR U, IND	ALL ELIGIBLE	REQ	IMMED					8.50%	3.50%	RET	65	70
PLAN COVERS— ALL EMPLOYEES												
TEACHERS COL, COLUMBIA U N Y	ASST PROF & ABOVE & EQUIV OFF	REQ	IMMED			FIRST $6600 BAL		9.00% 11.00%	.00% 4.00%	RET	65	NX
PLAN COVERS— FAC, OFF & DESIG CL	OTHER	REQ	3Y			FIRST $6600 BAL		9.00% 11.00%	.00% 4.00%	RET	65	NX
		VOL			ON RECOM							
TEMPLE BUELL COL, COLO	ALL ELIGIBLE	REQ	1Y &	30				7.00%	5.00%	RET	65	NX
PLAN COVERS— FAC, OFF												
TEMPLE U, PA	ASST PROF & ABOVE & EQUIV OFF	VOL	IMMED			FIRST $7800 BAL		6.75% 13.00%	4.50% 5.00%	RET	67	NX
PLAN COVERS— FAC, OFF, CLER & SEC	OTHER	VOL	18M			FIRST $7800 BAL		6.75% 13.00%	4.50% 5.00%	RET	67	NX
TENNESSEE, U OF	ASST PROF & ABOVE & EQUIV OFF	REQ	IMMED			FIRST $7800 BAL		3.00% 5.00%	3.00% 5.00%	RET	65	70
PLAN COVERS— ALL EMPLOYEES	OTHER	REQ	3Y &		$7800 SAL	FIRST $7800		3.00%	3.00%	RET	65	70
		VOL	3Y &		PERM APMT	BAL		5.00%	5.00%			
TENNESSEE WESLEYAN COL	ALL ELIGIBLE	REQ	3Y &		TENURE			7.00%	5.00%	RET	65	70
PLAN COVERS— FAC, OFF												
TEXAS CHRISTIAN U	FAC, OFF	VOL	2Y					10.50%	.00%	RET	67	70
PLAN COVERS— ALL EMPLOYEES	OTHER	VOL	2Y					5.50%	5.00%	RET	67	70
THEOLOGY AT CLAREMONT, SCH OF, CALIF	ALL ELIGIBLE	REQ	1Y &	30		FIRST $6600		4.20%	.00%	RET	65	69
PLAN COVERS— FAC, OFF		VOL	6M &	30		BAL		8.50%	.00%			
THIEL COL, PA	FAC, OFF	REQ	1Y					12.00%	.00%	65	65	70
PLAN COVERS— ALL EMPLOYEES	OTHER	REQ	1Y					5.00%	5.00%	65	65	70
THOMAS COL, ME	FAC, OFF	VOL	1Y &	30		FIRST $7800		5.00%	5.00%	RET	65	70
PLAN COVERS— CONTINUED ON NEXT PAGE						BAL		10.00%	5.00%			

INSTITUTION	PROVISIONS APPLY TO	REQ &/OR VOL	WAITING PERIOD TIME AGE	OTHER	TIAA-CREF CONTRIBUTIONS SALARY AGE	YRS	INST	INDIV	END AT	NOR RET AGE	MAX EXT TO
ALL EMPLOYEES	OTHER	VOL	3Y & 30		FIRST $7800 BAL		5.00% 10.00%	5.00% 5.00%	RET	65	70
THOMAS MORE COL, KY PLAN COVERS- FAC, OFF	ALL ELIGIBLE	REQ VOL	3Y & 30 2Y				5.00%	5.00%	RET	65	70
TRANSYLVANIA COL, KY PLAN COVERS- ALL EMPLOYEES	FAC, OFF	REQ	2Y & 30		FIRST $10000 BAL		10.00% 20.00%	.00% .00%	RET	65	NX
	CLER. & SEC	REQ	2Y & 30		FIRST $10000 BAL		10.00% 20.00%	.00% .00%	RET	65	NX
	OTHER	VOL	2Y & 30		FIRST $10000 BAL		10.00% 20.00%	.00% .00%	RET	65	NX
TREVECCA NAZARENE COL TENN PLAN COVERS- FAC, OFF	ALL ELIGIBLE	REQ VOL	3Y & 30 1Y				5.00%	5.00%	RET	65	70
TRI-STATE COL, IND PLAN COVERS- FAC, OFF	ASST PROF & ABOVE & EQUIV OFF	REQ	IMMED		FIRST $24000 BAL		10.00% .00%	.00% .00%	RET	65	70
	OTHER	REQ	3Y &	ON RECOM	FIRST $24000 BAL		10.00% .00%	.00% .00%	RET	65	70
TRINITY COL, CONN PLAN COVERS- FAC, OFF	ALL ELIGIBLE	REQ	30		FIRST $6600 BAL		6.00% 10.00%	5.00% 5.00%	RET	65	70
TRINITY COL, D C PLAN COVERS- FAC	ALL ELIGIBLE	REQ VOL	3Y & 30 2Y				6.00%	6.00%	RET	65	70
TRINITY COL, VT PLAN COVERS- FAC	ALL ELIGIBLE	VOL	3Y				5.00%	5.00%	RET	65	70
TRINITY U, TEX PLAN COVERS- FAC, OFF	ALL ELIGIBLE	REQ VOL	3Y & 30 1Y				10.00%	3.00%	RET	65	70
TUFTS U, MASS PLAN COVERS- ALL EMPLOYEES	FAC, OFF	REQ	1Y		FIRST $6600 BAL		7.50% 15.00%	1.50% 3.00%	RET	65	70
	OTHER	REQ	2Y & 30				4.00%	2.00%	RET	65	70
TULANE U, LA PLAN COVERS- FAC, OFF, CLER & SEC	FAC, OFF	REQ	IMMED				12.00%	.00%	RET	65	70
	DESIG NONACAD CL	VOL		ON RECOM			12.00%	.00%	RET	65	70
TULSA, U OF, OKLA PLAN COVERS- ALL EMPLOYEES	ASSOC PROF & ABOVE & EQUIV OFF	REQ VOL	1Y	TENURE	ALL PARTICIPANTS: FIRST $4800 NEXT $2400		7.50% 7.50%	7.50% .00%	RET	65	70
CONTINUED ON NEXT PAGE	ASST PROF & INSTR & EQUIV OFF	REQ VOL	3Y	TENURE	BAL		1.00%	.00%	RET	65	70

INSTITUTION	PROVISIONS APPLY TO	REQ &/OR VOL	WAITING PERIOD			TIAA-CREF CONTRIBUTIONS					END AT	NOR RET AGE	MAX EXT TO
			TIME	AGE	OTHER	SALARY	AGE	YRS	INST	INDIV			
	OTHER	VOL	3Y								RET	65	7C
TUSCULUM COL, TENN PLAN COVERS- FAC, OFF	ALL ELIGIBLE	REQ	2Y &	30					5.00%	5.00% #	RET	65	7C
TUSKEGEE INSTITUTE, ALA PLAN COVERS- FAC, OFF, CLER & SEC	ALL ELIGIBLE	REQ VOL	3Y &	30	CONTRIB ACCUM 1ST 3 YEARS AND TO AGE 30 BEFORE APPLIED TO CONTRACT	FIRST $7800 BAL FIRST $7800 BAL	 30 30	 3 3	.60% 5.00% 5.00% 7.50%	.60% 5.00% 5.00% 7.50%	RET	65	7C
UNION COLLEGE, KY PLAN COVERS- FAC, OFF, CLER & SEC	FAC, OFF OTHER	VOL VOL	2Y 2Y &	 30 OR 5 YEARS					7.00%	5.00%	RET RET	7C 70	NL NL
UNION COL, N Y PLAN COVERS- FAC	ALL ELIGIBLE	REQ VOL	1Y & 1Y	30					10.00%	5.00%	RET	65	NL
UNION THEOLOGICAL SEM, N Y PLAN COVERS- FAC, OFF	ALL ELIGIBLE	REQ			RANK OF ASST PROF				15.00%	.00%	RET	65	68
U S DEPT OF AGR GRADUATE SCH, D C PLAN COVERS- OFF, CLER & SEC	ALL ELIGIBLE	REQ	IMMED						15.00%	6.00%	RET	65	7C
UPPER IOWA U PLAN COVERS- ALL EMPLOYEES	FAC, OFF OTHER	VOL VOL	1Y 5Y						5.00% 5.00%	5.00% 5.00%	RET RET	65 65	7C 7C
UPSALA COL, N J PLAN COVERS- ALL EMPLOYEES	FAC DESIG NONACAD CL OTHER	REQ VOL REQ VOL VOL	5Y 2Y 5Y 2Y 5Y &	 30					7.00% 7.00% 7.00%	5.00% 5.00% 5.00%	RET RET RET	7C 65 65	NL NL NL
URBANA COL, OHIO PLAN COVERS- ALL EMPLOYEES	ALL ELIGIBLE	REQ VOL	2Y & IMMED	30					5.00%	5.00%	RET	65	7C
URSINUS COL, PA PLAN COVERS- ALL EMPLOYEES	FAC OTHER	REQ VOL	2Y OR 27 5Y &	 27					5.00% 5.00%	5.00% 5.00%	RET RET	68 68	72 72
URSULINE COL, KY PLAN COVERS- ALL EMPLOYEES	ALL ELIGIBLE	REQ VOL	3Y & 1Y	30					5.00%	5.00%	RET	65	7C
UTAH STATE U PLAN COVERS- FAC, OFF	ALL ELIGIBLE	REQ			$6000 SAL				5.00%	5.00% #	RET	65	7C

INSTITUTION	PROVISIONS APPLY TO	REQ &/OR VOL	WAITING PERIOD TIME AGE	WAITING PERIOD OTHER	TIAA-CREF CONTRIBUTIONS SALARY AGE YRS	INST	INDIV	END AT	NOR RET AGE	MAX EXT TO
UTAH, U OF PLAN COVERS— ALL EMPLOYEES	ALL ELIGIBLE	REQ	IMMED			5.00%	5.00%	RET	65	68
VALLEY CITY STATE COL, N D SUPPL PLAN COVERS— FAC, OFF & DESIG CL	ASSOC PROF & ABOVE & EQUIV OFF	REQ	IMMED		FIRST $20000 BAL	5.00% .00%	5.00% .00%	RET	65	70
	OTHER	REQ	2Y		FIRST $20000 BAL	5.00% .00%	5.00% .00%	RET	65	70
VALPARAISO U, IND PLAN COVERS— FAC, OFF & DESIG CL	ASST PROF & ABOVE & EQUIV OFF	REQ	IMMED			7.50%	7.50%	RET	70	NL
	OTHER	REQ	6Y			7.50%	7.50%	RET	70	NL
VANDERBILT U, TENN PLAN COVERS— ALL EMPLOYEES	ASSOC PROF & ABOVE & EQUIV OFF	REQ	IMMED			10.00%	5.00% #	RET	65	70
	ASST PROF	REQ	3Y			10.00%	5.00% #	RET	65	70
		VOL	IMMED							
	DESIG NONACAD CL	VOL	5Y			10.00%	5.00% #	RET	65	70
	OTHER	VOL		VARIES		5.00%	5.00% #	RET	65	70
VASSAR COL, NY PLAN COVERS— FAC, OFF	ALL ELIGIBLE	REQ	2Y & 30			13.00%	.00%	RET	65	NX
VERMONT, U OF PLAN COVERS— ALL EMPLOYEES	FAC	REQ		TENURE & $2000 SAL		8.00%	5.00%	RET	65	70
		VOL	2Y							
	OFF	VOL	2Y			8.00%	5.00%	RET	65	70
	FEM CLER & MAINT	VOL	3Y & 30 & $2500 SAL			6.00%	4.00%	RET	65	70
	OTHER	VOL	3Y & 30 & $3500 SAL			6.00%	4.00%	RET	65	70
VILLA MARIA COL, PA PLAN COVERS— FAC, OFF	ALL ELIGIBLE	VOL	1Y			5.00%	5.00%	RET	65	70
VILLANOVA U, PA PLAN COVERS— FAC, OFF	ALL ELIGIBLE	REQ	2Y			5.00%	5.00%	RET	65	70
VIRGINIA UNION U PLAN COVERS— ALL EMPLOYEES	ALL ELIGIBLE	REQ	3Y			3.50%	3.50%	RET	65	70
		VOL	IMMED							
VIRGINIA, U OF PLAN COVERS— FAC, OFF	ALL ELIGIBLE	REQ	IMMED		FIRST $5500 BAL NO CONTRIBUTIONS ARE MADE ON SALARY ABOVE $19800.	.00% 15.00%	5.00% # 5.00% #	RET	70	NX
VIRGINIA WESLEYAN COL PLAN COVERS— FAC, OFF, CLER & SEC	FAC, OFF	REQ	30			5.00%	5.00%	RET	68	70
	OTHER	REQ	6M & 30			5.00%	5.00%	RET	68	70

INSTITUTION	PROVISIONS APPLY TO	REQ &/OR VOL	WAITING PERIOD			TIAA-CREF CONTRIBUTIONS					END AT	NOR RET AGE	MAX EXT TO
			TIME AGE		OTHER	SALARY AGE		YRS	INST	INDIV			
VITERBO COL, WIS PLAN COVERS- FAC, OFF	ALL ELIGIBLE	REQ VOL	3Y & 30 1Y						5.00%	5.00%	RET	65	70
WABASH COL, IND PLAN COVERS- ALL EMPLOYEES	FAC, OFF OTHER	REQ VOL	1Y 1Y						6.00% 5.00%	.00% 5.00%	RET RET	NL NL	NL NL
WAGNER COL, N Y PLAN COVERS- FAC, OFF & DESIG CL	FAC, OFF OTHER	REQ VOL	1Y & 30 1Y & 30						7.00% 7.00%	5.00% 5.00%	RET RET	65 65	70 70
WAKE FOREST U, N C PLAN COVERS- FAC, OFF & DESIG CL	ASST PROF & ABOVE & EQUIV OFF OTHER	REQ VOL VOL	3Y & 30 1Y & 30 5Y						7.50% 7.50%	2.50% 2.50%	7C 7C	70 70	NL NL
WASHBURN U OF TOPEKA, KAN PLAN COVERS- ALL EMPLOYEES	FAC, OFF OTHER	REQ VOL	3Y OR 3Y		TENURE				5.00% 5.00%	5.00% 5.00%	RET RET	65 65	NX NX
WASHINGTON AND JEFFERSON COL, PA PLAN COVERS- FAC, OFF	ALL ELIGIBLE	REQ VOL	3Y & 30 3Y			FIRST $4800 BAL			6.66% 10.00%	3.33% 5.00%	RET	68	70
WASHINGTON AND LEE U, VA PLAN COVERS- ALL EMPLOYEES	ALL ELIGIBLE	VOL	2Y OR		ON RECOM				7.50%	7.50%	RET	65	NL
WASHINGTON COL, MD PLAN COVERS- FAC, OFF, CLER & SEC	ALL ELIGIBLE	REQ	1Y & 30						5.00%	5.00%	RET	65	68
WASHINGTON SCH OF PSYCHIATRY, D C PLAN COVERS- OFF, CLER & SEC	ALL ELIGIBLE	VOL	1Y & 30			FIRST $6600 BAL			5.00% 7.50%	5.00% 7.50%	RET	65	70
WASHINGTON STATE U PLAN COVERS- ALL EMPLOYEES	ALL ELIGIBLE	REQ VOL	2Y IMMED						5.00%	5.00%	70	65	70
						FIRST $7800 BAL FIRST $7800 BAL FIRST $7800 BAL	35 35 50 50		VOL AD .00% VOL AD 2.50% 5.00% 7.50% VOL AD 1.20% VOL AD 2.50%	.00% 2.50% 5.00% 7.50% 1.20% 2.50%			
WASHINGTON U, MO PLAN COVERS- ALL EMPLOYEES	FAC OFF OTHER	REQ VOL REQ VOL REQ VOL	5Y OR IMMED 5Y & IMMED 5Y & IMMED		TENURE $6000 SAL $6000 SAL		45 50 45 50 45 50		6.00% 7.50% 11.50% 6.00% 7.50% 11.50% 6.00% 7.50% 11.50%	5.00% 5.00% 5.00% 5.00% 5.00% 5.00% 5.00% 5.00% 5.00%	RET RET RET	68 65 68	NL NX NL

INSTITUTION	PROVISIONS APPLY TO	REQ &/OR VOL	WAITING PERIOD TIME AGE	OTHER	SALARY	AGE	YRS	INST	INDIV	END AT	NOR RET AGE	MAX EXT TO
WASHINGTON, U OF PLAN COVERS— FAC, OFF & DESIG CL	ALL ELIGIBLE	REQ	2Y OR 35					5.00%	5.00%	RET	70	NX
		VOL		ON RECOM								
					FIRST $4800	35		5.00%	5.00%			
					BAL	35		7.50%	7.50%			
						50		10.00%	10.00%*			
					OPTIONAL RATE IF EMPLOYMENT STARTS AFTER AGE 40.							
WAYNE STATE COL, NEB PLAN COVERS— ALL EMPLOYEES	FAC, OFF	REQ	IMMED					6.00%	6.00%	RET	65	68
	OTHER	REQ	3Y & 30 OR					3.00%	3.00%	RET	65	68
WAYNE STATE U, MICH PLAN COVERS— ALL EMPLOYEES	FAC, OFF	REQ	2Y & 30					10.00%	5.00%	RET	70	NX
	OTHER	REQ	2Y & 30					7.50%	5.00%	RET	70	NX
WAYNESBURG COL, PA PLAN COVERS— FAC, OFF	ALL ELIGIBLE	REQ	1Y & 30					7.00%	7.00%	RET	65	NL
		VOL	1Y									
WEBB INSTITUTE OF NAVAL ARCHITECTURE, N Y PLAN COVERS— FAC, OFF	ALL ELIGIBLE	REQ	2Y					7.00%	7.00%	RET	65	NL
		VOL	IMMED									
WEBER STATE COL, UTAH PLAN COVERS— FAC, OFF	ALL ELIGIBLE	VOL		$5000 SAL				5.00%	5.00%	RET	65	70
WEBSTER COL, MO PLAN COVERS— FAC	ALL ELIGIBLE	REQ	3Y & 30					5.00%	5.00%	RET	65	70
		VOL		ON RECOM								
WELLESLEY COL, MASS PLAN COVERS— FAC, OFF & DESIG CL	ASST PROF & ABOVE & EQUIV OFF	REQ		APMT MORE THAN 3Y	FIRST $7800 BAL			7.00% 12.00%	5.00% 5.00%	RET	65	NX
	INSTR & EQUIV OFF	REQ	4Y		FIRST $7800 BAL	APMT 3Y		12.00% 17.00%	0.00% 0.00%	RET	65	NX
		VOL	2Y									
WELLS COL, N Y PLAN COVERS— FAC, OFF	ALL ELIGIBLE	VOL	1Y				UP TO	7.50%	7.50%	65	65	NL
WESLEY THEOLOGICAL SEM D C PLAN COVERS— ALL EMPLOYEES	FAC	VOL	IMMED					10.00%	5.00%	RET	72	NX
	OTHER	VOL	2Y					5.00%	5.00%	RET	72	NX
WESLEYAN COL, GA PLAN COVERS— FAC, OFF	ALL ELIGIBLE	REQ	2Y					10.00%	.00%	RET	68	NL
WESLEYAN U, CONN PLAN COVERS— ALL EMPLOYEES	FAC, OFF	REQ		38 OR TENURE				15.00%	.00%	RET	68	NL
		VOL	IMMED		BEFORE PARTICIPATION IS REQUIRED, INDIVIDUAL MAY ELECT TO TAKE ADDITIONAL 7.50% IN SALARY IN LIEU OF 15% CONTRIBUTION TO ANNUITY.								

CONTINUED ON NEXT PAGE

INSTITUTION	PROVISIONS APPLY TO	REQ &/OR VOL	WAITING PERIOD TIME AGE	OTHER	SALARY	AGE	YRS	INST	INDIV	END AT	NOR RET AGE	MAX EXT TO
	DESIG PRO CL	REQ	30					10.00%	.00%	RET	70	NL
	OTHER	REQ	5Y & 30					10.00%	.00%	RET	70	NL
WEST LIBERTY STATE COL, W VA SUPPL PLAN COVERS– ALL EMPLOYEES	ALL ELIGIBLE	VOL	30 & $4800 SAL		FIRST $4800 BAL			.00% 5.00%	.00% 5.00%	RET	65	70
					FIRST $4800 BAL	35 35		.00% 6.00%	.00% 6.00%			
					FIRST $4800 BAL	45 45		.00% 7.50%	.00% 7.50%			
WEST VIRGINIA INSTITUTE OF TECHNOLOGY SUPPL PLAN COVERS– ALL EMPLOYEES	ALL ELIGIBLE	VOL	30 & $4800 SAL		FIRST $4800 BAL			.00% 5.00%	.00% 5.00%	RET	65	NL
					FIRST $4800 BAL	35 35		.00% 6.00%	.00% 6.00%			
					FIRST $4800 BAL	45 45		.00% 7.50%	.00% 7.50%			
WEST VIRGINIA STATE COL SUPPL PLAN COVERS– ALL EMPLOYEES	ALL ELIGIBLE	VOL	30 & $4800 SAL		FIRST $4800 BAL			.00% 5.00%	.00% 5.00%	RET	65	NL
					FIRST $4800 BAL	35 35		.00% 6.00%	.00% 6.00%			
					FIRST $4800 BAL	45 45		.00% 7.50%	.00% .50%			
WEST VIRGINIA U SUPPL PLAN COVERS– ALL EMPLOYEES	FAC	REQ VOL	30 & TENURE & $4800 SAL 30 & $4800 SAL		FIRST $4800 BAL			.00% 5.00%	.00% 5.00%	RET	65	70
					FIRST $4800 BAL	35 35		.00% 6.00%	.00% 6.00%			
					FIRST $4800 BAL	45 45		.00% 7.50%	.00% 7.50%			
WEST VIRGINIA WESLEYAN COL PLAN COVERS– ALL EMPLOYEES	FAC, OFF OTHER	REQ VOL VOL	1Y OR 30 IMMED 5Y					6.00% 6.00%	6.00% 6.00%	RET RET	65 65	70 70
WESTBROOK JUNIOR COL, ME PLAN COVERS– FAC, OFF	ALL ELIGIBLE	REQ VOL	3Y & 30 1Y		FIRST $4800 BAL			3.00% 5.00%	3.00% 5.00%	RET	65	70
WESTERN COL FOR WOMEN OHIO PLAN COVERS– ALL EMPLOYEES	ALL ELIGIBLE	VOL	IMMED					5.00%	5.00%	RET	65	NL

INSTITUTION	PROVISIONS APPLY TO	REQ &/OR VOL	WAITING PERIOD			TIAA-CREF CONTRIBUTIONS					END AT	NOR RET AGE	MAX EXT TO
			TIME	AGE	OTHER	SALARY AGE	YRS	INST	INDIV				
WESTERN MARYLAND COL PLAN COVERS- FAC, OFF	ALL ELIGIBLE	REQ	2Y &	30 OR TENURE				10.00%	5.00%		65	65	70
WESTERN NEW ENGLAND COL, MASS PLAN COVERS- ALL EMPLOYEES	ALL ELIGIBLE	REQ VOL	3Y & 25 9M					5.00%	5.00%		RET	65	70
WESTERN WASHINGTON STATE COL PLAN COVERS- FAC, OFF	ALL ELIGIBLE	REQ VOL	2Y		RANK OF ASSOC PROF	FIRST $4800 BAL		4.50% 7.50%	4.50% 7.50%		RET	67	70
WESTMAR COL, IA PLAN COVERS- FAC, OFF	ALL ELIGIBLE	VOL	IMMED					5.00%	5.00%		RET	65	70
WESTMINSTER CHOIR COL, N J PLAN COVERS- FAC, OFF	ALL ELIGIBLE	REQ	2Y & 30					10.00%	5.00%		65	65	70
WESTMINSTER COL, PA PLAN COVERS- ALL EMPLOYEES	ASSOC PROF & ABOVE & EQUIV OFF	REQ	1Y					7.50%	5.00%		RET	65	70
	ASST PROF & INSTR	REQ	3Y					7.50%	5.00%		RET	65	70
	OTHER	VOL	3Y					7.50%	5.00%		RET	65	70
WESTMINSTER COL, UTAH PLAN COVERS- ALL EMPLOYEES	FAC, OFF	VOL	IMMED					5.00%	5.00%		RET	65	70
	CLER & SEC, MAINT & SERV	VOL	2Y					5.00%	5.00%		RET	65	70
WESTMONT COL, CALIF PLAN COVERS- FAC, OFF	ALL ELIGIBLE	REQ VOL	5Y & 30 2Y					7.00%	3.00%		RET	65	70
WHEATON COL, ILL PLAN COVERS- ALL EMPLOYEES	ALL ELIGIBLE	VOL	1Y & 30				VCL AD	3.00% 3.00%	3.00% 3.00%		65	65	NL
WHEATON COL, MASS PLAN COVERS- FAC, OFF & DESIG CL	ALL ELIGIBLE	REQ VOL	3Y		RANK OF ASST PROF	FIRST $7800 BAL		5.00% 7.50%	5.00% 5.00%		RET	65	NL
WHEELING COL, W VA PLAN COVERS- ALL EMPLOYEES	FAC, OFF	REQ VOL	3Y & 30 IMMED					5.00%	5.00%		RET	65	70
	OTHER	VOL	4Y & 30					5.00%	5.00%		RET	65	70
WHEELOCK COL, MASS PLAN COVERS- FAC, OFF, CLER & SEC	ALL ELIGIBLE	REQ VOL	3Y & 30 1Y & 25					10.00%	.00%		65	65	NX
WHITMAN COL, WASH PLAN COVERS- FAC, OFF	FAC	VOL			TENURE			5.00%	5.00%		RET	65	NX
	OFF	VOL			TENURE			5.00%	5.00%		RET	NL	NA
WHITWORTH COL, WASH PLAN COVERS-	ALL ELIGIBLE	VOL	3Y OR		ON RECOM			5.00%	5.00%		RET	65	NX

CONTINUED ON NEXT PAGE

INSTITUTION	PROVISIONS APPLY TO	REQ &/OR VOL	WAITING PERIOD			TIAA-CREF CONTRIBUTIONS						NOR RET AGE	MAX EXT TO
			TIME	AGE	OTHER	SALARY	AGE	YRS	INST	INDIV	END AT		
WICHITA STATE U, KAN PLAN COVERS- FAC	ALL ELIGIBLE	REQ	2Y						5.00%	5.00%	RET	70	NX
WILBERFORCE U, OHIO PLAN COVERS- ALL EMPLOYEES	FAC	REQ	2Y & 30			FIRST $7800 BAL			5.00% 7.50%	5.00% 7.50%	RET	65	70
	NONACAD PERS	VOL	2Y & 30						5.00%	3.00%	65	65	70
WILKES COL, PA PLAN COVERS- FAC	ALL ELIGIBLE	REQ	2Y						6.00%	5.00%	RET	65	70
WILLAMETTE U, ORE PLAN COVERS- ALL EMPLOYEES	FAC, OFF	REQ VOL	2Y & 30 1Y						6.66%	3.33%	RET	65	70
	OTHER	VOL	4Y & 35						6.66%	3.33%	RET	65	70
WILLIAM PENN COL, IA PLAN COVERS- ALL EMPLOYEES	ALL ELIGIBLE	REQ VOL	3Y & 30 1Y						5.00%	5.00%	RET	65	70
WILLIAM SMITH COL, N Y PLAN COVERS- ALL EMPLOYEES	ALL ELIGIBLE	REQ VOL	IMMED		TENURE				5.00%	5.00%	RET	70	72
WILLIAMS COL, MASS PLAN COVERS- FAC, OFF	ASST PROF & ABOVE	REQ	IMMED						10.00%	5.00%	RET	65	68
	OTHER FAC & OFF	REQ VOL	3Y IMMED						10.00%	5.00%	RET	65	68
WILMINGTON COL, OHIO PLAN COVERS- FAC, OFF	ALL ELIGIBLE	REQ VOL	5Y IMMED						5.00%	5.00%	65	65	NL
WILSON COL, PA PLAN COVERS- FAC, OFF & DESIG CL	ASST PROF & ABOVE & EQUIV OFF	REQ	IMMED						7.50%	7.50%	RET	65	70
	OTHER	REQ	2Y & 30						7.50%	7.50%	RET	65	70
WINDHAM COL, VT PLAN COVERS- ALL EMPLOYEES	FAC	VOL	IMMED						10.00%	5.00%	RET	65	70
	OTHER	REQ VOL	5Y & 30 1Y & 30						5.00%	5.00%	RET	65	70
WITTENBERG U, OHIO PLAN COVERS- FAC, OFF & DESIG CL	ALL ELIGIBLE	REQ VOL	1Y & 26		TENURE				10.00%	5.00%	RET	68	NL
WOFFORD COL, S C PLAN COVERS- FAC, OFF	ALL ELIGIBLE	VOL	2Y						6.00%	5.00%	RET	65	NX
WOMANS MEDICAL COL OF PENNSYLVANIA PLAN COVERS- FAC	ALL ELIGIBLE	REQ	IMMED						5.40%	5.40%	RET	65	71

INSTITUTION	PROVISIONS APPLY TO	REQ &/OR VOL	WAITING PERIOD			TIAA-CREF CONTRIBUTIONS					END AT	NOR RET AGE	MAX EXT TO
			TIME AGE		OTHER	SALARY AGE		YRS	INST	INDIV			
WOOSTER,COL OF, OHIO	FAC	REQ	3Y OR		TENURE				10.00%	.00%	RET	68	NL
PLAN COVERS— ALL EMPLOYEES		VOL	IMMED										
	OFF	REQ	3Y OR		PERM APMT				10.00%	.00%	RET	68	NL
		VOL	IMMED										
	NONACAD	REQ	3Y						10.00%	.00%	RET	65	NL
		VOL	IMMED										
	VOL PARTIC	VOL	IMMED						5.00%	5.00%	RET	68	NL
WORCESTER POLYTECHNIC INSTITUTE, MASS	ALL ELIGIBLE	VOL	IMMED			UP TO VOL AD			4.00% 2.00%	4.00% 1.00%	RET	65	70
PLAN COVERS— FAC, OFF													
XAVIER U, LA	ALL ELIGIBLE	REQ	5Y			FIRST $4800 BAL			7.50% .00%	7.50% .00%	RET	65	70
PLAN COVERS— FAC, OFF													
XAVIER U, OHIO	FAC, OFF	REQ	1Y & 30						5.00%	5.00%	RET	65	70
PLAN COVERS— ALL EMPLOYEES													
	OTHER	REQ	5Y & 30						4.00%	2.00%	RET	65	70
		VOL	3Y										
YALE U, CONN	ASST PROF & ABOVE	REQ	IMMED						10.00%	5.00%	RET	68	NX
PLAN COVERS— FAC, OFF													
	OFF	VOL	IMMED						10.00%	5.00%	RET	68	NX
	OTHER	VOL	IMMED						10.00%	5.00%	RET	68	NX
YANKTON COL, S D	ALL ELIGIBLE	REQ	3Y & 30						5.00%	5.00%	RET	65	70
PLAN COVERS— ALL EMPLOYEES													

Appendix 5

STATE TEACHER AND
PUBLIC EMPLOYEE
RETIREMENT SYSTEMS

This appendix summarizes the principal provisions of the seventy-two state teacher and public employee retirement systems covering employees of institutions of higher education. The provisions described are those currently applicable to new entrants and do not include former or closed out plans. The descriptions have been verified by the executive directors of the respective plans.

The column headings are generally self-explanatory. Member institutions are listed in the first column, along with an indication as to whether the Social Security program covers plan participants. A separate column is devoted to vesting provisions, since the great majority of plans described vest only after participants have met stated service and/or age requirements.

Most of the abbreviations used in this appendix are self-explanatory, except for EE and ER, which mean, respectively, employee and employer.

STATE, PLAN, AND MEMBER INSTITUTIONS	PROVISIONS APPLY TO	REQ &/OR VOL	WAITING PERIOD	CONTRIBUTIONS		PENSION BENEFIT FORMULA	PRERETIREMENT DEATH BENEFIT	VESTING PROVISIONS	RETIREMENT AGE
				INDIV	INST				
ALABAMA: Teachers' Retirement System of Alabama Alabama A & M College Alabama College Alabama State College Auburn U Florence State College Jacksonville State U Livingston State College Troy State College U of Alabama* U of South Alabama* OASDHI	Fac, admin & cler *Faculty covered under TIAA-CREF plan.	Req	None	4% of salary	4% or balance necessary to provide formula benefit, if greater	Highest of: (a) money purchase plan; (b) 1¼% of average of 5 highest salary yrs out of 10 yrs preceding retirement for each yr of serv; (c) $6.00 per month for each yr of serv to a maximum of 25 yrs for classroom teachers; (d) $4.00 per month for each yr of serv to maximum of 25 yrs for nonclassroom teachers.	Return of EE contribs with interest. Disability After 10 yrs serv, annuity based on EE contribs and pension equal to 75% of retirement income payable at age 65, or 75% of formula plan.	Return of EE contribs without interest up to 3 yrs. 50% interest, 3 to 16 yrs; 16 to 21 yrs, 60%; over 21 yrs, 70% interest. Full vesting of ER contribs at age 55 with 10 yrs serv or at any age with 25 yrs serv.	Compulsory at 70; vol at 60. Formula benefit actuarially reduced for retirement under 65.
ALASKA: Teachers' Retirement System U of Alaska OASDHI	Fac, admin & pro staff EE eligible only if he can complete 15 yrs serv by age 65, 10 of which are in Alaska	Req	None	5% optional additional 1% to provide for survivor benefits	Amount equal to ½ EE contribs	1½% of the average salary of the highest 3 yrs serv in the last 10 yrs for each yr of serv. Benefit actuarially reduced for retirement under age 60. Postretirement pension adjustment not to exceed 1½% each yr. Cost of living adjustment for retired teachers remaining in Alaska, 10% of annual retirement benefit.	Return of EE contribs plus $1,000 plus $100 for each yr of serv, plus $500 if one or more children survive but in no event shall the benefit, excluding membership contrib, exceed $3,000. If EE has made optional additional contrib for 1 yr or more, additional monthly benefit for spouse aged 60 or more equal to 50% of retirement income EE would have received had he retired on date of death.	Return of EE contribs, with interest if withdrawal is in 3rd yr or later. After 15 yrs serv, EE may elect to leave contribs on deposit and receive deferred annuity at age 60 or later based on benefit formula. Disability After 5 yrs serv, disability income of 50% of prior base salary plus 10% of salary for each minor child (40% maximum). Income continues to age 60, when it is recomputed as for serv retirement with yrs of disability counted as yrs of serv.	Normal retirement at age 60 with 15 yrs serv. Early retirement after age 55 with 15 yrs serv. No mandatory retirement age.
ARIZONA: Arizona State Retirement System Arizona State U Northern Arizona U U of Arizona OASDHI	All EEs	Req	None	5% of salary	5% of salary, deposited to EEs account	Money purchase	Total annuity accumulation (ER-EE) paid to beneficiary as lump sum or under income option	Return of EE contribs with interest. After 5 yrs, EE may leave contribs on deposit and elect deferred annuity based on ER-EE contribs payable at age 60 or later. Disability After 5 yrs serv, an annuity based on total ER-EE accumulation at date of disability, or $50 per month, whichever is greater.	Normal, age 65. Early, age 60 with 5 yrs serv, with benefit actuarially reduced. Compulsory at age 70.

STATE, PLAN, AND MEMBER INSTITUTIONS	PROVISIONS APPLY TO	REQ &/OR VOL	WAITING PERIOD	CONTRIBUTIONS		PENSION BENEFIT FORMULA	PRERETIREMENT DEATH BENEFIT	VESTING PROVISIONS	RETIREMENT AGE
				INDIV	INST				
ARKANSAS: Arkansas Teachers Retirement System A & M Colleges at Pine Bluff* College Heights Arkansas Polytechnic College* Arkansas State College Arkansas State Teachers College* Henderson State Teachers College* Southern State College* OASDHI	Fac, adm staff, & cler staff (University of Arkansas in TIAA-CREFF plan) *May elect TIAA-CREF as alternate	Req for fac; vol for others	None	5% of first $6,600 of salary	Balance necessary to provide benefit	2% of first $3,500 of final average salary for each yr of serv before July 1, 1957; plus 2% of final average salary up to $5,000 for each yr of serv between July 1, 1957, and July 1, 1961; plus 1¼% of final average salary up to $5,000 for service between July 1, 1961, and July 1, 1965; plus 1¼% of final average salary up to $6,600 for each yr of serv after June 30, 1965. (Final average salary is highest during any 5 consecutive yrs of the 10 yrs preceding retirement.)	Return of EE contribs with interest. After 5 yrs serv, $100 a month to a widow with 1 or 2 children under 18, $150 for 3 or more, to a spouse 62 or over the greater of $50 per month or half EE earned annuity to date; after 15 yrs serv, to widow age 50 or over the greater of $50 per month or half EE earned annuity to date.	Return of EE contribs with interest. After age 60 and 10 yrs serv, or at any age with 25 yrs serv, EE may leave contribs on deposit for deferred annuity based on yrs of serv and final average salary. Disability After 10 yrs serv, benefit formula applied to serv to date of disability.	Normal at age 60 with 10 yrs or more serv (2% formula applies at age 60). Compulsory at age 72.

CALIFORNIA: California State Teachers' Retirement System
 	
California State Colleges at
  Dominguez Hills
  Fullerton
  Hayward
  Kern County (Bakersfield)
  Long Beach
  Los Angeles
  San Bernardino
California State Polytechnic Colleges at
  Pomona (Kellogg-Voorhis)
  San Luis Obispo
Chico State College
Fresno State College
Humbolt State College
Sacramento State College
San Diego State College
San Fernando Valley State College
San Francisco State College
San Jose State College
Sonoma State College
Stanislaus State College
 	
OASDHI
	Fac not in Public Employee's System. All other EEs covered under Public Employee's Retirement System)	Req	None	On basis of sex and age at time of entry into System; for men, ranges from 6.50% at age 25 to 11.09% at age 59 or over	Balance necessary to provide benefits; contrib approximates half the total cost	At age 60, 1/60 of highest average monthly salary of any consecutive 3 yrs for each yr of serv. Actuarially reduced for retirement under age 60, increased to a maximum of 137% of 1/60 at age 65.	(1) Return of EE contribs with interest plus 1/12 of current annual salary for each yr of serv to a maximum of 6.
							(2) If EE is age 55 with 5 yrs serv, monthly benefit in lieu of the above of ½ of retirement EE would have received had he retired instead of died.
							(3) EEs with at least 1 yr of serv and with benefits payable under (1) above are eligible for monthly survivor benefits for spouse with children under 18 (1 child, $180; 2 children, $250), widow or dependent widower age 62 or over ($90), dependent parents ($90).
								Return of EE contribs plus interest. After 5 yrs serv, EE may leave contribs on deposit and elect deferred annuity based on benefit formula.
								
								Disability
								After 5 yrs serv, disability income equal to 1½% of average of highest 3 consecutive yrs of membership. Members with 10 yrs serv guaranteed 25% of final compensation (with certain exceptions).
									Normal retirement at 60 with 5 yrs serv. Early, age 55 with 5 yrs serv. No compulsory age; "tenure" ceases at age 65.

STATE, PLAN, AND MEMBER INSTITUTIONS	PROVISIONS APPLY TO	REQ &/OR VOL	WAITING PERIOD	CONTRIBUTIONS		PENSION BENEFIT FORMULA	PRERETIREMENT DEATH BENEFIT	VESTING PROVISIONS	RETIREMENT AGE
				INDIV	INST				
CALIFORNIA: Public Employee's Retirement System California State Colleges at Dominguez Hills Fullerton Hayward Kern County (Bakersfield) Long Beach Los Angeles San Bernardino California State Polytechnic Colleges at Pomona (Kellogg-Voorhis) San Luis Obispo Chico State College Fresno State College Humboldt State College Sacramento State College San Diego State College San Fernando Valley State College San Francisco State College San Jose State College Sonoma State College Stanislaus State College OASDHI	All EEs (A few EEs—less than 3%—belong to State Teachers' Retirement System, which covers teachers in primary and secondary schools and junior colleges.)	Req	None	Per cent of salary according to age at entry, and sex, e.g., 5.54% for men age 25; 7.95%, age 45. Rate is reduced by 1/3 on first $400 of monthly salary for EEs covered by Social Security.	Balance necessary to provide benefit (7.11% of EE compensation)	EEs covered by Social Security: 1/90 of first $400 of final average salary plus 1/60 of balance times number of yrs serv. EEs not covered by Social Security: 1/60 of final average salary times number of yrs serv. Final average salary is the average of the 3 highest consecutive yrs of membership. Minimum benefit of $100 per month at age 60 with 20 yrs serv.	Basic death benefit: If no qualified survivors, and under age 55, return of EE contribs and interest plus 1 month's salary for each yr of serv to a total of 6, payable in lump sum or monthly installments. EE may prior to death elect life annuity with 120 months certain. If EE was age 55 or over and had 5 yrs serv, qualified survivor may choose basic death benefit or life annuity equal to ½ of EE annuity computed as of date of death.	Deferred right to a future formula benefit occurs when EE contribs total $500, or when EE has 20 or more yrs of serv and contribs and interest remain on deposit. Disability At any age, with EE contribs of $500 or more, or 10 or more yrs of serv: (1) 100% of serv retirement if age 60 or over; (2) if under age 60, 1½% of final average salary per yr of serv extending serv to age 60. Allowance cannot exceed retirement allowance receivable at age 60. If extensions to 60 produce more than 1/3 of final average salary, 1/3 is paid. If actual serv produces more than 1/3, more than 1/3 is paid. No OASDHI offset.	With $500 contrib or 20 yrs serv: Minimum age 55, actuarially reduced; normal age 60; actuarial increase to age 65; compulsory at age 70.
COLORADO: Public Employees' Retirement Association of Colorado Adams State College Colorado School of Mines Colorado State College Colorado State U Fort Lewis College Metropolitan State College Southern Colorado State College U of Colorado (nonacademic EEs) Western State College of Colorado No OASDHI	All EEs (Fac & adm off of U of Colorado covered by TIAA-CREF)	Req	None	6% of salary including overtime and pay for additional duties	6% of salary (not credited to individual accounts)	2½% of average salary of highest 5 consecutive yrs within last 10 yrs of serv times number of yrs of serv not to exceed 20 yrs. Reduction for those retiring prior to 60 if annuity exceeds $300 per month.	Return of EE contribs without interest. If 3 yrs of more of serv, dependent widow with children under 18 receives $200 per month. Widow without children under 18 receives at age 62 annuity of approximately 25% of final average EE salary depending on serv and salary. If 15 yrs or more serv, widow receives at age 50 annuity of approximately 25% of final average EE salary depending on serv and salary.	Less than 5 yrs serv, return of EE contribs. After 5 yrs, EE may elect to leave contribs on deposit and receive at age 65 or over annuity based on pension benefit formula. Disability Benefits payable if EE has 15 yrs consecutive serv. If at least 5 yrs serv, benefits payable for serv incurred disability.	Age 65 with 5 to 20 yrs serv; age 60 or higher with 20 or more yrs serv; age 55 with 30 yrs serv.

STATE, PLAN, AND MEMBER INSTITUTIONS	PROVISIONS APPLY TO	REQ &/OR VOL	WAITING PERIOD	CONTRIBUTIONS		PENSION BENEFIT FORMULA	PRERETIREMENT DEATH BENEFIT	VESTING PROVISIONS	RETIREMENT AGE
				INDIV	INST				
CONNECTICUT: Connecticut Teachers' Retirement System Central Connecticut State College Eastern Connecticut State College Hartford State Technical Institute Norwalk State Technical Institute Southern Connecticut State College U of Connecticut Waterbury State Technical Institute Western Connecticut State College No OASDHI	Fac (optional participation in State Employees Retirement System)	Req	None	6% of salary	Balance needed to provide benefit	40% of highest 3 yrs average salary for 20 yrs serv plus 2% for each yr thereafter (75% maximum). For serv under 20 yrs at age 65-70, 2% formula reduced by 0.1% for each yr under 20.	If 5 yrs serv or less, $500. Over 5 yrs serv, $500 plus $100 per yr of serv over 5 ($1,000 maximum) plus, for eligible survivors and dependents, annual benefit to widow of $1,500 and benefits to dependent children, with total family benefits not to exceed $300 per month. If no eligible survivors, EE contribs plus interest paid to beneficiary or estate.	Vested rights after 10 yrs Connecticut serv payable at age 60. Disability After 10 yrs serv, 1/65 of highest 3 yrs average salary for each yr of serv to date of disability.	Age 60 with 20 yrs Connecticut serv. Any age with 35 yrs serv. Actuarially reduced benefits for retirement under age 60 after 25 yrs serv.
CONNECTICUT: State Employees Retirement System Central Connecticut State College Eastern Connecticut State College Hartford State Technical Institute Norwalk State Technical Institute Southern Connecticut State College U of Connecticut Waterbury State Technical Institute Western Connecticut State College No OASDHI	All EEs Fac may join either Teachers' Retirement System or State Employees System	Req	None	EEs not covered by Social Security, 5%. EEs covered by Social Security, 2% on OASDHI earnings base, 5% above.	Balance necessary to provide benefit	After 25 yrs serv, 25% of average salary on which OASDHI taxes were paid (but not over $4,800 regardless of the OASDHI maximum) or would have been paid were he eligible for and included in OASDHI coverage during the 10 yrs preceding retirement, plus 50% of balance of average salary for 3 highest paid yrs. For serv in excess of 25 yrs, the percentage on the OASDHI base salary (up to $4,800) will be increased 1% and the percentage on salary above will be increased 2% for each additional yr. The above applies at age 65. The full 50% of the base salary is paid until that age.	Return of EE contribs without interest	Return of EE contribs without interest. After 10 yrs serv, EE may elect to leave contribs on deposit for deferred annuity at age 50 for a woman, or age 55 for a man, or later, based on benefit formula. Disability Nonoccupational: after 10 yrs serv, benefit formula is applied to yrs of serv to date of disability. No serv requirement for occupational disability.	With 25 or more yrs of serv, compulsory at 70, and voluntary for men at 55, for women at 50. Less than 25 yrs of serv, compulsory at 70, and voluntary for men at age 60 with 10 yrs serv; for women at 65 with 5 yrs serv, or at 55 with 10 yrs serv.
DELAWARE: Delaware State Retirement System Delaware State College U of Delaware* OASDHI	All EEs *Fac & adm off participate in supplementary plan at age 40 with TIAA-CREF or New England Mutual.	Req	None	5% on salary between $6,000 and $12,000	Amount necessary to purchase benefit	1/60 of average monthly salary during last 5 yrs for each yr of serv. Minimum of $150 and maximum of $500 monthly benefit.	Return of EE contribs without interest. After 15 yrs serv, benefit to spouse of ½ of benefit EE entitled to had he retired instead of died.	Return of EE contribs without interest. Disability After 15 yrs of serv, benefit based on application of retirement formula to yrs of serv to date of disability, not reduced actuarially for yrs under normal retirement age.	Compulsory at age 70; voluntary at age 60 with 15 yrs serv, or at any age with 30 yrs serv.

STATE, PLAN, AND MEMBER INSTITUTIONS	PROVISIONS APPLY TO	REQ &/OR VOL	WAITING PERIOD	CONTRIBUTIONS		PENSION BENEFIT FORMULA	PRERETIREMENT DEATH BENEFIT	VESTING PROVISIONS	RETIREMENT AGE
				INDIV	INST				
FLORIDA: Teachers' Retirement System Florida A & M U Florida Atlantic U Florida State U U of Florida U of South Florida No OASDHI	Fac & adm personnel	Req	None	6% (¼% additional for survivors' benefit fund)	Balance necessary to provide benefit	2% of average of highest 10 yrs salary (out of final 15 yrs serv) for each yr of serv.	Return of EE contribs with interest. Survivor's benefit: $500; additional $250 per month if survived by 2 or more children under age 18. After 1 day's serv or, if widow age 65, 10 yrs serv, widow receives $100 a month beginning at age 50, plus return of EE contribs. If EE is eligible for retirement, beneficiary receives annuity based on survivor option for EE retirement benefit.	Refund of EE contribs with interest. Full vesting of ER contribs after 10 yrs serv. Disability After 10 yrs serv, minimum benefit of 25% of final average salary; maximum benefit of amount EE would have received had he continued to age 55 and retired.	Normal at age 62 to receive 2% benefit formula. Compulsory at age 70. Reduced formula benefit available at age 55 with 10 yrs serv.
GEORGIA: Teachers' Retirement System of Georgia Abraham Baldwin Agr College Albany State College Armstrong State College Brunswick College Columbus College Fort Valley State College Georgia Institute of Technology Georgia Southern College Georgia Southwestern College Georgia State College Medical College of Georgia Middle Georgia College North Georgia College Savannah State College South Georgia College U of Georgia Valdosta State College West Georgia College Woman's College of Georgia OASDHI	All EEs	Req	None	6% of salary	8½% of aggregate salary of covered EEs, not credited to individual accounts	1¾% of average salary of highest 5 consecutive yrs for each yr of serv up to 40 yrs	Return of EE contribs with no interest under 5 yrs, ¾ of credited interest between 5 and 15 yrs, and full interest after 15 yrs. After 15 yrs serv or eligibility for retirement, survivor annuity based on benefit formula and age of beneficiary. Disability After 15 yrs serv before age 65, benefit formula is applied to yrs of serv to date without actuarial reduction for yrs EE is under age 65.	Return of EE contribs with interest as under death benefit. After 20 yrs serv, EE may elect to leave contribs in plan and receive deferred annuity at age 60 based on benefit formula.	Normal at age 63. Benefit actuarially reduced for retirement under 63. Early retirement at age 55 with 35 yrs serv or age 60 with 10 yrs serv.

STATE, PLAN, AND MEMBER INSTITUTIONS	PROVISIONS APPLY TO	REQ &/OR VOL	WAITING PERIOD	CONTRIBUTIONS		PENSION BENEFIT FORMULA	PRERETIREMENT DEATH BENEFIT	VESTING PROVISIONS	RETIREMENT AGE
				INDIV	INST				
HAWAII: Employees' Retirement System of Hawaii U of Hawaii OASDHI	All EEs	Req	None	6½% of salary	Actuarially determined	At age 55 or higher, 2% of average of highest 5 yrs salary for each yr of serv. Benefit actuarially reduced for retirement under age 55. Automatic annual increase of benefit of 1½% to provide postretirement living cost adjustment.	(1) Return of EE contribs with interest. (2) If 1 to 10 yrs serv, additional lump sum equal to ½ of previous yrs salary. (3) If over 10 yrs serv, additional benefit of 5% of salary for each yr of serv over 10, up to 1 yrs salary. (4) If EE is age 55 with 5 yrs serv, or has had 25 yrs serv, spouse may elect income option payable as if EE had retired. (5) If death is due to serv-connected accident, EE contribs are returned with interest and a pension of ½ final average salary (regardless of age or serv) is paid to widow, or if no widow to children under 18, or if no children to dependent parents. In no event does beneficiary receive less than a yrs salary inclusive of contribs.	Return of EE contribs plus interest. After 5 yrs serv EE may leave contribs on deposit and elect deferred annuity beginning at age 55, based on benefit formula. Disability (1) Nonserv-connected disability benefit after 10 yrs serv. Allowance is 25% of average final salary plus 1% for each yr of serv beyond 15. (2) Serv-connected disability benefit is 66 2/3% of salary offset by Social Security and Workmen's Compensation benefits.	Voluntary at age 55 with 5 yrs service, or at any age on completion of 25 yrs serv. Compulsory at age 70.
IDAHO: Public Employee Retirement System of Idaho Idaho State U U of Idaho OASDHI	All EEs	Req	1 yr	3% of 1st $400 of monthly salary. 6% of monthly salary above $400.	7.5% of gross EE salary.	Membership service. Annual allowance equal to 1/3 of EEs total contribs to the plan, exclusive of interest	Return of EE contribs with interest. (Separate group life insurance furnished by state.) Disability After 10 yrs credited serv, disability income (service or nonserv-connected) equal to the retirement income that would have been paid had EE continued serv to age 65. 6-month waiting period. Workmen's Compensation deductible.	Return of EE contribs with interest for separation before vesting. After 10 yrs membership serv, EE may leave contribs on deposit and elect benefit at age 55 or after based on actuarial equivalent of accrued serv retirement allowance.	Age 65 with 5 yrs serv including 6 months membership serv. Serv may be extended annually with ER consent to July 1 following attainment of age 70. Early retirement at age 55 with 5 yrs serv, including 6 months membership serv, benefit actuarially reduced.

STATE, PLAN, AND MEMBER INSTITUTIONS	PROVISIONS APPLY TO	REQ &/OR VOL	WAITING PERIOD	CONTRIBUTIONS		PENSION BENEFIT FORMULA	PRERETIREMENT DEATH BENEFIT	VESTING PROVISIONS	RETIREMENT AGE
				INDIV	INST				
INDIANA: Indiana State Teachers' Retirement Fund Ball State U* Indiana State U** OASDHI	Fac (other EEs participate in Public Employes' Retirement Fund). *May elect TIAA-CREF as alternate or supplement. **Fac & adm off also participate in TIAA-CREF supplementary plan.	Req	None	3% of salary up to $8,500	Balance necessary to provide benefit	Money purchase annuity provided by EE contribs, plus pension of 0.6% of salary over any 5-yr period up to $3,000 and 1.1% of all earnings above $3,000 using the best 5-yr period or average since April 1, 1959, times yrs of serv. Any serv in excess of 40 yrs earned before age 65 is credited as 1½ times actual serv.	If EE has less than 15 yrs of serv, return of EE contribs with interest to beneficiary. After 15 yrs serv, survivor benefit for spouse (married 3 or more yrs) based on benefits earned to date of death.	Return of EE contribs with interest. After 10 yrs serv EE may leave contribs on deposit and receive deferred annuity based on benefit formula. EE aged 50 with 15 yrs serv must leave contribs on deposit for deferred annuity. Disability EE with 7 yrs of creditable serv is eligible for disability benefit of $100 per month plus $1 per month for each yr of serv above 7 yrs.	Normal age 65, with minimum of 10 yrs of serv, extensions to age 70. Early retirement at age 50 with 15 yrs of serv. Benefits actuarially reduced for retirement under age 65.
INDIANA: Public Employes' Retirement Fund Ball State U* Indiana State U** Indiana U*** Purdue U*** OASDHI	EEs not elegible for Indiana Teachers' Retirement Fund *TIAA-CREF supplementary plan for fac & adm off. **TIAA-CREF alternate or supplementary plan for fac & off. ***Only nonpro EEs in state plan; all others are in TIAA-CREF plan.	Req	Vol immediately; req after 1 yr.	3% of first $8,500 annual salary	Balance necessary to provide pension benefit	Money purchase annuity from EE contribs, plus pension based on highest 5 yr salary over last 10 yrs: 0.6% of first $3,000 of average salary plus 1.1% of balance times number of yrs of credited serv.	Return of EE contribs plus interest. After 15 yrs serv, survivor benefit for spouse (if married 3 yrs) based on benefit earned to date of death.	Return of EE contribs with interest if not eligible for retirement. After 10 yrs serv, EE may leave contribs on deposit for deferred annuity based on benefit formula. If age 50 with 15 yrs serv, contribs must be left on deposit for deferred annuity. Disability After 10 yrs of serv, EE eligible for disability benefit of $70 per month plus $1 per month for each additional yr of serv over 10 yrs. Receives retirement benefit based on actual serv if disabled to age 65.	Normal, age 65 with minimum of 10 yrs serv. Early retirement permitted at age 50 with 15 yrs of serv. Benefit actuarially reduced for retirement under 65.
IOWA: Public Employees' Retirement System Iowa State U U of Iowa U of Northern Iowa OASDHI	Nonfac, nonadm staff (Fac & adm off participate in TIAA-CREF plan). All EEs of U of Iowa and Iowa State U participate in TIAA-CREF plan, except EEs under stated salary level.	Req	None	3½% of 1st $7,000	3½% of 1st $7,000	1¼% of average annual salary times yrs of covered serv	Return of EE and ER contribs with interest	Return of EE contribs with interest. After 8 yrs serv or attainment of age 55, EE may leave contribs on deposit for deferred formula annuity at age 55 or later. Disability Early retirement at age 55 or later, based on benefit formula actuarially reduced for ages under 65.	Normal age 65 with at least 5 yrs serv. Benefit actuarially reduced for retirement under 65. Compulsory at age 70 with provision for annual extensions. If less than 5 yrs serv, money purchase benefit substituted for formula.

STATE, PLAN, AND MEMBER INSTITUTIONS	PROVISIONS APPLY TO	REQ &/OR VOL	WAITING PERIOD	CONTRIBUTIONS		PENSION BENEFIT FORMULA	PRERETIREMENT DEATH BENEFIT	VESTING PROVISIONS	RETIREMENT AGE
				INDIV	INST				
KANSAS: Public Employees' Retirement System Fort Hays Kansas State College Kansas State College of Pittsburg Kansas State Teachers College Kansas State U U of Kansas Wichita State U OASDHI	Non-academic staff (Fac in TIAA-CREF plan)	Req	1 yr	4% of salary	4.5% of payroll	1% of final average salary for each yr of serv. Final average salary is the average of highest 5 of last 10 yrs of serv.	Return of EE contribs with interest. Lump sum life insurance benefit of 50% of final average salary if member under age 61. Insured benefit reduced between 61 and 65. No insured benefit after 65. Serv-connected: survivor annuity of 50% of final average salary to widow. Nonserv-connected: if member was age 60 or over with at least 10 yrs serv, either EE contribs with interest or survivor annuity to widow based on serv to date of death.	Return of EE contribs with interest. After 10 yrs serv, EE may leave contribs on deposit for deferred annuity based on formula, payable at age 60 or later. Disability Serv-connected: 50% of final average salary for life. Nonserv-connected: insured disability benefit of 42% of final average salary payable after EE totally disabled for 180 days. Also continued life insurance coverage at no cost to member and serv credit while disabled.	Normal retirement at 65. Early retirement at 60 with 10 yrs serv. Mandatory retirement at 70, with provision for extension. Formula benefit actuarially reduced for retirement below age 65.
KENTUCKY: Kentucky Employes Retirement System Eastern Kentucky U Kentucky State College Morehead State U Murray State U U of Kentucky* Western Kentucky U OASDHI	EEs other than fac & adm staff (fac & adm staff in Teachers' Retirement System, except in U of Kentucky). *Fac & others with educationally related duties covered under TIAA-CREF plan.	Req	None	4% of salary	Balance necessary to fund benefit	1.47% of average of highest 5 yrs annual compensation times yrs of serv	Refund of EE contribs with interest. After 8 yrs, survivor (spouse or dependent) benefits based on retirement annuity earned to date of death. Disability (1) Serv-connected: after 8 yrs serv, benefit formula applied to yrs of serv to date of disability without actuarial reduction for age below 65. (2) Nonserv-connected: after 8 yrs serv same as (1) except benefit is reduced actuarially for age below 65.	Return of EE contribs with interest. After 8 yrs, EE may leave contribs on deposit for deferred annuity based on benefit formula.	Normal, 65. Early, at age 55 with minimum of 8 yrs of serv, with benefit actuarially reduced.

STATE, PLAN, AND MEMBER INSTITUTIONS	PROVISIONS APPLY TO	REQ &/OR VOL	WAITING PERIOD	CONTRIBUTIONS		PENSION BENEFIT FORMULA	PRERETIREMENT DEATH BENEFIT	VESTING PROVISIONS	RETIREMENT AGE
				INDIV	INST				
KENTUCKY: Teachers' Retirement System of the State of Kentucky Eastern Kentucky U Kentucky State College Morehead State U Murray State U Western Kentucky U 　OASDHI	Fac & adm EEs (Fac & others educationally related duties at U of Kentucky covered under TIAA–CREF plan.)	Req	None	7% of salary	7% of aggregate salary, not credited to individual accounts	2% of average annual salary for the highest 5 yrs. 1% annual automatic increase in benefit after retirement.	$1,000 plus refund of EE contribs with interest. After 3 yrs serv, beneficiary may elect survivors benefits in lieu of refund: Spouse　　　$100 1 child　　　100 2 children　　160 3 children　　185 4 children　　195 (Reduced by income from other sources in excess of $2,400 per yr.)	Return of EE contribs with interest. After 10 yrs serv, EE may elect to leave contribs on deposit and receive deferred annuity at age 60 based on formula. Disability After 10 yrs serv, benefit of 50% of final average salary. EE entitled to 1 yr of disability income for every 4 yrs serv, minimum of 5 yrs income.	Any age after 30 yrs serv; age 60 and 10 yrs serv; age 70, any amount of serv. Actuarial reduction for ages under 60.
LOUISIANA: Teachers' Retirement System of Louisiana Francis T. Nicholls State College Grambling College Louisiana Polytechnic Institute Louisiana State U McNeese State College Northeast Louisiana State College Northwestern State College of Louisiana Southeastern Louisiana College Southern U and A & M College U of Southwestern Louisiana 　No OASDHI	Fac (others covered by State Employees' Retirement System)	Req under age 50 if certain serv conditions are met	None	Plan A: 7% of salary that does not exceed $7,500 per yr. Plan B: 7% of salary that does not exceed $16,000 per yr.	Balance necessary to provide benefit	(1) Money purchase benefit from accumulation, plus* (2) pension which together with (1) provides 2% of final average salary times number of yrs of serv limited to 37½ yrs, plus (3) a pension of $150 per yr or as much thereof as may be needed to provide not over $2,400 per yr. Final average salary is average of highest 5 consecutive yrs of annual salary on which contribs are made up to $7,500 per yr under Plan A and $16,000 per yr under Plan B. *Other supplemental benefits are provided for members whose retirement income is less than $2,640 per yr.	Return of EE contribs with interest. After 30 yrs serv and age 55, survivor option available to beneficiary.	Over 20 yrs of serv, EE may leave contribs in System and receive deferred annuity and pension beginning at age 60. Disability After 5 yrs of serv: (1) money purchase benefit on member's accumulation, plus (2) pension equal to 75% of the pension that would have been paid had member remained in serv until age 60.	Compulsory at age 68; optional at age 60 with 15 yrs serv; or age 55 with 30 yrs serv. ER may terminate EE serv at end of any fiscal yr following 65th birthday. Formula benefit actuarially reduced for retirement under age 60 under certain conditions.
LOUISIANA: State Employees' Retirement System Francis T. Nicholls State College Grambling College Louisiana Polytechnic Institute Louisiana State U McNeese State College Northeast Louisiana State College Northwestern State College of Louisiana Southeastern Louisiana College Southern U and A & M College U of Southwestern Louisiana 　No OASDHI	All EEs except fac who are covered under the Teachers' Retirement System of Louisiana	Req	None	6% of salary	Balance necessary to provide benefit	(1) Money purchase benefit provided by member's accumulation; and (2) an ER annuity which together with the member's annuity shall equal: 2% of average compensation (highest average compensation during any period of of 60 consecutive months) for each yr of credited serv, plus the sum of $300.	Return of EE contribs with interest, except: after 5 yrs, child or children under 18 or spouse with care of such child or children receives 75% of average compensation to maximum of $150 monthly. After 15 yrs, monthly benefit of 50% of average compensation (maximum $100 monthly) to widow at age 50. With 25 yrs serv or if member was age 60 or older, surviving spouse receives annuity as if member had retired under annuity with survivorship option. Reduced by 3% for each yr member was under age 55.	Return of EE contribs with interest. Over 15 yrs, EE may leave contribs on deposit for deferred annuity and pension at age 60 or later. Disability After 10 yrs serv: (1) money purchase benefit from EE contribs and (2) 75% of earned retirement allowance as if EE had continued serv to age 60.	Normal at age 65; compulsory at age 70. Early retirement at age 60 with 10 yrs of serv or age 55 with 30 yrs of serv. Formula benefit actuarially reduced for retirement under age 60.

STATE, PLAN, AND MEMBER INSTITUTIONS	PROVISIONS APPLY TO	REQ &/OR VOL	WAITING PERIOD	CONTRIBUTIONS		PENSION BENEFIT FORMULA	PRERETIREMENT DEATH BENEFIT	VESTING PROVISIONS	RETIREMENT AGE
				INDIV	INST				
MAINE: Maine State Retirement System Aroostook State College* Farmington State College* Fort Kent State College* Gorham State College* Maine Maritime Academy Washington State College* No OASDHI	All EEs *Applies only to EEs hired before May 27, 1968. Fac & off hired after that date participate in TIAA-CREF, other EEs in U of Maine self-administered plan. EEs hired before May 27, 1968, may elect to remain in State Retirement System or to come into TIAA-CREF (fac and off) or self-administered plan (other EEs).	Req	None	5% of salary	Balance necessary to provide benefit	1/70 of average annual salary during highest 5 yrs compensation for each yr of serv.	Return of EE contribs with interest. After 10 yrs serv, $100 per month paid to spouse to death or remarriage. For children under 18 (22 if full-time students) additional monthly benefit of $100 for 1 child, $150 for 2, $200 for 3. After age 60 or 30 yrs serv, survivor benefit based on earned retirement benefit to date of death	Return of EE contribs plus interest. After 10 yrs serv, EE may elect to leave contribs on deposit and receive deferred annuity at age 60 or later based on benefit formula. Disability With 10 yrs serv or over, 25% of average salary during highest 5 yrs preceding disability or, if greater, 90% of 1/70 of average final salary for each yr of serv to date of disability. Refigured at age 60 to determine if higher allowance applicable. If disability is serv-connected, benefit is 2/3 of final average salary, and there is no serv requirement.	Compulsory at 70; vol at age 60 or after 30 yrs serv. Benefit actuarially reduced for retirement under age 60.
MARYLAND: Employees' Retirement System of the State of Maryland Bowie State College Coppin State College Frostburg State College Morgan State College Salisbury State College Towson State College U of Maryland OASDHI	Nonfac EEs	Req	None	Percentage varying according to age of entry and sex, e.g., for males, ranges from 5.65% at age 30 to 7.40% at ages 59 and over	Balance necessary to provide benefit	Money purchase benefit provided by EE contribs plus pension of 1/140 of average final compensation for each yr of creditable serv. (Average final compensation is average of the 5 highest consecutive yrs of salary.) Minimum benefit of 1/70 of average final compensation for each yr of serv.	Return of EE contribs with interest; if over 1 yr of serv, amount in addition equal to 50% of average annual compensation or, if eligible for serv retirement or age 55 with 15 yrs serv, survivor benefit to spouse based on benefits earned to date of death.	Return of EE contribs with interest. After 20 yrs serv, EE may leave contribs in plan for deferred money purchase and pension benefit. Disability 5 yrs serv and under age 60, allowance equals 1/70 of average final compensation for each yr of serv, minimum of ¼ of average final compensation.	Normal, 60; compulsory, 70; optional, 30 yrs of serv regardless of age. Benefit actuarially reduced for ages under 60. No reduction with 35 yrs.
MARYLAND: Teachers' Retirement System of the State of Maryland Bowie State College Coppin State College Frostburg State College Morgan State College Salisbury State College Towson State College U of Maryland OASDHI	Fac	Req	None	Percentage varying according to age of entry and sex, e.g., for males, ranges from 5.60% at age 30 to 8.25% at ages 59 and over	Balance necessary to provide benefit	Money purchase benefit provided by EE contribs plus pension of 1/140 of average final compensation for each yr of creditable serv. (Average final compensation is average of the 5 highest consecutive yrs of salary.) Minimum benefit of 1/70 of average final compensation for each yr of serv.	Return of EE contribs with interest; if over 1 yr of serv, amount in addition equal to 50% of average annual compensation or, if eligible for service retirement or age 55 with 15 yrs serv, survivor benefit to spouse based on benefits earned to date of death.	Return of EE contribs with interest. After 20 yrs serv, EE may leave contribs on deposit for deferred money purchase annuity and pension. Disability 5 yrs serv and under age 60, allowance equals 1/70 of average final compensation for each yr of serv, minimum of ¼ of average final compensation.	Normal, 60; compulsory, 70; optional, 30 yrs of serv regardless of age. Benefit actuarially reduced for ages under 60. No reduction with 35 yrs.

STATE, PLAN, AND MEMBER INSTITUTIONS	PROVISIONS APPLY TO	REQ &/OR VOL	WAITING PERIOD	CONTRIBUTIONS		PENSION BENEFIT FORMULA	PRERETIREMENT DEATH BENEFIT	VESTING PROVISIONS	RETIREMENT AGE
				INDIV	INST				
MASSACHUSETTS: The State Board of Retirement/State Teachers Retirement Board Lowell Technological Institute Massachusetts College of Art Massachusetts Maritime Academy Southeastern Massachusetts Technological Institute State Colleges at Boston Bridgewater Fitchburg Framingham Lowell North Adams Salem Westfield Worcester U of Massachusetts No OASDHI	Fac, State Teachers Retirement Board. All other EEs, the State Board of Retirement	Req	None. Persons initially employed at age 60 or over not eligible.	5% of salary	Balance necessary to provide benefit	At age 65 or over, 2.5% of average of highest 3 yrs of annual compensation times yrs of serv not to exceed 80% of the 3-yr average annual salary	Refund of EE contribs with interest or beneficiary may receive retirement allowance of 2/3 of the amount the EE would have received under the Joint and Last Survivor provisions to which member should have been entitled had he retired. Or, widow of male member, $100 per month; 1st child, $50 per month; each additional child, $35 per month. Children's benefits cease at age 18. Widow's continues unless she remarries. Or, child or children of female member: 1 child, $50 per month; each additional child, $35 per month. Benefits cease at age 18.	Refund of EE contribs with interest. After age 55, EE is eligible for retirement benefit and may not withdraw his contribs. Disability Nonserv-connected: after 15 yrs serv (10 yrs if a veteran), 1.5% of average of highest 5 yrs of annual compensation times yrs of serv to date of disability. Serv-connected: 2/3 of salary plus an annuity based on EE contribs plus $312 annually for each child until attainment of age 18, but not totaling more than 100% of salary.	Compulsory at 70; optional at 55, or before age 55 with at least 20 yrs serv. Benefit actuarially reduced for retirement under age 65.
MICHIGAN: Board of Trustees Retirement Plan Michigan State U OASDHI	Non-academic EEs not covered by TIAA-CREF* (EEs hired over age 53 not eligible) *All other EEs covered by TIAA-CREF.	Req	None	None	Amount required to provide benefit	1% of average of highest 5 yrs annual salary for 1st 10 yrs of employment and 2% for each yr thereafter. Maximum $3,000.	None, unless death occurs after the first day of July following date of EEs 65th birthday. After such date, survivor benefit for spouse based on benefit earned to date of death.	None Disability After 15 yrs serv, pension based on formula application to yrs of serv to date of disability.	At any age following 25 yrs serv. Benefit actuarially reduced for retirement under age 65. Normal, age 65. Compulsory, age 68.
MICHIGAN: Michigan Public School Employees' Retirement Fund Central Michigan U Eastern Michigan U Ferris State College Northern Michigan U Western Michigan U OASDHI	All EEs Michigan State U—fac & adm staff in TIAA-CREF. Other EEs in U Board of Trustees Retirement Plan. U of Michigan—fac & off and other designated nonacademics with salaries above $10,000 are in the TIAA-CREF plan. Other EEs in U of Michigan Employees Retirement Plan (see self-administered plans). Wayne State U—all EEs in TIAA-CREF. Grand Valley State College—fac & off in TIAA-CREF plan; others in self-administered plan.	Req	None	3% up to $4,200 of salary; 5% above	11% of total payroll, not credited to individual accounts	1% of 1st $4,200 of salary plus 1½% of excess for each yr of serv. Salary base is computed as average for highest 5 consecutive yrs.	Return of EE contribs with interest. After 15 yrs serv, a survivor allowance is payable to wife and dependents based on benefit earned to date of death. Disability After 10 yrs serv, EE receives normal retirement benefit based on serv to date of disability, not reduced for age.	Return of EE contribs with interest. After 10 yrs serv and age 50, or 25 yrs at any age, EE may leave contribs on deposit for deferred formula annuity at age 60 or later.	Age 60 and 10 or more yrs of serv; at age 55 and 30 or more yrs serv, with benefits actuarially reduced for ages below 60.

STATE, PLAN, AND MEMBER INSTITUTIONS	PROVISIONS APPLY TO	REQ &/OR VOL	WAITING PERIOD	CONTRIBUTIONS		PENSION BENEFIT FORMULA	PRERETIREMENT DEATH BENEFIT	VESTING PROVISIONS	RETIREMENT AGE
				INDIV	INST				
MINNESOTA: Minnesota State Retirement System U of Minnesota Bemidji State College Mankato State College Moorhead State College St. Cloud State College OASDHI	Non-academic EES (Fac & adm staff in Minnesota Teachers Retirement Association.) (All fac EEs of U of Minnesota in Northwestern National Minnesota Mutual plan. All Civil Service EEs of U of Minnesota covered by State Retirement System.)	Req	None	3% of salary for EEs under Social Security or 6% of salary for EEs not under Social Security	Amount equal to EE amount plus additional 2/3 of such amount for EEs paying 3% or additional 1/6 for EEs paying 6%	Average salary times 1% per yr of serv for first 10 yrs, plus 1% per yr of serv for second 10 yrs or completed months of serv, plus 1.66% per yr of serv for third 10 yrs or completed months, plus 1.75% per yr of serv for subsequent yrs or completed months of serv. Actuarially reduced if retirement before age 65. Same formula applies to those not under Social Security but percentages are 1%, 2%, 2½%, and 3%, respectively.	Return of EE contribs with interest. For EEs not under Social Security with 18 months of serv, dependent spouse receives monthly 30% of average monthly salary not to exceed $65 plus 20% of average monthly salary for each minor child, not to exceed $45 per month. Maximum of $250 monthly. After age 55 and 10 yrs serv, dependent spouse receives survivor annuity based on EEs earned benefit to date of death.	Return of EE contribs without interest. Deferred annuity payable at age 65 with 10 yrs serv based on EE and ER contribs. Disability Benefit of 50% of average salary, not reduced if EE has at least 10 yrs serv and disabled prior to age 65.	Age 65 with 10 yrs serv or age 58 with 20 yrs serv. Formula benefit actuarially reduced for retirement under 65. Compulsory at age 70.
MINNESOTA: Teachers Retirement Association Bemidji State College Mankato State College Moorhead State College St. Cloud State College Winona State College Southwest Minnesota State College OASDHI	Fac & adm staff (Other EEs in Minnesota State Retirement System.) (All EEs of U of Minnesota in Northwestern National Minnesota Mutual Plan.) Supplemental Retirement Fund for certain personnel employed by State College Board.	Req	None	3% of salary Individual must make additional contribs of up to $450 per yr (5% of salary between $6,000 and $15,000) which are matched by the State, and paid into a separate Minnesota Supplementary Retirement Fund, under which EE may elect "income" or "growth" share accounts, with accumulated funds payable at retirement in cash or as a fixed-dollar annuity.	4½% of salary	Money purchase	Return of EE contribs plus interest, or after age 55 and 20 yrs serv, or 30 yrs serv at any age, member may elect a joint and survivor annuity for a dependent spouse.	Return of EE contribs without interest. Benefits vest after 10 yrs serv, with deferred annuity payable at age 55 or later. Disability After 10 yrs serv, or after 5 yrs serv and age 50, benefit of double the benefit that EE contribs would have purchased had he continued employment to age 65. In the new Supplemental Retirement Fund, full vesting is possible at death or disability or if withdrawn at age 65.	Normal retirement at any age with 30 yrs serv. Early retirement at age 55 with 10 yrs serv. No compulsory retirement age.
MISSISSIPPI: Public Employees' Retirement System of Mississippi Alcorn A & M College Delta State College Jackson State College Mississippi State College for Women Mississippi State U Mississippi Valley State College U of Mississippi U of Southern Mississippi OASDHI	All EEs	Req	None	4½% of salary above $1,200 up to $15,000	3% of total salary up to $15,000, 3% of total payroll (up to $15,000 salary) of covered EEs; not credited to individual accounts	Annuity based on EE contribs with interest; plus ½% of average annual salary (less $1,200) for 5 highest consecutive yrs for each yr of serv.	Return of EE contribs with interest. After 20 yrs serv, survivor benefits paid to widow based on total benefit earned to date of death.	Return of EE contribs with interest. After 16 yrs serv, EE may elect to leave contribs on deposit and receive benefit at age 60 based on EE contribs plus a proportion of ER contribs starting at 20% for 16 yrs, increasing 20% per yr to 100% after 20 yrs serv. Disability After 10 yrs serv, benefit of 1½% times yrs of serv to date of disability plus yrs to age 60 times highest 5 consecutive yrs average annual salary times 85% times 75%.	Normal at 65; 1-yr extensions to age 70. Vol at 55 with 30 yrs serv or at 60 with 10 yrs serv. Actuarial reduction of benefit for each yr retirement is under 65.

STATE, PLAN, AND MEMBER INSTITUTIONS	PROVISIONS APPLY TO	REQ &/OR VOL	WAITING PERIOD	CONTRIBUTIONS		PENSION BENEFIT FORMULA	PRERETIREMENT DEATH BENEFIT	VESTING PROVISIONS	RETIREMENT AGE
				INDIV	INST				
MISSOURI: Missouri State Employees' Retirement System Central Missouri State College Northeast Missouri State Teachers College Northwest Missouri State College Southeast Missouri State College Southwest Missouri State College Lincoln U* U of Missouri** OASDHI	Nonacademic EEs *All EEs covered under State Employees' Retirement System. **All EEs covered under self-administered system.	Req	None	4% of salary below $7,500	Balance necessary to provide benefit (not to exceed 4% of payroll)	5/6 of 1% of average salary over 5 highest consecutive yrs (not to exceed $7,500) times the number of yrs of serv	Return of EE contribs with interest. After 20 yrs serv and age 60, survivor benefit based on serv to date of death.	Return of EE contribs with interest. After 20 yrs serv and attainment of age 60, EE may leave contribs on deposit for formula annuity. Disability After 15 yrs serv, 5/6 of 1% of average compensation times yrs of credited serv.	Normal, age 65; extensions to 70. Early, age 60 and 20 yrs serv. Benefits actuarially reduced for retirement under age 65.
MISSOURI: Public School Retirement System of Missouri Central Missouri State College Northeast Missouri State Teachers College Northwest Missouri State College Southeast Missouri State College Southwest Missouri State College OASDHI	Fac & certified EEs—state colleges and state teachers colleges other than U of Missouri and Lincoln U (other EEs covered by Missouri State Employees' Retirement System)	Req	None	6% of annual salary. Members covered by OASDHI pay 2/3 of contribs and receive 2/3 of benefits.	6% of payroll credited to reserve account	$.60 plus 1½% of final average salary for each yr of serv. Benefit increased by ¾ of 1% for each month retirement is over age 60 but under age 65. Final average salary is average of highest 10 yrs of compensation.	Return of EE contribs with interest if EE not eligible for retirement allowance (30 yrs serv or age 60 with 5 yrs serv). After 2 yrs serv or after eligible for disability allowance, survivor may elect survivor benefits if (1) a female spouse age 60 or on attainment of age 60 (male dependent spouse age 65), $200 per month to death or remarriage; (2) a widow with dependent child under 18 or, if a student, 22, $200 per month plus $100 for each child; (3) a child alone, $150 per month per child; (4) a dependent parent 65 or over, $150 per month.	Return of EE contribs. After 5 yrs, return of contribs plus interest. After 20 yrs, EE may leave contribs on deposit for deferred formula annuity at age 65. Disability After 8 yrs serv, 90% of retirement allowance payable at age 65 had EE continued active serv to 65, or 50% of 1/12 of last complete yrs salary, whichever is greater.	Normal at age 60 with 5 yrs serv. Early after 30 yrs serv. Benefit actuarially reduced for retirement under age 60.
MISSOURI: The Public School Retirement System of the City of St. Louis Harris Teachers College OASDHI	All EEs	Req	None	3% of salary to a maximum of $12,180 plus 2% of salary in excess of Social Security earnings base. Additional voluntary contribs.	Balance necessary to provide benefit	1% of final average salary plus ½ of 1% of that part above Social Security earnings base times yrs of serv (not to exceed 35). Final average salary is average of highest 5 consecutive yrs in the last 10 to a maximum of $12,180.	Return of EE contribs with interest, or survivor benefit based on serv to date of death. Benefits to widow cease when oldest child reaches 18 and resume when widow reaches age 62.	Return of EE contribs with interest. After 5 yrs of serv, may elect deferred annuity based on formula benefit earned to date. Disability After 10 yrs serv, computed in same manner as serv retirement, with a minimum of 25% of average final salary.	Normal, age 65. Early, age 55 with 30 yrs serv or age 60 regardless of yrs of serv. Compulsory at age 70. Benefits actuarially reduced for retirement under age 65.

STATE, PLAN, AND MEMBER INSTITUTIONS	PROVISIONS APPLY TO	REQ &/OR VOL	WAITING PERIOD	CONTRIBUTIONS		PENSION BENEFIT FORMULA	PRERETIREMENT DEATH BENEFIT	VESTING PROVISIONS	RETIREMENT AGE
				INDIV	INST				
MONTANA: Public Employees' Retirement System Eastern Montana College Montana College of Mineral Science and Technology Montana State U Northern Montana College U of Montana Western Montana College OASDHI	Nonacademic EEs	Req	None	5.75% of salary	3.8% of payroll	1/70 of the average of the 3 yrs of highest salary for each yr of serv.	Return of EE contribs with interest, plus 1 month's salary for each yr of serv up to 6. After 10 yrs serv, beneficiary receives annuity based on ER and EE contribs to date of death.	Return of EE contribs without interest. After 10 yrs serv, return of EE contribs with interest, or EE may elect to leave contribs on deposit and receive deferred annuity based on ER and EE contribs at age 60 or later. Disability Nonserv-connected: after 10 yrs serv, payment of annuity income based on age at disability, minimum of 25% of final average salary. Serv-connected: annuity income of 50% of final average salary regardless of age or serv.	Normal retirement at age 65 with 10 yrs serv; early retirement at age 60 with 10 yrs of serv, reduced actuarially for ages under 65. No compulsory retirement age.
MONTANA: Teachers' Retirement System of the State of Montana Eastern Montana College of Education Montana College of Mineral Science and Technology Montana State U Northern Montana College U of Montana Western Montana College OASDHI	Fac & adm off (other EEs covered by Public Employees' Retirement System).	Req	None	5% of salary	4% of payroll not credited to individual accounts	Money purchase annuity benefit provided by EE contribs plus pension of 1/140 of average salary times yrs of serv. Average salary is average of 3 highest consecutive yrs.	Return of EE contribs with interest if less than 5 yrs serv. Over 5 yrs serv, beneficiary may elect a refund of EE contribs with interest or a monthly life income based on EE yrs of serv, average salary, contribs, and beneficiary's age. Additional benefit of $50 per month for each minor child.	Return of EE contribs without interest if less than 5 yrs serv. After 5 yrs serv, EE may leave contribs on deposit for deferred annuity and pension at age 60 or later. Disability After 5 yrs serv, 25% of average salary of 3 highest consecutive yrs for serv up to 20 yrs. Percentage increase for each additional yr of serv beyond 20, to maximum of 43.71% for 35 yrs serv.	Normal retirement at age 60 with 5 yrs of serv. Compulsory retirement at age 70. Early retirement same as normal retirement.
NEVADA; Public Employees Retirement System of the State of Nevada U of Nevada No OASDHI	All EEs	Req	None	6% of gross salary plus 24¢ per month administrative fee	6% of total payroll not assigned to individual accounts	2.5% of average of 3 yrs highest salary for each yr of serv up to 20, plus 1.5% of highest 3 yrs average salary for each yr of serv over 20 to a maximum of 10 additional yrs. Cost of living increase 1½% each year after retirement. after taxes. If member had 15 yrs of serv, widow will get $100 per month at age 60; 25 yrs, $125 per month at age 60. After 25 yrs serv, EE beneficiary is entitled to benefits EE would have had if he had retired instead of died.	Less than 2 yrs of serv, return of member's contribs, without interest. 2 or more yrs of serv, $75 per month for each child under 18 but no more than $210 monthly. Widow without children, $100 per month; widow with children, $100 per month as long as income is below $3,600 per year	Return of EE contribs. After completion of the following serv requirements, EE may leave contribs on deposit for deferred formula annuity: (a) after 10 yrs and attainment of age 60, or (b) after 25 yrs of serv regardless of age, or (c) after 20 yrs, in which case the benefits are reduced by 4% for each yr between the date of attainment of 20 yrs of accredited serv and the attainment of retirement age 60, provided that the reduction shall not exceed 20% of the formula benefit. Disability On completion of 10 yrs of continuous serv, the pension benefit formula is applied to the yrs of serv that have been completed.	Normal at age 60 with 10 yrs of serv, or at age 55 with 30 yrs of serv.

STATE, PLAN, AND MEMBER INSTITUTIONS	PROVISIONS APPLY TO	REQ &/OR VOL	WAITING PERIOD	CONTRIBUTIONS		PENSION BENEFIT FORMULA	PRERETIREMENT DEATH BENEFIT	VESTING PROVISIONS	RETIREMENT AGE
				INDIV	INST				
NEW HAMPSHIRE: New Hampshire Retirement System Keene State College* New Hampshire Vocational Institutes Manchester Portsmouth Plymouth State College* U of New Hampshire* OASDHI	All EEs at vocational institutes; all EEs except fac and adm off at U of New Hampshire and State Colleges *Fac & adm off in TIAA-CREF plan.	Req	None	Per cent of salary based on age at entry and sex, e.g., for men, 7.60% at age 30; 9.75% at age 59, reduced by half on Social Security earnings base.	Balance needed to provide benefit	Annuity based on EE contribs, plus pension which together with the annuity, equals 1/60 of final average salary for each yr of serv not in excess of 30 yrs, plus 1/120 of final average salary for each yr of serv over 30. After EE reaches age 65, benefit is reduced by 1/120 of final average salary up to the Social Security earnings base ($7,800) for each yr of serv up to 30, and by 1/240 for each yr over 30. (Average final salary is average of highest 5 yrs salary.)	Return of EE contribs plus interest. If death accidental in serv, pension to widow or dependent children of 25% of final average salary up to $7,800, plus 50% of final average salary in excess of $7,800. Total, including Social Security benefits, of not less than 50% of final average salary.	Return of EE contribs with interest. After 15 yrs serv, EE may leave contribs on deposit for formula deferred annuity payable at the minimum age of 60 but based on the 65 payment. Disability After 10 or more yrs of serv: (a) for ordinary disability, 90% of the retirement allowance that would have been payable prior to attainment of age 65 based on serv and average salary to date of disability, but not less than 25% of final average salary. Reduced by Social Security benefits payable on an unreduced basis. (b) accidental disability, 50% of final average salary until eligible for Social Security benefits then pension equal to retirement allowance payable at age 65 based on 30 yrs serv and final average salary at date of retirement.	Normal, age 65 for teachers; age 60 for EEs. Required at age 70.
NEW JERSEY: Public Employees' Retirement System of New Jersey Glassboro State College Jersey City State College Montclair State College New Jersey College of Medicine and Dentistry Newark College of Engineering Newark State College Paterson State College Rutgers U Trenton State College OASDHI	Nonfac EEs and also fac at Rutgers who have not elected TIAA-CREF alternate plan.	Req	None	Varies according to age of entry into plan and sex, e.g., 5.19%, male age 30; 7.12%, male age 50; reduced 2% on salary subject to Social Security. EE may make additional voluntary contribs up to 10% to New Jersey Supplemental Annuity Program for (1) fixed annuity, (2) variable annuity, or both.	Balance necessary to provide benefit	1/60 of average of highest 5 fiscal yrs times yrs of membership.	Benefit of 150% of last yrs salary (group life insurance plan) plus return of EE contribs with interest after 3 yrs, without interest less than 3 yrs. Accident in the course of employment: widow receives annual pension of ½ of final average salary plus refund of EE contribs with interest. (If deceased was married female, benefit to child or children.) Member may purchase additional 1 times salary as insurance at a premium of 1% of salary.	Return of EE contribs without interest. After 3 yrs, with interest. After 15 yrs, EE may elect to leave contribs on deposit and receive deferred formula benefit annuity at age 60. Disability After 10 yrs serv, 1½% of final average salary for each yr of serv to date of disability, minimum of 40% of the average salary for the 5 yrs preceding retirement or the highest 5 fiscal yrs providing it does not exceed 90% of the the serv retirement benefit he would be entitled to had he remained in serv to age 60. Serv-connected: 2/3 of salary at time of accident, plus payments based on EE contribs to system.	Age 60 or 25 yrs of serv. Compulsory at age 70. Formula benefit actuarially reduced for retirement at ages under 60.

STATE, PLAN, AND MEMBER INSTITUTIONS	PROVISIONS APPLY TO	REQ &/OR VOL	WAITING PERIOD	CONTRIBUTIONS		PENSION BENEFIT FORMULA	PRERETIREMENT DEATH BENEFIT	VESTING PROVISIONS	RETIREMENT AGE
				INDIV	INST				
NEW JERSEY: Teachers' Pension and Annuity Fund of New Jersey Glassboro State College Jersey City State College Montclair State College Newark College of Engineering Newark State College Paterson State College Trenton State College OASDHI	Fac (Nonfac covered by Public Employees' Retirement System of New Jersey.)	Req	None	Varies according to age at entry into plan and sex (e.g., 4.8% male age 19; 8.45% male age 59), reduced 2% on salary under Social Security earnings base. Additional voluntary EE contribs may be made to the fixed and variable annuities of the Supplemental Annuity Collective Trust of N.J.	Balance necessary to provide benefit	1/60 of final average compensation for each yr of serv. Final average compensation is average annual compensation received during the member's last 5 yrs of serv or any 5 fiscal yrs of membership.	Return of EE contribs with interest plus a benefit equal to 1½ times the compensation received in the last yr of creditable serv, or 3 times salary if EE contributes to insurance plan. Serv-connected: for widow, ½ of EE final average salary during widowhood.	Return of EE contribs without interest; with 2% interest after 3 yrs. After 15 yrs serv, EE may leave contribs on deposit for deferred annuity at age 60 based on benefit formula. Disability After 10 yrs serv, 1½% of final average salary for each yr of serv to date of disability, minimum of 40% of final average salary. Serv-connected: 2/3 of salary at date of disability plus annuity based on EE contribs.	Age 60 or 25 yrs serv. Benefit actuarially reduced for retirement under age 60. Compulsory at age 70.
NEW MEXICO: New Mexico Educational Retirement System Eastern New Mexico U New Mexico Highlands U New Mexico Institute of Mining and Technology New Mexico Military Institute New Mexico State U U of New Mexico Western New Mexico U OASDHI	All EEs *Professionals-teachers, nurses, and adm EEs.	Req for pro;* all other EEs vol	None	4% of salary	6½% of total salaries of plan members	1½% of the first $6,600 of the average salary of the last 5 yrs, or any other consecutive 5 yrs, whichever is higher, plus 1% over $6,600 of such average, multiplied by number of credited yrs of service.	Return of EE contribs plus interest. After 15 yrs serv, beneficiary may receive income based on actuarial equivalent of benefit EE would have received had he retired instead of died, if the EE elects this option prior to death.	Return of EE contribs without interest. After 15 yrs, EE may elect to leave contribs on deposit and receive deferred annuity at age 60 based on pension benefit formula. Disability After 10 yrs of credited serv, eligibility for disability allowance computed in same manner as retirement benefits. If serv less than 30 yrs, benefits are actuarially reduced to account for age.	Age 60 if EE has 15 yrs of credited serv; age 65 with 10 yrs of credited serv; after 30 yrs of credited serv regardless of age.
NEW YORK: Employees' Retirement System of the City of New York City U of New York Brooklyn College City College Graduate Studies Division Hunter College John Jay College Queens College Richmond College York College OASDHI	Nonacademic EEs	Req	None	Percentage of salary varying according to sex, age at entry into plan, and plan selected, reduced by 5% (paid by City into reserve for increased take-home pay).	Balance necessary to provide the benefit, plus 5% to reserve for increased take-home pay	An annuity payable from member's contribs and reserve for increased take-home pay, plus a pension payable from City contribs dependent on the plan selected. (a) 60-yr 1/140th plan: 1/140 of final average salary for each yr of serv. (b) 55-yr 1/120th plan: 1/120 of final average salary for each yr of serv. (c) 55-yr 1/100th plan: 1/100 of final average salary for each yr of serv. Final average salary is average annual compensation during last 5 yrs of serv.	Return of EE contribs and reserve for increased take-home pay, plus ½ yrs salary if under 10 yrs serv and 1 yrs salary if over 10. If eligible for retirement, survivor benefit equivalent to allowance payable had EE retired instead of died.	Return of EE contribs. Disability After 10 yrs of allowable serv and continuous membership, a combined annuity and pension equal to a minimum of 25% of final average salary, more if serv retirement for same length of serv would have been greater.	Age 60 or later, or age 55 or later under Age 55 plans. Required at age 70.

STATE, PLAN, AND MEMBER INSTITUTIONS	PROVISIONS APPLY TO	REQ &/OR VOL	WAITING PERIOD	CONTRIBUTIONS		PENSION BENEFIT FORMULA	PRERETIREMENT DEATH BENEFIT	VESTING PROVISIONS	RETIREMENT AGE
				INDIV	INST				
NEW YORK: Employees' Retirement System of the State of New York State U of New York OASDHI	All EEs (Fac, adm & executive off may elect to participate in the Teachers' Retirement System of the State of New York or TIAA-CREF.)	Req	None	Non-contributory	Rate fixed by the actuary which shall be computed to be sufficient to provide benefits	1/60 of final average salary for each yr of serv, guaranteed benefit for serv after 4/1/60. Final average salary is based on the 5 highest consecutive yrs. A 1-yr cost of living increase, beginning in October of any yr of retirement in which the ratio of the average of the 12 monthly Consumer Price Indexes of the Bureau of Labor Statistics (all items-U.S. city average) at the end of the preceding yr to the index for the yr of retirement, minus 1, and expressed as a percentage, is at least 3%. The increase percentage is multiplied by retirement income up to $7,000 and is recalculated each yr. This provision, along with certain others in the plan, must be renewed annually by the New York State Legislature.	1/12 of final salary for each yr of serv up to 36 yrs. (Maximum of 3 yrs, minimum of ½ yrs salary for EE with 90 days serv or more but not to exceed $10,000.) NOTE: Minimum is a benefit of Dept. of Civil Service. If EE was eligible for retirement, survivor benefit is equal to reserves. May be taken as annuity or lump sum payment.	After 10 yrs serv, member may vest and get a deferred pension at age 55 based on 1/120 of final average salary for each yr of serv. Disability After 10 yrs of serv, an allowance of 1/60 of final average salary for each yr of serv.	Age 55 or thereafter, regardless of length of serv.
NEW YORK: New York State Teachers' Retirement System State U of New York OASDHI	Fac, adm & executive off (may elect participation in New York State Teachers' Retirement System, New York State Employees' Retirement System, or TIAA-CREF).	Req	None	5% of salary for superannuation plan or 8% for special service plan, reduced by 8% under increased take-home pay provision (8% is credited to EEs reserve for take-home pay). Superannuation plan for retirement at any age after 35 yrs serv, or age 60 after 25 yrs serv, or age 70 with 1 or more immediately preceding yrs serv. (Special serv plan for retirement at age 55 with 20 yrs serv or age 65 or later with 1 or more immediately preceding yrs serv.) An additional annuity is also available under a voluntary additional contribution plan.	Balance necessary to provide benefit, plus 8% to Reserve for Take-Home Pay	Annuity from any accumulated EE contribs plus state contribs in lieu of EE contribs (reserve for increased take-home pay) plus a pension equal to: (1) 1/100 of final average salary for each yr of credited serv through the 25th, plus (2) 1/120 of final average salary for each yr of serv between 25 and 35, plus (3) 1/140 of final average salary for each yr of serv over 35. Final average salary is average salary for the highest salaried 5 consecutive yrs of serv.	Return of any EE contribs with interest; plus an ordinary death benefit of 1/12 of last yrs salary for each yr of credited serv up to 12 yrs. Maximum of 2 yrs salary, plus a benefit from the reserve for increased take-home pay, if due.	Return of EE contribs with interest. After 10 yrs serv, EE may leave contribs on deposit for deferred formula benefit at age 55 or later. Disability After 15 yrs serv, annuity from any accumulated EE contribs and State contribs to reserve for take-home pay, plus pension of 1/5 final average salary, or regular retirement benefits, whichever is greater.	See contributions column. SUNY retirement age is 70 for fac, 65 for adm staff.

STATE, PLAN, AND MEMBER INSTITUTIONS	PROVISIONS APPLY TO	REQ &/OR VOL	WAITING PERIOD	CONTRIBUTIONS		PENSION BENEFIT FORMULA	PRERETIREMENT DEATH BENEFIT	VESTING PROVISIONS	RETIREMENT AGE
				INDIV	INST				

NEW YORK: Teachers Retirement System of the City of New York
 	
City U of New York
  Brooklyn College
  City College
  Graduate Studies
    Division
  Hunter College
  John Jay College
  Queens College
  Richmond College
  York College
 	
    OASDHI
	Fac & adm off (non-academic EEs participate in Employees' Retirement System of the City of New York). Fac may elect TIAA–CREF as alternate.	Req	None	Per cent of salary depending on age at entry, sex, and plan selected, reduced by 5% under increased take-home pay provision. EE may elect to put 50% or 100% of EE contribs and reserve for take-home pay contribs into separate variable annuity program account. If 100% is elected, member may transfer all or part of prior contribs to the variable annuity program.	At rate required to produce an annual allowance equal to 1% for each yr of serv multiplied by the average salary of last 5 yrs plus 5% to reserve for take-home pay	Annuity based on EE contribs and increased take-home pay reserve, plus pension of 1% of average highest 5 yrs salary for each yr of serv.	Lump sum payment equal to 5% of average salary for each yr of City serv but not less than 50% or greater than 100% of average salary plus return of EE contribs and the reserve for increased take-home pay.
							
							Disability
							Disability retirement up to age 65 to members with a minimum of 10 yrs City serv who are physically or mentally incapacitated for the performance of duty. A member retired for disability receives a pension of 20% of his average salary for the first 10 yrs of City serv and an additional 1/5 of 1% of his average salary for each yr of City serv in excess of 10. In no event shall the total pension for disability retirement exceed 25% of average salary.
								Return of EE contribs with interest. After 15 yrs serv, EE may leave contribs on deposit for deferred benefit formula at age 60 or later.	Age 65 or after 35 yrs serv at any age, or at age 55 with 25 or more yrs serv. Optional retirement after 30 yrs serv at any age at reduced benefits. Required at age 70.

NORTH CAROLINA: Teachers' and State Employees' Retirement System
 	
North Carolina Agr and
  Technical U
Appalachian State U
Asheville-Biltmore
  College
East Carolina U
Elizabeth City State
  College
Fayetteville State
  College
North Carolina College
  at Durham
Pembroke State College
U of North Carolina at
  Chapel Hill
North Carolina State U
  at Raleigh
U of North Carolina at
  Charlotte
U of North Carolina at
  Greensboro
Western Carolina U
Wilmington College
Winston-Salem State
  College
 	
    OASDHI
	All EEs	Req	None	5% of 1st $5,600 and 6% of the balance	Balance necessary to provide benefit	1¼% of the first $5,600 of average final compensation and 1½% of the balance for each yr of credited serv. Final average salary is average of highest 5 consecutive yrs in the last 10 yrs of serv.	Return of EE contribs with interest plus lump sum payment equal to the salary paid in the last calendar yr. After age 55, or 30 yrs serv, survivor benefit based on earned credits to date of death.
							
							Disability
							After 10 yrs of serv, if under age 60, disability allowance equal to the service allowance payable at 60, minus the actuarial equivalent of the contribs made during continued serv.
								Return of EE contribs with ½ interest earned if less than 12 yrs serv; after 12 yrs, EE contribs with full interest, or EE may leave contribs on deposit and receive deferred annuity at age 60 or later based on benefit formula.	Compulsory at age 65; voluntary at age 60. Benefit actuarially reduced for retirement under 60; early retirement after age 50 and 20 yrs serv.

STATE, PLAN, AND MEMBER INSTITUTIONS	PROVISIONS APPLY TO	REQ &/OR VOL	WAITING PERIOD	CONTRIBUTIONS INDIV	CONTRIBUTIONS INST	PENSION BENEFIT FORMULA	PRERETIREMENT DEATH BENEFIT	VESTING PROVISIONS	RETIREMENT AGE
NORTH DAKOTA: North Dakota State Employees Retirement Plan Dickinson State College Minot State College North Dakota School of Forestry North Dakota State School of Science North Dakota State U U of North Dakota Valley City State College Mayville State College OASDHI	Nonacademic EEs (other EEs covered by Teachers' Insurance and Retirement Fund).	Req	5 mos	4% of salary	4% of each member's salary to maximum of $300 per yr	Money purchase based on 100% of EE contribs and 75% of ER contribs, plus interest earnings.	Lump sum benefit of EE contribs with interest plus 75% of total ER contribs with interest. **Disability** Money purchase benefit based on age at disability.	Return of EE contribs with interest. After 3 yrs serv, EE may elect to leave EE contribs on deposit and receive deferred annuity based on EE contribs plus percentage of 75% of ER contribs based on serv, as follows: 3-7 yrs 20% 7-11 30 11-15 40 15-18 60 18-20 80 over 20 100 Under age 55, EE may elect to take above combination of ER and EE contribs as a lump sum.	Normal, 1st day of month following attainment of age 65. Benefit actuarially decreased for earlier retirement, increased for later retirement.
NORTH DAKOTA: Teachers' Insurance and Retirement Fund Dickinson State College Minot State College North Dakota School of Forestry North Dakota State School of Science North Dakota State U U of North Dakota Valley City State College Mayville State College OASDHI	Fac (other EEs covered by North Dakota State Employees Retirement Plan). Not compulsory for persons employed after age 50. All fac also under TIAA–CREF supplementary plan.	Req	None	1st 8 yrs serv, 4% of 1st $3,000; 2nd 8 yrs serv, 5% of 1st $3,600; thereafter, 6% of 1st $3,333 of salary.	1st 8 yrs serv, 4% of 1st $1,250; thereafter, 4% of 1st $3,000 of salary (percentage contrib is of total covered payroll, not credited to individual accounts).	Annual pension of 2% of teacher's total earnings on which contribs have been made during 1st 25 yrs of serv. Minimum of $720 increased by $100 per yr of serv after 25 yrs until $1,200 is reached. ($1,200 is maximum benefit for 25 yrs serv.) $60 increase per yr of serv beyond 25. Early retirement benefit is 2% of total earnings but no more than $48 for each yr of serv.	Return of EE contribs without interest. After 25 yrs of serv, survivor may receive income under survivor option as if member had retired.	Return of EE contribs without interest. **Disability** EE must have 15 yrs of serv. Benefit is 2% of total earnings with maximum of $1,200 annually and minimum of $300 annually	Normal retirement at age 55 with 25 yrs of serv of which 18 yrs including last 5 were in North Dakota. Early retirement at age 55 with at least 10 yrs of serv in North Dakota.
OHIO: Public Employees Retirement System of Ohio Bowling Green State U Central State U Cleveland State U Kent State U Miami U Ohio State U Ohio U Toledo State College of Medicine U of Akron U of Toledo Youngstown State U No OASDHI	Nonfac EEs, except for Cleveland State U and Toledo State College of Medicine, at which all EEs are in Ohio Public Employees Retirement System	Req	None	7% of salary	Balance needed to provide benefit	1.75% of final average salary for each yr of serv, or $76 for each yr of serv, whichever is greater, not to exceed 75% of final average salary for retirement at 65, or 80% at 70. Benefit actuarially reduced for retirement under age 65, increased (to age 70) for retirement over age 65. Final average salary is average compensation of any 5 yrs. Widow at 62 — Min. $81 / Max. $96 Widow at 65 — 81 / 96 Widow and 1 child — 156 / 186 Widow and 2 or more children — 156 / 236	Return of EE contribs with interest. If eligible for retirement or deferred retirement benefit, survivor annuity based on EE serv to date of death. After 18 months serv, in lieu of return of EE contribs or serv based survivor annuity, the following monthly survivor benefits are paid:	Return of EE contribs with interest. After 5 yrs serv, EE may leave contribs on deposit for deferred formula annuity at age 60. **Disability** After 5 yrs serv, the greater of 1.75% of final average salary, or $76, for each yr of serv to date of disability plus yrs to age 60, but no more than 60% of final average salary. 1 Orphan — Min. $81 / Max. $96 2 Orphans — 156 / 156 3 or more orphans — 156 / 216 Each dependent parent — 81 / 96	Age 60 with 5 or more yrs serv, age 55 with 25 or more yrs serv, any age after 35 yrs serv. ER may require retirement at age 70.

STATE, PLAN, AND MEMBER INSTITUTIONS	PROVISIONS APPLY TO	REQ &/OR VOL	WAITING PERIOD	CONTRIBUTIONS		PENSION BENEFIT FORMULA	PRERETIREMENT DEATH BENEFIT	VESTING PROVISIONS	RETIREMENT AGE
				INDIV	INST				
OHIO: School Employees Retirement System U of Akron U of Toledo No OASDHI	Nonfac EEs	Req	None	7% of salary (optional on any salary in excess of $25,000)	Balance needed to provide benefit	Money purchase annuity from EE contribs plus pension to bring total benefit to 1.75% final average salary for each yr of serv. Minimum of $76 times yrs of serv. Final average salary is average of highest 5 yrs of compensation, not to exceed $25,000.	Return of EE contribs with interest, or, after 1½ yrs serv, survivor may elect survivor benefits as follows: (1) widow 62 or over, or widower 65, $96 per month to death or remarriage; (2) widow age 50, or dependent widower, $106 per month if EE had 15 yrs serv; (3) if children under 18: 1 child, $186 per month; 2 or more, $236 per month. If EE eligible for retirement, survivor may elect survivor income option based on formula and age.	Return of EE contribs with interest. After 5 yrs serv, EE may elect to leave contribs on deposit for a deferred annuity at age 60 or later. Disability After 5 yrs serv before age 60: benefit is an annuity based on EE accumulated contribs plus a pension to bring income up to that which would be provided for him had he retired at age 65 without actuarial reduction from the 1.75% formula.	Age 60 with 5 yrs serv. Early retirement at age 55 with 25 yrs serv or any age with 35 yrs serv. Benefit actuarially reduced for ages under 65 unless serv period is 35 yrs or more.
OHIO: State Teachers Retirement System of Ohio Bowling Green State U Central State U Kent State U Miami U Ohio State U Ohio U U of Akron U of Toledo Youngstown State U No OASDHI	Fac (other EEs in Public Employees Retirement System of Ohio or, for U of Akron and Toledo, the School Employees Retirement System of Ohio) (Fac, adm staff, & noncivil service EEs of the U of Cincinnati in TIAA-CREF plan; civil service EEs in City Retirement System)	Req	None	7% (optional on amounts of salary in excess of $25,000 Since 1/1/67, any adjustments required in the total rate of contribs computed by the actuary shall be divided equally between members and their ERs.	Balance necessary to provide benefit.	1.75% of average salary of 5 highest yrs for each yr of serv. Minimum of $76 times yrs of serv. Maximum of 75-80% of final average salary. Final average salary limited to $25,000.	Return of EE contribs with interest earned through 8/31/59. Subsequent to 8/31/59 interest is credited only at retirement. After 1½ yrs of serv (with ¼ yr earned within 2 yrs prior to death), monthly survivor benefit payable in certain classifications to widows, financially dependent widowers, widows with children, dependent children, and financially dependent parents, ranging from $96 for widow or child under 18 to $236 for widow with children under 18. If EE was eligible to retire, the properly designated spouse or other person financially dependent on the member may have the option of lifetime income equal to the joint survivorship amount had the member retired before death.	Return of EE contribs with interest earned through 8/31/59. Subsequent to 8/31/59, interest is credited only at retirement. After 5 yrs serv, EE may leave contribs on deposit for deferred formula benefit at age 60 or later. Disability Under age 60 with 5 yrs serv: benefit is lesser of 1.75% of 5 highest yrs (or $76 if greater) times number of yrs obtained by adding EE yrs of serv credit and yrs until age 60. Benefits limited to 60% of average salary.	Normal at age 65 with 5 or more yrs serv, or at any age with 35 yrs serv (without benefit reduction). Early retirement at age 55 with 25 yrs serv, with benefit actuarially reduced, or at age 60 with benefit actuarially reduced.

STATE, PLAN, AND MEMBER INSTITUTIONS	PROVISIONS APPLY TO	REQ &/OR VOL	WAITING PERIOD	CONTRIBUTIONS		PENSION BENEFIT FORMULA	PRERETIREMENT DEATH BENEFIT	VESTING PROVISIONS	RETIREMENT AGE
				INDIV	INST				
OKLAHOMA, Teachers Retirement System of Oklahoma Cameron State Agr College Central State College Connors State Agr College East Central State College Langston U Murray State Agr College Northeastern Oklahoma A & M College Northeastern State College Northern Oklahoma College Northwestern State College Oklahoma College of Liberal Arts Oklahoma Military Academy Oklahoma State U Panhandle A and M College Southeastern State College Southwestern State College U of Oklahoma OASDHI	All EEs	Req for pro staff; and for cler and maintenance EEs	None	4 % of salary up to $12,000 per yr. Contribs cease at the end of school yr in which EE attains age 65.	At retirement the state matches the amount of EE contribs which have accumulated at interest	Money purchase	Return of EE contribs with interest	Return of EE contribs without interest if less than 3 yrs; with 70% interest for serv from 3 to 16 yrs; 80%, 16 to 21 yrs; 90%, 21 to 26 yrs; 100% after 26 yrs. After 20 yrs serv, EE is eligible to leave contribs on deposit and receive deferred annuity at age 60 or later based on EE plus ER contribs. Disability After 10 yrs serv, annuity based on EE contribs to date of disability plus pension (based on ER contribs) which would have been payable at age 60 had EE continued working at salary on date of disability.	Optional at age 60 or after 30 yrs of serv. No compulsory retirement age; institutions may adopt compulsory age.
OREGON: Public Employees Retirement System U of Oregon Oregon State U Oregon College of Education Portland State College Southern Oregon College Eastern Oregon College Oregon Technical Institute OASDHI	All EEs	Req	6 mos	(¼ or ½ of EE contribs may be made to Oregon variable annuity fund.) Academic EEs may elect to contribute to TIAA-CREF on salary above $4,800 in lieu of full participation in PERS. Matching PERS contribs accumulated for 1st 5 yrs before applied to annuity contract. Per cent of monthly salary: Less than $500, 4%; $500-$1,000, 5%; $1,000-$1,500, 6%; $1,500 or more, 7%.	Such amounts as are actuarially computed to be necessary to provide pension portion of benefit	Pension: 0.67% of final average salary (5 highest yrs of last 10) multiplied by each yr of serv, not to exceed 30, plus $4 per month for each yr of serv before July 1, 1946, plus Annuity: money purchase equivalent of EE contribs to plan, including variable annuity benefit, if any.	Return of EE contribs with interest and 1 month's salary for each yr of membership (not to exceed 6 months' salary or amount of EE contribs, whichever is less).	Return of EE contribs with interest. After 5 yrs, EE may elect to leave contribs on deposit and receive deferred pension and annuity at age 60. Disability (Serv-connected): annuity from EE contribs plus pension equal to what he would have received at 65. After 10 yrs serv, disability need not be serv-connected to qualify.	Early at age 60 with actuarially reduced pension. Normal at age 65; extensions to 70.

STATE, PLAN, AND MEMBER INSTITUTIONS	PROVISIONS APPLY TO	REQ &/OR VOL	WAITING PERIOD	CONTRIBUTIONS		PENSION BENEFIT FORMULA	PRERETIREMENT DEATH BENEFIT	VESTING PROVISIONS	RETIREMENT AGE
				INDIV	INST				
PENNSYLVANIA: Pennsylvania Public School Employees' Retirement System Bloomsburg State College California State College Cheyney State College Clarion State College East Stroudsburg State College Edinboro State College Indiana U of Pennsylvania Kutztown State College Lock Haven State College Mansfield State College Millersville State College Shippensburg State College Slippery Rock State College West Chester State College OASDHI	All EEs (EEs may choose State Employees' Retirement System)	Req unless EE cannot render 5 yrs of credited serv before age 70 is reached	None	5½% of salary	Balance necessary to provide benefit	1/60 times final average salary times yrs of serv. Final average salary is the average annual salary for the 5 highest yrs.	Return of EE contribs with interest. After 10 yrs serv, lump sum benefit of 2-4 times the amount of member's contribs plus interest.	Return of EE contribs with interest. After 10 yrs serv, EE may leave contribs on deposit for formula pension benefit. Disability After 10 yrs serv, 1/60 of final average salary times yrs of serv, but not less than 1/3 of final average salary.	Age 62 with 5 yrs serv or any age after 35 yrs serv; age 60 with at least 30 yrs serv. Early retirement after 25 yrs serv but less than 35 yrs serv for those under age 62. Benefit actuarially reduced for early retirement. Compulsory retirement at age 70.
PENNSYLVANIA: Pennsylvania State Employees' Retirement System Bloomsburg State College California State College Cheyney State College Clarion State College East Stroudsburg State College Edinboro State College Indiana U of Pennsylvania Kutztown State College Lock Haven State College Mansfield State College Millersville State College Pennsylvania State U Shippensburg State College Slippery Rock State College West Chester State College OASDHI	All EEs EEs of state colleges may choose Public School Employees' Retirement System	Req	None	Varies according to age of entry into plan and sex (e.g., male age 25, 5.51%; male age 50, 7.86%)	Balance necessary to provide benefit	1/50 of average of 5 consecutive yrs of highest annual compensation for each yr of serv. Benefit composed of a member's money purchase annuity provided by EE contribs and interest earnings plus pension from state contribs.	Return of EE contribs with interest to beneficiary. After 10 yrs serv or attainment of age 60, EE contribs with interest plus per cent value of state pension paid to beneficiary or annuity based on benefit earned.	Return of EE contribs with 4% interest on a deferred annuity based on accumulated EE contribs at time of withdrawal. No interest credited after termination of employment or during leave without pay. On involuntary termination of employment after 10 yrs serv or on voluntary termination after 25 yrs serv, deferred annuity at age 60 or later based on member's accumulation plus pension of 1/100 of highest 5 yrs average annual compensation for each yr of serv. Disability After 5 yrs serv, benefit formula applied to yrs of serv to date of disability.	Age 60 or older for full formula benefit. No compulsory retirement age.

STATE, PLAN, AND MEMBER INSTITUTIONS	PROVISIONS APPLY TO	REQ &/OR VOL	WAITING PERIOD	CONTRIBUTIONS		PENSION BENEFIT FORMULA	PRERETIREMENT DEATH BENEFIT	VESTING PROVISIONS	RETIREMENT AGE
				INDIV	INST				
RHODE ISLAND: Employees' Retirement System Rhode Island College U of Rhode Island OASDHI	All EEs (fac & adm off participate in TIAA–CREF plan instead of State plan)	Req	None	5% of salary	Balance necessary to provide benefit	1 2/3% of average of 3 consecutive yrs of highest salary for each yr of serv (maximum of 45 yrs serv considered).	Return of EE contribs without interest, plus $250 times yrs of credited serv from a minimum of $1,000 to a maximum of $5,000.	Under 10 yrs serv, return of EE contribs without interest. Over 10 yrs serv, EE may leave contribs in System and receive earned retirement benefits at age 60. Disability With at least 7 yrs serv, 1 2/3% of average compensation times yrs of serv; 25% of compensation minimum. Occupational 66 2/3% of salary at time of disability less Workmen's Compensation payments.	Compulsory at age 70; vol at age 60 and 10 yrs serv or at age 55 with 30 yrs serv. Benefit actuarially reduced if retirement occurs before age 60. Retirement at any age with no reduction after 35 yrs serv.
SOUTH CAROLINA: South Carolina Retirement System The Citadel Clemson U Medical College of South Carolina South Carolina State College U of South Carolina Winthrop College OASDHI	All EEs	Req	None	4% on first $4,800, 6% above $4,800	Balance necessary to provide benefit	1% of average of 5 consecutive yrs of highest salary of 10 yrs preceding retirement up to $4,800; 1½% of average salary above $4,800 times yrs of creditable serv.	Return of EE contribs with interest. If death of active EE occurs after age 65, after 35 yrs serv, or after age 60 with 20 yrs serv, survivor annuity based on benefit EE would have received had he retired just before his death.	Under 15 yrs serv, return of EE contribs with interest; over 15 yrs, EE may leave contribs in the System and receive earned benefits at age 60. Disability Retirement allowance after 10 yrs serv: benefit payable at age 60 less actuarial equivalent of contribs he would have made. After age 60 or 35 yrs serv, a serv retirement benefit is payable.	Compulsory at 65 unless extensions are approved. Optional at age 60 or after 35 yrs serv. Benefit actuarially reduced if retirement is under age 65.
SOUTH DAKOTA: South Dakota Public Employees Retirement System Black Hills State College General Beadle State College Northern State College South Dakota School of Mines and Technology South Dakota State U Southern State College U of South Dakota OASDHI	Nonacademic EEs	Req	3 months and age 30, or 1 yr and age 25, or 3 yrs and age 17	3½% of first $6,000 salary	Matches EE contribs	1% of total salary on which contribs have been made.	Return of EE contribs with interest.	Return of EE contribs with interest. Benefits are vested gradually, beginning with 50% after 10 yrs serv and increasing by 5% each yr to full vesting after 20 yrs serv.	Normal at age 65 or, if hired after age 55, after 10 yrs participation. Early retirement after age 55 with 20 yrs serv. Extensions with permission of ER, but no further contribs are made.

STATE, PLAN, AND MEMBER INSTITUTIONS	PROVISIONS APPLY TO	REQ &/OR VOL	WAITING PERIOD	CONTRIBUTIONS		PENSION BENEFIT FORMULA	PRERETIREMENT DEATH BENEFIT	VESTING PROVISIONS	RETIREMENT AGE
				INDIV	INST				
TENNESSEE: Tennessee State Retirement System Austin Peay State College East Tennessee State U Memphis State U Middle Tennessee State U Tennessee A & I State U Tennessee Technological U OASDHI	All EEs except fac (fac covered under Tennessee Teachers' Retirement System) Class A covered by OASDHI; Class B not in OASDHI; Class C commissioned members of Department of Safety Fac and all other EEs of U of Tennessee under TIAA-CREF plan.	Req	None	Class A: 3% of 1st $6,600, 5% of excess; Class B: 7% of salary, optional above $4,200; Class C: 11.73% of total salary	Balance necessary to provide benefit	Class A: 1 1/8% of average of highest 10 yrs annual earnings subject to OASDHI tax, plus 1 ¾% of the average annual earnings above the OASDHI base for each yr of credited serv. Class B: 1 ¾% of the average of highest 5 yrs annual salary for each yr of serv (maximum of 75% of average salary). Class C: 2 ¼% of average of highest 5 yrs salary for each yr of serv (maximum of 75% of average salary).	Return of EE contribs with interest Disability Class A after 10 yrs. Class B and C after 5 yrs. Benefit formula percentages applied in Class A to the lesser of 20 yrs serv or serv EE would have had to age 65; in Class B and C, to yrs of serv to date of disability. Formula not reduced actuarially.	Return of EE contribs without interest; with interest if over 5 yrs serv. Over 10 yrs serv, EE can elect to leave contribs in System and receive deferred benefit as computed under formula.	Compulsory at 70 for A and B; at 65 for C. Normal at 65 for A; at 60 and 20 yrs serv for B; and at 50 and 25 yrs serv or after 30 yrs serv for C.
TENNESSEE: Tennessee Teachers' Retirement System Austin Peay State College East Tennessee State U Memphis State U Middle Tennessee State U Tennessee A & I State U Tennessee Technological U OASDHI	Fac (other EEs covered by State Retirement System) Class A covered by OASDHI. Class B not covered by OASDHI Fac and all other EEs of U of Tennessee under TIAA-CREF plan.	Req	None	Class A, 3% of OASDHI earnings base, 5% above; Class B, 7%. EE may elect to stop contribs after age 60 and upon completing 35 yrs of serv	As necessary to fund benefit	Class A, 1% of average final compensation times total yrs of credited serv plus ¾% of average final compensation above $6,600 times yrs of serv before 1/1/66 plus ¾% of average final compensation above the compensation covered by Social Security for each yr of credited serv after 1/1/66. Class B, 1 5/8% of average final compensation times yrs of credited serv. (Average final compensation is average salary during 10 yrs of highest earnings.)	Return of EE contribs with interest.	Under 10 yrs of serv or under 4 yrs of serv in institutions of higher learning, return of EE contribs with interest. Over, may elect to leave contribs in System and receive earned retirement benefit at age 60. Disability After 10 yrs of serv, Class A and B: 9/10 of an allowance computed as an unreduced serv retirement allowance based on average final compensation and credited serv to date of retirement.	Compulsory at at age 70; normal, age 65; voluntary, age 60 or 30 yrs serv. Benefit actuarially reduced for retirement earlier than 65.

STATE, PLAN, AND MEMBER INSTITUTIONS	PROVISIONS APPLY TO	REQ &/OR VOL	WAITING PERIOD	CONTRIBUTIONS		PENSION BENEFIT FORMULA	PRERETIREMENT DEATH BENEFIT	VESTING PROVISIONS	RETIREMENT AGE
				INDIV	INST				
TEXAS: Teacher Retirement System of Texas Angelo State College East Texas State U Lamar State College of Technology Midwestern U North Texas State U Sam Houston State College Southwest Texas State College Stephen F. Austin State College Sul Ross State College Texas A & M U 　Prairie View A & M College 　Tarleton State College Texas College of Arts and Industries Texas Southern U Texas Technological College Texas Woman's U U of Houston U of Texas 　Arlington State College 　U of Texas at El Paso West Texas State U 　OASDHI	All EEs	Req, vol for EEs hired at age 60 or over	None	6% of salary up to $8,400 plus $5.00 annual membership fee	Matches EE contribs	1½% of average salary (not to exceed $8,400) of highest 10 yrs times yrs of serv.	Beneficiary may select one of the following: Death Benefits (1) 1 yrs salary up to $8,400, or (2) 60 mos of annuity payments based on serv to date of death, or (3) a reduced life annuity based on serv to date of death and age of beneficiary, or (4) return of EE contribs with interest. Survivor Benefits (4½ mos serv required.) A $500 lump sum plus (1) widow only, $75 per month from age 65 to death or remarriage, or (2) widow and 1 or more children under 18, $150 per month until youngest reaches 18, or (3) 1 child under 18, $75 per month, or (4) 2 children or more under 18, $150 per month.	Return of EE contribs with interest. After 10 yrs serv, EE may leave contribs on deposit and receive formula benefit at age 65, or at age 60 with 20 yrs of serv. Disability 10 yrs or less: $50 per month for a time equal to the number of creditable months of serv. 10 yrs or more: an annuity for life based on benefit formula reduced according to age at disability, or $50 per month for life, whichever is greater.	Normal, age 60 and 20 yrs serv, or age 65 and 10 yrs serv. Early retirement at age 55 with 15 yrs serv (benefit reduced from age 65); or at age 55 with 25 yrs of serv (benefit reduced from age 60); or at any age with 30 yrs serv (benefit reduced from age 60).
U.S. GOVERNMENT: Civil Service Retirement System Agricultural Extension Services District of Columbia Teachers College U.S. Department of Agriculture Graduate School U.S. Air Force Academy U.S. Air Force Institute U.S. Coast Guard Academy U.S. Judge Advocate General's School U.S. Merchant Marine Academy U.S. Military Academy U.S. Naval Academy U.S. Naval Postgraduate School 　No OASDHI	All civilian EEs	Req	None	6½% of salary	An amount equal to amount withheld from EEs	(1) 1½% of highest average salary in any consecutive 5 yrs times 5 yrs of serv, plus (2) 1 3/4% of "high-5" salary times yrs of serv over 5 and up to 10, plus (3) 2% of "high-5" salary times yrs of serv over 10. Whenever the cost of living nationwide goes up by at least 3% over the Consumer Price Index for the month used as a base for the most recent cost of living increase and stays up for 3 consecutive months, an increase equal to the percentage rise is granted. The increase becomes effective the 1st day of the 3rd month after the price index has gone up by 3% and stays up for 3 consecutive months.	Return of EE contribs with interest if EE had less than 5 yrs serv and no dependent survivors. After 5 yrs serv, widow or dependent widower paid 55% of annuity EE had earned at death but not reduced for EE under age 55. Benefit for each eligible child is the lesser of 40% of "high-5" average salary divided by number of children, or $1,938.60 divided by number of children, or $661.20. If no wife or husband survives, benefit for each eligible child is 50% of EEs "high-5" average salary divided by number of children, or $2,380.32 divided by number of children, or $793.44.	Return of EE contribs with interest. After 5 yrs, EE may leave contribs on deposit for deferred formula annuity payable at age 62. Disability After 5 yrs serv, minimum basic annuity of the lesser of 40% of "high-5" average salary, or regular pension formula figured as if EE had reached age 60.	Compulsory at age 70 after 15 or more yrs of serv. Optional at age 62 and 5 yrs of serv, age 60 and 20 yrs of serv, or age 55 and 30 yrs of serv. Benefit actuarially reduced for retirement under age 55.

STATE, PLAN, AND MEMBER INSTITUTIONS	PROVISIONS APPLY TO	REQ &/OR VOL	WAITING PERIOD	CONTRIBUTIONS		PENSION BENEFIT FORMULA	PRERETIREMENT DEATH BENEFIT	VESTING PROVISIONS	RETIREMENT AGE
				INDIV	INST				
UTAH: Utah State Retirement System College of Southern Utah College of Eastern Utah U of Utah Utah State U of Agr and Applied Science Snow College Weber State College OASDHI	All EEs (TIAA–CREF is alternative)	Req	None	7/1/67-4% sal 7/1/69-4¼% sal 7/1/71-4½% sal 7/1/73-4¾% sal 7/1/75-5% sal	An amount equal to the total of EE contribs, not assigned to individual accounts	1% of average annual salary (5 highest consecutive yrs in the last 10 yrs) for each yr of serv after 7/1/67. Serv before 7/1/67 limited to 1% times yrs of serv before 7/1/67 times $6,000 salary average.	If beneficiary is spouse or dependent child, return of EE contribs with interest plus 50% of average annual salary using last 5 yrs earnings. Minimum benefit payable is $600. If deceased age 55-59 with 30 yrs serv, age 60-64 with 20 yrs serv, or age 65 with 10 yrs serv, spouse may receive survivorship annuity.	Return of EE contribs with interest, less withdrawal fee. After 4 yrs serv EE may leave contribs on deposit and receive deferred annuity at age 65 based on pension formula. Disability After 10 yrs serv: if under age 60, benefit of 90% of 1% of final average salary times yrs of serv to date of disability; if over 60, benefit of 80% of 1% of final average salary times yrs of serv. If benefit is less than 25% of final average salary, yrs of serv from date of disability to age 65 are added for calculation; if added, maximum benefit is 25% of final average salary.	Normal retirement at age 65 and at least 4 yrs serv. Benefit actuarially reduced if retirement is under age 65; early retirement permitted at ages 55-59 with 30 yrs serv; 60-61, 20 yrs; or 62-64, 10 yrs.
VERMONT: State Teachers' Retirement System of Vermont Castleton State College Johnson State College Lyndon State College Vermont Technical College OASDHI	Fac & off hired prior to establishment of TIAA-CREF plan in 1963 (other EEs in Vermont Employees' Retirement System)	Req	None	Percentage of salary based on sex and age at time of entry into plan (e.g., male age 30, 6.82%; age 59 and over, 8.98%)	Percentage of payroll determined by annual actuarial valuation	Annuity which is actuarial equivalent of EE contribs plus pension to provide a total benefit of 1/70 of average final compensation multiplied by number of yrs of membership serv not in excess of 35 yrs. (Average final compensation is average of highest 5 consecutive yrs.)	Refund of EE contribs plus interest. After 1 yr of serv, or before 1 yr for accidental death, survivor benefit of $50 per month paid to each dependent child (not exceeding 3) until age 18. Death at 60 or over, or with 35 yrs serv, surviving spouse receives survivor annuity in lieu of cash benefit.	Return of EE contribs with interest. Disability With 15 yrs serv including last 5 preceding disability: annuity which is actuarial equivalent of EE contribs plus pension equal to 9/10 of 1/70 of average final compensation multiplied by number of yrs of membership serv not in excess of 35.	Normal at 60; compulsory at 70; voluntary after 35 yrs serv or age 60 regardless of serv. Benefit actuarially reduced for retirement under age 60.
VERMONT: Vermont Employees' Retirement System Castleton State College Johnson State College Lyndon State College U of Vermont Vermont Technical College OASDHI	EEs other than fac & adm off (Fac & adm off participate in TIAA–CREF plan) Nonacademic EEs at the U of Vermont have the option to participate in TIAA–CREF plan.	Req	3 yrs of continuous serv	Percentage of salary based on sex and age at time of entry into plan (e.g., male age 30, 5.4%; age 64 and over, 27.31%)* *An EE may reduce his contribs to 4% of salary. Benefits are correspondingly reduced.	Balance necessary to provide benefit	(1) An annuity provided by the member's contribs, plus (2) a pension equal to 1/140 of average of highest 5 yrs annual salary times yrs of serv as a member of VERS plus 3 yrs to a maximum of 35 yrs.	Before age 65, return of EE contribs with interest. After age 65, or 25 yrs serv, survivor benefit to dependent spouse in lieu of cash settlement.	Return of EE contribs with interest. After 10 yrs serv, member may leave contribs in System and receive allowance at age 65. Disability After 12 yrs of serv: (1) an annuity provided by his contribs; (2) a pension equal to 9/10 of pension payable as of date of disability.	Compulsory at 70; vol at 65. Early at age 60 if male, 55 if female, with 10 yrs serv. Benefit actuarially reduced for retirement under age 65.

STATE, PLAN, AND MEMBER INSTITUTIONS	PROVISIONS APPLY TO	REQ &/OR VOL	WAITING PERIOD	CONTRIBUTIONS		PENSION BENEFIT FORMULA	PRERETIREMENT DEATH BENEFIT	VESTING PROVISIONS	RETIREMENT AGE
				INDIV	INST				
VIRGINIA: Virginia Supplemental Retirement System College of William and Mary Longwood College Madison College Medical College of Virginia Old Dominion College Radford College Richmond Professional Institute U of Virginia* Virginia Military Institute Virginia Polytechnic Institute Virginia State College OASDHI	All EEs *(Fac & adm off of U of Virginia may participate in a TIAA-CREF plan rather than in State plan)	Req for those under age 60 at time of employment	None	5½% on salary in excess of $1,200	Balance necessary to fund benefit	1 3/8% of average annual salary of highest 5 consecutive yrs serv, in excess of $1,200, for each yr of serv	Under 60, refund of EE contribs with interest. Over 60, same as above or optional monthly survivor benefit to beneficiary if death is between age 60 and 65 or EE has credited at least 30 yrs serv. Disability (1) 10 yrs of serv; (2) under age 65. Disability retirement allowance computed under retirement formula except that credited serv smaller of (a) twice actual period of credited serv; or (b) period of serv the member would have completed at age 60 had he remained in serv. Annual disability allowance with Social Security is guaranteed to be not less than the larger of (a) $1,000 or (b) 25% of the average final compensation.	Refund of EE contribs with interest. After 10 yrs serv, EE may elect to leave contribs on deposit and receive deferred retirement benefit after age 60 based on benefit formula.	65; optional after age 60, with benefit formula actuarially reduced if service is less than 30 yrs.
WASHINGTON: Washington Public Employees' Retirement System Central Washington State College Eastern Washington State College U of Washington Washington State U Western Washington State College OASDHI	Non academic EEs	Req	None	5% of salary	6% of salary	Money purchase annuity based on EE contribs, plus $100 per yr, plus 1/120 of average final compensation over highest 5 yrs serv for each yr of serv	Return of EE contribs with interest; after 10 yrs serv, spouse eligible for retirement benefit based on benefit EE had earned to date of death. Disability (1) Nonduty-connected: money purchase annuity purchased to date of disability, plus pension based on application of benefit formula to yrs of serv to date of disability, not actuarially reduced because of age. Total not to exceed lesser of $1,800 or ½ of final average compensation. Pension portion may not exceed $1,500 annually. (2) Duty-connected: under age 60, benefit of 2/3 of average final compensation, not exceeding $2,400. At age 60, benefit is recomputed to provide money purchase annuity EE would have received had he continued serv to age 60 at salary on date of disability, plus pension based on formula.	Return of EE contribs with interest; after 10 yrs serv, EE may elect to leave contribs on deposit and receive deferred annuity at age 60 or later based on benefit formula.	Vol at age 60 and at least 5 yrs serv; any age and 30 yrs of serv; age 55 with 25 yrs of serv; compulsory at 70. Full formula benefit payable at 60 or after
WASHINGTON: Washington State Teachers' Retirement System Central Washington State College Eastern Washington State College Western Washington State College OASDHI	Fac members who at time of employment are participating in Washington State Teachers' Retirement System (other fac, and all fac at U of Washington and Washington State U, participate in TIAA-CREF plan)	Req	3 mos	5% of salary	Balance needed to fund benefit	Money purchase annuity on EE contribs, plus pension of 1/120 average salary for highest paid 5 yrs in last 10 for each yr of serv.	Return of EE contribs with interest, plus $300 death benefit. After 15 yrs serv, $50 per month for widow, or, if EE is eligible to retire (30 yrs serv or age 60 and 5 yrs serv), spouse eligible for survivor annuity based on earned benefits to date of death.	Return of EE contribs with interest. After 10 yrs serv, EE may elect to leave contribs on deposit for deferred benefit based on formula. Disability After 15 yrs serv, annuity from EE contribs to date of disability, plus pension based on yrs of serv to disability, actuarially reduced for age under 60, with minimum of $4 per month per yr of serv. Temporary disability $120 per month for minimum of 60 days and maximum of 2 years.	Age 60 with 5 yrs serv or 30 yrs serv.

STATE, PLAN, AND MEMBER INSTITUTIONS	PROVISIONS APPLY TO	REQ &/OR VOL	WAITING PERIOD	CONTRIBUTIONS		PENSION BENEFIT FORMULA	PRERETIREMENT DEATH BENEFIT	VESTING PROVISIONS	RETIREMENT AGE
				INDIV	INST				
WEST VIRGINIA: West Virginia Teachers Retirement System Bluefield State College Concord College Fairmont State College Glenville State College Marshall U Potomac State College of West Virginia State U Shepherd College West Liberty State College West Virginia Institute of Technology West Virginia State College West Virginia U OASDHI	All EEs (all EEs also covered by a supplementary TIAA–CREF plan)	Req	None	4½% of salary not to exceed $216 annually (higher education limit—EEs also participate in TIAA–CREF)	Matches EE contribs	Plan A or B whichever is greater. **Plan A** (1) Money purchase benefit based on matched contribs, plus (2) $24 for each yr of serv as teacher, plus (3) $6 for each yr of serv as teacher to a maximum of $192, plus (4) prior serv. **Plan B** 1% of average annual salary (average of highest 5 in last 15 to a maximum of $12,000) times yrs of serv; $4,800 is maximum salary on which calculations are based for EEs at institutions of higher education. (Plan B has a limit of $4,800 salary for those in higher education.)	Total EE and ER contribs with interest. If death after age 50 and 25 yrs serv, beneficiary elects income option.	Refund of EE contribs with interest. After 20 yrs serv, EE may leave contribs on deposit for deferred formula pension at age 60. **Disability** After 10 yrs serv, calculated as if EE had retired instead of become disabled. If EE is under 50 he is credited with EE and ER contribs as if he had contributed until age 50.	Compulsory at age 65 unless ER requests retention. Optional at age 60 after 5 yrs serv; optional at age 55 with 30 yrs serv losing 10% of prior serv credit. Benefit actuarially reduced for retirement under age 65.

WISCONSIN: Wisconsin Retirement Fund
 	
U of Wisconsin
Wisconsin State U at
  Eau Claire
  La Crosse
  Oshkosh
  Platteville
  River Falls
  Stevens Point
  Superior
  Whitewater
Stout State U
 	
OASDHI
	All EEs except fac & adm	Req	6 mos	4.5% on salary subject to Social Security, 7% on balance. (Of above, 2% of salary is currently paid by ER.)	Amount required to assure formula benefit on a fully funded basis.	(1) Formula: A life annuity guaranteed to return EEs credit accumulations of: 6/7% of average earnings for 5 highest yrs during last 10 yrs of creditable serv plus 3/7% of such earnings in excess of the Social Security base times yrs of creditable serv. May participate in variable annuity program (up to ½ of EE contribs and an equal amount from ER). Participation in the variable annuity increases or decreases formula benefit depending on whether variable accumulation is greater or less than a corresponding fixed fund accumulation. Or, (2) an annuity purchased by the accumulations of EEs contribs plus ½ of (1).	Before age 60, return of EEs contribs with interest as a single payment or as an annuity. After age 60, the above or a survivor's benefit payable to spouse, minor or handicapped child or dependent beneficiary, as if the EE had retired the day of death on a joint and survivorship annuity.	Under age 55, EE may elect to withdraw his own contribs with interest except the portion based on the 2% currently contributed by ER or leave contribs on deposit and elect deferred annuity payable at age 55 or later based on benefit (1) or (2). After age 55 EE may not withdraw deposits, automatically qualifies for deferred benefit (1) or (2).
								
								Disability
								After 5 yrs of serv (immediately if disability is serv-connected) but before age 65, disability benefit is the lesser of annuity income of: (1) 50% of average monthly earnings during highest 5 consecutive yrs or (2) 1½% of average monthly salary during highest 5 yrs times number of yrs of serv, including yrs between date of disability and 65th birthday.
									Normal age 65. Benefit (1) actuarially reduced for retirement under normal retirement age.

STATE, PLAN, AND MEMBER INSTITUTIONS	PROVISIONS APPLY TO	REQ &/OR VOL	WAITING PERIOD	CONTRIBUTIONS		PENSION BENEFIT FORMULA	PRERETIREMENT DEATH BENEFIT	VESTING PROVISIONS	RETIREMENT AGE
				INDIV	INST				

WISCONSIN: Wisconsin State Teachers Retirement System
 	
U of Wisconsin
Wisconsin State U at
  Eau Clare
  La Crosse
  Oshkosh
  Platteville
  River Falls
  Stevens Point
  Superior
  Whitewater
Stout State U
 	
  OASDHI
	Fac & adm	Req	None	4½% on salary subject to Social Security tax, 7% of salary in excess of Social Security base	Same amount as EE plus additional amount required to provide formula benefit	(1) Formula: A life annuity with 5 yrs certain of: 6/7% of average earnings for the 5 highest yrs during the last 10 yrs of creditable serv plus 3/7% of such earnings in excess of the Social Security base times yrs of creditable serv. EE may put up to ½ of his contrib and an equal amount from ERs in variable annuity. Participation in the variable annuity increases or reduces amount of formula benefit, depending on whether variable accumulation is greater or less than corresponding fixed fund accumulation. Or, (2) an annuity of twice the amount purchasable by the accumulation of the contribs of EE.	Before age 60, return of EE contribs with interest as a single payment or as an annuity. After age 60, the above or a survivor's benefit, payable to spouse, minor or handicapped child or dependent beneficiary, as if the EE had retired the day of death on a joint and survivorship annuity.	Under age 50, EE may elect to withdraw his own deposits with interest or elect deferred annuity payable at age 50 or later based on benefit (1) or (2). After age 50 EE may not withdraw deposits, automatically qualifies for deferred benefit (1) or (2).
								
								Disability
								After 5 yrs serv (within 7 yrs preceding disability), (1) annuity of 50% of final average salary, or (2) 1½% of final average salary for each yr of serv, including yrs from date of disability to 65th birthday, whichever is the lesser.
									Normal age 70; EE may begin benefit of type (2) any time after age 50, or type (1) on a reduced basis between ages 50 and 65 and on a full basis after age 65. EE contribs not required after age 70. Serv after age 70 not counted in formula.

WYOMING: Wyoming Retirement System U of Wyoming OASDHI	All EEs	Req	None	3% of 1st $8,600 of salary to July, 1969; 5% of 1st $8,600 thereafter	Same as individual contrib	Money purchase	Return of EE contribs with interest. Disability After 15 yrs serv, benefit equal to that which would have applied had serv continued to age 60.	Return of EE contribs with interest, providing the member has less than 4 yrs serv. After 4 yrs of serv, EE may leave contribs on deposit and receive deferred annuity at age 60 based on EE and ER contribs.	Normal at age 60 with 4 yrs serv, or at any age (with actuarially reduced benefits if under 60) with 25 yrs serv. Extensions beyond 65 with ER consent.

Appendix 6

SELF-ADMINISTERED
OR TRUSTEED
RETIREMENT PLANS

This appendix summarizes the principal provisions of the self-administered or trusteed retirement plans in institutions employing 100 or more full-time faculty. The plans of smaller institutions are not described because of limited space.

The two largest plans in this appendix are the University of California Retirement System and the State Universities Retirement System of Illinois. The great majority of the rest of the plans cover clerical-service employees and are accompanied by a TIAA-CREF plan for faculty and administrative groups.

Most of the abbreviations used in this appendix are self-explanatory, except for EE and ER, which mean, respectively, employee and employer.

INSTITUTION	PROVISIONS APPLY TO	REQ &/OR VOL	WAITING PERIOD	CONTRIBUTIONS		PENSION BENEFIT FORMULA	PRERETIREMENT DEATH BENEFIT	VESTING PROVISIONS	RETIREMENT AGE
				INDIV	INST				
Amherst College Amherst, Massachusetts Self-Administered Plan	Nonacademic EEs in the maintenance and serv areas All other EEs covered by TIAA-CREF plan.	Req	None	None	Amount necessary to fund benefit. (Money is taken from current operating budget)	2% of final salary times yrs of serv less receipts from primary Social Security, up to a maximum of $6,000 per yr. (No benefit provided if EE does not work until age 65.)	None	None	Normal at age 65; extensions permitted with College's approval.
Antioch College Yellow Springs, Ohio Supplemental Pension Plan	Fac and adm off (these EEs also covered by TIAA-CREF plan)	Req	None	None	Amount necessary to fund benefit	¾% of the average of the 3 highest yrs salaries times the number of yrs of serv	None	EE eligible for a deferred annuity equal to 2/3 of benefit payable at 65 after 10 yrs of serv increasing each yr to 100% of earned benefit after 15 yrs of serv.	Normal at age 65. Early at age 60 or after.
Boston University Boston, Massachusetts Staff Retirement Plan	All full-time nonacademic EEs hired on or before their 55th birthday. Fac and adm staff covered by TIAA-CREF or insurance company plans.	Vol	3 yrs of serv and attainment of age 30	Approximately 2% of salary within the Social Security wage base and 4% of the excess	Balance necessary to provide benefit	A yearly benefit equal to one-half of the sum of his contribs	Return of EE contribs with interest	Return of EE contribs with interest. After 15 yrs of serv and attainment of age 55, EE may leave contribs on deposit and receive an annuity at age 65.	Normal, 65.
Bryn Mawr College Bryn Mawr, Pennsylvania Self-Administered	Full-time maintenance and serv EEs. All other EEs covered by TIAA-CREF plan.	Req	None	None	Amount necessary to provide benefit	1% to 2.5%, depending on yrs of serv, of average of final 5 yrs salary times yrs of serv. After 30 yrs of serv, benefit increased by $1 per month for each yr of serv over 30. Benefit payable only at age 65 with 10 or more yrs of serv.	None	No vesting before retirement	Normal at age 65; no extensions. 10 yrs serv required.
Bryn Mawr College Bryn Mawr, Pennsylvania Trusteed by Philadelphia Savings Fund Society	Full-time fac, adm and cler EEs. (TIAA-CREF is alternative.)	Req	None	None	10% of salary	Money purchase	Return of full accumulation	Immediate full vesting Disability Benefit may begin at any age in event of disability.	Normal at age 65; extensions to age 68.
University of California University of California Retirement System includes Berkeley Davis Irvine Los Angeles Riverside San Diego San Francisco Santa Barbara Santa Cruz No OASDHI	All EEs	Req Req	Basic plan: none. Supplemental plan: 1 yr & age 30 (vol immed).	(Supplemental plan.) Per cent of salary based on age of entry and sex, e.g., men: age 30, 7.35%; age 50, 9%; women: age 30, 8.48%; age 50, 10.96%. Reduced by 3% for instructors and professional ranks. In addition to the basic and supplemental plans, the staff member may contribute any amount of $10 monthly or more (by payroll deduction only) to the voluntary Fixed Annuity Plan or to the voluntary Variable Annuity Plan, but not to both at once. There is no ER contrib to these plans.	(Basic plan 8.25% of aggregate staff salary, not credited to individual accounts	At age 65 and after, 2.17% of highest average salary of any 3 consecutive yrs for each yr of serv, but not more than 80% of highest 3 yrs average salary. Benefit reduced to account for any yrs in which individual contribs were not made. Formula percentage reduced for retirement under age 65.	(1) Up to 8 yrs serv, $130 per month for spouse plus children's benefits. (2) 8 yrs or more serv, monthly benefit for spouse of 1/3 of benefit EE would have received at age 67 based on salary at death, plus children's benefit. (3) Age 55 & 20 yrs serv, or age 62: monthly benefit for spouse of 75% of benefit EE would have received at retirement on date of death. (4) 6 months salary for each yr serv, up to 6. (5) Balance of annuity accumulation to extent it exceeds value of 75% benefit in (3).	Under 5 yrs serv, refund of EE contribs with interest. After 5 yrs serv and age 30, may elect to leave contribs in system and receive deferred annuity based on the regular retirement formula, to begin between ages 55 and 67. Disability After 2 yrs of credited serv, monthly benefit equal to 1½% of highest consecutive 3 yr monthly salary rate times yrs of credited serv. Member with 10 yrs of serv or accumulation of $2,500 will receive benefit equal to one-half single life annuity he would have received at age 67.	Mandatory July 1 next following 67th birthday. Vol after age 62, or at age 55 with 5 yrs serv.

INSTITUTION	PROVISIONS APPLY TO	REQ &/OR VOL	WAITING PERIOD	CONTRIBUTIONS		PENSION BENEFIT FORMULA	PRERETIREMENT DEATH BENEFIT	VESTING PROVISIONS	RETIREMENT AGE
				INDIV	INST				
Carleton College Northfield, Minnesota Self-Administered Plan	All full-time EEs between the ages of 30 and 56	Vol	Minimum of 6 months; enrollment is on Sept 1 of each yr.	5% of salary	Amount necessary to fund benefit	1½% of average salary times number of yrs serv. Maximum 50% of final salary.	25 times last monthly salary	Return of EE contribs; EE may leave contribs on deposit and receive benefit at normal retirement age based on total accumulation.	Normal at age 65; early at age 60; year-to-year extensions beyond age 65.
Carnegie-Mellon University Pittsburgh, Pennsylvania	All non-academic EEs Fac and adm staff covered by TIAA-CREF plan.	Req	None	None	Amount necessary to provide benefit	Benefit equal to 2% of salary times yrs of serv up to 20 plus 1% of salary times yrs of serv over 20. Reduced by amount of Social Security benefit. Maximum 50% of final salary.	None	None	Normal at age 65.
Chicago College of Osteopathy Chicago, Illinois Self-Insured	All full-time non-academic EEs Fac covered by TIAA-CREF plan.	Req	1 yr	None	Amount necessary to provide benefit	$2 per month times yrs of serv	None	Full after 15 yrs if under age 45 when employment commenced; full after 10 yrs of serv if employed at age 45 or over.	Normal at 65. May be extended.
University of Chicago Chicago, Illinois Retirement Income Plan for Employees	All full-time EEs except fac Fac in TIAA-CREF plan.	Req	EEs under age 30, vol after 2 yrs; req after 2 yrs and age 30. EEs age 30 to 65, vol immediately; req after 2 yrs.	1 2/3% of salary to $6,600; 5% of salary above $6,600	Balance necessary to provide benefit	Annual benefit of 60% of the total of EE contribs made at the 1 2/3% rate plus 40% of the total of EE contribs made at the 5% rate.	Return of EE contribs with interest. If death after age 55, dependent spouse receives annuity payments for 5 yrs in an amount equal to EE benefit according to the benefit formula and based on contribs to date of death.	Return of EE contribs with interest. After 5 yrs serv and age 40, or 10 yrs of serv regardless of age, may elect deferred retirement income at age 65 in accordance with benefit formula. Retirement may be postponed with consent of Board of Directors. No contribs are made after age 65 and retirement benefit is same as EE would have received at 65.	Normal, age 65. Early, age 55 and 10 yrs serv with consent of University. Benefit reduced by 5% for each yr under age 65.
Colby College Waterville, Maine Self-Administered Plan	Nonacademic EEs in the cler, maintenance, and serv areas.	Req Fac and adm staff covered by TIAA-CREF plan.	15 yrs	None	Amount necessary to fund benefit	1% of average final 5 yrs salary times the number of full yrs of serv. Salary in excess of $5,000 per yr not counted in calculating the benefit. Minimum benefit is $200 per yr; there is no maximum.	None	None	Optional at 65; compulsory at 70.
Columbia University New York, New York Self-Administered Plan	All full-and part-time (20 hours per week or more) nonfac EEs hired before age 55. Academic staff covered by TIAA-CREF plan.	Req	Age 30	None	Amount necessary to fund benefit	1% of annual salary up to $6,600 and 1½% of salary in excess of $6,600 for each yr of serv. Salary on July 1, 1960, applies to all prior serv.	None (separate life insurance furnished by University)	EE eligible for deferred annuity after 10 yrs serv. Disability If EE is age 55 with 15 yrs of serv, disability income based on yrs of serv to date of disability.	Normal at age 65; extensions with University approval up to age 70. Early retirement with reduced benefits at age 62 with 10 yrs serv.

INSTITUTION	PROVISIONS APPLY TO	REQ &/OR VOL	WAITING PERIOD	CONTRIBUTIONS		PENSION BENEFIT FORMULA	PRERETIREMENT DEATH BENEFIT	VESTING PROVISIONS	RETIREMENT AGE
				INDIV	INST				
Cornell University Ithaca, New York Self-Administered	Endowed division EEs who are cler, secretarial, maintenance or serv EEs. Fac and adm staff covered by TIAA-CREF plan.	Req	None	None	Funded currently; University pays each retired EE out of current funds	1% of average of 5 highest yrs of earnings times yrs of serv plus ½ of 1% of salary above average Social Security wage times yrs of serv.	None	EE age 60 with 10 yrs of serv may receive actuarially reduced pension.	Normal at age 65; no limit on extensions.
Duke University Durham, North Carolina	Non-academic EEs Fac and other pro staff covered by TIAA-CREF plan.	Req	Age 30 and 3 yrs serv	None	4.73% of total wages, including overtime	An annual amount equal to the sum of (1) ¾ of 1% of the first $4,800 of the individual's annual salary, and (2) 1% of any excess, for each yr of employment.	None	Age 55 and 15 yrs serv	Normal at age 65. No extensions.
Harvard University Cambridge, Massachusetts Retirement Income Plan For Hourly Employees	Nonacademic EEs, hourly.	Req	3 yrs	Approximately 1.5% of salary	Amount necessary to provide benefit	Annual benefit equal to 1.8% of total salary	Return of EE contribs with interest	Return of EE contribs with interest. After 10 yrs and age 40, EE may elect a deferred annuity commencing at normal or early retirement date.	Normal at age 65. Early at 55 with 10 yrs of serv.
Retirement Income Plan For Salaried Employees	Nonacademic EEs, salaried. Academic staff covered by TIAA-CREF or separate self-administered plan.	Req	3 yrs	None	Amount necessary to provide benefit	Annual benefit of 1.5% of total salary	None	After 10 yrs and age 40, EE may elect a deferred annuity commencing at normal or early retirement date.	Normal at age 65. Early at 55 with 10 yrs of serv.

Harvard University Cambridge, Massachusetts
 	
Retirement Plan for Officers of Instruction and Administration
	Fac and adm off (TIAA-CREF is alternative)	Req	1 yr; immediate if appointment is for more than 1 yr.	None	12.5% to 20% of salary depending on age	Money purchase. Supplemental retirement income for plan participants who are in Harvard serv upon their normal retirement date (age 66), or actual retirement date, if earlier, and have 15 or more yrs of such serv. Supplemental benefit is the amount, if any, by which the individual's "minimum pension" benefit exceeds his "basic retirement income," where:
						  Minimum pension is a single life annuity of 2% of final average salary (average salary for fiscal yr in which EE retires and the 5 preceding fiscal yrs) for each yr of serv, but not exceeding a benefit of 50% of final average salary. Special formula used if ER or EE contribs required under the plan have been made to CREF.
						  Basic retirement income is the amount of single life annuity commencing with normal retirement date under the regular operation of the Harvard retirement plan(s).
							Benefit equal to full accumulation	Purchase of immediate or deferred annuity with amount of total accumulation on withdrawal.	Normal at age 66. Extensions, but contribs cease at 66.

INSTITUTION	PROVISIONS APPLY TO	REQ &/OR VOL	WAITING PERIOD	CONTRIBUTIONS		PENSION BENEFIT FORMULA	PRERETIREMENT DEATH BENEFIT	VESTING PROVISIONS	RETIREMENT AGE
				INDIV	INST				
College of the Holy Cross Worcester, Massachusetts	All EEs except fac. Lay faculty covered by TIAA-CREF plan.	Req	3 yrs	None	Amount necessary to provide benefit	¾ of 1% of annual salary within the Social Security base plus 1½% of salary in excess of Social Security base for each yr of participation in the plan. Minimum benefit $2 per month for each yr of serv.	None	10 yrs of serv and attainment of age 55.	Normal at age 65. Early at age 55 with 10 yrs serv.
Illinois State Universities Retirement System Eastern Illinois University Illinois State University Illinois Teacher Colleges, Chicago Northern Illinois University Southern Illinois University University of Illinois Western Illinois University No OASDHI	All EEs	Req	None	6% of basic annual salary for retirement; 1% of salary but not more than $80 per year for survivors' benefits.	Balance to provide benefits; estimated to be 10.09% of total payroll	At age 60 or later, 1 2/3% times number of yrs serv times average earnings during period of 5 consecutive highest 5 yrs salary (including summer session earnings). Between ages 55 and 60 with reduction of ½ of 1% for each month that annuity begins prior to age 60.	After 1½ yrs serv, monthly survivor annuity of up to $250 to widow at age 55 and before 55 if dependent children are in her care, plus $1,000 lump sum benefit plus refund of EE contribs with interest. Before 1½ yrs serv, $2,000 to $5,000 lump sum depending on salary plus refund of EE contribs with interest.	Under age 60, refund of EE contribs with interest. After 60, only if annuity payable is less than $30 per mo. After 5 yrs serv, EE may leave contribs on deposit for deferred formula annuity at age 62, or after 10 yrs serv for a deferred annuity at age 60. Disability Disability benefit after 2 yrs serv for illness and immediately for accident of 50% of the greater of: (1) basic monthly salary, or (2) average monthly earnings during the 24 months immediately preceding the month in which disability occurs. Benefit continues until payment total equals 50% of total earnings received during serv to date of disability.	Age 60 (age 55 with reduced benefits) with 10 yrs serv or 8 yrs serv if terminates after age 55. Age 62 with 5 yrs serv. Compulsory retirement at age 68.
Jefferson Medical College Philadelphia, Pennsylvania	All EEs except fac, senior adm staff, department heads. Fac and other pro Staff covered by TIAA–CREF plan.	Req	July 1 following employment.	None on first $6,600 of annual salary; 5% of salary in excess of $6,600	Balance necessary to provide benefit	Higher of: (1) 40% of average salary over highest consecutive 5 yrs, minus primary Social Security benefit, or (2) monthly benefit equal to $2 times yrs of serv	Return of any EE contribs with interest	Return of any EE contribs with interest tensions to age 70 permitted. Retirement date for EEs employed after age 55 is 10 yrs after employment date.	Normal at age 65. Early at age 55 with 15 yrs of serv. Annual ex-
Louisiana State University Baton Rouge, Louisiana	All regular EEs not in Federal Civil Service or State Retirement Systems	Req but EE may elect to participate in the Teachers Retirement System (fac) or the State Employees' Retirement System (other EEs) instead.	None	None	Amount necessary to provide benefit	Percentage of highest 5 yrs average salary according to chart, varying by age and yrs of serv from a minimum of 11.22% at age 65 with 10 yrs serv to a maximum of 33.33%. No benefit if EE has less than 10 yrs serv.	None	None Disability 10 yrs serv required. Benefit is amount specified on chart for EEs actual serv, but the "age 65" column is used rather than the EEs actual age.	Normal at age 65. Compulsory at age 70. Prior to age 65 with 20 yrs serv and Board approval.

INSTITUTION	PROVISIONS APPLY TO	REQ &/OR VOL	WAITING PERIOD	CONTRIBUTIONS		PENSION BENEFIT FORMULA	PRERETIREMENT DEATH BENEFIT	VESTING PROVISIONS	RETIREMENT AGE
				INDIV	INST				
Loyola University Chicago, Illinois	All full-time EEs	Req	No waiting period (90 days for staff and maintenance EEs only)	3½% of first $4,200 annual salary plus 5% of excess	Balance of cost, but not less than EE contribs	1% of salary up to $4,200 plus 1½% of excess salary for each yr of serv	Return of EE contribs plus interest. In addition, if EE was age 50 with 10 yrs serv, pension paid to widow of ½ the amount of husband's normal retirement allowance.	Return of EE contribs with interest. After 10 yrs of serv or age 50, EE may leave contribs on deposit and receive retirement allowance at early or normal date.	Early at age 55, actuarially reduced. Normal at 65; compulsory at 70.
Loyola University New Orleans, Louisiana Loyola Retirement Plan	(1) Lay full-time fac. (2) Staff members with fac rank. (3) Personnel with full-time contracts. (4) Others as determined by committee appointed by Board of Directors.	Vol	1 yr	3 % of salary	3% of salary	Money purchase	Return of total accumulation Disability Return of total accumulation	Return of percentages of EE and ER contribs with interest as shown below: Years Participation / Per Cent Less than 1 / 50 1-2 / 60 2-3 / 70 3-4 / 80 4-5 / 90 5 and over / 100	Normal at age 65 or later. Early at age 55 or later with consent of ER.
University of Maine Plan covers University of Maine at Orono Augusta Bangor Portland Aroostook State College Farmington State College Fort Kent State College Gorham State College Washington State College	Nonacademic EEs under age 55 at time of employment. State College EEs employed before May 27, 1968 may elect to remain in Maine State Retirement System.	Req	3 yrs and age 30	None	Amount necessary to provide benefit	1¼% of career average salary for each yr of participation	None Disability Early retirement in case of total disability is permitted after 10 yrs of participation and attainment of age 45.	None	Age 65 or anytime at or over age 55 with 15 yrs participation
Massachusetts Institute of Technology Cambridge, Massachusetts Trusteed Plan	All EEs	Req Req Vol	Fac, none. Nonfac EEs, after 5 yrs serv. Nonfac EEs over age 30—immediately; under age 30—1 yr serv.	5% of salary	Approximately 10% of salary	Money purchase, may include variable annuity. Formula for determining minimum benefit based on yrs of membership and average of last 10 yrs salary. Plan also provides separate spouse benefit inclusive of widow's benefit under Social Security.	Return of EE contribs with interest plus ER contribs equal to 200% of EE contribs with interest. Disability After 2 yrs participation, 60% of the first $1,000 of monthly salary plus 50% of excess. Maximum monthly benefit $1,500. Benefits reduced by primary Social Security disability benefits, and any other disability benefits from the Institute. Benefits begin after 6 mos of disability.	Return of EE contribs with interest. EE may elect a deferred benefit based on EE contribs plus a percentage of ER contribs according to yrs serv. Fully vested after 10 yrs serv.	Normal at age 65.

INSTITUTION	PROVISIONS APPLY TO	REQ &/OR VOL	WAITING PERIOD	CONTRIBUTIONS		PENSION BENEFIT FORMULA	PRERETIREMENT DEATH BENEFIT	VESTING PROVISIONS	RETIREMENT AGE
				INDIV	INST				
University of Miami Coral Gables, Florida Retirement Plan for Faculty Members and Staff Personnel (Annuity contracts purchased at retirement from Aetna Life Insurance Company.)	All EEs except those 57 or older at date of employment	Req	None	None	Amount required to provide benefits	7/8% of first $4,800 of final average salary plus 1 3/8% of the balance times number of yrs serv based on life annuity with 10 yrs certain. Final average salary is average of the highest 5 consecutive yrs of last 10.	Beneficiary receives life annuity with 10 yrs certain in the amount provided by the higher of: (1) a lump sum equal to EE basic compensation at time of death, or (2) the actuarial equivalent of his retirement income accrued to date of death. Disability Retired with a life annuity with 10 yrs certain that can be provided by the higher of: (1) a lump sum equal to his basic compensation at time of disability, or (2) the actuarial equivalent of his retirement income accrued to the date of disability.	None with serv of less than 5 yrs. With 5 yrs serv or more EE will receive the monthly income which can be provided by the actuarial equivalent of his retirement income accrued to date of termination and accumulated to his normal retirement date.	Normal at 65. Actuarially increased for retirement above 65 but serv beyond 65 not counted in determining benefits. Early at 55 with 10 yrs serv. Actuarially reduced for ages under 65.
University of Michigan Ann Arbor, Michigan Employee's Retirement Plan	EEs not eligible for the TIAA–CREF faculty retirement plan	Req Vol	3 yrs serv and age 30 Immediately	On Social Security earnings base: age 39 or less 8% age 40-49 9% age 50-69 10% less OASDHI tax Above Social Security earnings base: age 39 or less 5½% age 40-49 6½% age 50-69 7½%	Same as individual	Money purchase	Return of EE and ER contribs with interest	Return of EE contribs with interest. After 5 yrs, EE may leave contribs on deposit for deferred annuity based on EE contribs plus 28% of ER contribs, increasing to 100% for 10 yrs participation. if accumulation is less than $1,000, a lump sum benefit is paid. If over, purchase of life annuity from Connecticut General Life Insurance Company.	Normal, age 65; early, age 60; compulsory, age 70. Benefit actuarially reduced for retirement under age 65.
University of Missouri University of Missouri Retirement System includes Columbia Kansas City Rolla St. Louis	All EEs	Req	None	None	Amount required to provide benefit	1% of final average salary plus 0.6% of final average salary in excess of $4,800 for each yr of serv not to exceed 30. Final average salary is the average of the highest 5 consecutive yrs in the last 10.	Widow may receive life pension of ½ of disability benefit EE would have been entitled to if he had become disabled instead of dying. An additional 10% of widow's benefit is payable for each dependent child under 18. If no widow survives, each dependent child under 18 is eligible to receive a monthly benefit of 10% of the member's disability benefit as long as eligible.	Deferred annuity payable at age 68 or later if EE leaves system at age 55 or over with serv of 20 or more yrs Disability Same as retirement benefit, except, if EE has less than 15 yrs serv, his benefit is computed on basis of lesser of 15 yrs or amount of serv he would have had if he had continued in serv until age 70. Actuarial reduction on benefit in excess of 1% final average salary per yr serv if EE not eligible for Social Security disability benefits.	Optional at age 65; compulsory at age 70. Early retirement at age 60 or above, but benefits normally deferred until age 68.

INSTITUTION	PROVISIONS APPLY TO	REQ &/OR VOL	WAITING PERIOD	CONTRIBUTIONS		PENSION BENEFIT FORMULA	PRERETIREMENT DEATH BENEFIT	VESTING PROVISIONS	RETIREMENT AGE
				INDIV	INST				
University of New Hampshire Durham, New Hampshire University of New Hampshire Keene State College Plymouth State College	Nonacademics	Req; Entry not permitted after age 60.	None	None	Amount necessary to provide benefit	1½% of first $2,500 for each of first 10 yrs serv; 1% of first $2,500 for each yr between 10 and 30. Single life annuity only.	None	None	Normal at age 70 or at age 65 with 20 yrs serv or at any age with 35 yrs serv.
New York University New York, New York	All serv EEs not covered by separate union contracts Fac, adm and cler staffs covered by TIAA-CREF plan.	Req	None	None	Funds necessary to provide benefit	Final average salary times yrs of serv times .007. Final average salary is average of final 10 yrs salary.	None	Age 60 and 15 yrs of serv	Normal at age 65. Early after age 60.
Northwestern University Evanston, Illinois Noncontributory Staff Retirement Plan (Also has TIAA-CREF plan.)	All full-time EEs at least age 35, but under age 50	Req	None	None	Amount necessary to provide benefit	Unit benefit plan. Annual pension determined from pension table by actual salary paid during each yr of serv from age 35 to age 68.	None	None	Normal at 68. Extensions to age 70. Early at age 60.
University of Notre Dame South Bend, Indiana Self-Administered Plan	Full-time lay nonacademic EEs Lay fac and adm staff covered by TIAA–CREF plan.	Req	EE must attain age 35.	None, unless EE has annual salary of $7,500 or more, then EE must contrib 5% of total salary.	Balance necessary to fund benefit	Depends on yrs of serv and average last 10 yrs salary; e.g., (a) 15 yrs of serv, 20% of last 10 yrs average salary minus $539; (b) 20 yrs of serv, 26 2/3% of last 10 yrs average salary minus $539; (c) 25 yrs of serv, 33 1/3% of last 10 yrs average salary minus $539; (d) 30 yrs of serv, 40% of last 10 yrs average salary minus $539.	Return of EE contribs with 3% interest	None	Normal age 65.
Ohio Wesleyan University Delaware, Ohio	All full-time EEs other than fac and adm staff Fac and adm staff covered by TIAA-CREF plan.	Req	5 yrs and age 35	None	Amount necessary to provide benefit	1/50 of highest average 5 yrs salary times yrs of serv; maximum of 30 yrs serv; minimum of 15 yrs serv.	None	Full vesting after 15 yrs	Normal, 65. Early at 62, benefit actuarially reduced.
Princeton University Princeton, New Jersey Retirement Income Fund for Staff Employees	All full-time EEs except fac, adm, and pro staff. EEs hired after age 57 are not eligible. Academic and pro staff covered by TIAA–CREF plan.	Req	Age 30 and 1 yr serv	None	Amount necessary to fund benefit	1¼% of first $4,200 annual salary plus 1¾% of excess for each yr of participation.	If EE was age 55, benefit to widow age 50 or above in amount equal to amount payable to her under 50% survivor option, as if EE had retired on disability at time of his death.	50% after 10 yrs increasing 5% each yr thereafter. Full vesting after 20 yrs. Disability After age 55, normal retirement income accrued to date of disability.	Normal at age 65. Early after age 55 with reduced benefits with ER permission.

INSTITUTION	PROVISIONS APPLY TO	REQ &/OR VOL	WAITING PERIOD	CONTRIBUTIONS		PENSION BENEFIT FORMULA	PRERETIREMENT DEATH BENEFIT	VESTING PROVISIONS	RETIREMENT AGE
				INDIV	INST				
Rhode Island School of Design Providence, Rhode Island	All non-academic EEs Fac and adm staff covered by TIAA-CREF plan.	Req	2 yrs	None	Amount necessary to provide benefit	1¼% of salary for each yr of serv	None	Partial vesting after 10 yrs and attainment of age 45, increasing to full vesting after 15 yrs of serv.	Normal at age 65; earlier or later with ER consent; no credit is earned for participation after age 65.
Rice University Houston, Texas	All EEs (TIAA-CREF is an alternative.)	Req for assistant professors and above; others optional until 5 yrs serv and age 35. Those hired after age 55½ are not eligible.	None for assistant professors and above; 2 yrs serv and age 30 for others (waiting period may be waived by trustees).	5% of salary	5% of salary If member has attained tenure or age 35, institution will make additional contrib of 5% of salary in excess of Social Security wage base.	Money purchase. For those retiring at age 70 with 20 yrs serv, minimum benefit is smaller of $200 or ½ final salary.	Total accumulation including ER contribs paid to beneficiary as lump sum or annuity.	Upon termination, accumulated contribs purchase a single premium deferred annuity. If accumulation is under $2,000, return of EE contribs. Disability Early retirement (excluding ER contribs in excess of Social Security wage base).	Normal at age 70; no extensions. Early after age 60 with 5 yrs serv.
University of Rochester Rochester, New York	Full-time EEs who are cler, maintenance, serv, junior adm staff, or junior pro assistants. These EEs also covered by Metropolitan Insured Retirement plan. Fac and adm officers covered by TIAA-CREF plan.	Req	None	None	Amount necessary to purchase pension benefit each yr	Variable annuity:* each yr annuity purchased by 3/8% of salary up to Social Security base plus ¾% of salary above. In no event will variable annuity during retirement yr be less than 80% of annuity of previous yr. *See Insurance Company plan for fixed annuity portion of benefit.	None	After 10 yrs of serv, EE entitled to receive a pension at age 65	Normal at age 65; extensions permitted to age 70. Early with ER consent if age 55 or over.
St. Lawrence University Canton, New York Self-Administered Plan	Nonacademic EEs Academic staff covered by TIAA-CREF plan.	Req	15 yrs	None	Amount necessary to fund benefit	$600 per yr	None	None	Normal at age 65.
Smith College Northampton, Massachusetts Supplementary Pension Program for Members of the Service and Domestic Staffs	EEs of the buildings and grounds, garden, dormitory and laundry staffs. All other EEs covered by TIAA-CREF plan.	Req	5 yrs	None	Amount necessary to provide benefit	$2.50 a month for each 12 months of serv. The minimum qualifying period is 5 yrs; the maximum is 30 yrs.	None	100% after 25 yrs serv and age 55	June 30 next following the attainment of age 65 or, if the EE wishes, the first day of the month following his 65th birthday

INSTITUTION	PROVISIONS APPLY TO	REQ &/OR VOL	WAITING PERIOD	CONTRIBUTIONS		PENSION BENEFIT FORMULA	PRERETIREMENT DEATH BENEFIT	VESTING PROVISIONS	RETIREMENT AGE
				INDIV	INST				
Smith College Northampton, Massachusetts Supplementary Pension Plan for Faculty and Administrative Officers	Fac and adm staff who have not passed their 55th birthday at time of appointment Supplements TIAA-CREF plan	Req	10 yrs	None	Amount necessary to provide benefit	$10 per yr for each yr of serv	None	None Disability Regular benefits will be payable provided Social Security has made a monthly award and the individual has had 10 yrs of serv.	Normal at age 65. Early retirement after age 62 but prior to age 65, on a reduced basis in the same manner Social Security reduces benefits for retirees age 62–65.
Stephens College Columbia, Missouri Self-Administered Plan	Full-time EEs in the maintenance and serv area. Academic staff covered by TIAA-CREF plan.	Req	2 yrs if EE is hired prior to age 40; 1 yr if EE is hired after age 40	None	Amount necessary to fund benefit	½% of salary for each yr of credited serv	None	Vested after 10 yrs of serv and attainment of age 55, or after 20 yrs of serv, whichever occurs first.	Normal at age 65.
Syracuse University Syracuse, New York Self-Administered Plan	All full-time EEs in the cler, secretarial, maintenance and serv areas. Contributory TIAA-CREF plan is an alternative; fac and adm staff covered by TIAA-CREF plan.	Vol	None	None	Benefit paid out of current funds as individuals retire	After 15 yrs of serv, eligible for $2 per month for each yr of serv	None	None	Normal at age 65; extensions to 70.
Teachers College Columbia University New York, New York Trusteed Retirement Plan	Full-time nonacademic. Academic staff covered by TIAA-CREF plan.	Req	1 yr	None	Amount necessary to fund benefit	¾ of 1% of final average salary below $6,600 plus 1¼% of salary in excess of $6,600 times number of yrs serv. Final average salary is the average salary paid during the 5 highest consecutive yrs of the last 10. A maximum of 40 yrs serv is considered.	None	None Disability After 10 yrs of serv and attainment of age 40, full pension benefits will be provided if the member is totally disabled.	Normal at age 65. Early at age 60 with 10 yrs serv with reduced benefits.
Union College Schenectady, New York	Full-time EEs in the cler, maintenance or serv areas. Fac covered by TIAA-CREF plan.	Req	Eligible after 10 yrs serv	None	Unfunded retirement pension from college funds	1% times average salary for best 10 yrs out of final 15 times number yrs serv	None	No vesting until retirement	Normal at age 65; 1 yr extensions to age 70.
Vassar College Poughkeepsie, New York Self-Administered	Full-time EEs in the cler, maintenance, and serv areas. Fac and adm staff covered by TIAA-CREF plan.	Req	None	None	Amount necessary to provide benefit	1 1/8% of average of final 5 yrs of salary times yrs of serv minus ½ primary Social Security benefit. Minimum benefit of $3 per month for each yr of serv to a maximum of 15 yrs of serv.	None	After 10 yrs serv and attainment of age 45, may have reduced pension at age 65.	Normal at age 65. Extensions only under special circumstances.

INSTITUTION	PROVISIONS APPLY TO	REQ &/OR VOL	WAITING PERIOD	CONTRIBUTIONS		PENSION BENEFIT FORMULA	PRERETIREMENT DEATH BENEFIT	VESTING PROVISIONS	RETIREMENT AGE
				INDIV	INST				
Wellesley College Wellesley, Massachusetts Pension Plan for Classified Office and Service Employees	All EEs except adm off. EEs hired after age 55 are not eligible. Fac and adm off covered by TIAA-CREF plan.	Req	None	None	Amount necessary to provide benefit	¾ of 1% of basic pay up to Social Security base plus 1½% of excess	After 10 yrs or more of serv, a death benefit of $400 will be paid to the beneficiary.	None Disability Reduced retirement income will be paid if EE is age 50 and has 10 yrs serv.	Normal at age 65.
Wheaton College Norton, Massachusetts	All non-demic EEs. Fac and adm staff covered by TIAA-CREF plan.	Req	3 yrs and age 30	None required. Individual has the option of supplemental contribs if he earned more than $4,800 in the previous yr. Contrib is based on previous yrs earnings.	Amount necessary to provide benefit	A benefit based on salary is purchased during each yr of participation. For example, an annual benefit of $43.40 is purchased each yr for each EE whose salary is between $6,000 and $6,400. The benefit increases $2.80 per yr for each $400 salary increment.	None	None until early retirement	Normal at age 65. Early with reduced benefits at age 50 with 10 yrs of serv. Later with permission of College.
Williams College Williamstown, Massachusetts	All full-time non-academic staff members. Academic staff covered by TIAA-CREF plan.	Req	None	None	Amount necessary to provide benefit	A benefit including that from Social Security equal to 2% of final salary for each yr of serv up to 25; maximum benefit $3,300 per yr.	None	None	Normal 65; permissible at 60. Extensions with approval of College.
Yale University New Haven, Connecticut	All non-academic EEs. Fac and adm officers covered by TIAA-CREF plan.	Req	None	None	Amount necessary to fund benefit	1% of final salary up to $5,000 plus ½% of final salary in excess of $5,000 times yrs of serv.	None	None	Normal, 65. Early at 60 with 10 yrs of serv, if necessary for health. Later with permission of University.

Appendix 7

COMMERCIAL
INSURANCE COMPANY
RETIREMENT PLANS

This appendix describes commercial insurance company plans covering employees of colleges and universities. As in Appendix 6, only plans in institutions employing 100 or more full-time faculty are included.

Most of the abbreviations used in this appendix are self-explanatory, except for EE and ER, which mean, respectively, employee and employer.

INSTITUTION	PROVISIONS APPLY TO	REQ &/OR VOL	WAITING PERIOD	CONTRIBUTIONS		PENSION BENEFIT FORMULA	PRERETIREMENT DEATH BENEFIT	VESTING PROVISIONS	RETIREMENT AGE
				INDIV	INST				
Abilene Christian College Abilene, Texas Prudential Insurance Company of America	Fac and adm staff	Req	After 3 yrs serv (waived for professors and higher) for fac; upon tenure for adm staff.	None	10% minus cost of $5,000 group life coverage	Money purchase. 25% or 50% of premiums may be applied to variable annuity.	Single sum payment to beneficiary equal to the then current value of account; or survivor has option to select annuity within 2 yrs of death of insured.	(1) Return of any EE contribs with interest, plus (2) return of percentage of ER contribs increasing from 50% with under 6 yrs serv to 100% with 10 yrs or more. Disability Total accumulation is fully vested.	Normal at 68. Early at 58 with College consent (benefit actuarially reduced). Compulsory at 72.
Albion College Albion, Michigan Massachusetts Mutual Life Insurance Company	Housekeeping, grounds, maintenance and food serv EEs. Other EEs covered by TIAA–CREF plan.	Req	None	None	$.128 per hour of work	$2.50 per month times credited yrs of serv. Minimum of 10 yrs of serv required for benefits.	None if less than 10 yrs serv	¼ after 10 yrs grading upward to full after 25 yrs	Normal at age 65. Early at age 55, actuarially reduced.
Beloit College Beloit, Wisconsin New England Mutual Life Insurance Company	All non-academic EEs except those employed above age 50. Academic EEs covered by TIAA–CREF plan.	Req	5 yrs	None	Amount necessary to provide benefit	Pension which, when added to primary Security benefit, equals 60% of final average salary. Final average salary is average of highest consecutive 5 yrs prior to age 60. Benefit is reduced 1½% for each yr less than 25 yrs of serv. Minimum pension is $20 per month.	Payment to beneficiary of amount of insurance equal to 100 times pension EE would have received had he remained employed until 65.	Less than 5 yrs serv, none. 5 yrs serv, 50% of cash value of policy. 5–10 yrs serv, additional 10% of cash value of policy is vested each yr. 10 yrs serv or more, full cash value of policy.	Normal at age 65.
Brigham Young University Provo, Utah Beneficial Life Insurance Company (Plan offered as alternative to TIAA–CREF)	All full-time EEs	Vol Req	Fac and adm off immediately, all others after 2 yrs of serv. 4 yrs serv	5% of salary	5% of salary	Money purchase	Total annuity accumulation (EE–ER) paid to beneficiary as lump sum or under an income option	Immediate full vesting	Normal at age 65; early retirement allowed. Extensions to age 70.
Bucknell University Lewisburg, Pennsylvania Connecticut General Life Insurance Company	EEs compensated on a biweekly basis who are age 50 and under as of date of employment. Fac and adm staff covered by TIAA–CREF plan.	Req	None	None	Amount necessary to fund benefit	Yearly benefit equal to $12 plus 1% of last 5 yrs average annual salary above $4,800 times yrs of credited serv	None	After age 55 and 15 yrs credited serv, annuity beginning at age 65 or, with the consent of the University, actuarially reduced annuity beginning immediately.	Normal, age 65 or later. Early, age 55 with 15 yrs serv, with consent of the University. Benefit actuarially reduced.

INSTITUTION	PROVISIONS APPLY TO	REQ &/OR VOL	WAITING PERIOD	CONTRIBUTIONS		PENSION BENEFIT FORMULA	PRERETIREMENT DEATH BENEFIT	VESTING PROVISIONS	RETIREMENT AGE
				INDIV	INST				
California Institute of Technology Pasadena, California Prudential Insurance Company of America	Nonacademic EEs. EE may not become plan member after age 67. Fac and adm staff covered by TIAA-CREF plan.	Vol Req	1 yr serv and age 30. 3 yrs serv and age 30.	2½% of monthly earnings under $350; and 3¾% of the excess. EE may elect to have 50% of the ER's contribs allocated to the purchase of the variable annuity.	Balance necessary to provide benefit	EE may elect fixed dollar annuity or combination of fixed and variable annuity. If all contribs have gone into fixed dollar annuity, benefit will be 1 1/6% of monthly earnings up to $350 plus 1 ¾% of excess times yrs serv.	Return of EE contribs with interest	Return of EE contribs with interest, or EE may leave contribs in plan and receive at age 68 an annuity based on EE contribs plus a percentage of ER contribs as follows: Yrs in Plan % of ER Contribs Vested 5–10 33 1/3 10–15 66 2/3 15 or more 100	Normal at age 68. Early retirement after age 58 with consent of ER.
Calvin College Grand Rapids, Michigan Occidental Life Insurance Company	Cler and maintenance staff. Fac and adm staff covered by TIAA-CREF plan.	Vol	1 yr and age 30	None	9% of salary	Money purchase	Benefit based on age and salary	According to formula. Full vesting after 20 yrs.	Normal at age 65. Early retirement, benefits actuarially reduced.
Clarkson College of Technology Potsdam, New York Clarkson College Pension Trust Connecticut Mutual Life Insurance Company (Plan offered as alternative to TIAA–CREF)	All full-time EEs. EE may not become member after the age of 60 yrs and 6 months.	Req for academic EEs, vol for others after 3 to 5 yrs	3 yrs plus attainment of age 29 yrs and 6 months. Waiting period waived for associate professors and higher (or adm equivalent).	2½% of salary	7½% of salary	Money purchase	100 times monthly pension or cash value of contribs paid. Life insurance part of contract is payable as lump sum or periodic payments.	Full, immediate vesting	Normal, age 65; early at age 60 with 20 yrs serv.
Cranbrook Academy of Art Bloomfield Hills, Michigan New England Mutual Life Insurance Company	All full-time EEs between age 25 and 60	Vol	1 yr	5% of salary to Social Security base; 7½% of excess.	5% of salary to Social Security base; 7½% of excess.	Money purchase	$1,000 of benefit for each $10 of guaranteed monthly income at age 65, or the cash value, if larger, at date of death Disability Early retirement.	Immediate full vesting	Normal at age 65. Early retirement, with benefits actuarially reduced.
Dartmouth College Hanover, New Hampshire The Equitable Life Assurance Society of the United States	All EEs except fac and adm off. Fac and adm off covered by TIAA–CREF plan.	Req	3 yrs and age 30. EEs over the age of 60½ are not eligible.	None	Amount necessary to provide benefit	Monthly benefit equal to approximately 1.17% of the first $300 of monthly salary, plus 2% of monthly salary above $300, for each yr of membership in plan	None	After 15 yrs serv and age 45, member will be eligible for a deferred annuity.	Normal at age 65. Early at age 55 with consent of College. Benefit actuarially reduced. Extensions to age 70.

INSTITUTION	PROVISIONS APPLY TO	REQ &/OR VOL	WAITING PERIOD	CONTRIBUTIONS		PENSION BENEFIT FORMULA	PRERETIREMENT DEATH BENEFIT	VESTING PROVISIONS	RETIREMENT AGE
				INDIV	INST				
David Lipscomb College Nashville, Tennessee American National Insurance Company	Fac, adm staff, cler and secretarial staff	Vol	1 yr	5% of salary	5% of salary	Money purchase	Return of ER and EE contribs	Return of EE contribs	Normal at age 65. Early at age 62.
Fordham University, Bronx, New York Equitable Life Assurance Society	All full-time EEs in the maintenance, serv and cler areas. Fac and adm staff covered by TIAA–CREF plan.	Vol	3 yrs	5% of basic annual earnings	Match EE contribs	Money purchase	Return of EE and ER contribs with interest	Return of EE contribs with interest. At age 45 with 10 yrs serv, EE may elect a deferred annuity based on full accumulation at age 65.	Normal, age 65; earlier permitted with University's consent.
Gustavus Adolphus College St. Peter, Minnesota National Life Insurance Company	All regular full-time EEs compensated on an annual salary basis. EE may not become a member after age 60.	Req	3 yrs or age 30	None	10.53% of salary. (Half is charged to member's salary account)	Money purchase	$2,500 to $20,000 according to age at which EE joins plan and sex. If cash reserve of EEs annuity contract exceeds this amount, the death benefit is the cash reserve of the annuity contract.	Depends on yrs of participation as follows: Yrs Participation / Less than 1 / 1–2 / 2–3 / 3–4 / 4–5 / 5 or more	Normal at age 70. Earlier with consent of College. % of Pension Benefit Vested in EE / 50 / 60 / 70 / 80 / 90 / 100
Hofstra University Hempstead, New York Massachusetts Mutual Life Insurance Company	Full-time EEs of plant department and security staff. All other EEs covered by TIAA–CREF plan.	Req	Coverage begins when EE reaches 30 yrs of age.	None	Amount necessary to provide benefit	1/12 of 1% of average annual salary during last 3 yrs of serv times yrs of credited serv (up to 35)	None	None	Normal at 65. Early at age 62, actuarially reduced.
Illinois Wesleyan University Bloomington, Illinois Contracts available from several companies (TIAA–CREF is alternative)	Fac, adm, and cler staff	Vol	None for fac and adm; 10 yrs for cler staff.	5% of salary during first 3 yrs, no contribs thereafter	5% of salary during first 3 yrs, 10% thereafter	Money purchase	Refund of total accumulation	Immediate full vesting	Normal at 65. Extensions to age 68.
Ithaca College Ithaca, New York Massachusetts Mutual Insurance	Full-time EEs in the cler, maintenance, and serv areas. Fac and adm staff covered by TIAA–CREF plan.	Vol	3 yrs of serv and attainment of age 30	3% of first $333 of monthly earnings plus 5% of excess	3% of first $333 of monthly earnings plus 5% of excess	Money purchase	Return of EE contribs with interest	50% of ER contribs vested after 5 yrs participation plus an additional 10% for each yr over 5 until full vesting after 10 yrs participation.	Normal at age 65; extensions permitted to age 70.

INSTITUTION	PROVISIONS APPLY TO	REQ &/OR VOL	WAITING PERIOD	CONTRIBUTIONS		PENSION BENEFIT FORMULA	PRERETIREMENT DEATH BENEFIT	VESTING PROVISIONS	RETIREMENT AGE
				INDIV	INST				
Johns Hopkins University Baltimore, Maryland Connecticut General Life Insurance Company	All full-time EEs	Vol	None for associate prof and above and staff of comparable rank; other EEs, age 35.	Related to salary and to age at entry. Increases when salary increases. E.g., entry at age 40, 5.2% of $7,500 salary, 5.7% of $12,000 salary, 6.1% of $18,000 salary. Entry at age 45, 5.8% of $7,500 salary, 6.9% of $12,000 salary, 7.4% of $18,000 salary.	Balance necessary to provide benefit	Fixed benefit based on number of yrs of serv (maximum of 30) and salary classification (average base salary during last 5 yrs or average base salary during entire participation in plan, whichever is greater). E.g., after 30 yrs serv, Single Life Annuity of 35.2% of $7,500 final average salary, 41.5% of $12,000, 44.6% of $18,000. Annual cost of living increase equal to increase in Consumer Price Index, but not more than 2% per year.	Surviving spouse will receive income based on combined EE and ER contribs. Any other beneficiary will receive only EE contribs with interest.	Return of EE contribs with interest. Associate professors and above and staff of comparable rank: may leave contribs on deposit for deferred annuity. All other EEs, if age 55 or 5 yrs serv, may elect deferred annuity.	Normal at 65. Early at 55. 1 yr extensions at age 70.
University of Minnesota Minneapolis, Minnesota Faculty Retirement Plan Northwestern National Life Insurance Company of Minneapolis and The Minnesota Mutual Life Insurance Company of St. Paul	Full-time staff members under age 60 who are instructors or research fellows and above, or holders of other positions designated by Regents, and Civil Service staff in designated pay categories	Vol	Assoc prof and above, October 1 following 1 yr of serv; asst prof or research assoc, October 1 following 2 yrs serv; instructor or research fellow, October 1 following 3 yrs serv; Civil Service staff, October 1 following 3 yrs serv.	2½% of salary	2½% of 1st $5,000 plus 7½% of excess. EE may elect variable annuity under which 50% of ER contribs are applied to the variable annuity. Only ER contribs may be so applied.	Money purchase	Beneficiary receives total ER plus EE contribs or termination value of retirement annuity, whichever is greater.	EE may elect to receive cash value of both EE and ER contribs or a deferred annuity based on EE and ER contribs. Disability If totally disabled for more than 4 continuous months, all premiums waived until recovery or October 1 nearest 65th birthday, if later.	June 30 following 68th birthday. Early retirement at any age.
Mount Holyoke College South Hadley, Massachusetts Aetna Life Insurance Company	Nonacademic EEs Fac and adm staff covered by TIAA–CREF plan.	Vol	July 1 after 4½ yrs of serv and the attainment of age 30	3% of salary up to $6,600	Balance necessary to provide benefit	A benefit equal to 1¼% of the first $6,600 of salary for each yr of participation in the plan	Return of EE contribs with interest	Return of EE contribs with interest. After 15 yrs serv and the attainment of age 50, EE may elect to leave contribs on deposit and receive a deferred annuity at the normal retirement age.	Normal, at age 70. EE may retire after age 60 with consent of College with a reduced benefit.
New England Conservatory of Music Boston, Massachusetts New England Mutual Life Insurance Company	All full-time fac and adm staff members	Vol	Fac, none. Adm staff, 2 yrs and age 28.	2¼% of the first $5,400 plus 4½% of excess	Balance necessary to provide benefit	¾% of the first $5,400 of salary plus 1.5% of salary in excess of $5,400 for each yr of participation in the plan	Return of EE contribs with interest	Return of EE contribs with interest. EE may elect to leave contribs on deposit for deferred benefit based on formula.	Normal at age 65.

INSTITUTION	PROVISIONS APPLY TO	REQ &/OR VOL	WAITING PERIOD	CONTRIBUTIONS		PENSION BENEFIT FORMULA	PRERETIREMENT DEATH BENEFIT	VESTING PROVISIONS	RETIREMENT AGE
				INDIV	INST				
University of Pennsylvania Philadelphia, Pennsylvania The Equitable Life Assurance Society of the United States	All full-time EEs. Fac and adm staff covered by TIAA–CREF plan.	Req	3 yrs or age 25, whichever is later. Must be able to complete 13 yrs serv by normal retirement date.	None	Amount necessary to fund benefit	1½% of basic annual salary for each yr of participation	None	Eligible for deferred annuity after 20 yrs of serv. Disability Early retirement benefits after age 50 and 15 yrs of serv.	Normal at age 65. Later with University approval. Early at age 62 after 13 yrs of participation.
Quinnipiac College Hamden, Connecticut Continental Assurance Company	Fac	Vol	2 yrs	5% of salary	5% of salary	Plan A: money purchase. Plan B: money purchase with term life insurance to age 65.	Plan A: return of EE and ER contribs with interest. Plan B: Life insurance equal to 100 times estimated monthly benefit.	ER contribs vest after 3 yrs participation.	Age 65. Early retirement permitted at age 55 or over with reduced benefits. Benefit begins at age 65 even if EE continues to work.
Rensselaer Polytechnic Institute Troy, New York Bankers Life Company	All full-time EEs: Group 1: Fac above instructor and off of adm. Group 2: Instructor, research assistant, members of adm staff. Group 3: members of cler, secretarial, maintenance, and serv staffs.	Req for Groups 1 and 2; vol for Group 3.	Group 1: October 1, March 1, or July 1 following employment. Group 2: Vol; October 1, March 1, July 1, following employment. Req; October 1, March 1, or July 1 after completion of 2 yrs serv. Group 3: Vol on October 1 following completion of 3 yrs continuous serv. EEs 55 yrs and 6 mos or older may not enroll in plan.	6% of salary	Balance necessary to provide benefit	(1) 2% of monthly salary as of each October 1 times number of yrs participation, plus (2) variable annuity benefit from equity investment of the surplus earnings of the fund	(1) Return of EE contribs with interest, plus (2) benefit representing equity investment of surplus earnings of the fund	Return of EE contribs with interest. After 3 yrs of serv, EE may elect deferred annuity in accordance with pension benefit formula.	Normal at age 65. Early at age 55, payment actuarially reduced. Later with consent of Institute.

INSTITUTION	PROVISIONS APPLY TO	REQ &/OR VOL	WAITING PERIOD	CONTRIBUTIONS		PENSION BENEFIT FORMULA	PRERETIREMENT DEATH BENEFIT	VESTING PROVISIONS	RETIREMENT AGE
				INDIV	INST				
University of Rochester Rochester, New York Metropolitan Life Insurance Company	Full-time EEs who are cler, maintenance, serv, junior adm staff, or junior pro assistants. These EEs also covered by trusteed plan. Fac and adm off covered by TIAA–CREF plan.	Req	None	None	Amount necessary to purchase pension benefit each yr	Fixed annuity.* Each yr an annuity is purchased equal to 3/8% of salary up to Social Security base plus ¾% of salary above. *See self-administered plan for variable annuity portion of benefit.	None	After 10 yrs of serv, EEs entitled to receive pension at age 65.	Normal at age 65, extensions permitted to age 70. Early with ER consent if age 55 or over.
Saint Mary's College Notre Dame, Indiana The Sisters of the Holy Cross Retirement Income Plan	All EEs except fac. Fac and some adm staff covered by TIAA–CREF plan.	Vol	3 full yrs of serv and age 30	$1.73 per week plus 4½% of monthly salary in excess of $400	Balance necessary to fund benefit	Monthly benefit will equal $2.50 plus 1½% of monthly salary in excess of $400 multiplied by total yrs of serv (maximum credit will be 35 yrs).	Full amount of EE contrib with 3% interest	EE contribs with 3% interest. If age 60 and 15 yrs of serv, EE may elect to receive all accrued benefits at normal retirement age. Disability If EE is age 50 and has 15 yrs of serv, then eligible for monthly benefit of $50.	Normal age 65 if EE is age 55 or less at time of joining plan. If between ages 55 and 60, normal retirement is after 10 yrs of serv. If over age 60, normal retirement is age 70. Early, age 60 and 15 or more yrs of serv.
Samford University, Birmingham, Alabama Protective Life Insurance Company	All full-time EEs	Req	Fac, 1 yr; others, 1 to 5 yrs depending on age.	None	Amount necessary to fund benefits	1% of salary up to $4,800 plus 2% of excess times number of yrs serv	None	After 20 yrs serv, EE is eligible for a deferred annuity at age 65.	Normal at age 65.
Seton Hall University South Orange, New Jersey Phoenix Mutual Life Insurance Company	All lay EEs except fac and adm staff. Lay pro staff covered by TIAA–CREF plan.	Req	None	None	Amount necessary to fund benefit	1% of average of final 5 yrs salary times yrs serv	None	None before early retirement Disability Reduced benefit payable after age 55 with 10 yrs serv.	Normal at age 65 with 10 yrs serv. Reduced benefit payable after age 55 with 10 yrs serv.
South Dakota State System of Higher Education (Bankers Life Company) Black Hills State College General Beadle State College Northern State College South Dakota School of Mines and Technology South Dakota State University Southern State College University of South Dakota	Pro EEs	Vol	None	3½% of first $6,000 of salary	3½% of first $6,000 of salary	Money purchase group annuity	Return of EE contribs with interest	Return of EE contribs with interest. After 4 yrs serv, EE may elect to leave contribs on deposit and receive deferred annuity based on EE contribs and 40% of state contribs, increasing 10% for each additional yr of serv. Full vesting on 10 yrs serv. Disability Benefit payments based on total accumulation to date of disability.	July 1 following attainment of age 65. Extensions on a year-to-year basis.

| INSTITUTION | PROVISIONS APPLY TO | REQ &/OR VOL | WAITING PERIOD | CONTRIBUTIONS | | PENSION BENEFIT FORMULA | PRERETIREMENT DEATH BENEFIT | VESTING PROVISIONS | RETIREMENT AGE |
				INDIV	INST				
Stanford University Stanford, California The Prudential Insurance Company of America	All regular non-teaching EEs, except pro and managerial staff earning $8,400 per year or more. Fac and pro staff covered by TIAA–CREF plan.	Req	Vol after 1 yr of serv. Req after 2 yrs of serv, and attainment of age 35.	2½% of the first $300 of monthly salary and 5% of salary in excess of $300 per month	Balance necessary to fund benefit	If EE elects fixed dollar annuity only, monthly retirement income will be 3% of EEs total contribs. (Earlier formulas apply to contribs made before 1966.) If EE elects variable annuity option, depends on investment results of investment fund.	Return of EE contribs with interest	Return of EE contribs plus interest or, if EE has 15 yrs of serv or 10 yrs of serv and has reached age 45, may leave his contribs in plan and receive added retirement income purchased by ER.	Normal 65. Earlier retirement may be elected within 10 yrs of normal retirement date. Later retirement permitted only with ER consent.
Stevens Institute Hoboken, New Jersey The Prudential Insurance Company of America	All full-time non-academic EEs. Pro EEs covered by TIAA–CREF plan.	Req	None	None	Amount necessary to fund benefit	A monthly amount which, when added to primary Social Security, will guarantee the individual $200 per month for life.	None	None	65 for men, 62 for women.* *Until common retirement age can be resolved or until Congress clarifies rules on different retirement ages.
Trinity College Hartford, Connecticut Retirement Plan for Nonacademic Personnel Connecticut General Life Insurance Company	All non-academic EEs. Fac and adm staff covered by TIAA–CREF plan.	Vol until age 30. Req at age 30 and over.	1 yr	5% of salary	6% of salary within Social Security base plus 10% of salary in excess of Social Security base	Money purchase	Return of EE contribs with interest	Return of EE contribs with interest. After 3 yrs serv, EE may elect to leave contribs on deposit and receive a deferred annuity based on total accumulation.	Normal at age 65; early at age 55 with consent of ER
Worcester Polytechnic Institute Worcester, Massachusetts Connecticut General Life Insurance Company	All non-academic EEs. Academic staff covered by TIAA–CREF plan.	Vol	1 yr	3% of salary	Balance necessary to provide benefit	A benefit of 2% of annual salary is earned during each yr of participation in the plan.	Return of EE contribs with interest	Return of EE contribs with interest, or EE may leave contribs on deposit and receive deferred annuity at age 65. In addition, benefits purchased by ER contribs will be credited in accordance with the following schedule: Yrs of Serv and Age at Termination / % of ER Contribs Used To Purchase Benefits 5 yrs and age 45 — 50 10 yrs and age 50 — 75 15 yrs and age 55 — 100	Normal at age 65.

Appendix 8

CHURCH PENSION PLANS

Church pension plans cover certain employees in the church-affiliated colleges and universities. In seminaries, all ordained and lay employees may be covered by the church plan. In other institutions, membership in the church plan is usually provided for the ordained faculty or staff, while lay faculty and other employees participate in the regular college retirement plan. The plans of twelve church organizations cover at least some employees in higher education.

Most of the abbreviations used in this appendix are self-explanatory, except for EE and ER, which mean, respectively, employee and employer.

PLAN AND MEMBER INSTITUTIONS	PROVISIONS APPLY TO	REQ &/OR VOL	WAITING PERIOD	CONTRIBUTIONS		PENSION BENEFIT FORMULA	PRERETIREMENT DEATH BENEFIT	VESTING PROVISIONS	RETIREMENT AGE
				INDIV	INST				
AMERICAN BAPTIST CONVENTION New York, New York Ministers and Missionaries Benefit Board *Ottawa U, Kansas Alderson-Broaddus College, W.Va. Andover-Newton Theological School, Mass. Berkeley Baptist Divinity School, Calif. California Baptist Theological Seminary Central Baptist Theological Seminary, Kansas *Colgate-Rochester Divinity School, N.Y. Crozer Theological Seminary, Pa. Fuller Theological Seminary, Calif. Linfield College, Ore. Northern Baptist Theological Seminary, Ill. *U of Redlands, Calif. *Sioux Falls College, S.D. *Also has TIAA-CREF plan.	All EEs	Vol	None	Usually none	Usually 13% of salary	Variable annuity. Guarantee of 2% interest compounded annually on the 10% of salary allocated to retirement benefits.	(1) Single payment benefit of twice last (average, if higher) salary if EE was under age 61. Reduces after age 61 to a minimum benefit of one times average salary after age 65. Increased by 50% for accidental death, plus (2) widow annuity based on total accumulation (minimum of 50 annuity units) with additional 50 annuity units for each child under age 18. If no widow or child survives, the current value of the accumulation units is paid to EEs estate.	Immediate full vesting Disability Waiver of premium plus variable annuity which begins at 1/3 final salary plus 50 annuity units for each child under 18. Income begins after 1 yr of disability. Maximum initial basic benefit is $3,600. Minimum basic benefit is $1,200.	Any age.
THE AMERICAN LUTHERAN CHURCH Minneapolis, Minnesota Pension Plan for Clergymen Lay Workers Pension Plan *Augsburg College, Minn. *Augustana College, S.D. *California Lutheran College *Capital U, Ohio *Dana College, Neb. Evangelical Lutheran Theological Seminary, Ohio *Luther College, Iowa Luther Theological Seminary, Minn. *Pacific Lutheran U, Wash. *St. Olaf College, Minn. Texas Lutheran College Wartburg College, Iowa Wartburg Theological Seminary, Iowa *Also has TIAA-CREF plan.	Clergy All lay EEs	Vol	None	None 3% of salary **Includes 2% of salary set aside for major medical benefits. Any unused portion of this amount will be credited to the accumulation accounts of the members.	12%** of salary 9%** of salary	Money purchase	Lay EEs: Return of EE contribs plus interest. All EEs: Annuity for widow based on total accumulation plus supplement if necessary to provide minimum pension established by the Board of Pensions plus $25 monthly or $25 monthly for each eligible child. If no widow, the total accumulation shall be applied for the benefit of eligible children. If no children survive, the entire accumulation may be paid to any other dependent of the EE. After 1 yr in plan, cash benefit of 3-24 months salary, depending on age plus (if widow is or would have been eligible for pension) $500 per yr for each child under 25 for first 4 yrs of higher education.	Lay EEs: Return of EE contribs with interest. All EEs: After 5 yrs serv, may elect to leave contribs on deposit and receive a deferred annuity. Disability After 3 yrs serv, a minimum pension established by the Board of Pensions to age 65 plus waiver of future contribs. If member is not eligible for this benefit, he may use his total accumulation for a disability annuity according to actuarial rates established by the Board.	Normal at 65 or later, early at 62.

PLAN AND MEMBER INSTITUTIONS	PROVISIONS APPLY TO	REQ &/OR VOL	WAITING PERIOD	CONTRIBUTIONS		PENSION BENEFIT FORMULA	PRERETIREMENT DEATH BENEFIT	VESTING PROVISIONS	RETIREMENT AGE
				INDIV	INST				
CHRISTIAN CHURCHES DISCIPLES OF CHRIST) Indianapolis, Indiana Pension Fund Atlantic Christian College, N.C. *Bethany College, W.Va. Butler U, Ind. Chapman College, Calif. Christian Theological Seminary, Ind. Culver-Stockton College, Mo. *Drake U, Divinity School, Iowa *Drury College, Mo. Eureka College, Ill. *Hiram College, Ohio Lexington Theological Seminary, Ky. Lynchburg College, Va. Manhattan Bible College, Kan. Milligan College, Tenn. Missouri School of Religion Northwest Christian College, Ore. Phillips U, Okla. *Texas Christian U *Transylvania College, Ky. William Woods College, Mo. *Also has TIAA-CREF plan.	All EEs	Vol	None	Total contribs of 12% salary, often divided equally between individual and institution		1/70 of total salary on which dues have been paid. pension of greater of $300 a yr or ½ accrued pension credits, plus (4) $100 for each child under age 18 (if in school, under age 21) up to amount of widow's pension, plus (5) scholarship benefits of $500 per yr for up to 4 yrs higher education for each child. If both parents die, widow's pension is divided between eligible children.	(1) $1,000, plus (2) 6–18 mos salary depending on age, plus (3) widow's	Under 5 yrs serv, return of EE contribs plus interest. 5 yrs serv or more, (1) return of EE contribs plus interest plus portion of ER contribs not actuarially required for protection, or (2) EE may leave contribs on deposit and receive a deferred annuity, or (3) EE may continue full or partial membership by continuing to pay all or part of dues. Disability After 1 yr membership, up to $1,200 per yr to age 65 plus waiver of dues.	65 or later. Early retirement at 62 or later with reduced benefits.
CHURCH OF THE BRETHREN Elgin, Illinois Ministerial and Missionary Pension Plan *Bridgewater College, Va. *Elizabethtown College, Pa. *LaVerne College, Calif. *Bethany Theological Seminary, Ill. *Juniata College, Pa. *Also has TIAA–CREF plan.	All EEs	Vol	None for clergy. 1 yr for lay EEs.	4% of salary; if under OASDHI, member may reduce contribs to 3%, 2%, or 1%.	8% of salary; for lay EEs, ER contribs may be reduced by OASDHI ER tax.	Money purchase. Minimum of $50 per month after 30 yrs serv. If annuity payments to member and widow total less than EEs contribs plus interest, balance will be used for the benefit of children or paid to EEs estate.	Widow's annuity based on combined accumulation and actuarially determined. If no widow, EEs contribs plus interest will be used by Pension Board for the welfare of surviving children. Any portion of EE contribs plus interest left after payments (if any) to widow and children will be paid to contingent beneficiary or EEs estate. Disability Annuity determined by attained age and combined accumulation.	Clergy: After 1 yr not under covered employment, EE may withdraw contribs with interest only if total accumulation will not purchase monthly benefit of $25 at age 65. Otherwise he must leave contribs on deposit if he is a minister in good standing. Lay EEs: Return of EE contribs with interest; after 5 yrs serv, EE may elect to leave contribs on deposit and receive deferred annuity.	65 or later. After age 65, EE may receive annuity while receiving salary if ER continues contribs of 8% of salary to Supplemental Fund—EE has nothing more credited to his account.

PLAN AND MEMBER INSTITUTIONS	PROVISIONS APPLY TO	REQ &/OR VOL	WAITING PERIOD	CONTRIBUTIONS		PENSION BENEFIT FORMULA	PRERETIREMENT DEATH BENEFIT	VESTING PROVISIONS	RETIREMENT AGE
				INDIV	INST				
GENERAL CONFERENCE OF SEVENTH-DAY ADVENTISTS Washington, D.C. Sustentation Fund Andrews U, Mich. Atlantic Union College, Mass. Columbia Union College, Md. Loma Linda U, Calif. Oakwood College, Ala. Pacific Union College, Calif. Southern Missionary College, Tenn. Southwestern Union College, Tex. Union College, Neb. Walla Walla College, Wash.	All EEs hired before the age of 50 who are church members	Req	None	None	1¼% of payroll	The family rate of workers eligible for sustentation shall be 24% of the regular 100% salary level for 15 yrs of serv, and for each yr of serv from 15 to 40 there shall be added 1.6% of the 100% salary level, making a maximum of 64% of the regular 100% salary level for 40 or more yrs of serv. Single workers receive benefits equal to ¾ of the family rate. EEs hired between the ages of 40 and 50 have benefits reduced by 2% for each yr their age exceeds 40 yrs.	Institution continues salary to widow for 6 mos. Widow may receive assistance from Fund if she has dependent children or if she has been the wife of a worker while in active serv for at least 15 yrs and if she is not employed or otherwise capable of self-support.	Worker leaving within 5 yrs of retirement who has at least 20 yrs serv may be eligible for deferred pension at retirement age. If he leaves more than 5 yrs before retirement he loses 1 yr serv credit for each yr above 5 away from covered work. Disability Minimum serv requirement for temporary or regular benefits is 15 yrs. EE continues salary for 6 mos before sustentation benefits begin under benefit formula. Exception: sustentation benefits begin immediately for workers age 50 or above with 25 or more yrs of serv. A specific total sum may be granted to workers with less than 15 yrs of serv who become incapacitated by serious physical disability.	Minimum age 65 for men, 60 for women. Men may retire at age 60 with 32 yrs serv.
LUTHERAN CHURCH IN AMERICA Minneapolis Minnesota Board of Pensions Ministerial Pension and Death Benefit Plan Any institution affiliated with the Lutheran Church in America which employs pastors	Clergy	Vol	None	4% of salary. If under OASDHI, member may pay only on salary in excess of ½ the salary subject to Social Security self-employment tax.	8% of salary	Money purchase—may include variable annuity.	Widow receives a life annuity based on member's combined accumulation. If she dies or remarries before receiving an amount equal to the total accumulation, a pension shall be provided for the member's minor children in an amount totaling ½ the amount the member would have received if he had retired on the date of his death. This pension ceases when the accumulation is exhausted or when the youngest child reaches 21. If total payments to the widow and children are less than the EE contribs plus interest, the remaining amount will be paid to the contingent beneficiary or the member's legal representatives.	Return of EE contribs with interest. If this amount is $1,000 or more, EE may elect to leave his contribs on deposit and receive a deferred annuity. Disability Money purchase annuity based on assumption that ER contribs continue at the average rate of the last 4 yrs of employment until age 60. Interest on actual and presumed contribs is calculated on a fixed income basis, then the portion of ER accumulation previously elected by the member is converted to variable pension credits.	Normal at 65, early at 62.

PLAN AND MEMBER INSTITUTIONS	PROVISIONS APPLY TO	REQ &/OR VOL	WAITING PERIOD	CONTRIBUTIONS		PENSION BENEFIT FORMULA	PRERETIREMENT DEATH BENEFIT	VESTING PROVISIONS	RETIREMENT AGE
				INDIV	INST				
LUTHERAN CHURCH IN AMERICA Minneapolis, Minnesota Board of Pensions Lay Pension Plan *Augustana College, Ill. *California Lutheran College *Lenoir Rhyne College, N.C. Lutheran School of Theology at Chicago, Ill. Lutheran Theological Seminary, Pa. Midland Lutheran College, Neb. *Muhlenberg College, Pa. Northwestern Lutheran Theological Seminary, Minn. *Susquehanna U, Pa. *Also has TIAA–CREF plan.	All lay EEs	Vol	None	2% of salary	6% of salary	Money purchase—may include variable annuity.	Widow receives a life annuity based on member's combined accumulation. If she dies or remarries before receiving an amount equal to the total accumulation, a pension shall be provided from the excess for the member's minor children in an amount totalling ½ the amount the member would have received if he had retired on the date of his death. This pension ceases when the accumulation is exhausted or when the youngest child reaches age 21. If total payments to the widow and children are less than the EEs contribs plus interest, the remaining amount will be paid to the contingent beneficiary or the member's legal representatives.	Return of EE contribs with interest. If this amount is $500 or more, EE may elect to leave his contribs on deposit and receive a deferred annuity. Disability Money purchase annuity based on total accumulation at time of disability. If EE has at least 4 yrs serv, he is credited with the amount the ER would have contributed had he continued at a salary equal to the average of his last 4 yrs salary until age 60, plus interest which would have accrued to age 60 on a fixed income basis. This amount then may be wholly or partially converted to variable pension credits.	Normal at age 62. Early at age 55 with consent of ER or in case of involuntary separation.
LUTHERAN CHURCH– MISSOURI SYNOD St. Louis, Missouri Concordia Retirement Plan *Concordia College, Minn. Concordia Seminary, Mo. Concordia Senior College, Ind. Concordia Teachers College, Ill. Concordia Teachers College, Neb. Concordia Theological Seminary, Ill. *Also has TIAA–CREF plan.	All regular full-time EEs (EEs hired over age 60 not eligible.)	Req	First day of calendar quarter coinciding with or next following date of employment.	None	8% of salary for single EE or 10% of salary for EE with family. Reduced by ERs share of OASDHI tax.	1½% of final average salary times yrs of serv to maximum of 50% final average salary. This amount is reduced by 1 2/3% of the EEs benefit from Social Security per yr of serv to a maximum of 50% in those cases in which contribs to the Plan are offset by amount of contribs to Social Security. Final average salary is based on the 20 consecutive calendar quarters in the last 15 yrs which give the highest average.	Monthly benefit to the widow of 40% of the average monthly compensation received by the EE in the last 4 calendar quarters plus 10% of this final salary to each child except that the total of all payment plus any amount payable shall not exceed 60% of final salary.	Percentage of benefit vested according to age and yrs of serv. Full vesting for EE terminating at age 55 or over regardless of serv. Disability After 1 yr disability, benefit equal to what EE would have received had he continued at present salary to normal retirement age, except that the benefit shall not be reduced for Social Security unless EE is actually receiving Social Security disability benefits. Worker becoming member after age 50 must complete 2 yrs serv before becoming eligible.	Later of (1) age 65 or (2) 30 yrs serv but not beyond age 70. Early at age 55—EE may choose actuarially reduced benefit or may defer benefits until age 65 and receive full formula benefit based on serv from age 30 to date of actual retirement. Benefits must begin not later than age 72.

PLAN AND MEMBER INSTITUTIONS	PROVISIONS APPLY TO	REQ &/OR VOL	WAITING PERIOD	CONTRIBUTIONS		PENSION BENEFIT FORMULA	PRERETIREMENT DEATH BENEFIT	VESTING PROVISIONS	RETIREMENT AGE
				INDIV	INST				
PRESBYTERIAN CHURCH IN THE UNITED STATES Atlanta, Georgia Ministers' Annuity Fund Agnes Scott College, Ga. *Arkansas College *Austin College, Tex. Austin Presbyterian Theological Seminary, Tex. Belhaven College, Miss. Columbia Theological Seminary, Ga. *Davidson College, N.C. *Davis and Elkins College, W.Va. *Florida Presbyterian College *Hampden-Sidney College, Va. *King College, Ky. Louisville Presbyterian Theological Seminary, Ky. New Brunswick Theological Seminary, N.J. *Presbyterian College, S.C. Presbyterian School of Christian Education, Va. *St Andrews Presbyterian College, N.C. *Southwestern at Memphis, Tenn. *Stillman College, Ala. *Union Theological Seminary, N.Y. Union Theological Seminary, Va. *Also has TIAA-CREF plan.	Clergy	Vol	None	2½% of salary. ER may pay all or part of EEs contribs	7½% of salary	1/80 average salary per yr serv	$1,000 plus annuity to widow of ½ the age retirement annuity EE would have received based on his serv from their marriage to his death with a minimum of $300 a yr plus annuities of $100 a yr each to minor children until age 18 (21 if in school). Total annual payments to widow and children may not exceed annuity which member would have received.	Return of EE contribs plus interest. With 5 or more yrs serv, EE may leave contribs on deposit and receive a deferred annuity at age 65 or later based on 50% of benefit formula with 5 yrs serv and increasing gradually to the full formula benefit with 10 yrs serv or more. Disability After 1 yr serv, benefit of 40% of average salary earned during last 5 yrs (or total serv if less than 5 yrs) payable to age 65. Maximum benefit of 90% age annuity which would be earned if EE continued at present salary to age 65.	Normal at 65. Early retirement at 60 or later with benefits actuarially reduced.
PRESBYTERIAN CHURCH IN THE UNITED STATES Atlanta, Georgia Employees' Annuity Fund Austin Presbyterian Theological Seminary, Tex. Columbia Theological Seminary, Ga. Louisville Presbyterian Theological Seminary, Ky. *Presbyterian College, S.C. Presbyterian School of Christian Education, Va. *Also has TIAA-CREF plan.	All lay EEs	Vol	None	4% of salary. ER may pay all or part of EEs contribs	4% of salary	Money purchase	Return of EE contribs plus interest. If spouse or child survives, total accumulation shall be used to provide survivor annuity. Disability Early retirement.	Return of EE contribs plus interest or EE may leave his contribs on deposit and receive a deferred annuity.	60 or later.

PLAN AND MEMBER INSTITUTIONS	PROVISIONS APPLY TO	REQ &/OR VOL	WAITING PERIOD	CONTRIBUTIONS		PENSION BENEFIT FORMULA	PRERETIREMENT DEATH BENEFIT	VESTING PROVISIONS	RETIREMENT AGE
				INDIV	INST				
REFORMED CHURCH IN AMERICA New York, New York Contributory Annuity Fund New Brunswick Theological Seminary, N.J. Northwestern College, Iowa. Western Theological Seminary, Mich.	Fac, adm staff, and cler staff	Vol	None	1½% of salary	6½% of salary	Money purchase	Return of EE contribs with interest. If spouse or other beneficiary survives, the accumulation may be used to provide annuity based on age of beneficiary. If there are minor children but no spouse survives, the accumulation may be applied by the Board of Pensions for the benefit of the children. Disability Annuity based on member's attained age and total accumulation.	Immediate full vesting. Lay EE who leaves church serv or clergyman who loses ministerial standing may elect to withdraw his own contribs with interest	Normal at age 65 or later. Early at age 60.
SOUTHERN BAPTIST CONVENTION Dallas, Texas Southern Baptist Protection Program Baylor U, Tex. Belmont College, Tenn. Blue Mountain College, Miss. California Baptist College *Campbell College, N.C. Campbellsville College, Ky. U of Corpus Christi, Tex. Cumberland College, Ky. East Texas Baptist College *Georgetown College, Ky. Golden Gate Baptist Theological Seminary, Calif. Grand Canyon College, Ariz. Hardin-Simmons U, Tex. *Houston Baptist College, Tex. Howard Payne College, Tex. *Judson College, Ala. Louisiana College Mary Hardin-Baylor College, Tex. *Mercer U, Ga. Midwestern Baptist Theological Seminary, Mo. Mississippi College *Mobile College, Ala. New Orleans Baptist Theological Seminary, La. *Oklahoma Baptist U Ouachita Baptist U, Ark. Southeastern Baptist Theological Seminary, N.C. Southern Baptist Theological Seminary, Ky. Southwestern Baptist Theological Seminary, Tex. *Stetson U, Fla. Tift College, Ga. Union U, Tenn. *Wake Forest U, N.C. Wayland Baptist College, Tex. William Carey College, Miss. William Jewell College, Mo. *Also has TIAA-CREF plan.	All EEs EE may choose to participate in any combination of plans A, B, and C, except that he may not participate only in plan C.	Vol	None	Elective Plan A has a maximum contrib of $600 per yr. ERs maximum total contrib is 20% of salary.	Elective	Plan A: 10% of total dues paid. Plan B: Money purchase. Plan C: Variable annuity.	Plan A: Pension to widow (or dependent parent if no widow) of 40% of EEs potential pension at age 65 plus child's benefit of 15% of EEs potential pension at age 65 to each child (maximum of 4 children), plus up to $600 per child per yr for up to 4 yrs of college. Plans B and C: Benefit equal to total accumulation. Disability Plan A: After 1 yr in plan, benefit equal to potential age pension at 65. Plans B and C: Benefit based on total accumulation to date of disability.	Immediate full vesting	Plan A: Normal at age 65. Early at age 60 with benefit actuarially reduced. Plans B and C: Optional at any age.

PLAN AND MEMBER INSTITUTIONS	PROVISIONS APPLY TO	REQ &/OR VOL	WAITING PERIOD	CONTRIBUTIONS		PENSION BENEFIT FORMULA	PRERETIREMENT DEATH BENEFIT	VESTING PROVISIONS	RETIREMENT AGE
				INDIV	INST				
UNITED CHURCH OF CHRIST New York, New York Annuity Fund for Congregational Ministers Membership is on an individual rather than an institutional basis. Retirement Fund for Lay Workers Andover Newton Theological Seminary, Mass. Dillard U, La. Eden Theological Seminary, Mo. Fisk U, Tenn. Huston-Tillotson College, Tex. LeMoyne College, Tenn. Talladega College, Ala. Tougaloo College, Miss.	Clergy All Lay EEs	Vol	None	Total contribs of 6% to approximately 11% of salary		Money purchase. Annuitants may receive regular and special dividends expressed as a percentage of the basic annuity if investment returns are favorable. Clergy may also receive bonuses to bring annuities to a specified minimum (currently $50 annually per yr of serv for retirees age 70 or above). Bonuses are financed by the world giving of the churches and are not guaranteed. Disability Early retirement benefit based on actuarial value of the accumulation at the member's attained age.	Return of total accumulation in member's account. If beneficiary survives, the accumulation will be used to provide an annuity for the beneficiary. If beneficiary is under age 50, a refund of the accumulation in a specified number of installments may be made instead of a life annuity.	Clergy: May withdraw own contribs with interest or an amount based on contribs of 3% of salary if higher only if ministerial standing is lost during first 5 yrs of membership. Others must leave contribs on deposit for deferred annuity at 65. Those with ministerial standing may continue contribs on their own. Lay EEs: Return of regular EE contribs with interest or an amount based on contribs of 3% of salary if higher, plus any additional personal contribs. EE is encouraged to leave contribs on deposit for a deferred annuity at 60 or later based on total accumulation.	Clergy: Normal at age 65. Lay EEs: Age 60 or later.
THE YMCA RETIREMENT FUND New York, New York The Secretarial Plan Savings and Security Plan *George Williams College, Ill. *Springfield College, Mass. *Also has TIAA-CREF plan.	Pro EE groups determined by ER. Nonpro groups determined by ER. EEs age 60 or over are not eligible.	Vol	None	5% of salary 3% or 5% of salary	7% of salary Matches EE contribs	Money purchase	Return of EE contribs with interest plus death benefit of approximately 10 times EE contribs during 1 yr period before death. Death benefit doubles to 20 times last yrs contribs after 5 yrs serv.	Return of EE contribs with interest. Secretarial Plan: After 10 yrs serv, EE is eligible for deferred annuity at 65 from own contribs plus additional 4% of this amount per yr of serv up to 100%. If age 55 or older with 10 yrs serv, EE eligible for annuity at age 60 or later double what his own contribs will purchase. Savings and Security Plan: After 5 yrs serv, EE may elect deferred annuity at age 65 based on total accumulation. Disability Disability Secretarial Plan: After 5 yrs, benefit equal to projected age retirement at age 60 if salary had continued equal to average of last 5 yrs salary. Savings and Security Plan: After 10 yrs, benefit based on total accumulation. If less than 20 yrs serv, allowance is raised as if EE had participated for 20 yrs or until age 65, whichever is less.	Secretarial Plan: Normal at 60 or later. Savings and Security Plan: Normal at 65 or later. Early at 50 or later after 5 yrs serv and with ER consent.

INDEX

Washburn University of Topeka, Kans., 230, 385
Washington and Jefferson College, Pa., 244, 385
Washington and Lee University, Va., 247, 385
Washington Bible College, Washington, D.C., NI
Washington College, Md., 232, 385
Washington Public Employees' Retirement System, 419
Washington School of Psychiatry, Wash., D.C., 385
Washington State Teachers College, Me., 232, 402, 429
Washington State Teachers' Retirement System, 419
Washington State University, 247, 385, 419
Washington University, Mo., 235, 385
Washington, University of, 247, 386, 419
Waterbury State Technical Institute, Conn., 396
Wayland Baptist College, Tex., 452
Waynesburg College, Pa., 244, 386
Wayne State College, Nebr., 236, 386
Wayne State University, Mich., 234, 386
Webb Institute of Naval Architecture, N.Y., 239, 386
Weber State College, Utah, 246, 386, 418
Webster College, Mo., 235, 386
Wellesley College, Mass., 233, 386, 434
Wells College, N.Y., 239, 386
Wesleyan College, Ga., 227, 386
Wesleyan University, Conn., 226, 386
Wesley Theological Seminary, Washington, D.C., 226, 386
Westbrook College, Me., 232, 387
West Chester State College, Pa., 243, 414
West Coast University, Calif., 225
Western Baptist Bible College and Theological Seminary, Calif., 225
Western Carolina College, N.C., 410
Western College for Women, Ohio, 241, 387
Western Connecticut State College, 226, 396
Western Illinois University, 229, 428
Western Kentucky University, 400, 401
Western Maryland College, 232, 388
Western Michigan University, 234, 403
Western Montana College of Education, 236, 406
Western New England College, Mass., 233, 388
Western New Mexico University, 408
Western State College of Colorado, 225, 395
Western Theological Seminary, Mich., 234, 452
West Virginia Teachers' Retirement System, 22, 420
Western Washington State College, 247, 388, 419

West Georgia College, 227, 397
West Liberty State College, W.Va., 248, 387, 420
Westmar College, Iowa, 230, 388
Westminster Choir College, N.J., 237, 388
Westminster College, Mo., 235, 388
Westminster College, Pa., 244
Westminster College, Utah, 246, 388
Westminster Theological Seminary, Pa., 244
Westmont College, Calif., 225, 388
West Texas State University, 246, 417
West Virginia Institute of Technology, 248, 387, 420
West Virginia State College, 248, 387, 420
West Virginia University, 248, 387, 420
West Virginia Wesleyan College, 248, 387
Wheaton College, Ill, 229, 388
Wheaton College, Mass., 233, 388, 434
Wheeling College, W. Va., 248, 388
Wheelock College, Mass., 233, 388
Whitman College, Wash., 247, 388
Whittier College, Calif., 225
Whitworth College, Wash., 247, 388
Wichita State University, Kans., 230, 389, 400
Widow benefits, 124; in AAUP-AAC Statement, 18, 19; in group life insurance plans, 122; under Social Security, 122, 123 (table); in public employee and state teacher retirement systems, 124; in church retirement plans, 447–53
Wilberforce University, Ohio, 241, 389
Wiley College, Tex., NI
Wilkes College, Pa., 244, 389
Willamette University, Oreg., 242, 389
William and Mary, College of, Va., 419
William Carey College, Miss., 235, 452
William Jennings Bryan University, Tenn., 245
William Jewell College, Mo., 452
William Mitchell College of Law, Minn., NI
William Penn College, Iowa, 230, 389
Williams College, Mass., 233, 389, 434
William Smith College, N.Y., 389
William Woods College, Mo., 235, 448
Wilmington College, N.C., 410
Wilmington College, Ohio, 241, 389
Wilson College, Pa., 389
Wilson, Woodrow, 10
Windham College, Vt., 246, 389
Winebrenner Theological Seminary, Ohio, 241
Winona State College, Minn., 234, 404
Winston-Salem College, N.C., 240, 410
Winthrop College, S.C., 244, 415
Wisconsin, 64
Wisconsin Conservatory, 248
Wisconsin Retirement Fund, 60, 420
Wisconsin State Teachers Retirement System, 60, 421